D1139018

Modern American Society

READINGS IN THE PROBLEMS OF ORDER AND CHANGE

116

KINGSLEY DAVIS · *Columbia University*

HARRY C. BREDEMEIER · *New Jersey College for Women*

MARION J. LEVY, Jr · *Princeton University*

RINEHART & COMPANY, INC · *Publishers* · *New York*

Printed in the United States of America
Designed by Stefan Salter

INTRODUCTION

Social science frequently suffers two rather contradictory criticisms: first that it is too academic and too remote from the basic problems of our time; and second that it is too subjective and controversial to be scientific, being merely a hodgepodge of dubious information about social issues. Both criticisms are to some extent valid; the teacher of sociology will recognize in them, in part, the old dichotomy between theory and description. But the contradictory character of the criticisms suggests that something is wrong with the "public relations" side of social science. Since most people first encounter this field in the classroom, part of the trouble perhaps lies there.

Obviously social science, like any other science, must have a body of theory if it is to convey fundamental knowledge. It must have a conceptual framework and a system of empirical generalizations applicable to all societies before it can explain any particular society such as our own. It cannot therefore be a disorganized empirical miscellany. But unfortunately social theory is often taught in its "pure" form with no attempt to show its relevance to things familiar and important to the student. As a result the novice often acquires nothing more than some meaningless abstractions and a complicated vocabulary. As a reaction to this procedure many teachers have gone to the opposite extreme of teaching social science as merely a collection of facts about various social problems with no consistent organization or central theme. Nearly everyone realizes, of course, that both extremes are unsatisfactory, but the ideal solution—a formula that will combine systematic theory with empirical investigation, and science with human interest—is hard to find.

In the present book of readings the editors have sought one kind of solution. They have tried to bring social theory and empirical knowledge to bear upon the major problems of our own society by focusing on a central question profoundly important from both the theoretical and the practical points of view: the question of unity and continuity in American society. All the materials in the book are designed to help the student understand what gives order and disorder, unity and disunity, to our society as a whole. What are the forces giving continuity to the system and what are the forces responsible for deflection and discontinuity? How does our system retain a certain amount of consistency in the face of extremely rapid and pervasive social change? What are the sources of stress and strain?

We believe this focus to be an extremely practical as well as a significant device for organizing the study of society. It necessarily requires the integration of a very wide range of material, because our social order rests not on one but on many foundations. The contributions of sociology, social psychology, social anthropology, economics, and political science are essential to an understanding of the topics discussed, and an opportunity is thus provided for demonstrating the interrelation of the various aspects of social science. At the same time the organization of material around the problem of unity and continuity in American society permits the examination of many specific and pressing social maladjustments. It requires discussion of most of our major social problems—race relations, class antagonisms, religious friction, educational policy, recreational changes, and family disorganization. Finally, the necessity for a theoretical and analytical approach to the problems of society has been continually emphasized by the selection of materials which relate directly to the basic concept of the book.

The most convenient approach to the problem of unity and disunity in American society has seemed to us to lie in the relation between our system of values as it is expressed in the American ethos and as it is reflected in the actual functioning of our society. Therefore, the book takes as its point of departure the dominant values shared by Americans generally, because these values, these articles of faith of the American credo, furnish the main source of unity and cohesion in our society. Early in the book the reader will find the principles of American social philosophy stated in their classic form, including such doctrines as free speech, individual initiative, political democracy, equal opportunity, and fair play. Although these have the ring of slogans, they give expression to deeply rooted patterns of conduct and social organization which lie at the base of our institutional structure. Their nature and effects must be understood if American society is to be understood.

Teachers of sociology are painfully aware of the tendency of the student, when first invited to consider social values in relation to social institutions, to become moralistic. They have watched him abandon analysis and description of fact in favor of airing his opinions and speaking in terms of what ought to be rather than of what is, while at the same time deluding himself into believing that he is practicing social science and that his opinions as to what ought to be somehow have the weight of science behind them. To discourage this tendency we have placed at the very beginning, before the American credo is given, a chapter on the relation of science to value. Here it is made clear that values may be subjected to scientific study, but that they cannot be derived from such study; that science, in other words, deals with things as they are (including the values that people carry in their heads), while morality deals with things as they ought to be (according to somebody's subjective feeling of preference). The point of view underlying the present work is, therefore, that the American system of values is itself a fact—and one that plays an important role in defining the character of American society—but that whether these values are good or bad is a matter of subjective preference rather than objective fact. They could be scientifically regarded as efficient or inefficient if they were treated simply as means to more ultimate ends, but these values are taken as ultimate by most Americans, and it is precisely for this reason that they are important. As editors we have no intention of introducing gratuitously our own subjective values, regardless of whether or not these agree with the American credo. We have included some readings (such as a passage from *The Communist Manifesto*) that clearly uphold values contrary to the American system, but they have been chosen simply to clarify the alternatives and thereby to highlight the distinctive character of American ideals. If the student learns nothing more from these readings than the necessity of suspending judgment, of substituting factual scrutiny for the airing of opinions, he will have overcome the greatest single obstacle to the learning of social science.

The important characteristic of values, from the standpoint of the social scientist, is not the extent to which they are held, but the extent to which they are embodied in action. In what ways, for example, does the American social order carry out the social ideals for which it supposedly stands? In what ways does it fail to carry out these ideals? In so far as it fails, of course, something else besides these ideals is obviously at work—contrary principles, perhaps, or possibly nullifying conditions, or an inconsistency in the original value system itself. Hence we have tried to select materials that would illustrate both the embodiment of the central values and the failure to embody them in our social organization. Above all it has seemed necessary to sketch the changing conditions that have transformed the agricultural setting in which our values originated; to describe the urbanization that has inevitably brought new conditions and new values into conflict with the traditional ones; to include materials on the economic framework of our society, together with changes in this framework; and, wherever possible, to illustrate the sources of instability in American institutions. Like any other social system, the American system fails to embody its values perfectly in practice. In every aspect the social order is undergoing fundamental change. It should be clear that our purpose is neither to criticize nor to praise the American system of values, neither to debunk nor to absolve. It is rather to make possible, from a factual and analytic point of view, an examination of the sources of unity and disunity in American society in terms of the relation between the values we profess to live by and those which we actually do live by.

The materials are in large part descriptive, but some of them are analytical and others are argumentative. Their bearing on the central problem of the book should at all points be clear. This book furnishes the illustrative material; the instructor or reader himself should bring out their full significance by relating them to the central problem of unity and disunity in American society.

The selection of modern American society as the subject-area of this book should be self-explanatory. There is no society more interesting or more complex than our own. There is none which is more familiar or more important to all of us or which, conversely, students are more likely to know in small segments rather than as a whole. If the major task of social science is to evolve concepts and generalizations applicable to all societies, the most important use of these tools is for the analysis and explanation of our own social system. It is the editors' hope that this somewhat novel approach to the science of society will be particularly useful in courses in general sociology, social problems, and social science orientation, both by making the entire field of social science more meaningful to the student without sacrificing its systematic character and by leading him toward an understanding of the fundamental character of our own society.

The editors in no wise believe that the approach used in this book is the only possible one. American society and its relation to basic social theory can be approached from numerous points of view; the problem of unity and disunity in our society has simply seemed to us the most convenient and most fruitful point of departure. It is the general approach, the integration of theory and descriptive analysis, that seems to us fundamental, and we offer this attempt at integration in the hope that it will prove useful in bringing the teaching of sociology to the level that research and theoretical development have now made possible.

K. D.
May, 1949 H. C. B.
M. J. L., Jr.

ACKNOWLEDGMENTS

For indispensable work in the preparation of this volume, greatest acknowledgment is due Miss Mary Treyz, who, in excellent fashion, did most of the typing and all of the secretarial work.

A book of readings would of course be impossible if it were not for the kindness of publishers and authors in giving permission to use copyrighted materials. Although acknowledgment is given at the place in the volume where each selection is used, we are appending below a list of the publishers and publications who have been kind enough to let us use their materials, and to whom we express our great appreciation:

The American Academy of Political and Social Science
American Anthropologist
American Council on Education
American Journal of Sociology
American Sociological Review
Barnes & Noble, Inc.
The Catholic World
Christian Century Foundation
Columbia University Press
Conference on Science, Philosophy and Religion
F. S. Crofts & Co.
Thomas Y. Crowell Co.
Doubleday & Company
ETC: A Review of General Semantics
Harcourt, Brace and Company
Harper & Brothers
Harvard University Press
D. C. Heath and Company
Henry Holt and Company
Houghton Mifflin Company
Journal of Legal and Political Sociology
Alfred A. Knopf, Inc.
J. B. Lippincott Company
The Macmillan Company
Milbank Memorial Fund
William Morrow & Company
The Nation
New Centuries Publishers, Inc.
Prentice-Hall, Inc.
Psychiatry
Public Affairs Committee
Public Affairs Press
G. P. Putnam's Sons
Quarterly Journal of Studies on Alcohol
Random House, Inc.
The Rice Institute
Rinehart & Company, Inc.
Russell and Volkening, Inc.
Charles Scribner's Sons
Social Forces
Stanford University Press
The University of Chicago Press
University of Oklahoma Press
University of Pennsylvania Press
The Viking Press
John Wiley & Sons, Inc.
Yale University Press
Law and Contemporary Problems

CONTENTS

PART EIGHT: *Recreation: Leisure and Escape*

PART NINE: *Modern Marriage and the Family*

PART ONE

Scientific Understanding and American Values

CHAPTER I

Science, Value, and Social Analysis

One of the major problems facing social science today is that of settling the relation of science to value. This is a problem which arises in a doubly acute form in the social sciences. Like the natural sciences, the social sciences have to distinguish between questions asking "what is" and those asking "what ought to be." Unlike the natural sciences, however, the social sciences must, in addition, take into consideration the fact that questions of "what ought to be" seriously condition the phenomena under observation; namely, the actions of men in society. So far as is known no "values" alter in any way the phenomena under consideration from the point of view of physics or chemistry or geology or astronomy. But the values held by men do affect the actions of men, and a change in values does change their action. The two selections in this initial chapter were chosen in an effort first to distinguish clearly for the student science on the one hand and value or ethics or morals on the other; and second to indicate to the student that the impossibility of an ethic derived purely from science (in the sense of sharing the basic methodology of physics, chemistry, etc.) does not eliminate the possibility of a purely scientific treatment of the manner in which ethics affect the actions of men.

ETHICS AND SCIENCE *

In the last half of the 19th century people often dreamed of creating a scientific ethic. They were not content to praise the educational value of science, the advantages which the human soul gains for its own improvement by contact with truth seen face to face. They counted on science to place ethical truths beyond dispute as it had done for the theorems of mathematics and the laws affirmed by the physicists.

* Adapted from Poincaré, Henri, *Dernières Pensées* (Paris: Ernest Flammarion, Editeur, 1913), pp. 223–226, 241–243.

There are people who realize that religion can have great power over believers, but everyone is not a believer. Faith only imposes itself upon some; reason imposes itself upon everyone. It is to reason that we must turn, and I am not speaking of the metaphysician whose constructions are like soap bubbles which are amusing for a moment and burst. Such people feel that science alone builds solidly: it has built astronomy and physics; it is building biology today; by the same methods it will build ethics tomorrow. Its prescriptions will reign undisputed; no one will be able to whisper against them, and one will no more care to revolt against the moral law than anyone cares today to revolt against the theorem of the three perpendiculars or the law of gravity.

And on the other side there are persons who think the worst possible of science, who see in it a school of immorality. It is not only that it accords too great a place to the material sphere; but it removes the sense of respect because one respects only those things which one dares not investigate. They feel its conclusions become a negation of ethics. A famous author whose name I have forgotten has said that it extinguishes the lights of heaven or at least strips them of what mystery they have by reducing them to common gas burners. It unveils the tricks of the Creator who will lose to it some of his prestige. It is not good for children to look behind the scenes; that would cause them to doubt the existence of the Bogeyman. If one lets the scholars alone, there will be no more ethics.

What must we think of the hopes of the one and the fears of the other? I do not hesitate to answer: the one is as vain as the other. It is not possible to have a scientific ethic, but it is no more possible to have an immoral science. And the reason is simple; it is, how shall I put it, for purely grammatical reasons.

If the premises of a syllogism are both in the indicative, the conclusion will be equally in the indicative. In order for the conclusion to be put in the imperative it is necessary that at least one of the premises be in the imperative. Now the principles of science, the postulates of geometry, can only be in the indicative; experimental truths are also in this same mode, and at the foundations of the sciences there is not, cannot be, anything else. Moreover the most subtle dialectician can juggle with these principles as he wishes, combine them, pile them up one on the other; all that he can derive from them will be in the indicative. He will never obtain a proposition which says: do this, or don't do that; that is to say a proposition which confirms or contradicts values.

And this is the difficulty which the moralists have encountered for a long time. They have tried to prove the moral law; we must pardon them because it is their métier; they wish to rest ethics on something, as if it could rest on anything except itself. Science shows us that man can only degrade himself in a given manner; but what if I am not concerned about degrading myself, what if I call progress what you call degradation. . . .

There is still another manner of viewing the connections between science and value; there is no phenomenon which cannot be the object of science, since there is none which cannot be observed. Ethical phenomena escape no more than others. The naturalist studies societies of ants and bees, and he studies them calmly; similarly the scholar seeks to consider men as if he were not a man, to put himself in the place of some far away inhabitant of Sirius so that towns will be only ant hills. It is his right; it is his métier as a scholar.

The science of customs will be at first purely descriptive; it will teach us the customs of men and tell us what they are without telling us what they should be. Later it will be comparative; it will lead us in space to compare the customs of different people, those of the savage and the civilized man, and also in time it will lead us to compare those of yesterday with those of today. It will seek finally to become explanatory, and this is the natural evolution of all science. . . .

This science of customs is not a value, it can never be one; it can no more replace value than a treatise on the physiology of digestion can replace a good dinner. What I have already said above makes it unnecessary to labor this point further.

VALUES AND SOCIAL SCIENCE*

When we assign a value of any kind to an object or situation, we are making a value judgment. Illustrations may clarify the difference between such judgments and what are often called judgments of fact. When we say for instance, that a picture called "Aurora" was painted by Guido Reni, that the quantum theory accounts for certain phenomena of light, or that the Russian Revolution occurred in 1917, we are merely stating that certain situations exist, without giving them any value whatever. If we add that the "Aurora" is not a good painting, that the quantum theory is a beauti-

* Selected from Mary J. Shaw, "Social Valuation" in *Man and Society,* edited by Emerson P. Schmidt (New York: Prentice Hall, 1937), pp. 753–760, 762–763, 774–784, 786.

ful example of scientific reasoning, or that the Russian Revolution was a disaster, then we are making judgments of value. We are affirming that some object or state of affairs is good or bad, beautiful or ugly, or better or worse than some other possible situation.

Every language has such direct value terms as we have used in these judgments. In addition, many words which were once purely descriptive have become value terms through long use. The current slang and the current situation make new, if transitory, additions. Illustrations of such indirect terms for expressing approval or disapproval are good only for limited times and places, but for the United States in 1937, we may safely list "democratic," "practical," "vulgar," "modern," "un-American," "individualism," and "politician" as examples of the kind of thing we mean. Indeed there are so many of these indirect value terms that the social scientist who is trying to state the facts of social life without a coloring of approval or disapproval is forced either to define painstakingly the common words he uses or to invent a new vocabulary.

VALUE JUDGMENTS BASED ON PREFERENCE

The large number of value terms and the frequency of value judgments arise from the fact that preference is a fundamental human trait. Perhaps nothing about man is more conspicuous or more important than the obvious truth that he does not view the world of nature and society impartially. To him it is never a colorless and neutral scene. Some aspects of the environment interest him more than others and, among those that interest him, some attract and some repel. He pronounces them good or bad, better or worse, beautiful or ugly. He sees heroes and villains in natural forces and conceives a world nearer to his heart's desire.

These preferences are based on our own interests as biological and social individuals. All of the things which we judge to be good or desirable seem to us to make their contribution to satisfactory living. Some are more important than others, some fulfill permanent needs, some are transitory. Each person develops a pattern of living in which some goods are subordinated to others, and as many as possible are achieved. This is not easy, for the goods of life are limited, while those which can be had are not always compatible with each other. Furthermore, since no two men are the same, no two sets of values can be identical. Yet each has to take the other's evaluation as real and adjust himself to it as best he can, since all human beings are born into a society which they cannot leave and would not leave if they could.

Because nature and society do not furnish all of the good things which men's interests can suggest to their imaginations, we set up standards to which we try to make the world conform. Most men agree that this is not the best of all possible worlds and are reformers, on a small scale at least. They wish to change nature or social institutions, here a little, there a little, until a better situation is produced. A few bold souls, not content with such piecemeal improvement, hope to bring about wide-sweeping reorganizations of society. In any social group, therefore, imaginary utopias are as natural as any other social product.

Standards, like values, are constantly expressed in language. "There ought to be a better bridge over this river." "We should not allow our natural resources to be squandered." "No one should starve in the midst of plenty." "Examinations should be abolished." "Those who will not work should not eat." "The best government is a dictatorship of the proletariat." Every "ought," every "should" or "should not" in these judgments implies some ideal, some standard of values.

JUDGMENTS OF VALUE IN THE SOCIAL SCIENCES

So strong is this tendency to value and to set up standards, that it is only in exceptional cases, and after careful discipline, that most of us are able to view even a small area of the universe in an unprejudiced way. If the scene is very remote from our own life, we can look at it with little emotion, and perhaps abstain from passing judgment upon it. What the Chinese do, we may say, makes little difference to us. Or when we devote ourselves to the pursuit of science, we make a rigorous effort to exclude, for the time at least, all other interests except the interest in truth. The emphasis on scientific method, on scientific objectivity, in this book and elsewhere, is evidence that this is a difficult accomplishment. Even when we succeed we are still exhibiting preference, the preference for truth rather than falsehood.

Men have always valued knowledge; even those who do not rate it highly will agree that, within limits, it is a good thing. The limitation of its popularity is partly due to the fact that it is exclusive of other interests, at least for the time being. One who wishes to learn what the truth is about a subject must forget other preferences, leave out of consideration his likes and dislikes and questions of good and bad. The individual who classifies only some of the facts he is investigating to that extent defeats his own interest in truth. . . . The social scientist believes that, in order to treat social facts with impartiality, he must omit evaluations.

Values, moreover, are in some important ways quite different from matters of fact and, therefore, according to many social scientists, not suitable subject matter for scientific inquiry. A prominent sociologist says:

> The principal task of ethics in the past has been an elaboration of the prescription of *what ought to be* and *what ought not to be*. . . . So far as sociology professes that its scientific task consists in the study of social phenomena *as they have existed, do exist and will exist*, there is no direct connection between the two disciplines. . . . Natural sciences and other real sciences study the reality as it is, irrespective of whether it is "good" or "bad." [1]

This point of view has had its critics. One of them makes this comment:

> Some sociologists have banished from their program all questions of value and have sought to restrict themselves to the theory of social happenings. This effort to look upon human actions with the same ethical neutrality with which we view geometric figures, is admirable. But the questions of human value are inescapable, and those who banish them at the front door admit them unavowedly and therefore uncritically at the back door.[2]

Perhaps the social scientist does admit values at the back door; that is, he must take some of them for granted whether he considers them a part of his subject matter or not. But on the whole, as long as he consistently holds to his own idea of what the scientific method requires, he refuses to commit himself as to what he thinks is good or bad. Is communism worse than capitalism? Is the profit motive good for society as a whole? Should freedom of speech be curtailed? The scientist as a human being, an American, a Baptist, a Republican, or a philosopher may answer; as a scientist he has nothing to say. He will tell you what, as a matter of fact, the consequences are when freedom of speech is not allowed, how the profit motive operates in a market; he will not otherwise help you to choose between alternatives. And if anything in the presentation of his material gives the reader an inkling as to which side he is taking, his scientific colleagues are likely to bring him to book for wandering from

---

[1] Sorokin, Pitirim A., "Sociology and Ethics," in *The Social Sciences and Their Interrelations*, edited by Ogburn, William F., and Goldenweiser, Alexander, p. 311 (Houghton Mifflin Company, Boston, 1927).

[2] Cohen, Morris R., "The Social Sciences and the Natural Sciences," *op. cit.*, p. 453.

the narrow path of scientific rectitude, and accuse him of becoming a philosopher.

There is only one way in which the social scientist believes that he can safely treat of values and retain scientific impartiality; namely, he can discuss them as facts. For example, the anthropologist and the sociologist will necessarily include man's judgments of values, his ideals, and his standards as part of his non-material culture. The moral code of the Plains Indians is an important part of their whole culture pattern and, as such, is part of the subject matter of cultural anthropology. Beliefs of contemporary Americans about the desirability of divorce, about the value of going to church, or about the importance of discipline in bringing up children are all parts of the culture pattern and will be noted by the sociologist. . . .

CRITICAL REFLECTION AND SOCIAL VALUES

Because it is undeniably difficult, if not impossible, to come to final conclusions about questions of value, there is a tendency to assume that no intelligent methods can be applied to them. Here, as we sometimes say, one man's ideas are as good as another's. Yet even those who make this claim are likely to betray the fact that it is impossible to maintain such a point of view consistently. For if no comparison of values can be made, then we should not feel the necessity of giving reasons for our preferences. And yet we constantly do give reasons, and thereby imply that there are bases for our judgments of value which should convince reflective people. If we were consistent in the denial that any reasons could be given, we should be reduced to exclamation rather than to argument. "This is good" or "that is bad" would then be the last word about the matter. . . .

The preferences and values of an individual depend largely upon the groups to which, as we say significantly, he *belongs*. Inasmuch as he is a member of the group and participates in its activities, the interests of the group are necessarily his interests. The member of a family, of a church, of a trade union, of a fraternity, or of a nation, in so far as he is functionally part of the group, has accepted its standards, at least in part. For those standards express interests that the members have in common—the very thing that makes them a group.

Furthermore, everyone is born into one of these groups, the family, becomes an involuntary member of others, a school or possibly a church, and is trained in childhood to accept the standards of his group, long before he is in a position to make his own choices. From his elders, who express in their judgments of approval and disapproval the values of the group, he learns what he may successfully do as a member of his family and his neighborhood. It has always been a function of education to train the younger members of society in the behavior that is acceptable to those in control. Thus, education, particularly the training given by parents, brothers, or sisters, is conservative in the original meaning of the term. It conserves or saves the values of the group. In some societies this is the only function of education; in all societies schools are limited in the amount of criticism of the prevailing tradition which they dare introduce. . . .

As long as we stay at home, either physically or mentally, this business of taking our own code for granted, with little reflection upon it, works fairly well. But standards are sharply challenged when we move from one group into another. The student who leaves a small town to attend a university, the businessman who represents his firm abroad, the tourist who spends a summer in England or Russia—each finds himself among people whose loyalties are different from those to which he has given allegiance. The experience may be enlightening, but it is unlikely to be comfortable. If the contrast is marked, the individual feels lost, or on the defensive for the values which he holds. It is not difficult then to understand the astonishment of the South Sea islanders when they first heard from Christian missionaries that the amount of clothing one wears is an index to his moral condition. . . .

Modern civilizations are characterized by the complexity of the groupings that make them up. The individual is not merely a member of one unit, but of many. This is true, though to a much lesser degree, of all societies, even the primitive ones. But the increase of what we call civilization has brought division of social activity among many types of groups, each of which serves a slightly different purpose from that of any other. The membership of these groups necessarily overlaps. In a democratic state, lesser organizations are largely voluntary; the state regulates relations between them only to the extent that regulation is necessary to preserve the basic social system. Consequently any adult member of society is a member, by virtue of birth or of choice, of several groups.

The individual may have the good fortune to belong to social groupings that do not conflict; but inasmuch as the purpose of every organization differs from that of every other, it is likely that at times he will be confronted with the problem of bringing into harmony his own many-sided interests, of comparing standards which are incompatible and possibly irreconcilable. . . .

FREEDOM AS A SOCIAL VALUE

Liberty or freedom is a social value which has been highly prized in many societies, particularly in modern democratic nations. It has been conceived both as a right and as an ideal or standard for evaluating institutions and laws. So highly is it rated, in name at least, that even those governments which seem to restrict it most feel called upon to justify themselves on the ground that they are promoting "real" liberty as opposed to the supposedly spurious article to be had in nations that boast of their free institutions. . . .

When we analyze the notion of freedom as it has existed in the minds of those who have waged conflicts to gain it, two things become evident. It has usually been limited in the range of its application, and in the breadth of its meaning. Men have fought, not for the liberty of everyone, but for the liberty of a particular group, and they have had in mind, not liberty in general, but some partial aspect or particular embodiment of freedom.

It would be very difficult to say whether for the mass of the people there is more liberty today than there was, for instance, in the twelfth century. In any case, every historic struggle for freedom, no matter how wide its claims, resolved itself into the contest of a particular group to gain recognition of its own right to liberty. The Magna Charta of England, sometimes spoken of as a basic charter of English rights, as a matter of fact guaranteed protection of the barons against the encroachments of the king. The French Revolution, with its emphasis upon the rights of the common man, was at the same time a denial of most of the liberties of the nobility. The American Revolution was fought and won by the rather small part of the British Empire represented in the thirteen colonies in order to obtain relief from economic and political restrictions such as were almost universally imposed upon colonies in the eighteenth century. It did not attempt to free other colonies from those restrictions.

The appeal for greater liberty is thus usually the demand of one group for the right to compete on equal terms for the goods of life with other groups which have previously had an advantage. This motive often comes out clearly when an insurgent group gains its point, for frequently its success leads to its suppression of other helpless groups. The history of religious persecution furnishes numerous cases in which one oppressed sect gains its freedom, only to inflict persecution upon all dissenters within its own ranks.

We have stressed the fact that practical struggles for liberty have usually been carried on by groups interested in their own increased freedom. This fact is frequently overlooked and it is easy to forget, when we are promoting some form of liberty, that our aim may not be as broad as we are likely to believe. Nevertheless there has been here and there in European and American history the achievement of some types of liberty for very large groups of individuals, if not literally for everyone. In democratic nations, some kinds of freedom for almost all persons are guaranteed by law. The liberties are in fact often infringed upon, yet the theory is that any person can appeal for redress, since his rights are assured by the constitution of the state. The constitutional guarantee is designed to protect the individual or the group against aggression from others acting in behalf of their own selfish or unenlightened interests. Freedom of speech, of the press, and of religious worship, the right to trial by jury and to vote are among such liberties in the United States and England; the right to work is stressed in the new Russian constitution.

These illustrations bring us to the second limitation upon liberty. The liberty for which men struggle is usually specific, even though they state their ideal in general terms. The particular form of freedom demanded depends upon the circumstances and groups involved. The most conspicuous conflicts in European and American history have been described in terms of struggle for political and civil liberties. Sometimes, however, the more obvious struggle undoubtedly was for economic freedom. While the liberties which were finally guaranteed to Negroes during the American Civil War were civil and political, the underlying conflict was between two economic systems, neither of which seemed able to succeed without encroaching upon the other. A group which demands freedom may be thinking of the right to vote without coercion, of the right to think independently, to write and speak without fear of imprisonment, to hire and fire laborers without outside control, to strike against employers, of the right to work, or even to eat. . . .

In 1923 Mussolini stated the fascist attitude toward freedom in a manner which has since become familiar. "The plain truth that must stare into the eyes of anyone not blinded by dogmatism, is that men are perhaps tired of liberty. They have had an orgy of it. Today liberty is no longer the chaste stern virgin for whom the generations of the first half of last century fought and died. For the youth that is intrepid, restless and hard, that faces the dawn of the new history, there are other words of much greater power, and they are: order, hierarchy, discipline. . . . Let it be known therefore once and for all that fascism knows no idols and worships no fetishes; it has already passed over and if necessary will turn once more and quietly pass over the more or less decayed corpse of the Goddess Liberty." [3]

The liberties abolished by fascism are chiefly the rights to vote without coercion, to speak one's mind on controversial issues, and to ally oneself freely with organizations within the state. We shall consider here freedom of speech as a specific liberty which is conceived in democratic countries as, with few limitations, the right of all men.

Up to this point we have used the words "liberty" and "right" interchangeably. It would be well to consider briefly the relation between the two in order to avoid misunderstandings. First, a right is effective only in the society that guarantees it. The citizen of Germany in 1936 had, for instance, no effective right to freedom of speech, because the society in which he lived not only had failed to set up machinery for protecting such freedom, but actually forbade and punished its exercise. During the World War effective right to freedom of speech in the United States was much less than in times of peace.

What then do we mean when we say that we have the right to freedom even if that freedom is not operative in the society in which we live? To avoid confusion and unprofitable debate we need to take account of one fact, which is clear regardless of underlying ethical theory. When we say we have a right that we are not allowed to exercise within our existing group, we mean that the right in question is a valuable activity and that our society would be better if it guaranteed that value. We appeal, in other words, to an ideal situation which we think should be made actual in society. The German, for instance, who believed that he had a right to declare his convictions on political questions judged the existing state in the light of a social and ethical standard not exemplified in practice.

FREEDOM OF SPEECH

If the right is thus viewed as potential social value or good, the best rational defense of it lies in an exposition of the further social goods to which it leads. In terms of our previous analysis, this means that we treat the particular value as a mediate or instrumental good which leads to other goods about which agreement may exist. We shall consider freedom

[3] Mussolini, Benito, "Forza e Consenso," *Gerarchia,* March, 1923. Quoted in Schneider, Herbert W., *Making the Fascist State,* p. 342 (Oxford University Press, New York, 1928).

of speech from this point of view. Our question will be: What further social values does such freedom lead to, and what social evils does it guard against?

Let us begin with one of the more superficial justifications that have been given. It is often stated that free speech should be allowed because it furnishes a safety valve for dissatisfied elements within society who would otherwise be more dangerous to the stability of the social order. Particularly have the English been praised for the tolerance with which Hyde Park soap-box orators are allowed to say what they please, whether they advocate new religions, new governments, or new economic systems. The argument is good within limits, but it certainly is not a very profound one. For it seems to suggest either that social discontent is trifling and may therefore be taken out in talk, or that, if there is a fundamental social disharmony and discontent, it may evaporate in words. Both assumptions are false. The validity of such defense of free speech lies in the fact that there are minor discontents which free speech renders less violent.

A more basic justification, and perhaps the one most frequently offered, is that freedom of speech is ultimately a safeguard against the tyranny of the government and of smaller groups within the state. Free speech therefore guarantees and preserves many other goods which can flourish only in the absence of tyranny. In a state which allows free criticism of the groups in power, there is at least the possibility of pointing out abuses and arousing an effective public opinion against them. The force of this argument is attested to by the fact that wherever tyrannical governments arise, freedom of speech is one of the first social values attacked. It is not to the interest of the ruler to have his action subject to criticism, however valuable such criticism might be to the citizens. Conversely, when freedom of speech is abolished, there is reason to suspect that the government recognizes its own tyrannical character, although, of course, it rationalizes its tyranny as an interest in the public welfare.

There is need for free speech not only under autocratic governments but also in those countries in which a constitution and a long tradition guarantee many civil liberties. Oppression of individuals and of groups by others is always possible, and the only recourse against it may lie in public opinion aroused by the free speaking of those who know and resent these wrongs. Illustrations of this need for free speech could be given at great length. In the United States, to take an obvious example, where trial by jury is guaranteed in criminal cases, Negroes are sometimes lynched. At the same time an active minority is engaged in arousing general opposition to this clear case of injustice and has had a large measure of success.

There are, however, more positive gains from free speech in a democratic country than the ones we have so far discussed. Democracy implies a large degree of free discussion if it is to exist as such, for democracy involves a decision of many important questions by a majority. If the decision is to reflect a majority opinion, there must be the widest possible discussion of the issues involved. And since the majority may be wrong —and undoubtedly it often is wrong—the minority has the social value of continuing to point out another course which might better have been followed. This remains true in spite of the notorious faults of the method by which a majority decision is reached. Free discussion does not insure a wise decision, but it does furnish a basis on which it is possible to improve the character of decisions. It has been suggested frequently that a body of experts should present facts to the people so that they might have a sound basis for their vote upon issues. This, however, would not change the essential situation which we are discussing here, for freedom must be guaranteed to those experts if their statements are to be of use. Every such scheme therefore includes elaborate precautions against even indirect pressure upon such a group, as this might prevent their giving a complete and unbiased account of their findings. . . .

LIMITATIONS UPON FREEDOM OF SPEECH

If freedom of speech has the social values which we have indicated, does it follow that no limitations should be set upon it? Some ardent advocates say yes. If, however, free speech is defended as a social good, as it has been throughout this discussion, then it is impossible to decide, before examining the facts, whether it should sometimes be subject to limitation. For although it leads to social consequences which are undeniably good, it is after all not the only social value. We should expect that in practice, where it must take its chances with other social goods, it would sometimes have to be limited.

If we examine the kinds of situations in which it is actually limited, we discover that the other social good with which it most frequently comes into conflict is order, or stability. Speech is closely linked to action; those who desire freedom in its exercise do so because they hope to influence the behavior of other men. In practice every society, therefore, when it feels its existence or its stability endangered, places a ban upon free speech. War times furnish the clearest examples, but peace times have their illustrations as well. In Russia, for example, when pressure from the outside world upon the Soviets appeared most dangerous, restrictions upon thought and opinion were most severe. Can public order and social stability in a democratic country ever be so threatened by free speech that a ban should be placed upon it? This cannot be decided beforehand. When war comes, most of us at least acquiesce in restrictions which we would not tolerate in times of peace. In England in 1936 it seemed necessary to the authorities to prevent the free speaking of the organized fascist group, because in parts of London it led to violence against citizens who were entitled to protection.

While we may say that there are circumstances in which it is necessary that one liberty must be curtailed for the sake of other things, it is well to remember as a practical maxim that it is unwise to give up any value lightly. Freedom of speech will at times be subject to attack by any selfish group which feels that its private good is endangered by free criticism. The burden of proof for restriction of such freedom of speech lies upon those who attack it.

The difficulties inherent in resolving conflicts of rights suggest that, in the last analysis, the balancing of values which come into conflict is an art, not a science. Because values are not accurately measurable and consequences can be only partially foreseen, we are forced to act without complete assurance regarding the value of the outcome. And yet we are forced to act. Reflection upon values and knowledge about the social world are better guides than blind prejudice, but even when they are most complete and discriminating, there is still a large area of uncertainty. To complain about the existence of this difficulty would be to misunderstand completely our human situation. For that which is true of action in the social field is true of action of any kind. Whatever we do, we make assumptions about a future state of affairs which is in a measure unpredictable. We act upon probabilities and take risks. If we refused to do so, we should, of course, cease to live. Risk is a necessary condition of all action. Risks may be taken after much reflection or after little, but the outcome is usually favorably affected by previous thought. It is not a criticism of thinking to point out that it is never final or absolute.

The complete objectivity which the social scientist tries to achieve in his study of social facts may be necessary to discover fact and distinguish it from fiction. Outside of the scientific field, complete objectivity is an inappropriate ideal, perhaps a contradiction in terms. For objectivity means exclusion of all interests except one, the interest in truth. Yet the fact that we are living beings means that we have many interests, preferences, and aims. They must seek fulfillment in an uncertain world. . . .

CHAPTER II

The American Credo

What is "Americanism"? The answers have been so nearly legion, and so many of them have been cloaks for the pursuit of special interests, that the term itself has become suspect to many thoughtful Americans. Nevertheless, there *is* a core of sentiments and ideas, of values and principles, of beliefs and ideals, that nearly all Americans would agree to. These are "what America stands for."

Like every other society the United States has a creed stating the ultimate convictions of its members—convictions that are regarded as beyond question, as naturally basic truths. It is this creed which gives the society its integration—its order. It is also the pursuit of this dynamic creed that leads to drastic changes in the environment, changes that affect the creed in turn; yet whatever the changes that occur, they are always evaluated in terms of the existing value system.

In short, there is forever going on a process of mutual adaptation between our values and our social organization. Neither can be understood without the other; behavior apart from motives and motives apart from behavior are meaningless. In the present book we start with the values, with the American Credo, because it is here that the motives of Americans are summed up. It is here that the basic principles of our society receive their dynamic expression.

In the sections that follow, some of the great and crucial statements of the American value system are presented. They illustrate the essential features of the American Creed, as well as the profound problems connected with its application. The statements range in time from 1775 to 1947, and in subject from freedom of speech to American rules of pugnacity. The ultimate faiths evidenced and reported are the framework within which the remaining parts of the book must be understood. Along with these statements from the literature is included such discussion as may illuminate the implicit assumptions and social significance of the statements. The reader is asked to reflect carefully on the values here delineated and discussed. They are *his* values, but so often are they taken for granted and acted upon unconsciously that their full meaning is not usually understood.

FREEDOM AND INDEPENDENCE

When one speaks of America, one thinks in the first place of a nation, the United States, a sovereign and independent country. National independence is a strong ingredient in the American conception of freedom and liberty, and Americans have always been traditionally in favor of peoples or groups struggling for nationhood.

National independence is not, however, viewed as solely an end in itself. It is also a means to other ends, especially to another kind of freedom and liberty which is that of the individual with respect to his government. Americanism implies a certain kind of political democracy in which governmental power is viewed as securing the private person in his pursuit of ends that he considers good. This conception gives a certain structure to our national political institutions. The idea that men should be free, that *all* men should be *equally* free, and that one of the most important goals of social change should be an ever-greater increase of freedom, is an idea that both limits and directs the course of social action. The ideal of liberty through democracy is dramatically expressed, in words that Americans are taught to venerate, in the Declaration of Independence.

We hold these truths to be self-evident, that all men are created equal, that they are endowed by their Creator with certain unalienable Rights, that among these are Life, Liberty and the pursuit of Happiness. That to secure these rights, Governments are instituted among Men, deriving their just powers from the consent of the governed, That whenever any Form of Government becomes destructive of these ends, it is the Right of the People to alter or to abolish it, and to institute new Government, laying its foundation on such principles and organizing its powers in such form, as to them shall seem most likely to effect their Safety and Happiness.

Prudence, indeed, will dictate that Governments long established should not be changed for light and transient causes; and accordingly all experience hath shewn, that mankind are more disposed to suffer, while evils are sufferable, than to right themselves by abolishing the forms to which they are accustomed. But when a long train of abuses and usurpations, pursuing invariably the same object, evidence a design to reduce them under absolute Despotism, it is their right, it is their duty, to throw off such Government, and to provide new Guards for their future security.

And yet, the difficulty of defining the condition of freedom is notorious. The burden of the dictionary definition is that freedom is the condition of being without obligation to, or coercion by, any outside agent or agency. And, interestingly enough, this negative conception of freedom—that is, as freedom from restraint—seems to be the dominating theme in the articles of the Constitution that guarantee the basic "rights" of Americans:[1]

Article I. Congress shall make no law respecting an establishment of religion, or prohibiting the free exercise thereof; or abridging the freedom of speech, or of the press; or the right of the people peaceably to assemble, and to petition the Government for a redress of grievances. . . .
Article IV. The right of the people to be secure in their persons, houses, papers, and effects, against unreasonable searches and seizures, shall not be violated, and no Warrants shall issue, but upon probable cause, supported by Oath or affirmation, and particularly describing the place to be searched, and the persons or things to be seized.
Article V. No person shall be held to answer for a capital, or otherwise infamous crime, unless on a presentment or indictment of a Grand Jury, except in cases arising in the land or naval forces, or in the Militia, when in actual service in time of War or public danger; nor shall any person be subject for the same offence to be twice put in jeopardy of life or limb; nor shall be compelled in any criminal case to be a witness against himself, nor be deprived of life, liberty, or property, without due process of law; nor shall private property be taken for public use, without just compensation.
Article VI. In all criminal prosecutions, the accused shall enjoy the right

[1] Richardson, ed. *Messages and Papers,* Vol. I, p. 21 ff.

to a speedy and public trial, by an impartial jury of the State and district wherein the crime shall have been committed, which districts shall have been previously ascertained by law, and to be informed of the nature and cause of the accusation; to be confronted with the witnesses against him; to have compulsory process for obtaining witnesses in his favor, and to have the Assistance of Counsel for his defence.

Article VIII. Excessive bail shall not be required, nor excessive fines imposed, nor cruel and unusual punishments inflicted.

Article IX. The enumeration in the Constitution, of certain rights, shall not be construed to deny or disparage others retained by the people.

Article XIII. Sec. 1. Neither slavery nor involuntary servitude, except as a punishment for crime whereof the party shall have been duly convicted, shall exist within the United States, or any place subject to their jurisdiction.

Sec. 2. Congress shall have power, by appropriate legislation, to enforce the provisions of this article.

Article XIV. Sec. 1. All persons born or naturalized in the United States, and subject to the jurisdiction thereof, are citizens of the United States and of the State wherein they reside. No State shall make or enforce any law which shall abridge the privileges or immunities of citizens of the United States; nor shall any State deprive any person of life, liberty, or property, without due process of law; nor deny to any person within its jurisdiction the equal protection of the laws.

Article XV. Sec. 1. The right of citizens of the United States to vote shall not be denied or abridged by the United States or by any State on account of race, color, or previous condition of servitude.

Sec. 2. The Congress shall have power to enforce this article by appropriate legislation.

It is not surprising that the people of the 17th and 18th centuries, who found old values and institutions thwarting their efforts to follow newly emergent lines of action, should conceive of freedom as the absence of restraining influences. But neither is it surprising that the conception of freedom they worked out should in many cases prove inapplicable to conditions of a later date.

If freedom is defined as the absence of limitations upon either the ends that men might pursue or the means for achieving those ends, then it follows that the individual is the freer, the more alternative ways of behaving he has available—that is, the wider his range of ends and the greater his available means.[2]

But freedom also involves the ability to *act;* and since action requires decision, freedom must include the possession of criteria for choosing among the alternatives. An abundance of alternatives without criteria for choice may leave the individual helpless and impotent. On the other hand, the possession of criteria for choosing among ends automatically eliminates some ends from the running, as it were. Ultimately, then, freedom is limited to freedom of choice among means, some means being immediate ends sought in order to achieve a further end, but all means being weighed, accepted, or rejected on grounds of whether or not they contribute to the realization of the ultimate end in view.

It follows from this that, objectively speaking, the individual whose goals, or standards of preference, rule out the smallest number of possible means is the freest individual, other things being equal. Thus, for example, the individual whose goal, let us say, is wealth and who considers that murder is a legitimate means of satisfaction, is freer, other things being equal, than the individual with the same goals but with the *additional* end of avoiding murder.

If we now regard the individual as a member of society, there are additional limits to freedom that we must note. Since the satisfaction of many of his goals is dependent upon the performance of other members of society, the individual is the freer, the more nearly others do what is most instrumental to his ends. There are two types of situations in which others might behave so accommodatingly: (1) They may have values the satisfaction of which leads them to behave in a manner that contributes to the achievement of our individual's ends; or (2) the individual in question may be able to control the others so that, regardless of their values, they behave instrumentally for his goals. Now, the "other members" of society are by definition not free in the

---

[2] "Availability" should be understood to mean that the means are *known* to the actor, that he is *allowed* to use them, and that he *can obtain* them. For example, the consumer who does not know that the ten dollar shirts in Sax Bros. sell for three dollars at Mabels is, in so far, unfree. (Ignorance.) The teacher who is prevented from assigning James Joyce's *Ulysses* to her classes is, in so far, unfree. (Proscription.) And the New York worker who knows of a better job in Chicago and is legally and morally free to move but who lacks the railroad fare is, in so far, unfree. (Unobtainability.)

second case, and may or may not be *as* free as our individual in the first case.

If individuals in a society are to be *equally* free, the freedom of each must be limited not only by the ultimate values shared in common, but also by the condition that no one be free to acquire more control over others than the others have over him. The latter condition is met when two further conditions are met—namely, (1) when no individual has more alternatives than any other individual; and (2) when the intensity of desire for goals is the same for all persons. But it needs little reflection to see that these are impossible conditions for a society to realize fully. They are capable of only partial embodiment in the social structure. In the United States there are not only great inequalities in the access to means, but also great inequalities in the urgency and strength with which people cling to certain ends. Many of the legal, political, and economic conflicts in American life arise from the constant reinterpretation and redefinition of the ambiguous concept, freedom, in an effort to approach the conditions necessary for equality of freedom, which is one of the supreme American goals.

FREEDOM OF SPEECH

The perennial problem of free speech, for example, plagues every generation of Americans. One of the major perplexities in the maintenance of this value is that it is self-contradictory. Shall the person who does not believe in the value of "free speech" be allowed to speak freely in a way that will undermine this value? If so, then this great goal is being abandoned to possible self-elimination. If, on the other hand, free speech is to be denied to those who, if given power, would eliminate this goal, then the goal itself is being limited, at least partially. Some people have tried to solve this dilemma by asserting that it will do no "harm" to let people who detest free speech utilize this freedom to undermine it. But such a solution is logically fallacious, because it implies that speech itself is harmless, a proposition which, if true, means that it makes no difference whether speech is free or not.

Not only is absolute free speech self-contradictory, but it also conflicts with other major values. Americans say that they believe in racial and religious equality, but we know that one of the most damaging ways to perpetuate and expand racial and religious inequality is to permit one group to circulate false rumors about another. Americans also wish to maintain a certain amount of decency in matters concerning the family, the nation, and the individual. They will not, therefore, tolerate absolute free speech the effect of which would be, in their view, to undermine morals, to affront the symbols of national dignity, or to invade the rights of the individual to protection and security. In the last analysis, absolute freedom of speech, like absolute freedom of action, would make it impossible to have a society, because it would make it impossible to have a system of basic values held in common. Thus there is a contradiction between the belief that everyone should have the same chance to say what he thinks and the belief that everyone should have the same basic values—or at least, that certain basic values should always reign supreme over others.

The solution of this dilemma lies, it seems, in accepting the fact that no value can be absolutely supreme. Each value, however absolutely it may be stated in words, is actually limited in practice by the fact that the community has *other* values that are also important. If free speech is held as a major value, then it is presumably maintained so far as possible, but only to the extent that it does not do irreparable damage to the other major values cherished by the community. One of the classic statements along this line was formulated by Supreme Court Justice Oliver Wendell Holmes in a decision [3] reprinted below as a concrete illustration of the kind of compromise that comes to establish, for a time, a pattern for action. The case in question concerned the constitutionality of the Espionage Act of June 15, 1917. The defendants alleged that the act violated the First Amendment of the Constitution.

Holmes, J. This is an indictment in three counts. The first charges a conspiracy to violate the Espionage Act of June 15, 1917 . . . by causing and attempting to cause insubordination, &c., in the military and naval forces of the United States, and to obstruct the recruiting and enlistment service of the United States, when the United Sates was at war with the German Empire, to wit, that the defendants wilfully conspired to have printed and circu-

[3] Opinion of Mr. Justice Holmes in *Schenck v. United States.* 249 U. S. 47, 1919.

lated to men who had been called and accepted for military service under the Act of May 18, 1917, a document set forth and alleged to be calculated to cause such insubordination and obstruction. The count alleges overt acts in pursuance of the conspiracy, ending in the distribution of the document set forth. . . . They set up the First Amendment to the Constitution forbidding Congress to make any law abridging the freedom of speech, or of the press, and bringing the case here on that ground have argued some other points also of which we must dispose.

It is argued that the evidence, if admissible, was not sufficient to prove that the defendant Schenck was concerned in sending the documents. . . . Without going into confirmatory details that were proved, no reasonable man could doubt that the defendant Schenck was largely instrumental in sending the circulars about. . . .

The document in question upon its first printed side recited the first section of the Thirteenth Amendment, said that the idea embodied in it was violated by the Conscription Act and that a conscript is little better than a convict. In impassioned language it intimated that conscription was despotism in its worse form and a monstrous wrong against humanity in the interest of Wall Street's chosen few. It said, "Do not submit to intimidation," but in form at least confined itself to peaceful measures such as a petition for the repeal of the act. The other and later printed side of the sheet was headed "Assert Your Rights." It stated reasons for alleging that anyone violated the Constitution when he refused to recognize "your right to assert your opposition to the draft," and went on "If you do not assert and support your rights, you are helping to deny or disparage rights which it is the solemn duty of all citizens and residents of the United States to retain." It described the arguments on the other side as coming from cunning politicians and a mercenary capitalist press, and even silent consent to the conscription law as helping to support an infamous conspiracy. It denied the power to send our citizens away to foreign shores to shoot up the people of other lands, and added that words could not express the condemnation such cold-blooded ruthlessness deserves, &c., &c., winding up "You must do your share to maintain, support and uphold the rights of the people of this country." Of course the document would not have been sent unless it had been intended to have some effect, and we do not see what effect it could be expected to have upon persons subject to the draft except to influence them to obstruct the carrying of it out. The defendants do not deny that the jury might find against them on this point.

But it is said, suppose that that was the tendency of this circular, it is protected by the First Amendment to the Constitution. . . . We admit that in many places and in ordinary times the defendants in saying all that was said in the circular would have been within their constitutional rights. But the character of every act depends upon the circumstances in which it is done. . . . The most stringent protection of free speech would not protect a man in falsely shouting fire in a theatre and causing a panic. It does not even protect a man from an injunction against uttering words that may have all the effect of force. . . . The question in every case is whether the words used are used in such circumstances and are of such a nature as to create a clear and present danger that they will bring about the substantive evils that Congress has a right to prevent. It is a question of proximity and degree. When a nation is at war many things that might be said in time of peace are such a hindrance to its effort that their utterance will not be endured so long as men fight and that no Court should regard them as protected by any constitutional right. It seems to be admitted that if an actual obstruction of the recruiting service were proved, liability for words that produced that effect might be enforced. The statute of 1917 in sec. 4 punishes conspiracies to obstruct as well as actual obstruction. If the act, (speaking, or circulating a paper,) its tendency and the intent with which it is done are the same, we perceive no ground for saying that success alone warrants making the act a crime. . . .

Another attempt to state the limits of freedom of political speech and action is contained in a statement of the famous Dies Committee on Un-American Activities.

TREATMENT OF SUBVERSIVES *

There is at present taking place in the world a struggle between democracy on the one hand and dictatorship on the other, upon the outcome of which the future of human liberties in the next few centuries may well depend.

As long as this struggle continues the American Nation, along with other true democracies in the world, faces a serious dilemma. It is of primary importance to prevent the growth or spread of influence of any

* Report of the Dies Committee on Un-American Activities (January 3, 1940), U. S. 76th Congress, 3d Session, *House Report,* No. 1476.

organization or group which seeks to undermine democracy and substitute dictatorship of whatever sort for it. But it is at least equally important that in combating subversive groups of this character nothing be done which would undermine the fundamental structure of constitutional liberty itself.

One method which can and should from time to time be used is the method of investigation to inform the American people of the activities of any such organizations in their nation. This is the real purpose of the House Committee to Investigate un-American Activities. By un-American activities we mean organizations or groups existing in the United States which are directed, controlled or subsidized by foreign governments or agencies and which seek to change the policies and form of government of the United States in accordance with the wishes of such foreign governments. . . .

The Committee conceives its principal task to have been the revelation of the attempts now being made by extreme groups in this country to deceive the great mass of earnest and devoted American citizens. The Committee finds that the danger to American democracy lies not only in the rather remote possibility that Communists, Nazis, or Fascists will succeed in a frontal attack on our Constitutional government and overthrow it, but also in the much greater chance that each extreme totalitarian group seeking by deception to advance its own cause and pad its ranks will succeed in convincing a really substantial number of people that their only defense against violence from the opposite extreme is to accept the violence of the one they find least objectionable.

The Committee condemns without reservation the evident willingness of some supposedly responsible people to endanger the very civil peace of their country by encouraging, for purely political purposes, suspicion, fear, and bigotry of the worst sort. Those on the right of political center cannot in the long run be benefited nor can they save their country by attempting to brand as Communists all those on the left of that center. Conversely, those on the left cannot advance their cause nor save their country by leveling the charge of fascism and attempting to brand as tools of Hitler all who would proceed more slowly than themselves.

The Committee's work should result in freeing the progressive and labor movements from Communist control or domination and in preventing sincere conservatives from temporizing with essentially Fascist or Nazi groups or philosophies. If the findings of this Committee were to be used as a pretext for the building of an un-American movement of any sort on the excuse that such a movement were "necessary to combat such-and-such a danger to the country," clearly a disservice to our democratic institutions would have been done. The Committee wishes to state emphatically that the only proper and democratic method whereby un-American activities can be effectively combated is by the duly constituted law-enforcing bodies of America operating under our Constitution and with the support of an informed public opinion. . . .

American labor has borne the brunt of the Communist efforts to pursue the policy of penetration of mass organizations in the past 4 years and, to the degree that that effort has been successful, American labor has a task of great seriousness and importance on its hands. The serious factor in the situation, from the standpoint of the Nation as a whole, lies not so much in the purely economic views which the members of labor organizations may hold, as in the foreign control over Communist Party members, which might in time of stress lead to sabotage and to espionage, and in the Communist rule-or-ruin policy so disruptive to the labor organizations themselves.

The Committee believes that the American labor movement must, and will, as speedily as possible, free itself of Communist leadership and control wherever it exists.

The Committee is emphatic in its belief that a strong and vigorous labor movement is an element of strength in the life of our democracy. But the Committee must assert that the Communist Party is interested in trade-unions primarily for the purpose of attempting to utilize those labor organizations for the benefit of the Russian dictatorship and its foreign policies.

NAZI-FASCIST ORGANIZATIONS

The Committee heard numerous witnesses and received a large volume of documentary evidence concerning the extent, nature and activities of a number of Nazi-Fascist groups, individuals and organizations which are presently operating in the United States, or which have recently been active in this country. . . .

From the evidence which has been heard, the primary aims of these groups appear to be (1) a radical change in the American form of government, and (2) the collection of dues from such misguided citizens as will contribute to their support. The evidence also reflects that these various groups are engaged in a form of racketeering as well as in subversive activities. When the money ceases to flow into the coffers of one organization they abandon it and start another one. These groups and organizations make their chief appeal to the basest forms of religious and racial hatred. They promise to deliver this country from the menace of communism; they heap scorn upon the institutions of democracy; and they urge the short cuts of force and violence.

FREEDOM FROM SPECIAL PRIVILEGE

Whenever conditions defining the relationships among men change, as change they inevitably do in as dynamic and unstable a society as the United States, the concrete denotation of such a value symbol as *freedom* must change also. The new situation calls for a new interpretation of the old values, but it is still the old values in terms of which the new situation is appraised. Witness, for example, the linkage between traditional faiths and changed circumstances made by Woodrow Wilson shortly before World War I.*

No matter how often we think of it, the discovery of America must each time make a fresh appeal to our imaginations. . . .

How always have men's hearts beat as they saw the coast of America rise to their view! How it has always seemed to them that the dweller there would at last be rid of kings, of privileged classes, and of all those bonds which had kept men depressed and helpless, and would there realize the full fruition of his sense of honest manhood, would there be one of a great body of brothers, not seeking to defraud and deceive one another, but seeking to accomplish the general good!

What was in the writings of the men who founded America,—to serve the selfish interests of America? Do you find that in their writings? No; to serve the cause of humanity, to bring liberty to mankind. They set up their standards here in America in the tenet of hope, as a beacon of encouragement to all the nations of the world; and men came thronging to these shores with an expectancy that never existed before, with a confidence they never dared feel before, and found here for generations together a haven of peace, of opportunity, of equality.

* From: *The New Freedom* by Woodrow Wilson, copyright 1913, 1933, by Doubleday & Company, Inc., pp. 277–288, 290–292.

God send that in the complicated state of modern affairs we may recover the standards and repeat the achievements of that heroic age!

For life is no longer the comparatively simple thing it was. Our relations one with another have been profoundly modified by the new agencies of rapid communication and transportation, tending swiftly to concentrate life, widen communities, fuse interests, and complicate all the processes of living. The individual is dizzily swept about in a thousand new whirlpools of activities. Tyranny has become more subtle, and has learned to wear the guise of mere industry, and even of benevolence. Freedom has become a somewhat different matter. It cannot,—eternal principle that it is,—it cannot have altered, yet it shows itself in new aspects. Perhaps it is only revealing its deeper meaning.

What is liberty?

I have long had an image in my mind of what constitutes liberty. Suppose that I were building a great piece of powerful machinery, and suppose that I should so awkwardly and unskilfully assemble the parts of it that every time one part tried to move it would be interfered with by the others, and the whole thing would buckle up and be checked. Liberty for the several parts would consist in the best possible assembling and adjustment of them all, would it not? If you want the great piston of the engine to run with absolute freedom, give it absolutely perfect alignment and adjustment with the other parts of the machine, so that it is free, not because it is let alone or isolated, but because it has been associated most skilfully and carefully with the other parts of the great structure.

What is liberty? You say of the locomotive that it runs free. What do you mean? You mean that its parts are so assembled and adjusted that friction is reduced to a minimum, and that it has perfect adjustment. We say of a boat skimming the water with light foot, "How free she runs," when we mean, how perfectly she is adjusted to the force of the wind, how perfectly she obeys the great breath out of the heavens that fills her sails. Throw her head up into the wind and see how she will halt and stagger, how every sheet will shiver and her whole frame be shaken, how instantly she is "in irons," in the expressive phrase of the sea. She is free only when you have let her fall off again and have recovered once more her nice adjustment to the forces she must obey and cannot defy.

Human freedom consists in perfect adjustments of human interests and human activities and human energies.

Now, the adjustments necessary between individuals, between individuals and the complex institutions amidst which they live, and between those institutions and the government, are infinitely more intricate today than ever before. No doubt this is a tiresome and roundabout way of saying the thing, yet perhaps it is worth while to get somewhat clearly in our mind what makes all the trouble today. Life has become complex; there are many more elements, more parts, to it than ever before. And, therefore, it is harder to keep everything adjusted,—and harder to find out where the trouble lies when the machine gets out of order.

You know that one of the interesting things that Mr. Jefferson said in those early days of simplicity which marked the beginnings of our government was that the best government consisted in as little governing as possible. And there is still a sense in which that is true. It is still intolerable for the government to interfere with our individual activities except where it is necessary to interfere with them in order to free them. But I feel confident that if Jefferson were living in our day he would see what we see: that the individual is caught in a great confused nexus of all sorts of complicated circumstances, and that to let him alone is to leave him helpless as against the obstacles with which he has to contend; and that, therefore, law in our day must come to the assistance of the individual. It must come to his assistance to see that he gets fair play; that is all, but that is much. Without the watchful interference, the resolute interference, of the government, there can be no fair play between individuals and such powerful institutions as the trusts. Freedom today is something more than being let alone. The program of a government of freedom must in these days be positive, not negative merely.

Well, then, in this new sense and meaning of it, are we preserving freedom in this land of ours, the hope of all the earth?

Have we, inheritors of this continent and of the ideals to which the fathers consecrated it,—have we maintained them, realizing them, as each generation must, anew? . . .

The answer must be, I am sure, that we have been in a fair way of failure,—tragic failure. And we stand in danger of utter failure yet except we fulfill speedily the determination we have reached, to deal with the new and subtle tyrannies according to their deserts. Don't deceive yourselves for a moment as to the power of the great interests which now dominate our development. They are so great that it is almost an open question whether the government of the United States can dominate them or not. Go one step further, make their organized power permanent, and it may be too late to turn back. . . .

I do not believe that America is securely great because she has great men in her now. America is great in proportion as she can make sure of having great men in the next generation. She is rich in her unborn children;

rich, that is to say, if those unborn children see the sun in a day of opportunity, see the sun when they are free to exercise their energies as they will. If they open their eyes in a land where there is no special privilege, then we shall come into a new era of American greatness and American liberty; but if they open their eyes in a country where they must be employees or nothing, if they open their eyes in a land of merely regulated monopoly, where all the conditions of industry are determined by small groups of men, then they will see an America such as the founders of this Republic would have wept to think of. . . .

The welfare, the happiness, the energy and spirit of the men and women who do the daily work in our mines and factories, on our railroads, in our offices and ports of trade, on our farms and on the sea, is the underlying necessity of all prosperity. . . . Their physical welfare affects the soundness of the whole nation. How would it suit the prosperity of the United States, how would it suit business, to have a people that went every day sadly or sullenly to their work? How would the future look to you if you felt that the aspiration had gone out of most men, the confidence of success, the hope that they might improve their condition? Do you not see that just so soon as the old self-confidence of America, just so soon as her old boasted advantage of individual liberty and opportunity, is taken away, all the energy of her people begins to subside, to slacken, to grow loose and pulpy, without fiber, and men simply cast about to see that the day does not end disastrously with them?

So we must put heart into the people by taking the heartlessness out of politics, business, and industry. We have got to make politics a thing in which an honest man can take his part with satisfaction because he knows that his opinion will count as much as the next man's, and that the boss and the interests have been dethroned. Business we have got to untrammel, abolishing tariff favors, and railroad discrimination, and credit denials, and all forms of unjust handicaps against the little man. Industry we have got to humanize,—not through the trusts,—but through the direct action of law guaranteeing protection against dangers and compensation for injuries, guaranteeing sanitary conditions, proper hours, the right to organize, and all the other things which the conscience of the country demands as the workingman's right. We have got to cheer and inspirit our people with the sure prospects of social justice and due reward, with the vision of the open gates of opportunity for all. We have got to set the energy and the initiative of this great people absolutely free, so that the future of America will be greater than the past, so that the pride of America will grow with achievement, so that America will know as she advances from generation to generation that each brood of her sons is greater and more enlightened than that which preceded it, know that she is fulfilling the promise that she has made to mankind.

INDIVIDUALISM IN THE AMERICAN CREDO

Closely related to freedom is the thesis of individualism—the feeling that each person has an intrinsic merit of his own, that each individual's own aims and attitudes are important above all else. This value manifests itself in a hundred ways and is expressed in countless verbal formulae. Sometimes it is said that man is the measure of all things; that institutions are created for man, not man for institutions; that man's own conscience is his truest guide; that being oneself, self-expression, individual happiness are among the greatest goods of life.

An excellent expression of the doctrine of individualism is the following impromptu statement by David E. Lilienthal, made in response to a question before the Congressional Committee on Atomic Energy. The Committee was examining Mr. Lilienthal on his fitness for the post of Chairman of the Atomic Energy Commission. A Congressman who had charged Lilienthal with incompetence and with Communist sympathies, at one point criticized him for not "carrying in his head" certain statistics. Mr. Lilienthal's declaration of principles was made with immediate reference to this criticism, but was primarily designed as a defense against the charge of Communism.*

This I do carry in my head, Senator. I will do my best to make it clear. My convictions are not so much concerned with what I am against as what I am for; and that excludes a lot of things automatically.

Traditionally, democracy has been an affirmative doctrine rather than merely a negative one. I believe—and I do so conceive the Constitution of the United States to rest upon, as does religion—the fundamental proposition of the integrity of the individual; and that all Government and all private institutions must be designed to promote and to protect and defend the integrity and the dignity of the individual; that that is the essential

* *New York Times,* February 5, 1947.

meaning of the Constitution and the Bill of Rights, as it is essentially the meaning of religion.

IMPORTANCE OF MEN SUPREME

Any form of government, therefore, and any other institutions which make [men] means rather than ends, which exalt the State or any other institutions above the importance of men, which place arbitrary power over men as a fundamental tenet of government or any other institutions, are contrary to that conception, and therefore I am deeply opposed to them.

The communistic philosophy, as well as the communistic form of government, fall within this category, for their fundamental tenet is quite to the contrary. The fundamental tenet of communism is that the state is an end in itself, and that therefore the powers which the state exercises over the individual are without any ethical standard to limit them. That I deeply disbelieve.

It is very easy simply to say one is not a Communist. . . . It is very easy to talk about being against communism. It is equally important to believe those things which provide a satisfying and effective alternative. Democracy is that satisfying affirmative alternative.

Its hope in the world is that it is an affirmative belief, rather than being simply a belief against something else and nothing more.

One of the tenets of democracy that grow out of this central core of a belief that the individual comes first, that all men are the children of God and their personalities are therefore sacred, carries with it a great belief in civil liberties and their protection, and a repugnance to anyone who would steal from a human being that which is most precious to him—his good name; either by impugning things to him by innuendo or by insinuations.

And it is especially an unhappy circumstance that occasionally that is done in the name of democracy. This, I think, can tear our country apart and destroy it if we carry it further.

DEMOCRACY A DAILY NEED

I deeply believe in the capacity of democracy to surmount any trials that may lie ahead, provided only we practice it in our daily lives. And among the things we must practice is that, while we seek fervently to ferret out the subversive and anti-democratic forces in the country, we do not at the same time, by hysteria, by resort to innuendo and smears, and other unfortunate tactics, besmirch the very cause that we believe in, and cause a separation among our people, cause one group and one individual to hate another based on . . . mere unsubstantiated attacks upon their loyalty.

I want also to add that . . . it is the very basis . . . of . . . this country, . . . that the strictest rules of creditability of witnesses be maintained and hearsay and gossip shall be excluded in courts of justice. And that, too, is an essential of our democracy.

And, whether by administrative agencies acting arbitrarily against business organizations, or whether by investigating activities of the legislative branches, whenever those principles of the protection of an individual and his good name against besmirchment by gossip, hearsay and the statements of witnesses who are not subject to cross-examination are not maintained, then, too, we have failed in carrying forward our ideals in respect to democracy. That I deeply believe.

> Like the concept of liberty, the notion of individualism tends to be stated in absolute terms. We dwell at length on "the rights of the individual." But in practice, and in ethical opinions in which some other sentiment is uppermost in our minds, we limit individualism drastically. Then we take into account the duties, as well as the rights, of the individual, and we often place nation, church, family, and party above the individual. Moreover, the manner in which the individual expresses himself is positively channelized by the local organizations. As Wilbert E. Moore has noted, ". . . we have not in fact looked with the same favor upon the development of individual aesthetic or mystical talents as we have upon shrewd economic rationality. . . . It is thus *not* the complete and unrestrained individual who is the center and measure of modern industrial society, but rather the individual whose character most closely conforms to the ideals established in traditional doctrine." *

COMPETITION AND INDIVIDUALISM

The American faith that the pursuit by each individual of his own interests in his own way will result in the best possible use of all resources, then, is in a sense only half true. Its truth depends in

* Moore, Wilbert E., *Industrial Relations and the Social Order* (New York: The Macmillan Company, 1946), p. 52.

the first place, of course, on how one defines "best." But in the second place its truth depends on each individual's being *taught* to have *certain* "interests" rather than others, and to consider as his "own" way of pursuing those interests whatever the Credo defines as "proper."

Margaret Mead has given a very clear description of how the particular kind of conformity that Americans mean by individualism is developed in the typical American.*

INDOCTRINATION OF INDIVIDUALISM

Each civilization conveys different things to its children. The Balinese mother [1, 2] mimicking a desperate fear as she calls the wandering child back to her side teaches him forever after to fear the unknown, to cling, he knows not why, to well-trodden paths. *"Aroh',"* she shrieks, "Wild cat!" or "Witch!" or "Snake!" or "Fire!", making no effort to adapt the scare word to the circumstance. If she screamed "Snake" when the child went into the grass, and "Scorpion" when he climbed the wood-pile, he might learn to look and find patches of grass without snakes and piles of wood without scorpions. But instead any scare word in any context will do; the child gets no chance to test reality out, he remains frightened of an unknown.

"He's so strong," says the Iatmul mother. "He runs so fast. I can't catch him." "When I catch him I will hit him and kill him," she says, as she pretends to chase and fails to catch her erring two-year-old. She acts as if the child were as strong and fleeter of foot than she, and the terrified baby, pushed beyond his endurance into an assertive role for which he is not ready, learns that safety lies in stamping and shouting and pretending to be bigger and stronger and fiercer than one really is.

Not with a single phrase or a single gesture, not with one punishment alone, but in every tone of the voice, in each turn of the head, these nuances are conveyed to the child, and as the Balinese baby learns that the unknown is always to be avoided and the Iatmul baby learns to play at being strong, the American baby learns that its parents' love—even if they are his par-

* From *And Keep Your Powder Dry,* by Margaret Mead, copyright 1942 by Margaret Mead, by permission of William Morrow and Company, Inc., pp. 89–95, 107–109, 139–146, 193–197, 201–202.

[1] Mead, Margaret. Character Formation in Two South Seas Societies, *Proceedings, American Neurological Association,* 1940.

[2] Administrative Contributions to Democratic Character Formation at the Adolescent Level, *Journal, Association of Deans of Women,* Vol. IV, No. 2, pp. 51–57, Jan., 1941.

ents and he isn't adopted—is conditional upon the way in which he compares with others. "He's such a poor eater. I don't know what to do with him. I just can't get him to eat like other children." His mother thinks he isn't listening, as he digs with his shovel under the park bench, but the "won't eat" and the depreciating tone in which she says it gets through to him—she is not worrying because her beloved child does not take the food which she has lovingly prepared for him, but because he is showing himself inferior at being a growing child. At his next meal he looks guiltily at his carrots. If he rejects them again that same depreciatory note will recur tomorrow in his mother's voice.

So while the child is learning that his whole place in the world, his name, his right to the respect of other children—everything—depends upon his parents and on what kind of a house they have been able to build or buy or rent, what kind of a car they are able to drive, what kind of toys they are able to buy him, he also learns that his own acceptance by these parents, who are his only support, is conditional upon his achievements, upon the way in which he shows up against other children and against their idea of other children. To the anxiety with which small boys in many if not all cultures of the world view grown men and wonder if they will ever be as tall and strong, is added in America, for both boys and girls, the anxiety as to whether they will be successful in keeping their parents' love as children. American girls of college age can be thrown into a near panic by the description of cultures in which parents do not love their children. Against the gnawing fear that their personal achievement has made them unworthy of love, they have placed a vague persistent belief in "mother love," a belief that somehow or other their parents won't be able to get out of loving them some—because they are parents, and theirs. Any evidence that destroys their faith in this "maternal instinct" is profoundly disturbing. . . .

So the young American starts life with a tremendous impetus towards success. His family, his little slender family, just a couple of parents alone in the world, are the narrow platform on which he stands. . . .

The initial condition inserted into the mother's simplest kiss, that "I will love you only if you achieve as much as other people's babies. I can't love you if you don't," survives into every competitive situation in life. What was his handicap? Ha, and nevertheless he made it? . . .

Cultures have patterned aggression in many different ways: they have regarded it as primary and rewarded it; regarded it as incidental and undesirable and extinguished it; regarded it as primary and punished it; regarded it as secondary and developed it. . . . Almost all societies . . .

are, in some measure, concerned with the problem, with staying the baby's hand, with slapping the baby's hand, or with reinforcing the baby's aimless slap by a cheer or the comment: "How fierce and cruel he is!" And there is a definite relationship between the expectancy, the fear, the disapproval, the cheer in the parent's voice and the later fighting behavior of those babies grown to manhood.

What kind of pattern of aggressive behavior have we, as Americans? When is aggression justified in our eyes and when is it condemned? Who can be aggressive to whom, where? And with the answers to such questions as these we can look at the present world scene which calls for the exercise of certain types of aggression and ask: Have we, as Americans, got the kind of aggression that the present world developments demand? If not, what has to be done to alter the way we see the world—something actually easier to do than to alter the form of American aggressiveness.

A good place to study the American pattern is a playground where each mother is shouting her admonitions at her child. "Stand up for yourself! Don't come crying to me when he takes your shovel. Get it back. You're big enough to look after yourself." "Jimmy! Look out, he's just a little baby, don't hit him." "Well, hit him back if he hits you. Don't stand there like a sissy and take it." "Go on, make him learn he can't hit you without getting hurt." "Tommy, don't pull that little boy's hair. He's smaller than you are. He doesn't know any better. If you want to fight, pick on someone your own size." "Billy, don't tear that nice little girl's dress. Big boys don't hit little girls." "No, I won't ask his mother to make him give it back. Go and get it yourself if you want it. He's not much bigger than you are. Go and take it away from him! Show you've got what it takes." And as each mother leads her dirt-smeared champion home, she thinks to herself either: "He can stand up for himself all right. He can take it, and he can dish it out. He's got what it takes," or in a worried unadmitted undertone: "I wish he'd stand up for himself more. He's brave enough when it comes to teasing kids smaller than he is or pulling the girls' hair, but he won't stand up to anything his size."

When the children get a little older, when it is a teacher instead of a parent, a playground director instead of a nurse, a new note, the notion of rules, enters in more prominently: "Play fair." "It's his turn now." "Let him have it for a while now, Jimmy. You've had it a long time." "No, boys, turn about is fair play." "It's not fair to take the little boy's ball, Jimmy, he's smaller than you are." "Billy! Do you think it's fair to grab everything just because you're bigger than the others? I'm ashamed of you."

FAIR PLAY

Educators commenting on the contradictory threads in our culture have stressed that we confuse children about aggression; that we teach them to be tough and to stand up for themselves, and, at the same time, teach them that aggression is wrong and should be suppressed and, if possible, repressed. But actually there is a pattern which underlies these contradictory orders, and a very clear one. . . . [According to] Anglo-Saxon institutions . . . fair play means certain definite things. It means "obeying the rules," and the "rules" are thought of as a device for keeping people from bullying or taking an unfair advantage of the other person. One's character is defined by the way in which the rules are embodied in one's behavior—and "That's not cricket" may be applied to making love to the wife of a man who is in a weaker position than oneself. Our games traditions, although altered and transformed, are Anglo-Saxon in form; and fair play does mean for us, as for the English, a standard of behavior between the weak and the strong—a standard which is curiously incomprehensible to the German. During the last war, articles used to appear in German papers exploring this curious Anglo-Saxon notion called "fair play," reproduced without translation—for there was no translation.

Now the element which is so difficult to translate in the idea of "fair play" is not the fact that there are rules. Rules are an integral part of German life, rules for behavior of inferior to superior, for persons of every status for every formal situation. Rules for the hunter, who is ashamed if he does not hit his quarry in the appointed, difficult and honorable spot; rules for the man of honor who must know when to be insulted or be forever disgraced. Rules are common enough. The point that was incomprehensible was the inclusion of the other person's weakness inside the rules so that "fair play" included in it a statement of relative strength of the opponents and it ceased to be fair to beat a weak opponent. Something had to be done about a weak opponent so that he became a strong opponent, and if possible, a slightly stronger opponent, else there could be no fairness, and hence no honor in winning. The crude idea that the point of strength is to triumph over weakness simply doesn't fit in. The rules of the game always include at least two players. When one's opponent is stronger than oneself, maximum effort is no longer compatible with fair play. The Anglo-Saxon fear that a boy will be a coward contains in it the fear that he will also be a bully—for bullying is seen as a sign of responding to the same wrong stimulus—a difference in strength. The "fair play" character always finds the greater strength of his opponent a stimulus.[3] When the other is stronger, he puts out more effort, is "braver," and when the other is weaker, he reduces his effort, is "gentle." The coward, however, doesn't see the situation that way at all—another person's greater strength is a signal to him to cringe; and such an attitude finds its counterpart in bullying whenever the chance occurs. . . .

VIRTUE IDENTIFIED WITH SUCCESS

We have a certain kind of character, the American character, which has developed in the New World and taken a shape all its own; a character that is geared to success and to movement, invigorated by obstacles and difficulties, but plunged into guilt and despair by catastrophic failure or a wholesale alteration in the upward and onward pace; a character in which aggressiveness is uncertain and undefined, to which readiness to fight anyone who starts a fight and unreadiness to engage in violence have both been held up as virtues; a character which measures its successes and failures only against near contemporaries and engages in various quantitative devices for reducing every contemporary to its own stature; a character which sees success as the reward of virtue and failure as the stigma for not being good enough. . . .

It takes very special circumstances to back up a belief in the close connection between virtue and success. Most other cultures have had to construct their ethical systems on a less exacting model. The peoples have suffered for the sins of their kings; one evil deed has corrupted the land. Theories of reincarnation have permitted the notion that the luck fluctuates from one incarnation to another, or the whole problem of success was shelved altogether and each man took the fortune which a blindfold fate meted out to him. Christianity traditionally dealt with the problem in terms of heaven and hell, and those whose lot in no sense matched their effort or their deserts might flourish or suffer on earth; but all these inequalities were righted in heaven. The belief in the after-life was a particularly flexible method of reconciling a man who was exhorted to goodness, to a life without earthly rewards. But the essence of puritanism, although it retained all the color and terror of hell fire, was a belief that there was a relationship here on earth between good behavior and good deserts. God prospered the good man and withdrew from the evil man, and success could be taken as an immediate outward and visible sign that one had so lived as to find

[3] Bateson, Gregory. Equilibrium and Climax in Inter-Personal Relations. Paper read at Conference of Topologists, Smith College, Northampton, Mass., Dec. 31, 1940–Jan. 2, 1941.

favor in the sight of God. Very few peoples have ever trafficked long with such an unmanageable moral code, but the peculiar conditions of American life promoted this attitude rather than diminished it. In Europe if one were born one of ten sons, and one's neighbor was an only son, and the inheritance consisted of farms of the same size, nine of the ten, if it were entailed—all of the ten, if it were not—were desperately unlucky. But in America, the nine could go somewhere else and often prosper more than the brother who remained at home. The favors conferred by birth were obscured by the opportunity to wrest favors by hard work and enterprise.

LUCK AND HARD WORK

The American version of luck, best exemplified in the press stories of Hollywood success which have been analyzed by Rosten,[4] point up our essential puritanism by insisting that when sudden, undreamed-of, unheard-of success and fame befalls some unknown movie star, she should have no birthright claim to it. She was not, the careful press stories explain, even pretty—they had to alter the molding of her nose. She is not the right height—when she plays with the stars she prefers she has to stand on a box. Her success, her luck, is an artifact pure and simple, synthetic from start to finish. It might have happened to anybody. It might have happened to you and me. This is an excellent example of what the anthropologist means by the regularity of culture: that an apparent contradiction, like these tales of great and absolutely undeserved good fortune, when it is analyzed more closely nevertheless fits in with other ideas in the culture which it appears to contradict. The American logic is: Be intelligently good and you will be successful. As for those who cannot in any sense be shown to have been specially good, who have not worked or saved or slaved or supported their widowed mothers while they burnt the midnight oil and finished night school—when they succeed, we represent their great good fortune as due to a capricious turn of a wheel rather than tolerate the notion that those who benefited so greatly had some single initial advantage. The assumption that men were created equal, with an equal ability to make an effort and win an earthly reward, although denied every day by experience is maintained every day by our folklore and our daydreams.

Running through this emphasis that work brings its own rewards and that failure is squarely the fault of him who fails is another thread for

[4] Rosten, L. C. Hollywood: The Movie Colony; the Movie Makers. New York: Harcourt, Brace, 1941.

which the sanction is not guilt, but shame. Shame is felt perhaps most strongly over the failures of other people, especially one's parents,[5] who have not been successful, have not worked hard enough to have an inside bathroom or an automobile or to send one to a private school, to live on the right street, or go to the right church. As class is an expression of economic success, then it follows that to belong as a child or adolescent in a class below others is a statement that one's parents have failed, that they did not make good. This is bad enough when they have not risen, unbearable if they have started to fall even lower. Deeper than our disapproval of any breaking of the ten commandments lies our conviction that low economic estate is something dreadful and that a failure to keep moving upward is an unforgiveable sin. If one analyzed the novels of American life and the case histories of adolescents which have been collected by American sociologists, this terrible shame of children over their parents' failure—a failure which the parents themselves may well handle in terms of guilt rather than shame—comes out very strongly. Success and conformity—outward conformity made possible by economic success—these are the marks that one is a good American. . . .

We talk about saving the American way of life—and this stands for a number of vague things such as refrigerators and automobiles and marrying whom you like and working for whom you like and not having to be regimented and wrapped up in yards of governmental red tape. Or it may mean something more; it may mean saving that dynamic principle which associates success and goodness. Our character structure is based upon having a job to do which can be done, just as the Manus savage's goodness was based upon associating his failure to work with a disease from which he got well. If we cannot again work and move in a world where there is some relationship between our success and our effort and willingness to work, this American character is doomed to disappear with the physical frontier which fostered it. This insistence upon a relationship between what we do and what we get is one of our most distinguishing characteristics. On it is based our acceptance of men for what they have become rather than for what they were born. On it is based our faith that simple people, people like ourselves, are worthy of a hearing in the halls of the great. On it is based our special brand of democracy. Americans who are once convinced that it's all a matter of pull, of who you know, that working hard doesn't get you anywhere nowadays, that it's all a racket anyhow—which is the

[5] My understanding of this aspect of shame in America I owe to a conversation with Helen Lynd, who was stressing our lack of techniques for handling shame.

cynical obverse of believing that effort and success are linked—are not a desirable breed. No one who was interested in building the world anew would conceive of asking such people to help. Once we lose our moral keystone to an orderly world, the whole structure comes crashing down about our heads, leaving us with a type of American who has neither vision nor humility, who lacks the will and the purpose which have helped us shape a great country from an untouched wilderness, who lacks even the constructive fire which might come from bitterness and a genuine hatred of those who have brought him to such a pass.

LABOR RELATIONS AND INDIVIDUALISM

The American meaning of individualism, in brief, is that the individual should be *successful* in ***competition*** with other individuals under quite rigid rules of the game (including the ethical judgment that everyone should start with "equal opportunity"), and in certain materialistic, or secular, directions. Not only (the American Credo has it) does the individual have a *right* to compete for "success"; he *must* compete. If he succeeds, he is virtuous; if he is virtuous, he will succeed. If he is not virtuous, he will not succeed; if he fails, the fault is his own.

In later chapters, we shall see more of the implications of this Credo—its implications for the industrial order, in urban areas, for the American personality, for marriage and the family, for recreation, and for education. What should be noted now is the fact, observed above in respect to freedom, that even in such an "individual-centered" culture as our own, it is the system of social values that gives direction to people's actions, that limits their "freedom" and "liberty" and "individualism," that defines their "success" and "virtue."

As in the case of "freedom," so in the case of "individualism" there are always pressures at work to alter or modify the rules in the light of changed conditions and from the perspective of the Credo. Is it, for example, an interference with individual liberty to prevent an employer from working his employees more than ten hours a day? Less than fifty years ago, the answer was *yes,* as indicated in the majority opinion written by Supreme Court Justice Peckham in the case of Lochner v. New York, printed below.*

* *Lochner* vs. *New York,* 198 U. S. 45, 1905.

Today the answer is *no,* as foreshadowed by the dissenting opinion of Justice Holmes in the same case.

Peckham, J. . . . . The statute necessarily interferes with the right of contract between the employer and employees, concerning the number of hours in which the latter may labor in the bakery of the employer. The general right to make a contract in relation to his business is part of the liberty of the individual protected by the Fourteenth Amendment of the Federal Constitution. . . . There are, however, certain powers, existing in the sovereignty of each State in the Union, somewhat vaguely termed police powers, the exact description and limitation of which have not been attempted by the courts. These powers, broadly stated and without, at present, any attempt at a more specific definition, relate to the safety, health, morals and general welfare of the public. . . .

It must, of course, be conceded that there is a limit to the valid exercise of the police power by the State. There is no dispute concerning this general proposition. Otherwise the Fourteenth Amendment would have no efficacy and the legislatures of the States would have unbounded power, and it would be enough to say that any piece of legislation was enacted to conserve the morals, the health, or the safety of the people; such legislation would be valid, no matter how absolutely without foundation the claim might be. The claim of the police power would be a mere pretext—become another and delusive name for the supreme sovereignty of the State to be exercised free from constitutional restraint. This is not contended for. In every case that comes before this court, therefore, where legislation of this character is concerned, and where the protection of the federal Constitution is sought, the question necessarily arises: Is this a fair, reasonable, and appropriate exercise of the police power of the State, or is it an unreasonable, unnecessary, and arbitrary interference with the right of the individual to his personal liberty or to enter into those contracts in relation to labor which may seem to him appropriate or necessary for the support of himself and his family? Of course the liberty of contract relating to labor includes both parties to it. The one has as much right to purchase as the other to sell labor. . . .

The question whether this act is valid as a labor law, pure and simple, may be dismissed in a few words. There is no reasonable ground for interfering with the liberty of person or the right of free contract, by determining the hours of labor, in the occupation of a baker. There is no contention that bakers as a class are not equal in intelligence and capacity to men in other trades or manual occupations, or that they are not able to assert their rights and care for themselves without the protecting arm of the State, interfering with their independence of judgment and of action. They are in no sense wards of the State. . . .

It is a question of which of two powers or rights shall prevail—the power of the State to legislate or the right of the individual to liberty of person and freedom of contract. . . .

We think the limit of the police power has been reached and passed in this case. There is, in our judgment, no reasonable foundation for holding this to be necessary or appropriate as a health law to safeguard the public health, or the health of the individuals who are following the trade of a baker. If this statute be valid, and if, therefore, a proper case is made out in which to deny the right of an individual, *sui juris,* as employer or employee, to make contracts for the labor of the latter under the protection of the provisions of the federal Constitution, there would seem to be no length to which legislation of this nature might not go. . . .

Holmes, J., dissenting. . . . The case is decided upon an economic theory which a large part of the country does not entertain. If it were a question whether I agreed with that theory, I should desire to study it further and long before making up my mind. But I do not conceive that to be my duty, because I strongly believe that my agreement or disagreement has nothing to do with the right of a majority to embody their opinions in law. It is settled by various decisions of this court that state constitutions and state laws may regulate life in many ways which we as legislators might think as injudicious, or if you like as tyrannical, as this, and which, equally with this, interfere with the liberty to contract. Sunday laws and usury laws are ancient examples. A more modern one is the prohibition of lotteries. The liberty of the citizen to do as he likes so long as he does not interfere with the liberty of others to do the same, which has been a shibboleth for some well-known writers, is interfered with by school laws, by the post-office, by every state or municipal institution which takes his money for purposes thought desirable, whether he likes it or not. The Fourteenth Amendment does not enact Mr. Herbert Spencer's Social Statics. . . . United States and state statutes and decisions cutting down the liberty to contract by way of combination are familiar to this court. . . . Some of these laws embody convictions or prejudices which judges are likely to share. Some may not. But a constitution is not intended to embody a particular economic theory, whether of paternalism and the organic relation of the citizen to the state or of *laissez faire*. It is made for people of fundamentally differing views, and the accident of our finding certain opinions natural and familiar, or novel, and even shocking, ought not to conclude our judgment upon the question whether statutes embodying them conflict with the Constitution of the United States.

General propositions do not decide concrete cases. The decision will depend on a judgment or intuition more subtle than any articulate major premise. But I think that the proposition just stated, if it is accepted, will carry us far toward the end. Every opinion tends to become a law. I think that the word "liberty," in the Fourteenth Amendment, is perverted when it is held to prevent the natural outcome of a dominant opinion, unless it can be said that a rational and fair man necessarily would admit that the statute proposed would infringe fundamental principles as they have been understood by the traditions of our people and our law. It does not need research to show that no such sweeping condemnation can be passed upon the statute before us. A reasonable man might think it a proper measure on the score of health. Men whom I certainly could not pronounce unreasonable would uphold it as a first instalment of a general regulation of the hours of work. Whether in the latter aspect it would be open to the charge of inequality I think it unnecessary to discuss.

AS OTHERS SEE US

Americans, as the people of any culture, tend to see their value system and their social structure with an "of course" attitude—as a natural, inevitable, scarcely to-be-thought-about part of the environment. It is instructive sometimes to note that the same objective phenomena may appear in an entirely different light to observers who do not wear the same spectacles—who perceive the complex activities of a society from a *different* value point of view. For this reason, we end the present chapter by printing below the observations of Jean-Paul Sartre, the French "existentialist," who expresses a not uncommon evaluation of Americanism.*

There are the great myths, the myths of happiness, of progress, of liberty, of triumphant maternity; there is realism and optimism—and then

* Sartre, Jean-Paul, "Americans and Their Myths," *The Nation*, Vol. 165 (October 18, 1947), pp. 402–403.

there are the Americans, who, nothing at first, grow up among these colossal statues and find their way as best they can among them. There is this myth of happiness: black-magic slogans warn you to be happy at once; films that "end well" show a life of rosy ease to the exhausted crowds; the language is charged with optimistic and unrestrained expressions—"have a good time," "life is fun," and the like. But there are also these people, who, though conventionally happy, suffer from an obscure *malaise* to which no name can be given, who are tragic through fear of being so, through that total absence of the tragic in them and around them.

There is this collectivity which prides itself on being the least "historical" in the world, on never complicating its problems with inherited customs and acquired rights, on facing as a virgin a virgin future in which everything is possible—and there are these blind gropings of bewildered people who seek to lean on a tradition, on a folklore. There are the films that write American history for the masses and, unable to offer them a Kentucky Jeanne d'Arc or a Kansas Charlemagne, exalt them with the history of the jazz singer, Al Jolson, or the composer, Gershwin. Along with the Monroe doctrine, isolationism, scorn for Europe, there is the sentimental attachment of each American for his country of origin, the inferiority complex of the intellectuals before the culture of the old Continent, of the critics who say, "How can you admire our novelists, you who have Flaubert?" of the painters who say, "I shall never be able to paint as long as I stay in the United States"; and there is the obscure, slow effort of an entire nation to seize universal history and assimilate it as its patrimony.

There is the myth of equality—and there is the myth of segregation, with those big beach-front hotels that post signs reading "Jews and dogs not allowed," and those lakes in Connecticut where Jews may not bathe, and that racial *tchin,* in which the lowest degree is assigned to the Slavs, the highest to the Dutch immigrants of 1680. There is the myth of liberty—and the dictatorship of public opinion; the myth of economic liberalism—and the big companies extending over the whole country which, in the final analysis, belong to no one and in which the employees, from top to bottom, are like functionaries in a state industry. There is respect for science and industry, positivism, an insane love of "gadgets"—and there is the somber humor of the *New Yorker,* which pokes bitter fun at the mechanical civilization of America and the hundred million Americans who satisfy their craving for the marvelous by reading every day in the "comics" the incredible adventures of Superman, or Wonderman, or Mandrake the Magician.

There are the thousand taboos which proscribe love outside of marriage—and there is the litter of used contraceptives in the back yards of coeducational colleges; there are all those men and women who drink before making love in order to transgress in drunkenness and not remember. There are the neat, coquettish houses, the pure-white apartments with radio, armchair, pipe, and stand—little paradises; and there are the tenants of those apartments who, after dinner, leave their chairs, radios, wives, pipes, and children, and go to the bar across the street to get drunk alone.

Perhaps nowhere else will you find such a discrepancy between people and myth, between life and the representation of life. An American said to me at Berne: "The trouble is that we are all eaten by the fear of being less American than our neighbor." I accept this explanation: it shows that Americanism is not merely a myth that clever propaganda stuffs into people's heads but something every American continually reinvents in his gropings. It is at one and the same time a great external reality rising up at the entrance to the port of New York across from the Statue of Liberty, and the daily product of anxious liberties. The anguish of the American confronted with Americanism is an ambivalent anguish, as if he were asking, "Am I American enough?" and at the same time, "How can I escape from Americanism?" In America a man's simultaneous answers to these two questions make him what he is, and each man must find his own answers.

PART TWO

The New Urban Environment

CHAPTER III

The Growth of Cities

THE American system of values originated in a rural society. Its principles of government and economics, of religion and recreation, of family and community all arose in and were adapted to a rural setting. Quickly, however, the setting has changed. The growth of cities has been phenomenal, and the American people are now predominantly urban rather than rural. One of the great questions in American society is therefore this: Can the old values be adapted to the new urban setting without changing their essential nature? We know that the specific applications of the values must change, because the setting has changed. We know that the attainment or instrumentation of democracy, free speech, religious tolerance, equal opportunity, material welfare, and family integrity must be different, but we cannot be sure that the values themselves must change. Instrumentation, however, is as important as the values themselves; and nobody can understand the problem of unity and change in American life who does not understand the special demands of the new urban environment.

The readings that follow show the speed with which urbanization has taken place in the United States, and the probable course of future urbanization. They also describe some of the conditions and problems that city life presents. Throughout the rest of the book the urban setting must be kept constantly in mind. The present chapter and the next one form a background for the understanding of what is happening in nearly every aspect of American social organization, from government and the class structure to religion and family life.

URBAN VERSUS RURAL POPULATION GROWTH *

The growth and development of cities in the United States is one of the most striking population phenomena of all time. In 1790, of the twenty-four urban places [1] in the United States, only two, New York and Philadelphia, had a population of 25,000 or more. At that time only 200,000 persons, or approximately 5 per cent of the total population, were living in urban areas. By 1920 there were 2,722 urban places in the United States containing a total of over 54 million inhabitants—more than half the population of the United States. By 1940, the 3,464 urban places in the United States comprised over 74 million people, which constituted 56.5 per cent of the total population of the country. Included in these urban places were 5 with populations of a million or more and 92 with populations of 100,000 or more.

Along with the rapid concentration of population in urban areas came a considerable shrinking in the proportion which the rural farm population constituted of the total population in the United States. In 1920 the rural farm population numbered 31 million and made up 29.7 per cent of the total population. By 1940 it had shrunk to a total of slightly over 30 million or 22.9 per cent of the population. By the end of 1944 the farm population had declined still further, to about 20 per cent of the national total. The rural non-farm population changed from 20 million or 19.1 per cent of the population in 1920 to 27 million or 20.5 per cent in 1940. . . .

The interstate wartime movement of population has been accompanied by large-scale shifts of population from rural to urban areas. The movement of population from farms was larger than that recorded for any previous period of similar length. This movement, in large part, appears to represent an accentuation of former trends rather than a sharp break with the past. Under the circumstances, it is hardly to be expected that the postwar period will lead to a back-to-the-land movement of sufficient size to bring the farm population back to its 1940 level. Unless economic conditions are so unfavorable that migration from farms is drastically retarded or that large numbers of persons seek subsistence on the land, as they did im-

* Hauser, Philip M., and Taeuber, Conrad, "The Changing Population of the United States," *The Annals of the American Academy of Political and Social Science,* Vol. 237 (January 1945), pp. 16–17.

[1] As defined by the Census, the urban area, in general, is made up of cities and other incorporated places having 2,500 inhabitants or more. See Sixteenth Census of the United States, *Population—Number of Inhabitants,* Vol. I, pp. 20 ff.

mediately after 1929, it is probable that the number of persons living on farms in this country in the near future will be smaller than it has been in the recent past.

PAST AND FUTURE URBANIZATION *

The historical pattern of urban growth is tied to irregular social and economic changes. The course of urbanization in the United States has been somewhat uneven and erratic—precipitate in one period, quiescent in another. There has been some correspondence between rates of population growth and rates of urban growth and some correspondence between economic prosperity and urban expansion. Despite discernible associations of this type, it is quite possible that the very factors that have drawn people into cities in the past may in the future disperse them. Technological advance, which stimulated industrial concentration, may in another phase decentralize the economic operations of our society. Such a development could make it possible for the population to eat its cake and have it too, in the sense of living more spaciously while losing none of the advantages of urbanization. On the dark side, there is even now, in the atomic bomb, a technological threat to concentrated living, a threat which may scatter the population hastily and without the satisfactions of urban "culture." . . .

In spite of the short-run fluctuations in urban growth in the United States, fairly definite overall trends are discernible. The proportion of the population living in urban places has increased during every decade since 1790, except the decade 1810 to 1820 (probably the aftermath of the war of 1812). The percentage increase in urban population has been greater than the percentage increase in total population during every decade except 1810 to 1820. The increase in the percentage urban has varied from a high of 6.9 percentage points, 1880 to 1890, to a low of 0.3 percentage points, 1930 to 1940; (there was a loss of 0.1 percentage point from 1810 to 1820) with no apparent pattern beyond the fluctuations coinciding with troughs and peaks of economic activity. The percentage increase in the proportion urban has shown some tendency to decline slightly since the turn of the century, but because the last few decades have been characterized by economic extremes (from prosperity in the 'twenties, to extreme depression in the 'thirties, and back to prosperity in the 'forties) it is difficult to guess to

* Hauser, Philip M., and Eldridge, Hope T., "Projection of Urban Growth and Migration to Cities in the United States," *Postwar Problems of Migration* (New York: Milbank Memorial Fund, 1947), pp. 160–163, 165, 170–173.

what extent urban growth rates are representing aberrations and to what extent they are reflecting an alleged secular trend (see Table 1 . . .). . . .

TABLE 1

GROWTH OF THE URBAN POPULATION OF THE UNITED STATES, 1790 TO 2000

Year	*Total Population*	*Urban Population*			
		Number	*Per Cent of Total*	*Number*	*Per Cent of Total*
1790	3,929,214	201,655	5.1		
1800	5,308,483	322,371	6.1		
1810	7,239,881	525,459	7.3		
1820	9,638,453	693,255	7.2		
1830	12,866,020	1,127,247	8.8		
1840	17,069,453	1,845,055	10.8		
1850	23,191,876	3,543,716	15.3		
1860	31,443,321	6,216,518	19.8		
1870	38,558,371	9,902,361	25.7		
1880	50,155,783	14,129,735	28.2		
1890	62,947,714	22,106,265	35.1		
1900	75,994,575	30,159,921	39.7		
1910	91,972,266	41,998,932	45.7		
1920	105,710,620	54,157,973	51.2		
1930	122,775,046	68,954,823	56.2		
1940	131,669,275	74,423,702	56.5		
1946 (Estimate)	141,229,000	84,753,000	60.0		
Projection *		*Medium*		*High*	
1950	145,460,000	89,022,000	61.2	90,476,000	62.2
1960	153,375,000	98,620,000	64.3	104,448,000	68.1
1970	159,847,000	107,897,000	67.5	119,246,000	74.6
1980	163,877,000	116,189,000	70.9	133,724,000	81.6
1990	164,585,000	122,616,000	74.5	147,139,000	89.4
2000	163,312,000	127,710,000	78.2	159,719,000	97.8

* Projected urban population of the United States, 1950 to 2000. [The low estimates are not given.]

The urban population of the United States under sustained conditions of high production and employment will be 104,000,000, or 68 per cent of the total population in 1960. Under conditions of low production and employment, the 1960 urban population is estimated at 93,000,000, or slightly more than 60 per cent of the total; and under conditions of medium production and employment at about 99,000,000, or 64 per cent of the total.

The figures for the year 2000 are merely a demonstration of what would happen if the assumed rates of change in the urban proportion should remain constant until the end of the century. Thus, in the high projections, about 98 per cent of the population is shown to be urban in the year 2000.

As the situation is today with respect to agricultural productivity, habits of living, suburban trends, industrial labor force potentialities, and related matters, this "high" estimate does not seem a very likely eventuality. On the other hand, by the year 2000 our patterns of living may have changed so radically that the present meaning of the term "urban" may have vanished and the universe of discourse we now employ in this connection may find no comparable application. . . .

CITIES OF 100,000 OR MORE

Urban growth within the United States, at the various levels of concentration, has been a fairly unified process. The proportion of the population living in places of 100,000 or more inhabitants has increased in much the same way as the proportion living in all urban places. In most decades, the increase in the proportion of the population in the large cities has proceeded at a more rapid rate than the proportion urban, but the overall pattern was very similar (see Table 2). . . . A "medium" projection of the population in cities of 100,000 or more has been made on the same basis as that used for the urban projections. . . . According to these data, more than 67,000,000 persons, or 41.2 per cent of the total population, will be living in cities of this size class by the year 2000, as compared with about 38,000,000, or 28.9 per cent in 1940.

DECENTRALIZATION

The general assumption used for the present projections, namely that urban concentration will continue, is of course subject to challenge. One popular theory with respect to urbanization is that the process of dispersion has already begun. Proof is offered in comparisons of the percentage increase in the cities proper with increases in surrounding areas. The latter

TABLE 2

POPULATION IN CITIES OF 100,000 OR MORE INHABITANTS, 1820 TO 2000

Year	*Number*	*Per Cent of Total*
1820	123,706	1.3
1830	202,589	1.6
1840	517,216	3.0
1850	1,174,668	5.1
1860	2,638,781	8.4
1870	4,129,989	10.7
1880	6,210,909	12.4
1890	9,697,960	15.4
1900	14,208,347	18.7
1910	20,302,138	22.1
1920	27,429,326	25.9
1930	36,325,736	29.6
1940	37,987,989	28.9
1950 *	45,674,000	31.4
1960	50,920,000	33.2
1970	55,946,000	35.0
1980	60,634,000	37.0
1990	64,188,000	39.0
2000	67,285,000	41.2

almost invariably show greater rates of growth. This kind of resettlement is often interpreted as the beginning of de-concentration which may eventually result in the reduction of the density of cities and a more even distribution of the population over the country. This may be the correct interpretation, but from another viewpoint, "suburbanization" may be regarded, not as de-concentration, but rather as a by-product of the process of concentration whereby a city grows by accretion at the periphery, while the center, the area of business activity and large daytime population, forms a residential hollow that enlarges as business activity increases and city growth progresses.

* Projected population in cities of 100,000 or more inhabitants, 1950 to 2000. (Medium assumption.)

CHANGES ACCOMPANYING URBAN GROWTH *

The shift of the population to urban areas carries with it a fundamental change in the occupational structure of the Nation, as is evidenced by the fact that in 1870, 52.8 percent of American workers were gainfully employed in agriculture, while in 1930 the percentage had fallen to 21.3. This suggests that in little more than a century our country has profoundly altered its mode of life and has been transformed from a rural frontier settlement into a full-fledged, urban industrial society.

This development is not peculiar to the United States, for other countries of the world, especially those of Western Europe that have been touched by the machine technology, have undergone similar changes. But while the Old World grew by degrees over a period of many centuries from a town economy into its present urban cast, this country started as a wilderness on the outskirts of civilization and took the leap from primitive agriculturalism to mature urbanism in little more than a single century.

The figures on the extent and rapidity of urbanization in the United States, dramatic as they are, fail to convey the full significance of what the rise of cities has done to our civilization. The crowding of an increasing number and proportion of our people into relatively restricted areas has meant for them a revolution both in the way of living and in the ways of making a living, and has in turn been reflected in the changed character of our national life. The degree of concentration of a large part of the urban population into a few great metropolitan areas is indicated by the fact that the 96 leading metropolitan centers of the United States, occupying only 1.2 percent of the land area of the Nation, contained in 1930 nearly 45 percent of its total population and 68 percent of its urban inhabitants.

CITIES AS CENTERS OF INDUSTRY

But the city is not merely the characteristic place of residence, it is also the workshop of American civilization. In 1929 there were concentrated in 155 counties, containing the larger industrial cities, 64.7 percent of all of the industrial establishments, 74 percent of all industrial wage

* National Resources Committee, *Our Cities* (Washington: Government Printing Office, 1937), pp. 2–4.

earners, 80.7 percent of all salaried officers and employees. Moreover, 78.8 percent of all wages and 82.9 percent of all salaries in the country were paid in these counties. The value of the products these establishments produced was 79 percent of the country's total. They had installed 64.2 percent of the total horsepower classed as "prime movers" and 72.5 percent of the electric motors. They were credited with 80.2 percent of all the value added to products by manufacturing. Eighty-three percent of all of the wholesale trade in the United States was carried on in 127 counties, and the counties containing the 11 largest cities alone accounted for over one-half of the total, while the 93 cities over 100,000 reported over three-fourths of the total. Not only are the cities, and especially the great cities, the industrial workshops of the Nation that produce the bulk of its manufactured products and employ and support the majority of its working population, but they are also the managerial, service, and commercial distributing centers.

CITIES AS TRANSPORTATION CENTERS

It is in the cities, furthermore, that the transportation and communication lines converge, and it is from the cities, which are the traditional home of invention, that the technical facilities characteristic of modern civilization are diffused to other areas. Thus, 73 percent of all railway traffic terminates in urban areas; the single metropolis of New York contains over 500 freight stations within a radius of 35 miles of the city. Half of all railroad passengers either begin or end their journeys in 12 metropolitan cities. The use of electric energy is confined almost entirely to cities, since 86 percent of the population for whom electric energy is available live in urban communities. The urban areas make the most use of aviation, of rapid transit, of telephones, and the telegraph. Nearly 40 percent of all the mail in the United States originates in 12 metropolitan cities.

CITIES AS CULTURAL CENTERS

Similarly, it is in the cities that we must seek the heart of contemporary cultural activity, for it is predominantly there that the institutions, the facilities, the personnel, the atmosphere and the conditions prevail from which a rich intellectual and cultural life can spring and through which it can be promoted and diffused. The newspaper, the motion picture, the radio broadcasting station, the theater, the library, the museum, the concert hall, the opera, the hospital and the clinic, the higher educational institutions, the research and publishing centers, the professional organizations, and the religious and welfare institutions—these and others of the same type which compose the cultural apparatus of modern civilized living are to be found exclusively or predominantly in the city, and it is from there that the influences which they generate radiate to mold the character of life throughout the country.

CITIES AND GOVERNMENT

Finally, the multiplication and growth of cities and their importance have brought in their wake an enormously enhanced significance of urban government. Urban governments have come to play a major role in the national economy. Municipalities of the United States employ 1¼ million persons, or 1 out of every 3 public servants and 1 out of every 30 gainfully employed persons in the United States. Correspondingly, the expenditures of urban government loom large in the economy of the Nation. In 1932 urban governments spent 4¼ billion dollars or one-third of the total Government expenditures of the country, a sum greater than the Federal, the State, or the local nonurban expenditures during that year. Manifestly, a preponderant share of the public services formerly nonexistent has fallen upon the shoulders of the city government which, unfortunately, did not at the same time acquire corresponding resources and powers.

URBANISM AND NATIONAL MATURITY

Clearly, it is through the changes symbolized by and associated with urbanization that the lives of our people and the character of our Nation have been revolutionized in the course of less than half a century. For while in 1880 we were still predominantly rural with less than 30 percent of our population in places of 2,500 and over, by 1930 our urban population was well over half of the total. The United States can no longer be regarded as an undeveloped rural frontier country dependent upon the Old World for its industrial products, its technical skill, and its cultural guidance. If urbanization is a measure of the maturity of a country, then the United States may be said to have come of age.

CITIES AND PUBLIC POLICY

Strange as it may seem, however, this dramatic change in our national life and the product that has emerged—namely, the city—have not been adequately recognized by Government, nor has the citizenry become fully aware that the urbanization of the Nation calls for explicit consideration of the city as an entity. Compared to the attention that has been devoted to agriculture and the rural phase of American life, that part of America which is symbolized by the city has been almost completely neglected and has never fully emerged into our national consciousness.

As long as the United States was principally a rural and agricultural country, as long as our economy was relatively primitive, local, and self-sufficient, as long as our rich natural resources were scarcely known or exploited, and as long as a relatively secure and expanding life was within the reach of even a rapidly increasing population, it was to be expected that our outlook and policies should have been largely rural. But since the city has come to play such a preponderant role in our national existence, it becomes imperative that it acquire a central position in the formulation of national policy.

THE CAUSES OF URBAN GROWTH *

All over the world until about one hundred and fifty to two hundred years ago, and even now in a large part of it, man had only his hands and a few crude implements and tools with which to make his living. Under such conditions he could spare very little food from the farm.

The proportion of the crop that could be spared from the sustenance of the agricultural worker for the nonagricultural population remained extremely limited until more scientific agriculture and more extensive tillage came into being. But, of course, this proportion varied from place to place according to the fertility of the soil, the favorableness of the climate, the type of crops raised, and finally, but not least, the density of the agricultural population. Under very favorable conditions the agricultural worker in an age of hand production may have been able to spare to the nonagricultural population from one-fifth to one-fourth of what he produced. Under less favorable conditions, often as the consequence of an increase in his own numbers on a limited area of land, he could not spare any of his crop without endangering his own existence. . . .

Even in the United States . . . we are not far from the time when 80 to 90 per cent of us lived on the land, or in the small villages which were farm and service centers for the agricultural community; nor did we at that time ship much agricultural produce abroad. There is no need to labor this point; obviously a hand agriculture and a hand industry with

* Thompson, Warren S., "It Was Not Always So," from *Cities Are Abnormal* edited by Elmer Peterson, copyright 1946 by the University of Oklahoma Press, Norman. Reprinted by permission of the publishers and copyright owners. Pp. 54–64.

poor or nonexistent transport between communities made it practically impossible to have more than a very small city population. This is the basic reason for our certainty that man has been a rural village dweller during practically all of his existence on earth as an agriculturist.

We are reasonably sure also that until quite recent times most of the cities that did exist were quite small. Even great cities like Rome and Peiping at the height of their power probably did not have as many as a million people, and they grew to this size only because they were the centers of great empires whose rulers could levy tribute on a great agricultural population, so that even a small surplus per capita came to a large absolute amount. Moreover, this surplus could be brought by water to within a few miles of these capitals. In the past, practically all large cities have had fairly good water transport even if, like Peiping, it involved building long canals. . . .

Modern urbanization was made possible by the increasing productivity of agricultural labor. Without an agricultural revolution, closely associated with the Industrial Revolution, there could have been no large increase in urban population. In addition, the improved transportation accompanying the Industrial Revolution made it possible to bring this larger agricultural surplus to the city from greater and greater distances at low cost. Thus the agricultural revolution which began in the West about 1700 made possible a great movement of population from agricultural to nonagricultural work, and modern steam transportation made possible the great city of today. . . .

In pre-steam days it was almost impossible to feed any large city which was not readily accessible by water; nor could the few manufactures the peasants could buy be distributed over a wide territory. The cost of carriage by pack horse, wheelbarrow, and shoulder pack was prohibitive beyond the radius of a few miles, except for very expensive goods, for example, spices and silks. Moreover, transport of goods by wheeled vehicles was, with only a few exceptions, impossible before 1700. There could be a certain amount of cartage within the local community, but it was very limited even there.

The advantage of water location was lessened with the coming of the railroad, but it must be remembered that the railroads operating before the middle of the nineteenth century were of almost negligible importance from the standpoint of moving goods, even in England. Most of the great cities of today, even those in the New World, were located in the days when water transport was, relatively, far more important than it is now. When railroads came, they were built and run in such a way as to encourage the growth of the cities already established rather than to encourage the development of new centers largely or wholly dependent on rail transportation. This is true in general, although some fairly large cities have since been built which have no water transport. But steam power not only made large cities possible, it also exercised a decisive influence on their structure and organization.

Steam has to be converted into usable power quite close to the point of generation, and it is most effectively generated in relatively large units. Thus steam as an agent of transportation favors shipping in large quantities and over relatively long distances. . . . This natural advantage of the large city when serviced by steam transport was generally supplemented by rate and by service advantages. Altogether there can be little doubt that steam transport was a potent factor in encouraging the growth of the larger centers already established either as commercial centers or as manufacturing centers. Railway transport also favored the highly centralized city by delivering large numbers of people and large freight consignments to a relatively small downtown area more expeditiously and, up to a certain point, probably more cheaply than smaller numbers and amounts to several scattered areas within the urban region.

The centralizing effect of the use of steam transport on city growth was, however, probably much less than that of its use as power to drive machines. Until about forty years ago power had to be transmitted from the steam engine to the machine by mechanical means—pulleys, shafts, and belts. This made it economical to build the factory around the power plant—no machine could be more than a hundred yards or so from the engine, and the engine had to be quite close to the boiler. Thus the very nature of steam encouraged the building of larger and larger factories around the power plant and concentrated more and more workers near it; for, as we have seen, steam was not well adapted to quick and cheap local transport.

It was not until about 1900 that a new structure of urban life became possible, and it was another two decades before the potentialities of electricity as the agent of a new industrial and social revolution were widely realized, if, indeed, it can be said that they are realized even now. With the development of the use of electricity for power and communication and with the perfecting of the internal combustion engine for automobiles and airplanes a whole new distribution of industry and commerce and, therefore, of population became possible.

Long after it ceased to be necessary and probably after it ceased to be economical to crowd an enlargement of a factory into the small radius within which steam power could be transmitted to the machine by shaft, belt, and pulley, habit and convention continued to dictate the location of new productive equipment. Likewise, long after the need for frequent and prolonged communication between the men managing the production and the commercial aspects of a business ceased to depend on their having offices next door, or in the same building, or even in the same city, the process of agglomeration went on. But even when it was realized that the telegraph and especially the telephone made the decentralization of a business possible, there was little or no effort to use this new power to decentralize population. When the top-flight management took the opportunity to escape from the horrible manufacturing centers it had created, it only left these to go to larger commercial and financial centers. Furthermore, it quite frequently took a large part of the clerical staff to the new home. The net effect of management's moving out of manufacturing centers was not to decrease population in these centers so much as to increase congestion in the great commercial and financial centers. This inevitably resulted in increasing still more the proportion of the nation's commerce and wealth flowing into such centers. There does not appear to have been any significant change in this pattern of urbanization in the United States until after 1930, if then.

The centralization of the higher-flight executives of concerns doing a national business seems to have gone ahead without interruption between 1920 and 1930; indeed, it seems to have been accelerated during this decade. There was a veritable stampede, by the larger concerns doing a national and/or international business, to establish headquarters in New York, Chicago, or some other great city and for concerns doing a regional business to do the same in the dominant city in their region. It is true that after 1920 the large cities themselves did not increase as rapidly as their suburbs, but the decentralizing effect of the increasing use of the auto, the telephone, and electric power did nothing to break up the congestion of the downtown portion of our great cities. All they did was to scatter the living quarters of a growing proportion of city workers over a larger area and to move some of the industry of large cities from downtown locations to peripheral areas.

Sometimes the effect of moving industries to the periphery of a city without making any plans for housing was to make it even more necessary for the workers to live in a central location from which they had ready access to all parts of the periphery. But the lack of planning in connection with the centrifugal movement of industry was only one factor in keeping population from decentralizing to the same degree. Another very important factor was the reluctance of the workers to move to a locality where they could not readily secure transportation to other factories. They do not like to become too dependent upon a single employer or even on a few employers.

Between 1920 and 1930 the ninety-six metropolitan districts of 1930, nearly all of which contained a city of over 100,000, increased over 28 per cent in population, while the rate of growth for the total population was only 16.1 per cent. The central cities in these districts, however, grew by only 22.3 per cent, while the districts outside these cities grew by 44.0 per cent, or practically twice as fast. All the cities not in these metropolitan districts increased by only 19.4 per cent, or at a significantly slower rate than the central cities and only about two-thirds as fast as the entire districts. The rural areas of the nation outside these districts increased by only 3.7 per cent. When the rural population is broken into farm and nonfarm, it is found that the farm population declined by about 1.2 million while the nonfarm population grew by 3.7 million.

Between 1930 and 1940 this trend towards the metropolitan districts continued, although at a slower rate. However, instead of the metropolitan districts growing almost twice as fast as the nation, the 133 metropolitan districts for which comparable data are available grew less than one-seventh faster than the nation (8.2 and 7.2 per cent, respectively), while the districts outside the central cities grew more than three times as fast as the central cities (15.8 and 5.0 per cent, respectively). For the first time the outside areas grew more in absolute numbers than the central cities. It should also be noted that the small cities (2,500–50,000) grew faster (11.3 per cent) than the metropolitan districts (8.2 per cent). Unfortunately we do not know just what this more rapid increase of small cities signifies. A great many of these lie within the bounds of the metropolitan districts already referred to, and their more rapid growth may be largely a consequence of the suburban movement. . . .

During this last decade, 1930–40, the farm population remained practically stationary in numbers, hence it declined proportionately. The rural-nonfarm population, however, increased by about 3,400,000 or by 14.2 per cent (see Table I). This is about twice the rate of the nation as a whole and considerably more than that of the metropolitan districts (8.2 per cent). This would seem to indicate a considerable movement of people out of cities or at least into less congested areas. . . . Preliminary results . . . seem to indicate that a considerable proportion of this nonfarm increase took place within metropolitan districts and must be regarded as part of the suburban movement.

TABLE I

PERCENTAGE INCREASE IN THE POPULATION, URBAN AND RURAL, UNITED STATES: 1920–40

Area	*1930–40*	*1920–30*
Total United States	7.2	16.1
Urban	7.9	27.3
Rural-nonfarm	14.2	17.4
Rural-farm	0.2	−3.9

Increasingly frequent reference to "blighted" areas in our large cities might lead one to conclude that there was a rather large net movement of population out of the central cities to the suburbs. This does not seem to be borne out by the facts. The central cities claim not only their own excess of births over deaths but still draw some people to them from smaller areas which have higher birth rates, although their drawing power is now less than that of their suburbs.

It would appear, therefore, that one's judgment as to whether the rather slight decentralization of population from 1930 to 1940 is of much significance will depend largely on his evaluation of this suburban movement. Does the suburban movement in its present form yield the results in improvement in living and in changes in social attitudes which we believe decentralization should yield if it is to contribute to the more fruitful development of human nature?

URBANISM AND THE BIRTH RATE *

The large cities of today and their environs in nearly all of the industrialized West have birth rates too low to maintain their present numbers. Furthermore, the lowest of these birth rates are found in the more comfortable economic and the better educated classes. If we assume that it is desirable to maintain about our present numbers, the rates of reproduction in the cities and their suburbs become matters of very great importance, and if there are significant differences between them, the suburban movement might turn out to be of the highest consequence.

* Thompson, *op. cit.*, pp. 66–74.

Unfortunately, up to the present, there is no clear evidence of any substantial difference between cities and their suburbs in rates of reproduction, hence we must assume that, as yet, suburban living is not exerting much influence on the social attitudes which determine reproduction.

The important differentials in reproduction of which we are certain today are: (a) the relatively high rate in the rural population, and particularly the rural farm population, as compared with the urban population; and (b) within the urban population the much higher rate of the poor and the unschooled as compared with the comfortable and well schooled. . . .

Table II shows the replacement rate of certain groups of our population as it was in 1930–40 and thirty years earlier (1,000 will just maintain numbers).

TABLE II

NET REPRODUCTION RATES, FOR THE UNITED STATES, URBAN AND RURAL, 1935 TO 1940, 1930 TO 1935, AND 1905 TO 1910

Area	*1935–40*	*1930–35*	*1905–10*
United States	978	984	1,336
Urban	726	747	937
Rural-nonfarm	1,150	1,150	1,499
Rural-farm	1,661	1,632	2,022

Source: U. S. Bureau of the Census Special Report Series P-1943, No. 5, November 11, 1943. A rate of 1,000 would just maintain population with birth rates and death rates as they were at the given date, with no migration. A rate of 726, therefore, means that under these conditions this group would decline to 72.6 per cent of its present size in a generation, while a rate of 1,661 means that this group would increase to 166.1 per cent of its present size in a generation.

The statement that large cities and their suburbs have birth rates too low to insure reproduction may seem exaggerated to one who has just read in his local paper that X had 500 or 5,000 or 10,000 more births than deaths in 1943. The joker here is that although most large cities still have more births than deaths, they have such a surplus only because they have a very high proportion of young adults. According to the 1940 Census, 26.5 per cent of the urban population is aged 20–34 as compared with only 21.2 per cent of the rural-farm population. . . . Thus the urban population in the most important reproductive ages is one-fourth larger than the farm population. This large difference is due to the heavy migration into the cities both from abroad and from the rural areas. Since a high proportion of young adults in any population has the effect of maintaining a relatively high birth rate and a relatively low death rate, the cities appear to have a natural increase long after the number of children born per mother is insufficient to replace the current population. At present it can be safely said that there is no city in the United States having over 100,000 population that would maintain its numbers for two generations if it were deprived of migrants, and after that time most of them would decline by 25 per cent or more in each generation. Many of our small cities are in the same situation but to a lesser degree, for it is generally true today that as the size of the community decreases the birth rate rises. But in spite of the somewhat higher birth rate in the small cities, the only part of our population which is unquestionably replacing itself is the rural population, and even in the rural population the nonfarm group, being rather highly urbanized in many parts of the country, has a comparatively low rate of increase. (See Table I.)

I would not give the impression that it is a new thing for cities to fail to reproduce. In fact it is usual rather than unusual for cities to depend on migrants for the maintenance and increase of their numbers. Throughout most of man's history, however, the natural *decrease* of cities came about by reason of their enormous death rates rather than by reason of their low birth rates as is the case today. It was not until quite recently, with the coming of the Industrial Revolution, that man learned enough about the control of disease to insure a natural growth of city populations. Prior to about 1750–1800 the sanitation of all cities was so horrible that death rates of fifty or more per 1,000 (they are now ten to eleven in the United States) were usual. A careful study of the registration of deaths in London between 1700 and 1750 led Miss Buer to conclude that the excess of deaths over births amounted to about 10,000 annually. But once even a small measure of sanitation became possible in the cities, the death rate was lowered so rapidly that there soon came to be a substantial excess of births over deaths, and this excess grew as better economic conditions and improved medical care came to supplement better sanitation. As a consequence there was a period in the West from about 1750 or 1800 to 1900, varying considerably both in time and in duration in different countries and cities, when cities had a true and fairly large excess of births over deaths. Their death rates came under control much sooner and faster than their birth rates. However, this period was relatively short. The birth rate, too, began to come under control in the cities after two or three generations and was soon under such complete control and had been reduced so greatly that most of the large cities no longer had enough births to keep up their numbers on a long-time basis, although their death rates are still declining. This situation, if not already present, is rapidly becoming common to most western lands.

Some facts recently published by our Census Bureau regarding the number of children ever born to different groups of women throw additional light on the failure of our cities to reproduce. In 1910 about 12.8 per cent of the urban white women 40–44 (born 1866–70), who had married and who reported on the number of children they had borne, were childless. In 1940 (women 40–44, born 1896–1900) this proportion had risen to 17.6 per cent or more than one-third; for the rural-nonfarm white women the proportions were 10.1 per cent and 13.7 per cent, respectively; and for rural-farm white women 6.0 per cent and 8.7 per cent, respectively, or just about half as large as among city women. If the women who never married are assumed to be childless, and the same proportion of the married women who did not report on number of children borne as of those who did report are added to the married women reporting no child, we get a total of 27.2 per cent of all urban white women 40–44 in 1940 who were childless, as compared with 24.5 per cent in 1910. A similar calculation yields 20.3 per cent for rural-nonfarm white women and 14.1 per cent for rural-farm white women, as compared with 19.0 per cent and 11.9 per cent respectively in 1910. The increase between 1910 and 1940 in the proportions of the married white women 40–44 reporting who had only one child was as follows: in the urban population, from 13.6 per cent to 21.0 per cent; in the rural-nonfarm, from 11.5 per cent to 17.9 per cent; and in the rural-farm population, from 7.8 per cent to 11.8 per cent.

In most of the large cities the proportions of married women who are childless are even higher than in the urban population as a whole. In 1940 in New York City 18.0 per cent of the white married women 40–44 reporting on number of children ever born were childless, in spite of the fact that a great many of these women were foreign born, among whom childlessness is less than among native born. In Chicago, the proportion childless rose to 18.9 per cent and in Los Angeles to 28.5 per cent. When a proportional number of married women 40–44 not reporting on number of children born and the unmarried women of the same age are added to this childless group, we find that about 29 per cent of the white women 40–44 in New York and Chicago never had a child, and about 36 per cent of those in Los Angeles. Since these percentages of childless women in 1940 relate to women born in 1896–1900 and who were having most of their children during the nineteen twenties, it is safe to assume some further increase both in childlessness and in one-child families among younger women.

It was not a serious matter for the city to depend on the country for the migrants to keep up its numbers, or even to increase them as long as only 10 to 20 per cent of the people lived there. The 80 to 90 per cent of country people could easily make up this deficit. Today, when many countries have half or more of their people living in cities, the situation is quite different. In 1940 over 56 per cent of the people of the United States lived in urban communities and another 4 or 5 per cent lived in the satellite rural areas of our metropolitan districts and can very properly be regarded as urban in birth rates. Thus about 60 per cent of our total population is now living under distinctly urban conditions and has a deficit of births of about 27 per cent, that is, if it maintained the birth rate and the death rate of 1935–39 and had no in-migration, it would begin to decline by over one-fourth in each generation after its present favorable age make-up had passed. Obviously if the entire nation is to maintain its numbers when our whole population has ceased to have a favorable age make-up and 60 per cent is failing to reproduce by 27 per cent, the remaining 40 per cent must not only maintain itself but add over 40 per cent to its numbers in each generation. In terms of the reproductive performance of an average woman in these two groups, assuming a continuance of 1935–39 birth rates in the urban group (60 per cent), maintenance of our population would require that for each child born to a woman in this group there be 1.92 children born to a woman in the 40 per cent group. Is this a desirable situation even if it would work?

This is not the place to enter into the question of the desirability of a growing, a stationary, or a declining population in the nation. One's judgment on this point will depend on many things which have little to do with the effect of city life on population growth. I do wish, however, to call attention to the fact that in all human history, community life has been organized to insure reproduction to all its members with only minor exceptions (vestal virgins, a celibate priesthood, sisters of mercy, eunuchs of the royal household, and a few other small groups). There have always been some sterile marriages, but they were few and carried a stigma. Furthermore, until quite recently in the West, social sanction was commonly given to a variety of arrangements to insure the perpetuation of the family where the marriage was childless (concubinage, etc.).

Now we come rather suddenly to a form of society in which a large proportion of the women have no children, about 30 per cent in our urban white population, or only one child, about 20 per cent in the same group. This indicates the growth of a new scale of values in our urban community, since the evidence shows that a considerable proportion of all childlessness and of one-child families is voluntary. If this reproductive failure is not voluntary, it indicates a physiological degeneration which is just as deadly. In either event, for any society to have its dominant classes, and no one will dispute the dominance of the well-to-do urban classes in our modern society, lose interest in reproduction, and as a consequence in the future of the community because they have little or no biological stake in it, is an extremely serious matter. If the leaders of any society rather suddenly cease to organize their lives around children and instead organize them around personal desires and the use of goods which they can buy with what they save by not having children, that society will have to face a situation in which it would seem to stand but little chance of surviving. Its people will cease to belong to "the meek who shall inherit the earth."

We know too little to say with any certainty what the social effects on our civilization will be if 30 per cent of our city people continue to have no children and another 20 per cent continue to have only one child. The demographic problem we have already noted. We do know, however, that it is the women with no children or with one child who, in general, set the mode-for-living considered most desirable by the urban community. They are creating a pattern of living which certainly cannot be considered good if we are thinking farther ahead than our own immediate personal interests. No pattern of living which does not include reproduction can be other than ephemeral. A preoccupation with personal ambitions, luxury, and ease of living so great that children have no place in life does not augur well for the future of our civilization. Obviously there is no future for any class, group, or even a nation, if any considerable part of its people persistently refuses to reproduce. There are, in the judgment of the writer, times when the population of a nation should be reduced in numbers in order to make decent living possible; but it is hard to believe that this is now the case in a country so liberally endowed with natural resources as the United States.

CHAPTER IV

The Urban Way of Life

THE effect of the city on the attitudes, emotions, and habits of the people is not easy to measure. Some of the objective indices —such as the birth rate—have already been indicated. More indices are available, and in addition it is possible by realistic description to convey the quality of life as it appears in the minds of those who spend their lives in the city. The readings in the present chapter help us to realize the full impact of urban living upon the American individual and his mental outlook.

CITY CIVILIZATION *

The beginning of what is distinctively modern in our civilization is best signalized by the growth of great cities. Nowhere has mankind been farther removed from organic nature than under the conditions of life characteristic of great cities. . . . The distinctive feature of the mode of living of man in the modern age is his concentration into gigantic aggregations around which cluster lesser centers and from which radiate the ideas and practices that we call civilization.

The degree to which the contemporary world may be said to be "urban" is not fully or accurately measured by the proportion of the total population living in cities. The influences which cities exert upon the social life of man are greater than the ratio of the urban population would indicate, for the city is not only in ever larger degrees the dwelling-place and the workshop of modern man, but it is the initiating and controlling center of economic, political, and cultural life. . . .

The shift from a rural to a predominantly urban society, which has taken place within the span of a single generation in such industrialized areas as the United States and Japan, has been accompanied by profound changes in virtually every phase of social life. . . . Since the

* Wirth, Louis, "Urbanism as a Way of Life," *The American Journal of Sociology,* Vol. 44, No. 1 (July 1938), pp. 1–3, 10–17, 21–23.

city is the product of growth rather than of instantaneous creation, it is to be expected that the influences which it exerts upon the modes of life should not be able to wipe out completely the previously dominant modes of human association. To a greater or lesser degree, therefore, our social life bears the imprint of an earlier folk society, the characteristic modes of settlement of which were the farm, the manor, and the village. This historic influence is reinforced by the circumstance that the population of the city itself is in large measure recruited from the countryside, where a mode of life reminiscent of this earlier form of existence persists. Hence we should not expect to find abrupt and discontinuous variation between urban and rural types of personality. . . .

Since the population of the city does not reproduce itself, it must recruit its migrants from other cities, the countryside, and—in this country until recently—from other countries. The city has thus historically been the melting-pot of races, peoples, and cultures, and a most favorable breeding-ground of new biological and cultural hybrids. It has not only tolerated but rewarded individual differences. It has brought together people from the ends of the earth *because* they are different and thus useful to one another, rather than because they are homogeneous and like-minded. . . .

The bonds of kinship, of neighborliness, and the sentiments arising out of living together for generations under a common folk tradition are likely to be absent or, at best, relatively weak in an aggregate the members of which have such diverse origins and backgrounds. Under such circumstances competition and formal control mechanisms furnish the substitutes for the bonds of solidarity that are relied upon to hold a folk society together. . . .

The multiplication of persons in a state of interaction under conditions which make their contact as full personalities impossible produces that segmentalization of human relationships which has sometimes been seized upon by students of the mental life of the cities as an explanation for the "schizoid" character of urban personality. This is not to say that the urban inhabitants have fewer acquaintances than rural inhabitants, for the reverse may actually be true; it means rather that in relation to the number of people whom they see and with whom they rub elbows in the course of daily life, they know a smaller proportion, and of these they have less intensive knowledge.

Characteristically, urbanites meet one another in highly segmental roles. They are, to be sure, dependent upon more people for the satisfactions of their life-needs than are rural people and thus are associated with a greater number of organized groups, but they are less dependent upon particular persons, and their dependence upon others is confined to a highly fractionalized aspect of the other's round of activity. This is essentially what is meant by saying that the city is characterized by secondary rather than primary contacts. The contacts of the city may indeed be face to face, but they are nevertheless impersonal, superficial, transitory, and segmental. The reserve, the indifference, and the blasé outlook which urbanites manifest in their relationships may thus be regarded as devices for immunizing themselves against the personal claims and expectations of others.

The superficiality, the anonymity, and the transitory character of urban-social relations make intelligible, also, the sophistication and the rationality generally ascribed to city-dwellers. Our acquaintances tend to stand in a relationship of utility to us in the sense that the role which each one plays in our life is overwhelmingly regarded as a means for the achievement of our own ends. Whereas, therefore, the individual gains, on the one hand, a certain degree of emancipation or freedom from the personal and emotional controls of intimate groups, he loses, on the other hand, the spontaneous self-expression, the morale, and the sense of participation that comes with living in an integrated society. This constitutes essentially the state of *anomie* or the social void to which Durkheim alludes in attempting to account for the various forms of social disorganization in technological society.

The segmental character and utilitarian accent of interpersonal relations in the city find their institutional expression in the proliferation of specialized tasks which we see in their most developed form in the professions. The operation of the pecuniary nexus leads to predatory relationships, which tend to obstruct the efficient functioning of the social order unless checked by professional codes and occupational etiquette. The premium put upon utility and efficiency suggests the adaptability of the corporate device for the organization of enterprises in which individuals can engage only in groups. The advantage that the corporation has over the individual entrepreneur and the partnership in the urban-industrial world derives not only from the possibility it affords of centralizing the resources of thousands of individuals or from the legal privilege of limited liability and perpetual succession, but from the fact that the corporation has no soul.

The specialization of individuals, particularly in their occupations, can proceed only, as Adam Smith pointed out, upon the basis of an enlarged market, which in turn accentuates the division of labor. This enlarged market is only in part supplied by the city's hinterland; in large measure it is found among the large numbers that the city itself contains. The dominance of the city over the surrounding hinterland becomes explicable in terms of the division of labor which urban life occasions and promotes. The extreme degree of interdependence and the unstable equilibrium of urban life are closely associated with the division of labor and the specialization of occupations. This interdependence and instability is increased by the tendency of each city to specialize in those functions in which it has the greatest advantage.

In a community composed of a larger number of individuals than can know one another intimately and can be assembled in one spot, it becomes necessary to communicate through indirect mediums and to articulate individual interests by a process of delegation. Typically in the city, interests are made effective through representation. The individual counts for little, but the voice of the representative is heard with a deference roughly proportional to the numbers for whom he speaks. . . .

On the subjective side, as Simmel has suggested, the close physical contact of numerous individuals necessarily produces a shift in the mediums through which we orient ourselves to the urban milieu, especially to our fellow-men. Typically, our physical contacts are close but our social contacts are distant. The urban world puts a premium on visual recognition. We see the uniform which denotes the role of the functionaries and are oblivious to the personal eccentricities that are hidden behind the uniform. We tend to acquire and develop a sensitivity to a world of artifacts and become progressively farther removed from the world of nature.

We are exposed to glaring contrasts between splendor and squalor, between riches and poverty, intelligence and ignorance, order and chaos. The competition for space is great, so that each area generally tends to be put to the use which yields the greatest economic return. Place of work tends to become dissociated from place of residence, for the proximity of industrial and commercial establishments makes an area both economically and socially undesirable for residential purposes. . . .

The different parts of the city thus acquire specialized functions. The city consequently tends to resemble a mosaic of social worlds in which the transition from one to the other is abrupt. The juxtaposition of divergent personalities and modes of life tends to produce a relativistic perspective and a sense of toleration of differences which may be regarded as prerequisites for rationality and which lead toward the secularization of life.[1]

[1] The extent to which the segregation of the population into distinct ecological and cultural areas and the resulting social attitude of tolerance, rationality, and secular mentality are functions of density as distinguished from heterogeneity is difficult to determine. Most likely

The close living together and working together of individuals who have no sentimental and emotional ties foster a spirit of competition, aggrandizement, and mutual exploitation. To counteract irresponsibility and potential disorder, formal controls tend to be resorted to. Without rigid adherence to predictable routines a large compact society would scarcely be able to maintain itself. The clock and the traffic signal are symbolic of the basis of our social order in the urban world. Frequent close physical contact, coupled with great social distance, accentuates the reserve of unattached individuals toward one another and, unless compensated for by other opportunities for response, gives rise to loneliness. The necessary frequent movement of great numbers of individuals in a congested habitat gives occasion to friction and irritation. Nervous tensions which derive from such personal frustrations are accentuated by the rapid tempo and the complicated technology under which life in dense areas must be lived.

The social interaction among such a variety of personality types in the urban milieu tends to break down the rigidity of caste lines and to complicate the class structure, and thus induces a more ramified and differentiated framework of social stratification than is found in more integrated societies. The heightened mobility of the individual, which brings him within the range of stimulation by a great number of diverse individuals and subjects him to fluctuating status in the differentiated social groups that compose the social structure of the city, tends toward the acceptance of instability and insecurity in the world at large as a norm. This fact helps to account, too, for the sophistication and cosmopolitanism of the urbanite. No single group has the undivided allegiance of the individual. The groups with which he is affiliated do not lend themselves readily to a simple hierarchical arrangement. By virtue of his different interests arising out of different aspects of social life, the individual acquires membership in widely divergent groups, each of which functions only with reference to a single segment of his personality. . . .

Partly as a result of the physical footlooseness of the population and partly as a result of their social mobility, the turnover in group membership generally is rapid. Place of residence, place and character of employment, income and interests fluctuate, and the task of holding organizations together and maintaining and promoting intimate and lasting acquaintanceship between the members is difficult. This applies strikingly to the local areas within the city into which persons become segregated more by virtue of differences in race, language, income, and social status, than

---

we are dealing here with phenomena which are consequences of the simultaneous operation of both factors.

through choice or positive attraction to people like themselves. Overwhelmingly the city-dweller is not a home-owner, and since a transitory habitat does not generate binding traditions and sentiments, only rarely is he truly a neighbor. There is little opportunity for the individual to obtain a conception of the city as a whole or to survey his place in the total scheme. Consequently he finds it difficult to determine what is to his own "best interests" and to decide between the issues and leaders presented to him by the agencies of mass suggestion. Individuals who are thus detached from the organized bodies which integrate society comprise the fluid masses that make collective behavior in the urban community so unpredictable and hence so problematical. . . .

The low and declining urban-reproduction rates suggest that the city is not conducive to the traditional type of family life, including the rearing of children and the maintenance of the home as the locus of a whole round of vital activities. The transfer of industrial, educational, and recreational activities to specialized institutions outside the home has deprived the family of some of its most characteristic historical functions. In cities mothers are more likely to be employed, lodgers are more frequently part of the household, marriage tends to be postponed, and the proportion of single and unattached people is greater. Families are smaller and more frequently without children than in the country. The family as a unit of social life is emancipated from the larger kinship group characteristic of the country, and the individual members pursue their own diverging interests in their vocational, educational, religious, recreational, and political life. . . .

On the whole, the city discourages an economic life in which the individual in time of crisis has a basis of subsistence to fall back upon, and it discourages self-employment. While incomes of city people are on the average higher than those of country people, the cost of living seems to be higher in the larger cities. Home ownership involves greater burdens and is rarer. Rents are higher and absorb a larger proportion of the income. Although the urban-dweller has the benefit of many communal services, he spends a large proportion of his income for such items as recreation and advancement and a smaller proportion for food. What the communal services do not furnish the urbanite must purchase, and there is virtually no human need which has remained unexploited by commercialism. Catering to thrills and furnishing means of escape from drudgery, monotony, and routine thus become two of the major functions of urban recreation, which at its best furnishes means for creative self-expression and spontaneous group association, but which more typically in the urban world results in passive spectatorism on the one hand, or sensational record-smashing feats on the other.

Being reduced to a stage of virtual impotence as an individual, the urbanite is bound to exert himself by joining with others of similar interest into organized groups to obtain his ends. This results in the enormous multiplication of voluntary organizations directed toward as great a variety of objectives as there are human needs and interests. While on the one hand the traditional ties of human association are weakened, urban existence involves a much greater degree of interdependence between man and man and a more complicated, fragile, and volatile form of mutual interrelations over many phases of which the individual as such can exert scarcely any control. Frequently there is only the most tenuous relationship between the economic position or other basic factors that determine the individual's existence in the urban world and the voluntary groups with which he is affiliated. . . .

It is largely through the activities of the voluntary groups . . . that the urbanite expresses and develops his personality, acquires status, and is able to carry on the round of activities that constitute his life-career. It may easily be inferred, however, that the organizational framework . . . does not of itself insure the consistency and integrity of the personalities whose interests it enlists. Personal disorganization, mental breakdown, suicide, delinquency, crime, corruption, and disorder might be expected under these circumstances to be more prevalent in the urban than in the rural community. This has been confirmed in so far as comparable indices are available.

THE WORLD OF FURNISHED ROOMS *

Back of the ostentatious apartments, hotels, and homes of the Lake Shore Drive, and the quiet, shady streets of the Gold Coast lies an area of streets that have a painful sameness, with their old, soot-begrimed stone houses, their none-too-clean alleys, their shabby air of respectability. In the window of house after house along these streets one sees a black and white card with the words "Rooms To Rent." For this is the world of furnished rooms, a world of strangely unconventional customs and people, one of the most characteristic of the worlds that go to make up the life of the great city.

* Zorbaugh, Harvey W., *The Gold Coast and the Slum* (Chicago: The University of Chicago Press, 1929), pp. 69–82, 86.

This nondescript world, like every rooming-house district, has a long and checkered history.

> The typical rooming-house is never built for the purpose; it is always an adaptation of a former private residence, a residence which has seen better days. At first, in its history as a rooming-house, it may be a very high-class rooming-house. Then, as the fashionable residence district moves farther and farther uptown, and as business comes closer and closer, the grade of the institution declines until it may become eventually nothing but a "bums' hotel" or a disorderly house.[1] . . .

An analysis of the *Illinois Lodging House Register* reveals the fact that there are 1,139 rooming- and lodging-houses on the Near North Side, and that in these houses 23,007 people are living in furnished rooms of one kind and another. Ninety blocks in the better rooming area north of Chicago Avenue were studied intensively, by means of a house-to-house census. This study revealed the additional facts that 71 per cent of all the houses in this district keep roomers; and that of the people who live in these rooms, 52 per cent are single men, 10 per cent are single women, and 38 per cent are couples, "married," supposedly with "benefit of clergy." The rooming-house area is a childless area. Yet most of its population is in the productive ages of life, between twenty and thirty-five. . . .

The population living in these rooming-houses is typically what the labor leader refers to as the "white collar" group—men and women filling various clerical positions—accountants, stenographers, and the like, office workers of various sorts. There are also students from the many music schools of the Near North Side. . . .

The constant comings and goings of its inhabitants is the most striking and significant characteristic of this world of furnished rooms. This whole population turns over every four months. There are always cards in the windows, advertising the fact that rooms are vacant, but these cards rarely have to stay up over a day, as people are constantly walking the streets looking for rooms. The keepers of the rooming-houses change almost as rapidly as the roomers themselves. At least half of the keepers of these houses have been at their present addresses six months or less. . . .

The rooming-house is not to be confused with the boarding-house.

> The characteristics of the old-time boarding-house are too well known to need recounting here. With all its shortcomings, it will be admitted that there was in it something of the home element. Boarders knew each other; they met at table two or three times a day, and lingered a few moments in

[1] Trotter, *The Housing of Non-Family Women in Chicago,* p. 5.

conversation after dinner in the evening. In summer they gathered on the front steps and piazzas, and in the winter often played euchre and whist in the landlady's parlor. Congenial temperaments had a chance to find each other. There was a public parlor where guests were received, and, in a reputable boarding-house at least, a girl would not have thought of taking a gentleman caller to her own room. The landlady of a good boarding-house took something of a personal interest, even if remote, in her boarders, and they often found themselves becoming a part of the family, even against their wills. There was a certain personal element in the relations between individuals; no one could be isolated and certainly shut up to himself.[2]

Here, at least, was a nucleus of opinion, set of personal relationships, which tended to define social situations. But the boarding-house has passed out of existence in the modern city. The rise of rents, the mechanization of life, and sharper definition of economic function resulting in the development of the café and restaurant business has reduced the former keeper of the boarding-house to the simpler employment of "taking lodgers." Not a dozen boarding-houses were found in this Near North Side district.

The rooming-house which has replaced the boarding-house is a very different sort of place to live. It has no dining-room, no parlor, no common meeting place. Few acquaintanceships spring up in a rooming-house.

> One gets to know few people in a rooming-house. All told, in the year and a half I lived there, I didn't come to know over twenty well enough to speak to them. And there must have been nearly three hundred people in and out in that time—for there are constant comings and goings; someone is always moving out; . . . People change so fast, and one is in so little—being at work all day, and out every evening as likely as not—that there is little chance to get acquainted if one wished. But one doesn't wish—there is a universal barrier of distrust in this rooming-house world. . . .

The keeper of the rooming-house has no personal contact with, or interest in, his roomers. He is satisfied to collect his rents and to make a living. It is an entirely commercial consideration with him. Consequently the average keeper of a rooming-house is not too particular about who rooms in his house, or what goes on in it, as long as the other roomers are not disturbed. . . .

A woman who was asked by one of the census workers how many married couples there were in her house said: "I don't know— I don't ask. I want to rent my rooms."

The rooming-house is a place of anonymous relationships. One knows

---

[2] A. B. Wolfe, *The Lodging-House Problem in Boston,* I, pp. 46–47.

no one, and is known by no one. One comes and goes as one wishes, does very much as one pleases, and as long as one disturbs no one else, no questions are asked. How complete this anonymity may be shown in the following document:

> I had occasion to inquire for a man living in a rooming-house. He had roomed there about a week. There was no 'phone in the place, so I had to call at his address. I went there about 7:30. After I had rung the bell for some time, a woman about forty-five answered the door. She wore a house apron, and was evidently the landlady. I asked for Mr. X. She said "Who?" I repeated the name. She shook her head, and said that she didn't know anyone of that name. I looked at the address in my notebook, to see if I had the address correct. I told her that this was the address he had given, and went on to describe him. She knew of two men in the house who might answer to his description. I then told her that he did a lot of work on the typewriter in his room. Then she knew whom I meant. She told me to go to the third floor front and see if he was there. He was not in. I knocked at several other rooms, but no one knew anything about him. When I got downstairs the lady had disappeared, and I could not leave a message.
>
> I came back a week later, and the same woman came to the door. I asked if Mr. X. was in. She said he had moved yesterday. I asked if she knew where he went, but she did not know. She said that he left when his week was up. He had left a note for her, saying he had to leave. I asked her if he might not have left a forwarding address for his mail. She said that he did not, that he never got any mail.[3]

Such complete anonymity could be found nowhere but in the city of today, and nowhere in the city save in the rooming-house.

The peculiar social relationships of the world of furnished rooms are reflected in the behavior of the people who live in this world. Nothing could bring this out more clearly and significantly than the story which follows, the life-story of a "charity girl."

> Emporia, Kansas, was my home until I was twenty-two. My father had a small business there. He was an upright, God-fearing man. . . . He taught us to obey the Ten Commandments, to go to church on Sunday, to do all the things the "respectable" do in a small, gossiping place.
>
> We were a large family but father managed to save enough to send me, the oldest, to a small college in the state. And from the time I was a little girl I had music lessons. It is about these music lessons that the story of my life revolves. . . .

[3] Document 16.

The first few weeks [in the city] went by like magic. It was all so strange and maddeningly stimulating to my smalltown soul. . . .

I soon found a rooming-house was the only place I could live. But it was hard to find a rooming-house where I wanted to live. The rooms I could afford were in gloomy old houses on La Salle Street, bleak and bare, and so large that usually I had to share them with one or two other girls. The beds were hard, and often vermin-infested. The landladies were queer-looking and dowdy, tight-lipped and suspicious of eye, ignorant and coarse. They rarely took any other interest in you than to see that you paid your week in advance. The men and women living in the house were mostly a tough lot. There were goings on that shocked me then—though I would pay scant attention to them now. . . .

I had come to the city in June. By Christmas my loneliness amounted almost to desperation. I had made no friends—a girl brought up on the Commandments doesn't make friends in rooming-houses or as a waitress very readily. I didn't talk the same language as the girls I worked with. At the theater or the restaurant men often came up to me and said things in a way that made me blush, though often I had no idea what they meant, unsophisticated little fool that I was. Mother was ill, and letters from home came less and less frequently. Shortly after Christmas she died, and the last tie that bound me to Emporia was gone. I was "on my own," and very nearly "on my uppers" as well. But I still had my ambition—I would some day be a great *artiste,* and all this loneliness and hardship would be forgotten. . . .

There were occasional little dramas—as when a baby was found in the alley, and when the woman in "the third floor back" took poison after a quarrel with her husband, or when police came to arrest a man who had eloped from Pittsburgh with his wife's sister, and a new trio of roomers robbed most of the "guests" on the second floor; there were these occasional little dramas when the halls and bathrooms were the scenes of a few minutes' hurried and curious gossip. But the next day these same people would hurry past each other on the stairs without speaking. . . .

[A year of this had gone by, when one day her music teacher told her there was no hope of her ever realizing her ambitions.] I turned dazedly from the piano . . . I scarcely heard him. I picked up my music and tossed it into a waste-basket in the corner; and then I walked out of the room. . . .

Then I began to look at my life in Chicago. What was there in it, after all? My music was gone. I had neither family nor friends. In Emporia there would at least have been neighborhood clubs or the church. But here there was neither. Oh, for someone or something to belong to!

My room-mate had been going to Sunday night services at the Fourth Presbyterian Church, over on the Lake Shore Drive. She told them about me, and one day some pastor's assistant's assistant came to call on me. I went one night after that. I was greeted with ostentatious and half-hearted civility. It was all so impersonal . . . I never went back; and no other church ever took an interest in me. The only other group I had had anything to do with, outside of my work, had been a social agency from which I had tried to get a little help in the spring. They treated me as impersonally as though I had been a rag doll. There was ringing of buzzers, long documents with endless questionings to be filled out—and not a human touch in it all. . . .

Of course, there were two ways out: I might slip into the lake, there, and end it all. But somehow I didn't think seriously of that. Or I might do as some of the girls in the house, become a "gold digger," play life for what there was in it, pay with what there was in me. The idea half-sickened me, yet I played with it for a while—for so long that I drew up startled at the unknown possibilities that lurked within me, cold at the thought that there was neither person nor thing to hold me back.

I never went back to music school. I had been working as a waitress of late, . . . and I kept on with it. But the days and nights were empty now—and at last I knew to the full what loneliness could be. One night a nice boy came into the restaurant—it was one of the larger downtown restaurants—and sat down at my table. He talked to me, as they all did; told me he was from a small town in Oklahoma, that he'd made money, and had come to see the big city. He was friendly, and ended by asking me to a show. I accepted, and we went to a cabaret afterward. In a spirit of reckless bravado, to show the small-town boy I was a city-wise woman, I smoked my first cigarette and took my first drink.

There's no use in making a story of it. He had an engaging smile, and was in search of adventure. I was unutterably lonely—and tired. He said that he loved me, and I was willing not to question too closely. I left the rooming-house, and we took a little flat out near Rogers Park. For a month I played at being respectable, got acquainted with young wives in other apartments, had lovely clothes, lazy hours, ate at the best restaurants, saw the best shows, shopped in smart shops, drove my own car. Then, one day, B. came home and told me he was going back to Oklahoma, and that I wasn't going with him. I said little; I had known it must come, of course, though I had hoped it wouldn't come so soon. There was a generous check. And I moved back into the rooming-house.

No, I felt no remorse. Life had cheated me. There was no one to care. Why slave and work when I might have the things I wanted? And not the least of these was the intimate touch and glance of a man—even if it were half make-believe. Someone to talk intimately with, someone to come home to, someone to ask where you've been—these, too, are things one can't live without. . . .

The conditions of life in the world of furnished rooms are the direct antithesis of all we are accustomed to think of as normal in society. The exaggerated mobility and astonishing anonymity of this world have significant implications for the life of the community. Where people are constantly coming and going; where they live at best but a few months in a given place; where no one knows anyone else in his own house, to say nothing of his own block (children are the real neighbors, and it is a childless world); where there are no groups of any sort—where all these things are true—it is obvious that there can be no community tradition or common definition of situations, no public opinion, no informal social control. As a result, the rooming-house world is a world of political indifference,[4] of laxity of conventional standards, of personal and social disorganization . . . a mobile, anonymous, individual world, a world of thwarted wishes, of unsatisfied longings, of constant restlessness; a world in which people, in the effort to live, are building up a body of ideas that free them from a conventional tradition that has become fixed, hard, and oppressive; a world in which individuation, so typical of the life of the city, is carried to the extreme of personal and social disorganization. People behave in strange and incalculable ways; quick and intimate relationships spring up in the most casual way, and dissolve as quickly and as casually. Behavior is impulsive rather than social. It is a world of atomized individuals, of spiritual nomads.

RACE, SUICIDE, THE FAMILY *

Throughout history cities have been known as the melting pots of races and cultures and American cities exhibit this function in a most striking fashion. In the United States the foreign-born and their offspring are concentrated almost wholly in urban areas, and particularly in the largest cities. The foreign-born and their children constitute nearly two-thirds of all of the inhabitants of cities of 1 million and over. Their proportion of the urban population declines as the size of the city decreases until in

[4] A precinct captain in a rooming-house precinct said it was useless to try to get the people from rooming-houses to go to the polls (Document 17).

* National Resources Committee, *Our Cities* (Washington: Government Printing Office, 1937), pp. 9–11.

the rural areas they comprise only about one-sixth of the total population. Their preponderance is less pronounced today than it was in past decades, for in 1870 only 23.1 percent of the native white population was urban, while by 1930 this proportion had risen to 54.6 percent. The proportion of foreign stock has never been quite as high in the smaller as in the larger cities, but it was not until 1930 that the native whites of native parentage constituted as much as half of the population of even the middle-sized cities (25,000–50,000). The rural population, on the other hand, has always been predominantly native white of native parentage.

In addition to the foreign immigrants and their children, American cities derive their racial and ethnic heterogeneity from the migration of the Negro from the southern rural areas to the large cities. The largest cities have increased the number of their Negro population since 1890 at the expense of the smaller cities and rural areas. In the rural areas, for instance, the proportion of Negroes declined from 14.8 percent of the total rural population in 1870 to 12.4 percent in 1930. Since most of this decline has taken place since 1910 it may be assumed that the cityward migration of Negroes has probably not yet reached its full stride. Aside from the European immigrants and the Negro, our city population contains a sprinkling of other racial groups. When in addition we consider the fact that the European immigrants and their children who constitute so large a portion of the city dwellers, are by no means homogeneous, but comprise a wide variety of ethnic, linguistic, and nationalistic groups, the great diversity of mankind that makes up the American urban world becomes apparent. Cities of different sizes and types in different parts of the country show, of course, great variation in their racial and ethnic makeup. But the facts cited will suffice to show that one major characteristic of the urban dweller is his dissimilarity to this fellow townsmen.

Never before in the history of the world have great groups of people so diverse in social backgrounds been thrown together into such close contacts as in the cities of America. The typical American city, therefore, does not consist of a homogeneous body of citizens, but of human beings with the most diverse cultural backgrounds, often speaking different languages, following a great variety of customs, habituated to different modes and standards of living, and sharing only in varying degrees the tastes, the beliefs, and the ideals of their native fellow city dwellers. In short, far from presenting a picture of a single unified body of human beings, the American city is a motley of peoples and cultures forming a mosaic of little worlds which in part blend with one another, but, in part and for a time, remain segregated or come into conflict with one another.

SUICIDE

Every year in the United States approximately 22,000 persons take their own lives. For the past 30 years the rate of suicide in urban places of 10,000 population and over has been about 50 percent higher than in the smaller cities and rural areas. The incidence of suicide for the country as a whole increases directly with the increase in the size of the city, from a rate of 15.9 per 100,000 population in cities 10,000 to 25,000 population to 19.9 in cities of 250,000 to 500,000 population. There is a noticeable decline in the suicide rate for cities over 500,000 population. A tendency has been noted for fast-growing cities to have a higher suicide rate, which might account for the fact, in part, that the highest suicide rates are on the Pacific coast. The lowest suicide rates are in the New England and East South Central regions.

Urban areas with the highest percentage of adults, old people, males, and particularly elderly males, tend to have a higher incidence of suicide than other urban or rural places. Similarly, communities with large percentages of foreign born, Japanese, Chinese, and Mexican, tend to have higher rates. However, the incidence of suicide among Negroes is extremely low; in 1930 their suicide rate was 5.1 per 100,000 population as compared with 15.6 for the total population. Suicides are more frequent at the extremes of the economic scale than in the middle, which might in part account for the rural and urban differences in suicides, since extremes in wealth and poverty are found more often in the city.

Suicides increase markedly with business depressions. The suicide rate in urban areas, and for that matter in the country as a whole, is likely to decline as the economic and social security of the population increases, as mental and physical health is improved, as wholesome recreational facilities are provided, as the population becomes more stable, and as family and community solidarity are furthered.

OCCUPATION, INCOME, RECREATION *

Generally, a larger proportion of the adult urban population is gainfully employed than is the case with the rural adult population. The same is true of women, but the reverse of children. That these are specific characteristics of contemporary urban life is indicated by the fact that the larger the city the more prominent these are found to be.

* National Resources Committee, *op. cit.*, pp. 17–18, 22–24.

The cities differ from the country and the large cities from the small, moreover, by the types of occupations in which the inhabitants engage. The white-collar workers, i.e., those employed in trade and in clerical and professional work, are proportionally more numerous in large cities. Of 12 professions—authors and journalists, artists, architects, actors, musicians, lawyers, dentists, clergymen, trained nurses, teachers and physicians—only two, teachers and clergymen, have a lower ratio in large cities than in small ones. Even more pronounced is the difference in these respects between cities lying within and cities lying outside the metropolitan regions. The large cities and metropolitan centers not only have the largest proportion of white-collar workers and of certain professions, but they also appear to be less favorable to self-employment, especially in trade and probably also in the professions. Workers in rural areas are more evenly distributed throughout the various age groups, whereas urban workers, particularly those in clerical and professional service, trade, transportation, and communication, are more concentrated in the age class from 18 to 39 years. The span of the working life of the person is considerably shorter in the city than in the country. Thus while the city offers a greater range of vocational opportunities than does the country, it also introduces elements which undermine economic security.

The incomes of urban dwellers are on the average higher than those of rural persons and very large incomes, especially characteristic of certain limited strata of the urban population, are scarcely ever found in rural areas. Very large incomes from rural enterprises are almost always diverted to urban residents. Similarly, the larger the city the higher the per-capita income, and the more industrialized the city the lower the income. . . .

RECREATION

Recreational activities tend to become an important and distinct segment of life in the city. Urban recreation is particularly distinguished from recreation in rural areas by a greater degree of specialization and commercialization. Opportunities for informal recreation in the city, especially where the cooperation of others is concerned, are restricted by the limited extent of intimate and personal social contacts. No accurate account of this type of recreation is now obtainable. Expenditures for commercial recreation, which constitute 25 percent of the total recreational expenditures, increase directly with city size. Less than 2 percent of the total is accounted for by the recreational expenditures of all governmental agencies—local, State, and Federal. Commercial recreational establishments tend to provide largely passive recreational pursuits, whereas the forms of recreation involving some measure of active participation are largely supported by public and private noncommercial agencies. Public expenditures for recreation by cities over 30,000 population increase with the size of the city. The average public expenditure for such cities was $1.63 per capita in 1931, or 3.5 percent of the total municipal budget, in addition to an average expenditure of $0.61 per capita devoted to libraries.

Aside from the support they contribute to libraries, municipalities expend little of public funds for cultural activities such as concerts, museums, artistic and educational exhibits, the opera, and the theatre. Although the number, variety, and quality of recreational facilities increase with city size, their ratio to population is highest in the smaller or medium-sized cities. Utilization of recreational facilities is also greater in these cities. The medium-sized cities have the highest ratio of park acreage to population, and the rural areas have, of course, the natural recreational facilities of the open country. The large urban centers, however, have their advantage in the more highly institutionalized forms of recreation such as the art gallery and the symphony orchestra. . . .

TALENT AND ACHIEVEMENT

The privileges and opportunities as well as the handicaps and hazards of life in the city as compared to the country may be thought of from many and varied points of view. They range from the biological and physical advantages of either mode of life—including the chances of maintaining health and prolonging life, access to decent housing, finding satisfying work, sufficient income to assure security and to maintain an adequate and expanding standard of living, and the enjoyment of wholesome leisure—to the less obvious but highly important social and psychological influences which include opportunity for stimulating and fruitful associations with people and for personal self-development and achievement.

Without entering the question of the relative importance of inherited capacity as contrasted with opportunity for self-development, it is of interest to discover whether significant differences in achievement exist between urban and rural groups and whether they can be attributed to differences in inherited qualities in the population. If these differences should be found to be due to inherited capacity, then the possibilities of balanced progress in the sense of raising one group to the level of the other is, of course, less than it would be if the differences were due to environmental factors.

Some of the advantages of urban life seem to be indispensable to men who would achieve the goals that modern society values. It may well be that the criteria of success which our contemporary society cherishes are predominantly those of urban civilization, and that the rural inhabitant must be judged according to other standards of achievement which are relevant to the world in which he lives. But for good or for ill that world seems to bear the imprint of urbanism in an ever-increasing degree.

MUNICIPAL GOVERNMENT AND CORRUPTION *

The men who framed the first state constitutions and the city charters of the period based their work on those twin dogmas of government, the theory of the separation of powers and the doctrine of checks and balances. According to their reasoning government was a "necessary evil," affording a few men the opportunity to crush the liberties of their fellows. Against this danger the people must be always on guard, dividing power into such minute particles and distributing it among so many individuals that no one man would be able to abuse his authority. Every power they granted must be checked and counterbalanced by some limitation on its use, so that no person, however anxious he might be to sweep aside constitutional safeguards, would be in a position to disregard them. The fathers applied these doctrines zealously wherever possible. In the field of state government they created legislative bodies of two houses, so that each would act as a check upon the precipitate action of the other. They restricted so narrowly the powers of the governors that Madison declared in 1787: "The executives of the states are in general little more than ciphers." [1]

And so in the drafting of city charters they applied those same principles, in which they so ardently believed. The two chambers of the council were designed as a check upon each other, and the independently elected mayor was intended to be a check upon them both. Yet the mayor must not be permitted to become too powerful, else he might become a despot. The supervision of administration had passed entirely out of the hands of the council in most cities by 1850, and this work might well have been given to the mayor. Instead, however, it was transferred to independently elected heads of administrative departments. In time the principle of

* Macdonald, Austin F., *American City Government and Administration* (New York: Thomas Y. Crowell Company, 1941), pp. 50–60.

[1] *Elliot's Debates*, Vol. V, p. 327.

electing the more important administrative officials received almost universal acceptance, and the era of unrestrained democracy was in full swing. Surveyors, engineers, marshals, street commissioners, and superintendents of markets were popularly chosen, not to mention the more important officers whose candidacy might with some reason be thought to awaken public interest. Responsibility for satisfactory administration was therefore scattered among a large number of unrelated agencies, and no attempt was made to coordinate their work. The mayor was the logical person to bring order out of this administrative chaos, but the people refused to trust him. They pinned their faith instead to numerous elective officials and to frequent elections. Yet they did give the mayor a qualified veto over the acts of the council,[2] Baltimore conferring the veto power upon its mayor in 1796. Other cities were slow to follow, however, and it was not until the middle of the nineteenth century that the mayor's veto power was firmly established. As the mayor became more distinctly an administrative officer he lost his right to preside over the sessions of the council.

By 1835 democracy was firmly established. It was not the mild-mannered, cultured democracy of Thomas Jefferson, but the uncouth, aggressive democracy of Andrew Jackson. Distinctly it was the triumph of the people. One might almost be tempted to dub it the rule of the rabble. The charters granted to the cities immediately following the Revolution had carefully retained control of municipal affairs in the hands of the property owners by the simple expedient of denying the franchise to all others. But one by one the restrictions on the right to vote were swept away, and in the early years of the nineteenth century universal white manhood suffrage became the rule. About the same time foreign immigration began to assume large proportions. In the year 1832 sixty thousand immigrants were admitted into the United States—nearly three times the average of the five preceding years. The newcomers were for the most part from the peasant class. They were ambitious but ignorant, without any experience in the art of self-government, and without any concept of its obligations. They were easily misled by plausible theories, though it must be confessed that in this respect they differed but little from their native-born neighbors. One of the most popular theories of the day was the doctrine of rotation in office. "Public office is a prize and not a trust," said the political philosophers in effect. "Any man is capable of filling any position in the public service, so let us give every man, as far as possible, the opportunity to hold office and live for a time at public expense. To that end let us provide short terms, and make office holders ineligible to succeed themselves." This

[2] In 1830 the mayor of New York was given the power of absolute veto.

doctrine received widespread approval, and everywhere its effects were felt. One-year terms were the rule, and seldom were men permitted to remain in office long enough to prove their worth. Everywhere the common man was glorified, and there can be little doubt that the men generally elected to office were sufficiently common to satisfy the most rabid partisans. The concept of public offices as prizes to be distributed among the faithful proved particularly intriguing. "To the victor belong the spoils of the enemy," declared Senator Marcy in 1832, and since that time his name has been linked with the spoils system, but he only expressed the sentiment of his day. In virtually every city the triumph of the opposition at the polls was the signal for a complete turnover in the municipal working force, from the mayor to the janitor of the city hall. Incompetents and numskulls were summarily dismissed to make way for other incompetents and numskulls who happened to have cast their lot with the winning faction. . . .

CORRUPTION IN CITY GOVERNMENT

During the two or three decades following the Civil War municipal government in the United States sank to its lowest level. Those were the days of utter inefficiency, of flagrant corruption, of complete indifference to public opinion. In nearly every city the government fell into the hands of a well-organized group of professional politicians, who used their power to enrich themselves at public expense. They resorted to every known trick in order to retain control. Even though a majority of votes might be cast against them, their subordinates counted the ballots; and a substantial majority was always returned in their favor. Crude giving and taking of bribes were everyday occurrences. Contracts for the construction of public buildings were awarded according to the size of the "commissions" given the city boss and his subordinates. In New York City the notorious Tweed Ring diverted fifty millions or more of public money to their own pockets between 1869 and 1871. A court house originally designed to cost $250,000 was finally completed with a total outlay in excess of ten millions, most of which was paid over to "Boss" Tweed and his associates. This result was accomplished by the simple process of compelling contractors to submit bills far in excess of what they desired or ever received, the surplus representing the profits of the Tweed Gang.[3] New York did not stand alone,

[3] The classic account of the Tweed Ring is found in Bryce's *American Commonwealth,* Vol. II, pp. 379–396. In 1927 appeared Denis T. Lynch's excellent volume, *Boss Tweed: The Story of a Grim Generation.*

however, in the debauchery and corruption of public officials. Virtually everywhere it was much the same. Persons seeking special favors from the cities were compelled to pay well for the privileges they desired. Businesses asking only to be let alone in the conduct of their affairs were forced to pay tribute to city bosses in order to escape persistent persecution, a persecution that often took the form of frequent arrests for alleged infractions of minor ordinances. Every person on the payroll of the average city, from mayor to scrub-woman, was regularly assessed "for party purposes." The city dwellers of America no longer controlled their government in those dark decades, just prior to the beginning of the present century. They were ruled by little oligarchies of professional politicians, for whose services they paid a heavy price.

A number of factors combined to produce this unwholesome state of affairs. The form of government was in itself a standing invitation to political manipulation. With responsibility divided among a score or half a hundred individuals and boards, some of them popularly elected, some chosen by the mayor with the consent of the council, and some selected by state officials, it was impossible to place the blame when things went wrong. Nor did the electorate often try to fix responsibility. The poorer classes, composed chiefly of recent immigrants, lent themselves readily to the schemes of the politicians, and the more prosperous groups were usually too busy to devote much time to civic matters. Private fortunes were in the making, and the industrial and commercial leaders, who ought also to have been the civic leaders, scarcely knew and cared not at all that government by the people had become only an empty phrase.

The cities were more prosperous than ever before in the years from 1865 to 1890. They were growing at a rapid rate, and property values were doubling and trebling almost overnight. At the same time city services were multiplying. Functions that had formerly been left to private initiative were coming to be regarded as properly within the sphere of government. Water supply and fire protection, for example, were transferred in most cities from private to public control. New York City took over its water supply system in 1845, and Boston followed three years later, but in most cities the change occurred during the seventies and eighties. It was during those two decades, also, that such matters as public health and hygiene first began to receive attention from municipal authorities. The cities were spending more money and employing more persons than ever before in their history. Small wonder, therefore, that corruption and maladministration were the rule. The spoilsmen were more active because the spoils were greater. The professional politicians were more determined to win elections because control of the government carried with it a vast patronage. American cities had sown the seed of unsound political theory, and at last they were reaping the harvest of unsound administration.

The development of public utilities in the period following the Civil War also had an unwholesome effect upon the tone of municipal government. These utilities—street railways, gas works, and the like—were in private hands, and their owners desired special privileges from the cities for which they could afford to pay well. Every utility was required to have a franchise or permit to do business, and the terms of that franchise were all-important. If they gave to a street railway company, for example, the exclusive right to serve a city for a long period of years, virtually free from governmental supervision and at liberty to charge what the traffic would bear, the owners of that company were well started on the road to wealth. Public utility operators, therefore, soon found that it paid to have the friendship of city officials, even if their friendship had to be purchased. Many resorted freely to bribery. Some utility operators, broader visioned or less scrupulous than their fellows, went directly into the game of politics and secured control of the city government. After that, when questions affecting the utilities came before the council, it was no longer necessary to parley with each member of the council. All the members were the creatures of private interests. . . .

THE PEOPLE REVOLT

But as matters went from bad to worse the smouldering resentment of the people burst into an open flame of revolt. In city after city the party leaders suffered defeat at the polls, and the control of government came into the hands of the reform group. The Tweed Ring of New York City was completely crushed at the election of 1871, and Tweed himself died in prison a few years later. In 1881 the Philadelphia Gas Ring was driven from power, honest Republicans and Democrats uniting to elect an upright, capable mayor. The reformers were similarly successful elsewhere. Yet their triumph was short-lived. If they carried one election they were virtually certain to lose the next. If they succeeded in arousing popular interest during an election campaign, that interest dwindled to the zero point soon after election day. "Government by indignation" proved no match for government by vested interests. Within five years after the reform victory of 1871 in New York Tammany was back in the saddle, slightly more responsive to public opinion, but holding as firmly as ever the reins of government.

Little by little, however, popular sentiment made itself felt. Against the wishes of the professional politicians many changes were made in the structure of city governments. The office of mayor gained most from these innovations. In the majority of cities the mayor became in fact as well as in name the head of the administration. New York, Boston,[4] St. Louis and some other municipalities gave him the power to appoint and remove department heads at pleasure. They increased his term of office to four years. Other cities followed more cautiously. Everywhere the tendency was to centralize authority and responsibility in the hands of the mayor, who had often proved a champion of good government; but many persons still feared to place too great authority in one man, lest he abuse his trust. So while the mayor was generally given power to appoint the heads of administrative departments, his appointments were commonly made with the consent of the council. Removals made by him were likewise subject to councilmanic approval in most cities. The mayor's term of office was commonly fixed at two years, although an increasing number of municipalities shifted to the four-year term.

Meanwhile the civil service reform movement was gaining headway. The public was beginning to tire of paying large salaries to incompetents. People were asking whether any man should be entrusted with important public administrative duties solely because of his ability to control the vote of some ward or precinct. They were questioning the soundness of the old maxim—"To the victor belong the spoils," and suggesting in its place a new precept—"To the competent belong the jobs." The merit system of selecting public employees was established by state law in the cities of New York State in 1884, and one by one the other cities, particularly the larger cities, fell into line. Today seventy-five per cent of the people living in cities of more than 100,000 inhabitants are protected by civil service regulations of some sort. The efficacy of these laws varies greatly from city to city. Some are strictly enforced; others are so administered as to make evasion easy. Some apply to all city employees; others refer only to certain groups in the city service. But everywhere popular opinion has come to regard municipal administration as a field for expert technicians, and not for the henchmen of political bosses.

THE PRESENT CENTURY

Radical changes have come about in the structure and in the spirit of American city government since the beginning of the twentieth century.

[4] In Boston, however, the mayor's nominations must be approved by the state civil service commission.

Virtually everywhere the bicameral council has been abolished,[5] and its place has been taken by a small, single-chambered body, with a membership seldom in excess of twenty-five. The tendency of the late nineteenth century to concentrate authority in the hands of the mayor has become even more pronounced during the last three decades. In cities that still retain the mayor-council type of government—and most cities are in this class—the prestige of the mayor continues to increase, while the influence of the council is waning. Many communities, however, disgusted with the waste and inefficiency of the old system, have discarded the mayor-council form of government root and branch. Several hundred have adopted in its place the commission plan, which concentrates all authority in the hands of a small number of commissioners, usually five, and makes them responsible for the conduct of municipal affairs. Many another city has taken a page from the book of business organization, and has placed in charge of its administration an appointed manager who is intended to correspond roughly to the general manager of an industrial enterprise. This is the council-manager plan, now in operation in four hundred and sixty-eight cities and towns.

For more than half a century the people of the cities have waged an incessant fight to free themselves from some of the most burdensome restrictions imposed by state legislatures. In this struggle they have been partly successful. A number of states, led by Missouri in 1875, have granted to their cities a measure of home rule. These cities are free, within the limits imposed by state constitutions and state laws, to frame their own charters and to regulate their own affairs. State authority is still supreme with regard to matters of state-wide concern. In other states, although the principle of municipal home rule has not been accepted, constitutions have been so amended as to restrict the power of the legislature over cities. One of the most common of such restrictions is that cities must be chartered by general law—a provision designed to prevent state legislatures from meddling with every petty detail of municipal administration, since no general law can be framed to meet every local problem. State legislatures still dominate the situation in large measure, however. They still possess considerable authority over matters that every city ought to settle for itself. Constitutional limitations have proved easy to evade. Even home rule amendments, for one reason or another, have failed in many states to give the people of the cities adequate control over their own affairs. It is easy

[5] New York is the most recent of the large cities to make the change. It adopted the unicameral plan in 1936.

to announce the principle of local self-government, but extremely difficult to apply that principle in a practical way.

All forms of corruption—graft, bribery, election frauds, underworld tribute—play a smaller part in the administration of American city governments than they did half a century ago. Corruption still exists, but it is less flagrant, less brazen. It no longer flaunts itself before the public eye, and asks defiantly: "What are you going to do about it?" Instead it skulks in dark corners. The professional politicians find it profitable to make at least a pretense of civic virtue. Election frauds occur far less frequently. In many municipalities the civic renaissance has carried into office men of unquestioned integrity and ability, whose work compares favorably with the work of highly trained, highly paid business executives. City employees are commonly chosen by a system of competitive examinations, though in some cities the civil service laws are regularly evaded and appointments are still made on a partisan basis. Even yet the boss is the dominant figure in municipal politics, but he is a very different type of person from the boss of fifty years ago. Today he makes an earnest bid for popular favor. He is "as sensitive to criticism as a prima donna," in Walter Lippmann's colorful phrase.

THE SHAME OF THE CITIES: AN EXAMPLE *

PHILADELPHIA

So sure was I now of the family resemblance of American cities that I went at Philadelphia with as much confidence as I had felt fear and doubt before Pittsburgh. I knew just what to look for. . . .

The system stood. There was the same old arrangement of a mayor, councilmen, and the usual elected officials, all described in the new Bullitt Charter, which had been drawn by an expert of experience, intelligence, and integrity, to meet and to defeat the typical evils of the corrupt politics of old. And yet, back of this charter and working with and through it, there were the same old boss, ring, and machine, governing Philadelphia as St. Louis, Minneapolis, New York, and Pittsburgh were governed. What shocked me most, however, was to learn right away that the famous Bullitt Charter had adopted a principle which I had formulated as a theory of re-

* From *The Autobiography of Lincoln Steffens,* copyright 1931, by Harcourt, Brace and Company, Inc., pp. 407–413.

form and offered urgently to Dr. Parkhurst and other New York reformers for their new Greater New York Charter. The Bullitt Charter centered power in the mayor, put him in a position to do either good or evil, but made him by the same token responsible, so that the voters might know whom to praise or blame, promote or throw out of office. I had to note a (to me) new and startling theory, viz.: that the form of government did not matter; that constitutions and charters did not affect essentially the actual government.

I put this in the place of the old American theory of checks and balances, and to anticipate a bit, I never myself thereafter read the charter of any city or State that I studied. The paper government did not count. And I found in Pennsylvania that the bosses there knew this. Some of them helped the reformers put over their new, anti-graft charter. Their purpose was not reform. The State boss, Senator Matthew S. Quay, had had difficulties with a city boss, and it was to beat him that he made his State Legislature pass the Bullitt Charter, as an ouster. He said that he would deal with the difficulties of that instrument when he came to them, and he did. The old city boss knocked out by Quay and the new charter, the Senator appointed Israel W. Durham, a ward politician, to be boss of Philadelphia. This was new to me; no State boss could have named the boss of any city I had seen. A boss is a natural growth, not a legal device like a mayor. And even Quay had had to choose a ward boss and help him to master the party machinery. There was something to study in all this. The present point, however, is that in spite of the new, wise charter and the all-powerful mayor, the system prevailed. Quay and his city lieutenant ruled, as before reform, the two machines of the two old parties and, therefore, the mayor and elected officers; and they made the government represent, not the people as a whole, but the business, the same old businesses which contributed to the corruption of—all the cities I knew.

All was regular, and, as usual, all was known to everybody. I asked the manager of the hotel where I registered for the names of the bosses and reformers. He was not interested in politics, not in the least; but he knew. . . . The parallel of Philadelphia with other cities was so perfect that it was comic. And yet—there were differences. . . .

My hotel man, for example, said that at the last election, when he went to the polls, he was challenged; he had "voted already." He answered that he had not voted; there was a dispute, and it developed that his name and his brother's name had been voted on by machine repeaters. "Lots of my friends had the same experience," he told me. "I kicked so hard that they let me vote, but they called in a couple of gangsters to offset my ballot by voting the other way—in the names of George Washington and Benjamin Franklin."

This humorous impudence was characteristic of Philadelphia; the gang voted "for fun" all the names of the signers of the sacred Constitution of the United States, of the new charter and the membership of the swell clubs. This joyous defiance of the holy of holies was only a sign of the novelty I saw in this fine old city. The novelty was the attitude of this hotel man and of other good citizens of Philadelphia toward their notorious, insulting, cynical political and business crooks.

He and his kind did nothing about it. "There is nothing to be done," the hotel man said. "We have tried reforms over and over again; we have striven to beat this game; and we never got anywhere." The reformers I saw took much the same view. They were still working, but only on details, not for a thoroughgoing reform of the government. They had facts. There was no difficulty at all about getting all the evidence one wanted of any of the many, many scandals that had been and still were disgracing the city. And the reformers were able, courageous men. One of the most persistent of these fighters was E. S. Van Valkenburg, the editor-in-chief of the Philadelphia *North American,* a great newspaper owned by Thomas B., the son of John Wanamaker. Van Valkenburg was a smiling, experienced newspaper man, who had reported or edited in other towns in Pennsylvania. He knew everybody and everything. He printed everything, too. Threatened with assassination, he simply moved his desk out of range of his window and went right on getting and publishing the evidence, the libelous, uncontradicted facts. The gang tried to blackmail the owner of the paper with an exposure of something personal; John Wanamaker answered with a public offer of $2,500,000 for a street railway franchise which the mayor was about to give away. The *North American* was not to be intimidated, but neither was the gang. Mayor Ashbridge met Wanamaker's cash offer by signing away the franchise, quick. And Van Valkenburg wanted to know from me how in the deuce the reformers got so far as they did in St. Louis and Minneapolis. He and he alone in his city seemed to have some hope of beating the system there. I could not tell him how to do it; he pumped and pumped, and he was "wise" in his questionings. But I did not know the answer he needed; I was full of questionings myself, not of answers. I must ask for answers myself, answers which none of the reformers could give.

In desperation one day I called at the office of the boss, Israel W. Durham. His secretary shook his head. "Don't think Mr. Durham will see you; too busy." He would ask. He came out with his eyes and mouth open in surprise. "Go in," he said, and I went in, and saw a man well worth knowing. . . .

There had been a burst, a volcanic eruption, of "steals" and "jobs," all in the administration of Mayor Ashbridge. I asked Durham how they dared do such a wild, wholesale business in such a short time. He did not mind the assumption, in my question, that the franchise grants were steals and that he knew it. He waited a moment; then asked me quietly if I meant to quote him.

No, I said. I was really puzzled and wanted only to understand the politics of the Ashbridge administration; technically it looked like bad politics, "bad bad politics," I remember saying. He shook his head slowly, thoughtfully, no.

"In the first place," he said, "Ashbridge wished it so. He wanted but one term in office, and having no further ambition, he wanted to crowd as much business as we would let him into that one term. And we—we talked it all over. With the mayor known to be for one term only we would have to stay here and take the permanent blame. The responsibility fell upon me. But we reasoned—"

"Well," I urged, when he halted there, "you could put over one of those steals in New York or anywhere else, but one would be enough to strain any machine I know of. And five—or more!" He smiled.

"We reasoned," he resumed, "we agreed among ourselves that it was exactly the five or—more that would save us."

He let me express my bewilderment; then he cleared it as by a lightning flash.

"If we did any one of these things alone the papers and the public could concentrate on it, get the facts, and fight. But we reasoned that if we poured them all out fast and furious, one, two, three—one after the other—the papers couldn't handle them all and the public would be stunned and —give up. Too much."

We sat there, he amused, I as stunned as his public.

"Well, you Pennsylvania politicians know something even Tammany doesn't know."

He nodded. "Yes," he said. "We know a lot they don't know. We know that public despair is possible and that that is good politics."

So that was why my hotel host, and the reformers, and the professors at the university, and the good citizens generally, said there was nothing to be done.

"Yes," Iz Durham answered. "The Bullitt Charter was a great thing for us. It was the best, last throw of the reformers, and when we took that charter and went right on with our business, we took the heart out of our reform forever."

"Then," I summed it up, "then Philadelphia is a city where reform is over."

He nodded, watching me humorously, while I went on theorizing out loud. Here was the difference I had felt in this city: that Philadelphia was in the condition St. Louis would be in after the graft system had recovered from Folk and his attacks. The people of a city would accommodate themselves to the revealed conditions and practices and rearrange their ideas and fit their minds to things as they are. The boss listened; he stopped smiling, but he nodded.

"Political corruption," I went on, "is, then, a process. It is not a temporary evil, not an accidental wickedness, not a passing symptom of the youth of a people. It is a natural process by which a democracy is made gradually over into a plutocracy. Treason, in brief, is not a bad act; it is an inevitable, successful policy, and the cities differ one from another according to age. Philadelphia is worse than St. Louis because it is older—in experience."

I soon had the boss bewildered and as puzzled and serious and shocked as I had been.

"If this process goes on," I said, "then this American republic of ours will be a government that represents the organized evils of a privileged class." I had forgotten Durham; I wasn't accusing him of wrong-doing. But I remember the awed tone in which he broke into my soliloquy to ask how it could be stopped. I saw that he cared. I said I didn't know. . . .

CONGESTION AND DISPERSION *

The problem of urban congestion arises from the fact that as the city spreads out at its periphery it almost invariably also rises at the center. The skyscraper is a visible symbol of this congestion. As it fills and empties, the streets and traffic facilities, which were designed for smaller cities and lower buildings, are no longer able to carry the load without friction and delays. The extensive remodeling of these facilities to bring them again in scale with the new and greatly more intensive use of private property is

* National Resources Committee, *op. cit.*, pp. 58–59.

inordinately expensive in most cases. For it is precisely at the center, where the region-wide functions of the city are concentrated, where the daily ebb and flow of the human tides converge and where the acquisition of every foot of additional space involves high land costs and building damages, that this remodeling is most needed and space is at a premium.

While the elimination of congestion would involve enormous costs, the aggregate cost of permitting this congestion in our cities to continue represents an imposing waste. Traffic delays where speed and promptness are at a premium, overcrowding of sites and buildings, dark and badly ventilated dwellings and offices, overtaxing of public facilities and services, deficiency in public open space combined with a surplus of unused private open space, undue concentration of land values, and unfair apportionment of the local tax burden—these and other detriments to urban well-being are present in varying degrees in practically every American city. These conditions generally accompany the type of urban growth which is characterized by uninterrupted accretion at the periphery and increasingly more intensive building development, concentration, and congestion in the center, seldom relieved for long, but rather aided and abetted by subways, traffic lights, one-way streets, and the staggering of office hours.

One of the most serious consequences of traffic congestion at the center of urban areas and of the high-speed radial traffic to their outskirts is the increasing rate of street-traffic accidents and the appalling number of fatalities. These constitute a hazard in present-day city life comparable in some respects with the plagues of old.

Just as extreme concentration is wasteful, so is extreme dispersion. The suburbanite aims to escape at least some of the disadvantages of living in the densely built city but by coming to the central city to earn his living, he creates new problems of overcentralization. The advantages of residential dispersion are coupled with the disadvantages of atomized administrative areas which tend to break up urban regions into suburban bailiwicks and dormitories independent of the central city.

The real difficulty with the dispersive tendencies of suburbanization and other centrifugal movements lies in the lack of planning and the consequent waste in public facilities, services, and the use of urban land and space. Urban expansion being left largely to the whim of the subdivider, discontinuous, sporadic, suburban settlements or ribbon developments along the highways, with large undeveloped interstices between them, greatly increase the cost and difficulties of providing the essential public facilities and services. On his part the subdivider has so thoroughly pursued his job—in many cases at the expense of either the land owner, the gullible home seeker, or the community—that even now enough land is subdivided in the outskirts of many of our larger cities to exceed any prospective need of these communities for building sites for a great many years to come. . . .

PART THREE

The Economic Framework

CHAPTER V

Industry and Society

THE economic structure is perhaps the most obvious facet of American society. It is certainly the facet that most impresses Americans and foreigners alike. The significance of this aspect of American society is borne out by the fact that the term "industrial," which describes the predominant form of American economic organization, is frequently used to describe the entire society. Although Americans like to emphasize the efficiency, as well as the great size and complexity of their economic system, the disinterested observer is likely to be impressed with its enormous wastefulness. In a sense, both of these views are correct. It is precisely the paradoxical combination of tremendous capacity for production and frightful waste of resources that needs serious thought, and it is to this general subject that the readings in this and the next chapter are addressed.

In order to understand the productive capacity of our economy, one must grasp the kind of economy it is. What is its social framework? What is its history? What is its relation to science and technology? These are questions that the first reading in the present chapter attempts to answer briefly. We know that productive capacity is more than minerals, more than tools, more than labor; it is coöperation and common will. But how secure this coöperation when one of the greatest issues shaking our society is the proper relation between employer and employee? This topic is treated in Part IV, "Social Stratification," but it is also dealt with here in the context of the industrial plant itself. The second reading deals with the human, or non-economic, factors affecting the working relations of employees. As such it deals with an aspect of our economy that has until recently been quite neglected, and which is still poorly understood.

FACTORY PRODUCTION*

In the latter part of the eighteenth century "modern" industry got its start in the factory system. Since contemporary industrial organization and production stems directly from the first crude attempts at mass production under a single roof, it is pertinent to review some of the economic circumstances that fostered the development, as well as some of the basic features that prompted contemporaries to think that the change was revolutionary.

The factory system did not suddenly unfold out of the invention of power-driven labor-saving machines. These were important, even essential, to industrial expansion. But the factory system and industrial reorganization were revolutionary only by subsequent judgment of their far-reaching effects. The elementary social relationships of employer and employee, of capitalist and laborer, had already been developed by the rise of the merchants and the use of the putting-out system. The relation of the worker to the machine and to raw materials and the market which we associate with modern industrialism was thus not a sudden innovation. Often even the machines of the early factories were precisely those already used in the putting-out system. The change in the place of work was about the only new element in the first establishment of factories. Looked at in retrospect, this change was scarcely any more important than any one of the series of minute changes that had preceded it. It was, however, an obvious change and one which entailed wide social transformations that no contemporary witness could over-look. Some of these nonindustrial consequences of factory production are discussed later. For the moment we may limit our view simply to the causes and conditions of the transfer of production from the home to the workshop.

Although economic historians tell us that forms of shop production (as opposed to home industry) are very old and very common in human society, and often involved rather large numbers of workers, the essentials of the factory in the modern sense are: (1) shop industry, requiring (2) fixed capital, and (3) free labor.

Shop production means unified and co-ordinated production within a single establishment for that purpose. Although usually thought of as de-

---

* Moore, Wilbert E., *Industrial Relations and the Social Order* (New York: The Macmillan Company, 1946), pp. 21–32. By permission of The Macmillan Company, publishers and copyright holders.

noting a small establishment, shop in this sense might apply to manufacturing units ranging from the very small to the extremely complex. It is not even necessary that all the operations take place "under the same roof" as long as the units are located in close proximity, are interdependent, and are subject to a unified control.

There are certain inherent advantages arising from the centralization and close supervision provided by shop production, particularly for large-scale production or for manufacturing that entails a series of closely related processes. Among the advantages which early (and modern) factories enjoyed over domestic production were: minimizing the transportation of goods, especially those at different stages of completion; saving of time and effort of agents and "factors"; reducing irregularities of quality and quantity resulting from inadequate supervision. It does not follow that these advantages were in every case crucial; often they were outweighed by the failure of other necessary conditions for factory production. They are, however, sufficiently important to merit the attention of those who think that the use of natural power alone "caused" the industrial revolution.

Actually the first factories were not large, but did combine several processes in manufacturing or else brought a number of similar machines together for centralized supervision. Often the interests of the entrepreneurs were technical as well as commercial; the "capitalist" was frequently his own technical designer both for machines and for shop arrangement. Others relied chiefly on managerial ability. In any event, the impetus to further specialization and elaboration was provided by making the shop, not the craftsman, the productive unit in society.

The term fixed capital refers to investments in productive goods that are not easily transportable from one locality to another, or broken up into small units. A water wheel, heavy machinery, or a series of smaller machines which can be effectively operated only as interdependent units are examples of fixed capital. It was the introduction of fixed capital which often prompted transferral of production from scattered homes to a unified productive establishment. Occasionally, it is true, other advantages of the factory system (or rather of shop production) made even the use of fixed capital unnecessary. However, once established—for whatever reason or combination of reasons—the buildings and equipment became fixed capital themselves.

The early development of textile manufacturing in England, which may be taken not as typical of industrial transformation, but rather as its vanguard, illustrates the early advantages gained through centralization of production. The introduction of the power loom, together with the utilization of nonhuman energy in the form of water power, made the decentralized putting-out system definitely outmoded. There is no need here to follow through the various important inventions and innovations which gave England its supremacy in industrial production. It is simply to be noted that the establishment of the "factory system" was actually the introduction of unified production with fixed capital in one manufacturing industry in one country—cotton production in England. Why this was so will become evident from the subsequent analysis of other characteristics of factory production and the essential conditions for its successful operation.

The characteristic use of free labor saved capital investments in slaves, removed the risk of such investments, and made possible an insistence on technical efficiency in the labor force. This is one of the chief distinctions between the modern factory system and the "factories" of the ancient world. Actually, of course, enterprising capitalists in England and western Europe did not have to face this issue; they simply benefited, especially in England, from the presence of a large supply of cheap labor.

In the gradual disestablishment of feudalism in western Europe the lot of the peasant fell out in quite different ways. In general, the French serf became in time a free tenant or even proprietor on the ancestral plot of land. Not so the English villein. His complete freedom from feudal obligations was achieved for the most part much earlier than on the continent. (The principle of mortmain whereby the property of a peasant dying without legitimate heirs reverted to the lord or patron was maintained in France until the time of the French Revolution.) As sometimes happens, the English freeman paid for his liberty by lack of economic security. "Enclosures" which removed communal areas from the use of tenants started as early as the thirteenth century, and the process went on at an accelerating rate until, with the complete collapse of feudalism, tenants were evicted from their ancestral holdings. The extent of poverty and unemployment in England is attested by the famous Elizabethan Poor Laws of the sixteenth and early seventeenth centuries. By 1750 the tenant evictions and general agricultural poverty had created such a large unemployed population that labor supply was no problem, at least in regard to quantity. These same considerations also guaranteed that it would be cheap.

Bitter things have been written about the exploitation of labor in the early factories. Some of the early social results of industrialism will be discussed in a subsequent part of this chapter. For the moment it is sufficient to repeat that an essential characteristic of modern factory production is the use of wage labor, and an adequate supply of such labor was at hand for the first factories established.

As previously noted, the establishment of factories did not simply grow out of the invention of power-driven machines. In the beginning, there was economic demand—a mass demand, fostered by the long-developing trade and commerce and greatly enhanced by colonial expansion and the opening of markets in the New World.

It was only in a large and steady demand that it was possible, or at any rate profitable, to tie up investments in land, buildings, and machinery. Although laborers could be dismissed during a slack season, the material investment could not. So far as the physical equipment was concerned, it would often cost almost as much to maintain the plant during a shutdown as during full operation. It is true, as we are often told today, that the economies achieved through organized and mechanized production tended to reduce prices and thus bring many manufactured products within the purchasing power of those formerly unable to buy. But the reverse relationship—the effect of actual (or reasonably certain) demand on industrial expansion—was certainly an important consideration in the early days of the factory system and cannot be lightly dismissed even today. Moreover, it is clear that whenever specialized production is established it presumes a monetary basis of exchange; the manufacturer must produce for the market, not for his own use. This is further evidence of the high importance to the factory system of a pre-existing commercial development. The routes of distribution had already been established, and the idea of purchasing at least part of the necessities and comforts of life, rather than producing these within the household, was no novelty.

Again it was primarily in England that these necessary conditions were most fully met. Not only were there large numbers of people who were no longer "tied to the soil" and economically self-sufficient, but the expansion of British trade and commerce, particularly in the New World, had been going on for about a century and a half. The "colonial economy," whereby outlying possessions furnished raw materials for English factories and provided part of the market for finished products, was already well established by the time of the American Revolution, and continued with respect to Southern cotton long after American independence. Small wonder, then, that England is regarded as the home of the industrial revolution.

Again contrary to the prevalent notion of a rapid and wholesale transformation of economic life with the introduction of the factory system, this type of production actually gained headway rather slowly until the middle of the last century. Early factories were limited by inadequate technical and scientific knowledge, particularly in the transition from human to natural sources of power, and in developing transportation and other marketing facilities. Inventions do not appear out of thin air to revolutionize industrial life, and complex inventions depend upon a combination of simpler mechanisms which precede them. Water power, for example, is limited in its usefulness as a direct source of power, not only because of possibly inadequate supply, but also because the factory locations which are satisfactory for supply of water power are not necessarily near the sources of raw materials, the markets, or transportation routes. It was thus not the application of nonhuman sources of power which was of primary importance to further expansion of mechanized production. Domestic animals, wind, and water had been used for thousands of years. It was transportable natural power in the form of coal which was of outstanding significance for industrial expansion, for which the invention of the steam engine heat could be transformed into energy for power-driven machinery. The power thus available was generally greater, more certain, and less restricted in use or location. Other more recent technical developments in industrial power, such as the use of petroleum products (either as an additional source of heat for steam or in the internal combustion engine) and electricity, share with coal the advantages just noted, and in a sense are simply refinements of the basic principle of transportable power.

The greater power made possible by harnessing steam and other sources of energy required more durable machines if rather large investments were to be protected without too much breakage and replacement. Although iron had previously been used fairly extensively for tools, weapons, and other consumption goods, it came into its own as a part of capital or productive goods. Iron, especially when alloyed to make steel of various types, became the primary material of mechanized production. The refinement and elaboration of steel is still going on, and now as in the last century is making possible higher speeds with less wear and greater standardization of products.

The introduction and development of durable machines has of course depended in large part upon another important outgrowth of factory production—the utilization and combination of new resources. In response both to the demand for more efficient production and to the pressure for diversified production, new materials have been developed, such as aluminum, the rarer metals, and the recent plastics, and old materials have been put in new combinations. Industrial research serves the interests of large manufacturing corporations, just as the early textile factories benefited from the availability of large quantities of short-staple cotton after the invention of the cotton gin, or from the perfection of new colors and dyes.

A final series of changes that started very early in the modern industrial era has been in the direction of technical specialization and co-ordination. Although early factories often represented but a single stage in the productive process and comprised a collection of nearly identical machines, the advantages of combining a number of processes under one roof and with unified supervision soon became apparent. The elaboration of the technical processes for various stages in the manufacture of such a complex mechanism as a modern bomber often still prevents a complete unification within one plant. What has happened is that specialization has proceeded by leaps and bounds, with co-ordination taking place within the plant or division of the plant and then further co-ordination being provided either by overall direction or more impersonally through contracts, agreements, or simply buying and selling on the market. It is the assembly line which symbolizes modern mass production of complicated mechanisms involving many distinct operations. Some of the units are made within the plant, some are manufactured by subsidiary plants, and some are purchased from other manufacturers. The factory system not only allows but fosters the integration of specialized activities.

A minute division of labor, directed, officially at least, toward a common goal, could scarcely be accomplished by any other system of production. Much of the remainder of this book will be concerned with the social significance of this outstanding characteristic of factory production. For it has not been simply a question of building the necessary specialized machines and putting them in the appropriate locations, but a problem, at least equally important, of organizing the human resources for production. Any industrial executive can assure you that this is a large undertaking. The factory system, in other words, has produced some concrete social situations which are fairly new in human society, and the process of adjustment to these innovations has been a good deal less than automatic.

EARLY RESULTS OF THE FACTORY SYSTEM

Hitherto we have examined the economic and technical changes which preceded the factory system and the transformations made possible by factory production. This is by no means the whole story. Aside from the cultural environment that made a diversified and monetary economic life possible, which will be outlined in the following two chapters, there were immediate social situations which helped and hindered the industrial changes. If specialization and mass production created new social relationships within the factory, they also created new problems within society as a whole.

In casting up the social balance sheet for the factory system one would, by general consent, put on the credit side such things as "store clothes" and tufted tooth brushes, to say nothing of radios, automobiles, telephones, and other items of modern urban living, and on the debit side industrial accidents and diseases, child labor, urban slums, and unemployment. But whether the net balance would be black or red cannot be scientifically determined. This is true for a number of reasons. There is not universal agreement as to the side of the ledger on which some items ought to be entered. For example, there are some who do not regard the almost universal use by women of finger-nail polish and silk hose as an unmixed blessing, or "child labor" as an unmixed evil. Even if such agreement could be found within our society, it would rest on value judgments rather than statements of fact. Not only that, but each item cannot count as one, for some are certainly considered more important than others. How these are weighted depends in general not upon scientific but upon ethical judgment. Even to speak of the "social problems" resulting from early factory production implies that situations existed which contemporary observers and subsequent reviewers found to be contrary to their conceptions of ethics, morals, or social order and stability. One must be very cautious here, for an impartial view has knowledge and understanding as its goal, not reform or pointing the finger of shame. In reviewing the social "problems" or "dislocations" resulting from the early adjustments to factory production it is therefore important to note: (1) the facts in regard to the disruption of previous patterns of social life and activities, without regard to the beneficial or harmful effects of such disruptions, and (2) what people have said and how they have acted in reference to the first set of facts, for these reactions are also important facts for an understanding of the relation of industrial production to the community and society. Rather than attempting to set off against one another the advantages and disadvantages, it will be more fruitful to examine the factors hindering factory production, and the community changes resulting from centralized direction of machines and labor.

The factory system, established well before 1800 in English textile manufacturing, proceeded rather slowly elsewhere and in other industries. We have already noted the convergence of economic and social transformations which facilitated factory production. However, it was not all smooth going. This represented a new type of investment, and one not regarded with particularly high favor by the wealthier classes whose chief interest was in land. Merchants who had accumulated a little capital under the putting-out system were the most numerous class of factory entrepreneurs, but others who had technical and managerial ability as well as enterprise often found it difficult to get the necessary capital. Apparently this caution of potential investors was not entirely mistaken, for the risk and uncertainty were certainly large. This risk was bound to be larger in the early days when transportation, the condition of distant markets, and other conditions beyond the capitalist's control but upon which he was dependent, were likely to be uncertain. Moreover, a small enterprise was scarcely equipped to weather heavy storms, since the margin of safety was often very small. The disruptive influence of wars and even piracies, of a poorly established credit system, and of capricious machines still in experimental stages of development contributed to a fairly high mortality rate for new industrial enterprises. Nor did the difficulties end there.

The factory system, it has been noted, is characterized by free contract labor, preferably cheap. In England, especially, the quantitative supply was certainly adequate. In America the availability of lands on the frontier was offset early in the nineteenth century by the recession of the frontier and a rising tide of immigration. But in neither area was there any guarantee that the quality of the labor would be adequate. Machines, especially the early machines, did not remove the necessity of skilled labor; rather they demanded workers with new skills for operating the machines. The factory system has long been charged with replacing skilled workers with machines. This is only one side of the picture, for the history of modern industrial development shows just as clearly the continual creation of positions requiring new technical abilities. The problem, however, is not completely dissolved by this observation, for the skills required are not those existing in the laboring population.

The transfer of production from the home to the factory frequently meant the necessity of drawing upon a much wider area and population than the local village or town in which the factory was located. In the early days of factory production in England there was a notable reluctance of workers to leave their homes and work in factories at some distance. During slack periods the workers had a tendency to drift back to their homes or former homes. The factories, even by standards prevalent at the time, were not exactly attractive places for work. Then, as until fairly recently, laborers were thought of as a cost of production, or at most as cogs in the industrial machine, and not as private persons. Factory discipline was harsh, the work often tedious, and the surroundings dismal. Lighting and ventilation were often rather primitive, and other conditions of work suffered by comparison with former home or shop production. Although the hours were long, this was by no means peculiar to factory production and became a grievance only because other working conditions were regarded as unsatisfactory. The wages also were low, but probably did not compare too unfavorably with incomes available to the same persons elsewhere. Then, as now, complaints about wages and hours were frequently made in view of working conditions considered unsatisfactory.

We have already observed that the basic social structure of the factory system, so far as the relations of capitalist and laborer, employer and employee are concerned, were established before work moved to the factories. The transformation up to that point had been gradual and unobtrusive. Many changes took place while things appeared to be about the same as ever. But the establishment of factories, with direct and insistent supervision of the laborer, made the relatively disadvantageous position of the employee apparent. He worked on the premises of another, often at a great distance from his home. He started work at a specified hour and stopped work when the plant closed for the day. The quality of his work was subject to constant scrutiny, as were his speed and general efficiency. If he lagged in one or the other he was reprimanded by his employer or one of his employer's representatives. The controls to which he had formerly been subject were often almost as great in net result, but they had been introduced gradually, and were in general more formal and impersonal. As an individual craftsman he was controlled by the impersonal market and the reality of hunger, not by particular persons. As an employee of a merchant under the putting-out system he was subject to the same controls, plus that of his employer whom he saw infrequently and to whom it still seemed that he was selling goods and not services. But with the factory system this illusion of liberty could no longer be maintained. That factory workers were newly conscious of their subserviencies is attested by many riots, acts of sabotage, disorderly strikes, and other signs of bitterness at their lot. Despite stringent laws attempting to suppress organizations of workers—some of which traced direct descent from independent guilds—machines were destroyed, tools broken, and factories burned around 1800 in England. The repressive power of the law, together with some greater regulation of working conditions, gradually reduced the effect of the opposition to industrialism on the part of labor.

One of the most spectacular results of the early development of manufacturing was the widespread redistribution of the population. Cities, even rather large cities, are by no means exclusively modern novelties, but the rapid growth of rather numerous large cities is certainly an outstanding accompaniment of industrialization. The movement of the population to the factory towns and cities has been significant in itself, and important in its wider results.

Early as well as recent factories were located chiefly in reference to sources of power, raw materials, markets, and the transportation facilities necessary to co-ordinate these essential factors in production. It was true that a labor supply was also necessary, but this was in general a relatively minor problem, since the mobility of labor resources could be counted on to a large degree, and not at the capitalist's expense. This meant that laborers seeking work crowded into villages, towns, and cities which were unprepared to house them. Crowded living arrangements, with meager sanitary facilities and a generally low level of living, combined to provide the dismal picture of early industrialism with which most of us are familiar.

Manchester, England, provides an interesting case in point. A center of textile products from around 1300, it saw the rise and fall of guilds and the domestic system. With a population of less than 5000 in 1650, the introduction of early factories, with a number of hand looms under a common roof, gave Manchester a population of 17,000 by 1750. The use of power looms, first with water power and subsequently with coal and steam, gave added impetus to factory development. By 1800 the population had reached 70,000. Another half century brought the number of inhabitants to 400,000. At no time during this period did housing or sanitary facilities keep pace with the expanding population.

Although the growth of American cities for the most part came later, it proceeded just as rapidly and with the same general consequences. The cluster of dwellings in the area surrounding the factory in a small community, or the tenement slums in the metropolitan areas, entailed many readjustments in patterns of living and social relationships for a hitherto predominantly rural population. This page in industrial history is ordinarily called black. Be that as it may, it is certainly full, for the problem has persisted with continued industrial expansion.

The social changes that accompanied these ecological shifts are too numerous to be reviewed here. . . . One basic change in the social structure was of sufficient importance to require a few words here. The character of the family, always a highly important segment of society, underwent a number of modifications with the introduction of new methods of economic production. The family under older systems of production had always been a producing unit. It actually continued to be so under the changed conditions of factory production. Although formally the same, it was in fact one thing for the whole family to engage in economic production under the domestic system, and quite another thing for the whole family to work from early morning until late at night in a factory. Although subsequent changes "reduced" the family to the role of consuming unit, early factories moved the family out of the home into the workshop. This was the beginning of the "problem" of the labor of women and children. It is against such a background of economic history that many modern industrial problems are to be understood.

CAPITALISM, SCIENCE AND TECHNOLOGY*

It is generally supposed that the development of the factory system and modern industrial organization was "inevitable." This is true. It is true in the sense that any historical change is inevitable when viewed in retrospect. The proof is that it happened. But difficulties arise when, with scant scientific justification, peculiar and primary significance is attached to some of the antecedent factors in the situation and other factors are persistently overlooked or dismissed as "unimportant." The preceding chapter emphasized the technological and economic changes, that is, changes in methods and relationships of production, which marked the unfolding of modern industrialism. Standard interpretation stops here, but all this took place within a wider social and cultural framework of ideas and values, knowledge and sentiments. And these ideas made, and continue to make, a difference.

The developments outlined in the preceding chapter were in a continual functional relationship with a system of ideas and values which prevailed, and were undergoing transformation, at the same time. These ideas are of continued import for modern industrial organization, for they form the general "climate of opinion" within which specific actions and attitudes are understandable. The cultural values and social institutions which converge their bearing on modern industrialism may be classified under the following heads: (1) capitalism, (2) science, (3) technology, (4) individualism, and (5) rational division of labor. Since these have been closely interrelated in fact, the lines of distinction between them are in particular cases likely to be a little artificial. This is more especially true since it is possible to expand the connotations of "capitalism" or "individualism" or "division of labor" to include all the others. Nevertheless,

* Moore, *op. cit.,* pp. 35–46.

we may make some reasonable separation, and proceed from the characteristics of capitalism to those of its close relatives.

CAPITALISM

If the factory system in its modern expansion constitutes the characteristic type of productive organization in our society, its cultural counterpart is to be found in a system of ideas and values known as capitalism. Capitalism has been talked and written about a great deal; it has become a slogan for some and an epithet for others. The present discussion is concerned only with a series of interrelated characteristics, their cultural origins, and their relation to other social elements.

The accumulation of fluid capital in the form of money (or bills of exchange) and the development of cost accounting and exact computation of profits were known in Europe long before the modern industrial period. It is to the merchants of medieval Italy, who not only engaged in a lively commerce in the Mediterranean area but were not too proud to use the Arabic numerical system, that we owe the establishment of banking and credit with profits and losses entered in record books. Not only was capital in money thus put to use in buying and selling, but risks were shared by the pooling of capital and the pro rata apportionment of profits or losses. Thus economic historians speak of commercial capitalism in distinction from modern capitalistic production. For early capitalism had practically nothing to do with production. How the goods were produced or where they came from was of small importance. It was in trade and in the equipment for trade (as storehouses, ships, and wharves) that money was invested and profit taken. This type of economic activity took on fairly large proportions unaided by mass production in factories. The Italians and Germans bought and sold, and kept the difference. With the colonization of the Americas and the beginning of sea trade with the Orient this commercial capitalism became very nearly world-wide in character, and wondrously full of romance. The line between legitimate trade and piracy was occasionally thin, but the trade went on. Even in the North American colonies "Yankee ingenuity" first manifested itself, not in the machine shop or factory, but in the shipyards and ports serving the traders. This international trade, because of its characteristics of great risks and great profits, as well as for its avid search for new products and new markets, has often been called adventure capitalism. It was remarked . . . that these commercial interests, already well established, preceded the factory system, and that the effective demand so created was a necessary economic condition for the establishment of unified and co-ordinated production. Indeed, the term capitalism is often limited to these commercial interests, and their union with machine technology to form the modern economy is called a marriage of convenience. Be that as it may, the interests of the trader and the interests of the mechanic were actually combined with a number of other elements to produce the system which we know as industrial capitalism.

The system of ideas and principles which underlay factory production and complex industrial organization had—and continues to have—a number of distinct but interrelated elements. In the most general terms these may be grouped under two principal characteristics: (1) free labor and (2) a free market. Because of the importance of these conceptions for an understanding of the social setting of industrial development, each will be considered in some detail in the following paragraphs. Some of the more important elements will then be considered in the remainder of this chapter. . . .

The expression free labor is here used in a very general sense to include not only free wage labor, but the independent economic activities of all classes of individuals in the production and distribution of economic goods. Perhaps a better term would be the customary catch phrase "individual initiative." For what is of fundamental significance in the culture of capitalism is its emphasis on the economic individual, that is, the rational, acquisitive, self-interested individual who goes about the pursuit of private ends (generally capable of expression in monetary terms in the forms of wages, rents, or profits) in the most efficient manner possible. His prototype is popularly supposed to be found in the ingenious Yankee, whether as an industrious laborer with reasonable hope of better things, the inventive manufacturer, or the shrewd trader.

This is so much a part of our philosophy that we have come to take it for granted as a part of "human nature." But acquisitiveness is a distinctly modern and Western phenomenon. It is associated, as we shall see more fully below, with the socially sanctioned dissatisfaction with what one has. It is based upon a moving goal, not a stationary one fixed by tradition. And its emphasis is on the individual, private character of production. Thus under the feudal regime one simply did the appropriate duties required of one's station. Even under the arrangement of the guilds, production was controlled in the interests of the guild as a whole. But under modern capitalism the emphasis has shifted to the individual productive unit, with each individual making the greatest possible effort to achieve a place in the economic world.

This meant that the physical means of production not only were greatly increased—in contrast with primary emphasis upon land or simple tools—but the instruments of production were henceforth to be considered as the disposable property of separate industrial enterprises. The world has always known a good deal about "private property," particularly in consumption goods and in individual tools and weapons. But the emphasis on private property in capital goods, that is, productive goods, is fairly rare, and fairly recent even in Western society. We hear a good deal about the "sacredness of private property," but modern industrial property is not so sacred but that it can be bought, sold, and traded to the advantage of one or the other or (in theory) all concerned. For free labor, or individual initiative, demands that the individual shall have access to the productive property of the community and is not to be kept out of the running by reason of lowly birth or lack of traditional rights.

In summary, then, the free labor characteristic of capitalism involves (a) emphasis upon the acquisitive individual, (b) individual technical efficiency, and (c) private ownership of productive goods.

Closely associated with the foregoing cultural values which we have grouped together under the general heading of free labor are other characteristics of capitalism which are implied by or follow from a "free market." Again in the most general terms a free market is one which is not positively regulated or manipulated by any social agency or organization, political or otherwise, but which is rather "determined" by the impartial operation of unregulated "supply and demand." Public regulation is presumably minimal and indirect, designed primarily to keep the market free. Without undue elaboration at this point, this simply means that individual consumers "come to the market" willing to buy at certain prices for certain qualities, whereas separate and discrete producers are willing to sell goods of a certain quality at a certain price. If the supply is small, demand remaining constant, the price goes up. If the demand is small, supply remaining constant, the price goes down. The important point in all this is that none of the three elements—demand, supply, price—is regulated from outside, but only by the operation of the other two. If one were to label the free market system with a catch phrase, it would be laissez faire.

It is not of present importance to worry about the ethics of laissez faire, or even to inquire into the failure of this set of ideas accurately to describe the actual operation of the market. It should simply be noted that this has constituted a basic "ideology" of industrial capitalism, and that to a significant degree a free market has in fact existed.

Not only does a free market imply freedom from regulation of any of the elements by governmental agency, by traditional restrictions upon demand, by traditional or other restrictions upon productive techniques, and so on, but it means that the market is not regulated or controlled through collaboration among consumers or among producers. Thus a consumers' boycott or a producers' "combination in restraint of trade" through monopoly or other price-fixing methods are violations of the tenets of the free market. Put more simply, and no less accurately, the free market involves free competition (within broad limits to ensure "fairness"). Thus the individual's efficiency is impartially and impersonally weighed (and presumably appropriately awarded) within the economic system itself.

Another aspect of the free market, or at least a conception closely related to it, is that of freedom of contract. This means that the individual is not only free to sell his goods or services to the one he wishes, or rather to the one with whom he can strike the best bargain, but is positively enjoined not to extend contractual obligations to more general and unspecified rights and duties. Thus in all economic relations, whether of employer and employee or buyer and seller, each interested person presumably acts as a free agent, bound only to those obligations to which he himself has willingly agreed. This is, for example, quite different from the feudal conception of customary duties associated with hereditary statuses, or from the traditional neighborly rights and obligations of peasant communities. The contractual relationship is voluntary, limited, explicit, and supposedly gives some advantage or "consideration" to all parties. All this in turn implies an official equality of opportunity. Without such equality of opportunity freedom of contract becomes a rather empty phrase, and bargaining in the market place a fairly one-sided affair. We shall later note that this has been a very sore spot in the relationships of employer and employee, and that this sore has been rubbed rather frequently of late.

As has already been observed, free labor implies and involves individual ownership of the means of production and individual initiative in their operation. The interrelationship of all these characteristics may once more be noted in view of the close dependence of a free market upon the commercialization and transferability of property. By commercialization of property we mean simply the conversion of property rights and their appropriate values into monetary terms. This has an immediate advantage in the market, for it subjects capital goods to the same measuring stick as all other economic values, and provides the basis for exchange. This was, in fact, a heritage from earlier commercial capitalism, which had already established a basis for rational capital accounting and the translation of property values into money, with paper symbols of ownership. Not only did this make it possible to compute "paper" profits and "paper" losses, but it gave to capital its modern fluid character whereby vast industrial empires may be bought and sold in New York or London without disturbing production at the various plants, and cotton and wheat "futures" can be transferred in Chicago between individuals who do not so much as walk on the grass or water a window box. A market could conceivably be "free" without this commercialization and cost accounting, but certainly could not be very active. For a genuinely free market in all its ramifications it is essential that the means of production be available to those who can afford them. This would be next to impossible without the commercialization of all property values. Thus not only are consumption goods transferred on the market, but, through absentee ownership and paper symbols of property, the means of production also are subject to the counterbalancing pressures of supply and demand. To use a far-fetched illustration, it is possible for a person with sufficient capital (that is, money) to face a decision between buying a new yacht or a new factory.

Finally, a necessary condition for the operation of a free market is that not only must the trader or the employer be protected from positive outside control so long as he stays within the two boundaries set by force and fraud, but the operation of the law must be certain and predictable. That is, the legal framework must be regarded as a constant condition, so that knowledge of its operation is alone sufficient in the rational calculation of means to the end of self-interest. Specifically, it means that legal and judicial favoritism, or uncertainty in the law, or purchasable "justice" destroy equality in the market place, as they destroy the possibility of reasonable prediction of results. The idea of reasonable certainty in the law, and impartial justice, is so much a part of our culture that we may be tempted to forget that it is fairly recent in origin and not too extensive in the world today. The arbitrary actions of a monarch, or of administrative officials, the practice of only reaching decisions on legality after the act, are all inimical to the operation of a free market. Whether the law is in fact certain, and whether it may not often be used as a means rather than a constant condition, are matters for future consideration. We are again here simply outlining the interrelated elements which converge to make up the "culture of capitalism."

In summary, the free market of industrial capitalism involves (a) free competition and impersonal judgment of efficiency; (b) freedom of contract and equality of opportunity; (c) commercialization and transferability of all property, including rational capital accounting, monetary exchange and paper symbols of ownership, and fluidity of capital; finally (d) the whole presupposes certainty and predictability in the operation of the law.

Many transformations have taken place in the machinery of production and in the social organization of industrial enterprise since the early days of capitalism. Some of these have forced modification in the underlying assumptions of capitalistic production, and others have led to demands for even further modification. These will be considered in the proper place. Nevertheless, modern economic life to a large degree operates under the assumptions which we have just outlined, and against a cultural background which has united ethical and normative conceptions with the demands of the market place. In short, modern industry is preeminently a social product.

SCIENCE AND TECHNOLOGY

An outstanding characteristic of modern industry is its wide-spread use of exact knowledge. Science and industrial production are separate yet related aspects of our civilization. Thus in tracing the cultural background of industrial organization it is fitting to sketch the development of science before turning to its union with production through technology.

Science rests as much upon metaphysical assumptions or "acts of faith" as does any other mode of orientation to the world about us. There is no need here, even were it possible, to examine the ultimate truth or falsity, or even the relative adequacy of those assumptions. It must be simply noted that among many types of "world views" science represents but one. It assumes, for example, a certain orderliness in natural events: that what happens is not simply the result of chance, or luck, or the whimsy of a facetious or malicious divinity. It assumes, moreover, that this order is knowable, or discoverable, through sensory experience. Reality is what one sees or hears or smells or turns about in one's hands. Subject to the refinements made possible by mechanical aids, and to the checks provided by the experiences of others, science must assume that "seeing is believing," that this is not an illusory dream world, but a world of fact. These may be said to constitute the basic assumptions of science concerning the nature of the universe—of reality. But one must add to this a further basic assumption which is normative in character, that is, a view concerning the obligations that follow from such a conception of reality. The ultimate ethical judgment that supports scientific inquiry is that it is good to know. For science as a part of our culture consists not simply of abstract metaphysical preconceptions; it is also a set of beliefs relating to action. If knowledge is possible, it is also good; it is better to know more than to know less. These are the dicta which transform a philosophical conception into a program of action.

It follows from the underlying "factual" and ethical assumptions of science that this sort of knowledge must place particular emphasis on doing things. The orderliness of nature is not revealed by sudden inspiration, or by long and quiet contemplation. It must be actively sought. Thus the validity of the oft-repeated assertion that science is essentially a method. Knowledge of worldly affairs is the result of doing certain things, of going through regular procedures. Scientific knowledge is distinguished from common-sense knowledge not only in that the former is more often "right" (within the assumptions noted), but that it is more orderly, precise, and organized. It is not simply a question of looking at lots of things, but of ordering, classifying, noting similarities, observing sequences, and drawing conclusions. Thus the primary test of the validity of a statement of fact is not its correspondence with some system of truth, but rather the repetition of the procedures whereby the phenomenon was observed. The importance of this aspect of science can scarcely be overemphasized, for it provides the key to an understanding of the active orientation to the knowable universe with which we are so familiar. More and more phenomena must be brought within the purview of the scientific observer, and the precision and exactness of the observations must be continually increased. Such are the conclusions to be reached from the basic assumptions of science.

Like many other important aspects of the culture which bear on the nature of modern industry, the preconceptions of science antedate capitalistic production. On the other hand, the modern rapid development of science and the expansion of industry have been not only parallel but also closely interdependent movements.

Medieval churchmen would have understood expressions such as "natural order" or the "orderliness in nature," but they would not have understood them in the same way as the modern scientist. The scholar versed in the Scripture and the writings of the Church Fathers knew the world as an exemplification of the handiwork of God, about which it was unnecessary to ask further questions. The important reality was that of the Heavenly City, not the forces of nature. To the untutored, natural events were largely mysterious or miraculous. The conceptions of knowledge and control were essentially magical, involving mystical associations and belief in the efficacy of ritual incantations. But the newer conceptions of time and space and movement made possible a new and mechanistic view of nature. Movements became connected through causation. The study of astronomy and discovery of order and regularity in the heavenly bodies which were amenable to quantitative expression provided the basis for "laws" based on observation, not on faith or philosophy.

But first and foremost there was a shift of interest from the perusal of sacred manuscripts and an other-worldly focus of attention to interest in natural events. Much of this development had taken place by slow accretions before the seventeenth century. The groundwork in basic conceptions had been laid through several hundred years. However, it is from the seventeenth century that we must date most of the rapid development of modern science.

While it is true that much of the voluminous work of that century may be represented as simply combining principles previously established and multiplying their applications, the development was given a tremendous impetus by the same transformations which contributed to the ideology of capitalism. Notably, the Protestant Reformation transformed scientific interests from preoccupations contrary to or barely suffered by the teachings of the church, to positive goods.

Much of the interest which has fostered scientific development has been primarily practical (technological), and only secondarily in knowledge for its own sake. Science may be either an intermediate or an ultimate value. For his protection, and with good grounds in view of the notable gaps at least in time between theoretical and practical importance, the scientist often insists on the ultimate value of scientific knowledge. It is certainly true historically that reservation of judgment concerning the value of "pure science" has borne subsequent fruit in practical applications to mechanical production or new consumption goods. Nevertheless, science has been tied up with technology during most of its recent history.

Technology, simply defined, is the application of scientific principles for the achievement of particular concrete ends, taken as given. These ends are "practical" within the given scale of values, although they may be regarded as illusory or wasteful according to different value schemes. For example, for approximately twenty years after 1918 the technology of armaments and destructive warfare was widely regarded in our society as wasteful, whereas during the second World War civilian production was often held to be wasteful of valuable resources, skills, and productive capacities needed in the war effort.

It is the utilization of science for technical organization and industrial production which has given modern industry its economic superiority over other systems of production. Whether this system is ultimately "better" than traditional handicrafts cannot be scientifically determined. What is of importance here is that a distinct body of culture, namely, technology, has been of profound importance in shaping the character of modern industry. Its particular manifestations include the large number of technical schools which not only carry on research of fairly immediate applicability to industrial processes and products, but the graduates of which find positions as technical specialists in manufacturing corporations. Although there are many actual, and more conceivable, varieties of "engineers," the large and growing profession of technologists finds its primary societal function in the service of productive enterprise. That science ought, sooner or later, to be useful is a widespread belief in our society. Contemporary industrial technology represents one fulfillment of that conviction.

The utilization of science in capitalistic production has taken three principal forms: increased complexity and coordination of semiautomatic (machine) production; increased and intensified production through greater and greater mastery of mechanical power; and multiplication and standardization of industrial products, giving a much wider range and larger quantity of articles of consumption.

The ideas and values embodied in capitalism, science, and technology should provide warning against any crude economic or technological determinism in the analysis of modern industry. Together with the ideas of individualism and a technical division of labor, they form a general climate of opinion which had major importance in the formative stages of factory production and continues to influence the organization of modern industry.

THE SOCIAL STRUCTURE OF INDUSTRY *

Too frequently the human activities of industry are conceived of as essentially economic. An industrial organization is assumed to be composed of a number of individuals entering into relations of contract for the promotion of their own individual economic interests. It is not easy to explain why this conception, which runs counter to everyday experience, should be so firmly entrenched in the minds of men and why it should be so difficult to eradicate. In many of the written decisions of management it lies as an implicit premise, unchallenged and absolute. Fortunately,

* Reprinted by permission of the publishers from F. J. Roethlisberger, *Management and Morale* (Cambridge, Mass.: Harvard University Press, 1941), pp. 46–66.

many executives in action are wiser than their theories and often make decisions in terms of factors not strictly economic. Yet few of them when challenged can resist the temptation to rationalize their practices in terms of this oversimplified theory of human motivation.

SOCIAL BEHAVIOR

To say that a more adequate way of conceiving of the human activities of industry is to view them as essentially social brings up the question of what is meant by "social." There are few words more overworked or more shot through with different meanings. For some people the word "social" applies only to those activities enjoyed after work in the company of one's friends. It calls forth ideas of social clubs, social sets, or social circles, of people who seek diversion through association with others, and of activities pertaining essentially to the pleasure-seeking world. For others, it may bring to mind people who are sociable by nature and in habit and who have a disposition for coöperative relations with their fellow men. Those who are more serious or "socially minded" may immediately think of social problems, such as crime, suicide, and divorce, or the conditions and welfare of different groups within the community—the poor, the alien, the neglected, the maladjusted. Their thoughts then may run to social legislation, social work, social diseases, social hygiene, and social security. Another group of serious students may think of social theories or social questions pertaining to the fundamental relation between capital and labor.

But in speaking of social or socialized behavior I shall not be referring to any of these high abstractions in particular, but to far more simple matters. From experience we know that individuals interact and that the expression of that interaction is commonly recognized as social behavior. Whenever a person is acting in accordance with the expectations and sentiments of some other person, or groups of persons, his behavior is social or socialized. Such behavior, it is easy to see, can occur in a bread line just as well as at a fox hunt. It is manifested by the millionaire socialite owner of a factory as well as by his most lowly skilled worker. It occurs just as much at work as it does outside of working hours. In fact, there are few acts of men that are not social in the way in which I have defined the word.

CUSTOMARY OR ROUTINE WAYS OF BEHAVIOR

One can hardly speak of socialized behavior without understanding customary, traditional, or routine ways of doing things. Strangely enough, custom has never been considered a subject of great scientific importance. For any one scientific book describing the folkways and customs of any locality there can be found at least ten books about what behavior in general is or should be. Compared with the dignity of exploring the inner workings of the brain, the study of customary behavior is likely to be thought of as undignified and commonplace. The reader would be bored if I should describe that mass of detailed behavior which goes to make up my daily existence. The facts about my shaving and washing before dressing in the morning, the articles of clothing I put on and the order in which I put them on, the kinds of foods I eat and when and how I eat them, the way in which the different objects on the table are arranged, the order in which the different members of my family sit—all this would probably soon elicit the comment, "So what? Roughly, everyone does the same things. These patterns of behavior which you so minutely describe are well-understood and recognized responses to rational or biological needs. Is there anything more to be said about them?"

In my opinion, there is. In the first place, it is a well-known fact that these routine patterns of behavior vary with different localities. We would all agree that coffee for breakfast and three meals a day are not universal routines of behavior. Yet, many of these routines are so close and fundamental to us that they lie outside the field of our conscious attention. As a result, we tend to identify our own particular local ways of behaving and thinking with behavior and thought in general. Our attention is directed to them only when we are brought into contact with groups whose customary ways of doing things are different from our own.

In the second place, these customary ways of doing things are frequently the occasion for the affirmation of our solidarity with groups. The family meal is more than an occasion for the satisfaction of biological needs. It also satisfies certain emotional needs of men. It is, for example, the occasion when the members of the family come together and when the father has an opportunity to see his children.

Now it can be seen that these customary ways of doing things constitute the framework within which the social life of groups is carried on. This framework is seldom completely coincident with biological needs. On biological grounds alone, a cup of hot water would be as good for me in the morning as a cup of coffee. A good case, in the name of science, could be made to the effect that some number other than three meals a day would be more appropriate to my sedentary way of living. Yet, were I to insist on such changes in family routines, it is probable that my wife would assume that something was wrong with me. I would be badgered with questions: "Aren't you feeling well? Don't you think you should see the doctor?" And, curiously enough, in spite of the fact that I should have science on my side, more often than not my wife would be right, not in sending me to the doctor but in feeling intuitively that my total disregard for the customary routines of behavior was symptomatic of a morbid preoccupation about my health. It is not entirely fortuitous that most neurotic ailments appear in connection with the breakdown of customary ways of doing things.

Socialized behavior, I have said, is behavior in accordance with the expectations and sentiments of others. Such behavior is expressed most often in terms of customary routines. These routines act as a sort of social cement. They bind men together in collaborative effort. Moreover, they change slowly and provide security for the individuals who perform them together.

ECONOMIC ASPECTS OF PRIMITIVE SOCIAL ORGANIZATION

Before looking at modern industry from the point of view of socialized behavior, I shall describe first the economic aspects of a more primitive type of society. By looking at a different culture we sometimes see more clearly certain uniformities of relationship that escape our attention when looking at our own.

Among the natives inhabiting a group of islands north and east of New Guinea, there exists a set of trade activities which has been interestingly described by Malinowski. Round these islands, which roughly are in the shape of a ring forming a closed circuit, two kinds of articles are constantly circulating; long necklaces of red shell travel about the islands always in a clockwise direction, and bracelets of white shell circulate always in the opposite direction. These articles are of no use to the natives except for ornamentation and are not used for this purpose to any extent. And yet these apparently worthless articles keep going round and round these islands. The natives of one island are continually giving gifts of red necklaces to the natives of another island on their clockwise side and receiving gifts of white bracelets in return. To their neighbors on their counterclockwise side, they are making gifts of white bracelets and receiving in return gifts of red necklaces.

This exchange of these two articles is known as the Kula. It takes place at definite times, in a definite manner, and between definitely prescribed partners. No Kula article remains in the hands of any one individual for any great length of time. At some future time and place it will be exchanged for some other article of equivalent prestige value. Each native knows just what these prestige value equivalences are, that is, for example, how many red necklaces of a particular kind are equivalent to a white bracelet of a particular kind. Every detail of the transaction is regulated by a set of traditional rules and conventions and is accompanied by elaborate public ceremonies. It would be irrelevant to describe in detail the rules and regulations of these ceremonial transactions; it is enough to say that they cover a complex of interrelated activities which are rooted in myth and backed by tradition. These Kula articles are prized very highly by the natives. Each necklace and bracelet has its own peculiar history and the natives spend much time in swapping stories about the individual fortunes or misfortunes of each article.

There are a number of other activities associated with the Kula. Along with the Kula system the natives carry on ordinary trade. Articles actually to be used are bartered from one island to another. Moreover, to go on these Kula expeditions to islands which are often separated by hundreds of miles of water, it is necessary for the natives to build seagoing canoes. So it can be seen that what we would regard as important economic activities—trade and canoe building—are going on in these islands in association with the exchange of necklaces and bracelets. An outsider looking on might think that these were the really important activities and that the Kula proper was only a secondary phenomenon, an indirect stimulus encouraging the natives to sail and trade. I can imagine that a modern industrial engineer entrusted with the economic reorganization of these islands might say, "Let's stop these 'Kula-shines' and get down to the real business of trade and canoe building." And he might substitute more modern incentives to get the natives about their "real" business.

Now, strange as it may seem to our own ways of thinking and behaving, to the natives themselves the Kula proper is the primary and chief activity; trading and canoe building are activities secondary to it. From studying the behavior of the natives and all their customs, Malinowski found that "the Kula is in all respects the main aim: the dates are fixed, the preliminaries settled, the expeditions arranged, the social organization determined, not with regard to trade, but with regard to Kula. On an expedition, the big ceremonial feast, held at the start, refers to the Kula; the final ceremony of reckoning and counting the spoil refers to Kula, not to the objects of trade obtained. Finally, the magic, which is one of the main factors of all the procedure, refers only to the Kula, and this applies even to a part of the magic carried out over the canoe. . . . The construction of the canoes is always carried on directly in connection with a Kula expedition."

The Kula, then, is more than a meaningless circulation of two worthless articles. It is a complex institution and as such plays a vital part in the lives of these savages. It is in this Kula setting that their productive activities gain meaning and significance, and to isolate these activities from this social setting is to give a completely erroneous and misleading picture of the economic life of these natives. Unthinking interference with a trading system such as this, which from our point of view may appear to be cumbersome and inefficient, would upset the entire social equilibrium and would rob the natives of those very social sentiments which provide an incentive to work. Yet very often by a failure to understand such social organizations, the white man deeply offends native belief and seriously affects capacity for work. The white man tends to divorce magic from work and is surprised when the suppression of one leads to inefficiency in the other.

This example of a primitive economic organization illustrates two points very clearly: In the first place, it shows that the forces which make collaboration possible among these natives are only in part economic; to a great extent they are essentially social and religious. Social motives, far more than expectations of economic gain, determine individual action. In the second place, these people are likely to assume that if the rules of the tribe imposed by tradition are rigidly upheld—that is, if all those ceremonials and rituals that play such an important role in maintaining the collaborative effort and unity of the group are seriously carried out—the economic problems will more or less take care of themselves.

Of course, this social philosophy could not be stated explicitly by any of the natives. If one were to talk to the older men of the tribe, however, one would find that most of their interest and attention is directed toward those matters pertaining to the social rather than to the economic organization of the group. Here, then, is a striking difference from the assumption of our civilization. The primitive leader assumes that if he maintains the discipline imposed by tradition there will be few economic problems. Today we make the contrary assumption. We assume that if we understand intelligently the conditions necessary for the getting of raw materials and the technical production and distribution of goods, we need to give but little attention to the problems involved in collaborative effort; that is, the human problems of effective and meaningful association at work will take care of themselves.

MODERN INDUSTRIAL ORGANIZATION

Now in stating this formulation I have oversimplified matters. There are, of course, certain individuals throughout the field of modern business who are giving attention to problems of human collaboration. It might even be argued that there are distinct groups of people—personnel organizations—who give their entire time to this problem. And yet if one looks carefully at these individuals or personnel organizations one is apt to find a strong tendency to separate the strictly technical problems of production and distribution from the human problems connected with work association. It would not be an exaggeration to say that the activities of most personnel organizations are largely based upon this very sharp separation of technical or economic matters from matters of human concern. Very seldom do such organizations act in an advisory capacity regarding technical practices of the company. From the economic viewpoint most personnel people are considered supernumeraries. Most of their duties are concerned with the routine carrying out of policies that have been settled by other groups or with settling as best they can human problems that have already been created. There is a tendency in modern industrial organization to separate the economic function from all the social interrelations and to believe that in the settlement of economic problems it is not necessary to consider any other aspect of human organization. The following are concrete examples from factory situations.

EXAMPLE NO. 1

A company in the process of reorganization found that it had on its hands approximately 200 people whose jobs had been so greatly simplified that their highly developed skill was no longer required. Fortunately, the company was then enjoying renewed business activity so that it was possible to reabsorb these people in other parts of the plant. The executives of the company felt that this problem could be solved by transferring these employees to new jobs whenever vacancies occurred in other types of work. At the same time management insisted that there should be no diminution in the "take-home." Workers should be transferred only to jobs on which they could earn as much money as they had been able to earn on their old jobs.

Now it can be seen that the logic of management was very simple. It assumed that inasmuch as the worker was primarily interested in the "take-home," any transference to another job, regardless of its nature, in which the weekly pay was not affected would be satisfactory to the employee. This logic holds in many instances primarily because two jobs whose earnings are more or less the same carry with them more or less the same social status in the company. In this particular case, however, this assumption did not hold. It happened that many of the jobs which had been affected by the reorganization were, in terms of the attitudes of the employees toward them, "superior" to those to which they were being asked to transfer. The reorganization meant transferring stock assemblers and storeroom keepers to simple machine operations or assembly work. The results were not satisfactory. Many employees who were given a choice of new jobs did not care to accept. Instead they preferred to stay on their existing jobs until conditions made it imperative to transfer, even though staying involved the risk of diminished earnings.

EXAMPLE NO. 2

Many times management makes certain changes based upon logical and economic considerations and then finds that the human interrelations which were also affected by the change create new and difficult problems. Let me take, for example, a company in which the primary manufacturing activities were divided into six functional units such as operation, inspection, production, etc. Each of these functional units had its own hierarchy of authority and interacted with the other functional units only at certain specified points in the manufacturing process. Although this type of organization secured excellent vertical control within each function, there still existed the difficulty of co-ordinating the activities of the various functions. This lack of co-ordination, particularly at the lower levels, resulted in manufacturing inefficiency. To obviate this difficulty, it became necessary to reorganize the company on new lines. A number of different shops were set up, the activities of each centering around a particular product which it manufactured from start to finish. Under this new plan each shop had its own inspection and production people, who were now expected to report to supervisors in the operating line organization. Logically, this new setup should produce the desired effect of co-ordination of functions and probably in time will do so. But at present the company is finding that it is much easier to co-ordinate these logical functions on paper than to co-ordinate the people carrying them out. It is easier to change the logical basis of organization than to change the routine human sentiments that are being violated by the reorganization.

Immediately following this reorganization, the production and inspection people, the former in particular, began to register many complaints. They found the lighting conditions in their new surroundings faulty; they did not like the common washrooms. They found fault with the lockers. Some of them went to extreme lengths in registering their dissatisfaction. One employee, for instance, refused to use the washroom on the floor where he worked and laboriously climbed several stories to use a washroom for office employees. But far more serious were the organizational difficulties that developed. There was a tendency for production clerks to short-circuit the new formal lines of authority. Instead of reporting directly to their immediate superiors—the operating supervisors—they were likely to go to production supervisors up the line.

An explanation of this situation may be found in the fact that the new organization had broken down the sharp distinction between office people and shop people that had existed under the old arrangement. In the old organization, production clerks had regarded themselves as office people. Their feeling of superiority to shop people was not merely a fanciful whim, for, although there were no written statements by the company to this effect, in all the minor distinctions and privileges which differentiated office people from shop people—lockers and washroom facilities, for example—production people were socially identified with office people. Under the new organization they felt that their status had been jeopardized; in terms of the customary interhuman relations they felt they had been demoted. Their complaints were an expression of this disruption in the social equilibrium to which they had become accustomed.

EXAMPLE NO. 3

The foundry department of a manufacturing concern employed some fifty men who were almost all highly skilled craftsmen and long-service employees. These workers prided themselves on their traditions and clung to certain privileges, such as smoking on the job, which were denied to other employees in the factory. According to the nature of their work, the foundry workers were differentiated into four groups. These job groups, according to the foundrymen themselves, were not of equal importance. Each had its own social values and its own rank in the social scale. One of these groups was dominant, and in this group three or four members rigidly controlled the rest.

About three or four years ago, in line with its general policy, the company put all the foundry employees on group piecework. Up to this time they had been on straight piecework. Management felt that, under group piecework, earnings could be distributed more equitably and that such an arrangement would divide among all the employees the responsibility for turning out a satisfactory product and for reducing the amount of scrap due to defective castings. Such was the logic of what should happen. What actually happened was something quite different. Total output, instead of increasing, went down. The problem of scrap, instead of being solved, tended to reappear and complicate other issues. The iron molders felt they were not getting what they earned. Those operators with high outputs felt they were carrying the less efficient men. Molders did not see why they should be penalized for parts that were broken by the chippers and grinders. Some of the men who had previously earned about $1.00 an hour now earned about $.75 an hour; this in spite of the fact that the new rates under the group payment plan were not in any way "tighter" than the old rates under straight piecework.

So management was faced with the problem of disentangling itself from the human complications of its own logic. The situation was far more complex than my simplified account has suggested. In essence, however, it was a situation of extreme resistance to a change introduced by management which failed to take into account the social sentiments of the foundrymen. To the foundry employees there were four different social groups—four different ways of life—which, under the new wage payment system, were no longer recognized. The foundry employees never ceased to petition management to put them back on straight piecework or, failing this, to divide them, at least for the purpose of payment, into the four natural job groups. However, for technical reasons, management found it impossible to make either of these two moves. As a result, the employees tried to force the hand of management by restricting output even at the expense of lowered individual earnings.

EXAMPLE NO. 4

Suggestion plans, according to the general logic of management, are intended to promote constructive thinking and cooperation of employees. In one company such a system was introduced. The method of administration was very simple. Suggestions handed in by the employees were considered by a committee, and suitable awards were made for accepted suggestions. Management believed that notice of these awards should be posted publicly on the bulletin boards in order to stimulate submission of suggestions and give the suggesters full recognition. However, the public posting of awards met with increasing dissatisfaction on the part of the workers. If a worker submitted a suggestion that either eliminated an operation, or so simplified or changed a work routine that rate revision was necessary, a great deal of social pressure was put on this operator by his fellow workers. Often a foreman discriminated against a worker who turned in a suggestion that improved a process for which the foreman himself was responsible. He tended to interpret such a suggestion as criticism of his work and either penalized the worker or tried to rearrange the process in such a way that the suggestion was no longer of value. Many disputes arose as to the distribution of the "windfall" when an award was made public. If the suggester owed money, claimants would appear and ask the company to effect a settlement. For these reasons, management finally had to publish awards by code number only, thereby nullifying in part the original intention of the plan. Management's logical method of promoting collaboration had failed to take into account other important aspects of this human organization.

THE SOCIAL ORGANIZATION OF INDUSTRY

These examples show that industry has a social organization which cannot be treated independently from the technical problems of economic organization. An industrial organization is more than a plurality of individuals acting only with regard to their own economic interests. These individuals also have feelings and sentiments toward one another, and in their daily associations together they tend to build up routine patterns of interaction. Most of the individuals who live among these patterns come to accept them as obvious and necessary truths and to react as they dictate.

If one looks at a factory situation, for example, one finds individuals and groups of people associated together at work, acting in certain accepted and prescribed ways toward one another. There is not complete homogeneity of behavior between individuals or between one group of individuals and another, but rather there are differences of behavior expressing differences in social relationship. Individuals conscious of their membership in certain groups are reacting in certain accepted ways to other individuals representing another group. Behavior varies according to these stereotyped conceptions of relationship. The worker, for example, behaves toward his foreman in one way, toward his first-line supervisor in another way, and toward his fellow worker in still another. People holding the rank of inspectors expect a certain kind of behavior from the operators; the operators from the inspectors. Now these relationships, as we all know from everyday experience, are finely shaded and sometimes become very complicated. When a person is in the presence of his boss alone, he acts quite differently from the way he acts when his boss's boss is also present. Likewise his boss acts toward him alone quite differently from the way he behaves when his own boss is also there. These subtle nuances of relationship are so much a part of our everyday life that they are commonplace. We take them for granted. We hardly realize the vast amount of social conditioning that has taken place in order that we can maneuver ourselves gracefully through the intricacies of these finely shaded social distinctions. We only pay attention to them when we blunder into new social situations where our past social training prevents us from making the necessary delicate interpretation of a given social signal and hence brings forth the socially wrong response.

In the factory, as in any social milieu, a process of social evaluation is constantly at work. From this process distinctions of good, bad, inferior, superior, etc., arise. This process of evaluation is carried on with simple and ready generalizations by means of which values become attached to individuals and to groups performing certain tasks and operations. It assigns to a group of individuals performing such and such a task a particular rank in the established prestige scale. Each work group becomes a carrier of social value. In industry, with its extreme diversity of occupations, there are a number of such groupings. Any noticeable similarity or difference, not only in occupation but also in age, sex, and nationality, can serve as a basis of social classification, as for example the married woman, the old-timer, the white-collared or clerical worker, the foreign element. Each of these groups too has its own value system.

Now the patterns of interaction that arise between individuals or between different groups can be graded according to the degree of intimacy involved in a relationship. Grades of intimacy or understanding can be arranged on a scale and expressed in terms of social distance. Social distance measures differences of sentiment and interest which separate individuals or groups from one another. Between the president of a company and the elevator operator, there is considerable social distance; more, for example, than between the foreman and the bench worker. Social distance is to social organization what physical distance is to physical space. However, physical and social distance do not necessarily coincide. Two people may be physically near but socially distant.

Just as each employee has a particular physical location, so he has a particular social place in the total social organization. But this place is not so rigidly fixed as in a caste system. In any factory there is considerable social mobility or movement. Movement can occur in two ways: The individual may pass from one occupation to another occupation higher up in the prestige scale. Or the prestige scale itself may change. It is obvious that these scales of value are never completely accepted by all groups in the social environment. The shop worker does not quite see why the office worker, for example, should have shorter hours of work than he has. Or the newcomer whose efficiency on a particular job is about the same but whose hourly rate is less than that of some old-timer wonders why service should count so much. The management group, in turn, from the security of its social elevation, does not understand what all the fuss is about. Advocates of a different social scale, therefore, are constantly trying to upset the existing social equilibrium and establish the supremacy of their own scale.

Any person who has achieved a certain rank in the prestige scale regards anything, real or imaginary, which tends to alter his status adversely as something unfair or unjust. It can be seen that any move on the part of the company may alter the existing social equilibrium to which the employee has grown accustomed and by means of which his status is defined. Immediately this disruption will be expressed in sentiments of resistance to the real or imagined alterations in the social equilibrium. In the case of the complaints of the production people previously given we have a good example of this phenomenon.

THE PROBLEM OF COMMUNICATION

In the technical organization of most companies there is very little explicit recognition given to these social distinctions. The blueprint organization plans of a company show the functional relations between working units, but they do not express these distinctions of social distance, movement, or equilibrium. This hierarchy of prestige values, which tends to make the work of men more important than the work of women, the work of clerks more important than the work at the bench, has no meaning for the technical organization. Nor does a blueprint plan show the primary groups, that is, those groups enjoying daily face-to-face relations. Logical lines of vertical and horizontal co-ordination of functions replace the actually existing patterns of interaction between people of different social places. From a technical standpoint, social place has no existence; only physical space exists. In place of all the sentiments of value residing in the social organization by means of which individuals and groups of individuals are differentiated, ordered, and integrated, there is substituted the logic of efficiency. Now it can be seen that this failure to recognize explicitly these human interrelations has certain consequences.

For example, the problem of communication is very important in the effective integration of any group or of a group of groups, of which industry is composed. Successful communication between individuals depends upon something more than a common language, a common set of words. People and groups with different experiences and social places, although having in common many of the same words, may vary widely in mental attitudes. These differences in modes of thought and ways of viewing things may make communication in some instances almost impossible. The trained expert with his precise and logical vocabulary has difficulty in communicating with the layman. The customary ways of thinking of the skilled toolmaker, for example, are quite different from those of the non-machine minded unskilled worker. They differ also from those of the engineer, the accountant, the marketing expert, the executive, or the administrator. As it is commonly expressed, people with different ways of thinking do not "get" each other.

If there is to be successful communication between the top and bottom of an industrial organization, these differences in modes of thought must be more clearly recognized. The same symbol does not necessarily have the same referent for different groups. Most symbols not only point out something, they also convey certain emotions. There is no better example than the case of the language of efficiency. The top of the organization is trying to communicate with the bottom in terms of the logical jargon and cold discriminations of the technical specialist, the engineer, the accountant, etc. The bottom of the organization, in turn, is trying to communicate with the top through its own peculiar language of social sentiments and feelings. Neither side understands the other very well. To the bottom the precise language of efficiency, instead of transmitting understanding, sometimes conveys feelings of dismay and insecurity. The bottom, in turn, instead of transmitting successfully its fears of social dislocation, conveys to the top emotional expressions of petty grievances and excessive demands.

The following situation is an example of what I mean. A company found it advisable to reduce the hourly rates of a number of long-service employees. This move was made not with the idea of reducing labor costs, but primarily with motives of "fairness and justice" in mind. It happened that the company had been left after the depression with a number of long-service people whose hourly rates were "out of line" with the grades of work they were doing. When business picked up and new employees were hired at hourly rates comparable to the grades of work to which they were assigned, and put into work groups with these longer-service people under the group payment plan, a situation to the disadvantage of the younger and newer men was created. In fairness to these new men, management felt something should be done. Clearly, the executives of the company had human values in mind when making this change. The purpose of their plan was to redistribute more equitably the total earnings of a group piecework department among its individual members. But here is the curious part of the story. When the company put in this change, it explained the move to the employees concerned in terms of the language of efficiency. The employees' response to this move was bitter and voluble. The more management tried to explain its reasons for making this change, the more resistance it met. Finally, one executive in conference with the employee representatives saw what had happened. The company had always had a policy favorable to its long-service employees. With this move, the long-service employees felt that the company had changed its policy with regard to them. It seemed to them that efficiency only, not service, now counted in the company. When the executive was able to reassure the employees that this move in no way had changed the basic company policy toward seniority, that long service was still valued and would be rewarded by certain considerations and privileges, the disturbance died down. The employees affected were satisfied to accept the change as long as the social values attaching to long service, which the company had upheld, had not been changed.

In conclusion, let me review briefly the points that I have made:

(1) Without misunderstanding, no particular economic activity can be torn apart from its surrounding social fabric and treated as a thing in itself. In the trade activities of the natives of the Melanesian Archipelago, for example, the economic functions of trade and canoe building cannot be adequately understood apart from the background of the Kula, a set of beliefs and attitudes expressing their social organization.

(2) Modern management tends to subsume the problems of group collaboration under the technical problems of production and efficiency. As a result, collaboration is conceived of as a logical contrivance for getting people to work together by appealing primarily to their individual economic interests.

(3) However, modern industry is built up of a number of small working groups. Between the individuals within these groups and between in-

dividuals of different groups, there exist patterns of behavior which are expressing differences in social relationship. Each job has its own social values and its rank in the social scale.

(4) Each industrial concern has a social as well as a physical structure. Each employee not only has a physical place but he also has a social place in the factory. Any technical change on the part of management may therefore affect not only the physical but also the social location of an individual or group of employees. This fear of social dislocation is likely to be a constant threat to the social security of different individuals and groups of individuals within the industry.

(5) The failure on the part of management to understand explicitly its social structure means that it often mistakes logical coordination for social integration. This confusion interferes with successful communication up and down the line as well as between different groups within the industry.

As I have said before, primitive man attaches primary importance to the social organization of the group; his economic life is completely subservient to it. Primitive belief assumes that by strict upholding of the tribal customs expressing social organization it can meet the exigencies of nature—a food shortage or drought, for example. Modern belief, on the other hand, assumes that by the efficient production and distribution of goods, it can fulfill the demands of human nature. As a result we have the goods but the natives have the morale.

It is needless to point out that neither position is tenable. However, it is much easier to see the absurdity of primitive belief than to see the absurdity of our own. It seems obvious to our logical ways of thinking that no ritualistic performance of certain ceremonials can bring forth the rain that is necessary for the successful growing of crops. It is less obvious that the application of science to agriculture does not in itself provide the basis for meaningful human association at work.

CHAPTER VI

The Business System

WHAT is the meaning of waste, and why is our economic system considered wasteful? What is the meaning of monopoly, and why is our system sometimes called monopolistic? The readings below give crucial answers to these questions. The first two selections describe the varieties of wastes—of resources, of manpower, of inventiveness—and explain how they come about. The next one depicts in superlative fashion the tendency toward concentration of economic power, and gives some of the reasons for and consequences of this tendency. Finally, the statement of President Roosevelt on economic concentration is the summation, by a practical but forward-looking statesman, of the political measures deemed necessary to avoid the wasteful faults of our system and keep the productive gains.

WASTE OF RESOURCES *

Resources are wasted or used ineffectively as parts of the [economic] organization get out of adjustment with each other, or as the organization fails to adjust to new conditions; as individuals fail to find, or are prevented from finding, the most useful field of activity; as material resources are unused, or as their effective use is impeded by human barriers; and as the most effective technology is not used or its use is prevented.

The waste of natural resources through misuse, or ruthless exploitation, is thoroughly familiar. The cutting of forests in a manner which delays or prevents reforestation, the farming of lands by methods which mine the soil of its fertility and encourage soil erosion, the extraction of petroleum by methods which blow into the air billions of cubic feet of natural gas daily,[1] these are specific resource wastes to which attention has already

* National Resources Committee, *The Structure of the American Economy,* Part I (Washington: Government Printing Office, 1939), pp. 1–3.

[1] *Report of National Resources Board,* December 1, 1934, p. 406.

turned and which reflect the inadequacies in our organization of resources.

Equally important, but less often thought of as a waste of resources, is the idleness of men and machines that could be productively employed. The power of individuals to produce is a resource like unharnessed water power. It is gone if it is not employed. It cannot be stored. If 10 million men are able and willing to work, but are forced to be idle for a year by lack of jobs, the community has wasted the valuable resources of manpower. And because of idleness, the individuals are likely to suffer a loss of skill and a breakdown of morale. The Nation is poorer both by the goods that could have been produced and by the frustration and loss of morale of the unemployed individual.

Idle machinery may also involve a waste of resources. When machinery is idle and accumulating rust or losing usefulness through becoming obsolete, when idle men are available to operate it and when its product would be useful to the community, its idleness is likely to constitute ineffective use of resources.[2] Digging a large building foundation with pick and hand shovel and leaving an available steam shovel idle may not be as wasteful of resources as keeping both men and shovel idle, but it nevertheless involves waste. Waste is also involved when obsolete equipment uses more manpower and materials in doing a particular job than would be required if improved techniques were employed, or when production is divided among so many plants in an industry that no plant can have enough volume to run efficiently. In all of these cases, failure to use the best-known technology consumes manpower or materials that might be released to be used elsewhere.

MAGNITUDE OF WASTES

The waste of resources from these three sources, ruthless exploitation, idleness of men and machinery, and failure to use the most effective known technology, all combine to give a tremendous total of wasted resources. How great this waste is it is impossible to estimate, but some suggestion of

[2] Standby equipment may, of course, be idle without involving waste of resources. Also, it should be noted that if a machine will be as much reduced in usefulness at the end of a year (or any period of time) regardless of whether it is used or left idle, a year's use of the machine is wasted by keeping it idle. Only where the machine will lose usefulness less rapidly by being idle than by being used is the waste from idleness likely to be less than the full use of the machinery. Likewise, when the machine will lose usefulness more rapidly if kept idle than if used, the waste through idleness may be more than the full current use of the machine. It should also be noted that an idle machine may not involve a waste of resources even when idle men are available to operate it and its product would be useful, if a superior machine is also idle or if a sufficiently superior machine could be built.

its magnitude can be given by estimating a single item: the depression loss in income through idleness of men and machines. . . . While no calculation can give a precise figure for the depression loss in income due to the idleness of men and machines, the figures do suggest that this loss through nonproduction was in the magnitude of 200 billion dollars worth of goods and services. Most of this represents sheer waste, though to some extent it reflects a smaller depletion of natural resources.

The significance of this figure of 200 billion dollars is hard to grasp, but some idea can be obtained by considering what 200 billion dollars would mean in terms of concrete goods. If all the idle men and machines could have been employed in making houses, the extra income would have been enough to provide a new $6,000 house for every family in the country. If instead, the lost income had been used to build railroads, the entire railroad system of the country could have been scrapped and rebuilt at least five times over. Of such is the magnitude of the depression loss in income through failure to use available resources. It meant a lower standard of living for practically every group in the community.

Even in the nondepression years there was extensive idleness of men and machines which would have been used had there been adequate organization. The Brookings Institution has estimated that in the peak year 1929 both production and national income could have been increased 19 percent by merely putting to work the men and machines that were idle in that year even without the introduction of improved techniques of production.[3] While it is not possible to establish such a figure with perfect accuracy, its magnitude suggests a very real waste of resources.

Wastes through the failure to use the best techniques of production and through faulty exploitation of natural resources likewise contribute their quota to the total waste. Few have attempted to make estimates in this highly uncertain field, but there can be little question of the magnitude of resource waste through using less than the best techniques and through faulty use of natural resources.

THE IMPACT OF WASTE

The full meaning of this failure to use resources effectively can only be realized by considering its impact upon individuals. Practically every individual in the community suffers as a result of these wastes. When the national income is 60 billion instead of 90 billion dollars, the worker suffers a lower income through unemployment or partial employment or through

[3] *America's Capacity to Produce*, Brookings Institution, p. 422.

wage rates lower than resources make possible; the farmer receives a lower income because of a reduced home market; the return on capital is reduced as a result of the partial use of equipment and the resulting increase in unit costs. For each group in the community this waste of resources means a lower standard of living than would clearly be possible.

Even more basically significant is the individual frustration resulting from the inability to find an effective use for one's skills. Without the satisfaction of useful activity, without the sense of security in a job well done, most men lose some of their self-reliance and some of their ability to be productive.

Moreover, as people become increasingly aware of the discrepancy between rich resources and poor results in living and as the ineffectiveness in the organization of resources becomes more clear, a sense of social frustration must develop and be reflected in justified social unrest and unavoidable friction. Individual frustration builds into social frustration. And social frustration is quite as likely to work itself out in socially destructive as in socially constructive ways.

THE OPPORTUNITY

At the same time this waste of resources presents a tremendous opportunity. Such resources hold the promise of a much higher standard of living than is now being obtained and present a challenge to this country, as a national household, to work out their effective use. It is a surprising comment on a Nation that prides itself on its skill in organization, in administration, and in management that such tremendous waste of resources can occur. The abundance of natural resources and the continental pioneering that has been necessary for their development may in part account for the past waste. With the continent spanned, the frontier shifts from the bringing of new resources into control to the more effective use of the resources already controlled. Here is the great challenge of today.

How long this opportunity will be open to the American democracy involves a serious question. The opportunity for a higher standard of living is so great, the social frustration from the failure to obtain it is so real, that other means will undoubtedly be sought if a democratic solution is not worked out. The time for finding such a solution is not unlimited.

STATING THE PROBLEM

This problem, the basic problem facing economic statesmanship today, can be stated as follows: How can we get effective use of our resources, yet, at the same time preserve the underlying values in our tradition of liberty and democracy? How can we employ our unemployed, how can we use our plant and equipment to the full, how can we take advantage of the best modern technology, yet in all this make the individual the source of value and individual fulfillment in society the basic objective? How can we obtain effective organization of resources yet at the same time retain the maximum freedom of individual action? This is a problem so large that no solution is likely to be arrived at except over a period of years and through the efforts of many people.

IMPEDIMENTS TO TECHNOLOGICAL CHANGE*

The acceptance or rejection of technological innovations depends to a large measure on whether they are introduced at a time when an economy is static, contracting or expanding; whether they appear in a setting of social stratification, of anarchic competition and class struggle, or in a planned industrial order. Within these varied frameworks there are other psychological and cultural factors that determine receptivity to technological innovation which can be brought into perspective by a study of specific cases of opposition to technological change. . . .

TRANSPORTATION

It is clearly to man's advantage to be able to traverse distances with facility and in ease, yet innovations permitting more comfortable and more rapid mobility generally have encountered apathy or overt resistance, and their utilization has repeatedly been restricted by vested interests. . . .

Automobile. The automobile propelled by the internal-combustion engine made its way slowly against ignorance, apathy, and competition. . . . One of the greatest sales obstacles the gasoline car had to overcome was the widespread conviction that Edison would invent a superior and cheaper electric automobile. As late as 1896, A. R. Sennett read a paper before the British Association for the Advancement of Science in which he maintained that the steam engine rather than the internal-combustion engine would prevail and that petroleum propulsion had to improve a great deal before heavy loads could be dealt with or passengers conveyed

* National Resources Committee, *Technological Trends and National Policy* (Washington: Government Printing Office, 1937), pp. 39, 43–45, 49–50, 59, 61–64.

"free from excessive vibration and offensive exhalations and with a degree of luxury at all comparable with that which we have come to identify with horse-drawn vehicles." He likewise contended that horseless carriages could not be widely used because they required great skill, inasmuch as the driver "has not the advantage of the intelligence of the horse in shaping his path." [1] In a communication to the city council in 1908, the mayor of Cincinnati declared that the driving of an automobile requires such qualifications that no woman is physically fit to undertake the task. . . .

Financiers were in nowise ahead of popular sentiment in reference to the automobile. They had no conception of its future development, and looked askance upon it. Both R. E. Olds and Charles E. Duryea testify as to the hostile reception they received in Wall Street where the bankers could not see the wisdom of investing a few thousand dollars in what they considered a plaything. Chauncey M. Depew confessed that he warned his nephew not to invest $5,000 in Ford stocks because "nothing has come along to beat the horse." W. C. Durant's prediction that some day 500,000 automobiles would be manufactured annually in the United States is said to have provoked George W. Perkins to declare "If he has any sense, he'll keep those notions to himself if he ever tries to borrow money." J. P. Morgan & Co. refused to buy for $5,000,000 in 1908 a block of securities which were later incorporated in General Motors and rose to a value of $200,000,000.[2] The financiers exaggerated the numerous mechanical imperfections that existed in the early cars, stressed the absence of good roads, were deterred by litigations over the early patents, and above all could not envisage a profitable market.

Changes in the automobile that would increase its sales possibilities by making its use simpler and its power greater were accepted slowly. The self-starter was invented in 1899, and installed on one brand of car in 1902. It was impossible, however, to get manufacturers to spend money on "refinements," and by 1912 less than 5 percent of the manufacturers were offering cars with self-starters as standard equipment.[3]

French auto manufacturers perfected a V-shaped eight-cylinder motor several years before American manufacturers showed the feasibility of producing an eight-cylinder car in quantity. In 1914, such a car was produced, yet by 1926, production still consisted of 64 percent fours, 34 percent sixes

---

[1] Quoted in Robbins, L. H., "Old Cry 'Get a Horse' Echoed in the Sky," in *New York Times Magazine,* Dec. 23, 1928, pp. 4, 13.

[2] MacManus, T. F., and Beasley, Norman, *Men, Money, and Motors* (New York, 1929), pp. 5, 113, 117.

[3] Epstein, R. C., *The Automobile Industry* (Chicago, 1928), pp. 105–107, 110.

and 2 percent eights. It was not until 1932 that Ford—who had likewise delayed adopting the standard selective three-speed transmission until December 1927—deserted the four-cylinder types to manufacture eights. By 1934, when fours practically ceased being manufactured, eight-cylinder cars still comprised only 40 percent of production.[4] A large portion of British automobiles were equipped with four-wheel brakes in 1923, when only 3 percent of American cars were so equipped; it was not until 1927 that as many as 90 percent had four-wheel brakes as standard equipment.[5] It required 7 years for the superior balloon tire to lead over the high-pressure tire. The large difference in costs between the closed car and the open car caused the manufacture of open cars to exceed closed until 1925; by 1935 the open car had practically disappeared.[6] The problem of disturbing the market, through depreciation of price of products, and the rigidity of large-scale enterprise, have been potent factors in delaying acceptance of innovations in automobile production.

The delay in the development of interurban bus transportation due to the competition of railroads has already been mentioned. The equally intense and discriminatory competition against busses by streetcar companies possessing "perpetual" franchises delayed the development of autobus transportation for decades. . . .

COMMUNICATION

The telegraph companies, once entrenched, did not encourage and were slow to respond to the innovations in their own and related fields. They did not encourage the invention of the cable and even after the first cable had been laid they continued their efforts to have transoceanic communication by way of Alaska and Siberia. Neither the telegraph nor the cable companies invented the telephone. Bell's offer to sell it to the Western Union Telegraph Co. for $100,000 was rejected. In 1883 eight leading business men in New York City met to decide whether to buy rights to the Bell telephone or the printing telegraph, both of which were offered at the same price, $300,000, and they decided to buy the latter.[7] When the telephone began seriously to compete with the telegraph, and to menace its interests, the telegraph companies accentuated public skepticism by a cam-

[4] *Automotive Industries* (Feb. 22, 1936), p. 239.

[5] Epstein, *op. cit.,* p. 110–115.

[6] Automobile Manufacturers Association, *Automobile Facts and Figures* (New York, 1935), p. 11.

[7] Fessenden, R. A., "The Inventions of Reginald A. Fessenden" in *Radio News,* vol. vi (1925), 1140–1142, 1851–1853, 1999.

paign of ridicule and disparagement. The inventor was characterized as a crank and a charlatan. His work was the devil's work, disturbing the tranquility of the countryside, and inducing break-downs among its users. The widespread currency of this attitude even among the sophisticated is seen in Thorstein Veblen's statement as late as 1914 that the use of the telephone "involves a very appreciable nervous strain and its ubiquitous presence conduces to an unremitting nervous tension and unrest wherever it goes."[8] Imperfections in the apparatus and in service were stressed. The plan to connect cities, villages, and isolated homes into one comprehensive system was denounced as folly.

The monopolistic control over the basic telephone patents which the Bell corporation acquired made it impossible to introduce improvements without its sanction. Thus when Edison, Blake, and Berliner improved the Bell telephone, their important contributions could not be utilized without the basic invention, and so they came under the control of the owners of Bell patents.[9] In 1937, the Federal Communications Commission declared that the Bell Telephone System suppressed 3,400 unused patents in order to forestall competition. Of these, 1,307, it said, were "patents voluntarily shelved by the American company and its patent-holding subsidiaries for competitive purposes." In answer to the company's declaration that the other 2,126 patents were not used because of "superior alternatives available," the Commission reported: "This is a type of patent shelving or patent suppression which results from excessive patent protection acquired for the purpose of suppressing competition. The Bell System has at all times suppressed competition in wire telephony or telegraphy through patents. It has always withheld licenses to competitors in wire telephony and telegraphy under its telephone and telephonic appliance patents, and this exclusion is extended to patents covering any type of construction. Moreover the Bell System has added to its . . . patents any patent that might be of value to its competitors. This policy resulted in the acquisition of a large number of patents covering alternative devices and methods for which the Bell System has no need. . . .

"Provisions tending to suppress development are found to be present in patent license contracts between the Western Electric Co. and independent manufacturing companies."[10]

Automatic telephone switchboards were introduced slowly. The chief

[8] Veblen, Thorstein, *The Instinct of Workmanship* (New York, 1914), p. 316.

[9] Vaughan, F. L., *Economics of our Patent System* (New York, 1925), p. 72.

[10] Federal Communications Commission, *Patent Study of Bell Telephone System*, Special Docket No. 1, 1937 (Washington, D.C., 1937).

engineer of a leading telephone company denounced the automatic system before the American Institute of Electrical Engineers. It was difficult for the public to orientate itself to the automatic system. The United States Senate, for example, had a new dial telephone system removed after a short trial. There were protests by workers against the installation in terms of technological unemployment. But the delay was chiefly occasioned by the depreciation costs on obsolete equipment. Similarly, the cradle or French telephones were long in use on the Continent before they were installed in the United States and then a service charge was added largely in order to retard their introduction. . . .

FACTORS EXPLAINING RESISTANCE TO INVENTION

Each example of opposition to technological innovation that has here been given has obviously its unique constellation of circumstances and causes. But comparable situations appear frequently enough to permit a tabulation of the basic factors involved in resistance to technological advance. In every case there are both cultural and psychological factors present, related in an inextricable manner, as aspects of the same situation; the cultural gives the historical and socio-economic setting which provoke a specific psychological response from the individuals participating. From the results of this study it is apparent that the psychological factors of habit, fear, desire for personality equilibrium and status, and the tendency of groups to coerce their members to conformity, are latent predisposing factors toward resistance to change. The manner and degree in which these factors function depend on forces in the cultural environment. . . .

Opposition to innovation is not invariably on a quasi-automatic level. Especially in economic and technological fields, there is involved conscious self-interest in the maintenance of status and, in some cases, even of life itself. Abstract "progress" usually rates insignificantly compared to the actual, immediate effects which an innovation has directly on the person or class involved.

Contemporary education in the United States appears to do little to facilitate or promote receptivity to technological innovation and is rather occupied with the organization and perpetuation of past experience and tradition. The majority of graduates, even of universities, remain ignorant of the relation of technology to contemporary culture, and few technologists are educated outside of the narrow limits of their specialities. With few persons equipped with the experimental or scientific method of verifying data, or accustomed or able to analyze proof as a criteria of truth, there must be recourse to authority. The virtue in such use of authority is counteracted by the fact that in the field of technology experts have been historically conservative, have been indifferent to and have lacked understanding of the social aspects of their work, and have often been too biased in terms of their own schooling and specific research to give deliberate and reasoned judgments.

There are factors involved in resistance to change that are implicit in group behavior. The collective behavior of groups is expedited by orderliness based on the ability to anticipate the behavior of their members. Innovations are disruptive in that they affect not isolated persons but members of groups who influence the behavior of all with whom they come in contact. There is in consequence group resentment against innovators because they disturb established relations, upset routines, and cause temporary confusion. Social pressure upon the deviant to conform follows. Caviling criticism, ridicule and disparagement, economic discrimination, social ostracism, and violence are utilized. In order to avoid such reprisals most persons endorse customary procedures and refrain from projecting or supporting innovations. Social approval gives the tone to personal adjustment, and the restraints imposed by group attitudes are thus powerful deterrents of change. The size of the community is a factor in determining the strength of its power of coercion. If it has many members, cohesion is not as close, and the innovator, finding some support, may be able to ignore detractors, but in a small community, contacts are more immediate and the influence tends to be more direct. The deterrent of group criticism functions not only in the general group life of the community, but within specific industrial organizations. To avoid the unpleasant, an individual tends to continue established routines rather than to venture with revolutionary innovations that will meet the resistance of his co-workers and superiors. "Not to venture, is not to lose," becomes a guiding principle unless incentives are strong.

In different cultures, opposition to technological change has varied in its character and strength. The factors inhibiting innovation in primitive societies, apply to a large extent to small isolated communities throughout history, and to rural communities in the modern world. Absence of a knowledge of writing in preliterate societies, and illiteracy in civilized societies, establish the need of conserving tradition through speech and behavior. Sparsity of the technological base, a relatively scant margin of safety and wealth which permits few risks, the conformity demanded within closely related groups, little division of labor which diminishes the possibilities of experimentation, dominantly nonempirical attitudes, isolation which limits horizons and experience and permits few collisions with novel concepts from without, and close integration of different aspects of the cultural configuration—all intensify conservatism.

In the ancient world, technological advances such as Hero's steam engine and mechanical appliances for construction work, were neglected mainly because of the abundance of the labor supply, because of the belief that it was degrading to science to put it to practical uses, and because of the disparaging social attitude toward artisans and manual labor.

The cultural retrogression of the Middle Ages in Europe, which made the situation prevailing in many medieval communities approximate in some respects that of primitive societies, was not conducive to innovation, least of all in the field of technology. The hierarchic social stratification that was sanctioned as divinely ordained by the Church, which spiritualized poverty and denounced materialism and experimentation, created an economic setting and authoritarian attitudes fatal to scientific progress and technological change. Medieval society was not entirely immobile and unprogressive. But local self-subsistence was a limiting economic frame, and the antiscientific attitude of the Church enforced by heresy trials afforded an environment hostile to scientific and technological innovations.

The revival of interest in classical science, slowly followed by the beginnings of the experimental methods; the discovery of new continents, the plunder of which brought vast new wealth to Europe; the rise of cities with consequent increasing power of the burghers formed the social setting of capitalism that accelerated change and led the way to increasing receptivity to technological progress. Delays were now occasioned not only by efforts of the aristocracy to check the rise of the industrial bourgeoisie, but factors, peculiar to the structure and functioning of capitalism, impeded technological advance.

Under capitalism, the almost exclusive incentive to the incorporation of technological improvements into industry has been the drive for profits. The profit motive undoubtedly served as a ferment, accelerating change, in the early days of capitalism in contrast to a relatively static feudal economy. Its effectiveness in this respect was and is dependent upon the availability of markets, and the need to acquire or maintain control of that market in competition with rival capitalists. When new continents were being opened as markets, and capitalism was an expanding economy, new machinery could more readily be used to supplement the old. Competition between entrepreneurs, although it led to wasteful anarchic production and marketing, to some extent stimulated a response to technological innovation to keep ahead of competitors. But in the degree to which monopoly in the setting of the profit system is able to control prices, standardize products, and restrict production, alertness to technological change is diminished, a brake is put on inventions and their applications.

William M. Grosvenor has, in *Chemical Markets,* expressed the sentiments of modern corporate management toward the utilization of new inventions:

> I have even seen the lines of progress that were most promising for the public benefit, wholly neglected or positively forbidden just because they might revolutionize the industry. We have no right to expect a corporation to cut its own throat from purely eleemosynary motives. . . . Why should a corporation spend its earnings and deprive its stockholders of dividends to develop something that will upset its own market or junk all its present equipment. . . . When development is directed by trained and experienced men responsible to stockholders for expenditures, they have little inducement to try to supersede that which they are paid to develop and improve.[11]

Harry Jerome, after a study of mechanization of industry under the auspices of the National Bureau of Economic Research, likewise formulated the principle that guides the relation of present-day capitalism to technological progress:

> Technical progress far outruns actual practice. This margin of nonuse is in part due to nonpecuniary factors, but the major explanation is simply that, on the whole, industry must be conducted with profits as the immediate goal; hence the first and major consideration in any choice of method is not merely, Will it do the work? but also Will it pay? [12]

The results upon technological invention of excessive rigidity of monopolistic enterprise, arising from its fear of imperiling its heavy investments, especially in durable goods, and from its elaborate mechanics of functioning, were noted before the Oldfield Hearings on Patents in 1912, by Louis D. Brandeis:

> These great organizations are constitutionally unprogressive. They will not take on the big thing. Take the gas companies of this country; they would not touch the electric light. Take the telegraph company, the Western Union Telegraph Co., they would not touch the telephone. Neither the telephone company nor the telegraph company would touch wireless telegraphy. Now, you would have supposed that in each one of these instances those concerns if they had the ordinary progressiveness of Ameri-

---

[11] Grosvenor, W. M., "The Seeds of Progress," in *Chemical Markets,* vol. xxiv (1929), pp. 23–26.

[12] Jerome, *op. cit.,* p. 33.

cans would have said at once, "We ought to go forward and develop this." But they turned it down, and it was necessary in each one of those instances, in order to promote those great and revolutionizing inventions, to take entirely new capital.[13]

Charles F. Kettering, vice president and director of research of the General Motors Corporations, likewise stated in this connection in 1927:

> Bankers regard research as most dangerous and a thing that makes banking hazardous, due to the rapid changes it brings about in industry. . . .[14]

Monopolies are themselves not only irresponsive to change, but through their control of basic patents and improvements, and also of kindred patents, only a few of which they utilize or develop, they prevent others from making technological changes in the fields which they preempt. Such is the testimony of the Inventors' Guild:

> It is a well-known fact that modern trade combinations tend strongly toward constancy of processes and products, and by their very nature are opposed to new processes and new products originated by independent inventors, and hence tend to restrain competition in the development and sale of patents and patent rights; and consequently tend to discourage independent inventive thought.[15]

Judicial decisions in United States courts have sanctioned the suppression of patents in decisions which are of primary importance when resistance to technological change in the United States is being appraised. In 1896 the judgment of the court was that the patentee "may reserve to himself the exclusive use of his invention or discovery. . . . His title is exclusive, and so clearly with the constitutional provisions in respect of private property that he is neither bound to use his discovery himself, nor permit others to use it." When this decision was reaffirmed in 1909, it was declared that "the public has no right to compel the use of patented devices or of unpatented devices when that is inconsistent with fundamental rules of property." [16] Technological progress is thus inextricably made dependent upon property rights interpreted in terms of individual rights and the rights of a specific industry as against the interests of the community. In practice, this interpretation benefits large corporations. For it is the consistent experience of inventors that they are helpless to promote their patents independently in fields which are dominated by such corporations. A chief obstacle is, of course, lack

[13] U. S. Congress, House, Committee on Patents, Oldfield Revision and Codification of the Patent Statutes: Hearings, 62d Cong., 2d sess. (1912), no. 18, p. 12.

[14] Address before Association of National Advertisers, in Detroit, May 9, 1927.

[15] Vaughan, *op. cit.*, p. 212.

[16] Vaughan, *op. cit.*, p. 161, 164.

of capital to put their plans in operation.[17] They find themselves involved in costly infringement suits, and harassed by interference procedures, which oblige them to sell their patents to the large-scale enterprises with concentrated capital resources, and in this way take a chance at their suppression. Patent pools often keep the benefit of patents within a small circle of corporations and restrain independents from their use, thus preventing broad technological advance. The rule of monopolies in technological change suggests at once an analogy with the restraining influence of the medieval guilds.

It is often argued that the establishment of laboratories and research associations by large corporations and cartels disproves the charge of inflexibility of giant industry. But these relatively few research departments give the corporations greater control over the innovations that might disturb the market. According to Grosvenor, only 12 out of the 75 most important inventions made between 1889 and 1929 were products of corporations' research.[18] Evidence that inventions under these auspices are not fully utilized is given in the British Report of the Committee on Industry and Trade, made in 1929, by Sir Arthur Balfour:

> It is when we come to consider the relation between the research associations and the industries themselves, and the extent to which these industries avail themselves in practice of the results of research by their own associations, that we find most cause for disquietude. . . . We have laid special stress on the importance of this aspect of the question of scientific research in relation to industry, because, in our opinion, it is the imperfect receptivity toward scientific ideas on the part of British industry which is at the moment the main obstacle to advance.[19]

The dominance of profit over these research activities is seen in the drastic retrenchment in research staffs concomitant with the economic crisis.

While in its early periods capitalism was more responsive to advance in technology, there have always been within it, forces which have checked maximum receptivity to technological innovations. Factors inherent in the structure of capitalism have often made technological innovation overwhelmingly, and sometimes exclusively, in the interests of a relatively few owners of industry, and to the disadvantage, sometimes temporary,

[17] Rossman, Joseph, *The Psychology of the Inventor* (Washington, 1931), pp. 161–162; Wyman, W. I., "Patents for Scientific Discoveries," *Patent Office Society Journal*, vol. xi (1929), p. 552.

[18] Grosvenor, *op. cit.*, p. 24.

[19] Great Britain, Committee on Industry and Trade, Final Report, Comd. 3282 (London, 1929), pp. 215, 218.

but often permanent, to the masses of the population. The technical innovations in the early phases of the industrial revolution were introduced with callous disregard of the havoc they wrought in the lives of the skilled artisans, as have such changes, with few exceptions, since. They have in fact been utilized repeatedly to curb the militance of labor. Andrew Ure acknowledged this already in 1835 when he called the invention of the self-acting mule "a creation destined to restore order among the industrious classes. . . ." and added "This invention confirms the great doctrine already propounded, that when capital enlists science in her service the refractory hand of labor will always be taught docility." [20] James Nasmyth is quoted to have declared that the desire to break strikes was a prime factor in the introduction of machinery:

> In the case of many of our potent self-acting tools and machines, manufacturers could not be induced to adopt them until compelled to do so by strikes. This was the case with the self-acting mule, the wool-combing machine, the planing machine, the slotting machine, Nasmyth's steam-arm and many others.[21]

Workers can hardly be expected to be receptive to technological changes in the specific fields in which they are employed, when they are cognizant that their skills will be rendered worthless and their status imperiled by resulting unemployment. It is opposition so motivated that has sometimes reached dramatic proportions, in many industries, particularly in the textile, mining, iron and steel, shoe, machinery, clothing, railroad, cigar, and glass industries.

The degree of trade-union or class consciousness determines the extent to which workers in a situation of technological change understand, articulate, and act upon their resentment at being the victims of such change. It also decides the form which their expression takes. Among unorganized workers, action is often directed against the machine itself as the immediate cause of their degradation, with the result that machine wrecking occurs. Trade-unions reject the tactic of destroying machinery and seek to substitute organized measures of bargaining with employers to lessen the impact of the tragedy of displacement through the more gradual introduction of the machine or process, and by demands for compensation to those displaced. Socialists and communists likewise discourage wrecking of machinery, support trade-union methods to get as much for the workers involved as is possible in a given situation, advocate social

[20] Ure, Andrew, *The Philosophy of Manufactures* (London, 1835), pp. 367–368.
[21] Smiles, Samuel, *Industrial Biography* (new ed. London, 1876), pp. 294–295.

insurance programs to take care of the unemployed, as do many trade-unionists, and at the same time seek to crystallize resentment in preparation for a seizure of power by labor to establish an economy in which technology will not be subject to the exigencies of a profit system but may be used to the fullest in the interests of the entire population.

THE CONCENTRATION OF OWNERSHIP *

Corporations have ceased to be merely legal devices through which the private business transactions of individuals may be carried on. Though still much used for this purpose, the corporate form has acquired a larger significance. The corporation has, in fact, become both a method of property tenure and a means of organizing economic life. Grown to tremendous proportions, there may be said to have evolved a "corporate system"—which has attracted to itself a combination of attributes and powers, and has attained a degree of prominence entitling it to be dealt with as a major social institution.

We are examining this institution probably before it has attained its zenith. Spectacular as its rise has been, every indication seems to be that the system will move forward to proportions which would stagger imagination today; just as the corporate system of today was beyond the imagination of most statesmen and business men at the opening of the present century. Only by remembering that men still living can recall a time when the present situation was hardly dreamed of, can we enforce the conclusion that the new order may easily become completely dominant during the lifetime of our children. For that reason, if for no other, it is desirable to examine this system, bearing in mind that its impact on the life of the country and of every individual is certain to be great; it may even determine a large part of the behavior of most men living under it.

Organization of property has played a constant part in the balance of powers which go to make up the life of any era. We need not resolve the controversy as to whether property interests are invariably controlling. The cynical view of many historians insists that property interests have at all times, visible or invisible, been dominant. Following this grim

* Adolf A. Berle, Jr., and Gardiner C. Means, *The Modern Corporation and Private Property* (New York: The Macmillan Company, 1935), pp. 1–9, 18–33, 40–46, 352–357. By permission of The Macmillan Company, publishers and copyright holders.

analysis, one commentator on the rise of corporations observed that they had become the "master instruments of civilization." Another expressed his depression at the fact that the system had at length reached a point definitely committing civilization to the rule of a plutocracy. Still others have seen in the system a transition phase towards ultimate socialism or communism. Acceptance of any of these beliefs may be delayed; but the underlying thought expressed in them all is that the corporate system has become the principal factor in economic organization through its mobilization of property interests.

In its new aspect the corporation is a means whereby the wealth of innumerable individuals has been concentrated into huge aggregates and whereby control over this wealth has been surrendered to a unified direction. The power attendant upon such concentration has brought forth princes of industry, whose position in the community is yet to be defined. The surrender of control over their wealth by investors has effectively broken the old property relationships and has raised the problem of defining these relationships anew. The direction of industry by persons other than those who have ventured their wealth has raised the question of the motive force back of such direction and the effective distribution of the returns from business enterprise.

These corporations have arisen in field after field as the myriad independent and competing units of private business have given way to the few large groupings of the modern quasi-public corporation. The typical business unit of the 19th century was owned by individuals or small groups; was managed by them or their appointees; and was, in the main, limited in size by the personal wealth of the individuals in control. These units have been supplanted in ever greater measure by great aggregations in which tens and even hundreds of thousands of workers and property worth hundreds of millions of dollars, belonging to tens or even hundreds of thousands of individuals, are combined through the corporate mechanism into a single producing organization under unified control and management. Such a unit is the American Telephone and Telegraph Company, perhaps the most advanced development of the corporate system. With assets of almost five billions of dollars, with 454,000 employees, and stockholders to the number of 567,694, this company may indeed be called an economic empire—an empire bounded by no geographical limits, but held together by centralized control. One hundred companies of this size would control the whole of American wealth; would employ all of the gainfully employed; and if there were no duplication of stockholders, would be owned by practically every family in the country.

SEPARATION OF OWNERSHIP AND CONTROL

Such an organization of economic activity rests upon two developments, each of which has made possible an extension of the area under unified control. The factory system, the basis of the industrial revolution, brought an increasingly large number of workers directly under a single management. Then, the modern corporation, equally revolutionary in its effect, placed the wealth of innumerable individuals under the same central control. By each of these changes the power of those in control was immensely enlarged and the status of those involved, worker or property owner, was radically changed. The independent worker who entered the factory became a wage laborer surrendering the direction of his labor to his industrial master. The property owner who invests in a modern corporation so far surrenders his wealth to those in control of the corporation that he has exchanged the position of independent owner for one in which he may become merely recipient of the wages of capital.

In and of itself, the corporate device does not necessarily bring about this change. It has long been possible for an individual to incorporate his business even though it still represents his own investment, his own activities, and his own business transactions; he has in fact merely created a legal *alter ego* by setting up a corporation as the nominal vehicle. If the corporate form had done nothing more than this, we should have only an interesting custom according to which business would be carried on by individuals adopting for that purpose certain legal clothing. It would involve no radical shift in property tenure or in the organization of economic activity; it would inaugurate no "system" comparable to the institutions of feudalism.

The corporate system appears only when this type of private or "close" corporation has given way to an essentially different form, the quasi-public corporation: a corporation in which a large measure of separation of ownership and control has taken place through the multiplication of owners.

Such separation may exist in varying degrees. Where the men ultimately responsible for running a corporation own a majority of the voting stock while the remainder is widely diffused, control and part ownership are in their hands. Only for the remaining owners is there separation from control. Frequently, however, ownership is so widely scattered that working control can be maintained with but a minority interest. The Rockefeller family, for example, is reported to have retained direct or indirect minority interests in many of the Standard Oil Companies; and in the case of the Standard Oil Company of Indiana, this interest, amounting to only 14.5 per cent combined with the strategic position of its holders, has proved sufficient for the control of the corporation. In such a case the greater bulk of ownership is virtually without control. Separation of ownership and control becomes almost complete when not even a substantial minority interest exists, as in the American Telephone and Telegraph Company whose largest holder is reported to own less than one per cent of the company's stock. Under such conditions control may be held by the directors or titular managers who can employ the proxy machinery to become a self-perpetuating body, even though as a group they own but a small fraction of the stock outstanding. In each of these types, majority control, minority control, and management control, the separation of ownership from control has become effective—a large body of security holders has been created who exercise virtually no control over the wealth which they or their predecessors in interest have contributed to the enterprise. In the case of management control, the ownership interest held by the controlling group amounts to but a very small fraction of the total ownership. Corporations where this separation has become an important factor may be classed as quasi-public in character in contradistinction to the private, or closely held corporation in which no important separation of ownership and control has taken place.

Growing out of this separation are two characteristics, almost as typical of the quasi-public corporation as the separation itself—mere size and the public market for its securities. It is precisely this separation of control from ownership which makes possible tremendous aggregations of property. The Fords and the Mellons, whose personal wealth is sufficient to finance great enterprises, are so few, that they only emphasize the dependence of the large enterprise on the wealth of more than the individual or group of individuals who may be in control. The quasi-public corporation commands its supply of capital from a group of investors frequently described as the "investing public." It draws these savings to itself either directly, as individuals purchase stocks or bonds, or indirectly, as insurance companies, banks, and investment trusts receive these saving and invest them in corporate securities. To secure these funds it must commonly avail itself of an open market in its securities—usually by listing shares on a stock exchange, or, less importantly, by maintaining a private or "unlisted" market. So essential, in fact, is the open market to the quasi-public corporation that it may be considered almost as characteristic of that type of corporation as the separation of ownership from control and the great aggregation of wealth.

These characteristics are not invariable. The private corporation may be, and in a few instances is, exceedingly large; witness the Ford Motor Company, still owned and directed by Mr. Ford and his immediate associates. Private or "close" corporations may and occasionally do avail themselves of a public market for their shares; the Aluminum Company of America, though most of its stock is closely held, has its shares listed on the New York Curb Exchange, and a small fraction of its stock is traded in there. But these instances are so exceptional as to prove the rule. In the overwhelming bulk of cases, corporations fall into the quasi-public class when they represent large aggregations of wealth and their securities are available in the open market; for in such corporations part or most of the owners have almost invariably surrendered control.

Though the American law makes no distinction between the private corporation and the quasi-public, the economics of the two are essentially different. The separation of ownership from control produces a condition where the interests of owner and of ultimate manager may, and often do, diverge, and where many of the checks which formerly operated to limit the use of power disappear. Size alone tends to give these giant corporations a social significance not attached to the smaller units of private enterprise. By the use of the open market for securities, each of these corporations assumes obligations towards the investing public which transform it from a legal method clothing the rule of a few individuals into an institution at least nominally serving investors who have embarked their funds in its enterprise. New responsibilities towards the owners, the workers, the consumers, and the State thus rest upon the shoulders of those in control. In creating these new relationships, the quasi-public corporation may fairly be said to work a revolution. It has destroyed the unity that we commonly call property—has divided ownership into nominal ownership and the power formerly joined to it. Thereby the corporation has changed the nature of profit-seeking enterprise. This revolution forms the subject of the present study.

Examination of the changes produced can properly commence with the new relationships between the owners on the one hand and control on the other, and it is these relationships with which this [section] will deal. This involves the area roughly termed "corporation finance"—the relations between the corporation as managed by the group in control, and those who hold participations in it—its stockholders, bondholders, and, to some extent, its other creditors. The change in internal organization—the relation of the corporation to its workers, its plant organization and its technical problem of production—we cannot consider at this time. Nor can we here deal with its external relationships, on the one hand with its customers

—the terms on which it furnishes to them its products or its services—and on the other hand, with the political state—the government by which it may be in some degree controlled, or over which it may have a measure of dominance. Here we are concerned only with a fundamental change in the form of property, and in the economic relationships which rest upon it.

Outwardly the change is simple enough. Men are less likely to own the physical instruments of production. They are more likely to own pieces of paper, loosely known as stocks, bonds, and other securities, which have become mobile through the machinery of the public markets. Beneath this, however, lies a more fundamental shift. Physical control over the instruments of production has been surrendered in ever growing degree to centralized groups who manage property in bulk, supposedly, but by no means necessarily, for the benefit of the security holders. Power over industrial property has been cut off from the beneficial ownership of this property—or, in less technical language, from the legal right to enjoy its fruits. Control of physical assets has passed from the individual owner to those who direct the quasi-public institutions, while the owner retains an interest in their product and increase. We see, in fact, the surrender and regrouping of the incidence of ownership, which formerly bracketed full power of manual disposition with complete right to enjoy the use, the fruits, and the proceeds of physical assets. There has resulted the dissolution of the old atom of ownership into its component parts, control and beneficial ownership.

This dissolution of the atom of property destroys the very foundation on which the economic order of the past three centuries has rested. Private enterprise, which has molded economic life since the close of the middle ages, has been rooted in the institution of private property. Under the feudal system, its predecessor, economic organization grew out of mutual obligations and privileges derived by various individuals from their relation to property which no one of them owned. Private enterprise, on the other hand, has assumed an owner of the instruments of production with complete property rights over those instruments. Whereas the organization of feudal economic life rested upon an elaborate system of binding customs, the organization under the system of the property owner—a self-interest held in check only by competition and the conditions of supply and demand. Such self-interest has long been regarded as the best guarantee of economic efficiency. It has been assumed that, if the individual is protected in the right both to use his own property as he sees fit and to receive the full fruits of its use, his desire for personal gain, for profits, can be relied upon as an effective incentive to his efficient use of any industrial property he may possess.

In the quasi-public corporation, such an assumption no longer holds. As we have seen, it is no longer the individual himself who uses his wealth. Those in control of that wealth, and therefore in a position to secure industrial efficiency and produce profits, are no longer, as owners, entitled to the bulk of such profits. Those who control the destinies of the typical modern corporation own so insignificant a fraction of the company's stock that the returns from running the corporation profitably accrue to them in only a very minor degree. The stockholders, on the other hand, to whom the profits of the corporation go, cannot be motivated by those profits to a more efficient use of the property, since they have surrendered all disposition of it to those in control of the enterprise. The explosion of the atom of property destroys the basis of the old assumption that the quest for profits will spur the owner of industrial property to its effective use. It consequently challenges the fundamental economic principle of individual initiative in industrial enterprise. It raises for re-examination the question of the motive force back of industry, and the ends for which the modern corporation can be or will be run.

GIANT CORPORATIONS AND THEIR DOMINANCE

The corporate system further commands attention because its development is progressive, as its features become more marked and as new areas come one by one under its sway. Economic power, in terms of control over physical assets, is apparently responding to a centripetal force, tending more and more to concentrate in the hands of a few corporate managements. At the same time, beneficial ownership is centrifugal, tending to divide and subdivide, to split into ever smaller units and to pass freely from hand to hand. In other words, ownership continually becomes more dispersed; the power formerly joined to it becomes increasingly concentrated; and the corporate system is thereby more securely established.

This system bids fair to be as all-embracing as was the feudal system in its time. It demands that we examine both its conditions and its trends, for an understanding of the structure upon which will rest the economic order of the future. . . .

The size of the modern giant corporation is difficult to grasp. Many people would consider large a corporation having assets of a million dollars or an income of $50,000. Measured by the average corporation this idea would be justified. In 1927 two-thirds of all corporations reporting net incomes earned less than $5,000 each. The average non-banking corporation in that year had an income of only $22,000, and gross assets of but $570,000. In comparison with the average corporation the million dollar company would be large. But in comparison to the great modern corporation both are pigmies. On the basis of assets, the American Telephone and Telegraph Company would be equivalent to over 8,000 average sized corporations and both the United States Steel Corporation and the Pennsylvania Railroad Company to over 4,000. A hundred million dollar company would be equivalent in assets to nearly 200 average corporations. Clearly such great organisms are not to be thought of in the same terms as the average company. Already the Telephone Company controls more wealth than is contained within the borders of twenty-one of the states in the country. . . .

These great companies form the very framework of American industry. The individual must come in contact with them almost constantly. He may own an interest in one or more of them, he may be employed by one of them, but above all he is continually accepting their service. If he travels any distance he is almost certain to ride on one of the great railroad systems. The engine which draws him has probably been constructed by the American Locomotive Company or the Baldwin Locomotive Works; the car in which he rides is likely to have been made by the American Car and Foundry Company or one of its subsidiaries, unless he is enjoying the services of the Pullman Company. The rails have almost certainly been supplied by one of the eleven steel companies on the list; and coal may well have come from one of the four coal companies, if not from a mine owned by the railroad itself. Perhaps the individual travels by automobile —in a car manufactured by the Ford, General Motors, Studebaker, or Chrysler Companies, on tires supplied by Firestone, Goodrich, Goodyear or the United States Rubber Company. He may choose among the brands of gas furnished by one of the twenty petroleum companies all actively seeking his trade. Should he pause to send a telegram or to telephone, one of the listed companies would be sure to fill his need.

Perhaps, on the other hand, the individual stays in his own home in comparative isolation and privacy. What do the two hundred largest companies mean to him there? His electricity and gas are almost sure to be furnished by one of these public utility companies: the aluminum of his kitchen utensils by the Aluminum Co. of America. His electric refrigerator may be the product of General Motors Co., or of one of the two great electric equipment companies, General Electric and Westinghouse Electric. The chances are that the Crane Company has supplied his plumbing fixtures, the American Radiator and Standard Sanitary Corp. his heating equipment. He probably buys at least some of his groceries from the Great Atlantic and Pacific Tea Co.—a company that expected to sell one-eighth of all the groceries in the country in 1930—and he secures some of his drugs, directly or indirectly, from the United Drug Company. The cans which contain his groceries may well have been made by the American Can Company; his sugar has been refined by one of the major companies, his meat has probably been prepared by Swift, Armour, or Wilson, his crackers put up by the National Biscuit Company. The newspaper which comes to his door may be printed on International Paper Company paper or on that of the Crown Zellerbach Corporation; his shoes may be one of the International Shoe Company's makes; and although his suit may not be made of American Woolen Company cloth, it has doubtless been stitched on a Singer sewing machine.

If he seeks amusement through a radio he will almost of necessity use a set made under a license of the Radio Corporation of America. When he steps out to the movies he will probably see a Paramount, Fox, or Warner Brothers' picture (taken on Eastman Kodak film) at a theatre controlled by one of these producing groups. No matter which of the alluring cigarette advertisements he succumbs to he is almost sure to find himself smoking one of the many brands put out by the "big four" tobacco companies, and he probably stops to buy them at the United Cigar store on the corner.

Even where the individual does not come in direct contact, he cannot escape indirect contact with these companies, so ubiquitous have they become. There are few articles of consumption to whose production one of the big companies has not to some extent contributed. The International Harvester Company and the Deere Company, plowmakers, have aided in the production of most of the bread that the American eats, to much of the cotton he wears and to many of the other agricultural products he consumes. It is almost impossible to obtain electric power from a local utility without receiving service from generating equipment supplied by one of the two big electric equipment companies. Few industrial products are made without the aid at some point in the process of steel derived from one of the big companies. And nearly every article involves transportation by one of the big railroads, either in the state of a raw material or that of a finished product.

While these companies play an integral part in the business of the country, their dominant position becomes apparent only when we seek to examine their importance in relation to the whole of the American economy. Here we must turn to the tool of statistics for only thus can we grasp the picture of our economic life as a whole. To make a statistical comparison of the relative importance of the large corporations, it is first necessary to decide upon a measure of importance. Since this study is primarily concerned with property, we have taken wealth, the economic equivalent of property, as the criterion of "importance" and have further assumed that the gross assets controlled by a corporation are roughly proportional to its wealth. Wherever possible, however, the results obtained have been checked by the use of a second measure of importance—net earnings.

In seeking to present a picture of the relative positions of these large corporations, four economic areas will be examined: (1) the New York stock market; (2) all corporate wealth; (3) all business wealth; and (4) the national wealth.

In the New York stock market there can be no question of the dominant position of the large corporation. Taking the list of stocks published weekly by the "Commercial and Financial Chronicle" and covering all but the most inactive stocks traded on the New York Stock Exchange in a normal week, 130 out of the 573 independent American corporations represented can be classed as huge companies, each reporting assets of over one hundred million dollars. These 130 companies controlled more than 80 per cent of the assets of all the companies represented. . . .

When we compare the combined assets of the two hundred largest non-banking corporations with the assets of all non-banking corporations, their dominant role is further emphasized. These companies, 42 railroads, 52 public utilities, and 106 industrials, each with assets over ninety million dollars, had combined assets at the beginning of 1930 of $81,074,000,000. According to an estimate based on Income Tax figures, the total assets of all non-banking corporations at the beginning of 1930 amount to $165,000,000,000. Thus the two hundred big companies controlled 49.2 per cent or nearly half of all non-banking corporate wealth, while the remaining half was owned by the more than 300,000 smaller companies.

The same dominant position of the large companies is shown when we compare the net income of the largest companies with the net income of all corporations. In 1929, the most recent year for which Income Tax statistics have been published, the largest two hundred non-banking corporations, each with an income of over $5,000,000, received 43.2 per cent of the income of all non-banking corporations.

Even this figure, however, tends to minimize the importance of the big companies. To a very considerable extent the Income Tax statistics, on which it is based, fail to include as part of the income of a big company all the income derived from property under its control. In compiling the figures of income the Treasury Department has tabulated as separate corporations all companies filing separate Income Tax returns, even when they were actually controlled by other companies. Since any subsidiary company controlled through ownership of less than 95 per cent of its stock (or of the voting stock) was required to file a separate return—and any subsidiary could file a separate return if it so desired—many companies are included as separate when actually they were controlled by other companies and for the present purpose should have their earnings consolidated with the latter.

For instance, the American Telephone and Telegraph Company was presumably represented in Income Tax returns as at least four companies, the parent company with assets over $3,000 million in 1928, the Pacific Telephone and Telegraph Company with assets over $379 million, the New England Telephone and Telegraph Company with $268 million assets and the Mountain States Telephone and Telegraph Company with $80 million assets. Even dividends received from these subsidiaries were not included in the statutory net income of the parent. Many other large corporations were in the same situation. For this reason the earned incomes reported by the large companies are frequently less than the earnings of property under their control.

A second factor tending to minimize the apparent importance of the large corporation, is the greater proportion of its income which is paid out as interest and therefore is not included as "statutory net income." It is fairly certain that large companies, particularly railroad and public ultilities, tend to have a larger indebtedness in proportion to their size than small companies. If the net income of all subsidiary corporations had been included in the net income of parents, and if income had included income represented by amounts paid out as interest, it is probable that the two hundred largest would have received well over 45 per cent of the net income of all corporations. This figure would therefore tend to give support to the figure derived on the basis of gross assets.

The income figures also indicated that the medium-sized corporation is not a particularly important factor. The 800 non-financial corporations next in size (according to net income) after the largest 200, received only 19.3 per cent of the net income of all corporations. This figure covers all corporations reporting income of over one million dollars and less than four and one-half million dollars, incomes representing assets ranging roughly from 18 to 80 million dollars. If all corporations had filed consolidated income accounts, the 800 corporations would have reported a still smaller proportion of corporate income since that of many important corporations would have been shifted into the higher group and only a slight balancing would come through addition from below.

In contrast to the medium-sized, the small corporation, reporting an income under one million dollars, makes an important showing. Such corporations accounted for 37.5 per cent of all corporate income, due, in large measure, to the sheer weight of numbers among the smallest units. This would seem to indicate that the bulk of corporate wealth was represented either by huge units having assets running into the hundreds of millions or by relatively small corporations having assets under four million dollars.

When we seek to compare the wealth of the big companies with that of all industry we get into difficulty since there appears to be no adequate basis for estimating the total business wealth in the country. A very rough estimate, however, indicates that at least 78 per cent and probably a larger proportion of American business wealth is corporate wealth. Since the two hundred largest corporations controlled approximately 49 per cent of all corporate wealth, the rough calculation would indicate that they controlled 38 per cent or more of all business wealth.

When we come to national wealth, we are necessarily dealing with estimates which can at best be only most approximate. The National Industrial Conference Board has estimated that the national wealth at the end of 1928 amounted to $360,062,000,000. If we assume an increase equal to the average of the previous six years we should have $367,000,000,000 as the national wealth in 1929. Since the total assets of the two hundred big companies in that year amounted to $81,077,000,000, they controlled roughly 22 per cent of the total wealth of the country. The lower relative importance of the large corporation in comparison to the national wealth is in large measure due to the importance of agricultural land and improvements, residential real estate, personal property including automobiles, and the large volume of government property.

To recapitulate, . . . [Table 1] gives the results of the foregoing analysis.

It is apparent from these figures that a very considerable portion of the industrial wealth of the country has been concentrated under the control of a relatively few huge units. There were over 300,000 non-financial corporations in the country in 1929. Yet 200 of these, or less than seven-hundredths of one per cent, control nearly half the corporate wealth.

It must further be remembered that the influence of one of these huge

TABLE I

RELATIVE IMPORTANCE OF LARGE CORPORATIONS

(ON OR ABOUT JANUARY 1, 1930)

	Results obtained by actual computation %	*Probable limits* %
Proportion of corporate wealth (other than banking) controlled by the 200 largest corporations	49.2	45–53
Proportion of business wealth (other than banking) controlled by the 200 largest corporations	38.0	35–45
Proportion of national wealth controlled by the 200 largest corporations	22.0	15–25

companies extends far beyond the assets under its direct control. Smaller companies which sell to or buy from the larger companies are likely to be influenced by them to a vastly greater extent than by other smaller companies with which they might deal. In many cases the continued prosperity of the smaller company depends on the favor of the larger and almost inevitably the interests of the latter become the interests of the former. The influence of the larger company on prices is often greatly increased by its mere size, even though it does not begin to approach a monopoly. Its political influence may be tremendous. Therefore, if roughly half of corporate wealth is controlled by two hundred large corporations and half by smaller companies it is fair to assume that very much more than half of industry is dominated by these great units. This concentration is made even more significant when it is recalled that as a result of it, approximately 2,000 individuals out of a population of one hundred and twenty-five million are in a position to control and direct half of industry.

The actual extent to which the concentration of power has progressed is striking enough. More striking still, however, is the pace at which it is proceeding. In 1909, the assets of the 200 then largest non-banking corporations amounted to only $26.0 billion. By 1919 they had reached $43.7 billion, an increase of 68 per cent in ten years. In the next ten years from 1919 to 1929 they increased to $81.1 billion, an increase of 85 per cent. . . .

To summarize the conclusions with relation to growth:

(1) On the basis of gross assets, the large corporations appear to have been growing between two and three times as fast as all other non-financial corporations.

(2) This conclusion is supported by the figures of corporate income.

(3) Since an increased proportion of industrial wealth presumably continues to come under corporate sway, the proportion of industrial wealth controlled by the large corporations has been increasing at a rate even faster than the proportion of corporate wealth controlled by them.

(4) Since estimates of national wealth are extremely approximate it is not possible to determine the growth in the proportion of national wealth controlled by the large corporations, but there can be little question that the proportion has been increasing at a rapid rate.

Just what does this rapid growth of the big companies promise for the future? Let us project the trend of the growth of recent years. If the wealth of the large corporations and that of all corporations should each continue to increase for the next twenty years at its average annual rate for the twenty years from 1909 to 1929, 70 per cent of all corporate activity would be carried on by two hundred corporations by 1950. If the more rapid rates of growth from 1924 to 1929 were maintained for the next twenty years 85 per cent of corporate wealth would be held by two hundred huge units. It would take only forty years at the 1909–1929 rates or only thirty years at the 1924–1929 rates for all corporate activity and practically all industrial activity to be absorbed by two hundred giant companies. If the indicated growth of the large corporations and of the national wealth were to be effective from now until 1950, half of the national wealth would be under the control of big companies at the end of that period. . . .

In conclusion, then, the huge corporation, the corporation with $90,-000,000 of assets or more, has come to dominate most major industries if not all industry in the United States. A rapidly increasing proportion of industry is carried on under this form of organization. There is apparently no immediate limit to its increase. It is coming more and more to be the industrial unit with which American economic, social, and political life must deal. The implications of this fact challenge many of the basic assumptions of current thought.

(1) Most fundamental of all, it is now necessary to think, to a very important extent, in terms of these huge units rather than in terms of the multitude of small competing elements of private enterprise. The emphasis must be shifted to that very great proportion of industry in the hands of a relatively few units, which can be studied individually and concretely. Such studies will reveal the operation of half of industry and

what is more important, that half which is likely to be more typical of the industry of the future.

(2) Competition has changed in character and the principles applicable to present conditions are radically different from those which apply when the dominant competing units are smaller and more numerous. The principles of duopoly have become more important than those of free competition.

(3) An increasing proportion of production is carried on for use and not for sale. With the increase in the large companies, a larger proportion of goods are consumed by the producing organization in the process of making further goods. To this extent the calculus of cost versus quality would presumably be solved in the interest of producing a product which would yield the maximum use per unit of investment. Under the latter incentive the consumer is only incidentally offered the product which will give him the most use per unit of cost unless he himself is easily able to measure usefulness. Adulteration, shoddy goods, and goods of lower quality than would be economically desirable are frequent under the incentive for profit. To the extent that production is for use by the producing organization there is no such incentive.

(4) The nature of capital has changed. To an increasing extent it is composed not of tangible goods, but of organizations built in the past and available to function in the future. Even the value of tangible goods tends to become increasingly dependent upon their organized relationship to other tangible goods composing the property of one of these great units.

(5) Finally, a society in which production is governed by blind economic forces is being replaced by one in which production is carried on under the ultimate control of a handful of individuals. The economic power in the hands of the few persons who control a giant corporation is a tremendous force which can harm or benefit a multitude of individuals, affect whole districts, shift the currents of trade, bring ruin to one community and prosperity to another. The organizations which they control have passed far beyond the realm of private enterprise—they have become more nearly social institutions.

THE NEW CONCEPT OF BUSINESS ENTERPRISE

Such is the character of the corporate system—dynamic, constantly building itself into greater aggregates, and thereby changing the basic conditions which the thinking of the past has assumed. . . .

Most fundamental to the new picture of economic life must be a new concept of business enterprise as concentrated in the corporate organization. In some measure a concept is already emerging. Over a decade ago, Walter Rathenau wrote concerning the German counterpart of our great corporation:

> No one is a permanent owner. The composition of the thousandfold complex which functions as lord of the undertaking is in a state of flux. . . . This condition of things signifies that ownership has been depersonalized. . . . The depersonalization of ownership simultaneously implies the objectification of the thing owned. The claims to ownership are subdivided in such a fashion, and are so mobile, that the enterprise assumes an independent life, as if it belonged to no one; it takes an objective existence, such as in earlier days was embodied only in state and church, in a municipal corporation, in the life of a guild or a religious order. . . . The depersonalization of ownership, the objectification of enterprise, the detachment of property from the possessor, leads to a point where the enterprise becomes transformed into an institution which resembles the state in character.

The institution here envisaged calls for analysis, not in terms of business enterprise but in terms of social organization. On the one hand, it involves a concentration of power in the economic field comparable to the concentration of religious power in the mediaeval church or of political power in the national state. On the other hand, it involves the interrelation of a wide diversity of economic interests,—those of the "owners" who supply capital, those of the workers who "create," those of the consumers who give value to the products of enterprise, and above all those of the control who wield power.

Such a great concentration of power and such a diversity of interest raise the long-fought issue of power and its regulation—of interest and its protection. A constant warfare has existed between the individuals wielding power, in whatever form, and the subjects of that power. Just as there is a continuous desire for power, so also there is a continuous desire to make that power the servant of the bulk of the individuals it affects. The long struggles for the reform of the Catholic Church and for the development of constitutional law in the states are phases of this phenomenon. Absolute power is useful in building the organization. More slow, but equally sure is the development of social pressure demanding that the power shall be used for the benefit of all concerned. This pressure, constant in ecclesiastical and political history, is already making its appearance in many guises in the economic field.

Observable throughout the world, and in varying degrees of intensity, is this insistence that power in economic organization shall be subjected to the same tests of public benefit which have been applied in their turn to power otherwise located. In its most extreme aspect this is exhibited in the communist movement, which in its purest form is an insistence that *all* of the powers and privileges of property shall be used only in the common interest. In less extreme forms of socialist dogma, transfer of economic powers to the state for public service is demanded. In the strictly capitalist countries, and particularly in time of depression, demands are constantly put forward that the men controlling the great economic organisms be made to accept responsibility for the well-being of those who are subject to the organization, whether workers, investors, or consumers. In a sense the difference in all of these demands lies only in degree. In proportion as an economic organism grows in strength and its power is concentrated in a few hands, the possessor of power is more easily located, and the demand for responsible power becomes increasingly direct.

How will this demand be made effective? To answer this question would be to foresee the history of the next century. We can here only consider and appraise certain of the more important lines of possible development.

By tradition, a corporation "belongs" to its shareholders, or, in a wider sense, to its security holders, and theirs is the only interest to be recognized as the object of corporate activity. Following this tradition, and without regard for the changed character of ownership, it would be possible to apply in the interests of the *passive* property owner the doctrine of strict property rights, the analysis of which has been presented above. . . . By the application of this doctrine, the group in control of a corporation would be placed in a position of trusteeship in which it would be called on to operate or arrange for the operation of the corporation for the *sole* benefit of the security owners despite the fact that the latter have ceased to have power over or to accept responsibility for the *active* property in which they have an interest. Were this course followed, the bulk of American industry might soon be operated by trustees for the sole benefit of inactive and irresponsible security owners.

In direct opposition to the above doctrine of strict property rights is the view, apparently held by the great corporation lawyers and by certain students of the field, that corporate development has created a new set of relationships, giving to the groups in control powers which are absolute and not limited by any implied obligation with respect to their use. This logic leads to drastic conclusions. For instance, if, by reason of these new relationships, the men in control of a corporation can operate it in their own interests, and can divert a portion of the asset fund of income stream to their own uses, such is their privilege. Under this view, since the new powers have been acquired on a quasi-contractual basis, the security holders have agreed in advance to any losses which they may suffer by reason of such use. The result is, briefly, that the existence of the legal and economic relationships giving rise to these powers must be frankly recognized as a modification of the principle of private property.

If these were the only alternatives, the former would appear to be the lesser of two evils. Changed corporate relationships have unquestionably involved an essential alteration in the character of property. But such modifications have hitherto been brought about largely on the principle that might makes right. Choice between strengthening the rights of passive property owners, or leaving a set of uncurbed powers in the hands of control therefore resolves itself into a purely realistic evaluation of different results. We might elect the relative certainty and safety of a trust relationship in favor of a particular group within the corporation, accompanied by a possible diminution of enterprise. Or we may grant the controlling group free rein, with the corresponding danger of a corporate oligarchy coupled with the probability of an era of corporate plundering.

A third possibility exists, however. On the one hand, the owners of passive property, by surrendering control and responsibility over the active property, have surrendered the right that the corporation should be operated in their sole interest,—they have released the community from the obligation to protect them to the full extent implied in the doctrine of strict property rights. At the same time, the controlling groups, by means of the extension of corporate powers, have in their own interest broken the bars of tradition which require that the corporation be operated solely for the benefit of the owners of passive property. Eliminating the sole interest of the passive owner, however, does not necessarily lay a basis for the alternative claim that the new powers should be used in the interest of the controlling groups. The latter have not presented, in acts or words any acceptable defense of the proposition that these powers should be so used. No tradition supports that proposition. The control groups have, rather, cleared the way for the claims of a group far wider than either the owners or the control. They have placed the community in a position to demand that the modern corporation serve not alone the owners or the control but all society.

This third alternative offers a wholly new concept of corporate activity. Neither the claims of ownership nor those of control can stand against the paramount interests of the community. The present claims of both contending parties now in the field have been weakened by the developments described in this book. It remains only for the claims of the community to be put forward with clarity and force. Rigid enforcement of property rights as a temporary protection against plundering by control would not stand in the way of the modification of these rights in the interest of other groups. When a convincing system of community obligations is worked out and is generally accepted, in that moment the passive property right of today must yield before the larger interests of society. Should the corporate leaders, for example, set forth a program comprising fair wages, security to employees, reasonable service to their public, and stabilization of business, all of which would divert a portion of the profits from the owners of passive property, and should the community generally accept such a scheme as a logical and human solution of industrial difficulties, the interests of passive property owners would have to give way. Courts would almost of necessity be forced to recognize the result, justifying it by whatever of the many legal theories they might choose. It is conceivable,—indeed it seems almost essential if the corporate system is to survive,—that the "control" of the great corporations should develop into a purely neutral technocracy, balancing a variety of claims by various groups in the community and assigning to each a portion of the income stream on the basis of public policy rather than private cupidity.

In still larger view, the modern corporation may be regarded not simply as one form of social organization but potentially (if not yet actually) as the dominant institution of the modern world. In every age, the major concentration of power has been based upon the dominant interest of that age. The strong man has, in his time, striven to be cardinal or pope, prince or cabinet minister, bank president or partner in the House of Morgan. During the Middle Ages, the Church, exercising spiritual power, dominated Europe and gave to it a unity at a time when both political and economic power were diffused. With the rise of the modern state, political power, concentrated into a few large units, challenged the spiritual interest as the strongest bond of human society. Out of the long struggle between church and state which followed, the state emerged victorious; nationalist politics superseded religion as the basis of the major unifying organization of the western world. Economic power still remained diffused.

The rise of the modern corporation has brought a concentration of economic power which can compete on equal terms with the modern state—economic power versus political power, each strong in its own field. The state seeks in some aspects to regulate the corporation, while the corporation, steadily becoming more powerful, makes every effort to avoid such regulation. Where its own interests are concerned, it even attempts to dominate the state. The future may see the economic organism, now typified by the corporation, not only on an equal plane with the state, but possibly even superseding it as the dominant form of social organization. The law of corporations, accordingly, might well be considered as a potential constitutional law for the new economic state, while business practice is increasingly assuming the aspect of economic statesmanship.

THE PRESIDENT'S STATEMENT ON ECONOMIC CONCENTRATION *

To the Congress of the United States:

Unhappy events abroad have retaught us two simple truths about the liberty of a democratic people.

The first truth is that the liberty of a democracy is not safe if the people tolerate the growth of private power to a point where it becomes stronger than their democratic state itself. That, in its essence, is fascism—ownership of government by an individual, by a group, or by any other controlling private power.

The second truth is that the liberty of a democracy is not safe, if its business system does not provide employment and produce and distribute goods in such a way as to sustain an acceptable standard of living.

Both lessons hit home.

Among us today a concentration of private power without equal in history is growing.

This concentration is seriously impairing the economic effectiveness of private enterprise as a way of providing employment for labor and capital and as a way of assuring a more equitable distribution of income and earnings among the people of the Nation as a whole.

THE GROWING CONCENTRATION OF ECONOMIC POWER

Statistics of the Bureau of Internal Revenue reveal the following amazing figures for 1935:

> *Ownership of corporate assets:* Of all corporations reporting from every part of the Nation, one-tenth of 1 percent of them owned 52 percent of the assets of all of them.

* S. Doc. 173, 75 Cong., 3 Sess.

> And to clinch the point: Of all corporations reporting, less than 5 percent of them owned 87 percent of all the assets of all of them.
>
> Income and profits of corporations: Of all the corporations reporting from every part of the country, one-tenth of 1 percent of them earned 50 percent of the net income of all of them.
>
> And to clinch the point: Of all the manufacturing corporations reporting, less than 4 percent of them earned 84 percent of all the net profits of all of them.

The statistical history of modern times proves that in times of depression concentration of business speeds up. Bigger business then has larger opportunity to grow still bigger at the expense of smaller competitors who are weakened by financial adversity.

The danger of this centralization in a handful of huge corporations is not reduced or eliminated, as is sometimes urged, by the wide public distribution of their securities. The mere number of security holders gives little clue to the size of their individual holdings or to their actual ability to have a voice in the management. In fact, the concentration of stock ownership of corporations in the hands of a tiny minority of the population matches the concentration of corporate assets.

The year 1929 was a banner year for distribution of stock ownership.

But in that year three-tenths of 1 percent of our population received 78 percent of the dividends reported by individuals. This has roughly the same effect as if, out of every 300 persons in our population, one person received 78 cents out of every dollar of corporate dividends, while the other 299 persons divided up the other 22 cents between them.

The effect of this concentration is reflected in the distribution of national income.

A recent study by the National Resources Committee shows that in 1935–36—

> Forty-seven percent of all American families and single individuals living alone had incomes of less than $1,000 for the year; and at the other end of the ladder a little less than 1½ percent of the Nation's families received incomes which in dollars and cents reached the same total as the incomes of the 47 percent at the bottom.

Furthermore, to drive the point home, the Bureau of Internal Revenue reports that estate-tax returns in 1936 show that—

> Thirty-three percent of the property which was passed by inheritance was found in only 4 percent of all the reporting estates. (And the figures of

concentration would be far more impressive, if we included all the smaller estates which, under the law, do not have to report.)

We believe in a way of living in which political democracy and free private enterprise for profit should serve and protect each other—to insure a maximum of human liberty, not for a few, but for all.

It has been well said that, "The freest government, if it could exist, would not be long acceptable if the tendency of the laws were to create a rapid accumulation of property in few hands and to render the great mass of the population dependent and penniless."

Today many Americans ask the uneasy question: Is the vociferation that our liberties are in danger justified by the facts?

Today's answer on the part of average men and women in every part of the country is far more accurate than it would have been in 1929 for the very simple reason that during the past 9 years we have been doing a lot of common-sense thinking. Their answer is that if there is that danger, it comes from that concentrated private economic power which is struggling so hard to master our democratic government. It will not come, as some (by no means all) of the possessors of that private power would make the people believe—from our democratic government itself.

FINANCIAL CONTROL OVER INDUSTRY

Even these statistics I have cited do not measure the actual degree of concentration of control over American industry.

Close financial control, through interlocking spheres of influence over channels of investment and through the use of financial devices like holding companies and strategic minority interests, creates close control of the business policies of enterprises which masquerade as independent units.

That heavy hand of integrated financial and management control lies upon large and strategic areas of American industry. The small businessman is unfortunately being driven into a less and less independent position in American life. You and I must admit that.

Private enterprise is ceasing to be free enterprise and is becoming a cluster of private collectivisms; masking itself as a system of free enterprise after the American model, it is in fact becoming a concealed cartel system after the European model.

We all want efficient industrial growth and the advantages of mass production. No one suggests that we return to the hand loom or hand forge. A series of processes involved in turning out a given manufactured product may well require one or more huge mass-production plants. Modern efficiency may call for this. But modern efficient mass production is not furthered by a central control which destroys competition between industrial plants each capable of efficient mass production while operating as separate units. Industrial efficiency does not have to mean industrial empire building.

And industrial empire building, unfortunately, has evolved into banker control of industry. We oppose that.

Such control does not offer safety for the investing public. Investment judgment requires the disinterested appraisal of other people's management. It becomes blurred and distorted if it is combined with the conflicting duty of controlling the management it is supposed to judge.

Interlocking financial controls have taken from American business much of its traditional virility, independence, adaptability and daring—without compensating advantages. They have not given the stability they promised.

Business enterprise needs new vitality and the flexibility that comes from the diversified efforts, independent judgments, and vibrant energies of thousands upon thousands of independent businessmen.

The individual must be encouraged to exercise his own judgment and to venture his own small savings, not in stock gambling but in new enterprise investment. Men will dare to compete against men but not against giants.

THE DECLINE OF COMPETITION AND ITS EFFECTS ON EMPLOYMENT

In output per man or machine we are the most efficient industrial nation on earth.

In the matter of complete mutual employment of capital and labor we are among the least efficient.

Our difficulties of employing labor and capital are not new. We have had them since good, free land gave out in the West at the turn of the century. They were old before we undertook changes in our tax policy or in our labor and social legislation. They were caused not by this legislation but by the same forces which caused the legislation. The problem of bringing idle men and idle money together will not be solved by abandoning the forward steps we have taken to adjust the burdens of taxation more fairly and to attain social justice and security.

If you believe with me in private initiative, you must acknowledge the right of well-managed small business to expect to make reasonable profits. You must admit that the destruction of this opportunity follows concentration of control of any given industry into a small number of dominating corporations.

One of the primary causes of our present difficulties lies in the disappearance of price competition in many industrial fields, particularly in basic manufacture where concentrated economic power is most evident—and where rigid prices and fluctuating pay rolls are general.

Managed industrial prices mean fewer jobs. It is no accident that in industries like cement and steel where prices have remained firm in the face of a falling demand pay rolls have shrunk as much as 40 and 50 percent in recent months. Nor is it mere chance that in most competitive industries where prices adjust themselves quickly to falling demand, pay rolls and employment have been far better maintained. By prices we mean, of course, the prices of the finished articles and not the wages paid to workers.

When prices are privately managed at levels above those which would be determined by free competition, everybody pays.

The contractor pays more for materials; the homebuilder pays more for his house; the tenant pays more rent; and the worker pays in lost work.

Even the Government itself is unable, in a large range of materials, to obtain competitive bids. It is repeatedly confronted with bids identical to the last cent.

Our housing shortage is a perfect example of how ability to control prices interferes with the ability of private enterprise to fill the needs of the community and provide employment for capital and labor.

On the other hand, we have some lines of business, large and small, which are genuinely competitive. Often these competitive industries must buy their basic products from monopolistic industry, thus losing, and causing the public to lose, a large part of the benefit of their own competitive policy. Furthermore, in times of recession, the practices of monopolistic industries make it difficult for business or agriculture, which is competitive and which does not curtail production below normal needs, to find a market for its goods even at reduced prices. For at such times a large number of customers of agriculture and competitive industry are being thrown out of work by those noncompetitive industries which choose to hold their prices rather than to move their goods and to employ their workers.

If private enterprise left to its own devices becomes half-regimented and half-competitive, half-slave, and half-free, as it is today, it obviously cannot adjust itself to meet the needs and the demands of the country.

Most complaints for violations of the antitrust laws are made by businessmen against other businessmen. Even the most monopolistic businessman disapproves of all monopolies but his own. We may smile at this as being just an example of human nature, but we cannot laugh away the fact that the combined effect of the monopolistic controls which each business group imposes for its own benefit inevitably destroys the buying power of the Nation as a whole.

COMPETITION DOES NOT MEAN EXPLOITATION

Competition, of course, like all other good things, can be carried to excess. Competition should not extend to fields where it has demonstrably bad social and economic consequences. The exploitation of child labor, the chiseling of workers' wages, the stretching of workers' hours, are not necessary, fair, or proper methods of competition. I have consistently urged a Federal wages-and-hours bill to take the minimum decencies of life for the working man and woman out of the field of competition.

It is, of course, necessary to operate the competitive system of free enterprise intelligently. In gaging the market for their wares, businessmen, like farmers, should be given all possible information by government and by their own associations so that they may act with knowledge, and not on impulse. Serious problems of temporary over-production can and should be avoided by disseminating information that will discourage the production of more goods than the current markets can possibly absorb or the accumulation of dangerously large inventories for which there is no obvious need.

It is, of course, necessary to encourage rises in the level of those competitive prices, such as agricultural prices, which must rise to put our price structure into more workable balance and make the debt burden more tolerable. Many such competitive prices are now too low.

It may at times be necessary to give special treatment to chronically sick industries which have deteriorated too far for natural revival, especially those which have a public or quasi-public character.

But generally over the field of industry and finance we must revive and strengthen competition if we wish to preserve and make workable our traditional system of free private enterprise.

The justification of private profit is private risk. We cannot safely make America safe for the businessman who does not want to take the burdens and risks of being a businessman.

THE CHOICE BEFORE US

Examination of methods of conducting and controlling private enterprise which keep it from furnishing jobs or income or opportunity for one-third of the population is long overdue on the part of those who sincerely want to preserve the system of private enterprise for profit.

No people, least of all a democratic people, will be content to go without work or to accept some standard of living which obviously and woefully falls short of their capacity to produce. No people, least of all a people with our traditions of personal liberty, will endure the slow erosion of opportunity for the common man, the oppressive sense of helplessness under the domination of a few, which are overshadowing our whole economic life.

A discerning magazine of business has editorially pointed out that big-business collectivism in industry compels an ultimate collectivism in government.

The power of a few to manage the economic life of the Nation must be diffused among the many or be transferred to the public and its democratically responsible government. If prices are to be managed and administered, if the Nation's business is to be allotted by plan and not by competition, that power should not be vested in any private group or cartel, however benevolent its professions profess to be.

Those people, in and out of the halls of government, who encourage the growing restriction of competition either by active efforts or by passive resistance to sincere attempts to change the trend, are shouldering a terrific responsibility. Consciously or unconsciously they are working for centralized business and finance or the other alternative—a growing concentration of public power in the Government to cope with such concentration of private power.

The enforcement of free competition is the least regulation business can expect.

A PROGRAM

The traditional approach to the problems I have discussed has been through the antitrust laws. That approach we do not propose to abandon. On the contrary, although we must recognize the inadequacies of the existing laws, we seek to enforce them so that the public shall not be deprived of such protection as they afford. To enforce them properly requires thorough investigation not only to discover such violations as may exist but to avoid hit-and-miss prosecutions harmful to business and government alike. To provide for the proper and fair enforcement of the existing antitrust laws I shall submit, through the Budget, recommendations for a deficiency appropriation of $200,000 for the Department of Justice.

But the existing antitrust laws are inadequate—most importantly because of new financial economic conditions with which they are powerless to cope.

The Sherman Act was passed nearly 50 years ago. The Clayton and Federal Trade Commission Acts were passed over 20 years ago. We have had considerable experience under those acts. In the meantime we have had a chance to observe the practical operation of large-scale industry and to learn many things about the competitive system which we did not know in those days.

We have witnessed the merging-out of effective competition in many fields of enterprise. We have learned that the so-called competitive system works differently in an industry where there are many independent units, from the way it works in an industry where a few large producers dominate the market.

We have also learned that a realistic system of business regulation has to reach more than consciously immoral acts. The community is interested in economic results. It must be protected from economic as well as moral wrongs. We must find practical controls over blind economic forces as well as over blindly selfish men.

Government can deal and should deal with blindly selfish men. But that is a comparatively small part—the easier part—of our problem. The larger, more important and more difficult part of our problem is to deal with men who are not selfish and who are good citizens, but who cannot see the social and economic consequences of their actions in a modern economically interdependent community. They fail to grasp the significance of some of our most vital social and economic problems because they see them only in the light of their own personal experience and not in perspective with the experience of other men and other industries. They therefore fail to see these problems for the Nation as a whole.

To meet the situation I have described, there should be a thorough study of the concentration of economic power in American industry and the effect of that concentration upon the decline of competition. There should be an examination of the existing price system and the price policies of industry to determine their effect upon the general level of trade, upon employment, upon long-term profits, and upon consumption. The study should not be confined to the traditional antitrust field. The effects of tax, patent, and other Government policies cannot be ignored.

The study should be comprehensive and adequately financed. I recommend an appropriation of not less than $500,000 for the conduct of such comprehensive study by the Federal Trade Commission, the Department of Justice, the Securities and Exchange Commission, and such other agencies of government as have special experience in various phases of the inquiry.

I enumerate some of the items that should be embraced in the proposed study. The items are not intended to be all inclusive. One or two of the items, such as bank holding companies and investment trusts, have already been the subject of special study, and legislation concerning these need not be delayed.

(1) *Improvement of antitrust procedure:* A revision of the existing antitrust laws should make them susceptible of practical enforcement by casting upon those charged with violations the burden of proving facts peculiarly within their knowledge. Proof by the Government of identical bids, uniform price increases, price leadership, higher domestic than export prices, or other specified price rigidities might be accepted as prima facie evidence of unlawful actions.

The Department of Justice and the Federal Trade Commission should be given more adequate and effective power to investigate whenever there is reason to believe that conditions exist or practices prevail which violate the provisions or defeat the objectives of the antitrust laws. If investigation reveals border-line cases where legitimate cooperative efforts to eliminate socially and economically harmful methods of competition in particular industries are thwarted by fear of possible technical violations of the antitrust laws, remedial legislation should be considered.

As a really effective deterrent to personal wrongdoing, I would suggest that where a corporation is enjoined from violating the law, the court might be empowered to enjoin the corporation for a specified period of time from giving any remunerative employment or any official position to any person who has been found to bear a responsibility for the wrongful corporate action.

As a further deterrent to corporate wrongdoing the Government might well be authorized to withhold Government purchases from companies guilty of unfair or monopolistic practice.

(2) *Mergers and interlocking relationships:* More rigid scrutiny through the Federal Trade Commission and the Securities and Exchange Commission of corporate mergers, consolidations, and acquisitions than that now provided by the Clayton Act to prevent their consummation when not clearly in the public interest; more effective methods for breaking up interlocking relationships and like devices for bestowing business by favor.

(3) *Financial controls:* The operations of financial institutions should be directed to serve the interests of independent business and restricted against abuses which promote concentrations of power over American industry.

(a) *Investment trusts.* Investment trusts should be brought under strict control to insure their operations in the interests of their investors rather than of their managers. The Securities and Exchange Commission is to make a report to Congress on the results of a comprehensive study of investment trusts and their operations which it has carried on for nearly 2 years. The investment trust, like the holding company, puts huge aggregations of the capital of the public at the discretion of a few managers. Unless properly restricted, it has potentialities of abuse second only to the holding company as a device for the further centralization of control over American industry and American finance.

The tremendous investment funds controlled by our great insurance companies have a certain kinship to investment trusts, in that these companies invest as trustees the savings of millions of our people. The Securities and Exchange Commission should be authorized to make an investigation of the facts relating to these investments with particular relation to their use as an instrument of economic power.

(b) *Bank holding companies.* It is hardly necessary to point out the great economic power that might be wielded by a group which may succeed in acquiring domination over banking resources in any considerable area of the country. That power becomes particularly dangerous when it is exercised from a distance and notably so when effective control is maintained without the responsibilities of complete ownership.

We have seen the multiplied evils which have arisen from the holding company system in the case of public utilities, where a small minority ownership has been able to dominate a far-flung system.

We do not want those evils repeated in the banking field, and we should take steps now to see that they are not.

It is not a sufficient assurance against the future to say that no great evil has yet resulted from holding company operations in this field. The possibilities of great harm are inherent in the situation.

I recommend that the Congress enact at this session legislation that will effectively control the operation of bank holding companies; prevent holding companies from acquiring control of any more banks, directly or indirectly; prevent banks controlled by holding companies from establishing any more branches; and make it illegal for a holding company, or any corporation or enterprise in which it is financially interested, to borrow from or sell securities to a bank in which it holds stock.

I recommend that this bank legislation make provision for the gradual separation of banks from holding-company control or ownership, allowing a reasonable time for this accomplishment—time enough for it to be done in an orderly manner and without causing inconvenience to communities served by holding-company banks.

(4) *Trade associations:* Supervision and effective publicity of the activities of trade associations, and a clarification and delineation of their legitimate spheres of activity which will enable them to combat unfair methods of competition, but which will guard against their interference with legitimate competitive practices.

(5) *Patent laws:* Amendment of the patent laws to prevent their use to suppress inventions, and to create industrial monopolies. Of course, such amendment should not deprive the inventor of his royalty rights, but, generally speaking, future patents might be made available for use by anyone upon payment of appropriate royalties. Open patent pools have voluntarily been put into effect in a number of important industries with wholesome results.

(6) *Tax correctives:* Tax policies should be devised to give affirmative encouragement to competitive enterprise.

Attention might be directed to increasing the intercorporate dividend tax to discourage holding companies and to further graduating the corporation income tax according to size. The graduated tax need not be so high as to make bigness impracticable, but might be high enough to make bigness demonstrate its alleged superior efficiency.

We have heard much about the undistributed-profits tax. When it was enacted 2 years ago, its objective was known to be closely related to the problem of concentrated economic power and a free capital market.

Its purpose was not only to prevent individuals whose incomes were taxable in the higher surtax brackets from escaping personal income taxes by letting their profits be accumulated as corporate surplus. Its purpose was also to encourage the distribution of corporate profits so that the individual recipients could freely determine where they would reinvest in a free capital market.

It is true that the form of the 1936 tax worked a hardship on many of the smaller corporations. Many months ago I recommended that these inequities be removed.

But in the process of the removal of inequities we must not lose sight of original objectives. Obviously, the Nation must have some deterrent against special privileges enjoyed by an exceedingly small group of individuals under the form of the laws prior to 1936, whether such deterrent take the form of an undistributed-profits tax or some other equally or more efficient method. And obviously an undistributed-profits tax has a real value in working against a further concentration of economic power and in favor of a freer capital market.

(7) *Bureau of Industrial Economics:* Creation of a Bureau of Industrial Economics which should be endowed with adequate powers to supplement and supervise the collection of industrial statistics by trade associations. Such a bureau should perform for businessmen functions similar to those performed for the farmers by the Bureau of Agricultural Economics.

It should disseminate current statistical and other information regarding market conditions and be in a position to warn against the dangers of temporary overproduction and excessive inventories as well as against the dangers of shortages and bottle-neck conditions and to encourage the maintenance of orderly markets. It should study trade fluctuations, credit facilities, and other conditions which affect the welfare of the average businessman. It should be able to help small businessmen to keep themselves as well informed about trade conditions as their big competitors.

No man of good faith will misinterpret these proposals. They derive from the oldest American traditions. Concentration of economic power in the few and the resulting unemployment of labor and capital are inescapable problems for a modern "private enterprise" democracy. I do not believe that we are so lacking in stability that we will lose faith in our own way of living just because we seek to find out how to make that way of living work more effectively.

This program should appeal to the honest common sense of every independent businessman interested primarily in running his own business at a profit rather than in controlling the business of other men.

It is not intended as the beginning of any ill-considered "trust busting" activity which lacks proper consideration for economic results.

It is a program to preserve private enterprise for profit by keeping it free enough to be able to utilize all our resources of capital and labor at a profit.

It is a program whose basic purpose is to stop the progress of collectivism in business and turn business back to the democratic competitive order.

It is a program whose basic thesis is not that the system of free private enterprise for profit has failed in this generation, but that it has not yet been tried.

Once it is realized that business monopoly in America paralyzes the system of free enterprise on which it is grafted, and is as fatal to those who manipulate it as to the people who suffer beneath its impositions, action by the Government to eliminate these artificial restraints will be welcomed by industry throughout the Nation.

For idle factories and idle workers profit no man.

Franklin D. Roosevelt

The White House, April 29, 1938

PART FOUR

Our Class System

CHAPTER VII

The Doctrine of Class Struggle

No matter what one's political faith, no matter what one's method of approach, an extremely important aspect of modern society is the class system. The existence of classes (groups of people who differ in status, prestige, and income from other groups) is undeniable. The relationships between them—their conflicts and mutual adjustments—tell us a great deal about the way our society operates.

Always, of course, there are at least two things to keep in mind about class organization. The first is the factual situation—the actual differences of income, occupation, education, opportunity, and prejudice between the different social layers. The second is the theory of class organization that people carry in their heads when they think about the class system as a whole. The theory, or doctrine, may or may not correspond with the factual situation. Often the theory is elaborated by intellectuals who have a political axe to grind. As such they are distortions with a strong propaganda element in them. One of the most extreme of such doctrines is that of the communists. Repeatedly, communistic and socialistic theorists have sought to give a picture of our society in terms of a bitter struggle that can have only one conclusion, the dictatorship of the proletariat. This is not the theory of class that the American people, or indeed the American intellectuals and statesmen, have held. The American view is that we have a system in which there are social and economic differences, to be sure, but in which every man has an opportunity to better himself. It denies the rigidity of class lines in this country and emphasizes peaceful competition rather than bitter struggle.

Neither the communistic nor the American theory of class is strictly true to the facts of American society. The American view, however, has the advantage of being the ideal, the myth, of the American people; it is the model to which we hope to make our society conform. As such, it has already been documented in Chapter II of the present volume, the chapter on the American

Credo. The whole American theory of political order, the American philosophy of social justice, is implicitly a theory of class organization. Having presented this theory already, we now must give in the present chapter the extreme opposite, the communistic doctrine of the class struggle. This will be followed by two chapters on the facts and scientific theories of our class system, furnishing a corrective to both doctrines, but especially refuting the straight Marxian dogma.

THE COMMUNIST MANIFESTO *

Modern bourgeois society with its relations of production, of exchange and of property, a society that has conjured up such gigantic means of production and of exchange, is like the sorcerer who is no longer able to control the powers of the nether world whom he has called up by his spells. For many a decade past the history of industry and commerce is but the history of the revolt of modern productive forces against modern conditions of production, against the property relations that are the conditions for the existence of the bourgeoisie and of its rule. It is enough to mention the commercial crises that by their periodical return put the existence of the entire bourgeois society on trial, each time more threateningly. In these crises a great part not only of the existing products, but also of the previously created productive forces, are periodically destroyed. In these crises there breaks out an epidemic that, in all earlier epochs, would have seemed an absurdity—the epidemic of over-production. Society suddenly finds itself put back into a state of momentary barbarism; it appears as if a famine, a universal war of devastation had cut off the supply of every means of subsistence; industry and commerce seem to be destroyed. And why? Because there is too much civilization, too much means of subsistence, too much industry, too much commerce. The productive forces at the disposal of society no longer tend to further the development of the conditions of bourgeois property; on the contrary, they have become too powerful for these conditions, by which they are fettered, and no sooner do they overcome these fetters than they bring disorder into the whole of bourgeois society, endanger the existence of bourgeois property. The conditions of

* Karl Marx and Friedrich Engels, *Manifesto of the Communist Party,* first published in German in 1848. The present selection is taken from an edition by Random House Publishers, New York, 1932, pp. 326–334.

bourgeois society are too narrow to comprise the wealth created by them. And how does the bourgeoisie get over these crises? On the one hand by enforced destruction of a mass of productive forces; on the other, by the conquest of new markets, and by the more thorough exploitation of the old ones. That is to say, by paving the way for more extensive and more destructive crises, and by diminishing the means whereby crises are prevented.

The weapons with which the bourgeoisie felled feudalism to the ground are now turned against the bourgeoisie itself.

But not only has the bourgeoisie forged the weapons that bring death to itself; it has also called into existence the men who are to wield those weapons—the modern working class—the proletarians.

In proportion as the bourgeoisie, *i.e.,* capital, is developed, in the same proportion is the proletariat, the modern working class, developed—a class of laborers, who live only so long as they find work, and who find work only so long as their labor increases capital. These laborers, who must sell themselves piecemeal, are a commodity, like every other article of commerce, and are consequently exposed to all the vicissitudes of competition, to all the fluctuations of the market.

Owing to the extensive use of machinery and to division of labor, the work of the proletarians has lost all individual character, and, consequently, all charm for the workman. He becomes an appendage of the machine, and it is only the most simple, most monotonous, and most easily acquired knack, that is required of him. Hence, the cost of production of a workman is restricted, almost entirely, to the means of subsistence that he requires for his maintenance, and for the propagation of his race. But the price of a commodity, and therefore also of labor, is equal to its cost of production. In proportion, therefore, as the repulsiveness of the work increases, the wage decreases. Nay more, in proportion as the use of machinery and division of labor increases, in the same proportion the burden of toil also increases, whether by prolongation of the working hours, by increase of the work exacted in a given time, or by increased speed of the machinery, etc.

Modern industry has converted the little workshop of the patriarchal master into the great factory of the industrial capitalist. Masses of laborers, crowded into the factory, are organized like soldiers. As privates of the industrial army they are placed under the command of a perfect hierarchy of officers and sergeants. Not only are they slaves of the bourgeois class, and of the bourgeois state; they are daily and hourly enslaved by the machine, by the over-looker, and, above all, by the individual bourgeois manufacturer himself. The more openly this despotism proclaims gain to be its end and aim, the more petty, the more hateful and the more embittering it is.

The less the skill and exertion of strength implied in manual labor, in other words, the more modern industry develops, the more is the labor of men superseded by that of women. Differences of age and sex have no longer any distinctive social validity for the working class. All are instruments of labor, more or less expensive to use, according to their age and sex.

No sooner has the laborer received his wages in cash, for the moment escaping exploitation by the manufacturer, than he is set upon by the other portions of the bourgeoisie, the landlord, the shopkeeper, the pawnbroker, etc.

The lower strata of the middle class—the small tradespeople, shopkeepers, and retired tradesmen generally, the handicraftsmen and peasants—all these sink gradually into the proletariat, partly because their diminutive capital does not suffice for the scale on which modern industry is carried on, and is swamped in the competition with the large capitalists, partly because their specialized skill is rendered worthless by new methods of production. Thus the proletariat is recruited from all classes of the population.

The proletariat goes through various stages of development. With its birth begins its struggle with the bourgeoisie. At first the contest is carried on by individual laborers, then by the work people of a factory, then by the operatives of one trade, in one locality, against the individual bourgeois who directly exploits them. They direct their attacks not against the bourgeois conditions of production, but against the instruments of production themselves; they destroy imported wares that compete with their labor, they smash machinery to pieces, they set factories ablaze, they seek to restore by force the vanished status of the workman of the Middle Ages.

At this stage the laborers still form an incoherent mass scattered over the whole country, and broken up by their mutual competition. If anywhere they unite to form more compact bodies, this is not yet the consequence of their own active union, but of the union of the bourgeoisie, which class, in order to attain its own political ends, is compelled to set the whole proletariat in motion, and is moreover still able to do so for a time. At this stage, therefore, the proletarians do not fight their enemies, but the enemies of their enemies, the remnants of absolute monarchy, the landowners, the non-industrial bourgeois, the petty bourgeoisie. Thus the whole historical movement is concentrated in the hands of the bourgeoisie; every victory so obtained is a victory for the bourgeoisie.

But with the development of industry the proletariat not only increases in number; it becomes concentrated in greater masses, its strength grows, and it feels that strength more. The various interests and conditions of life within the ranks of the proletariat are more and more equalized, in proportion as machinery obliterates all distinctions of labor and nearly everywhere reduces wages to the same low level. The growing competition among the bourgeois, and the resulting commercial crises, make the wages of the workers ever more fluctuating. The unceasing improvement of machinery, ever more rapidly developing, makes their livelihood more and more precarious; the collisions between individual workmen and individual bourgeois take more and more the character of collisions between two classes. Thereupon the workers begin to form combinations (trade unions) against the bourgeoisie; they club together in order to keep up the rate of wages; they found permanent associations in order to make provision beforehand for these occasional revolts. Here and there the contest breaks out into riots.

Now and then the workers are victorious, but only for a time. The real fruit of their battles lies, not in the immediate result, but in the ever expanding union of the workers. This union is furthered by the improved means of communication which are created by modern industry, and which place the workers of different localities in contact with one another. It was just this contact that was needed to centralize the numerous local struggles, all of the same character, into one national struggle between classes. But every class struggle is a political struggle. And that union, to attain which the burghers of the Middle Ages, with their miserable highways, required centuries, the modern proletarians, thanks to railways, achieve in a few years.

This organization of the proletarians into a class, and consequently into a political party, is continually being upset again by the competition between the workers themselves. But it ever rises up again, stronger, firmer, mightier. It compels legislative recognition of particular interests of the workers, by taking advantage of the divisions among the bourgeoisie itself. Thus the ten-hour bill in England was carried.

Altogether, collisions between the classes of the old society further the course of development of the proletariat in many ways. The bourgeoisie finds itself involved in a constant battle. At first with the aristocracy; later on, with those portions of the bourgeoisie itself whose interests have become antagonistic to the progress of industry; at all times with the bourgeoisie of foreign countries. In all these battles it sees itself compelled to appeal to the proletariat, to ask for its help, and thus, to drag it into the political arena. The bourgeoisie itself, therefore, supplies the proletariat with its own elements of political and general education, in other words, it furnishes the proletariat with weapons for fighting the bourgeoisie.

Further, as we have already seen, entire sections of the ruling classes are, by the advance of industry, precipitated into the proletariat, or are at least threatened in their conditions of existence. These also supply the proletariat with fresh elements of enlightenment and progress.

Finally, in times when the class struggle nears the decisive hour, the process of dissolution going on within the ruling class, in fact within the whole range of old society, assumes such a violent, glaring character, that a small section of the ruling class cuts itself adrift, and joins the revolutionary class, the class that holds the future in its hands. Just as, therefore, at an earlier period, a section of the nobility went over to the bourgeoisie, so now a portion of the bourgeoisie goes over to the proletariat, and in particular, a portion of the bourgeois ideologists, who have raised themselves to the level of comprehending theoretically the historical movement as a whole.

Of all the classes that stand face to face with the bourgeoisie today, the proletariat alone is a really revolutionary class. The other classes decay and finally disappear in the face of modern industry; the proletariat is its special and essential product.

The lower middle class, the small manufacturer, the shopkeeper, the artisan, the peasant, all these fight against the bourgeoisie, to save from extinction their existence as fractions of the middle class. They are therefore not revolutionary, but conservative. Nay more, they are reactionary, for they try to roll back the wheel of history. If by chance they are revolutionary, they are so only in view of their impending transfer into the proletariat; they thus defend not their present, but their future interests; they desert their own standpoint to adopt that of the proletariat.

The "dangerous class," the social scum (*Lumpenproletariat*), that passively rotting mass thrown off by the lowest layers of old society, may, here and there, be swept into the movement by a proletarian revolution; its conditions of life, however, prepare it far more for the part of a bribed tool of reactionary intrigue.

The social conditions of the old society no longer exist for the proletariat. The proletarian is without property; his relation to his wife and children has no longer anything in common with bourgeois family relations; modern industrial labor, modern subjection to capital, the same in England as in France, in America as in Germany, has stripped him of every trace of national character. Law, morality, religion, are to him so many bourgeois prejudices, behind which lurk in ambush just as many bourgeois interests.

All the preceding classes that got the upper hand, sought to fortify their already acquired status by subjecting society at large to their conditions of appropriation. The proletarians cannot become masters of the productive forces of society, except by abolishing their own previous mode of appropriation, and thereby also every other previous mode of appropriation. They have nothing of their own to secure and to fortify; their mission is to destroy all previous securities for, and insurances of, individual property.

All previous historical movements were movements of minorities, or in the interest of minorities. The proletarian movement is the self-conscious, independent movement of the immense majority, in the interest of the immense majority. The proletariat, the lowest stratum of our present society, cannot stir, cannot raise itself up, without the whole superincumbent strata of official society being sprung into the air.

Though not in substance, yet in form, the struggle of the proletariat with the bourgeoisie is at first a national struggle. The proletariat of each country must, of course, first of all settle matters with its own bourgeoisie.

In depicting the most general phases of the development of the proletariat, we traced the more or less veiled civil war, raging within existing society, up to the point where that war breaks out into open revolution, and where the violent overthrow of the bourgeoisie lays the foundation for the sway of the proletariat.

Hitherto, every form of society has been based, as we have already seen, on the antagonism of oppressing and oppressed classes. But in order to oppress a class, certain conditions must be assured to it under which it can, at least, continue its slavish existence. The serf, in the period of serfdom, raised himself to membership in the commune, just as the petty bourgeois, under the yoke of feudal absolutism, managed to develop into a bourgeois. The modern laborer, on the contrary, instead of rising with the progress of industry, sinks deeper and deeper below the conditions of existence of his own class. He becomes a pauper, and pauperism develops more rapidly than population and wealth. And here it becomes evident, that the bourgeoisie is unfit any longer to be the ruling class in society, and to impose its conditions of existence upon society as an over-riding law. It is unfit to rule because it is incompetent to assure an existence to its slave within his slavery, because it cannot help letting him sink into such a state, that it has to feed him, instead of being fed by him. Society can no longer live under this bourgeoisie, in other words, its existence is no longer compatible with society.

The essential condition for the existence and sway of the bourgeois class is the formation and augmentation of capital; the condition for capital is wage-labor. Wage-labor rests exclusively on competition between the laborers. The advance of industry, whose involuntary promoter is the bourgeoisie, replaces the isolation of the laborers, due to competition, by their revolutionary combination, due to association. The development of modern industry, therefore, cuts from under its feet the very foundation on which the bourgeoisie produces and appropriates products. What the bourgeoisie therefore produces, above all, are its own grave-diggers. Its fall and the victory of the proletariat are equally inevitable.

PREAMBLE TO CONSTITUTION OF THE AMERICAN FEDERATION OF LABOR *

Whereas, A struggle is going on in all the nations of the civilized world between the oppressors and the oppressed of all countries, a struggle between the capitalist and the laborer, which grows in intensity from year to year, and will work disastrous results to the toiling millions if they are not combined for mutual protection and benefit. It, therefore, behooves the representatives of the Trade and Labor Unions of America, in convention assembled, to adopt such measures and disseminate such principles among the mechanics and laborers of our country as will permanently unite them to secure the recognition of rights to which they are justly entitled. We, therefore, declare ourselves in favor of the formation of thorough Federation, embracing every Trade and Labor Organization in America, organized under the Trade Union system.

HUNGER AMIDST PLENTY †

Capitalism's criminally stupid economic system, both here and abroad, has caused more suffering, desolation and death than even its savage, in-

* *Report of Proceedings of the 52d Annual Convention of the American Federation of Labor*, Cincinnati, Ohio, 1932, p. xviii ff.

† Foster, William Z., *Socialism* (New York: Workers Library Publishers, Inc., 1941), pp. 7–8, 10–13, 15–17, 24–27.

terminable wars. All the major evils of the present social order originate in its rotten economic foundations.

The United States, occupying one of the most favored areas of the globe, has the objective requirements for an abundant prosperity for all its people—rich soil, boundless mineral resources, a great industrial system, a vast body of skilled workers. Yet, according to the latest Government survey, 66 per cent of American families live on slow starvation incomes of less than $825 a year, over 4,000,000 families having yearly incomes of but $312. Compare these pitiful incomes with the $1,958 yearly income necessary as a minimum for a family of five, as established by the Labor Research Association (February, 1941), on the basis of United States labor statistics. The Gallup Poll of December 22 says that four out of every ten families complain they do not get enough to eat. The bulk of the population live in slums or semi-slum houses and lack elementary medical care. John L. Lewis was correct in charging that there are 52,000,000 shrunken bellies in this country, and President Roosevelt made an understatement in declaring that one-third of our nation is ill-fed, ill-clothed and ill-housed. . . .

The exploitation of the workers and farmers is basically responsible for the tremendous inequality of wealth which prevails in this country and others. In 1928 less than 1 per cent of the population owned 46 per cent of this nation's income-yielding wealth, and now the disproportion is far greater. Sixty rich families practically dominate the vital resources of the United States. The Rockefeller, Mellon and du Pont families alone control over eight billion dollars worth of assets, while millions of families of workers and farmers own practically nothing. The country is being systematically robbed by a whole series of powerful and ever growing banker-controlled monopolies, each preying upon some vital social necessity, while ever greater numbers of workers and farmers, squeezed and exploited by these powerful corporations, sink deeper and deeper into poverty and misery. . . .

THE GENERAL CRISIS OF CAPITALISM

All the foregoing reactionary features of capitalism are rapidly growing worse, as Marx forecast generations ago. The rich are getting richer and the poor poorer. Since 1918 the industrial output per man-hour in the United States has doubled, while real wages for employed workers have made but slight advances. Millions of workers, through unemployment, have had their living standards reduced by one-half or more. Exploitation is growing more intense and the workers and farmers are steadily receiving a smaller proportion of what they produce. The C.I.O. research department says that from 1932 to 1940 the percentage of the national income going to wages has fallen from 77 per cent to 61 per cent. Monopolization of industry and farming is proceeding with giant strides. In 1919 there were ten corporations owning over one billion dollars in capital, totaling $10,000,000,000 in assets: by 1939 the figure had jumped up to twenty-eight of such giant corporations, with $58,000,000,000 in capitalization. In 1921 there was 30,812 banks with $50,000,000,000 in assets, but by 1937 the number of banks had been reduced to 15,724, while their assets had increased to $60,000,000,000. In 1909 the 200 largest corporations in this country owned $26,000,000,000 in assets; in 1937 they owned $122,000,-000,000. Similar examples of increased exploitation of the toilers and of the greater concentration of capital and industry exist in all the capitalist countries.

The periodic (cyclical) economic crises of capitalism are now becoming broader, deeper and more permanent. In the earlier period of capitalism it was possible for the capitalists to find outlets for the huge wealth they exploited out of the workers and farmers, by investing it in the expanding home market, by finding markets abroad, and by developing the raw material sources in the colonial countries. But now these means of capitalist expansion are rapidly drying up. The home market, because of the reduced purchasing power of the underpaid and unemployed masses, is steadily shrinking. And because of the sharpened competition of the other industrialized countries, the impoverishment of the colonial lands, the disruption caused by the interminable wars, and through the capitalist exploiters losing control over one-sixth of the world, the land of the Soviet Union, the foreign markets are less and less capable of absorbing the mounting surplus of commodities robbed by the capitalists from the workers in all capitalist countries, especially in the United States. In consequence, mass unemployment on a gigantic scale has become permanent; production is systematically reduced and commodities are destroyed while millions starve, the industrial crises have become more profound, more prolonged and more devastating. The only way the capitalist industrial system, including that of the United States, has been kept temporarily from collapsing altogether is by government make-work schemes—such as road building, housing, etc., and especially by the wholesale production of munitions of war.

The rapidly worsening world economic situation inevitably produces discontent, class consciousness, organization and revolt among the workers and other toilers. To counteract this, to hold the masses under the capitalist yoke, to intensify mass exploitation, and to facilitate their imperialist wars, the capitalists proceed to institute increased oppression of the toiling masses. In Germany, Italy, Japan, Spain, and now in France, Holland, Belgium, etc., they have, under fascist terrorism, abolished parliamentary government, broken up the trade unions, destroyed the toilers' political parties and cooperatives, cultivated anti-Semitism, and reduced the working population to near slavery. Similar fascist tendencies are to be found among the big capitalist circles in all countries, including the United States. Fascism is the goal they are striving for through their increased attacks upon the organizations, living standards, and civil rights of the people.

The breaking down of world capitalist economy inevitably intensifies the trade conflicts and wars between the great capitalist states. With more or less permanent economic crises in their respective countries, the aggressive drives of these imperialist powers to conquer markets, to secure sources of raw materials, to acquire colonies and world strategic positions, and especially to defeat, if possible, the socialist U.S.S.R., take on great sharpness. Consequently the international gold standard has broken down, solemnly agreed-upon treaties have come to mean nothing, the fiercest trade wars rage, normal methods of commerce are abandoned and barter systems adopted. These many growing conflicts and antagonisms culminate in wars of unheard of violence and brutality. . . .

A FREE PEOPLE

In a socialist America the people will enjoy freedom in its fullest sense and also the material well being which must serve as its base. The people will finally emerge from the capitalist jungle in which they now live. They will then have a country and a world indeed well worth living in.

The worker will have a steady job at the maximum rates of pay that the output of industry permits. There will be no capitalists to rob him and no industrial crises to plague him. The dread fear of unemployment will be banished completely from his life. He will work under conditions of maximum efficiency, comfort and safety. His family and himself will be thoroughly protected by social insurance against sickness, accident, old age and all other disabling contingencies. His health will be a major concern of the state. Periodic vacations will be his as a matter of right. He can look forward without fear to an old age of ease and well-earned rest after a life of pleasant and constructive labor. No longer will his life be harassed by the poverty and insecurity that are his and his family's lot under capitalism.

The farmer will be secure in the possession of his land under forms of collectivization adapted to American conditions and traditions. His returns for his labor will be honest and complete. There will be no landlords and trusts to gouge him. Tenancy, mortgages and sharecropping will be but bad memories of a barbarous capitalist age. The farms will be equipped with every known labor-saving device and the farmer himself will be a trained agriculturist. In his home and in his life generally he will enjoy the cultural advantages of the city.

The professional—the scientist, the doctor, the engineer, the artist, the writer and others—will enter upon a new period of efficiency and honor among his fellow men. No more will he be a mere servant of the rich, a mouthpiece of the oppressors. The professions will achieve the true respect that should be theirs. The professional, his economic status free from all worry, will have unexampled opportunity to develop his specialty. Under socialism the arts, sciences and professions, sedulously cultivated by the state and the people's mass organizations, will flourish to an extent undreamed of under capitalism. Lines of demarcation between workers, farmers and professionals will tend to disappear by the closer linking of the professions to the life of the people and by a great rise in the level of popular education.

The woman under socialism will, for the first time since most primitive days, be a free human being. All the tangible and intangible handicaps laid upon her during long centuries of oppression will be liquidated. In every respect she will occupy an equal position with men. Equal wages in industry, equal rights under the law, equal opportunity of entry into any profession or occupation, economic independence in the fullest sense of the word will be hers. Socialism will free woman from her double slavery which she shares with all workers and her special economic dependence upon her husband.

The youth, girls and boys alike, will also enter a golden era under socialism. Their childhood will be surrounded with every care by family and state to develop their health and individuality. They will be guaranteed the broadest general and technical education. Positions in their chosen vocations will be theirs by right—no more heart-breaking joblessness. Promotion will be wide open to them in every occupation—no more will they come up against the blank wall of finding all good jobs occupied by a favored few. The socialist youth will be able to marry and establish families at a normal age and will not be frustrated as most young people are under capitalism. Under socialism, for the first time in history, youth will come into its own. Its great vigor and creativeness will be called forth to the utmost.

Members of national groups will find freedom from persecution only under socialism. With no unscrupulous capitalist exploiters to profit by creating chauvinistic antagonisms among them, the many national groups that go to make up the nation as a whole will live harmoniously together, each making its own contribution to the general well being. The shameful oppression of the Negro people will cease outright and they will enjoy social equality in the fullest sense of the word. Anti-Semitism will also be unknown and Jews will have all the rights of other citizens. The Indians will be raised from their present status of government wards to that of real free men. Chauvinistic attitudes among all other national groups will be abolished. On the same principle, the American socialist government will live in friendly collaboration with all other governments.

Socialist citizens will enjoy rights and freedom of a kind and to a degree quite unknown under capitalism. They will possess the fullest liberties of speech and assembly, as well as the right to worship or not to worship as they choose. They will enjoy the right to the product of their labor, and the right to rest and education will be guaranteed them. In order to practice all their rights they will build trade unions, cooperatives, sport clubs and mass cultural organizations on a scale totally unknown under capitalism. The family, in this environment of freedom and prosperity, will take on new strength. Underlying and protecting these liberties will be a broad political franchise which, expressing itself under the leadership of the Communist Party, will create the most democratic government in the world.

Thus in socialism will be found the only answer to the mass starvation, brutal oppression, and savage slaughter that are increasingly being produced by the decaying capitalist system. Humanity faces the alternative of either advancing to peace, prosperity and freedom under socialism, or of sinking into undreamed of depths of pauperization, terrorism and murderous war under capitalism. This is the historic choice of our time and there can be no doubt but that socialism will eventually triumph in the United States and on a world scale.

CHAPTER VIII

The American Class Structure

WHEN one leaves the realm of doctrine and enters the real world of factual description and objective analysis, the American class organization appears much more complex and many-sided than it did before. Class affiliation is only one of the characteristics that each individual has and consequently, especially in our complex social order, the lines cannot be drawn as neatly as sheer doctrine would require. The following selections are designed to show the difficulties of handling the concept of class with reference to America and to give some notion of the relation of class lines to the rest of our social system.

WORK HABITS AND CLASS POSITION*

Just as the members of the higher skilled working class and of management act in response to their culture, to their system of social and economic rewards, so do the underprivileged workers act in accord with their culture. The habits of "shiftlessness," "irresponsibility," lack of "ambition," absenteeism, and of quitting the job, which management usually regards as a result of the "innate" perversity of underprivileged white and Negro workers, are in fact *normal responses* that the worker has learned from his physical and social environment. These habits constitute a system of behavior and attitudes which are realistic and rational in *that environment* in which the individual of the slums has lived and in which he has been trained.

My purpose is to trace the origin of these work habits in the social and economic system of the communities in which the underprivileged worker has to live. I shall be specific and concrete. I shall not take time to

* Davis, Allison, "The Motivation of the Underprivileged Worker," *ETC: A Review of General Semantics,* Vol. III (Summer, 1946), No. 4, pp. 243–53. This article was also reprinted in W. F. Whyte (ed.), *Industry and Society* (New York: McGraw-Hill Book Co., Inc., 1946), pp. 86–106. Permission to use this article was granted by both publishers.

indulge in sociological abstractions, but I shall try to deal with realities, with the habits of sleeping, of medical care, of joint communal living, of housing, of tavern and night-club life, of gambling, of sex, and of the social competition that the underprivileged worker learns from his slum environment.

The evidence will be taken from several studies of white and Negro working-class groups in the Chicago area, studies recently carried out by my colleagues and myself in the University of Chicago. They include evidence on 600 families, both white and Negro. Of these, 200 were middle class, and 400 were working class. In addition, the studies include intensive observation and interviewing of selected white and Negro working-class families in their homes, where they were observed several times a week throughout nearly a year. The intensive studies of Pearl, a white underprivileged worker, of Ruth, an even more underprivileged Negro worker, and of Clark, a lower class white worker, will be used to illustrate the findings of the statistical data on 600 families.

PEARL AND HER KIN

Pearl Elno, the white female worker, was born of old native stock in southern Indiana, the daughter of a coal miner. At the beginning of the great depression, her father came to Chicago to seek work, bringing his family. Here Pearl met Jim Elno, a young machinist, the son of a Polish laborer and a charwoman, and, like both his parents, extremely devoted to liquor in general and to schnapps in particular. At eighteen, Pearl married Jim Elno. Both youngsters were ambitious and smart. They were both good workers, anxious to buy a home of their own, and to get ahead in the world. Jim studied hard at his trade; and he bought a derby hat and a pair of spats—just to show his friends that he was a man who took himself seriously and intended to get somewhere in the world.

His young wife was always more practical and conscientious than Jim, and forced him to leave his mother's, set up a home of his own, and to work for goals more enduring than a derby and spats. All her efforts for a house of their own and for a decent standard of living were defeated, however, during the next ten years, by the rapidly increasing number of their children. Jim was a Catholic, and Pearl was a very fertile woman. In 9 years, she bore seven children.

Unable to secure work during most of the thirties, and presented annually with a new baby by Pearl, Jim began to drink heavily. Any father who has had to come home to five, or six, or seven small children, and has had to try to live and sleep with them, crowded into a three-room flat, will sympathize with Jim, I imagine. During the depression, four children were born to the Elnos. They had to flee to steadily smaller and poorer apartments, and the children were reduced to half-starvation rations, which kept them sorely undernourished and chronically ill. Unemployment and their hopelessly large family wore away the determination and the morale of the parents, especially of Jim. They separated twice, and Jim deserted once but returned. He was arrested two or three times for panhandling while drunk. He beat his wife several times, when he was drunk. The Elnos and their seven little children were on the rocks and seemed headed for the bottom.

But Pearl still had her own parental family. Her father and mother, and her sisters, together with their husbands, formed a closely organized and loyal clan, which repeatedly rescued her and her seven children. The sisters took them in, when Jim was violently drunk, or when they were evicted for inability to pay the rent. They bought the children clothes, and helped feed them. Pearl's mother, still able to hold a job at sixty, borrowed money on her home to lend to Jim, when he was employed by the Works Progress Administration. She came up from southern Indiana repeatedly to care for the children, so that Pearl could work as a waitress, and as a machine operator, to help feed the children while Jim was unemployed. One of Pearl's sisters opened a tavern recently and employed the mother, who in turn helped Pearl's family. Both the sisters and mother thus have continued to help Pearl.

The history of the Elno family illustrates in part how the organization, and the typical experiences of the white working-class family, control the motivation of the lower class worker. First, its size is typical of working-class families, and it is an important factor in their motivation. We found the average number of children in white *middle-class* families in Chicago to be only 2.2. In white working-class families, the average number of children is 3.3. This is a tremendous difference; along with the lower incomes that go with these much larger families, it changes the nature of family relationships in the working class, the methods of child training the standards of nutrition, of cleanliness, of education, and of sex behavior The actual daily pressure of 5 to 10 hungry stomachs to fill, backs to clothe and feet to cover forces the working-class parent to reduce his ambitions to this level of subsistence; to lower his sights as far as long-term planning and studying for better jobs and for finer skills are concerned; to narrow limit, and shorten his goals with regard to the care, nutrition, education and careers of his children.

This terrible pressure for physical survival means that the *child* in the average working-class family usually does not learn the "ambition," the drive for high skills, and for educational achievement that the middle-class child learns in his family. The working-class individual usually does not learn to respond to these strong incentives and to seek these difficult goals, because they have been submerged in his family life by the daily battle for food, shelter, and for the preservation of the family. In this sense, ambition and the drive to attain the higher skills are a kind of luxury. They require a minimum *physical security;* only when one knows where his next week's or next month's food and shelter will come from, can he and his children afford to go in for the long-term education and training, the endless search for opportunities, and the tedious apple polishing that the attainment of higher skills and occupational status requires.

Secondly, the Elno family's history illustrates the deprivations, the shocks of fortune, the drain of illness and malnutrition, as well as the social and psychological disorganization, that reduce the efficiency of the underprivileged worker. A society that pens families into this kind of physical and social environment actually cripples both the ability and the work motivation of its workers. If there is one thing that modern psychology makes clear, it is this: men cannot be motivated successfully to work hard, or to learn well, simply by putting the screws upon them. The starvation theory of wages may or may not have been abandoned in actual industrial practice, but it is certain that other theories of social punishment, and of economic pressure, other theories that men will work hard and well *only* when they are *compelled* to by economic or legal necessity are still very popular. But the analysis of our system of economic and social prestige, as well as the findings of psychologists, make it clear to any realist that men work hard and learn well only when they have been trained to work for increasing rewards.

To improve the underprivileged worker's performance, one must help him to learn *to want* and to be anxious to attain higher social goals for himself and his children. All one can get out of methods of starvation conditions in wages, or of threat and intimidations, is more of the same inferior work and more concealed resistance, as in the case of a man whipping a poorly trained mule. The problem of changing the work habits and motivation of people who come out of families like the Elnos' is far more complex than mere supervision and pressure. It is a problem of changing the goals, the ambitions, and the level of cultural and occupational aspiration of the underprivileged worker.

This change in his cultural motivation cannot be attained by getting him into the starvation box. For, as the Elno family illustrates, the average working-class family is a large economic unit, a clan of kin. They can depend upon *each other* for shelter and food in time of unemployment, or of reduced income, or of prolonged absenteeism, or when they simply quit the job. In this working-class culture, one may usually fall back upon his brothers, or sisters, or aunts, or nieces, or cousins for a bed and meals, in a way that middle-class people cannot. The middle-class adult person is ashamed to go to his relations or friends for food and shelter. "Respectability" prohibits such dependence. To avoid this embarrassing loss of "face," he will work harder, take more punishment of a mental and emotional kind on the job, and cling to the job more desperately than will the average lower class, underprivileged worker.

That is to say, the masses of working-class people, like the Elnos, cannot be frightened and forced into better work habits, simply through having the economic squeeze put on them, or through being threatened constantly with firing. Such threats do not intimidate them, as they do the middle-class clerk or schoolteacher, because the underprivileged worker is thoroughly accustomed to those conditions of life that middle-class people call "insecurity." Most important of all, he knows he can always "bunk in" with a relative, usually on his mother's side of the family, and he is certain that an extra plate will be filled for him and his, so long as his relatives have food. The harder the economic *noose* is drawn, the tighter the *protective* circle of the average working-class family is drawn. Thus economic intimidation is much less effective than with white-collar employees. Since most working-class people do not get the rewards of social and economic prestige in our society, they do not fear the loss of the job or the attendant loss of respectability in their communities nearly so deeply as do the white-collar workers.

RUTH IN A KITCHENETTE

One other example of this pattern of *group* economic help and solidarity should be included, before leaving the matter. In Negro families in the rural South, and generally in those which have migrated from the farms to Chicago, the circle of relations who help each other economically is even larger than in the average white working-class family. There are more children in these families; the average number of children in 300 Negro working-class families in the Chicago area is 4.9. The bonds of kinship, the closeness of feeling, and the number of mutual duties are also greater in the Negro working-class family, owing to its recent experiences as an integrated economic and social unit on the plantations.

There are also many broken white and Negro working-class families, of course. But these individuals, whose families have been scattered by death, disease, desertion, and immigration, are also provided with a communal group, which helps them in times of economic difficulty and illness. The life of Ruth, a Negro factory worker in Chicago, who was born in Mississippi, illustrates this point.

Ruth's parents were unskilled workers, far below the Elnos in both education and opportunity for occupational training—at the very bottom of the economic hierarchy. The family came to Chicago in 1935. For a long time, they were unable to secure either work or relief. Both then, and later when the father was given a job as an unskilled laborer on WPA, Ruth, her four sisters and brother, and her parents lived in the large cellar of an old tenement on the South Side. The cellar had been divided into nine rooms, one for each family. There was no kitchen, only an open corner at the back of the cellar, with a small gas stove and a faucet. The nine families shared this corner as their "kitchen." But they had an organized, cooperative system of sharing, which went far beyond the joint use of the so-called "kitchen." They shared their small stocks of furniture, their bedclothes, and their wearing apparel. Most important of all, they shared their food and even their money. When a family was both out of work and off relief, the other families put their money and food into a communal "pot," in which the destitute family shared. This is a hard system to beat, for those who believe in the effectiveness of economic intimidation in making good workers. When workers can survive at this level, and still have the social support and approval of their friends, they can scarcely be threatened or starved into better work habits. They will have to be led, by the offering of concrete rewards of better job opportunities and wages and better treatment and status on the job.

In 1942, when Ruth was fifteen, her parents separated, and her mother remarried. This marriage forced Ruth out of her home at once. The next year she had to leave school and go to work. After she had to leave her home, but before she could obtain her working papers, Ruth lived, slept, and ate with the families of her working-class school friends. Often she had little sleep because there was no bed available, but she had a roof over her and at least a meal a day. She also shared the clothes of her school friends.

This communal, group living has persisted, even though Ruth has now been working for more than two years. She is a hard and powerful worker, who carries a man's load. Foremen pick her for heavy, driving jobs that not 1 woman out of 10 can stand. She likes to do this heavy work thoroughly, but she also finds it exhausting. Moreover, she is still very young, and she has no responsibilities except herself. Therefore, she stays off the job rather frequently and sometimes misses several days in succession. She can continue this habit, because she still has her group of friends, her large social clique, who are really her "adopted" family and who will give her shelter and food and lend her clothes whenever they have them. Therefore, Ruth disappears from the job even when she has *no* money. Keeping her broke, by paying her only every two weeks or every three weeks, will not keep her on the job. She can always "bunk in" with her group of friends. This is a typical experience of underprivileged workers, both male and female, and both in the South and in the North. Groups of people, who have *no families,* live together, share food, money, clothes, and beds, and also share their work; for example, trading their ironing for another person's washing or cleaning.

It scarcely needs to be emphasized that this is a way of life that is demoralizing to the individual's habits of work. It is not realized generally, however, that the problem of increasing the efficiency of the underprivileged worker always involves two major kinds of difficulties that must be attacked. First his cultural goals must somehow be raised; his ceiling of aspiration for education, for respectability, for skills, and for better training of his children must become high enough to motivate him to work harder. Such efforts to change their cultural habits and their social status are the driving force behind those relatively few workers who do rise above the slum environments that I have been describing. Because this problem of motivating the lower class worker to strive hard for more respectable and complex ways of life is the more difficult problem, it will be considered last here.

The other, more immediate, more tangible task for our society in improving the efficiency of the labor supply is that of improving the underprivileged worker's standard of living. Workers who live under the conditions that I have described suffer heavy penalties in loss of sleep, malnutrition, and disease, which in turn greatly reduce their efficiency.

Worst of all, from the point of view of those who wish to change these poor work habits, the slum dwellers become accustomed and "adjusted" to their crippling standards of living. Like people in every class, every culture, they learn to regard their environment and their living habits as decent and satisfying. This is the circle that our society must break, in order *to increase the consciousness of economic needs among the masses of workers,* and thus lead to fuller production and better labor.

The miserable housing, and recurrent homelessness of the underprivileged workers are the most costly of all drains upon his efficiency. A study of working-class Negroes in Chicago in 1944–1945 revealed that most of them had less than five hours sleep per night. Children and adults must sleep three to five in a bed. Beds are usually filled day and night in Chicago's slums, as workers await their turn to sleep. The density of the population on the Negro South Side is the second highest in the United States.

Ruth sleeps in a kitchenette apartment rented by a mother with eight children. Ruth shares a bed with five other adolescents and children, sleeping crosswise the bed. She counts it a windfall when there are only three in the bed, and she may sleep lengthwise. A record of her hours of sleep was kept last winter, for two periods of two weeks each, one in November and one in January. She was in bed an average of 4½ hours out of each 24. During these 10 working days, she was absent 4. Her work was extremely heavy, so heavy that she was given a half hour's rest by the plant for each hour on the job. Without more sleep, she said, she could not stand the work even five days a week. She has been trying since Christmas to find a room to rent. Last fall she tried to find a kitchenette apartment, so that she could marry, but, as anyone who knows the South Side's residential "lock-in" understands, she had no chance.

Similar conditions prevail among white workers in many parts of the city, of course. In one large area restricted to whites on the South Side, the great majority of *families with children* live in single rooms, or in kitchenette apartments. No matter whether the people in these modern, urban ratholes in which human children and their parents must live are white or Negro the social and economic results are the same. The children are forced out into the streets, day and night; they are "movie children" or completely vagrant children. Life cannot be lived as a family group in these packed rooms; it has to be lived on the streets, in the motion-picture theaters, the taverns, the bars, and the night clubs. Under such unimaginable living conditions, all the effort, training, and money, which in the case of the middle-class worker goes into his home, is blocked and diverted to sex, recreation, and gambling. How can a worker be motivated to work to furnish or to improve his home, when he cannot get an apartment, or even a bed to sleep in? The most basic goal, the most powerful organizing control in our society, or in any Western society, is the establishment and maintenance of a living place and a home. A society, such as ours, that deprives great masses of the workers of this primary goal, deprives them thereby of the prime incentive, the most insistent drive for steady, determined work habits. In addition, it directly reduces their efficiency on the job by the steady drain of exposure, lack of sleep, and the diseases, such as tuberculosis, which are related to overcrowding.

The physical disabilities of underprivileged workers in Chicago are far more extensive than the favorite publicity concerning their lack of orange juice and milk, and the occasional ratbites, would suggest. Unemployment and inadequate income resulting in chronic malnutrition decrease both their physical resistance and their working efficiency. A series of recent scientific studies of the children of underprivileged workers, as contrasted with children of middle-class parents have revealed that the vitamin and chemical levels in the blood of working-class children are greatly below those of middle-class children and are seriously deficient. A study of the bone structure of children in two such groups, by means of X ray, revealed that these nutritional and other environmental deprivations of working-class people leave their marks upon the very bones, themselves. In Chicago, the rates of infection and death from tuberculosis are far higher among underprivileged working-class groups, both white and Negro, than among middle-class groups, as revealed by a survey made at the University of Illinois. At the same time, hospital and medical care is far more limited and is critically limited for Negroes.

For the employer, the most important consideration here is that the underprivileged worker becomes accustomed to these conditions; he learns to accept poor habits of nutrition and medical care and to accept physical impairment as a natural part of his life. Ruth, for instance, eats only one meal a day, even when doing heavy labor. She has never been to a physician, or an optician, or an ophthalmologist. Yet she is so nearsighted that she has to be within six inches of a newspaper or clock to read them; she is partly deaf from an early childhood accident, and she lived with a tubercular father for several years. But like Pearl, the white underprivileged worker, whose stamina is sufficient only for periods of a few weeks on a job, Ruth regards her physical impairment as "natural." She has not had the money nor the training requisite to secure good medical attention and to learn good health habits. Thus, both cultural attitudes toward nutrition and medical care, as well as severe limitations in housing and hospital facilities work together to reduce the efficiency of such workers. These social and economic drains accustom them to accept high absenteeism and chronic physical impairment as normal aspects of their work adjustment.

Education, as the underprivileged worker experiences it, likewise differs from the education of middle-class persons. It differs in its length, in its content, and in its value as a social and economic tool. In the Chicago area, the average number of grades completed by white *working-class* mothers is 8.6, whereas white middle-class mothers have completed an average of 14.2. White working-class fathers have finished the eighth (8.3) grade, on the average; by contrast, middle-class white fathers have completed an average of 16 grades. Among Negroes, the average for working-class parents is even lower, but is rapidly overtaking that for white workingmen.

On the whole, the Negro worker of the past generation in Chicago—that is, those who are grandparents now—was better educated than the white worker. Whereas 22.9 per cent of our sample of white working-class women in that generation had no schooling at all, only 11.1 per cent of the Negro working-class women had none. The proportion of both white and Negro working-class women who had finished grammar school was the same, 22 per cent. Among the working-class men of this older generation, the Negroes were nearly equal to the whites in years of schooling. Today, the Negro lower class workingman is practically on a par with the white worker with regard to grades completed in school. For example, if we consider those who have spent some time in high school, the proportion is higher among Negroes (34.8 per cent as compared with 32.7 per cent). For instance, in our *middle-class* Chicago sample, both white and Negro women had completed an average of 14 years in school. Negro middle-class men had completed 14.3 years, and white middle-class men 16.1 years. In the generation born since the First World War, moreover, Negroes have greatly increased their average level of schooling. In another decade, the Negro working class in the Chicago area probably will have a higher average grade attainment than the white working class. Their great handicap even now, in the fifteen to twenty year age group is the lack of opportunities for apprenticeship, from which they are barred generally by both management and unions.

Among the present adult generations of underprivileged workers, white or Negro, however, education has had little effect upon work habits. Nor does it "take" very successfully with the slum child of any color.

Whereas, for the skilled worker and the office person both their drive to work steadily and their interest in developing their skills are powerfully stimulated by their training in school, for the average underprivileged worker, on the other hand, our schools are unrealistic in their methods and in their attempts at motivation. Furthermore, the schools are staffed by highly protected middle-class persons, whose goals and whose economic opportunities are quite different from those of the families and children of the lower class. To the underprivileged adolescent, the words and the goals of his teacher—those words and goals to which middle-class adolescents react with respect and hard striving—mean very little. For the words of the teacher are not connected with the *acts of training in his home,* with the actual rewards in school, or with actual steps in moving toward a career, which alone can make the words effective in motivating him to learn good school habits. Thus our educational system, which next to the family is the most effective agency in teaching good work habits to middle-class people, is largely ineffective and unrealistic with underprivileged groups. Education fails to motivate such workers because our schools and our society both lack *real rewards* to offer underprivileged groups. Neither lower class children nor adults will work hard in school or on the job just to please the teacher or boss. They are not going to learn to be ambitious, to be conscientious, and to study hard, as if school and work were a fine character-building game, which one plays just for the sake of playing. They can see, indeed, that those who work hard at school usually have families that *already* have the occupations, homes, and social acceptance that the school holds up as the rewards of education. The underprivileged workers can see also that the chances of their getting enough education to make their attainment of these rewards in the future at all probable is very slight. Since they can win the rewards of prestige and social acceptance in their own slum groups without much education, they do not take very seriously the motivation taught by the schools.

CLARK GIVES UP TRYING

The impact upon the underprivileged worker of the physical and cultural environment that I have been describing is represented by the case of Clark, a twenty-four-year-old white man, who was intensively studied by an interviewer in the department of education. In 1939 and 1940, Clark was living in basement rooms, bunking in with friends. As conditions became too crowded even for that level of society, or as Clark wore out his welcome, he moved from one such refuge to another. He ate what he could buy with the change he made on odd jobs and what his friends could give him. Except for a meal from his friends two or three times a week he lived on two or three nickel frankfurters or hamburgers a day. For clothes, he had one frayed suit made of shoddy and a ragged half-cotton overcoat. He also had two pairs of trousers and two or three shirts, which he left for a time with various friends, and which were all eventually stolen.

In the fall of 1940, Clark went to work as a machine operator in a defense plant. He continued to bunk in with friends for several months. With the wages he earned the first three or four months, he bought chiefly food and clothes, paid his debts to his friends, and got drunk on week ends. As time went on, he spent about 75 per cent of his income on clothes, liquor, night clubs, and house parties. Less than a week after payday, he usually had to borrow his carfare to get to work, and to depend upon his friends for his meals, as well as for a place to sleep.

This behavior was part of a practical cultural system, however. His friends also depended upon him for loans and food, when *he* had just been paid. Thus, they actually had developed a system of getting money every Friday or Saturday, instead of only every second week, on payday. Each worker's payday was in reality a payday that he shared with one or two friends. Thus each man had a payday every week. Their ideal was a payday every day, so that they would have ready cash always.

Like most of his group, Clark had a regular week-end bout of drunkenness and a series of parties. These lasted through Sunday night, so that he almost never went to work on Mondays. On other nights, he always stayed up until twelve or one o'clock. Since he had to be up by six in order to reach work on time, he averaged less than five hours per night, including week ends. He missed an average of 1½ days on the job, out of every week; sometimes because he did not have carfare or food; sometimes because his rest was too broken.

After about 15 months of work, Clark fell in love with a girl, and he began to take more interest in his job. He wanted to become a foreman, and began getting up at five o'clock in the morning, so as not to be late for work. He decided to marry the girl and for the first time began to "save" his wages, paying on furniture. He and the girl set out to find a place to live. Finally they discovered a tenement on the railroad tracks where the landlady agreed to rent them two rooms. They returned with their suitcases to discover that the landlady had decided she would rent only to men. In two months, they were unable to find any other place to live.

Clark is still living with his friends, four to a room, and has given up his plan to marry. He still spends almost all his wages on clothes, liquor, and recreation. He still misses at least three days on the job out of every two weeks. During the four years he has been working, however, there have been three periods when he improved his work habits, his punctuality, and his motivation. The first was when he wanted to marry, and actually was buying furniture, and looking for a home. The second period of improvement occurred later, when Clark was trying to become a foreman, in order to convince his girl's mother that he was not an "ignorant bum," as she claimed. The third period followed his first visit to a meeting of his union, and his resultant interest in winning status within the union. Each of these situations was a powerful stimulus to Clark's motivation on the job. From them, we can learn what makes him ambitious, and what can make him work more effectively.

First, however, what made him *fail* to work well? During these three periods when he actually wished to become an efficient worker and tried to change his habits, why did he gradually lose his drive and return to his old habits? The reasons seem clear enough. First, like Ruth, the colored worker, he was influenced powerfully by the fact that he had no home and was unable to find one. The effort of both these workers to find a home, so that they could marry, was blocked by our chaotic housing situation. A society in which a large proportion of the population cannot find a home—cannot even rent a home from the people who own them—is in this basic respect less well organized than most "primitive" societies. If people cannot find a place for themselves and for their families to live as a group, and to live fairly decently, according to their lights, their motivation to work hard is severely weakened. If the young adults cannot find a home, they usually cannot marry. Since marriage is one of the most powerful drives in motivating workers to accept responsibility and to "settle down," our housing situation is demoralizing to work habits.

Secondly, Clark failed in his hopeless desire to become a foreman, because both the habits he had learned and especially his lack of education made him unfit for this responsibility. He had gone only to the sixth grade, and he had not learned well what was taught in those grades. Like millions of underprivileged workers, he could barely write a sentence, even an ungrammatical sentence. Simple addition and subtraction were laborious problems for him. This educational handicap, plus the great mental and nervous strain created by the improvement of his habits (of his hours of going to bed and getting up, of his application to his work, of making time *every* day), is too great for 9 out of 10 individuals in his position to overcome.

Third, the same educational deficiencies and cultural habits, which prevented his improving his status in the plant, likewise made it impossible for him to attain any status in his union. The local, he found, was run by workers who were a step above him in social status, who were at the *top* level of lower class groups and sometimes were in the lower middle class. They had skills and habits with which he could not compete. He soon gave up this hope also, and thus his third powerful incentive to change his work habits was extinguished.

The most powerful of all the forces that keep him in his present way of life and of work are the pleasures that he actually can attain by following his underprivileged culture. He gets strong biological enjoyment. He spends a great deal of his nights in sexual exploration, since he does not have to go to work the next day. He lives in a social world where visceral, genital, and emotional gratification is far more available than it is in a middle-class world. Recreation, relaxation, and pure laziness from Friday night through Sunday night are extremely satisfying experiences. If such a week end leaves the worker too exhausted to get on the job Monday or even Tuesday and causes him to lose $10 or $15, it nevertheless is so organically rewarding that he will repeat the experience the following week end, or certainly the following payday.

Such are the emotional, the cultural, and the economic determinants of the work habits of the underprivileged worker. He lives in a different economic and social environment from that in which the skilled and the middle-class workers live. Therefore the behavior that he learns, the habits that are stimulated and maintained by his cultural group, are different also. The individuals of these different socioeconomic statuses and cultures are reacting to different realistic situations and psychological drives. Therefore their values and their social goals are different. Therefore, the behavior of the underprivileged worker, which the boss regards as "unsocialized" or "ignorant," or "lazy," or "unmotivated" is really behavior learned from the socioeconomic and cultural environments of these workers. In a realistic view, we must recognize it to be perfectly normal, a sensible response to the conditions of their lives.

If we wish to change these habits—and they are a great burden upon our production, because about one-third of our total population falls into this group—we must offer the underprivileged worker real rewards. They must be sufficiently powerful to repay him for the hard work and self-denial required to change his old habits, and to compete with the rewards of a physical kind that he already gets.

What are these real goals, for which he will work harder? The first is a place to live, a place that is not merely a kitchenette apartment, or a basement room, or a corner in a cellar, with three to six people to a bed. It has to be a place that appears desirable in the eyes of the underprivileged worker, a place he will "go for." Thus the first goal to be set before him, as a real, attainable probability is a permanent, decent home. This means a more permanent family life. This in turn means acceptance of responsibility and the setting up of long-term goals. And these require good, steady work.

Neither a home for the rearing of a family nor the development of good work habits can be attained in a year or two. The underprivileged worker's goals are short term because his hold upon a job and upon clothes and upon food is short term. He knows well that he cannot establish a home, buy furniture, begin buying a house—all the endeavors that keep middle-class people busy and conscientious—in a year or two. He cannot educate his children, even through high school, on a few years of good wages. These basic social goals require a prospect of a steady job and good wages. This is what is meant by the words "economic and social security" to the middle-class person, namely, that there is an excellent chance that his work career and income will be steady and adequate to meet his standard of living. This is the kind of security possessed by middle-class people.

For the worker, short periods of good wages and plentiful jobs do not take the place of this security. One cannot change his way of living, or buy a home, or educate his children on this kind of income. To have a chance to develop stable habits of living, which means good work habits, people must have a stable job. The underprivileged worker is perfectly realistic when he asks, "Why should I try to save and get a little ahead in these times, when I'll be back on relief, anyhow, in a year or two?"

All this is to say that our society must offer the underprivileged worker a fair prospect, a better chance than he now has, of improving his status. It must convince him that he can secure a better life by hard work, and he can be convinced only when he *sees* a fair number of underprivileged *people like himself* getting reasonably secure jobs, a place to live, and a chance for promotion. I am *not* saying that society has to provide every such worker with permanent tenure and homeownership, and likewise make him a foreman, in order to motivate him to work harder. But I am saying that the underprivileged worker will not improve unless he finds that there is a chance of his getting the basic social and economic rewards that I have mentioned. He must be given the realistic hope that the game is worth the candle. If he *does change* his work habits, if he does become ambitious, if he does begin to crave respectability, then industry and society must have the homes and steady jobs and education to offer him in return for this great effort.

We see that middle-class people work like beavers and have an insistent conscientiousness. They have the craving for respectability to drive them, and the hope of a better home, or better job, or higher status for their children to pull them. In order to make underprivileged people anxious to work harder and willing to bear more responsibility on the job, our industry, business, and government must convince them that they can get more out of life than they now get. This means that our system of production must expand so as to offer a larger proportion of the working class steadier jobs, good wages, and a decent place in which to live and to rear a family. Otherwise, a third or more of our white and Negro labor supply will become increasingly demoralized. In a society where even wars are won by the side with the largest skilled labor supply and the most efficient industrial structure, this is a vital consideration. In the future, our survival as a nation very likely will depend upon what happens to this one-third of our labor supply.

CLASS AND CLASS CONSCIOUSNESS *

We derive many of our ideas of class from the study of Europe in the Middle Ages and afterward. As peasants emerged from serfdom, as craftsmen and tradesmen developed in the areas adjacent to the castles where the nobles, clergy, and knights dwelt, three broadly differentiated groups of people appeared. As their customs and manners became fixed, their relationships to each other well established in law and handed down from generation to generation, hereditary classes developed. The peasants bore a relationship to the land which they worked for the landlords; their movements were restricted, and their station was much below that of the burghers or towns-people. The latter were made up of two groups—tradesmen who transported and sold goods, and journeymen and their apprentices who moved about from place to place practicing their crafts. These burghers were money-handlers, owners of property, their incomes being derived from profits of trade. The upper class of nobles, clergy, and knights were an aristocracy, born into their status, possessing land which was worked by peasants or town property rented to the burghers. They, too, were dependent upon profit from property, but they took no active part in trade as such.

These three broadly different groups carried on through the Middle

* Reprinted from *Ballots and the Democratic Class Struggle* by Dewey Anderson and Percy E. Davidson with the permission of the authors and of the publishers, Stanford University Press, 1943. Pp. 206–212, 216–221, 224–226, 228–230, 232–236, 240–246.

Ages into the period of the industrial revolution, when the commercial-agrarian system began to disintegrate and the factory system developed to rearrange the people into modified economic and social groups.[1] Then in the towns appeared a fourth class, composed of peasants who got free of the land and burghers who could not make their way in the crafts or in trade and transportation. This fourth class was employed in the factories and mills at unskilled or semiskilled work, foredoomed by the very nature of the industrial system to remain apart from the guild artisans and the tradesmen. Denied apprenticeship, they became a hereditary proletariat.

It was largely from the farm and townspeople that the immigration came which settled the United States. Some indentured servants, usually of the farming class, but also some from the city proletariat, were included in the early immigration. Once established, the American colonies received a new batch of immigrants every year. But it was during the nineteenth century that great waves of immigrants sought homes in the new land. They came to states already banded together into a nation, where customs, habits, and beliefs had become stabilized to give characteristic form to American life. That these new immigrants added much from their heritage cannot be doubted; but they never came to any virgin territory where they were the only settlers, or in sufficient numbers to transplant an entire foreign culture to American soil. Instead, they were absorbed into the great American melting pot, a society evolving its own distinctive culture, its unique social system, and its particular type of capitalistic economy.

These great flood tides of immigration came first from northern, then from central, southern, and southeastern Europe. From 1850 to 1930 a net annual average of approximately 500,000 persons came to the United States. It was this immigrant population, totaling many millions, which made the greatest mass movement of people known to history. What happened to their social classes when these people came to the United States? Were they reshuffled, did they join new classes, or were conditions in this country so different from those of the older homelands that these immigrants became part of a classless society? The answers have considerable bearing on our discussion of class consciousness in the United States.

It will be recalled that the great bulk of immigration came in the nineteenth century, following or contemporaneous with middle-class revolutions in Europe. Our own Colonial revolution leaned heavily on the ideology of the French egalitarians. The free land and the virginal op-

---

[1] Franklin C. Palm, *The Middle Classes, Then and Now,* The Macmillan Company, New York, 1936, chapter i.

portunities of this country fitted well their concept of a free people surrounded by boundless opportunity to make their own way by their own efforts. Very naturally, immigrants, many of whom had been active in movements to achieve liberty, equality of opportunity, and fraternity, were absorbed into the American way of life and soon became its most ardent champions. The judgment of a representative writer on this subject, treating of the period from 1820 to 1850 when this American dream came closest to reality, is as follows:

> Neither an extreme of individualism nor uniformity. Class distinction became less obvious than in earlier days, but it did not quite disappear. There was absent the later bitterness of class feeling. . . . American aristocracy was not a closed caste, and it was everywhere firmly linked with the mass. . . . There was so close an approximation to economic equality to match the political that effort and ability could raise anyone to the top. . . . A fundamental element of a living was liberty, and all Americans were expected to look forward to becoming their own masters. . . . The agency of the national government was reduced to a minimum. . . . To deny that the American system of government would be immediately beneficial if adopted in China was to commit democratic treason; heredity availed not, opportunity plus effort would produce anything at once. . . . Free men could be trusted to want what was right, and to get it. The dominant and simple belief in equality, the vast demand for labor, and the individualistic conception of government, all re-enforced the sentiment that the United States was a refuge for the oppressed as well as an example in the world.[2]

Historians are in considerable agreement that whatever the decisive influences at work, the United States during the nineteenth century, especially its first half, did present this picture in good part. While there were noticeable differences among the people, especially in the older regions, the Deep South, and the more populous cities, yet the economy was still largely agrarian, there was still free or cheap land, industrialization had not yet proceeded far, and, until the last quarter of the century, enterprise was still largely conducted by individuals or partners who owned and operated their businesses. The American system of free and competitive enterprise was quite real. It is so today for a great many living Americans whose childhood came during the old century and who have risen to success through the exercise of talents and efforts developed in that atmosphere and tradition. It is still a guiding influence to many more who go through the free public-school system which is one of its great achieve-

[2] Extracts from *The Rise of the Common Man,* by Carl Russell Fish, 1912, pp. 8–12, 110, by permission of The Macmillan Company, publishers.

ments, who obtain training in skills and professions which give them preferred status, or who have access to capital and become independent businessmen. This picture of "self-made" success remains a realizable goal to so many in the population and a hope to so many more that it is established firmly in the cultural fabric of American society, a society presumably of open, not of closed or hereditary, classes.

Upon what, then, does the conclusion rest of those who consider all this only a historical moment in American life, squaring not at all with present class-like conditions which foredoom democracy to failure and deny great segments of the population any proportionate share in the good life? Their list is long: the passing of the geographical frontier, and the closing of free or cheap land to settlement; the excessive development of a profit economy; the rise of corporations to dominance over the business world and the heavy mortality among private enterprisers; the growth of monopoly; the entrenched power of hereditary fortunes; the concentration of control of industry in the hands of a few who manage it for a very few owners; the uneven distribution of national income and the gains from productive effort; the various devices such as a regressive tax system used to preserve the inequalities among income groups, and a use of the patent system which enables corporations to strengthen their stranglehold on independent creative effort and to exploit inventive genius; managed prices, restraints of trade, and control of the market place; the concentration of ownership of natural resources essential to industrial production; the relatively high costs of specialized schooling or professional training, which present an effective barrier against entrance of resourceless youths to the better-paid careers; artificial barriers raised by skilled-labor groups to entrance into their preferred status; subservience of political and social institutions, such as the church and the government, to the will of the propertied class; and weaknesses inherent in the democratic electoral system, which enable a small ruling class to maintain control while preserving a pretense of majority rule. These are among the reasons given to prove that class consciousness has aroused or must arouse Americans to an awareness of their condition and pit them one against another in a class struggle for power.

But does the existence of any or all of these conditions necessarily mean that the people are inevitably arrayed in distinct classes? So much depends on the answer that we suggest, first, a reference to the historical nature of "class." There were four broadly distinguishable European classes: aristocrats (nobles, knights, clergy); townspeople or bourgeoisie (at first including tradesmen and guild artisans, later made up of "businessmen"); peasants (at first fixed to the land, later free, but remaining a land-tilling class); and the proletariat (made up at first of the unskilled who served the tradesmen and artisans, later—with the development of factories and the periodic overproduction in agriculture—of farming people who were forced off the farms into cities to join the urban unskilled and semiskilled).

These European classes developed in a somewhat stable social economy over several centuries to become largely hereditary in character. Social institutions—such as class-differentiated school systems, the indenture-and-apprentice system, distinct forms of dress, the carrying of side arms or personal weapons, and particular training for class callings—firmly embedded these classes in a caste-like structure so powerful that it persists in substantial part in many European countries to this day, long after the economic systems which produced it have become obsolete and their governments destroyed or reformed.

But when members of these hereditary classes immigrated to the United States they found an environment uncongenial to the preservation of their rigid European class distinctions. A pioneer land required much co-operative effort for survival. Cultural accumulations were relatively meager, and, except for a very few of great wealth or possessed of large holdings, most of the colonists and early settlers perforce achieved common levels of dress, work, habits, and surroundings. . . .

What, then, became of the class groupings which these people brought with them from Europe? Did America develop a distinct class of "peasants," for example? On the contrary, the class as such vanished and even the word passed from our speech. The concept of a peasant class was entirely destroyed by the abundance of free land, the mastery of the tiller of the soil over his own destiny. The independent farmer emerged in this transformation—a being quite different from his European cousin still tied to the land in numerous ways, his place in society and government subservient to the will and whim of an aristocratic, land-owning class. As he settled the wilderness, the American farmer built towns, established schools, took an active part in self-government, and occupied for himself and his family a place in a society which stoutly affirmed his independence and which in the next generation permitted his offspring access to all levels of education and perhaps to positions as leaders even in the highest walks of life. If "scratch a Russian and you'll find a Tartar" aptly characterized one culture, "scratch an American and you'll find a farmer's son" fits our own.

The farmer maintains his independent status to this day, despite the numerous economic perplexities confronting him. These do not signify —as those who support the thesis of class conflict seem to believe—that farmers, or any particular group among farmers, are now a distinct class, conscious of class interests and banded together in conflict against other classes. It is true that farmers have certain fairly common interests which they seek to further through political means, using pressure groups for that purpose; but in such efforts are associated farmers of the widest range of material circumstances and culture, who differ on many other equally fundamental issues, who belong to opposing political parties, and who have little in common except specific agricultural problems. . . .

That agriculture in the United States is undergoing a long and painful reorganization is apparent. Perhaps self-mastery in the ownership of a farm which characterized the earlier period in the United States is giving way. But that does not mean necessarily or inevitably the degrading of free farmers to the level of peasants. It may mean for one thing, as appears to be the case in the manufacturing field, that corporation farming sets up a different agricultural hierarchy, with gradations of income for different levels of work ranging from seasonal harvesting of crops to year-around management of vast farm enterprise. If this be the prospect for any considerable part of agriculture, then "climbing" within this system will still be possible and will become the goal of this new type of farmer. Farming will still remain the way of life of those who follow agriculture. Political alignments will continue between face-to-face groups within agriculture whose common interests will transcend any inclusive working-class connections which might be agitated into existence by those seeking the revolutionary over-throw of the economic system.

BOURGEOISIE—THE AMERICAN MIDDLE CLASS

What happened to the European bourgeoisie in their transition to the United States? According to some social historians they found here conditions permitting them to flourish as in no other country, to become the dominant middle class of the nineteenth century, only to find themselves losing status in the twentieth and foredoomed to an early eclipse in the struggle between the powerful owners and the working-class masses.[3] According to an opposing school of thought, they are emerging from the corporate industrial revolution now under way transformed considerably

[3] See particularly Lewis Corey, *The Crisis of the Middle Class,* and Franklin C. Palm, *The Middle Classes, Then and Now.*

in relation to the economic structure but stronger and more certain of continued power on the days ahead.[4]

While the farmer was long the backbone of the nation, being largely responsible for the territorial expansion of the first quarter of the nineteenth century, it was the townspeople who made up the independent enterprisers in trade and the artisans and workers in manufacture who accounted for the great gains in population and in national income in the last half of the century. Much is hidden from view, and yet much is revealed, in the simple facts which follow: Between 1820 and 1850 the population of the country's four largest cities, New York, Philadelphia, Boston, and Baltimore, increased 400 per cent. In a single decade, 1840–50, while the United States population increased 36 per cent, that of the towns above 8,000 inhabitants grew 90 per cent. After the turn into the twentieth century these great centers of population gained so fast on the rural areas that by 1930 urban areas contained more people than rural areas.[5] In this growth of the cities is found the outward manifestation of an industrialization which expanded yearly following the Civil War, and which stemmed largely from the development of the corporate form of organization, the technological advance made in the use of machinery, new forms of energy, especially electricity, and mass-production methods.[6]

The revolutionary changes from the earlier stages of handicraft and independent enterprise to large-scale manufacturing made enormous differences in the status of the townspeople. In that earlier day it was property ownership and mastery over their own lives which characterized the burghers who settled in our cities. Enterprise was small, operated by its owner. Now enterprise became large, owned by shareholders and managed by hired persons who did not necessarily have vested rights in it. Thus, in this corporate revolution, which is still proceeding at a rapid pace, lately invading the distributive field of retail merchandising, the townspeople who characterized the middle class of free enterprisers have been and are being transformed. Many among them, more particularly the artisans, had already been absorbed in a factory system which destroyed craft skills and substituted the assembly-line operator for the mechanic of an earlier day.

[4] This is the view expressed by Alfred M. Bingham, *Insurgent America,* chapter ix; and by Leon Samson, *The American Mind,* Farrar and Rinehart, New York, 1932, and *Toward a United Front,* same publishers, 1934.

[5] Franklin C. Palm, *The Middle Classes, Then and Now,* pp. 216–217.

[6] Dewey Anderson, Lewis Lorwin, John Blair, *Technology in Our Economy,* Temporary National Economic Committee Monograph No. 22, Government Printing Office, Washington, D.C., 1941.

Many more were and are being faced with the necessity of becoming "hired workers."

This fact is regarded by some as proof of the degradation of the middle class and their eventual disappearance and absorption in the working class. But it may not have such an outcome; for within the corporate industrial structure there is a vertical dimension ranging from unskilled casual labor at the bottom to the highest managerial and administrative positions at the top. The remuneration, security, chance for advancement, recognition of success, community prestige, and influence possible under this system are most attractive goals. To conclude, as one of the apologists for the class-conflict thesis does, in the following statement, seems to neglect these powerful new motivating forces developing within modern industry:

> Thus, apparently, economic mobility has become a thing of the past, and stratification rather than mobility is becoming the norm of today. In view of the fact that our natural resources have already been appropriated, that there is no new territory to conquer and no more virgin soil to exploit, and that those who are in possession of these resources do not seem to be willing to utilize them for the development of an economy of abundance, economic stratification obviously becomes inevitable. The form of economic mobility still operative in our economic life tends to be in a downward direction—a mobility resulting from increased economic concentration. It would seem that only through precarious and speculative means such as stock gambling, prize fighting, sudden acquisitions of fabulous wealth, and so on, is it still possible for a rare and lucky individual to ascend the economic ladder.[7]

In fact, the writer quite misses the nature of climbing, or the qualitative and quantitative aspects of success. While American ideology pays allegiance to the belief in an open class system, it has obviously understood that relatively few would ever reach the top. It is not the number who gain such dizzy heights which proves the existence of open classes, or the essential "classlessness" of our economy, but that some do climb into higher status from below, on rare occasion even all the way up from the bottom.

Whether or not the channels of vertical mobility are sufficiently open to warrant our belief in a properly functioning democratic system which uses its best talents, regardless of their social origin, for its most exacting service, is another matter. But as the writers found in their study of oc-

[7] Zalmen Slesinger, *Education and the Class Struggle,* Covici-Friede, New York, 1937, p. 94.

cupational mobility,[8] facts do not justify the pessimistic conclusion that "economic mobility has become a thing of the past." There it was reported that 20 per cent of professional men had risen from homes where their fathers were skilled, semiskilled, or unskilled laborers, that 20 per cent of proprietors had come from such homes, that 18 per cent of white-collar clerical workers had been reared in the homes of semiskilled and unskilled fathers, and that 10 per cent of skilled artisans had had unskilled laboring fathers. Here is suggestion of substantial upgrading, resulting in economic and social differences of significant proportions between sons and fathers. . . .

Nor is rare success impossible today. Taussig and Joslyn disclosed such success in their unique study of American business leaders.[9] There are approximately 25,000 executives of "big business" in the United States, officers of concerns grossing over $500,000 annually. Of these the investigators studied a sample of 7,371. It was revealed that 44 per cent of them came from homes with fathers who had attained positions as major executives, large owners, or professionals, 11 per cent from homes of manual laborers, 44 per cent from homes of farmers, clerks, salesmen, minor business executives, or small proprietors. It was found that not more than 31 per cent of the fathers of the business leaders examined had been big-business executives in their generation. While this shows considerable inbreeding, even in the field where access to capital and command of complex business techniques are essential, over two-thirds of those who emerge as business leaders had made their way from homes where no such eminence had been achieved. . . .

It may really turn out on examination that no middle class exists in the United States. It may well be a stereotype, a "flash picture" deeply implanted in our minds subject to ready recall, the result of long training in an American ideology which does not necessarily square with the facts. Bingham hints as much when he says:

> We are what we think we are. And if the bulk of the people, in a modern capitalistic country like the United States, think of themselves as being of the middle class, having interests between those of "capital" and "labor," then there is such a middle class, or middle group of classes.[10]

---

[8] Davidson and Anderson, *Occupational Mobility in an American Community,* chapter ii.

[9] F. W. Taussig and C. S. Joslyn, *American Business Leaders,* The Macmillan Company, New York, 1932, chapter x.

[10] Alfred M. Bingham, *op. cit.,* p. 47.

Moreover, the word used to describe the middle class, bourgeoisie, is an importation from abroad which carries with it a historical connotation of a city-dwelling population composed of business and trades proprietors, artisan proprietors, and the banking fraternity. Such a conception of the middle class soon gave way to the influence of pioneer life in America. With a new division of labor, this middle class was considerably broadened, being augmented by a numerous professional and administrative personnel who achieved status above that of manual labor and were able to live on a plane easily recognized as "comfortable."

The factory system played havoc with the old idea that ownership was essential to middle-class status. Many higher-level clerical incomes afforded a middle-class status in the community, while some proprietor groups were apparently thrust out of the charmed circle of the middle class into a lower class. The "white collar" and the "business suit" increasingly clothe moderately circumstanced people in a wide variety of callings. As schooling differences between people have lessened, as mass production has somewhat standardized culture and has permitted a similar type of living to many people in the white-collar ranks whose income circumstances are quite dissimilar, so the gross distinctions between such people have lessened and the conception of a widespread membership in the American middle class has grown. But this description is most indefinite; it conceives of the middle class as a broad middle band drawn across the pyramid of gainful workers to include people in a general category above poverty and below luxury. It testifies to a belief in an essential "commonness" of circumstances, culture, attitudes, and aspirations. It can be pictured as an approximation to the normal curve into which so many measured traits of individuals and society seem to fall when examined scientifically, a curve wherein only a few are found below or above the vast majority. But such a conception destroys belief in a class-like, well-knit group. Nor does it stand up when differing incomes or scales of living are examined; for then it is revealed that the curve describing the circumstances of the people is decidedly skewed, a few at the top enjoying great luxury, a great mass at the bottom living miserably, a substantial body of citizens in the upper-middle range living decently. . . .

THE ARISTOCRACY—THE AMERICAN UPPER CLASS

What happened to the European upper class which came to the New World? Few among them did so, for their preferred status in the homeland did not spur them on to assume the trials and tribulations of the wilderness. Except for a very few who came here to establish colonies on grants from the Crown, or as Colonial governors sent out to manage the Crown interests, and some officers and clergy, there was no aristocratic class transplanted to our soil. It was necessary for us to develop our own. Having no peerage, no hereditary aristocracy, the rewards of eminence went more nearly to the swiftest in the race. As the New Englanders became established, they transmitted to their offspring goods and chattels and traditions of learning for the professions which enabled some among them to become leaders in government and business. Likewise the Southern aristocracy developed its plantation culture during a period when their possession of broad, fertile acres, slave economy, and a foreign market for cotton and tobacco entrenched the class as a leisured, ruling aristocracy. But even here the failure to make primogeniture function as in the old country, isolation from foreign enemies which prevented the development of a military caste, and the abundance of free land for settlement, coupled with the ever increasing immigration, westward migration, and growing industrialization, meant that families could not maintain very easily their aristocratic purity. Hence families broke up and scattered over the country —their offspring being socially resorted by the varying conditions—a process which so drastically disturbed genealogies that few among us can successfully trace our ancestry beyond a few generations.

This does not mean that there has been no aristocracy in the United States. It simply explains that the original aristocracy was supplanted or routed by newer aristocrats, the product of our economic development. The term "aristocracy" thus hardly fits our upper level; "plutocracy" would more nearly do so. For we early became a nation of money-makers. With each year's national income rising above the last, except for periodic depressions or panics, with seemingly boundless opportunity for profit to businessmen, it was inevitable that some among them had a combination of talent, good fortune, and business ruthlessness which brought outstanding success. The story of the development of the American millionaire is by no means a romance of clean adventure; many are the skeletons in the closets of the Four Hundred. Yet millionaires they became. Hereditary fortunes were built up and passed on to successive generations, until there is today a small but highly entrenched group of wealthy people in the United States whose position and power greatly exceed their numerical importance.

Nor is the process ended; for, as one of the writers has amply shown in his tax studies, there is little comfort to be gained from the present fiscal policy if it is presumed that the accumulation and bequeathing of fortunes is being prevented to any substantial degree by present tax levies. Yet there is reason to believe that in this direction will be found much of the adjustment necessary to equalize the economic conditions of our people, to ease the strains which lead to social conflict, and to distribute purchasing power more equitably in order to lessen the sharpness of the swings in the business cycle. The use of income, inheritance, and gift taxes, extensions of social-security programs, and adequate public-works schemes, brought together in a government public and fiscal policy geared to meet the changing conditions in the economy, give real hope for peaceful and satisfactory adjustment of life conditions for all groups without recourse to violence by any group in the population.

But the opportunity to make new fortunes still exists. . . .

THE PROLETARIAT—THE AMERICAN WORKING CLASS

The word proletariat is chiefly employed by historians and radical agitators. One must be on guard against the use of this word to designate a single class either in Europe or America. Certainly the term has not been commonly employed among manual workers as descriptive of themselves on either side of the Atlantic.[11]

During the American Colonial period and for a number of decades thereafter agriculture was the chief occupation; land was cheap or free and no large amount of capital was required for its cultivation. Restless or ambitious urban workers found it comparatively easy to "go west" and set up for themselves. Cheap labor, where it was required, was found in the North in the indentured servant, who canceled the cost of the sea voyage from Europe by binding himself to an employer for a term of years, at the conclusion of which he was free to try for himself in a field of wide opportunity. In the South the African Negro slave became the mainstay of the plantation system. Such manufacturing as existed in this early period was largely in the domestic and handicraft stage. The household on the frontier farm did most of its own manufacturing. The Southern plantation evolved its own manufacture by the use of Negro craftsmen.

During Colonial times manufacturing had been discouraged by British legislation. Following the Revolution some textile and other machine production was undertaken in the New England region, but its development had to await the settlement of the West and the increase of man power. The industrial revolution in this country really began about ten

[11] For a treatment of the proletariat and the relative absence of feudal vestiges in the United States, see the *Encyclopaedia of the Social Sciences,* under "Proletariat."

years prior to the Civil War, which hastened its advance. Its greatest strides followed the year 1866 in response to the needs of the agricultural West.

The sources of the industrial man power required for the enormous expansion of American manufacturing have been identified with certain fundamental conditions in Europe and America: (1) a high birth rate in settled foreign lands and teeming populations in need of opportunities; (2) an excess of agricultural workers in Europe due to the decline of landlordism and the coincident emergence of trade and manufacturing which were incapable of absorbing the displaced population; (3) an excess of journeymen and apprentices due to the supplanting of handicraft by the factory and the partial substitution of cheap child and female labor in the factories; (4) a similar excess of agricultural labor in the United States due to the high rural birth rate, diminishing cheap or free land, and the increasing productivity of the farm from better knowledge of farming methods and from the use of machines; (5) the availability of superabundant Negro labor in the South which was eventually drawn in considerable quantity to Northern industries; (6) the increasing use of female labor, especially of the younger adult ages; (7) and, most important of all, the appeal of opportunity and higher real wages to the impoverished or resourceless, and even to some of the more well-to-do, in Europe and other foreign lands.

This brief catalogue of the sources of the new American industrial working class shows it to be a conglomeration of all sorts and conditions, and not the transfer to America of an established European class with a self-conscious status. The European artisan, who came to this country in large numbers, had superior status in his homeland which he retained in the new, where he was welcomed for his needed craftsmanship. Common industrial labor was chiefly from foreign and domestic agriculture, often with recognized peasant or farming traditions and with no industrial solidarity. The new semiskilled factory labor came from both these groups, supplemented by new female labor from the homes of manual labor at large.

It is not strange, then, that until recent years not more than 10 per cent of American manual workers were organized, and this largely from the elite of labor, much of it under compulsion rather than voluntary. Only recently, with the advent of the Congress of Industrial Organizations, has systematic effort been made to bring the great masses of industrial labor into the unions. These are not indications of a well-defined "class" of manual workers in the country having a high degree of self-consciousness among them. Their conglomerate character and the recency of their industrial working status presumably explain the existing situation.

An enormous foreign immigration was the principal source of cheap labor for American industry in the heyday of its expansion. The net contribution of immigration from 1820 to 1930, a period of one hundred and ten years, has been put at more than twenty-seven million persons. Not all of this was "proletarian," for some among the peasant immigrants from foreign lands had a sufficient stake to set themselves up on good land and to compete with an initial advantage. Others were small traders, or even technical, clerical, or professional workers. But the great preponderance were without resources of any considerable amount.[12]

Upon their arrival these immigrants tended to settle in the manufacturing cities, at first on the Atlantic seaboard; then, as these areas became congested and as work opportunities beckoned from inland cities, they moved westward. As newcomers, they were usually forced to accept the lowest grade of labor. They were subjected to many indignities, their ignorance of our ways making them prey to many kinds of oppression and exploitation. Under such powerful drives they adjusted more rapidly and more completely than would be considered possible for classes which had had low status for generations in Europe. They soon accepted the habits of dress and manners of the community and, by the time a first generation of their children had been reared here, many traces of their foreign origin had already disappeared.

While the resourceless immigrant found no streets of our cities "paved with gold" as he had been led to believe, he did find a scale of pay, a freedom of movement, and a hope for his children far beyond anything he could ever have expected in his homeland. This was a substantial gain in status. It made him aware of still further gains ahead when he should acquire citizenship and exercise the franchise. Many among these immigrant workers were destined to move considerably above their original pick-and-shovel or machine-tending status, to own land, to become business proprietors, and to acquire skills and levels of competency and remuneration much higher than their first jobs in the United States. Many more believed it possible to do so. Even for those who never achieved any substantial measure of success, the relatively higher standard of living, available free schools, and the lack of outward distinctions of class among those with whom they came in contact all tended to create a sense of "belonging" which made it difficult to retain habits and thoughts of the

[12] On the origin and sources of a wage-earning class, see W. B. Catlin, *The Labor Problem,* revised, Harper & Brothers, New York, 1935, Part I.

European lower classes; for the occupational, social, and economic structure was sufficiently mobile to prevent severe class rigidity.

Moreover, the expansion of commerce and trade, the advanced technology which greatly increased man-hour productivity and real wages of labor, combined to alter the significance of the term "proletarian." The geographical and occupational mobility characterizing the American economy has been so great, the tempo of change so rapid, that the manual-labor groups have been regarded, with considerable warrant in the earlier generations, as a great common reservoir from which people "climbed" to varying levels of attainment. Only if it should be shown that this is now becoming a false picture of actual conditions, that manual laborers are mostly condemned to successive generations of existence on these levels, that the channels of vertical mobility have been drastically constricted, and that the circumstances of working groups are similar with no important gradations within these levels, can one suppose that there has developed in the United States a "working class" which may become conscious of its inferior status and seek to use the power of its dominant numbers to effect a change through class conflict. [See the excerpt from W. E. Moore, above, for a summary of the data on vertical mobility.] . . .

Again we return to the suggestion that any rise in the occupational scale is an indication of success to those who make it. The unskilled laborer who becomes a skilled artisan has achieved distinct gains, in both prestige and plane of living. So long as this channel of movement remains open to him, he cannot or does not regard himself as a member of an unskilled class. The skilled laborer, on the other hand, has such prestige, income, and living standards in the community that he often regards himself as part of the middle class. His lodge, church, and social activities are carried on in company with other moderately circumstanced people, cutting across occupational lines to a considerable degree. His union affiliations are usually along craft lines and his labor consciousness is confined to a struggle, not for class power and dominance, but for better pay and working conditions for his "craft." Even the vertical unionism of the C.I.O. has apparently not resulted in the class consciousness of the workers; for here, too, the chief concern is to wrest better pay and working conditions for themselves from the employing plant or industry rather than for their kind in all plants and all industries.

That there is a marked stability of the occupational structure from generation to generation, in spite of this substantial amount of vertical mobility among the workers, has been amply shown above and need not again be emphasized. And it may be that the trial-and-error approach from the first job to the regular occupation . . . is slackening; for when two age groups (age 10 to 34 with age 35 and above) are compared, there is a suggestion in our data of a somewhat greater measure of agreement of "first-job" status with that of the regular occupation in the younger group. This may be due to less floundering on the way to the regular occupation because of improved guidance in recent years or, more especially, to a more formal training in the schools for higher positions, which are entered directly from the completed training course.

This last condition does not imply a slackening of opportunity of access to the better jobs if the schools keep all young people enrolled and supply them equitably with suitable vocational training for all grades of labor. It merely makes school life a substitute field of vocational competition and selection. Unfortunately, the schools as yet have not gone far in this direction, and length of schooling is still in great part related to the economic status of the family. It must be noted, consequently, that there is a danger to equality of vocational opportunity if only the more fortunate young people are able to stay on in school for the higher vocational training and so enter the market on its higher levels, to the disadvantage of those who leave school early in the hope of climbing to the better jobs in the old way.

Some rather loose thinking is abroad to the effect that advancing technology inevitably means that more and more workers will be reduced to the level of semiskilled machine operatives, craft pride and status being lost in the process, and that their ensuing sorry plight will induce them to favor taking over the economic system in their own behalf. While technological change undoubtedly entails loss of skill for a great number of workers, it at the same time occasions a further division of labor, building up new skills into professions and semiprofessions, and rearranging labor into many new and different occupations outside of the customarily considered skilled group.[13] Within manufacture, where technological gains are most pronounced, the number of skilled workers increased from 3,821,000 in 1910 to 4,678,000 in 1930. But while skilled workers were 36 per cent of all workers in manufacturing industries in 1910, they were 33 per cent in 1930, a loss or "degrading" of some 3 per cent in the twenty years of intensive technological advance.[14] A consideration of the changes in percentage of the total gainfully occupied population found among the several occupational groups (as ranked by Edwards' classification) indicates the probability that a small loss in the skilled category from 1920 to

[13] Anderson and Davidson, *Occupational Trends in the United States,* pp. 40–43.

[14] Dewey Anderson, Lewis Lorwin, John Blair, *Technology in Our Economy,* pp. 143–44.

1930 was due to a net upgrading of such workers rather than to a degrading to the semiskilled level and that there was a net upgrading of the whole working force during the decade—if movement to white-collar work is to be regarded as upgrading.

Group	Percentage of All Workers			
	1920	1930	Difference in 1930 [a]	
			Net Gain	Net Loss
White-Collar				
Professionals	4.9	6.0	+1.1	
Business	6.7	7.5	+0.8	
Clerks, etc.	13.7	16.3	+2.6	
Farmers	15.3	12.3		—3.0
Manual Workers				
Skilled	13.4	12.9		—0.5
Semiskilled	16.0	16.3	+0.3	
Unskilled	30.0	28.7		—1.3
Total	100.0	100.0	+4.8	—4.8

[a] Note that 0.1 per cent of all gainful workers in 1930 is 48,829 workers, 1 per cent is 488,299, and 4.8 per cent is 2,343,836.

Since the only direction of change possible to the unskilled is upward, the net loss of 1.3 per cent means "upgrading" in that amount. If the entire net gain of the semiskilled came from the unskilled group, there would still remain one per cent of the upgraded unskilled to be accounted for. The net loss of one-half of one per cent by the skilled cannot then reasonably be charged to their being forced into semiskilled or unskilled labor. These workers were therefore, in all likelihood, upgraded to the growing white-collar populations, since these made significant gains. Whether or not this was an economic gain cannot be asserted; for many white-collar jobs are poorly paid. Essential degrading may have occurred, but the alleged submergence of the skilled within the lower levels of manual labor—with its encouragement of an intensified "proletarian" state of mind —is not indicated.

A marked shift in emphasis of the kind of work done has occurred since 1870. Then three-fourths of all workers were related to the production of physical goods, one-fourth to distribution and the services. By 1930 half of all workers in the United States were producing goods, half rendering services. In 1850 the proportions were three to one. While the total population in the United States increased 33 per cent from 1910 to 1930, the number of workers engaged in the combined branches of production, processing, and transporting goods increased only 6 per cent, and the physical goods which passed through their hands increased 86 per cent. During this time, those occupations concerned with merchandising, financing, managing, and serving increased 50 per cent. The division of labor increased so that there are over 20,000 recognized forms of labor, each with its own competency, pay scale, and conditions of labor.[15] The over-all change indicated here is from manual labor to white-collar work, ostensibly an improvement in "social status."

An attempt to stratify the 52,500,000 workers found in the United States in 1940 into class-conscious groups in such a highly mobile society is impractical. Even the emergence from this situation of a self-conscious "industrial working class" is doubtful. Moreover, dependence upon the industrial working class to accomplish the revolution, as Bingham rightly points out, is futile for the very reason that that class is declining in relative significance in the United States.[16] Workers in manufacturing industries reached their peak in proportion to all gainfully employed in 1900, and have been declining since. In actual numbers, they leveled off in 1930. As over a fourth of all workers, they include 13,600,000 persons—quite a sizable "army" for revolt if welded into a class intent upon the class struggle. But the enormous gains in white-collar workers engaged in numerous professional, clerical, public-service, and trading occupations now more than offset this industrial working group.

Peopled by the sons and daughters of industrial workers and workers from all levels in the occupational pyramid, white-collar groups are more often related to the consumer directly, more dependent for their own well-being on what happens in the consuming market. Theirs is not an industrial class interest. To quote Bingham: "Far from dividing society into two hostile camps, capitalism, as it developed, was bringing new classes and interests into consciousness."[17] Dependent on the consumer directly

[15] These data on occupational trends, unless otherwise indicated, are taken from the authors' work on that subject mentioned above.

[16] Alfred Bingham, *Insurgent America,* pp. 23–24.

[17] Alfred Bingham, *Insurgent America,* p. 24.

for their continued employment, their incomes, and their status, these greatly increased white-collar groups could hardly be expected to prove readily susceptible to the urging that they join with the industrial workers to achieve class ends when they feel no such class consciousness themselves, nor any such close affinity with the industrial workers as commonness of class would imply. Moreover, as some among them become unionized, they are no more inclined to become class-conscious than other members of unions, seeking rather to exert their influence as a pressure group within the democratic framework in order to secure limited and clearly defined ends, such as wage increases, closed shops, and better working conditions—ends far removed from class revolution, and calculated, to the degree that they are obtained, to remove these workers further from susceptibility to the blandishments of agitators.

Marxists welcomed the coming of the industrial union, for they had despaired of making any great headway with the middle-class-minded trade-unionists in the American Federation of Labor. The Congress of Industrial Organizations seemed to answer their wishes. Here craft status was disregarded and even the unskilled could be consolidated with their more highly skilled fellows. The Communists received their orders and set to work in key positions within the new organization. Everything seemed in their favor—a prolonged and stubborn depression, mass unemployment with work relief for not more than a fourth of the people needing it, a dole for the rest who could qualify for aid, financial assistance and leadership of several well-established unions, doubt and confusion among the people generally, the New Deal with its avowedly pro-labor sentiments, and the Wagner Labor Relations Act which guaranteed labor the right to organize and bargain collectively. The more ardent among the Communists thought they could already discern the gray morning when the barricades would be manned by their disciplined industrial unionists. Not to overlook any advantage, they thrust labor into politics directly, with the establishment of Labor's Nonpartisan League, to be used as a training ground for political action and for whatever political pressure they could exert to confuse and confound the democratic political process. With what results?

What happened is perhaps the best proof that the necessary ingredients for a class consciousness leading to a class conflict are not to be found in the American labor movement. For American workers are not living in a class-structured society. True, the C.I.O. filled a very real need for a type of unionism different from that found in the crafts, and it prospered rapidly. But, as soon as the first fire of enthusiasm cooled, the forces of conservatism within the C.I.O., springing from the very culture of which these people are a part, veered the course of its action toward narrowly conceived, practical goals—wages, hours, the closed shop, better conditions of labor, participation in dismissal procedures, grievance committees within the shop, etc. Interest in the political arm of labor, the Nonpartisan League, waned and union members began cutting down its financial support. Never strong, it sank to insignificance. Then began the purging of the Reds, in such spectacular drives as that which troubled the auto workers' union. This purge continued and reached its peak in the 1941 C.I.O. convention, with the rank-and-file viewpoint prevailing. Its program then toned down to the level of strictly unionist activities, formulated not with the intent of disciplining its members to carry out the Marxist appeal—"Workers of the world, unite"—but as a powerful pressure group working within the democratic framework, mindful of the democratic process, solicitous of public opinion, seeking the good-will and cooperation of even reactionary industrialists, anathema to Marxists.

With each victory won for labor, with each year added to its maturity, C.I.O. conservatism increases and its use as a nucleus for class-conscious revolt fades. For, we repeat, its cause rests not on class cleavage but on numerous "classes" in the nation with their diversity of interests, from whom a powerful temporary alignment can perhaps obtain, by way of compromise, substantial gains in the scramble for favors that goes on indefinitely.

CHAPTER IX

The Difference It Makes

In the study from which the following excerpts are reprinted, Alfred W. Jones * tried to discover differences in class beliefs concerning what is "right" behavior and whose "rights" are paramount. He made the investigation in Akron, Ohio, in late 1938 and early 1939, shortly after Akron had emerged from the violence of a successful drive to organize the rubber workers. The rights Jones chose to study were those relating to property; he focused on what is often called the conflict between "property rights and human rights."

The procedure was to describe to a large sample of the Akron population, seven cases of conflict between property rights and human rights, and then to ask the respondents for judgments of the behavior of those involved in the conflict. The same people were asked to express their attitudes toward the "proper shares" of each of several groups in the productive process. Some of the cases and questions are reproduced below.

CASE I

Anthracite coal mining in Eastern Pennsylvania was a "sick industry" even before the depression. In the 1930's still more mines shut down, the companies deciding to keep their coal in the ground until prices for it should go up. There was great unemployment and distress among the miners. In these years the unemployed miners began going into the idle mines and taking out the coal. They did this without the permission of the companies which own the mines, and without the interference of the local police, so that no violence resulted. They have both burned the coal themselves, and sold it.

---

* Jones, Alfred Winslow, *Life, Liberty, and Property* (Philadelphia: J. B. Lippincott Company, 1941), pp. 170–180, 250–255, 257–259, 261–269, 358–363.

Question: What do you think of this sort of action on the part of the unemployed miners?

Answers: 0. I approve

1. I think it may have been all right if they were really in distress, but I'm doubtful about it
2. I can't decide
3. I suppose it is wrong, but I must qualify my feeling. For example, I think it is wrong for them to sell the coal, but not if they merely burn it to keep warm
4. I disapprove, and cannot let my sympathies interfere

CASE II

In early 1938 negotiations took place between the Utility Workers' Organizing Committee, and the Consumer's Power Co., of Michigan. The union wanted a renewal of its contract with the company which was about to expire, and a year's guarantee against wage cuts. The company refused this and negotiations broke down at the same time as the contract expired. A strike followed, in which the workers took possession of the company's power plants, in the Saginaw Valley area, and expelled the company's superintendents and foremen. During the several days that this stay-in strike lasted, the property of the company was not damaged in any way. Nor was it a sitdown strike, since the workers continued to operate the power plant, so that the interests of the consumers did not suffer. Although the company officials were strongly opposed to this strike action, they settled with the union after a time and it is safe to say that the union won better terms by this action than they would have won in any other way.

Question: What do you think of the action of the workers in this case?

Answers: 0. I approve

1. I approve, but with qualifications
2. I cannot decide
3. I disapprove in general, but I find points in favor of this action
4. I disapprove

CASE IV[a]

During good times a farmer in the Middle West borrowed a considerable sum of money from a big Chicago bank, and gave a mortgage on his farm as security. When the depression came he could no longer meet the payments on this loan, and the bank, after waiting a reasonable time, foreclosed. They started legal proceedings and the local sheriff advertised a foreclosure sale. But on the day of the advertised sale, the neighboring farmers gathered on the property to be sold at auction, and acted in such a threatening way that no genuine bid could be made. The farmer himself bid one dollar, and since this was the highest bid, he bought his farm back for this amount, which was all the bank got in place of the mortgage. The mortgage was lifted and the farmer remained in possession instead of being driven off the land.

Question: What do you think of the action of the neighbors?

Answers: 0. I approve

1. I approve, but with qualifications
2. I cannot decide
3. I disapprove, but with qualifications
4. I disapprove

In the assessment of the results, weights were assigned to the answers in such a way that attitudes favorable to "human rights" received a low score, while those supporting property rights received a high score. The lowest possible score was zero; the highest, 32. Jones' analysis of the replies of two extreme groups—business men and C.I.O. workers—follows.

Surmounting the social heap in Akron are the leaders of the rubber industry—the chief beneficiaries of its progress. They tend to gain financially if their companies gain, whether in Akron or elsewhere, and they are probably more to be identified with the welfare of the industry than with the welfare of their community. If other things were equal, they would like to see Akron prosper. Only unfortunately for their city other things are not equal, and they must choose first to protect their wealth and that of the other stockholders, rather than the workers and people of Akron.

We studied a little of the background of thirteen of the top leaders, of whom eleven are still living. Seven of the thirteen are or were natives of this part of Ohio, and therefore oldtimers like George Potter and the

[a] Editors' note: Cases III, V, VI, and VII, which appear in the original of this work, have been omitted.

farmers. Three of the remainder are products of the urban East, and the others are much like the oldtimers in that they come from the Middle West. The names are mostly Anglo-Saxon. Three of the remainder are German and one Irish, but all of these last are from the old immigrant stock that has been two or more generations in this country. All but one were brought up as Protestants (the one has always been a Roman Catholic) but at least half have given up any active part in their religion. Three of them have had no college training, one a very meager education indeed. Two failed to finish college because of financial difficulties at home. Eight completed the four years of college and one of these went on for two years of business-school training. The average help which these men have had from the "position in life" of their parents has been considerable, but they have pushed ahead beyond this, it is safe to say, by virtue of the characteristics which have usually advanced individuals in our culture to wealth, prestige, and the exercise of power.

With respect to the element of struggle, Akron and the rubber industry may be no more than an extreme case. But in our understanding of the opinions of the rubber magnates we must remember, above all, the intensity with which they have fought—particularly against each other and the labor unions. They have gotten on in a world where you arrive only if you go straight ahead. To put yourself in the position of anyone else, or to see two sides to the argument in which you are involved, means to hesitate. And hesitation would have been fatal to any of these men.

We interviewed and scored eight of the top executives of the rubber companies. We also interviewed ten of the other business leaders of Akron. These were the heads of various local enterprises—a real estate man, a bank president, the head of a publishing company, and so on. There was so little difference in the scores of these two groups, and in the character of their remarks, that they can all be reported together.

The average score of the eighteen [1] was 29.1. It could hardly have been higher. In a possible range of zero to 32—where 32 indicates the highest regard for corporate property—six scored 32 and five scored 28. The lowest score was 22. In sum:

Scores:	Below 21	21–24	25–28	29–32
Number:	0	2	6	10

[1] This was the mean; the median was 29.5. The eight rubber executives taken by themselves had a mean score of 29.6 and a median score of 30. Standard deviation of the 18 scores was 2.61—the lowest of any group in the study.

On the individual stories, the magnates scored as [indicated below].

		Scores[b]					
		0	1	2	3	4	Mean
I.	Bootleg coal	..	1	..	3	14	3.7
II.	Utility stay-in strike	..	..	1	..	17	3.9
IV.	Farm mortgage foreclosure	..	..	..	2	16	3.9

[b] Editors' note: Cases III, V, VI, and VII have been omitted from the table, since the cases have been omitted from the text.

In the case of the bootleg coal story with seventeen disapprovals of the miners' action to one approval, outraged feelings for property plainly prevailed, but generally there was a countervailing pull of sympathy for the cold and hungry people that expressed itself in two ways. The first was in a certain fierceness. "I think the same as I would if you should go out to the warehouse and help yourself to tires for your car and your friends. It's plain stealing." Perhaps the speaker really felt it was not the same thing, but he wished to leave no crack in the door. "If such actions spread to other industries, we would be in a bad condition." The fierceness comes out in other remarks, as well. We say it is a form of sympathy, but perhaps it would be more correct to say that it is a substitute for the sympathy which was more directly expressed by some of the others; "There should be some way to take care of this situation." "It was up to the State of Pennsylvania to take care of the miners." The president of one of the rubber companies reduced his total score from 32 to 30 by refusing to commit himself on this issue. All he would say was that "preservation is the first law." Another said: "They had to live," but the action did not fail to be "confiscation of property," and "They have no right to help themselves to these resources."

In the mind of even the most property conscious of capitalists there is a slight emotional interference with judgment if the violation of property is the work of miserable, unorganized individuals. But where the activity is organized—as by a labor union—and where the human need is not immediately apparent, the decisions all lean in the same direction. The workers who took over the power plant in Michigan were condemned almost unanimously, and every one of this group of respondents scored four, except our bank president, who, for some reason, refused to commit himself on this story alone. The workers were condemned with a bitterness which sometimes resulted in long and rather irrelevant speeches. The surge of emotion carried along with it all the other sources of resentment —and lurking deep under all the remarks can be detected perhaps some sort of basic, nuclear fear—the fear which takes many forms and in these times is to be found in all classes of men.

The expression of the whole social philosophy of one of the very big rubber magnates was opened up by the story of the union in Michigan and how it took over for a time the management of the company's property. "That was damn foolishness just like the TVA, Guffey Coal Bill, Labor Relations Act, and all this union racket. Roosevelt has gone fishing today. The sooner he gets drowned the better it will be for the whole country. He is just like Hitler and the only reason he does not act like Hitler is because it would not be politically expedient."

"The trouble with the present times is that America does not need labor unions of European background. To meet our problems they will have to be American—derived from American tradition. The C.I.O. had its origin in coal—a natural resource—not a man-made industry like rubber. Because the rubber industry is man-made it is movable—not fixed as natural resources are."

It is not clear whether this last remark refers back to the bootleg coal story (where the answer was qualified) or expresses the respondent's feeling that, while labor unions may be justified in the coal industry, they are not in the case of rubber. It is certainly true that rubber is harder to organize than coal, just as we know that it is harder to organize any industry that can move away. But it can hardly be inferred that organization is more undesirable merely because it is more difficult. The speaker continued:

"The C.I.O. is foreign in its principles. Such unionism creates class feeling in large production industries. Such unionism stifles the freedom of an ambitious worker to rise to the top. There can be no easy give and take between labor and management because there is always the union committee between the two. This fact creates class consciousness on both sides. Both sides resent each other. The management therefore cannot spot the able, interested, or ingenious individual for promotion, or get the benefit of his ideas."

We cannot say that it is typical, but there came out later in this interview just a trace of yearning for the European relationships between classes —a wish for the resigned and contented recognition of "position in life" on the part of the workers. The same man went on:

"The United States is becoming more snobbish than European countries which have had admitted class distinctions for centuries. Ramsay Mac-

Donald was every bit as liberal as Roosevelt—more so. He took care of the interests of labor, but he did not allow labor to step into the management of business as Roosevelt has. The Democratic Party in this country has permitted incompetent persons to dictate the business policies of the country supposedly in the interest of labor.

"Yes, Akron is different from other industrial cities. We do not have many foreigners unless you count the West Virginia Snakes. Real foreigners are good workers. They are easy to handle in labor groups, at least at first, because they accept their position. They do not question authority. But not so with the Snakes. They are not used to authority. The unions will never be able to unify them because West Virginians will not accept the discipline of an orderly organization.

"The unions use the newspapers to create political pressure. Management has never been in politics. Business will not fight through politics."

This last comment is probably ingenuous, hard as this is to believe. He may mean that business is active in politics only in pursuit of something like "common welfare." It would be interesting to know how many big business men would express this belief so blandly. Our respondent continued:

"This spread-the-work principle is all hokum. It only results in lowered annual income for all the workers. And the workers have a reasonable income. The average working man in East Akron is better off than the average man on West Hill. The West Hill man has a salary of, say, $5,000 a year. It costs him $2,000 to pay interest on home investment, taxes, and so forth. He is the only one employed in his family. He is helping his relations. The East Akron worker earns $1,500, his wife is working and earns about $1,000, his son and daughter are working and earn about $600 a year each. The family pays $30 a month rent—no taxes, no interest—and have a net income of over $3,000. And all the relatives are on relief."

This picture of the fiscal paradise in which the hypothetical Akron worker lives is a far cry from a strike up in Michigan, but such verbalizations serve a valuable purpose for the thinker. It is important not to be sorry for the man you have to fight.

Other comments were more directly to the point. "This amounts to taking over the power plant and sounds like communism. I suppose if you asked the workers, they would approve such action—but ask them about somebody coming into their own house, and they would show the same feelings as I have about this case." For this man property is property, and, whether or not a corporation is a person, corporate property is merely a form of personal property. Another ventured the opinion that "the English system is coming. The unions should be made responsible and not allowed to strike unless the employer breaks his contract." Again, "They took over property that did not belong to them." "I do not believe in confiscating any man's property." "I am unalterably opposed to this action. The workers have a claim to their jobs, but they lose this claim when they violate the rules of their employment by sitting down or unlawfully possessing company property."

Beyond "property," "law," "unions," and "strikes," one comment was hung around the word "communism." Another was as general, and very interesting, if we could know just what the respondent meant by "system": "If you want to change the system, okay, but if not you have to bar lawlessness. You're breaking off bits of the foundation." . . .

In the case of the farm mortgage foreclosure only two qualified their answers, and all the rest of the scores piled up at four. "If it was legally wrong, it was wrong!" The same man who told us that he did not go to church because the "music is lousy," but that "the family goes and I support it with dues," called on the Almighty and, as treasurer of one of the big companies, put himself in the place of the bank: "Divine Providence operates against the farmer, causing crop failures, as it does against all others. The bank should not be expected to make good the farmer's loss." Another agreed: "The stockholders of the bank should not take this loss nor should the insurance companies. Neither should the farmer be permitted to buy a farm for that price." . . .

Whether or not we use the word conservative for the high scores in our interview as a whole, we should repeat that where 32 is the highest possible score, the business leaders in Akron averaged 29.1. This is the statistical summary of what came out also in their remarks, from which the quality of compassion is conspicuously absent. We do not know anything about the behavior of these men within their family circles, nor how they treat their chauffeurs, or caddies on the golf course on Saturday afternoon. We suspect that most of them are genial and sympathetic, and have established their authority by persuasion as well as by economic domination. Our stories, however, seem to have made them feel that their authority in the industrial sphere is not wholly secure, and to have brought out qualities of hardness and coldness, very little mitigated by feelings for the personal rights of others. . . .

We interviewed in Akron three different categories of rubber workers —(1) those that we knew belonged to the Employee Associations . . . , thirty-seven of them averaged 17.6 in their scores; (2) sixty-eight that we knew did not belong to the C.I.O. unions, although we did not know whether or not they were members of the Employee Associations, and who averaged 12.6 (virtually the same as the control group); and (3) 193 members of the C.I.O. union, the United Rubber Workers of America.

The last group scored an average [2] of 6.2. Thirty-six of them (19 per cent) scored a flat zero. There was no other tendency to cluster, and a steady falling off in the higher scores as follows:

Scores:	0–3	4–7	8–11	12–15	16–19	20–23	24–27	28–30	31–32
Number:	75	56	32	11	11	6	1	1	0

Our interview contains two stories calling for a reaction to the militant actions of labor unions—and two other stories in which unions play a part. Obviously we need make no investigation to know that the members of the C.I.O. in Akron tend to be in favor of labor unions, and even tend to be in favor of their militant action; that the non-members are at best neutral; and that the Red Apples [3] are hostile. The scores, therefore, in so far as they are influenced by the union stories, are just about what we might expect. However, the responses to the separate stories should be analyzed further.

The Michigan stay-in strike was the militant action of a labor union, and, compared with either the C.I.O. workers, or the control group, the Red Apples showed an extraordinary tendency to disapprove—that is, they had higher relative scores on this story than on the interview as a whole. The comparison between the C.I.O. and the Red Apples is as follows:

UTILITY STAY-IN STRIKE (STORY II)

	Approval (Scores 0 & 1)		Disapproval (Scores 3 & 4)	
	Number	*Per Cent*	*Number*	*Per Cent*
C.I.O.	153 *	79	34 *	18
Red Apples	11 *	30	24 *	65

(In this and the subsequent tables of the same sort the numbers seldom add up to 193, and the percentages seldom add up to 100. This is because of the few respondents who could not, or did not want to answer one way or the other, and who were scored 2.)

* The statistical reckoning, chi-square, for this table is 38.8, and indicates that the difference between the responses of C.I.O. and Red Apples is highly significant.

[2] Standard deviation was 5.91. The differences between the various means are highly significant.

[3] [Epithet applied by C.I.O. men to members of the Employee Association, a company union.]

This table demonstrates that there was a deep cleavage of opinion between these two groups, on this issue. If we could explain the difference we should be at least part way toward explaining the difference in attitude toward corporate property between two groups whose economic status and function differ little if at all. Such an explanation may be easier after we have examined the free comment made by the rubber workers.

We saw that the Red Apples were concerned with "the owner's consent" and with the protection of property, and that where they approved of the action it was because the consumers were considered and because the strike was not a sitdown.

The majority of the C.I.O. workers approved of the action, but commented in a variety of quite different ways. There were the militant, even rebellious ones:

"I think they should shoot more of our factory operators." "I sure agree with the workers. They fought for their rights. Do you think they were right?" (Asking the interviewer.) "I believe in the working men uniting together to protect themselves. I was one of the first in Akron to help organize a rubber union in the rubber shops in 1932. We have to work for our living and if we don't fight to hold our gains the rich men will make slaves out of all the workers." "Labor must use everything at their command to get a contract. I'm a strong union man and I think that sitdown strikes are justifiable. The workers have a right to use the strongest methods they can to win a strike. The shop owners do the same against the workers." "The workers were fighting for their existence. It does not matter what system they use in winning a strike. The workers must do the best for themselves. The manufacturers don't do it for them."

There was also a softer type of comment in which the speaker went out of his way to find a positive virtue in the action, or to explain it away. "I would say it was all right to put the superintendents out, but not the foremen, who are just workers like the rest. Some foremen are pretty good, and some are all for the company and against the men. Maybe there was a personal grudge and that's why they run the foremen out. Anyway, I think the workers were in the right." "As long as property was not damaged, I guess it was the only way to win." In this comment the property damage idea had little to do with property right, but the concern seemed rather to be with the physical injury to "property." Again: "What the workers did was okay. They gave service to the consumers and no damage was done." "As long as nobody suffered but the foremen and the superintendents, the strikers were justified. Even for them there was only a little humiliation; that was all."

Finally, there were those who had a somewhat longer view of the matter, and who in many cases were worried about the general use of sitdowns. "The sitdowns did a lot of good before the unions were organized and they were all right at that time. But I think they were not justified later on." "I approve of this, but I do not generally approve of sitdown strikes. Differences should be settled by conferences. [Then followed a cryptic remark, whose significance can only be guessed at.] If I was not a union man, I might give a different answer." "Action such as this may change precedents—may cause banks and legislators to act differently. That would certainly be a good thing."

The minority of 18 per cent that disapproved of the action had more to say in proportion to their number: "The workers and the company are both to blame; but if I was on strike I would not go as far as these strikers did." "They have no business taking possession of company property." "I don't believe in disorderly strikes. I don't say this merely because I am a union man, but I believe in fairness, and it is better for the unions if they are conducted fairly." "If someone would come and take my property, I would not like it." "The strikers were wrong. But I believe public utility activities should be run by the consumers. I come from a small place 120 miles from here. Most of the time the people there don't have to pay for their electricity, but get receipted bills because the plants are run by the city." "The government should take control instead of the workers." Whereas these last two disapproved because they wanted to see the government intervene, a few others were critical of what they thought were bad union tactics: "They should have struck without kicking out the superintendents and foremen. Should have picketed the plant." "These workers should have walked out and stopped work. That would get action and they wouldn't have to take over property." "The workers overstepped their authority by operating the plant without any supervision. If something should happen to the machinery or equipment, the workers would be criticized. It would be better to quit work until the question is settled." "They should strike." (That is, walk out.)

Still others were afraid of radicalism: "I don't believe in such strikes. Taking the shop and kicking out the foremen was too much like bolshevism." "I believe in the principle of unionism, but not in radicalism." "That is wrong. If such stuff is allowed we might as well go to Russia." "I think the union is all right; but it should carry on regularly. I don't like radicals." "It was something new to expel the bosses and take the shop over. That was too much. It was too radical." . . .

The three remaining stories have nothing to do with unions, and it will be important to see whether or not the C.I.O. members and the Red Apples differ significantly in their responses to them. We have already seen that there are such large differences in their answers to the above stories as to indicate beyond any reasonable doubt that the results did not come about by chance. This, however, is hardly to be wondered at. When it comes to stories of simple individual suffering there is no reason to believe that union and non-union men would differ—unless they really differ in their attitude toward corporate property even where the labor union issue is not involved.

BOOTLEG COAL (STORY I)

	Approval of Miners (Scores 0 & 1)		Disapproval of Miners (Scores 3 & 4)	
	Number	*Per Cent*	*Number*	*Per Cent*
C.I.O.	147 *	78	45 *	23
Red Apples	23 *	62	13 *	35

* Chi-square = 2.6, which means that the difference verges on significance (at about the 10% level). . . .

The story about the farmer and the bank that foreclosed the mortgage is another that has nothing to do with unions, but with a conflict between an individual and the "vested interests."

FARM MORTGAGE FORECLOSURE (STORY IV)

	Approval of Neighbors (Scores 0 & 1)		Disapproval of Neighbors (Scores 3 & 4)	
	Number	*Per Cent*	*Number*	*Per Cent*
C.I.O.	131 *	68	52 *	27
Red Apples	10 *	27	24 *	65

* Chi-square = 22.4, and the difference is highly significant.

The minority of the Red Apples that approved of the neighbors had little comment to make. One said: "During the depression the farmer should have protection." One who disapproved, added: "If the farmer was making the best effort he could, the bank should have been more lenient, although the bank can't wait too long. The farmer had everything to lose, while the bank had proportionally little."

The majority of Red Apples accepted authority throughout. "The neighbors had no right to interfere in somebody else's business." "That was not according to American ideals." "If the law was wrong, they should change the law. They were wrong to interfere with the due process of law."

The majority of the C.I.O. workers (68 per cent) that approved the action of the neighbors commented in some cases so as to show sympathy for the farmer. "I am for the poor people." "They must have had good reason for helping their neighbors. He must have been a good neighbor; they are hard to find." "I think the farmers did a good job. He would have lost all he had, and the bank would have still been able to operate." "My parents own a farm in West Virginia. I know the neighbors would have done the same for them at home." "The farmers were right. I know how I would feel if I was to lose what I worked for all my life."

But the comment of the majority more often took the form of anger —sometimes criticism of things as they are, and sometimes plain hostility to the banks. "The bank got hooked, but I'm glad. The money men all stick together and hold things up. The bank had probably gotten their part already anyhow." "The farmers done right in helping. Some of these banks are no good. You borrow a few dollars and they make you sign your life away." "Some of these bankers work for the almighty dollar instead of trying to help the community. I believe the banks should render a service to the people and help them when they are down and out, or the neighbors will have to take things in their own hands." "The banks don't want to give a man a chance. People must help each other. The banker won't help us." "These banks take back too many properties and forget the man that has an equity in the property." "They done a great thing. The trouble with us right now is the banks. They do crooked things and get away without punishment." "The banking institutions have wrecked too many people." "The banks want all the money and when they get it they won't turn it loose without a guarantee on your life as security." "I lost one home to the bank—they stole it."

Only a few went beyond a show of sympathy or anger and suggested what ought to be done: "The neighbors were of great help. The banks should be more liberal in extending time and lowering interest." "I approve of this sort of action or anything like it. It may change precedents and may cause banks and legislators to act differently."

One comment had nothing in common with any of the others, and is hard to interpret: "I still figure myself as a farmer in my feelings, and we farmers are a pretty good class of people. The neighbors used to look up to us."

There were critical ideas about the system and the way money operates: "The money system is all wrong. The government should loan the money without interest." "Well, I think interest is our biggest trouble today. I approve of the neighbors. I wish I could take some of these people to the district near my home town where the old Quakers or Amish people have some farms. They don't borrow money on interest but when a house or barn of one of them burns down they furnish the material and labor together and build up the building. The banks can't horn in there, and they are happy people."

Some of the opposition showed indignation, but against the neighbors. "They had no business in the thing, they should have kept away." "The neighbors should have been locked up themselves. The farmer should have known what he was getting into in the first place. I live in this shack and owe the government on it. But when I can't pay what I agreed to, they are welcome to it." "I don't approve of their action. It was too underhanded."

Again, there were some that disapproved who had the system as a whole in mind. "Tailspin of business is no excuse." "He owed the bank and they should have gotten more. This sort of thing breaks business; the banks couldn't stand many of these deals. It's an unfair way to do business." "The government should come to the farmer's aid."

There was only one recorded comment that brought the worker, as a worker, together with the farmer: "We need more cooperation on the part of the working people."

One disapproval was for a perverse reason: "We are now living in an extreme form of capitalism. The banks ought to take every penny coming to them. People won't find a remedy for their troubles until they have suffered more." . . .

Obviously the kind of rubber worker that joins the C.I.O. union differs from the Red Apples not merely in his ideas about unions. In two out of the three stories that have nothing to do with unions there is a "highly significant" difference between the two groups in the replies, and in the third story there is a difference that "verges on significance." The Red Apples have a higher regard for corporate property according to all of the standards that we have devised.

LIFE IN THE CLASSES *

Members of any one class . . . think of themselves as a group and have a certain unity of outlook. This is indicated by their frequent reference to "people like us" and to persons "not our kind." Expressions of this group solidarity are particularly prevalent when individuals are discussing groups immediately above and below them. When expressing resentment at exclusion from the class above and antagonism toward mobility from the class below, social classes betray unconsciously their sense of solidarity and "we-ness." It will be seen subsequently, too, that members of these classes and subclasses have a further unity through a common set of beliefs, a common pattern of overt behavior, and other traits which function as symbols of status.

While members of all class groups recognize classes above and below them, or both, the greater the social distance from the other classes the less clearly are fine distinctions made. Although an individual recognizes most clearly the existence of groups immediately above and below his own, he is usually not aware of the social distance actually maintained between his own and these adjacent groups. Thus, in all cases except that of members of the upper-lower class the individual sees only a minimum of social distance between his class and the adjacent classes. . . . Almost all other class divisions, however, are visualized as definite lines of cleavage in the society with a large amount of social distance between them.

In general, too, individuals visualize class groups above them less clearly than those below them; they tend to minimize the social differentiations between themselves and those above. This difference in perspective is partly explained by the fact that class lines in the society are not permanent and rigid and that upward mobility is fairly frequent. It is, further, due to the natural tendency in such a status system to identify with "superiors." In view of this situation it is not surprising that individuals in the two upper strata make the finest gradations in the stratification of the whole society and that class distinctions are made with decreasing precision as social position becomes lower.

Not only does the perspective on social stratification vary for different class levels, but the very bases of class distinction in the society are variously interpreted by the different groups. People tend to agree as to where people

* Davis, Allison; Gardner, Burleigh B.; and Gardner, Mary R., *Deep South* (Chicago: The University of Chicago Press, 1941), pp. 71–83.

are but not upon why they are there. Upper-class individuals, especially upper uppers, think of class divisions largely in terms of time—one has a particular social position because his family has "always had" that position. Members of the middle class interpret their position in terms of wealth and time and tend to make moral evaluations of what "should be." Both middle-class groups accept the time element as an important factor in the superordinate position of the "old aristocracy," but for the rest of the society they consider only individual wealth and moral behavior as differentiating factors. Lower-class people, on the other hand, view the whole stratification of the society as a hierarchy of wealth. The lower lowers think that all those above them on the social scale are progressively wealthy and that their own subordination is dependent upon this economic factor alone. While upper lowers have a similar idea of those above them, they frequently add a moral note in explaining the subordinate position of lower lowers.

The identity of a social class does not depend on uniformity in any one or two, or a dozen, specific kinds of behavior but on a complex pattern or network of interrelated characteristics and attitudes. Among the members of any one class, there is no strict uniformity in any specific type of behavior but rather a range and a "modal average." One finds a range in income, occupation, educational level, and types of social participation. The "ideal type" may be defined, however, for any given class—the class configuration—from which any given individual may vary in one or more particulars. Also, two individuals may belong to the same association, fall in the same occupational category, belong to the same church, or have the same ideas about local politics; but identity in any one or two such particulars does not necessarily indicate that both individuals belong to the same social class. Class position is determined rather by the configuration of traits which an individual possesses.

An important aspect of this configuration is "ideology"—the set of concepts and the complex of attitudes toward individuals and institutions which individuals exhibit. The members of any one class or subclass share the same general attitudes and beliefs—that is, the same ideology. The conceptions of class which have been described in this section represent one aspect of the class ideologies; and while no systematic cataloguing of the beliefs and attitudes of each class toward all social structures is given in this study, the ideology of each class will be characterized in terms of one or two distinctive and fundamental concepts which dominate the thinking of each group. These will then be related to the other traits in the class configurations.

THE UPPER-CLASS CONFIGURATION

The idealization of the past. The ideology of the upper class, as suggested above, is colored particularly by the concept of time. Stability in time is of supreme value to members of this class, and they conceive of the class structure as having its basis in lineage, in the stability of a family's social position. An individual is thought to have a certain class position because his family has always occupied that position. This emphasis on the past may be seen, furthermore, in almost all aspects of upper-class behavior. They display little interest in the community, today, except where particular activities reflect the past.

Although upper-class people, today, enjoy a certain amount of economic security, they are not all "wealthy" individuals, nor are they the most affluent group in the society. Most members of the upper-upper class, however, have been wealthy in the past, or at least their families have been. Their families, a generation or two ago, were a group whose economic position and standard of consumption far surpassed that of the rest of the community. Mostly large planters, owners of great tracts of land and of many slaves, they lived extravagantly, spent money freely, and entertained elaborately; and upper uppers, today, in spite of their diminished resources, try to preserve, as far as possible, this old pattern of behavior which their families established during a past period of opulence. Houses and furnishings reflect their erstwhile riches, and this particular reflection of the past is highly valued by them. Whenever it has been economically possible, the members of the "old aristocracy" have retained their plantation homes; and they take great pride in keeping them intact—just as they were in "the old days." Newly acquired furnishings are generally old, preferably "antebellum" rather than new and modern. In fact, one proof of their superordinate position is that members of the lower-upper class whose lineage would not, in itself, engender such reverence for the past, tend to pattern their behavior after that of the upper-upper class and to cultivate an appreciation for time, as a part of the process of seeking mobility into the upper-upper group.

Lack of interest in the community. As a group, members of the upper class seldom participate actively in contemporary community organizations or activities. There is almost no political activity among them, or even any pronounced effort to observe with care the laws of the community. Their regular attendance at church is apparently just a part of the ritual of upper-class behavior and does not signify any interest in theology or religious teachings. Their associational activity is limited almost entirely to participation in the Historical Club, the primary function of which is preservation and honoring of the past. Most of their informal social participation is in small groups whose memberships, especially in the older age ranges, often include upper-class persons exclusively.

Primacy of lineage. It is apparent from this brief summary of the upper-class configuration of attitudes and behavior that their concept of time, their value of the past, is a very important element in their ideology and one which has a very definite relation to specific behavior. Closely linked to this time concept, and an integral part of it, is the upper-class preoccupation with lineage. It may be said that an upper-class person is primarily a member of a group and is only secondarily an individual. He is a member of a kinship group and, as such, a bona fide member of his class. Variations in his individual behavior have little effect upon his membership or position in either his family or his class. Because of the high value placed on lineage, he maintains his position no matter what his individual pattern of behavior may be. Social control, pressure by the group to maintain uniform patterns of individual behavior among its members, is, therefore, at a minimum in the upper class. An individual is a member of the upper class because of the past—his family's past—and not because of what he has or what he does.

THE MIDDLE-CLASS CONFIGURATION

Importance of wealth and morality. The middle class, on the other hand, may be looked upon as a group in which special value is placed upon individual wealth and upon the observance of religious and moral precepts in individual behavior. Middle-class ideology is colored not by the past behavior of the individual's forebears but by his own present behavior, especially as that behavior reflects economic status and moral and religious attitudes. Not only the number of possessions, but their cash value also, is of significance to this group. It is here, especially in the upper-middle class, that "appearances" are particularly important. Both of the middle-class groups, while interpreting the class structure of the society primarily in terms of contemporary wealth, at the same time concede that the superiority of the upper class has its basis in past affluence. Also embodied in their interpretation of the society's stratification is a preoccupation with religious teachings, a concern with moral concepts of "right and wrong," "good and evil." These concepts, then—the high value of contemporary individual wealth and "moral" behavior—profoundly influence middle-class behavior.

In general, the configurations of upper-middle and lower-middle class are sufficiently similar so that they may be discussed together. Differences between them in regard to any one characteristic of behavior are generally differences in degree, so that upper middles are usually superordinate to lower middles only in a specific type of behavior or in a specific type of relation. Economic security is enjoyed to some extent by both groups but is achieved to a much higher degree in the upper-middle class, although lower-middle-class persons generally have a certainty of sufficient income to meet their physical needs. Members of the upper-middle class, however, on the whole, control more wealth, receive higher incomes, and are in occupations which have more prestige, thus giving them a security beyond the mere ability to care for fundamental physical needs. Upper-middle-class men are most frequently found in independent or supervisory occupations, as professional men or as employers and owners or managers of large businesses. Lower-middle-class men are much more often employees or the owners of small enterprises. The greatest wealth in the society today is centered in the upper-middle class, and it is in this group that the greatest emphasis on the display of wealth is found. Fine clothes, new cars, well-kept homes, and expensive furnishings are the rule. In neither middle-class group, however, do possessions suggest the time values of the upper class. Rather, there is an emphasis on modern styles and values, with concern for "quality" among upper middles and for "quantity" in the lower-middle group.

The informal social participation of the middle class is often characterized by organization into card clubs, a type of association not often found among the upper class and entirely absent from the lower-class configuration. Behavior in these informal groups is usually more restrained and more limited to a specific recreational activity than among the upper class, whose recreational behavior is condemned by the middle group as "indecent" and "immoral." Middle-class people refer to their own members as "good clean people," emphasize the fact that they "don't drink," often mention that their "women don't smoke," and are particularly vehement in stating that their married couples don't "carry-on" with one another's mates in the manner of the upper class.

"Self-improvement." In the middle class, furthermore, it is also important to "improve one's self," an attitude which has special significance for those individuals who are aware of the possibilities of social mobility. Every middle-class parent who is financially able attempts to educate his children beyond secondary school, at least to some extent. Specialized study, talent achievement, and organizations around talent, such as music and

study clubs, flourish on this social level. It is primarily the mobile middle-class individuals who want to "improve" themselves through study clubs and exercise of talent, although even the more stable members of the middle class attach considerable importance to self-improvement as a means of maintaining status (usually defended as a means of achieving a "better" community through "better" individuals).

"Community improvement." Community activities and organizations are the great participation field of this class. Both middle-class groups are active politically (the upper middles usually occupying the superordinate positions), and both groups feel it their "duty" to take an interest in this particular function of the community. Laws are taken much more seriously by them than by the upper class. Very active in churches and church associations, middle-class people are not content merely to participate but tend to concern themselves with discussions of theology and with a strict observance of religious teachings.

It is this group which supplies the majority of the members in formal associations, the upper middles usually occupying the positions of authority in them. A large proportion of these associations—men's and women's organizations alike,—profess to function in the interests of the community as a whole and concern themselves with various types of civic improvement, such as, promoting "better" business relations, "better" schools, and more "beautiful" public parks, streets, etc. Emphasis is pre-eminently on the community of today, and almost no middle-class associations are primarily interested in the past, the chief preoccupation of the upper-class Historical Club. In all their organized activity there is a moral note. It is one's "duty" as a member of the community to function actively in the Rotary Club, the Woman's Club, the Parent-Teachers Association, or in some associations concerned with "bettering" present conditions.

Social conformity. The importance of wealth and "moral" behavior is stressed with emphasis upon the individual and his expression of these values. In the middle class, a person's position is directly dependent upon his pattern of behavior, especially his appearance of wealth and his moral attitudes. His social status is not an inherent quality, as is that of an upper-class individual, but is dependent entirely upon his actions. He retains his position in the group only so long as his behavior conforms to the rules which the middle class has established. It appears, therefore, that behavior in this class is highly organized and closely controlled; and, much more than in any other group in the society, the members of this group complacently accept and abide by the "rules." The high development of associational behavior is the one outstanding expression of these controls, and the whole associational structure reflects the moral concepts of the middle class.

The middle class may, then, be interpreted as a group in which a high degree of organization and moral rules act to limit the amount and effects of individual variation. In other words, in a class where membership may be directly influenced by variations in individual patterns of behavior, the many rules and the extreme group pressure for enforcement may be seen as a technique for limiting individual variations and so strengthening class solidarity through enforced uniformity. Similarly, the large amount of organized activity in the middle class—in churches, associations, politics, etc.—is a means of controlling and limiting the disruptive effects of middle-class individualism.

THE LOWER-CLASS CONFIGURATION

Lack of integration into the community. In contrast to the upper class, the lower class is a relatively new group in the community. This is not to infer that the presence of some type of lower class is new but, rather, that it has only recently become a significantly large group and is composed of a type of people relatively new to the community. Now comprising about a third of all the white population, the lower class is composed mainly of mill and factory workers who have come into the community during the last thirty years. They are primarily an industrial group, a new occupational grouping in the society, and one which, as we have already pointed out, is generally ignored by the higher social classes.

The lower class in Old City does not take part in the formal associational activity found in the middle class. There are few associations and formal groups among them. They take no part in the organizations and group activities of the other classes or of the community as a whole, and seem but slightly interested. They participate but little in community politics except as voters; and the lower lowers, especially, have a conscious, thorough disregard for the laws of the community. Crimes of violence, public drunkenness, disturbing the peace, are frequent offenses among them. Lower-class people, too, generally have little church participation, although upper lowers do attend church services occasionally. By and large, lower-class behavior and ideology may be said to be characterized by a disdain for all the values of the higher classes, a disdain for the government and laws which they see as creations of the upper class and middle class, a disdain for churches and associations and for the moral and religious values. This contempt for all the mores and institutions of the upper classes, especially for those of the middle class, reaches a much higher intensity in the lower-lower group than among upper lowers. The latter group is more aware of the social position of the middle class, feels less socially distant from its members, and, in many cases, sees the possibility of mobility into this class.

Economic insecurity. Lower-class people generally do not have a high degree of economic security. Usually employees, working for wages by the hour or by the day, they have little certainty of sufficient income over any period of time to care for their physical needs. This insecurity is reflected in the number and type of their possessions and in their attitude toward them. One lower-lower-class family, for example, exhibited as its most prized possession a colored paper poster advertising some commercial product. One adult member of the family had found it in the city dump and had brought it home as a gift for his younger brother. There is a great deal of instalment-plan buying, and emphasis is entirely upon quantity without regard for quality. While upper-lower-class people take some interest in caring for such possessions as they have, lower-lower-class individuals are quite consistently improvident. They have little consideration for their future welfare; and they find it impossible to provide for the future, since immediate needs are so rarely satisfied.

Primacy of the job. The meaningful solidarities among the lower classes are neither those of association nor those of church, but rather those of occupation and neighborhood. Roughly, these "new people" divide themselves into three groups on the basis of their industrial affiliation: that is, workers in cotton mills, sawmills and planing mills. Members of each of these segments of the lower class have a certain amount of solidarity through their occupational relations and consider themselves somewhat different from members of the other occupational groups. This differentiation among themselves has some basis, too, in the backgrounds of the various groups, for cotton-mill workers (who, in actual fact, have had no common bond of employment, since the cotton mills closed some ten years earlier) came to the community mostly from other industrial cities in the eastern part of the state; planing-mill workers and many sawmill workers, on the other hand, are largely people of farming background—tenant-farmers and small farmers—and farm laborers from the surrounding territory. In addition to these industrial people who form the bulk of the lower class today, there are also some fishermen, artisans, and small shopkeepers. There are also a few tenant-farmers and small farm-owners who do not actually have a "place" in the urban society but who may have extensive urban contacts. Members of these latter urban occupational groups do not have occupational solidarities among themselves, as the industrial groups do. They do, however, have membership in other lower-class groupings based on the locality in which they live.

Importance of residential areas. Superimposed upon the industrial groupings in the lower class, and closely related to them, are distinctions made on the basis of specific localities in which individuals live. These localities are larger than neighborhoods, as that term is generally applied; and residents do not necessarily have the complex of one-to-one, face-to-face relations with one another which constitute the conventional neighborhood relation. There is, however, a certain solidarity among residents of the same district, a distinction between themselves and members of their class who live in other parts of town. Thus, Dunlap Street, on the "east side of town" near the planing mill, and the side streets and alleys running into it, constitute a locality whose residents have a sense of solidarity. Inhabited mainly by planing-mill workers, this district's solidarity embraces some residents who are not employed by that factory. Similarly, Crowder Street, inhabited largely by people who once worked in the cotton mills, is not limited to them entirely. A third, quite well-defined locality is that which includes factory workers and fishermen who, together, have a certain amount of solidarity because of common residence in this district. Sawmill workers generally live outside the urban area.

Not only does the lower class make distinctions and form groups on the basis of these industrial differences and locality differences, but there is also a definite ranking of residential areas.

This reflects a significant difference, for Crowder Street residents, and perhaps the bulk of cotton-mill workers in the community, have a general pattern of behavior somewhat different from the other lower-class population, a pattern which is upper-lower rather than that of the lower-lower-class people on Dunlap Street and the river front. The upper-lower-class people have a little church of their own, somewhat better housing, an interest in caring for their real and personal property, and a more complex code of ethics. Even within the lower lower-class there are distinctions in rank. Dunlap Street ranks higher than the river front; planing-mill workers are considered definitely above fishermen and houseboat dwellers. One woman, whose several husbands had been variously employed in several different industries and who had lived in almost every lower-class locality in Old City, felt that she had really reached the lowest rank when her husband moved her into a houseboat on the river front.

> I ain't never had to live like this and I ain't never going to do it for no man. I seen some mighty hard times, but I ain't never see nothing like this. He's just been trying to pull me down lower and lower ever since I took up with him. I'm down low enough, and I ain't going to have him nor no man pulling me down lower. . . . I told him just how it was, and I says to him, I says:
>
> "I'd jest as leave get out and scratch dirt with the chickens as live here like this with you!" And I would, too . . . I ain't never had to live like this. I just ain't going to put up with it. No, Honey, I ain't never had to live here before. I never did like it none down here. I seen some mighty hard times, but I always was able to get me a house up in town.

Summary. The inhabitants of Old City recognize the reality of class division within the society and, from their varied positions in the social structure, evaluate the class system from different perspectives. A synthesis of these perspectives and a study of overt behavior reveal three well-defined classes and three subclasses. The classes may be characterized by general patterns of behavior. The past is of prime importance to the upper class. Wealth and "morality" mark the aspirations of the middle class, as well as concern with making themselves and the community "better." Poverty, lack of formal organization, and isolation from the other classes distinguish the lower class, and the "job" and area of residence serve to differentiate segments within it.

CLASS DIFFERENCES IN FERTILITY*

Differences in the fertility of the social-economic classes probably became important only with the growth of our modern industrial urban culture. True, in every age of human history, students have observed the failure of the "upper classes" to reproduce as rapidly as the "lower classes." But such observations related to the educated and ruling classes which constituted the merest fringe of the entire population in agrarian and handicraft economies. Our present interest is not in the low fertility of powerful but numerically unimportant minorities, but in that of substantial sections of the population. Today, residents of urban communities constitute more than one half, and the white-collar classes perhaps one quarter of the total population. These groups are not sufficiently fertile to replace their own numbers. They are being recruited from the rural and laboring

* Notestein, Frank W., "Class Differences in Fertility," *The Annals* (Philadelphia: The American Academy of Political and Social Science, 1936), Vol. 188, pp. 26–36.

classes which, in a real sense, may be thought of as the nation's population reservoirs. Differential fertility on this scale appears to be modern.

CHINA AN EXCEPTION

Even now, fertility is not everywhere inversely associated with social-economic status. An inverse association is the characteristic one found in the industrial countries of Europe and America. Our knowledge of other populations is extremely limited, but in them some exceptions have been observed. China, for example, remains primarily an agrarian economy, and one in which unusual importance is attached to the perpetuation of the family. There Lamson, studying data for a series of small samples largely drawn from urban communities, finds that the educated and well-to-do have more children than the poor and ignorant. In the rural population of China differences in the fertility of economic groups appear to be relatively unimportant, but to the extent that they do occur, they also indicate a direct association between fertility and economic status. Data bearing on the subject have recently been collected for about forty thousand families located in 101 selected rural communities. These give no evidence that married women in the families of landowners are significantly either more or less fertile than those in the families of landlords or tenants. Apparently, however, there is a slight positive association between fertility and the crop area of the farm. . . . Married women in families with the largest farms of their own communities had borne more children than those in families with the smallest farms. Whatever the meaning of this direct association may be, it is clear at least that the differences in the fertility of the economic classes in China are quite different from those in the industrial West.

TREND IN LATTER PART OF THE NINETEENTH CENTURY

There is sound evidence that in England the inverse association of fertility and social-economic status was developing rapidly during the latter half of the nineteenth century. . . . The fertility of all classes was declining during the period. However, the decline was more rapid in the upper classes than in the lower, and more rapid in the urban classes than in the agricultural and mining populations. There is no mistaking the effect of these different trends on the relative fertility of the classes. Among women who married between 1851 and 1861 fertility and social-economic status were inversely related, but the differences between the classes were small. The data suggest that at a still earlier period they may have been even smaller. However that may be, after 1851 they increased rapidly until for marriages contracted between 1886 and 1891 the spread of the classes was more than two and one half times that at the beginning of the record. Since then the differences may have narrowed. . . .

A similar differentiation of the classes probably was going on in the United States during the last half of the nineteenth century, but the evidence of it is much less satisfactory. Data similar to those for England are available only for rather small samples of the Northern white population of native parentage. These suggest that the fertility of married women in the professional and business classes of the urban population was declining more rapidly than that of the wives of farm owners.

TREND IN THE PRESENT CENTURY

During the present century there probably has been a further strengthening of the inverse association between fertility and social-economic status in this country. Kiser, studying selected groups of the native white population of the East North Central States, found that the general decline in fertility between 1900 and 1910 resulted in an increased differentiation of both the urban and the rural classes. A similar increase in the differentials between 1900 and 1930 is suggested by Ogburn's study of the size of families in the same region. He found that the decrease in the size of the family among urban groups was largest in the professional class and smallest among the unskilled laborers, while the change in the size of rural families suggested little change in fertility. There is no conclusive evidence that the trend was towards increased differentiation during the entire period. Whelpton has advanced data which strongly suggest that the differences in the fertility of urban and rural groups have been declining recently. The same may have been true of the differences between the various classes of each group.

While the differences in the fertility of the social-economic classes may be decreasing somewhat, the inverse relation still persists. A number of recent studies have shown this to be true, not only for the country as a whole, but also for the populations of widely different types of communities, ranging from the open country and farm village to large cities, and even within the poorer sections of large cities where one might expect selective factors to make for greater homogeneity. . . .

Even in 1928 the unskilled laborers were the only non-agricultural group which was much more than replacing its numbers. The business and clerical groups were well below replacement level, and the fertility of the professional class was only about three quarters of that required for replacement. The fertility of the agricultural population, on the other hand, was well above that of the unskilled non-agricultural group.

THE FACTOR OF CONTRACEPTION

We have seen that the increased class differences in fertility have arisen primarily as the result of a decline in the birth rate which has been more rapid in the upper than in the lower classes, and in urban than in rural communities. It is becoming increasingly clear that these different trends have arisen chiefly through differences in the use and the effectiveness of contraception. Some observers have been inclined to attribute virtually the entire differential relation to a lag in the infiltration of contraceptive knowledge from class to class, and to look upon it as a temporary rather than a permanent relationship. It is reasoned that class differences will narrow or perhaps even reverse as the fertility of all classes comes more completely under control. If all births were "planned," the number of children might become proportionate to the ability of the parents to support them. Proponents of this view point out that this is exactly what has happened in Stockholm, where contraceptive information has been available for a long time and where the birth rate is now far below the level required for permanent replacement. . . .

Edin and Hutchinson have found that married couples of the Stockholm upper classes are more fertile than those of the lower classes. Income is a more important factor in this relationship than occupation. Within similar income groups the association between fertility and occupation disappears. On the other hand, within each occupational group except the industrial workers, fertility increases sharply with income. Somewhat similar reversals have been reported in a few other European cities, but none of them is based on as convincing evidence.

Whether or not Western communities in general will follow Stockholm to a reversal of existing differentials remains to be seen. However, the spread of contraception is a sufficiently important factor to warrant the prediction that class differences will become smaller as the general birth rate continues to decline.

To interpret the present inverse relation of fertility and social-economic status entirely in terms of a lag in the infiltration of contraceptive knowledge is to oversimplify a complex causal nexus. Contraception is undoubtedly the most important means by which fertility has been controlled.

But underlying differences in the prevalence and the effectiveness of contraceptive practice are differences in customs, habits, attitudes, and interests arising from complex differences in the environment of the classes. It is to these environmental differences that we must look for the fundamental causes of much of the class differences in fertility and their changes. Only a brief discussion of a few of these environmental factors need be presented here.

THE FACTOR OF EDUCATION

It has long been known that extensive education and low fertility go together. Any number of studies comparing the fertility of college graduates with that of non-college relations or other persons in roughly comparable "walks of life" point in that direction. However, these studies indicate that the low fertility of college groups comes primarily from the small proportions which marry and the later age of marriage, rather than from a conspicuously low fertility of marriage. . . .

First, school attainment and fertility are inversely associated, not only in the entire sample of each community, but also within each of the rather broad occupational classes. The differences between the college and high school groups are relatively small compared with those between the high school and common school groups. It appears that a moderate amount of education is accompanied by a substantially lowered fertility. Second, the inverse relation between fertility and broad occupational status holds even when the comparison is limited to similar educational groups. Third, the fertility of each educational and occupational class seems to be affected by the special characteristics of the community. Birth rates are highest in the poor areas of the five cities, and progressively lower in Columbus, Syracuse, and Bushwick. This relationship holds when the comparison is limited to similar occupation and educational groups.

THE FACTOR OF RELIGION

The same series of field studies also yields interesting data on the association of fertility and religious affiliation. . . .

It is clear that class for class, the Catholics are more fertile than the Protestants, although the differences are greater among the families of business men than among those of unskilled laborers. In the latter class the proportions of large families are the same. It is equally clear that both religious groups exhibit the characteristic inverse association between fertility and occupational status, although the association is stronger among Protestants than among Catholics. These results are in interesting general agreement with those obtained from a study of patients of a birth-control clinic located in New York City. That study showed that even among the selected group of Catholics who attended the clinic, contraceptive practice prior to clinic attendance was both less frequent and less effective than it was among Protestant and Jewish patients. These data strongly suggest, first, that fertility is less controlled among Catholics than among Protestants; but second, that the fertility of both religious groups reacts in the same direction to similar environments.

THE FACTOR OF INCOME STATUS

Fertility is also inversely correlated with income status. This is true even of the families selected from the poor areas of the five cities referred to in the discussion of education. . . . The data again relate to unbroken marriages in which both the husband and the wife were native white. The incomes are those reported by the families for 1929. In this case fertility is expressed as the total number of children born per hundred wives under 45 years of age. The rates have been standardized for age of the wife. Married women in families with incomes of less than $1,200 in 1929 were definitely more fertile than those in families with incomes of $2,000 or more. The same type of relationship was also found within the business class.

It must be remembered that the difference in the fertility of the poor and the well-to-do does not measure the influence of income *per se* on fertility, any more than differences in the fertility of the educational groups measure the influence of education *per se*. Since, broadly speaking, the poor are the uneducated and the manual workers, particularly of the unskilled class, classifications based on any one characteristic will uncover fertility levels associated with the others, and with many more which help to determine customs, habits, attitudes, and interests of the lower status groups. The characteristics are so interlocked that it is impossible to dissociate them completely.

It is especially important to remember the interlocking nature of class characteristics when one considers the relation of poverty to fertility. Too often it has been assumed that the high fertility of the poor demonstrates that an immediate effect of poverty or loss of income is the stimulation of fertility. The evidence is at best fragmentary. It seems probable that poverty is related to fertility through the modes of life which are both its causes and its consequences. These modes of life once established are slow to change.

On this view of the matter, one would not expect increased economic pressure to operate as an immediate stimulus to fertility.

THE FACTOR OF RELIEF

A widespread misunderstanding of the effect of the depression on fertility has resulted from the failure to differentiate between the inverse association of fertility and income status and the immediate effect of economic pressure on fertility. Reliable studies by Stouffer and Sydenstricker and Perrott showed that families receiving relief were more fertile than the families of roughly comparable groups not receiving relief. In spite of the care taken by the authors to avoid misunderstanding, these studies were immediately interpreted as indicating that families accepted for relief promptly increased their fertility. It was even suggested, on the basis of these studies, that the large number of persons on public relief might explain the rise of the birth rate in 1934.

Actually the studies yielded no evidence of the effect of relief on fertility, and were not intended to do so. That by Sydenstricker and Perrott indicated that the average birth rate for the period 1929 to 1932 was higher for families on relief in 1932 than for families not on relief with incomes under $1,200 in 1932. It is much more likely that the causal sequence ran from high fertility to the need for relief, than from relief to high fertility. Stouffer on the other hand showed that relief families were more fertile when on relief than non-relief families in similar broad occupational and religious groups. This difference would have been found if fertility increased during dependency, but it would also have been found if the fertility of relief families had simply remained high during dependency, which was probably what happened. Thus far no study has come to the writer's attention which shows that families increase their fertility after becoming dependent. . . .

GAPS IN OUR KNOWLEDGE

We know little enough of the differences in the fertility of the important classes of our population, but still less of the specific elements through which they arise. For example, there is little known of the influence of marriage age on differences in fertility. The most recent data relate to 1910. These indicate that among Northern women of native white parentage, marriage age varied directly with social-economic status, and further, that the entire inverse association between fertility and social economic status came from marriages contracted before the wife's twenty-fifth year.

Virtually nothing is known concerning differences either in the proportion of wives who remain permanently childless or in the proportion of women who marry. The 1910 data referred to above show that the proportion of childless married women ranged from 7 per cent in the farm laborer class to 18 per cent in the professional class. The largest differences, however, occurred between the urban and rural groups. There is even less information about differences in the proportion of women who marry. On the basis of data from the 1900 census and those from scattered special studies, it appears probable that they are not an important element in fertility differentials of the urban population. As between the agricultural and non-agricultural populations, however, both childlessness and the proportion married are important. Lorimer and Osborn indicate that had these factors been taken into account, their 1928 estimate of the net reproductive force of the agricultural population would have been 158 instead of 132 per cent of that of the non-agricultural population.

It is evident that much more must be known of the specific elements through which differences in the fertility of important groups arise before we can have any true understanding of the problem. Unfortunately this is not all. Our present knowledge of the differences themselves is far from precise. We should know their amounts more accurately, how much they vary from community to community and region to region, and how they are changing. More must be known of the influence of specific environmental situations on fertility. Most important of all, we must know much more of the origins and the attributes of the classes themselves.

Until these and many more problems can be solved, there can be no general agreement concerning the significance of differential fertility. Today, everyone who thinks about the matter at all agrees that the systematic recruiting of the nation's population from the working and agricultural classes may have an important bearing on the quality of the future population. Here agreement stops. Some view with alarm the failure of the most educated classes to reproduce. Others see with complacency the operation of a temporary adjustment, or the continuance of a time-honored relationship, depending on their reading of the available facts. Most students, however, look with an intense curiosity at a relationship so freighted with potentialities for our future culture and stock as to demand penetrating research rather than passing guesses.

PART FIVE

Race Versus Democracy

CHAPTER X

Race: Science and Prejudice

THE racial question in American society yields to no other problem its place as a primary source of embarrassment both at home and abroad. The contravention by racial discrimination of the values expressed in the American Credo is too obvious for any but the most encysted personalities to ignore. There are on all hands indications that those who visit these discriminations upon their fellow men are themselves upset by the inconsistency of their behavior. No study of the sources of order and change in American society can go forward without attention to an area of aggressive action serving as an outlet for some of the major sources of frustration in America. The readings on this problem are divided into four parts: (1) a statement of some of the basic fallacies and social usages of race; (2) the status of the Negro; (3) the status of the Spanish-American minority; and (4) the status of the Japanese-Americans in the United States in the last war.

The readings from the work of Dr. Ruth Benedict are presented in order to pose the problem set by the current racial discrimination and to expose briefly the invalid use of science to support the prejudices of men.

WHAT IS RACE? *

We may then ask: what is a race? In the first place, race designates a group of human beings set apart from others by one or more marks of physical difference. It is a taxonomic, zoölogical term and it is thus similar to such terms as variety, subspecies, species, genus. These terms designate groups of quite different inclusiveness. Thus we have the human race, the Caucasian race, the Caledonian race. But in all cases the word means a group of men set apart by certain physical traits implied in the qualifying

* Reprinted from THE RACIAL BASIS OF CIVILIZATION by Frank H. Hankins, by permission of Alfred A. Knopf, Inc. Copyright 1926 by Alfred A. Knopf, Inc. Pp. 262–270.

adjective. Thus when one speaks of the human race he means to set off all mankind as distinct in certain physical respects from the rest of the animal world. In this case the range of variability is very great and the elements found in common among all members of the group are general rather than specific. The terms Caucasian or Mongolian applied to races are likewise recognized as broad and general in nature. They call attention to certain obvious differences between some of the major ethnic stocks of mankind which include within themselves a variety of minor divisions. . . .

As Pritchard [1] said: "The different races of man are not distinguished from each other by strongly-marked and permanent distinctions. . . . All the diversities which exist are variable, and pass into each other by insensible gradations." Indeed, this same fact had been perceived by Blumenbach a generation earlier when he said: "The innumerable varieties of mankind run into one another by insensible degrees." Topinard [2] said: "Race in the present state of things is an abstract conception, a notion of continuity in discontinuity, of unity in diversity. It is the rehabilitation of a real, but directly unattainable thing." . . .

If we begin with the human race as the most inclusive group we can steadily narrow the number of individuals included and hence the range of variation by a more and more precise definition of requisite traits. If, for example, we add to the trait human, the trait white, or near-white, skin we set apart the Caucasian division. Let us add blond hair, and our group diminishes and the range narrows; if we add blue eyes, it contracts still further. It should be evident that we can go on adding traits of more and more specificity until we distinguish one stirps or kinship group from another; and in this we could set families off one from another; until, in the last analysis, we come to the individual, who is the only creature in the world like himself in all respects. We can thus arrange a series ranging down from Primates through humanity to such narrower groups as Caucasian, Nordic, Nordic varieties. and sub-varieties, or stirpes or clans and families to individuals. Such a series would be comparable to the zoologist's series: kingdom, phylum, class, order, genus, species, variety, individual.

The term race in the sense of a group with distinctive hereditary traits would apply to every category in such a series, except the last. Each category is included in the one which precedes it and to that extent bears

[1] *Natural History of Man*, 1885, p. 644.

[2] "De la notion de race en anthropologie," *Revue d'Anth.*, 1879, quoted by Ripley, *The Races of Europe*, pp. 111–112.

a fundamental resemblance to it; but each is also distinctive in possessing traits peculiar to itself. One may thus say that all men are human. . . . This would not be a denial of man's fundamental unity with the anthropoids but would emphasize his differences in certain respects. Similarly with each narrowing category. Hence one must beware of unconsciously assuming because all men are human that, therefore, their differences are negligible. There is probably no point of demarcation where the differences are negligible, even down to the individuals who represent the smallest possible sub-division. We may not, however, as yet be able to measure the significance for human affairs of some of these differences. It is thus apparent why the concept of race is so elusive. We can say only that, in its general meaning, the concept of race, first of all, includes the idea of distinctive hereditary traits.

In the second place, since the concept must allow for a certain variability among the members of the designated group, the two ideas of type and variation about the type become essential elements in the definition of race. If we think of a race as a group set apart by some *single* trait, as stature, these ideas may be represented in their simplest form by graphs for Japanese and American soldiers. The one group has a typical or average stature of 63.24 inches but varies in height from just under 56 inches to 69 inches; the other has an average stature of 67.51 inches and varies in height from under 62 inches to nearly 75 inches.

This simple illustration also serves to bring out the overlapping of races though the overlapping is here much less than will be found in most cases. If we had only stature to go by we should not be able to determine whether many of the individuals measured belonged to the taller or to the shorter race. This fact of overlapping constitutes, then, a third primary feature in our concept of race. . . . This is true of all the customary indices of racial difference, viz., stature, cephalic-index, hair-color, eye-color, skin-color, nasal-index, hair-form, alveolar-index, etc. As regards any one index, therefore, it is possible to arrange the types of man into a series with large overlapping areas so that it would be impossible to tell where one race ends or the next begins. This overlapping is primarily a consequence of the fact that all men may be traced back through hundreds of thousands of years to a common ancestral stem; in spite of their differentiation into varieties all men retain some combination of those traits which distinguish men from the other primates. The overlapping is due in part also to the universal tendency of all living things to vary about their own hereditary center. Thus Professor Jennings and his laboratory associates have shown that even in pure-line paramecia, bred from single individuals, there is a considerable variability, and a great deal of overlapping of strains nearest each other.[3]

It follows from this extensive overlapping of racial categories when only a single trait is measured, that we must combine a number of traits in order to distinguish one race from another. Even white and negro cannot be distinguished by stature or by cephalic index; even as regards skin-color and hair-form the border areas of distribution overlap. It is this overlapping that makes it necessary to think of a race as a complex of traits inherited together within a limited range of variability. Since tall shades into short, long into round, and dark into light, it must be shown that with tall stature are found also a certain head-form, eye-color, shape of hair, etc. But even with a combination of traits there is considerable difficulty in distinguishing one race from another in areas where the two have long been in contact with each other and produced intermediate types of varying degrees of composition.

And it is here that we come upon the central difficulty of race discrimination, namely, the fact that through geologic periods one human stem has crossed with another so that traits tend to spread widely from the center of their first specialization. In other words, as regards man, there is no such thing as a pure line in either modern or extinct races. There has always been a certain amount of cross-breeding, though among peoples living in great isolation, such as the extinct Tasmanians, this must have been slight. All peoples living in accessible, and especially all those living in fertile areas, have been so subject to immigration, war and conquest as well as wife stealing and other variations of matrimonial institutions as to make impossible the maintenance of racial purity in an unalloyed state. . . .

If Sir Arthur Keith[4] be correct in assuming that the human stem differentiated from the anthropoid stem about 2,000,000 years ago and that the fundamental types of modern men were differentiated from each other at least 400,000 years ago, there has been plenty of time for both race specialization and race crossing. White, Yellow, and Black—each during all this time has undergone mutation, variation and selection and varying degrees of geographic isolation for varying lengths of time. Groups have repeatedly split off from parent stems, undergone greater or less differentiation, and then crossed with other variates of the same general stock. Crosses have now been between closely related types and now between those widely

[3] See T. H. Morgan and others, *The Mechanism of Mendelian Heredity,* rev. ed. 1923; p. 284.

[4] *The Antiquity of Man,* London, rev. ed., 1925.

separated. They have taken the form sometimes of small infusions of alien elements, sometimes of large ones, and sometimes large, fairly heterogeneous groups have been absorbed into others. . . .

The result is that the populations found within any considerable geographical area will present a certain broad similarity which sets them off from the populations of other distant areas, as Africans from Europeans, Chinese or Hindus. But within each such area viewed by itself there is great diversity; these large areas may be broken up into smaller ones each showing a certain distinction from others, as is seen in the case of Europe where the south, northwest and east form more or less distinctive anthropological provinces. Then these provinces may be further sub-divided until one reaches those small and very special differences which distinguish the people of one mountain valley from their neighbors. Here again we see that the concept of race must vary constantly with the number of traits which are brought into consideration and the extent of their variation. . . .

And as we thus give definiteness and concreteness to the concept we meet with an increasing difficulty of finding perfect exemplars of it. Thus Ripley found that the European peoples were so mixed that any given combination of hair-color and eye-color would exclude two-thirds of the population in nearly every area. If to these two traits be added head-form, then only a small portion of the population in any European area would be found to combine all three traits. "Imagine a fourth trait, stature, or a fifth, nasal-index, to be added, and our proportion of pure types becomes almost infinitesimal." So that, when Ripley asked Ammon for a photograph of a pure Alpine type, the latter, although he had measured thousands of Rhenish recruits, replied that he had never found a specimen of the Alpine type perfect in all details. "All his round-headed men were either blond, or tall, or narrow-nosed, or something else they ought not to be." [5]

This means that when we define a race in terms of a series of physical traits we necessarily describe an idealized type. Thus the Baltic, Teutonic or Nordic race is said to have tall stature, long heads, narrow noses, clear blue, green or gray eyes and blond hair. All these traits are variable, even the blue eyes, though the range of variation is narrowly restricted in each case. If now, one studied the population of a presumably "Nordic" community he might begin by singling out all the tall people; among these he might select out those with long heads; and from among these in turn those with narrow noses, etc. He would end by having all those of his

[5] Ripley, *op cit.*, pp. 107–8.

assumed race, and they would be only a small fraction of those with whom he began. If now, these were judged by an exacting standard, such as is used in judging animals at the cattle show, an even smaller fraction of them, a truly infinitesimal portion of them, would exemplify the true or perfect type. It is much like the "average man" of common parlance. All of us represent him in some respect; many of us in more than one; but almost none, if any, of us represent him in all respects. He is purely ideal because so many variants of him are embodied in all sorts of persons.

In other words, when one speaks of a race he must bear in mind the following considerations. There is, first, the general fact of human variability. There is, secondly, the idea of type about which individual copies more or less inexact are grouped in a more or less regular manner. There is, thirdly, the overlapping with reference to any specific traits of the exemplars of one type and of related or contiguous types. This in itself would tend to prevent the easy separation of types but such is made immensely more difficult by the fact of race crossing. This brings it about, fourthly, that the determination of race types in any given area (except long isolated ones) becomes a process of the abstraction of traits from existing individuals and their recombination into a generalized or ideal type represented by few or no living individuals.

RACE CLASSIFICATION *

Granting that physical traits are important, it remains to be decided which trait is most important for purposes of classification; it is clear that the classifications will not be the same if, let us say, skin color is selected by one anthropologist and the shape of the head by another. Since there appears to be no objective way of deciding which trait is to be preferred, there are a great many different racial classifications, all of them equally subjective and equally arbitrary. . . .

Head shape is . . . made to unite the African and the North European, differing as to skin color, hair texture, nasal index and a host of other characteristics. On the other hand, if skin color is used as a criterion of race, there is very little difference between the North and the Central European, who differ markedly in cephalic index; the skin color of the Negro and the Australian is almost the same, but their hair texture is altogether dif-

* Klineberg, Otto, *Race Differences* (New York: Harper & Brothers, 1935), pp. 20, 22, 24–29.

ferent. If hair texture is used, the Australian and Mongolian belong together; but they differ in skin color, in the hairiness of the body, and in a great many other morphological features. It is hardly necessary to multiply instances of the discrepancies in the field of race classification. . . .

When it is said that the Scandinavian countries, for example, are Nordic, it is usually implied that almost all, if not all, Scandinavians are tall, blond and dolichocephalic. This is far from being the case. The Swedish anthropologist Retzius [1] found among recruits in the Swedish army only 11 per cent pure or "typical" Nordics. In another study using a somewhat less rigorous criterion, the figure was raised to 30 per cent. Even in a country like Sweden, which has frequently been described as 100 per cent Nordic, the typical Nordics still appear to be very much in the minority. The present writer had occasion in connection with a psychological investigation conducted in Europe some years ago [2] to visit certain regions which have been regarded as "purely" Nordic, Alpine and Mediterranean, respectively; he found only 20 to 25 per cent of boys between the ages of ten and twelve who conformed to the physical type supposedly predominating in their particular community. "Pure races," that is to say, populations all the members of which are of the same physical type, are occasionally found in small inbred communities (Boas [3]), but not as constituting any of the existing European nations. To preach in favor of race purity, as has been done so often in recent times, is therefore just anthropological nonsense. It is many thousands of years too late, not only for Europe and Europeans, but for other parts of the world as well; there are no longer any pure races to be kept pure.

It may be, however, that this whole manner of stating the problem is a misleading one. The relative rarity of pure racial types may be due to countless generations of race mixture; it may also be due to the fact that the pure race never existed in the form in which it has been described by the anthropologist. The type may be an entirely artificial creation, introduced for purposes of classification, but with little or no basis in reality. If we compare Swedes and Bavarians, we find the former to be on the average taller, fairer and more long-headed; if now we combine these three characteristics of tallness, blondness and dolichocephaly into a "type" or "race" and assume that originally it was a pure race, every member of which showed this same combination of characteristics, we are definitely

[1] Retzius, G., and Fürst, C. M., *Anthropologia suecica,* Stockholm, 1902.

[2] Klineberg, O. "A Study of Psychological Differences between Racial and National Groups in Europe." *Arch. Psych.,* No. 132: 1931.

[3] Boas, F. *Anthropology and Modern Life,* New York, 1928.

going beyond the evidence. We have no way of knowing whether such a homogeneous group ever existed.

RACE AND NATION

It follows from the above that to assume any sort of identity between race and nation is clearly unjustified. Race is a zoological concept; it refers to physical type; nation is a political concept implying boundaries and an independent government. The absurdity of identifying the two is clearest in the case of the American "melting pot" nations, each with an almost boundless heterogeneity of physical characteristics. Similarly among the European nations, it is at once clear that the political boundaries have nothing to do with physical type. References to a French or German or Italian race are meaningless. . . .

RACE AND LANGUAGE

There is even more confusion between race and language, and many terms which properly apply only to language have been used as if they had also a racial connotation. It is wrong, for example, to speak of a "Latin" race, in spite of the frequency with which that phrase appears in popular literature. Latin is of course a language, and "Latins" can mean only those groups whose languages are of Latin origin—among others, the French, Italians, Spaniards, Portuguese and Roumanians. Of these, the Spaniards and Portuguese are mostly Mediterranean in type, Roumanians are largely Alpine, Italians are partly Alpine and partly Mediterranean, and the French are a mixture of all three European types, with the Alpine predominating. Clearly, there is no race or physical type to which all Latins may be said to belong.

The term "Aryan" as applied to race is also meaningless. Students of linguistic science have given the name Aryan to the parent language from which most European languages presumably developed. Aryans, then, would be the people who speak a language derived from the original Aryan or Indo-European; if such a language is spoken by Negroes or Polynesians, they too may legitimately be called by that name. If it is preferred to restrict the term to those who were the first to use an Aryan language, it is still impossible to give it a precise racial significance, for no one knows to what physical type these original Aryans belonged. Max Müller, [4, 5] who

[4] Müller, M. *Lectures on the Science of Language.* London, 1864.

[5] Müller, M. *Biographies of Words and the Home of the Aryas.* London, 1888.

at one time believed that one could speak of the Aryans as a race, later realized his error, and gave it as his opinion that an ethnologist who speaks of Aryan race, Aryan blood, Aryan eyes and hair, is as great a sinner as a linguist who speaks of a dolichocephalic dictionary or a brachycephalic grammar. Dolichocephaly refers to physical type, and Aryan to language; the two categories require to be kept separate. It need hardly be added that the recent agitation in favor of preserving the purity of the Aryan race and rigidly excluding all non-Aryans has no foundation in anthropology.

There is no "Semitic" race; when Arabs and Jews are described as Semites, all that can legitimately be meant is that Arabic and Hebrew both belong to a group of languages known as Semitic. As to physical type, Arabs are predominantly Mediterranean. Many Jews belong to the same general type, but these are definitely in the minority; if there is any one type which occurs more frequently than another, it is the Alpine. There is clearly no one physical type which can be described as Semitic. As far as the Jews are concerned, a very large number of investigations have revealed so much variability in physical type, with skin color ranging from very blond to very dark, and cephalic index from extreme dolichocephaly to extreme brachycephaly, that almost all anthropologists (with the exception of those whose views are influenced by purely political considerations) agree that a distinctively "Jewish race" does not exist. In every country there seems to be a clearly marked tendency for Jews to approximate the physical type of the people among whom they live. Presumably distinctive Jewish characteristics, like the "Jewish" nose, are relatively rare, and, in any case, are probably due to intermixture with groups which were originally not Jewish. (See Ripley,[6] Dixon,[7] Fishberg.[8])

WHY THEN RACE PREJUDICE? *

As we have seen, all scientific knowledge of race contradicts the idea that human progress has been the work of one race alone or can safely be entrusted to a program of racial hygiene in the future. No great civilization has been the work of a pure race, and neither history nor psychology,

[6] Ripley, W. Z. *The Races of Europe.* New York, 1899.
[7] Dixon, R. B. *The Racial History of Man.* New York, 1923.
[8] Fishberg, M. *The Jews: A Study of Race and Environment.* New York, 1911.
* From *Race: Science and Politics,* by Ruth Benedict. Copyright 1940, 1943, 1945 by Ruth Benedict. Reprinted by permission of the Viking Press, Inc., New York. Pp. 140–162.

biology nor anthropology can render decisions about the future destiny of any present human breed. Racism has been a travesty of scientific knowledge and has served consistently as special pleading for the supremacy of any group, either class or nation, to which the pleader himself belonged and in whose permanent place in the sun he desired to believe.

Why then does racism have such social importance in our times? No discussion of race and racism can be complete without raising this problem; it is the really burning question, for upon our answer depend the measures we can trust to bring about a cure.

In answering this question we do not need to depend on fine-spun theories or self-communings; history has given the answers many times. We need only to obtain a little perspective. We have seen that racist dogmas as they are stated today are modern. But they express an old human obsession and only the "reasons why" have been altered. This old human obsession is that my group is uniquely valuable and, if it is weakened, all valuable things will perish. It were better therefore that a million perish than that one jot or tittle of that unique value should be lost. It becomes my divine mission to extirpate the challenger in whatever field.

The fields change, however. When one field has been won and tolerance and co-operativeness established in what was before an armed camp, we look back upon the episode as an example of human aberration. We think we are different and feel that progress has really been achieved—until other generations arise to look back upon us and decide that we have only shifted mutual intolerance to another area of life. For centuries the battlefield was religion. The Inquisition was not pure barbarism; it was the claim to unique value worked out with all its implications in a field where today we are willing to follow the precept of live and let live. We cannot see racism in perspective without reviewing the occasions and consequences of this earlier arrogance. The fact that it is in the field of religion instead of in the field of race is a reflection of the times; from every other point of view religious persecutions duplicate one another. Their proponents claimed similar sacred missions; they killed and looted and temporarily enriched themselves. From the standpoint of history both set up false fronts that served political purposes; they destroyed brilliant civilizations. In that one matter in which they differ, religion as over against race, the earlier persecution was at least as justified as the latter. The medieval world, convinced that man's existence was an infinitesimal episode in his everlasting life, thought it was common humanity to kill the Antichrist that would lead thousands of souls to damnation. Today we judge this a fallacy, but we must not under-estimate the worthy motives of those who believed that they alone had received the divine command; they were not actuated solely by arrogance but by their duty to keep the world faithful to the word of God and to ensure salvation to as many souls as possible. In many churchmen this must have been a worthy emotion, just as today we recognize that patriotism or pride of class is a worthy emotion. However, the judgment of history is that, when either of these worthy emotions is carried into a campaign of extermination of all who belong in other camps, the exterminators suffer with the exterminated and the result is social tragedy.

It was so in the Inquisition. Between 1200 and 1250 the Roman Church was at the apex of its political and temporal power, and these were the great years of the Inquisition. Heresy hunting was, like Jew-baiting in this decade in Germany, an eruption of minority persecution. It held out the same short-range advantages to the persecutors; it could be used as a front for political purposes; the confiscation of the victims' property enriched the persecutors; and the campaign of hate distracted attention from real issues. The real issues, as they appear in the perspective of history, were two. The first was the issue of freedom of conscience, a freedom which all the tortures of the Inquisition were powerless to uproot and which eventually triumphed in spite of bishops and of kings. The second was the worldliness and in some cases the corruption of the Catholic clergy of the period. Even in the highest Council of the Church itself this had been for some time a grave issue, and under Hildebrand (Gregory the Great) and the monk Bernard of Clairvaux there had been valiant efforts toward reform. The times, however, were not auspicious, and the heretics took up the cry of licentiousness against the Church. In stamping out the heretics, the Church embarked upon a campaign of extirpation that absorbed the attention of the faithful and postponed reform in its own ranks.

As a front for political purposes the Inquisition was used in southern France to break the opposition to the growing power of the Capetian kings, and in Florence its terrible severities under Fra Ruggieri crushed also the Ghibelline revolt. Wherever the Inquisition flourished—in France, in Italy, and in Spain—it made common cause with power politics. The full extent of this common cause depended upon the practice of confiscating the heretics' property. The Inquisition is linked in popular thought with the burning of heretics and the use of torture to obtain confessions, but the confiscation of property was sociologically more important. Originally such property confiscated by the Inquisition belonged not to the Church but to the kings and secular rulers; the right of the Papacy, and hence of the Inquisitors, to a share of these riches was not accepted until almost 1250, and the lion's share went always to secular authorities. Heresy hunting was profitable, and all those who sought riches and power eagerly took advantage of the opportunity, masking their satisfactions behind the dogma that the heretics were guilty of treason against the Almighty.

The most celebrated campaign of the Inquisition "in the name of God" was against the heretics of southern France in the first half of the thirteenth century. These heretics were known as the Albigenses and their home in Provence was a region on which the Roman Church had a comparatively small hold. In those days Provence had little in common with northern France, and her barons were not vassals of the French king. The house of Toulouse in southern France had had an especially brilliant history. For two centuries its court had been famous for its love of art and literature, for its wealth and gallantry, and it had established its sovereignty throughout half of Provence. Its cities were the most wealthy and independent in all of France, and their culture was greatly influenced by interchange of goods and ideas with the Saracens of Palestine and the Moors of Spain—cultures in many ways more enlightened than any others in the Western World at that time.

The heresy of the Albigenses was one of the many medieval cults of Manichaeism which taught the strictest asceticism in order that man might free himself from original evil. Manichaean cosmology was an all-embracing dualism of good and evil, of light and darkness, and only eating the light contained in plants and by eschewing the darkness in meat, only by eliminating the darkness of sensual acts, could righteousness be achieved. "Finished" ascetics, as in many Oriental religions, became divinities and objects of worship to the laity. The dualism of these heresies was simple to grasp and offered an explanation of the evils of the world which had a strong appeal in those troubled times. But we know little of the teachings of the Albigensian sect; most of our knowledge is of their protest against the corruption of the contemporary clergy of the Church. Though Provence lay between great Catholic strongholds to the south and to the north, within its territories the Church was weak; the roots of Provençal culture were not in Rome. The rising burgher class in the towns especially espoused the heresy, and the growing independence of this class made the threat increasingly serious to the Church which was then at the height of its temporal power. The Papacy ordered the faithful clergy of northern France to preach a campaign of extermination against heretical Provence, and the crusade became one of the most implacable of religious wars. Its conclusion established the Capetian kings of northern France as monarchs in Provence after mass executions had decimated the independent burghers of the cities and had destroyed the civilization that had flourished in southern France. The burning of heretics continued for a hundred years, and at last the cult was exterminated.

The Inquisition did not survive into the modern period, but religious persecution did. One of the longest and most disastrous of these conflicts occurred in France in the sixteenth and seventeenth centuries. French Protestants of that time were called Huguenots; by the middle of the sixteenth century they had grown greatly in numbers. Like the Albigensian heretics they were mainly prosperous bourgeois, and the bourgeois of the sixteenth century were opposed to concentration of power in the hands of the French kings. The bloody wars of a generation (1562–1593) were fought in the name of religion, but they masked a conflict which was in great part economic and political. After the renegade Huguenot leader, Henry of Navarre, was crowned king of France as Henry IV in 1594, the Edict of Nantes proclaimed full civil rights for the Protestants without withdrawing these from the Catholics. It was a signal victory. The law of the land now guaranteed religious and political freedom but, as has happened before and since that time, conflict continued. The Crown was Catholic and the Catholic clergy never accepted the Edict of Nantes. Cardinal Richelieu was the greatest power in France; he was both Cardinal and member of the royal council. His domestic policy was to concentrate power in the hands of the king, and to this the Huguenots were opposed. Therefore his internal policy was dominated by his ruthless opposition to the Huguenots, whom he could persecute in the name of religion. Louis XIV, after the death of Richelieu, exercised these royal powers to the full; his dream of absolute monarchy could be realized only if the Huguenots were removed. He carried on a legal persecution, discriminating against them in the exercise of their religion and their civil rights, and the terrible dragonnades used torture to compel their acceptance of the "king's religion." It was then, in 1685, that Louis XIV revoked the Edict of Nantes, declaring it was now unnecessary since all his subjects were Catholics. The Protestants emigrated or were sent to the galleys. His act left Louis absolute monarch and enriched his coffers with the expropriated wealth of the Huguenots. It also bled France of more than 400,000 of its inhabitants, intelligent and courageous people who enriched with their abilities the countries which received them.

The Albigensian crusade and the expulsion of the Huguenots are only two high spots in the long story of the suppression of minority groups before the rise of racism.

This suppression of minorities has been continued in the persecutions and nationalistic wars of the twentieth century. In the thirteenth century and in the sixteenth, as in the world today, new economic and social necessities were starting new ferments. Groups arose which opposed some aspect of the old order. The party in power answered by using torment, death, and confiscation of property. Parties in power can always do this, but in the eyes of history these suppressions have puchased an empty triumph. The great period of the Inquisition marked the downward-turning point in the temporal power of the Church no less than the ruin of Provençal civilization, and the Huguenot expulsion gave France only the disastrous and temporary splendor of the reign of Louis XIV. Persecution stopped neither the growing demand for freedom of conscience nor the rise of the bourgeoisie.

For a theory of racism there are two conclusions to be drawn from the whole matter. The first is that, in order to understand race persecution, we do not need to investigate race; we need to investigate persecution. Persecution was an old, old story before racism was thought of. Social change is inevitable, and it is always fought by those whose ties are to the old order. These ties may be economic or they may be religious, as in medieval Europe, or those of social affiliation, as with Roman patricians. Those who have these ties will consciously or unconsciously ferret out reasons for believing that their group is supremely valuable and that the new claimants threaten the achievements of civilization. They will raise a cry of rights of inheritance or divine right of kings or religious orthodoxy or racial purity or manifest destiny. These cries reflect the temporary conditions of the moment, and all the efforts of the slogan-makers need not convince us that any one of them is based on eternal verities. The battle cries of Nordicism belong with "Keep Cool with Coolidge" and "He Kept Us Out of War" of American presidential campaigns, and with slight changes in social necessities they will be as evanescent. All slogans are useful in the degree to which they express the faiths and discontents of the hour. Religious varieties were politically useful in eras and regions which had powerful religious interests; when these were overshadowed by secular privileges and when cleavages along religious lines became less important, religious slogans no longer justified the persecution of minorities as they had in earlier days.

Racial slogans serve the same purpose in the present century that religious slogans served before, that is, they are used to justify persecution in the interests of some class or nation. This racial slogan is peculiarly congenial to our times. Science is a word to conjure with in this century; unfortunately it is often used to conjure. It is not alone racism that has turned to so-called science for its arguments. A manufacturer of cosmetics conducted not long ago an investigation of various advertisements of his wares. He found that the two words which had most sales-appeal were "immediately" and "scientific." Every rouge, every face powder must claim a "scientific" uniqueness, and by this ballyhoo millions are impressed. It was the same with fake medicines, with drug-store drinks, and with health foods until it became necessary to defend the public by federal supervision of manufacturers' claims. The slogan of "science" will sell most things today, and it sells persecution as easily as it sells rouge. The scientist repeatedly points out that the advertised rouge is indistinguishable from others or even that he has found it especially harmful in a laboratory test; he points out that no race has a monopoly of abilities or of virtues and that, as science, the racists' claims have no validity. For the scientist, science is a body of knowledge; he resents its use as a body of magic. But he knows that scientific is the word our civilization conjures with—in no matter what cause.

The choice of racial slogans to justify conflict is rooted in still another manner in the conditions of the modern age. Racial reasons for persecution are convenient just because in Western civilization today so many different breeds live in close contact with one another. The racist cries are raised not because those who raise them have any claim to belong to pure races, but because they do not; in other words, because today several ethnic groups occupy one city or one state, or states that share in one civilization are engaged in nationalistic wars. Hence comes the paradox that has been so often pointed out: that it is the most mongrel peoples of the world who raise the war cry of racial purity. From the point of view of race, this makes nonsense, but from the point of view of persecution it is inevitable. No group raises battle cries against people whose existence is of no moment to it; for conflict to arise, there must first be contact. Racial slogans arose therefore in Europe in class and national conflicts. The old religious slogans for persecution had lost their hold, and the racists evolved in their stead a bastard version of contemporary science. Racism remains in the eyes of history, however, merely another instance of the persecution of minorities for the advantage of those in power.

Once we have recognized that race conflict is only the justification of the persecution that is popular at the moment, the strangest paradox in all racist theory becomes clear. The racists have over and over again derived race prejudice from a race repulsion instinctive in mankind, and historians and biologists and anthropologists have as repetitiously pointed out that such a theory is impossible in view of the universal mixture of races. "Why, if Nature abhors race-crossing, does she do so much of it?" But repulsion to inter-marriage accompanies any conflict of two groups, however the groups may be defined. They need not be racial. The patricians of Rome recoiled from marriage with plebeians in the same way, the Catholics of France from marriage with the Huguenots. It is not that man has a set of instincts which make only his own race sexually attractive, but that in-groups are unwilling to give status to the outsider. They do not want to share prerogatives with him. If this in-group is defined racially as Anglo-Saxons have defined it in their contact with native peoples of the world, their desire to maintain the in-group will bring about selective mating in marriage, but it notoriously does not prevent mating outside of marriage. The great numbers of half-castes in India and mulattoes in America are testimony to the fact that the antipathy is not instinctive aversion to members of another race.

Those theorists also who have explained race prejudice by visible racial differences are similarly confused. They have said that race prejudice is caused by obvious and striking contrasts in face and color. They are, however, mistaking a momentary feature of persecution for a causal one. There was no differentiating skin color or nose shape in a Huguenot, or in the Albigensian victims of the Inquisition. On the other side of the picture, poverty sets groups as visibly apart as the color of their hair or the shape of their heads. Groups may be set apart by any number of things besides race—by whether they go to Mass or by whether they drop their h's. Members of a primitive tribe have been known to kill at sight members of a neighboring tribe of the same race and language because they felt that the way they carried their burden baskets was an insult to human beings. Not the fact of "visibility" of skin color but the fact that racial characteristics are transmitted over so many generations makes racial prejudice a new problem in the world. A man can stop going to Mass or a Huguenot can take the sacrament because "Paris is worth a Mass" or the heroine of Pygmalion learn to enunciate her mother tongue in the Oxford fashion, but too dark a Negro cannot "pass" and not even his children's children may be born light enough to do so. This is a problem of relative permanence of distinctions, not specifically of "visibility." In the long course of history persecution has been now more, now less intense; but these variations do not correlate with the presence or absence of racial visibility.

Mistaken explanations of the nature of race prejudice are of minor importance so long as they are concerned with theoretical points like instinctive antipathies or the role of racial visibility. There is a far more important issue. The fact that to understand race conflict we need fundamentally to understand conflict and not race, means something much more drastic. It means that all the deep-seated causes of conflict in any group or between groups are involved in any outbreak of race prejudice. Race will be cried up today in a situation where formerly religion would have been cried up. If civilized men expect to end prejudice—whether religious or racial—they will have to remedy major social abuses, in no way connected with religion or race, to the common advantage. Whatever reduces conflict, curtails irresponsible power, and allows people to obtain a decent livelihood will reduce race conflict. Nothing less will accomplish the task.

For the friction is not primarily racial. We all know what the galling frictions are in the world today: nationalistic rivalries, desperate defense of the status quo by the haves, desperate attacks by the have-nots, poverty, unemployment, and war. Desperate men easily seize upon some scapegoat to sacrifice to their unhappiness; it is a kind of magic by which they feel for the moment that they have laid the misery that has been tormenting them. In this they are actively encouraged by their rulers and exploiters, who like to see them occupied with this violence, and fear that if it were denied them they might demand something more difficult. So Hitler, when his armament program cut consumers' goods and increased hours of work and lowered real wages, exhorted the nation in 1938 to believe that Germany's defeat in 1919 had been due to Jewry, and encouraged racial riots. And this served two purposes: It gave an undernourished people an outlet harmless to the government, and it allowed the government treasury to appropriate to itself the wealth of the Jews.

In this sequence of events the Third Reich is but following a long series of precedents in European anti-Semitism. During the Middle Ages persecutions of the Jews, like all medieval persecutions, were religious rather than racial. Intermarriage between Jews and Gentiles was condemned, not as a racist measure, but in the same manner as marriages between Catholics and heretics were condemned. The pogroms of the time of the Crusades were carried out by stay-at-home mobs imitating the Crusaders in avenging the death of Christ; the mobs killed Jews, the Crusaders fought the Arabs and Turks. The link between Jews and Turks was not racial; in the period of the Crusades the two were equated because the first had crucified Christ and the second owned his tomb. Nor were persecutions other than those set in motion by the Crusaders directed toward eliminating a racial breed; apostate Jews purchased safety. A renegade Jew denounced or concealed his religion, not his race. The Popes and rulers favorable to the Jews promulgated laws directing that "they should not be baptized by force, constrained to observe Christian festivals nor to wear badges." Even up to the First World War some German racists advocated as the cure for conflict, not extinction of the Jewish race, but a racial merger. This was especially true of the great nationalist historian Treitschke, who was one of Germany's foremost advocates of racist salvation at the turn of this century.

As racist persecutions replaced religious persecutions in Europe, however, the inferiority of the Jew became that of race. By the 1800's a tidal wave of pogroms and persecutions swept over large parts of Europe. To the people it everywhere appeared that the bourgeoisie were in the saddle, and the Jews, owing to earlier segregation in city ghettos and to restrictions against land-owning, were all bourgeoisie. They were hated for this reason, and persecution was reinforced by the old tradition of religious animosity against the Jews. Racial anti-Semitism was all too easy to arouse. In Germany in the eighties an anti-Semitic demagogue of evil repute was cynically encouraged by members of the Conservative Party in order to strengthen with his following their opposition to the Social Democrats; synagogues were burned and violence against the Jews went unpunished. The charge of Jewish ritual murder was revived. In France, the anti-Semitic movement came to a climax in the 1890's with the famous Dreyfus affair. It marks probably the climax of prewar anti-Semitism in Europe. The reactionary party was most strongly represented in the Army, and the "framing" of a prominent Jewish staff officer, Captain Alfred Dreyfus, and his conviction of treason on forged evidence, were the occasion for a year-long conflict that rocked the nation. To the honor of France, the plot was laid bare, Dreyfus was exonerated, and it was shown that those who were really guilty of the treason had attempted to hide themselves behind a Jew because of popular anti-Semitism.

The more closely one studies European anti-Semitism in its modern racial guise, the less it appears that the conflict is racial; it is the old problem of unequal citizenship rights. Whenever one group, whether industrial workers or a religious sect or a racial group, is discriminated against before the law or in equal claims to life, liberty, and jobs, there will always be powerful interests to capitalize on this fact and to divert violence from those responsible for these conditions into channels where it is relatively safe to allow. In the case of the Jews we inherit from the old era of religious persecution all the necessary shibboleths of hate, and these are easily turned to account in a new setting. In addition there is exceptional profit; unlike most discriminated-against minorities, the Jews often provide rich contraband and are therefore marked objects for persecution to a poverty-stricken government or populace.

The cure for anti-Semitism, therefore, logically lies, as in all minority conflicts, in the extension to all men of full citizenship rights and of full opportunity to make good in any field. There would have been no Dreyfus case if certain traitors had not felt that a framed Jew would be found guilty by the courts. There would have been no nationwide pogroms in Germany in 1938 if all those who took part in them had known the state would hold them accountable. It is not only for the sake of the persecuted that the full rights of minorities need to be maintained. The minorities may be only martyrs, but the persecutors revert to savagery. If we are unwilling or unable to pay the price of equality in human rights, we, the persecutors, suffer brutalization in ourselves whenever we fall into the trap set for us.

The case of the Negro since the Civil War in America points the same social lesson. The only trustworthy objective in any color-line program is the ultimate elimination of legal, educational, economic, and social discriminations. The fact that such elimination is not accepted even as an ultimate objective in most parts of the South is due to the persistence of slave-owner attitudes on the one hand and, on the other, to the degrading conditions under which great numbers of Negroes have lived in the United States. Granted that great numbers of Negroes are not ready for full citizenship, the social conditions which perpetuate their poverty and ignorance must be remedied before anyone can judge what kind of citizens they might be in other, more favorable circumstances. To be able to live a decent life and be respected for it, without being subjected to a blanket damnation that one's personal life cannot remove, is a human right, the granting of which would have immense social repercussions.

In periods and places where social institutions have made this possible for the Negro in the New World, the results have been incomparably better than those in the United States since the Civil War. Lord Bryce, an excellent observer, said of Brazil: "Brazil is the one country in the world, besides the Portuguese colonies on the east and west coasts of Africa, in which a fusion of the European and African races is proceeding unchecked by law or custom. The doctrines of human equality and human solidarity have here their perfect work. The work is so far satisfactory that there is little or no class friction. The white man does not lynch or maltreat the Negro; indeed I have never heard of a lynching anywhere in South America except occasionally as a part of a political convulsion. The Negro is not accused of insolence and does not seem to develop any more criminality than naturally belongs to any ignorant population with loose notions of morality and property. What ultimate effect the intermixture of blood will have on the European element in Brazil I will not venture to predict. If one may judge from a few remarkable cases it will not necessarily reduce the intellectual standard."

Such conditions were possible in Brazil only because of the extreme lack of racial discrimination which the Portuguese everywhere showed in their post-Columbian colonization; with the growing influence of non-Portuguese cultures in modern Brazil, the Negro has to some extent suffered. With growing discrimination against his race, the usual effects have followed, small though these consequences are in Brazil in comparison with the United States. But while discrimination was at a minimum, the social results were good.

To minimize racial persecution, therefore, it is necessary to minimize conditions which lead to persecution; it is not necessary to minimize race. Race is not in itself the source of the conflict. Conflict arises whenever any group—in this case, a race—is forged into a class by discriminations practiced against it; the race then becomes a minority which is denied rights to protection before the law, rights to livelihood and to participation in the common life. The social problem does not differ whether such a group is racially distinguished or whether it is not; in either case the healthy social objective is to do away with minority discriminations.

We are so far from doing this in the modern world that it is likely to seem a program impossible of achievement. Even so, this is not the total program for a world free of race conflict. It is not enough merely to legislate human rights for the minorities. The majorities, also—the persecutors—must have solid basis for confidence in their own opportunity to live in security and decency. Otherwise, whatever the laws, whatever the guarantees, they will find out a victim and sacrifice him as a scapegoat to their despair. Everything that is done in any nation to eliminate unemployment, to raise the standard of living, to ensure civil liberties, is a step in the elimination of race conflict. Whatever is done to fasten fear upon the people of a nation, to humiliate individuals, to abrogate civil liberties, to deny coveted opportunities, breeds increased conflict. Men have not, for all their progress in civilization, outgrown the hen yard; a hen who is pecked at by a cock attacks, not the cock, but a weaker hen; this weaker hen attacks a still weaker, and so on down to the last chicken. Man too has his "pecking order," and those who have been victims, even though they belong to the "superior race," will require victims.

The truth of the matter is that these two aspects of a program for preventing the ravages of racism—democratic opportunity for the privileged and for the underprivileged—cannot be separated from one another. They are web and woof. One of the great political advantages of racist slogans is that the underprivileged may use them. Therefore the unemployed and the low-income groups can vent, through this alleged racist "superiority," the hatred that is engendered by their fear and insecurity. Studies in America have many times shown that anti-Semitism is strongest among low-income groups and that the high peaks of racial persecution have coincided with the low troughs of depression periods. While we raise Negro standards of living, of health, and of education in the South, therefore, it is necessary also to raise the standards of the Southern poor whites. Until we have "made democracy work" so that the nation's full manpower is drafted for its common benefit, racist persecution will continue in America. Until housing and conditions of labor are raised above the needlessly low standards which prevail in many sections of the country, scapegoats of some sort will be sacrificed to poverty. Until the regulation of industry has enforced the practice of social responsibility, there will be exploitation of the most helpless racial groups, and this will be justified by racist denunciations.

Hard-boiled economists and statesmen recognize today the shortsightedness of policies which allow such conditions to continue and to become intensified. Those who fight to perpetuate them are repeating the errors of the Albigensian crusade and the Huguenot expulsion; they are gaining a false and temporary advantage at the expense of their own permanent welfare. National prosperity, however thin you cut it, has two surfaces: ability to sell means ability to buy; employment means production. Whatever groups battle with each other, under conditions of modern industry and finance, the most important condition of either one's getting more is that the other shall also get more. Since their conflict is truly suicidal, it is necessary for the benefit of the contestants themselves that far-sighted regulations should be imposed on both parties.

In the last decade we have grown to recognize much more fully the responsibility that rests on the state for achieving satisfactory national conditions, and from the standpoint of history it is likely that this role of the state will in the long run be extended rather than curtailed. A democratic state, when it lives up to its minimum definition at all, is the one institution which represents all the parts of the body politic. It can propose for itself programs which will eventually benefit the whole body. It is hard to see how this responsibility for the whole can be taken today except by the national government, and in the past decade state regulation has increased, national treasuries all over the Western World have been opened for the relief of the unemployed, and compulsory old-age insurance is in operation in many nations. These and other national undertakings can be used to minimize economic discrimination. Equality in the matter of civil liberties is closely bound up with such programs, and so long as civil liberties are made more, rather than less, equal for different groups, there is no historical reason for fearing the increased role of the state. For the true goal in any program for a better America is that all men may be able to live so that self-respect is possible and so that they may have confidence that prosperity will spread its benefits widely over the population.

The cultural anthropologist has the best reason in the world to know that conflict is eliminated only as men work together for common benefits, and obtain them in common. In most of the tribes the anthropologist knows, he can study side by side two different codes of ethics: one is that of open-handed hospitality and liberality and sharing, along with condemnation of aggressions like stealing and murder; the other is death at sight, torture, and the exaltation of robbery. The first code a man applies to those whose economic and social activities benefit him; these form an in-group within which none but moral reprobates are penalized. No matter who is successful in the hunt, the whole in-group benefits; any special skills any man may possess are an asset to the group as a whole. The priests conduct ceremonies for the good of the tribe and for common advantages like increase of plants and animals; warriors defend the little group against predatory outsiders. The second code a man applies to tribes with whom his tribe makes no common cause. No activities of theirs feed or house or bless or defend him. They are outside the pale. It is only a question of whether he kills his enemies first or they kill him.

The in-group code of ethics arises, however, only as the institutions of a society provide for shared advantages. When increase of food supply is not a common benefit, but something one man must get at the expense of another; when supernatural power is not used for general blessings, like rain, which falls on all, but for charms to use for personal ends against a neighbor; when legal or economic or political institutions put one man at the mercy of his neighbors, persecution develops. The gain or loss of all men is no longer my own gain or loss and the tribe is no longer a unit within which in-group ethics operate. The persecution that develops is most often sorcery. Sorcery is a very evil thing and when society does not officially punish it the victim has no redress. Unchecked sorcery societies are like modern nations with Ogpus and Gestapos, and they act out in deeds Hitler's dictum: "We need hatred, hatred, and then more than hatred."

In-group ethics is therefore a reflection of the fact that all members share in their tribal enterprises and do actually profit from one another's activities. In-group mutual support is as native to the human race as out-group hostility; it is not something precarious and achieved only by isolated individuals at the end of a long social evolution. It arose long before the higher ethical religions with their teachings of altruism and duty. It occurs automatically whenever the social order makes it advantageous. It is at home among the lowest savages, and the one essential contribution modern civilization has made has been to enlarge the size of the in-group. In this there has been incomparable progress. Millions today recognize their common cause as citizens of a great nation, or as members of a party, or as financiers, or as workers, whereas in past history some little territory might be divided into a dozen hostile groups recognizing no common bonds. Today the increasing complexity of the processes of production, the ease of transportation, the interdependence of financial systems have brought it about that people in the remotest part of civilization suffer from catastrophe in another part.

The very progress of civilization, therefore, has laid the foundation for a vast extension of in-group mutual dependency and mutual support. Mankind has not yet adjusted its institutions to the real requirements of the world it has created, and this cultural lag today threatens the very bases of international life. Many serious students of human affairs have been driven to despair. The world of our fathers, they conclude, has been destroyed because it tried to ignore the real facts of human nature; it tried to impose a peaceful social order on a predatory animal. The lesson we should learn from recent events, they say, is that man is by nature a beast of prey who will always tear and rend his weaker neighbors; we must recognize that wars and racial persecutions are inevitable in human destiny. To the anthropologist such a counsel of despair is demonstrably false. In-group ethics are as "innate" as out group ethics, but they occur only when certain social conditions are fufilled. We cannot get in-group ethics without meeting those conditions. In our own country this means that a better America will be one which benefits not some groups alone but all citizens; so long as there is starvation and joblessness in the midst of abundance we are inviting the deluge. To avert it, we must "strongly resolve" that all men shall have the basic opportunity to work and to earn a living wage, that education and health and decent shelter shall be available to all, that regardless of race, creed, or color, civil liberties shall be protected.

The elimination of race conflict is a task of social engineering. But what of education? It is often said that our school systems must make themselves responsible for ending race prejudice, and attempts have been made to achieve tolerance by special instruction. This is of great importance, but we should be quite clear about the limits of its effectiveness; otherwise, in the end we shall cry that we were betrayed because it has not succeeded. All education, whether of children or of adults, is important and necessary because it makes for an enlightened mind and for unbiased impulses.

These are essential because without them discriminations may not be done away with at all and barriers to opportunity may never be thrown down. But good impulses are socially effective only when they have accomplished these results. "Hell is paved with good intentions"—intentions which were blindly regarded as ends in themselves and not as mere preliminaries. This is a platitude, but one which is often forgotten in discussions of the role of our schools in racial matters. If we are to make good use of the great powers of education in combating racism, two goals should be kept clearly distinct. On the one hand, it is desirable to teach in the regular social studies the facts of race and of the share of different races in our civilization. On the other hand, it is necessary to hold up ideals of a functioning democracy; it is necessary to help children to understand the mutual inter-dependence of different groups; it is necessary to encourage comparison of our social conditions with conditions which are better than ours as well as with those that are worse. It is necessary that they should be taught to think of unsatisfactory conditions not as inescapable facts of Nature, but as ones which with effort can be done away with. Only through such education can school instruction lay the basis for the amelioration of race conflict. We cannot trust to teaching them about the glories of Chinese civilization or the scientific achievements of the Jews. That is worth doing, but if we leave it at that and expect them to become racially tolerant we have deceived ourselves. The fatal flaw in most arguments which would leave to the schools the elimination of race conflict is that they propose education instead of social engineering. Nothing but hypocrisy can come of such a program.

The program that will avail against racism is called today "making democracy work." In so far as it is achieved in America it will produce the kind of behavior it has always produced in a mutually supporting in-group. Change, we must recognize, is always difficult and produces dislocations. But if we know the direction in which we must move, we can resolve to pay the necessary costs of change. The Arabians have a proverb " 'What will you have?' said the Prophet, 'take it and pay for it.' " We must pay for a democracy that works, but fortunately in this case we can reassure ourselves with the knowledge that, even in financial accounting, government investments in rehousing and rebuilding America, in soil conservation, in health and education, and in increasing the nation's purchasing power through insurance benefits, pay their own way with handsome returns. A price is exacted also for a social order like Nazi Germany, and that price, in lowered standard of living, in brutalization, in denial of human rights, in sabotage of science and the intellectual life, is higher than any costs of democracy. In persecuting victims, the Nazis were themselves victimized.

Our Founding Fathers believed that a nation could be administered without creating victims. It is for us to prove that they were not mistaken.

CHAPTER XI

The American Caste System

THE position of the Negro is unique in the racial problem of American society. It is the case of racial discrimination carried to an extreme, that is, to the erection of a caste barrier. Within that barrier the people so categorized may hope to rise, but the more attractive goals are closed to them insofar as the caste barrier holds fast. It is the treatment of the American Negro which serves America's critics as the example par excellence of inconsistency in American ideals and American actions.

CASTE AND CLASS IN SOUTHERNTOWN *

A discussion of caste and class in Southerntown may well begin with a classic story on race relations. A Negro was found by the conductor sitting in the white car of a southern train. He was challenged and told to go to the Jim Crow car. He objected, said he belonged in the white car, and gave as his reason, "Boss, I'se resigned from de colored race." This story is a play on the most serious issue in Southerntown; and it illustrates how futile it would be to pretend that one can study Negro personality without reference to white society. The incredulous white conductor is quite as necessary to the anecdote as the ingenuous Negro. Every fact about Negroes is likely to have an obverse side with meanings for the whites.

Description of social life in Southerntown inevitably involves a discussion of the nature of caste and class. Caste and class distinctions are ways of dividing people according to the behavior expected of them in the society. Caste and class show the relations in which people stand to one another in Southerntown; they organize local life securely and make social coöperation possible. They deserve a detailed discussion in order that th

* Dollard, John, *Caste and Class in a Southern Town* (New Haven: Yale University Press 1937), pp. 62–97.

emotional patterns appropriate to them may come into clear outline. We do not have here any racial soul or genius defending its heritage, as is often alleged; what we see is a moral and status order in operation, whose operators safeguard and perpetuate their positions in it.

Caste has replaced slavery as a means of maintaining the essence of the old status order in the south. By means of it racial animosity is held at a minimum. Caste is often seen as a barrier to social contact or, at least, to some forms of social contact. It defines a superior and inferior group and regulates the behavior of the members of each group. In essence the caste idea seems to be a barrier to legitimate descent. A union of members of the two castes may not have a legitimate child. All such children are members of the lower caste and cannot be legitimated into the upper caste by the fact that they have an upper-caste father or mother. Caste in Southerntown is also a categorical barrier to sexual congress between upper-caste women and lower-caste men, within or without the married state. It does not result in such a barrier between upper-caste men and lower-caste women. In this it seems to be modeled on the patriarchal family with its possessive prerogatives of the male; it has a double standard of the same type. Nothing else seems absolute about the caste barrier. It does not totally exclude social contact and seems to have no other mark so distinctive as the marriage and sexual prohibition.

It is necessary to remind ourselves that American democratic mores are set in quite another current. They do not recognize barriers to legitimate descent or preferential rights to sex relationships. Democratic society guarantees equal opportunity to enjoy whatever goods and services society has to offer; there are no arbitrary limitations based on race or color. This is the sense in which northerners seem theoretical to southerners when the Negro is discussed. Northerners look at the Negro through the constitutional window; southerners look at him through the caste window. In the train of the barriers to legitimate descent and sexual contact come other limitations. The caste line works out also as an automatic block to social advancement for the Negro and this means that the highest prestige prizes are not accessible to him. For example, we bring millions of boys into the world who are in training as future presidents of the United States; no one expects, however, that Negro boys are really included. Their caste membership silently excludes them from such high hopes.

American caste is pinned not to cultural but to biological features—to color, features, hair form, and the like. This badge is categorical regardless of the social value of the individual. It is in this sense that caste is "undemocratic" since it accepts an arbitrary token as a means of barring

Negroes from equal opportunity and equal recognition of social merit. Negroid body form was at one time a mark of a Negro culture and is still to some degree a mark of an inferior assimilation of white culture; but both of these differentiating marks of Negroes are rapidly diminishing and in the course of time the physical stigmata may be left isolated as the only warrant of caste difference. The cultural stigmata of the past seem likely to disappear altogether.

Inferior caste results in a degree of social isolation for the individuals concerned. It tends to limit the personal development of members so that it is more difficult for them to compete for the highest social rewards and position. American policy is somewhat contradictory on this score, since we really do not keep the caste barrier fixed by the most effective methods. Slavery in this sense is much superior as a method of holding a population as a subject group. The upper caste would be more secure if the inferior caste were to have a separate language, or at least if its acquisition of our speech were limited. It would be safer also if lower-caste members were not able to read, if there were no social or religious sharing, and if the group were geographically immobile and extremely limited in social participation. The leaven of our dominant democratic mores has, however, made such a firm adjustment impossible; war broke up the southern approximation of it and we have a system of subjugation which is, for all its seeming firmness, shaky and contradictory.

Caste members tend to develop a distinctive psychology. This is nc less true of the white caste than of the Negro, and we must never forge that we have two castes in the South and not just one. Southern whit solidarity is caste solidarity. Nor should we overlook the fact that most o us, in the North as well as South, are members of the white caste, that w do, in practice, define the Negro as something categorically inferior an demand special privileges for ourselves and fellow whites. Our sympath also tends to run along caste lines, even if it is not so acute in the North b virtue of the absence of the problem in a crucial form; northern Negroe are not numerous enough to be designated as out-groups in most norther communities.

The slogans of the white caste are among the most common expre sions in Southerntown: "Niggers are all right in their place." "Would yo want your sister to marry a nigger?" "Whenever whites have come in cor tact with blacks the world over, they have always been the dominant race, etc. Here is certainly a situation in which prediction is possible in the soci sciences because these beliefs may be elicited at will from high and low i the southern white caste. Their repetition can in fact become tedious, an one is surprised at the sense of originality which those who repeat them often seem to feel. These expressions are always heavily supported from the emotional side and are impressive in the actual situation. White-caste members exhibit an appropriate pride in the achievements of their caste and like to stress its superiority in management and social responsibility. In the Negro caste also a distinctive emotional set tends to develop, a psychology which is an accurate response to the caste position of the Negro.

The solidarity of the white caste on sexual and social issues has been widely noticed. When southern white people tell a northerner that after a few years in the South he will feel about Negroes just as southerners do, they are making the point that he joins the white caste. The solicitation is extremely active, though informal, and one must stand by one's caste to survive. Negroes, of course, know the power of white solidarity better than anyone else. A Negro put it this way: Although white men often appear to be good friends to Negroes, if a Negro commits a crime against a white man, the white friend will invariably turn against him; whereas if a white man has any little trouble, all his white friends flock to him and defend him. He says it is different with Negro friends: they stick by you better. Raper has cited the case of a white infantryman who actually used a bayonet in defending a Negro charged with rape. This white man was never able to keep a position in his town thereafter; his white fellow workers forced him to leave for one reason or another.

A feature of white solidarity, as has been noted, is the harsh term that brands the caste traitor—"nigger-lover." Such a man enjoys the benefits of white solidarity, but does not stand by his caste. In the epithet there is an implication of inferiority and perhaps a threat of being classed with the scorned Negro.

To the Negro, of course, the caste barrier is an ever present solid fact. His education is incomplete until he has learned to make some adjustment to it, usually the one preferred by the white caste. Since our democratic society is built on equal opportunity to achieve the highest social distinction, highest class position, and highest financial rewards, the caste barrier is obviously in contradiction with it. The Negro must haul down his social expectations and resign himself to a relative immobility in contrast to the dominant spirit of our society. This dominant spirit is well expressed by the notion of "beginning at the bottom and working to the top." Moton has pointed out that the Negro may begin at the bottom but, on the average, he may expect to stay there, or pretty close to it.

There was no lack of appreciation of this fact among my informants. A Negro plantation manager, a very rare specimen, said that the Negroes on his plantation tend to improve faster under a Negro manager. They say to themselves that what he can do, they can do; whereas with a white boss they feel that the gulf is too great and make no effort to improve. My informant believed that white men cultivate this sense of intrinsic superiority of the whites and use it to keep the Negroes in their places, as the whites see them. A woman Negro informant said that white people do not like to see Negroes get along well. For example, her mother has a very pleasant house with flowers in the yard and pretty decorations in and around it. A white man who came there to bring her some laundry saw how attractive the place was, and then went to a miserable Negro cabin next door and called her mother over there. The informant said that he was so mean he did not like to go to a Negro house that was nice. She had to add in all truthfulness that white people have come to the house, have gone through it, and complimented her mother on it. A third Negro explained that he had been talking with a white man that morning; they had leaned over the fence and gossiped for about an hour. The white man discussed political candidates, asked the Negro his opinion of this one and that one. The informant felt this was all well and good, but rather ironical since he could not vote. He thought the white people in America have their minds pretty well made up about the Negro; they are determined not to let him get anywhere. By "getting anywhere" he meant they will not let the Negro have full opportunity for social advancement and do not expect of him the efforts appropriate to it.

On the other hand, Negroes, like other Americans, pursue the goals and ideals which are characteristic of America and cannot in these days ignorantly accept their "place" as once they could. The Negro shares inevitably the values of the dominant group and aspires to full participation in it. Many Negroes also have white blood which gives them another type of claim to social consideration.

Since our social values are best represented by white persons, the Negro aspires also to whiteness. As Reuter says, the "center of gravity of the hybrid group is outside itself." This presents a difficulty, however, because, while white culture may be assimilated, whiteness itself cannot be imitated. For Negroes there is a definite pull toward all the identifying marks of the white caste, cultural and physical. It is not believed that Negroes want to be "white" in any abstract sense; what they want is to be indistinguishably full participants in American society. For the present, to be white seems to be the best guarantee of this complete human status. Such a discussion as the following brings out the issue clearly.

A Negro schoolteacher remarked that Negro babies often change their color after they are born, and asked me what changes white babies undergo. I answered that their hair and eyes often change color, the nose form changes, and the ratio of the head to the body becomes smaller as they grow. Informant said regretfully that Negro babies frequently become darker as they grow and the hair changes texture. Colored babies' hair is likely to be very fluffy. If the baby has a lot of thick hair when small, it will probably turn out later to be bad; but if it has thin hair or none at all, it is more likely to be good. By "bad" and "good" she meant farther from or nearer to the straight hair of the white type. The above is enlightening in that it indicates the anxiety which exists about the future caste marks of the child.

The same woman also commented upon one of her students who is very sullen and mean, but whose older brother has a much better disposition. She thought the younger one sensitive because his lips are heavy and he is so much darker than his brother, and she felt the boys' mother might be at fault, since she is said to show open favoritism toward the lighter brother. It is impossible to know how much of a role this sensitivity to caste characteristics plays, but it must be very great in a Negro family since the fact of good or bad caste marks plays such an important part in the future success of the child.

Another of my informants was discussing with his wife the question of children they might have. He told her he supposed that one of their children would be dark (that is, much darker than they were—his wife is also brown-skinned and a bit darker than he). The idea that one of their children should be dark infuriated the wife and she became much upset over it. He thinks the reason is that her mother was very dark and that she is afraid his prediction is all too true.

First caste awareness apparently occurs very early. One Negro said he used to hear his parents and their guests talking; the conversation would always be about the bad treatment received by the Negroes, their hard lot, etc. Still another source of racial awareness occurred in the family because his brothers and sisters were of different shades. The darker ones would assume that the lighter ones wanted to be white and, if they showed any arrogance in behavior, it was said of them that they were trying to act like whites; in fact the lighter children did not have to be nearly as bold as the darker ones to draw this reproach.

Another informant was taught by his mother to prefer "brighter" Negro girls. He is fairly light himself. When he thought of marrying, he could not consider any real dark girls. He said his mother felt like this because the brighter people are treated more like men and women and get more concessions from the whites; it was obvious, too, that this informant wished to advance his own status by marrying a light woman.

The principle here seems very simple. Whiteness represents full personal dignity and full participation in American society. Blackness or darkness represents limitation and inferiority; and sometimes even animal character is imputed to it. The Negroes share sufficiently in American society to want to be fully human in the American sense and to this end they prefer to be as light as possible, since the white caste seems to grant some recognition, informally of course, to the lighter colors. Consciousness of color and accurate discrimination between shades is a well-developed Negro caste mark in Southerntown; whites, of course, are not nearly so skilful in distinguishing and naming various shades.

The question of color comes up constantly in reference to marriage within the Negro group. A woman informant said her mother objected to her marriage to a very dark man. Informant did not know the reason at the time and the mother did not press her objections. Later, however, it became clear that the mother did not like the fact that the husband was so dark. She was extraordinarily sensitive to color and preferred the lighter people. The same informant stated that light Negro men frequently like darker women, whereas very dark men like lighter women. She says this belief is widely held by colored people. A professional man in particular likes to have a very light wife. It is believed that, if a man is very dark and his wife very light, he is likely to be madly in love with her.

There is, of course, no absolute rule on this score. Personal qualities undoubtedly interfere with the tendency to "marry light." Since the marriage choice remains so often with the man in our society, it usually follows that the woman is lighter than the man, since he has the chance to choose. Class considerations, however, enter here also. A man may marry a darker woman because she is of a better class than he; she may have, for example, some exceptional skill or talent, like being a nurse, a teacher, a singer, a caterer, or what not. Another informant said that her mother was quite dark, much darker than her father. She added that this always seemed to be a sore point with the mother. She never seemed to be able to forgive the father for being a light-skinned man, and wanted the girls to marry light men. The mother eventually divorced the father, the informant thought because of their difference in color. It seemed possible in this case that the lighter husband had superior social advantages which humiliated his wife or made her jealous.

A Negro man said that his father, who was very light and could almost pass for a white man, was often used as a peacemaker between the races because of his light color. His mother and his mother's side of the family were dark, but she always preferred light people. She thought they received much better treatment than dark Negroes: "The black man always gets the worst of it." The whites like Negroes with white features or skin color and tend to trust them more than dark Negroes. He said that white employers have a tendency to separate the light from the dark Negroes, as, for example, when a foreman will assign all the darker Negroes to work in a cluster and will separate out the lighter ones in the same way. I asked him how it was that a man as light as his father married a woman as dark as his mother, since I had been told that men usually marry lighter women. He said that this was not always the case and that sometimes lighter people preferred darker people; but he himself seemed puzzled on this point. The same informant stated that mulatto families in his childhood community were always at a social premium. For instance, the light-colored men had many more sexual opportunities than darker men would have, that is, opportunities with Negro women. His father, he said, was so light that he was constantly mistaken for a white man; this was embarrassing to him and was one of the reasons he stayed away from church, since when he went to church, people would begin to show him the courtesies accorded to white people.

This emphasis on whiteness as a means to achieve full human dignity has been repeatedly noted. Delusions of being white in color are quite common in Negro psychotics and have been noted by many researchers.

As an hypothesis it might be worth saying that the whites may prefer on a straight narcissistic basis those Negroes who look most white. He who looks most like me is most entitled to my love and confidence; he who is strange is more likely to be dangerous. The presence of "white" hair and features is a kind of guarantee of good relations between the white and the Negro.

As a result of caste pressure, there is a sort of passive solidarity within the Negro caste. This is illustrated by a complaint often made by the police in Southerntown. They say that Negroes will not testify against other Negroes; that often, for example, those who have been right at the scene of a murder will not talk and will pretend to know nothing about it. Then the police have to use third-degree methods to get the truth out of them. The Negroes have a reputation with whites of shielding, hiding, and aiding criminal members of their race. The degree of solidarity is disappointingly small, though, from the standpoint of middle-class Negroes. One of my informants stated that a certain prominent Negro scholar was a talented man, but that many Negroes were disappointed in him because he did not take a stronger attitude of leadership for the "group." She said that one of the constant disappointments with Negro leaders is that they work for their own selfish interests and forget the group which they represent.

Another Southerntown Negro showed how membership in the Negro caste is forced on the Negro, not chosen by him. He illustrated this statement by referring to the contrary behavior of the Negroes in the North. On one occasion in Ohio he was riding on a bus in which were two white people and a Negro girl. The white people sat up in front, as did the informant, but the girl went to the back of the bus. He felt this was somewhat characteristic of northern Negroes; they do not want to cluster with other Negroes. He later found out that she came from an Ohio town where there were only eight or nine Negro families. These families all go to different churches and live in different parts of the town; they do not want to be grouped together by the whites. The dispersion is explained by the fact that, if they cluster by their own wish, then the whites will make them cluster legally. They had best stay apart and view themselves as individuals and not as members of a group. In the South, on the contrary, Negroes have no choice; an appearance of solidarity is forced on them by segregation but it does not result in sentiments of being bound together.

It is frequently alleged, and with truth, that the social arrangement of having two castes in the South is a means of limiting conflict between the races, a conflict which is always potential whenever the races use the same schools, trains, amusement facilities, etc. There is another and less desirable feature of the caste arrangement: It limits the possibility of sympathetic contact. Middle-class Negroes are especially sensitive to their isolation and feel the lack of a forum in Southerntown where problems of the two races could be discussed. It is often something of a discovery when white people learn that there are Negro people of refined feeling and noteworthy talent, because they stand in such sharp contrast to the white-caste stereotype of the Negro.

Caste as a barrier to social equality between the races will be discussed in another connection. The word "social" is here used in the narrow sense of polite social participation and not in the sociological sense of any traditionally guided contact. Negroes are not admitted on equal terms to the amusements and entertainments of the whites. How completely this is understood by the Negroes is illustrated by the following sinister story. A Southerntown white girl of exceptional warmth and sensibility had a Negro friend of whom she was very fond, and often said that she wished this Negro woman were white. Once she asked her friend whether she might bring a man she knew to her house and whether the Negro woman would have some of her good fruit cake for them. The latter said "Gladly," and as she was leaving asked, "Do you want me to put clean sheets on the bed?" The girl, somewhat startled, said "No." When they got there, the Negro woman took them into her own room, a combination bedroom and sitting room with a radio. After a while she left them there alone. The girl was appalled to notice on a tray near the bed an outfit of contraceptive materials. After an hour or two the Negro woman came back, knocked on the door, and served them a light supper. The behavior of the white girl in this case was certainly unconventional, but the Negro woman's interpretation was ruthlessly according to the code; the only way she could understand it was to think that the white couple had made an excuse to use her house for a rendezvous.

The full implications of the caste concept will be worked out steadily throughout the study. It is important now to discuss the classes within each of the castes, white and Negro, classes which are so obvious a feature of life in Southerntown.

The existence of social classes in the South has been noted by many observers despite the convention that social class is not a feature of our American democratic society. We are not accustomed to think in these terms, and to be sure, the class hierarchy is not so clearly marked in the northern states. At least three classes may be noticed which we designate briefly as lower, middle, and upper. The existence of these classes was quite clear in the South even before the War. It may be that this picture is clearer to Negroes than to others; at least, an astute Negro writer has commented on the class problem and asserted that Negroes have characteristic attitudes toward each one of the classes in the white group.

The existence of the lower-class whites or poor white group has been one of the continuous features of southern social organization. One might say of them that they have neither capital, talent, nor ancestry to give them preferential claims on income or prestige. From the standpoint of social usefulness, they have arms and legs and minimum skills, usually of the agricultural type. Biologically they are old Americans. In the area surrounding Southerntown they seem to have a certain amount of diffuse resentment against upper-class white people and some resentment against Negroes, especially the middle-class Negroes. They seem to face the greatest difficulties in gaining status because they do not have the capital to begin making any kind of advance, nor do they have the resolute and tormented determination of some of the immigrant groups. Since their chances of social advancement are relatively low, they have little to lose in status or economic reward by lax behavior and in general they do not maintain the personal standards of the middle-class whites. Apparently in some areas they play an unusual role in forceful demonstration against the Negro. If it is said that the Negroes do not have social equality in the South, it is equally true that this class of white people does not have it either, unless it be at infrequent political picnics and barbecues. In an economic sense their competitors are the lower-class Negroes and, since the whites have the political instrument to work with, they are enabled to gain some advantages over their rivals; on the other hand they face economic disadvantages in the form of the alliance between the field Negroes and the white owners which tends to exclude them from plantation work. A shred of statistical information on this issue indicates that the lower-class people, white and Negro, are numerous in this state since it is one in which fewest families have radios and telephones, perhaps a mark of middle-class status.

In contrast to the lower-class white people, and distinct from them, is the middle-class group. In general, middle-class members have risen from the lower class rather than fallen from the upper. Their class membership is based on small capital holdings, or on the possession of social skill, managerial or professional, which enables them to make a claim on a larger income and gives them a higher position in the eyes of others. One feels their spirit to be energetic and acquisitive. In the main they intend to make their way by their exertions and personal contributions to the welfare of the community. Their personal standards of behavior, on questions of drinking, divorce, and profanity, seem to be more rigorous than those of the classes above or below them. They seem to be religious and are in fact faithful churchgoers. These people are the best demonstrations of the "equal chances" offered by American society. Their class position itself is a way station to still higher prestige levels. Usually some degree of education is combined with capital when the latter is present; if not, the capital may be invested in the education of the children and thus win for the family line a secure middle-class position. It should be noted that there is a limit to our democratic possibility of social advancement for any and every individual; this limit is reached when previous acquisition and use of capital by others constitute a barrier to the advancement of new group members.

Middle-class white people in Southerntown seem to have a great deal of contempt for the lower-class whites, and this contempt often flares into open animosity. They also have vigorous hostile attitudes toward the Negroes and are seldom found in the ranks of those who take the friendly attitude toward the Negro evinced by the white aristocracy. They hold that the main tormentors of the Negro are the lower-class whites, a statement which the Negroes tend to confute. Negroes, especially the most vocal of the middle-class Negroes, say that their real antagonists are not the whites of the highest or the lowest status; the former have too much to be jealous and the latter get from the upper-class whites the same treatment as the Negroes. A number of informants believed, on the contrary, that the lower-class whites sympathized with the Negroes. The Negroes have a name for the middle-class white group which corresponds remarkably well with their position in the eyes of the sociological analyst; they call them "strainers," those who are pressing forward and straining to get on in the world. Middle-class people must stress sharply the differences between themselves and the lower-class whites and Negroes because they are none too sure that the differences are very important or permanent.

Often in the face of economic reverses middle-class families will cling bitterly to their class standards, one of which is education for their children. They will endure great hardships and humiliation to make this education possible rather than risk demoting the family line to a lower-class position. They will struggle to maintain their children in the same class, to see that they marry appropriate persons, that the daughter has the right kind of a wedding, and so on.

Most of the businessmen in Southerntown fall in the group of middle-class people. The following note on a Rotary Club meeting will give an idea of what they hear on such an occasion:

> Attended Rotary Club luncheon today; the speaker talked about how much bigger profits one can make if one takes a human attitude toward one's employees, considers them not as automatons but as persons. We should have work for our hands to do, clean thoughts for our minds, love in our hearts, etc. Much emotion on part of speaker, fluent speech full of clichés and quotations from inspirational sources. The chairman said in his speech of thanks, and in justification of Rotary, that it was only in a Rotary Club that one could hear such a speech.

There seems to be, on the whole, a much better disciplining of members within the middle-class group than is the case with the other two classes. As "strainers" they are on the march to higher status position and, like an army on the march, they are provident, industrious, vigilant, and determined. For example, the professional wing has to maintain careful personal standards in order not to suffer in public estimation. Teachers must "watch their step" since they have a certain idealized role before the young. There seems to be in this group a sense of insecurity which acts as a goad to abstemious behavior and close control of impulse.

A person who has fallen from his class position is in a sorry state. One of the middle-class families was widely sympathized with because it had such a member. This man could not be made to work consistently and all class pressure (shame) put on him to do so was ineffectual. He drank a great deal, more than was tolerated or perhaps possible to a middle-class man. Finally he completely dropped his claims on middle-class and upper-caste consideration by living more or less *openly* with a Negro concubine. He has finally become a dependent individual who is supported by his relatives, is socially disgraced, and has no claims on the esteem accorded to other members of his middle-class family.

This is not to say that all middle-class members do or are able to conform to the strictest standards. The picture presented here is the one which middle-class individuals strive toward and which most of them manage to approximate. Disordered personalities exist in this class, secret drinkers will be found, sex delinquencies are not unknown, although there is usually the attempt to keep them secret. In considering the "strains" of modern life in reference to nervous and mental disorder, one might well note those imposed on individuals in this class where the pressure toward individual achievement and advancement, which require exceptional impulse renunciation, is so great.

So powerful is the strain toward a democratic uniformity in our society that the emerging lower and middle classes have tended to replace the old aristocratic upper class in social significance; but it will still be worth while to identify this class group. It is the remains of the ruling group against which the Civil War was fought, a group whose claims to precedence were heavily discredited by defeat in the War. Since it is but little represented in Southerntown, we will try to characterize it for the culture area of the South as a whole. Although it has lost its actual grip on the social machine to a very great extent, it has maintained the momentum of its social prestige and assimilation into it is still a great value in the South.

To be an upper-class person is to have a certain kind of memory of the past and to hold a certain role in the eyes of others with similar memories. If, on meeting a southern person, the stranger could by chance open a history book and ask him to thumb through it, and if the southerner stopped now and then tosay, "Oh, yes, that is Governor So-and-So; he was my grandmother's brother," or "General Blank married a second cousin of my mother, she was of the South Carolina Blanks, you know," he would be dealing with an upper-class person. Originally, no doubt, membership in this class was based on a strong position in the economic system and entry to it was often secured by possession of special social skills and money. Like all aristocratic traits, however, class membership tends to be socially inherited and does not continually need the underpinning of actual economic pre-eminence. In its day this was a functioning class leading in statecraft and agriculture, and disciplining its individuals for leadership. Nowadays it seems to be based largely on memories of interrelationship with other leading families of the past, rather than on current achievement. It still differentiates sufficiently the behavior of those who are born into it so that it is a formative force in the culture.

The immediately striking thing at a dinner party of upper-class people is the astonishing degree of interrelationship of the members. There are echoes of old transactions, such as whose relative sold what house and piece of land to whose grandfather, and there is an amazing knowledge of the tangled genealogies of all the leading families. One is much impressed by the poise and social readiness of the group, their ease in conversation, and the grace and certainty with which they receive a stranger. They know that they are placed definitely in the social world by the strings which bind them to their ancestors and that they have a form of personal security which cannot be taken away by economic disaster or by anything short of death or destruction to those who remain. The ancestors are potentially present every time an upper-class group gathers; even though in the case of the younger members of this class these is less frequent trading of memories and old associations.

With this class, which is sure of itself socially, a freer measure of impulse expression is possible than with the stressful middle-class group. There is a more tolerant attitude toward religion and drinking and a less intensive sense of scandal about personal delinquencies.

A number of times in seeking Negro informants I was advised by upper-class white people to consult this or that aristocratic planter who had lived with the Negroes all his life and knew them well; he would refer me to several intelligent Negroes on his place who could tell me the situation. I did indeed avail myself of these sources of information, but realized too that I was being passed on from one class member to another and it was presumed to be guaranteed that by these means I would get "safe" information from this class standpoint. As a matter of fact, the information was, for the most part, extremely good and realistic in the sense that it checked with other observations, but it tended to have an inevitable class bias.

Here is a note made on a visit with a young southern man whom I met on a train:

> Met a young man on the train last night and fell into conversation. Apparently he comes of a well-known family here. Says grandfather told him about having been a courier for General Hood in the Civil War. Says when they say "war" down here, they mean the Civil War, not the World War. Says northern people feel that southerners are mean toward Negroes; says this is not so, his family have always had Negro slaves and servants and have loved them. Gives example of personal services to Negroes. Feels people have not gotten over the Civil War. He wanted me to learn about the "real South," says southern hospitality is not a myth but exists in the small upper group. Wishes I could see it as he knows it from his own home. Said that he wished that his family were still prosperous so that he could take me to his home and show me the real thing. Despaired of communicating the real South to me by word.

My friend above commented on the affection of his family for Negroes, undoubtedly correctly. One finds this quite regularly as an upper-class mark, this tolerant, poised affection. But the Negroes have to be the right kind, the "old-timy" ones who draw out this friendliness in the class to which they were once related as slaves. Still, in all cases the upper-class attitudes toward Negroes seem mild and there is no sense of being challenged or threatened by them. An upper-class woman in Southerntown commented on the hostility of certain middle-class whites, whom she named, for the Negroes, and said that she came from the upper group who like Negroes. In actual life, she was known to be rather foolish and indulgent in her treatment of them, at least according to prevailing standards in Southerntown. This lenient attitude is undoubtedly an historical resultant in the upper class who have had long accommodative relations with Negroes as master to slave, have many personal memories of them, and have been freed from the competition which middle- and lower-class people have experienced. Raper has noted this cordial relationship between Negroes and the wealthiest whites, a relationship which is very important to understand since it can be transferred also to the white factory owner or employer in the North. The indulgent upper-class attitude toward Negroes is shown by many of the stories written about them since the War. Chesnutt has captured the spirit very well, as has also Judge Moore. Page refers to this love of old-timy Negroes, a love which was indeed well-deserved in view of the role which the Negroes had to play in serving the upper-class white people of the South.

The lower- and middle-class whites are indeed in some ways not so near to upper-class white people as the Negroes, perhaps again for the reason that class antagonism separated the white groups in earlier days and some relics of it still exist despite present-day solidarity against the Negro caste. The mammy tradition is frequently thought of as a criterion of upper-class membership; it is a point which whites like to remember and Negroes like to forget.

It seemed, from my small contact, that the upper-class group, on the whole, is less bound by the southern mores and folkways than the other classes. They are, of course, likely to be more traveled, better read, and even acquainted with some social movements which it would be almost a scandal to know about in the other classes. My experience is too limited to make the following statement as a confirmed impression, but the only protestors against white solidarity and the current treatment of the Negro whom I encountered were upper-class people.

As already observed, we have a situation in Southerntown where there are not only castes, but classes within the two castes. It seems reasonable also to posit three classes within the Negro group, although only two of them will be discussed here. There was no chance for me to examine the criteria for the upper-class Negroes, although undoubtedly such a designation is worth making in view of what is known of Negroes in Philadelphia, Washington, Charleston, New Orleans, and other cities. Here we will discuss only the lower- and middle-class Negro groups as they are actually represented in Southerntown.

The Negro lower class is the same "arms and legs" group with the simplest of agricultural skills and personalities adapted to continue peaceably a subordinate role in the plantation economy. It is at the bottom of the economic and social system and forms a broad base on which society in this area rests, a fact by no means true for the whole South. Attention would be called to the class, in the first place, by the type of observation made by one of my Negro informants who was a teacher. This man told me that his disciplinary problems are much more severe with children who come from tenant homes; the children who come from Negro landowning families submit more easily to school routine. An example from the tenant group is the case of a little girl of twelve who became very hostile toward a ten-year-old girl. The father of the twelve-year-old girl was at the State Prison farm. Saying, "Well, I want to see my father anyway, so I am going to kill you and get sent up there," she chased the ten-year-old with a pair of scissors, and when the child got safely away she threatened to kill her the next day. Presumably the landowning Negroes are in or on the edge of the middle class and have acquired the refinements of behavior and personal repressions characteristic of that class. It is this lower class whom southerners hold up to northerners as the reality of the problem with which the South has to deal in contrast with the northerners' idealized picture of the Negro. This peasant class of Negroes has been very well described by Johnson who observes among them also a pressure to escape the limitations of their class status by means of educating their children. Reuter also posits among them a wish to cross the caste barrier, at least in the sense of arranging life so that they will be as much in contact with lighter people as possible and have lighter children. It is in this class also that the presence of the mother-centered family has been noticed by Frazier. It is apparently more difficult to stay alive in this group of Negroes because we learn that in this state the rural Negro death rate is markedly higher than the rural white death rate, and the infant mortality per thousand live births for rural Negroes is almost twice as high as for rural whites. The behavior of middle-class Negroes is differentiated from that of the lower-class group; when a southerner says "Negro" he refers invariably to his stereotype of the lower-class Negro. It is this group which draws and seems to deserve the low opinion of the whites.

The class grouping, as we shall see, tends to be similar in the two castes, with the crucial exception that the hope of social advancement in the Negro middle class is emphatically limited by the caste barrier. Another differentiation is that social advancement in the Negro middle class seems more often due to developed talent or skill than to capital accumulation. Not infrequently, too, Negroes are aware of a family lineage and family tradition, although there is also a widespread consciousness of plantation cabin background. Frequently awareness of white blood and corresponding lightness of color play a role among the middle group of Negroes.

The impression one gets from Southerntown is that the Negro middle-class people are mostly teachers and ministers of the gospel, apparently a characteristic finding. There are two physicians, no lawyers, and a few businessmen including only two people who control a considerable acreage of land.

The attempt of the middle class to mark itself off from the pilloried lower-class Negroes seems constant. For example, the wife of a professional man said that she recently started her four-year-old son off to kindergarten in the Negro school. One day he came home from school and said, "Me wants something to eat." She told him that he had never learned that at home and he would not get it if he asked for it that way. She deplores the fact that she must send her son to school with children of illiterate families who get him into such ways of talking, but there is nothing else to do. She is a woman of college grade. It may be that historically the Negro middle (and upper) classes are derived for the most part from the house servants and the free Negroes who formed one-ninth of the total Negro population in 1860. Undoubtedly, too, this class contains more mixed blood than the lower-class Negroes. The bi-racial arrangement has probably provided a social role for the middle-class Negro which he would not have if he were exposed to the direct competition of the white middle-class group. It is easy, in Southerntown at least, to observe the presence of persons of mixed blood in the middle class by talking to a group of county teachers or taking the frequently offered opportunity to "say a few words" at a rural Negro church. The teacher group is markedly more Caucasoid in its characteristics.

Middle-class Negroes follow, at least as an ideal, the highest standards of sexual morality. It is not certain that they measure up to them any better than do the whites, but it is certain that they appreciate them. One of my informants said, for example, that her stern conscience probably came from her mother and father; she mentioned her father in particular in this connection, saying that he had never done anything low or mean and never had any illegitimate children. He always took pride in the fact that, although the family had little in the way of possessions, they had integrity and were persons of high standards. As a bad example, she cited a man in the community who had formerly been a peasant Negro but had become well-to-do. He was known to have had a number of illegitimate children by different mothers and was judged to be not really of the middle class for this reason.

Another Negro woman refused a man who proposed to her several times because she did not like his family. He had a sister who was "very careless in her social relationships" and lived with a number of men successively without marrying them or getting support from any of them; meanwhile her brother supported her. He disapproved what his sister did but continued to support her; and the informant felt his sister would always come first, that is, his allegiance would remain fixed to lower-class standards. This same conflict was represented several times in Negro middle-class families, one of the partners holding to middle-class standards and fearing that the other would drag down the family status by behavior appropriate to the lower class.

Education is, of course, a passion with the middle-class Negroes, as has been frequently noted. The most extraordinary sacrifices may be made by parents to give their children opportunities for status advancement through education.

There is a good deal of shame among middle-class Negroes over the caste marks which whites take to be typical of all Negroes. Resentment of the mammy tradition has already been indicated. One of my woman informants told me of a Negro woman who made candy in a southern town and who put a dummy of herself outside her store as an advertisement. The dummy showed a very dark woman with a bandana around her head. The Negroes resented this fiercely and my informant thought the reason was that it reminded them of the mammy stereotype of the whites which they so much resent. For herself, she did not see why the resentment was so great, because she thought if the woman could make candy better than anyone else, it was all to the credit of the race. Again, there seems to be antagonism to spirituals since they are reminders of the slave situation. The same informant said that she thought it was foolish for her group to be ashamed of the spirituals; they ought to be proud of anything they could do better than anyone else. Middle-class Negro churches tend to be more sedate than the lower-class churches. The reason probably is that the emotionalism of the lower-class churches has become associated in white minds with primitive and animal behavior, and the middle-class Negroes wish to deny such a trait in themselves. It is often irritating to the spiritual-loving northerner to go to a concert in Southerntown. He wants spirituals and still more of them. All he will get will be a small group, usually beautifully sung. And he has to bear with a soprano soloist who sings "Trees" in a sentimental manner, various other vocal solos of indifferent quality, and a lot of piano playing, some good and some bad. This is probably what he might find in any small town; but after all, most small towns do not have and cannot sing spirituals. The fact seems to be that the classical part of the entertainment is stressed to show what the group can do and that it is not deficient in appreciation of "the best" in music.

The better discipline of the middle-class group in respect to aggression is another feature by which it is differentiated from the lower class. It is a point of pride that no one has been in jail or arrested.

Observation indicates also that middle-class Negro men take pride in the fact that their wives do not work outside the home. In this, of course, they follow the valuations of their class, white or colored. Women at home are much better protected against sexual temptation than those who work out, which in turn is probably effective in helping to consolidate the middle-class family.

It is the Negro middle class which feels most bitterly the pressure of the caste barrier with its damaging effect on individual self-esteem; this barrier sets the Negro outside the possibility of achieving personal dignity in the fullest American sense. It seems likely that this fact, rather than a desire to be white in any physical sense, is at the bottom of the distress of so many people with mixed blood. Their sense of injustice is all the more keen since the personal achievement characteristic of middle-class Negro people is categorically superior to the large lower-class white group and to some of the middle-class whites.

Be it noted that a blank appears in the description of the Negro class pattern where the upper class ought to be. I will not attempt to fill this in from memory or imagination, but will leave it to better informed researchers. Very likely it can be made a useful concept. One detects in some Negroes in Southerntown a stress on lineage similar to that found among upper-class white people. Family connections appeared frequently in one such conversation, "my grandfather's grandfather," "my granduncle," etc. On the other hand, among Negroes, there must be a strong tendency against remembering ancestry. It tends to remind Negroes of slavery days, a remembrance which is bound to be painful while the pattern of Negro subordination persists as it does today. Let us remember the negative value often placed on the beautiful spirituals—"slave songs." And while some Negroes may count their own light color as an asset, they cannot escape the bitterness of our social judgment on bastardy which inevitably accompanies the memory of a white ancestor. No such ancestor can, of course, be legitimate. In one or two cases recourse was taken to memories, legendary or factual, of descent from African princes who never did work, who were brought over to boss other Negroes. In another case the ancestor was a Seminole chieftain and the Negro stressed that he had free blood in his veins. The problem of ancestry, however, is bound to be a complex and painful one for Negroes when they become fully aware of the dominant American moral standards.

The advantage of outlining clearly a scheme of caste and class distinctions is that it enables one to place people and to have some systematic expectations of them. Let us practice a little by reminding ourselves that the "poor whites" are upper caste but lower class, that the researcher is upper caste but middle class, that my best Negro informant was middle class but lower caste, and so on. It is within such a frame of reference that personality differences achieve their right perspective. Comparisons of psychological facts are only truly effective when the subjects are similar as to caste and class. A murder done by a lower-class Negro is a different kind of fact from a similar act by the president of the Rotary Club, who is, of course, upper caste and middle class; and in real life the two acts are treated differently by the group itself. Strain on the individual personality undoubtedly differs as between the castes and classes. An hypothesis, which needs to be tested, is that it is greatest in the middle-class Negro group for the reason that severe impulse restriction is enjoined without appropriate compensation from the status side. The more clearly the necessity of making out the systematic form of the social life comes home, the more one sees how qualified must be any social psychology which is developed by members of a single class.

One useful result of clarifying the class and caste picture is to learn that white middle-class people show some loyalty for their Negro classmates across the caste line. Observations to this effect come from both white and Negro sides. This loyalty really should be described as an ambivalent relationship: hostility along caste lines, loyalty along class lines. A Negro informant says that educated colored people get much better treatment than uneducated ones. White people tend to be more respectful and friendly. This is the positive side of class loyalty. Still and all, she says, they seem to resent seeing a colored person dressed up and looking nice. She often feels criticized by white eyes when she goes out in a tastefully designed dress. This is the negative side of caste hostility.

A grandson of a Negro, highly placed in an economic sense, reported the civilities that his grandfather had received in contrast to other Negroes. He was said to have had good white friends in Southerntown. Three or four of these friends had his picture on their office walls and in their offices they somewhat relaxed the severity of caste conventions in talking to him. The grandson thinks that white people in the town show him deference because of his family and economic background. On the other hand, the grandfather had still to submit to galling restrictions, was addressed by his first name, and could not share in civic enterprises on equal terms.

It has sometimes seemed, in explanation of this ambivalence, that the class conflict centers around economic position and advantage, whereas the caste conflict centers around social, and ultimately sexual, contact. The white man can have a certain loyalty to members of his class in the Negro group providing the barriers against more intimate contact are maintained. The argument against "marrying a nigger" would come up as quickly against a middle-class as against a lower-class Negro.

The explanation of the class loyalty does not seem far to seek. After all, the middle-class Negro buys more gas, better groceries, more insurance, more medical services, sees the lawyer oftener, and is in general a good customer. Since there is competition among white people in performing these services, some deference tends to be doled out to the middle-class Negroes as a bid for their business. It is important, furthermore that Negro employers should follow the customs of white landowners, and it is worth something in the way of respect to keep the Negro landowners in line. One Negro owner says that the whites put pressure on him to treat his tenants as they do theirs; otherwise it would create discontent because tenants would come to the whites and talk about the especially good treatment they receive at a Negro's place. Since the informant conforms and does not set a bad example to Negro tenants, the white people are very nice to him.

In another case also the reason for the superior rapport between the middle classes was clear. A Negro informant told me that he had consolidated himself with the whites in the following way. A number of Negroes were killed by a railroad train. Through his influence they did not sue the railroad, and it might have been a costly suit. In return for this favor informant received special protection of various types, for example, police protection. Once, he had hit a car driven by a white woman who chanced also to be pregnant, an especially unfavorable detail; the chief of police declared it a mere accident and let him go, whereas the officer on the spot had been abusive and was about to take him to jail.

A young middle-class Negro man told me what it felt like to come back to Southerntown from a northern city. He got into the Jim Crow car at Chicago instead of at Cairo, Illinois, where the Jim Crow line begins. The accommodations were as good for Negroes as for whites. When he passed out of Cairo he wished he could turn back north. He had a gloomy anticipation of his stay in Southerntown and resolved to keep out of contact with the white people when possible. Contrary to expectation, he has been rather flattered by the reception he has received. The whites have taken a friendly interest in him and have gone out of their way to lead him into conversation. He has not minded being here and is not especially anxious to return North in the fall. He agrees that the good treatment is probably due to high-class status.

Another Negro man says he found little difficulty in getting along with white people once he got a bit of money together and made a start. He thinks they did try to prevent him from getting a start, but after he got it, they encouraged him. This implies simply a generalized middle-class resistance against competition from lower-class Negroes, but a recognition of similarity once middle-class status is achieved.

In accounting for the alliance between the middle classes in the two castes one should not overlook the cultural and personality similarities which they share. As already noted, southern white people are occasionally surprised when they have their first real contact with a middle-class Negro person. The surprise is evidence of their recognition of similarity in culture, if not in color.

Another question of interest that arises from this classification is the way in which lower-class white people in the North differ from lower-class Negroes in the South. Since I have not studied the class question in the North I can offer only a guess. In so far as the lower class in the North has been recruited steadily for a century from foreign immigrants, it differs greatly from Negroes for obvious reasons. Whereas the Negroes have little hope of highest status because of the caste barrier, the immigrants have every hope of it, have come here expressly to strive for personal advancement and constantly see members of their own groups winning recognition. This hope of advancement tends to middle-class-ify all of northern society. The immigrants, further, were not all in the same class position in their home lands. Undoubtedly many of them already had middle-class standards and left their home lands under middle-class pressures toward advancement. Once in the northern status structure, they show the energy and drive characteristic of a mobile class. The immigrants are, in one manner of speaking, our "Negroes," but they are temporary Negroes.

A comparison of the lower-class whites in the South and the lower-class Negroes is also important. One can say that the whites are much like the Negroes in respect to economic position, but have superior social status. They are able to affect the operations of the state by their votes and get a kind of noisy, if ineffectual, political representation. They are not categorically debarred from rising in the white-status scale, as are the Negroes. It is an impression, which should be checked, that direct sexual and aggressive expression, though freer among lower-class whites than in the upper classes, is still less common than with the Negroes. This aspect of the problem must be definitively studied.

The hostility between the middle-class and lower-class whites is striking around Southerntown. Informant after informant from the middle-class group came forward with derogatory opinions relating to the poorer whites. A landowner told how mean his white tenants are, how spiteful and gossipy they are toward one another, how they always complain and demand things of him. He is going to replace them next year with Negroes. Another said that the white tenants are mean and disagreeable and contrasted them unfavorably with the Negroes who "know their place." Another said that the white tenants are not tractable at all, as are the Negroes, and that planters much prefer Negroes. A result is that there are many more poor whites than Negroes on the federal relief budget. This informant felt that the federal relief people are too easy, that there should be some hard-headed men in the relief office instead of soft-hearted women. He said the poor whites are a very mean class; they will come into a store, order something, and say, "Charge it to Tom Smith"; they will not even have enough respect for their boss to say "Mr. Smith." He said that the poor whites around Southerntown are the worst class he knows of, worse than in other sections of the South. They do not even dress up on Sunday, have no respect for others' property, and will curse a man going by in a car just because he has something and they have not.

Often these attitudes toward the lower-class whites will come out in the gossip which circulates at the time of a political campaign. A middle-class informant referred to one of the candidates as a "redneck" and a "peckerwood." He said that the candidate was just trash and he was not going to vote for him; and added scornfully that the candidate's father was still a tenant just outside of town. The man had been disloyal to his friends and benefactors and was in general an ungracious upstart. These attitudes are obviously intended to resist the emergence of the candidate in question from his class and they show the ordinarily strong class antagonism in lurid exaggeration.

Another informant referred to two classes of white tenants, the "sorry" white tenants and the others. He thinks the sorry ones are mainly poor whites with a long lower-class tradition; the others are probably persons who have been pressed down through misfortune to the level of the tenant farmer. The latter have more orderly habits of work and some "culture." Here middle-class loyalty extends to those who have lost class status but still conform more nearly to middle class standards.

Something should be said in detail about class structure in Southerntown. The white population is composed largely of middle-class persons. The Negro population is divided between a great mass of lower-class Negroes and a film of middle-class people. There seem to be very few upper- or lower-class whites in Southerntown, although probably more of the latter than of the former. This was expressed by a white informant who claimed that the white people in this town are *nouveau riche* or climbers, and not the real old southern type. The Southerntown area has not been settled as long as older regions of the South and still has a trace of the frontier social structure. It has been so prosperous at various times within recent years that a man who could get hold of land, even rent it, could make himself more or less independent with a very few crops. The result has been the advancement to middle-class status of considerable numbers of people, formerly less secure. In this sense "white superiority" in Southerntown really turns out to be the superiority of the white middle class which is automatically protected against competition from the Negroes by the caste barrier. It is difficult to make out from the statistics on gainful occupations for the county just how people may be divided by classes. There are only a few such data for Southerntown. One cannot tell how many Negro landowners there are, but they must be few; the number of Negro farm managers and foremen is negligible. Negroes comprise 80 percent of the farm laborers. The number of Negroes in skilled trades is also negligible. Only one out of forty persons in the postal service is a Negro. Activities connected with telephone and telegraph companies are a white monopoly. One out of twenty persons in banking and brokerage is a Negro, one out of five in insurance and real estate, and one out of seven in wholesale and retail trade; and it seems likely that in these cases the Negroes do the roustabout work. One out of ten of the employees in public service is a Negro but 97 percent of the women listed under "domestic and personal service" are Negro women. In a county where about three quarters of the people are Negroes it can be seen that they are decisively underrepresented in occupations which might lead to inclusion within middle-class status. This accords absolutely with personal observation and opinions of informants, white and Negro. It tends to justify the conclusion that we are dealing in Southerntown with a white middle-class group and a Negro group largely of the lower class. This conclusion is quite important for the sake of the logical structure of the research and should be carefully noted. It is, however, asserted to be true only of Southerntown.

AMERICA AGAIN AT THE CROSS-ROADS *

THE NEGRO PROBLEM AND THE WAR

The three great wars of this country have been fought for the ideals of liberty and equality to which the nation was pledged. As a consequence of all of them, the American Negro made great strides toward freedom and opportunity. The Revolutionary War started a development which ultimately ended slavery in all Northern states, made new import of slaves

* Myrdal, Gunnar, *An American Dilemma* (New York: Harper & Brothers, 1944), pp. 997–1018.

illegal and nearly accomplished abolition even in the South—though there the tide soon turned in a reaction toward fortification of the plantation system and of Negro slavery. The Civil War gave the Negro Emancipation and Reconstruction in the South—though it was soon followed by Restoration of white supremacy. The First World War provided the Negro his first real opportunity as a worker in Northern industry, started the Great Migration out of the South, and began the "New Negro" movement —though the end of the War saw numerous race riots and the beginning of a serious decline in employment opportunities. After the advances on all three occasions there were reactions, but not as much ground was lost as had been won. Even taking the subsequent reactions into account, each of the three great wars in the history of America helped the Negro take a permanent step forward. . . .

SOCIAL TRENDS

What we usually call "social trends" have their main significance for the Negro's status because of what is in white people's minds. It is true, for instance, that the decreasing relative demand for unskilled work, compared with skilled and semi-skilled work, and the change of much dirty and heavy labor to clean and easy labor, have dangerous implications for the Negro's employment opportunities. But if these technological and economic trends have disastrous effects on the Negro, the cause of this is the persistency with which white people want to keep him out of skilled and pleasant work. It is also true that the trend toward mass unemployment in America tends to turn Negro labor into a relief burden. But, again, the concentration of unemployment upon the Negro people is explainable only as the direct and indirect effects of discrimination. The restricted immigration of white Europeans to America and other population changes are reversing the century-old trend, in which the Negro was becoming a smaller portion of the total population of the United States, into a trend in which the Negro is becoming a slightly increasing proportion of the population. But if this change of trend will disappoint some white Americans and perhaps tend to increase racial friction, the cause is again race discrimination. . . .

In the field of "social" relations we traced a slow but visible decrease of discrimination in the South during recent decades up until the outbreak of the present War. The racial etiquette was gradually loosening. White people were beginning to take cognizance of distinctions in education and class within the Negro community and becoming prepared to treat Negroes somewhat differently according to their individual worth. The "no social equality" theory was not quite so rigid as in earlier generations. The entire Jim Crow apparatus was maintained, but its motivation was no longer so self-evident. Southern liberals were demanding with increasing courage and determination that the doctrine "separate, but equal" should be followed out in its "equality" aspect as well as in its "separateness" aspect—that segregation should not be utilized as a means of discrimination.

The separation of the two groups in the South was, meanwhile, becoming more and more perfected as the frequency of personal master-servant relations was decreasing and as the segregated Negro institutions and Negro professions were being built up. There even seemed to be a growing mental isolation between whites and Negroes. Behind this potentially most dangerous development was not only the exclusionist policy of the whites, but also the sullen dissatisfaction and bitter race pride of the Negroes themselves. They were "withdrawing" themselves as a reaction to the segregation and discrimination enforced by the whites.

In the North the sudden influx of Southern Negroes during the Great Migration caused a temporary rise in social discrimination. Since, in spite of this, there was much less of it in the North than in the South, the migration meant a decrease of social segregation and discrimination for the Negro people as a whole. It also seemed that, despite the sharp temporary rise on account of the migration, the trend in the North, too, was toward decreasing race prejudice.

In the administration of *justice* there was a definite improvement in the South, even if Negroes in that region are still far from enjoying equality before the law. There was a slow rise in the quality of the police and the courts. Lynching, peonage, and other conspicuous aberrations of justice were becoming stamped out. This development was spurred by the increasing interest and interference in the judicial order of the region, shown by the federal courts and other federal agencies, and also by the state governments. The activity of such private organizations as the N.A.A.C.P. and the Interracial Commission were also of paramount importance for this development. More fundamentally the prestige of law was rising in the South and people were becoming more law-abiding. These changes were related to a general rise in education of the Southerners and to their fuller participation in the larger American culture.

In the North the Negro continued to enjoy full equality before the law. There was some strain in the North during the Great Migration, sometimes mounting to race riots during which the arm of the law was not always just and impartial. But on the whole the judicial order of the region was upheld, and equality in justice was not a major problem.

In the *political* sphere, the South continued to disfranchise the Negro, contrary to the clear precept of the American Creed and the Constitution. The masses of whites were also kept from political participation. Real issues were kept out of politics and there was a great amount of corruption. But these things proved increasingly difficult to keep up. Economic and ideological changes, related to the region's rapid industrialization, urbanization, and labor unionization, stepped up by the Great Depression and the New Deal, caused political splits in the Southern Democratic party machines. The splits usually remained latent, but here and there, now and then, they forced themselves into the open. The "Solid South" seemed definitely endangered. The poll tax was under fierce attack in all Southern states, and some had already abolished it.

Meanwhile such things as the rise of the price level since the nineties and the improved educational level of Southern Negroes made the statutory devices to keep Negroes from the polls—by property and literacy requirements as well as by the poll tax—less and less effective. Negro disfranchisement came increasingly to depend upon extra-legal and illegal sanctions. We viewed this situation as extremely unstable for several reasons: the legal culture of the South was rising; there were no more loopholes left for legalizing Negro disfranchisement; the Solid South was showing signs of breaking up; the liberal forces in the North were getting increasingly exasperated with the South; and the Supreme Court was starting to enforce the Constitution as it applied to voting in the South. Southern liberals were standing up, not only against the poll tax, but often also against the one-party system and the exclusion of Negro voters from the primaries. . . .

In the North the Negro enjoyed uninfringed his right to vote, and the steadily continuing migration to the North meant that the Negro vote was growing.

In the enjoyment of *public services* the Negro was discriminated against severely in the South in blunt repudiation of the Constitution and the state laws. But even in this sphere we saw a slow improvement of his status as a result of the rising legal culture of the region; the pressures from the Negroes, from public opinion in the North, from the federal courts and administration as well as from the white Southerners' own better conscience. It was becoming somewhat less unusual that a playground or even a little park was arranged for Negroes in some cities. The Negro schools were greatly improved even if they usually still remained inferior. Without question the New Deal was of tremendous importance for the Negro in respect to the share he received of public services. It is true that the Washington administration did not dare and, in any case, did not succeed in stamping out discrimination in relief, agricultural policies, or anything else in the South, but it definitely decreased it. It also brought a new kind of public servant to the South, educated and zealous officials who were not primarily interested in "keeping the Negro in his place" but in encouraging and advancing him. This introduced a new and wholesome type of public contact for the Negro people in the South, and Negroes got a feeling that public authority could be other than arbitrary and suppressive.

In the North public services were, on the whole, granted to Negroes as to other citizens in similar circumstances. . . .

Meanwhile, the new unions in the mass production industries gave Negro workers hope by organizing them together with whites in fields in which Negroes were already working. But, with few exceptions, they did not open up new industries for Negro employment during the 'thirties, neither did they pave the way for Negroes to rise by promotion from the level of unskilled workers to that of the semi-skilled and skilled. Negro business did not flourish either, and the small gains made in a few professions were quantitatively insignificant. There is no question but that the development in the economic sphere was grave. But as discrimination was slowly decreasing in all other spheres, as there were good prospects that national politics would remain liberal and progressive, as Negro defense organizations and Negro advisors in the federal administration were hammering on the inequalities, and as the new unions were pledged to nondiscrimination, there seemed to be good prospects that even the threatening trends respecting the Negro's economic status could have been turned, if the country had got out of the long stagnation in a normal way and had entered a new era of continued industrialization. Some of the economic policies of the New Deal were poorly thought out and badly integrated; in some respects they were damaging to the Negro. But administrators and experts were eager to learn from their mistakes and could be expected to accomplish better economic planning and direction when they were relieved of the pressure of emergency and improvisation. . . .

THE DECAY OF THE CASTE THEORY

We need to take a still broader perspective and ask: what has happened to white opinions on the Negro problem in the span of three generations since Emancipation?

In the South three generations ago white people had for their defense a consistent and respectable theory, endorsed by the church and by all sciences, printed in learned books and periodicals, and expounded by the South's great statesmen in the Capitol at Washington. The Negro's subordinate status was a principle integrated into a whole philosophy of society and of human life. The Negro was a completely different species of mankind: undeveloped, "child like," amoral, and much less endowed with intellectual capacities than the white man; he was meant by the Creator to be a servant forever; if kept in his "place" he was useful or at least tolerable, and there he was also happy; "social equality" was unthinkable as it implied intermarriage which would destroy the white race and Anglo-Saxon civilization. Much of this theory—which acquired an elaborate structure to satisfy the specific needs to justify discrimination in various spheres of life—remained through Reconstruction, and it was again hailed in the Restoration of white supremacy. Indeed, much of it remained until a couple of decades ago. But now it is almost destroyed for upper class and educated people. Its maintenance among lower class and uneducated people meets increasing difficulties. The gradual destruction of the popular theory behind race prejudice is the most important of all social trends in the field of interracial relations.

It is significant that today even the white man who defends discrimination frequently describes his motive as "prejudice" and says that it is "irrational." The popular beliefs rationalizing caste in America are no longer intellectually respectable. They can no longer, therefore, be found in current books, newspapers or public speeches. They live a surreptitious life in thought and private remarks. There we have had to hunt them when studying the matter in this inquiry. When they were thus drawn out into the open they looked shabby and ashamed of themselves. Everybody who has acquired a higher education knows that they are wrong. Most white people with a little education also have a hunch that they are wrong. There is today a queer feeling of *credo quia absurdum* hovering over the whole complex of popular beliefs sustaining racial discrimination. This makes the prejudiced white man nearly as pathetic as his Negro victim.

The white man is thus in the process of losing confidence in the theory which gave reason and meaning to his way of life. And since he has not changed his life much, he is in a dilemma. This change is probably irreversible and cumulative. It is backed by the American Creed. The trend of psychology, education, anthropology, and social science is toward environmentalism in the explanation of group differences, which means that the racial beliefs which defended caste are being torn away. It also means, by implication, that the white majority group in power is accused of being the cause of the Negro's deficiencies and unhappiness. Authority and respectability are no longer supporting the popular beliefs. The beliefs are no longer nourished from above. Instead they are increasingly fought. There is a considerable time-lag between what is thought in the higher and in the lower social classes. But as time passes the lower social strata also will change their beliefs. These ideas are spread by the advance of education.

All of this is important. People want to be rational, and they want to feel that they are good and righteous. They want to have the society they live in, and their behavior in this society, explained and justified to their conscience. And now their theory is being torn to pieces; its expression is becoming recognized as a mark of ignorance.

On the other side of the caste gulf the development leads to increased bitterness. To the Negro the white man's trouble with his conscience cannot but seem to be insincerity or something worse. The Negro protest is rising, spurred by the improvement in education. The Negro group is being permeated by the democratic and equalitarian values of the American culture. Since at the same time there has been increasing separation between the two groups, Negroes are beginning to form a self-conscious "nation within the nation," defining ever more clearly their fundamental grievances against white America.

America can never more regard its Negroes as a patient, submissive minority. Negroes will continually become less well "accommodated." They will organize for defense and offense. They will watch their opportunities ever more keenly. They will have a powerful tool in the caste struggle against white America: the glorious American ideals of democracy, liberty, and equality to which America is pledged not only by its political Constitution but also by the sincere devotion of its citizens. The Negroes are a minority, and they are poor and suppressed, but they have the advantage that they can fight wholeheartedly. The whites have all the power, but they are split in their moral personality. Their better selves are with the insurgents. The Negroes do not need any other allies.

This moral process had proceeded far when the Second World War broke out.

NEGROES IN THE WAR CRISIS

This War is an ideological war fought in defense of democracy. The totalitarian dictatorships in the enemy countries had even made the ideological issue much sharper in this War than it was in the First World War.

Moreover, in this War the principle of democracy had to be applied more explicitly to race. Fascism and nazism are based on a racial superiority dogma—not unlike the old hackneyed American caste theory—and they came to power by means of racial persecution and oppression. In fighting fascism and nazism, America had to stand before the whole world in favor of racial tolerance and cooperation and of racial equality. It had to denounce German racialism as a reversion to barbarism. It had to proclaim universal brotherhood and the inalienable human freedoms. The fact that the Japanese utilize anti-white feelings in Asia and elsewhere made it even more necessary to stress the racial equality principle.

In the internal political struggle before America became involved in the War, the isolationists had worked up the idea that there was much to improve at home without trying to improve the rest of the world. They did not disdain even to point to the injustices inflicted upon the Negro; many isolationists to the left put the Negro cause to the forefront. A Georgia senator who had made a lengthy talk about the danger to democracy abroad was challenged by an isolationist co-senator with the question whether the fight for democracy should not begin in Georgia. The plight of the Negro sharecropper and the presence of peonage and lynching were brought up to stress the unsolved tasks at home and to win Negro sympathies for the isolationist cause. One permanent result of this pre-war discussion was that, in this War, the promises to establish the full democratic liberties, not only abroad but also in America, played an even more prominent role than in the First World War.

For the Negroes this new War carried unpleasant reminiscences of the earlier one. The situation looked bitterly ironical. This time too, the Negro had to fight desperately to get the right to fight for his country. In the armed forces Negroes were discriminated against in the usual ways and to almost the same extent. Mobs had attacked Negro soldiers and war workers, and a Southern senator had requested the Army to keep Negro soldiers out of the South. Negroes also had to fight to get into the war industries and had only partial success. In the First World War they actually made considerable advances in industrial employment, and the Great Migration was a welcome consequence. But this time the nation was well stocked with unemployed whites at the beginning of the defense boom. A technological development had also intervened, decreasing the industrial demand for unskilled labor—the type of jobs for which Negroes are least unwelcome. Up to the time when this is being written (August, 1942), the Negro has been almost excluded from the great bulk of the war industries. Discrimination is the rule practically everywhere.

Under the threat of a Negro march on Washington, skillfully staged by A. Philip Randolph, the President made a solemn proclamation against discrimination in the defense industries and government agencies and appointed a committee, having both Negro and white members, to see that it was observed. Other branches of the Administration made declarations and issued orders against discrimination: some of these statements were apparently sincere in their intention, some were face-saving moves, and most had their locus somewhere in the wide range between. The Republican National Committee resolved that racial discriminations are "wrongs under the Constitution" and pledged the opposition party to work to correct them. The national labor unions also lined up for nondiscrimination. The Negroes heard and read the kindly promises. They again noted the public acceptance of their own reading of the Constitution and the American Creed. But they knew the grim reality.

In the twenty years between the two World Wars the general level of education of the American Negroes had become considerably higher, and so had their capacity for democracy. The Negro press had become better equipped, and it reached farther. The Negro organizations had grown in strength. The national Negro leaders had become firmer, and they were more resentful. This time they were not willing cheerfully to postpone their complaints until the War was over. The elderly Du Bois renounced with bitterness the credulous advice he once gave his people in the First World War to "close ranks." In this new War the Negro leaders advertised freely—and sometimes provocatively—the danger of a low morale among Negroes.

In this War there was a "colored" nation on the other side—Japan. And that nation started out by beating the white Anglo-Saxons on their own ground. The smoldering revolt in India against British rule had significance for the American Negroes, and so had other "color incidents" in the world conflict: the wavering sympathies of several native populations in the Dutch and British possessions in the Pacific, the mistrust against Great Britain among the Arab peoples, the first abandonment of Ethiopia, and the ambiguity of the plans for the colonial chessboard of Africa. Even unsophisticated Negroes began to see vaguely a color scheme in world events, although their thoughts are usually not yet organized in a definite pattern. In a "letter to the editor" by a Negro, which crept into a liberal white paper in the Upper South, the concluding sentences read:

> The Negro races on earth are very suspicious of the white man's good intentions. This is very likely to be the last war that the white man will be able to lead humanity to wage for plausible platitudes.

And this low-toned threat from a single Southern Negro became occasionally more shrill in the North: all colored people should be united in their interests against the whites, and the aim should not be "national unity" but a real color war which would definitely end white imperialism and exploitation.

But this was exceptional. World politics and the color issue are, in the final analysis, of secondary importance to American Negroes, except as avenues for the expression of dissatisfaction. The American Negro is thoroughly Americanized; his complaint is merely that he is not accepted. What really matters to him is his treatment at home, in his own country. A Negro journalist, explaining the feeling of the Negro to the white public, has this to say:

> Because he must fight discrimination to fight for his country and to earn a living, the Negro to-day is angry, resentful, and utterly apathetic about the war. "Fight for what?" he is asking. "This war doesn't mean a thing to me. If we win, I lose, so what?"

Reading the Negro press and hearing all the reports from observers who have been out among common Negroes in the South and the North convince me that there is much sullen skepticism, and even cynicism, and vague, tired, angry dissatisfaction among American Negroes today. The general bitterness is reflected in the stories that are circulating in the Negro communities: A young Negro, about to be inducted into the Army, said, "Just carve on my tombstone, 'Here lies a black man killed fighting a yellow man for the protection of a white man.'" Another Negro boy expressed the same feeling when he said he was going to get his eyes slanted so that the next time a white man shoved him around he could fight back. Their caste status being what it is in America, Negroes would, indeed, not be ordinary human beings if such dissatisfaction and bitterness were not their reaction to all the morale talk about democracy, the four freedoms, the American way of life, all the violent denunciations of Nazi race hatred and the lack of freedom under totalitarian rule. We should also remember, however, that, even if Negroes are still mainly excluded from work in the manufacturing industries and from employment offering much future prospect, the war boom has created a lot of secondary employment for Negroes, too. There is more money in circulation and some trickles down to the Negroes. With a little money in his pocket even the poor Negro day laborer or domestic worker feels that he can afford to stiffen himself. Many white housewives notice strange thoughts and behavior on the part of their Negro servants these days.

The loyalty of the American Negro in war and peace is, however, proverbial. The only thing Negroes ask for is to be accepted as Americans. The American Constitution is even dearer to them than to their white compatriots. They are more unreservedly anti-fascist. Few American Negroes want the Axis powers to win the War. But this is not much of an issue to Negroes, as they, about as much as white Americans, are convinced of the invincibility of their country. Negroes have never doubted the strength and resourcefulness of the whites. Even more, they know that America offers more possibility of democracy, even for themselves, than do the Axis nations. In one of the most thoughtful statements on the question of Negro loyalties since the beginning of the war crisis, Ralph Bunche says:

> There should be no illusions about the nature of this struggle. . . . The fight now is not to save democracy, for that which does not exist cannot be saved. But the fight is to maintain those conditions under which people may continue to strive for realization of the democratic ideals. This is the inexorable logic of the nation's position as dictated by the world anti-democratic revolution and Hitler's projected new world order.

But it is quite common that Negroes feel a satisfaction in the temporary adversities and want the War to become as serious a matter as possible to the white people in power. There have been reports that poor Negro sharecroppers in the South sometimes indulge in dreams of a Japanese army marching through the South and killing off a number of "crackers." They do not want them to land in the North, though, and they certainly do not want them to stay. But much more common is a glowing ill-concealed satisfaction over the war adversities on various fronts. Practically every issue of any Negro newspaper gives proof of this attitude. It must be conceded that Negroes have also some good rational reasons for this feeling. They know, of course, that, as a Northern Negro social scientist explains:

> . . . the graver the outside danger to the safety of this country, the more abundant the gains will be likely to be [for the Negroes]. But until such time as this country is actually in grave danger most of the attention given to the problem of [Negro] morale will be that of conjuring up the right type of propaganda to allay their discontent.

A white commentator complained some months ago that the Negro press is something of a fifth column. He received the unanimous and angry answer in all Negro papers that this is exactly contrary to the truth. Negroes are standing only for the democratic principles, to defend which

America is waging war. They are dissatisfied because these principles are ignored in America itself. They are just the opposite of war dodgers and traitors: they pray to have the right to fight and die for their country and to work in the war industries, but they are excluded. They can, with new reason, point to the inconsistency between American ideals and practices, as does one of their wisest editors, Elmer A. Carter: ". . . this strange and curious picture, this spectacle of America at war to preserve the ideal of government by free men, yet clinging to the social vestiges of the slave system." This ideological attack is so clear-cut and simple and so obviously to the point that it appeals even to the least educated Negro. The cause of the American Negro has supreme logical strength. And the Negro is better prepared than ever before in his history to fight for it.

THE WAR AND THE WHITES

This simple logic is, of course, apparent to white Americans, too. And the whites were on the way, even before the War, to lose their caste theory and their complacency in the face of obvious abuses of the American Creed. They were also stirred up by the War and the great cause of human liberties at stake. In the North the question can be publicly approached in only one spirit, that of the American Creed. A newspaper editorial reads like this:

> If the United Nations win this war the principle of the world-wide legal equality of races will have to be recognized. Since this is largely a war of ideas, and since racial equality before the law has become one of the central ideas on the democratic side, we can almost say that this principle, in itself, may be the deciding factor. The Chinese, the East Indians, the numerous African peoples and many other groups are on our side, or would be so if they were completely convinced that we mean what we say by equality just as unreservedly as the Nazis mean what they say by inequality. But we Americans cannot very well talk convincingly in these terms unless we prove our sincerity in our own country. Our largest recognizable racial minority is the Negro.

The titular leader of the Republican party, Wendell Willkie, speaking in July, 1942 at the annual conference of the N.A.A.C.P. in Los Angeles, California had this to say:

> Today it is becoming increasingly apparent to thoughtful Americans that we cannot fight the forces and ideas of imperialism abroad and maintain a form of imperialism at home. The war has done this to our thinking. . . . So we are finding under the pressures of this present conflict that long-

standing barriers and prejudices are breaking down. The defense of our democracy against the forces that threaten it from without has made some of its failures to function at home glaringly apparent. Our very proclamations of what we are fighting for have rendered our own inequities self-evident. When we talk of freedom and opportunity for all nations the mocking paradoxes in our own society become so clear they can no longer be ignored.

The world conflict and America's exposed position as the defender of the democratic faith is thus accelerating an ideological process which was well under way. In this dramatic stage of the American caste struggle a strategic fact of utmost importance is this, that the entire caste order is extra-legal if not actually illegal and unconstitutional. The legal order of the land does not sanction caste but, on the contrary, is framed to guarantee equality and to suppress caste. The only important exceptions are the Jim Crow laws in the Southern states. But even they are written upon the fiction of equality, although, if equality were enforced, they would not only lose in efficacy as means of expressing caste subordination, but also become tremendously burdensome economically for society and, consequently, the whites would be robbed of one of their main interests in upholding them.

The whites are aware of the tremendous social costs of keeping up the present irrational and illegal caste system. Among other things, this anomaly is one of the main factors keeping the respect for law and order and the administration of laws at such a low level in America. The whites investigate these irrationalities and the consequent social wastage; they build scientific systems to explain their social causation, in fact, they know all about it and deplore it. They have the political power to make caste legal and orderly, whether with Negro consent or without it. But practically never will whites be heard making such proposals, and still less will they seriously discuss and plan for such a change. They cannot afford to compromise the American Creed.

Caste may exist, but it cannot be recognized. Instead, the stamp of public disapproval is set upon it, and this undermines still more the caste theory by which the whites have to try to explain and justify their behavior. And the Negroes are awarded the law as a weapon in the caste struggle. Here we see in high relief how the Negroes in their fight for equality have their allies in the white man's own conscience. The white man can humiliate the Negro; he can thwart his ambitions; he can starve him; he can press him down into vice and crime; he can occasionally beat him and even kill him; but he does not have the moral stamina to make the Negro's subjugation legal and approved by society. Against that stands not only the Constitution and the laws which could be changed, but also the American Creed which is firmly rooted in the Americans' hearts.

THE NORTH MOVES TOWARD EQUALITY

In the North the Creed was strong enough long before the War to secure for the Negro practically unabridged civic equality in all his relations with public authority, whether it was in voting, before the courts, in the school system or as a relief recipient. But he is discriminated against ruthlessly in private relations, as when looking for a job or seeking a home to live in. The white Northerner, in his private dealings with people to whom he does not feel akin, has dangerous traditions derived from the exploitation of new immigrants. But even in those nonpublic spheres, and particularly in the problem of breadwinning, the white Northerner is becoming prepared, as a citizen, to give the Negro his just opportunity. But apparently, as a private individual, he is less prepared to feel that he himself is the man to give the Negro a better chance: in his own occupation, trade union, office or workshop, in his own residential neighborhood or in his church. The social paradox in the North is exactly this, that almost everybody is against discrimination in general but, at the same time, almost everybody practices discrimination in his own personal affairs.

It is the cumulation of all these personal discriminations which creates the color bar in the North and for the Negro causes unusually severe unemployment, crowded housing conditions, crime and vice. About this social process the ordinary white Northerner keeps sublimely ignorant and unconcerned. This aloofness is, of course, partly opportunistic but it can be fought by education. When now, in the war emergency, the Negro is increasingly given sympathetic publicity by newspapers, periodicals, and the radio, and by administrators and public personalities of all kinds, one result is that the white Northerner is gradually waking up and seeing what he is doing to the Negro and is seeing also the consequences of his democratic Creed for his relations with Negroes. We have become convinced in the course of this inquiry that the North is getting prepared for a fundamental redefinition of the Negro's status in America. The North will accept it if the change is pushed by courageous leadership. And the North has much more power than the South. The white South is itself a minority and a national problem.

Also working in favor of the Negro is another trend, namely, the concentration of responsibility. Particularly in the crucial economic sphere this trend is rapid. Labor relations are coming increasingly to be planned and regulated by broad union policies and by national legislation and administration. The War will force this change forward step by step. After the War, in the great crisis of demobilization and liquidation, mass unemployment will be a main problem. Large-scale public intervention will be a necessity. In this endeavor no national administration will dare to allow unemployment to be too much concentrated upon the Negro.

The average white Northerner will probably agree with a policy which holds open employment opportunities for Negroes, because, as we said, he is against economic discrimination as a general proposition. There is also—together with all opportunistic ignorance and unconcernedness—a bit of rational defense for the distance he preserves between his political and his private opinion. In the individual shop where he works or the residential section where he lives, he sees the danger in admitting a few Negroes, since this will bring an avalanche of Negroes on his shop or his neighborhood. This danger is, of course, due to the fact of the Negro's general exclusion. It is part of the vicious circle holding the Negro down.

If government policy prevents general discrimination, however, there will be no avalanche of Negroes on any one white employer or group of employers. The Negroes, who comprise less than 10 per cent of the population, must be given their chance in private enterprise or be supported by public funds. "Buck-passing" is no longer possible when the problem comes to be viewed nationally. And the planning and directing agencies will be compelled to make the white public see the problem nationally in order to get public support for the policy they must pursue. As private relations are increasingly becoming public relations, the white Northerner will be willing to give the Negro equality.

These are the reasons why we foresee that the trend of unionization, social legislation, and national planning will tend to break down economic discrimination, the only type of discrimination which is both important and strong in the North. Other types of discrimination will then tend to decrease according to the law of cumulative causation which has been frequently referred to in this book.

TENSION IN THE SOUTH

The situation in the South is different. Unlike the white Northerner, who is most inclined to give the Negro equality in public relations and least inclined to do so in private relations, the white Southerner does not differentiate between public and private relations—the former as well as the latter have significance for prestige and social equality. Moreover, he is traditionally and consistently opposed to Negro equality for its own sake, which the Northerner is not. He may be privately indulgent much more than the white Northerner, but he is not as willing to give the Negro equal treatment by public authority. This is one of the romantic principles behind the legal inequity in the South. But the Southerner is a good American, too, and the region has been becoming rapidly "Americanized" during the last generation.

The ordinary conservative white Southerner has, therefore, a deeper split in his moral personality than does the white Northerner. The War is stirring up the conflict in his soul. The air is filled with reminders of the great cause of democracy and the equality of peoples, which is the main issue in the War America is waging against nazism, fascism, and Japanese imperialism. His "own Negroes" are making some money, reading the Negro press and getting restless. The N.A.A.C.P. and other protest organizations are fighting ever more daringly in his own cities. In his newspapers he reads how the national leaders, from the President down, come out with blunt denunciations of racial discrimination. He is finding that Northern leaders are increasingly getting interested in the poll tax, the white primary, Negro disfranchisement, injustices against Negroes, and other peculiar institutions of the South which he guards behind the doctrine of "states' rights."

What is he supposed to do? Give up Jim Crow and so perhaps allow a Negro to marry his daughters; build good schools for Negroes, though the schools are not too good for his own children; punish white invaders of Negro rights, though they otherwise may be perfectly good and upright citizens; relinquish white supremacy? Is he supposed to retreat from all "Southern traditions"? He sees "outside aggression" wherever he turns.

This is an old story and a phase of a mental cycle through which the unfortunate South has often passed before. The fact that this time the white Southerner's caste theory is weaker than ever and does not inspire much of his own intellectual confidence makes his dilemma worse. His emotions on the color issue are less stable also because his personal ties to the Negro group have been decreasing, and racial isolation has been intensified during the last generation. He "knows the Negro" less well than did his father and grandfather, though he continues to pretend that he knows him well, because to "know the Negro" is also a Southern tradition. Having fewer personal contacts with Negroes he is likely to exaggerate the signs of opposition from the Negroes, for he feels that the Negroes have good reason to develop opposition. The presence in Southern communities of Negro soldiers, many from the North, increases his uneasiness. Du Bois, writing about the First World War, talks about:

> . . . the deep resentment mixed with the pale ghost of fear which Negro soldiers call up in the breast of the white South. It is not so much that they fear that the Negro will strike if he gets a chance, but rather that they assume with curious unanimity that he has *reason* to strike, that any other persons in his circumstances, or treated as he is would rebel. Instead of seeking to relieve the cause of such a possible feeling, most of them strain every effort to bottle up the black man's resentment.

In the present crisis, Guion G. Johnson, a liberal Southern white historian, could already in July, 1941, report from the South that

> . . . there has been some uneasiness that "our Negroes" are being tampered with, and white advocates of racial goodwill have occasionally found it more difficult within the last year to speak out boldly. White persons who have for decades been working toward interracial cooperation may now find themselves charged with fifth column activity and Negro leaders may be denounced as communists or nazis.

Another prominent white Southern liberal describes in a letter to the author the mental state of the white South as of summer, 1942:

> . . . we are in the midst of a situation in the South where we seem to have been thrown back with great losses where we had expected great gains: and . . . the situation in the South may be of the proportions of a crisis greater than we have had in many years. For the first time in my experience the situation is so complex that we do not know how to proceed to next steps. Just a few years ago we almost had unanimity in plans for cooperative arrangements, in which Negroes and whites were enthusiastic and in which representatives of nearly all phases of the South were participants. We had worked into entirely new patterns of fellowship and participation, and there were many evidences that the South was beginning to be proud of this progress. Today, as far as I know, there is practically none of this left. The South is becoming almost unanimous in a pattern of unity that refers to white unity. The thousands of incidents and accidents in the South are being integrated into the old pattern of Southern determination against an outside aggression.

In the approaching conflict between the Negro and the South, this writer sees that

> . . . a South which was just coming into its own, getting ready for an enriched agriculture, a more balanced economy, a more liberal viewpoint will

sacrifice all this in a pathetic blood and sweat episode reminiscent of the Civil War and Reconstruction.

Similar to this deeply concerned statement of a liberal white Southerner, we may cite the equally troubled view of a Negro clergyman, Dr. J. S. Nathaniel Tross:

> I am afraid for my people. They have grown restless. They are not happy. They no longer laugh. There is a new policy among them—something strange, perhaps terrible.

The situation is so critical in the South today that fifty Southern Negro leaders have seen fit to gather together, deliberately excluding Northern Negroes, to plead for racial amity. They accept social segregation, but request the elimination of all other inequalities. This development was made necessary by the fearful backing away of some Southern liberals—notably Mark Ethridge, John Temple Graves, and Virginius Dabney—from the social segregation issue. The meeting of the Southern Negroes serves both as an attempt to prevent the racial lines from being drawn more sharply and as a disclaimer of responsibility for future violence.

An important element in the situation is that the Southern Negroes, if they are attacked, are more prepared to fight this time than they have ever been before. A competent Negro social scientist, who has recently been studying conditions in the Upper South, confirms this view and, in May, 1943, confides that he expects the outbreak of serious race riots in the South within the next year.

The situation is grave, and the years to come will provide a serious test of the political resourcefulness of white public authorities and of other white and Negro leaders. But regardless of what happens, we do not believe that this is a turn for the worse in race relations in the South. Even if there are going to be serious clashes and even if their short-run effects will be devastating to the Negroes involved and, perhaps, to Negroes in the whole region, we believe that the long-run effect of the present opinion crisis in the South, because it is a catharsis for the whites, will be a change toward increased equality for the Negro. When we make this judgment, we recall a remark once made in a conversation by a prominent and conservative Negro social scientist in the South. He stated as his considered opinion that tensions are not necessarily bad and that under certain conditions even race riots may have wholesome effects in the long run. He continued in about the following way: "They stir up people's conscience. People will have to think matters over. They prevent things from becoming settled. If the race situation should ever become fixed, if the Negro were really accommodated, then, and only then, would I despair about a continued great improvement for Negroes. As long as there is friction and fighting, there is hope."

At this juncture the white North is moving in a direction contrary to the South. The white South is becoming increasingly isolated. There has not been such a great distance in the views of the Negro problem between the white majority groups in the two regions since Reconstruction. Though it is seldom expressed clearly, the outside observer feels convinced that an increasing number of white Northerners mean business this time. It is true, as James Weldon Johnson once observed, that "essentially the status of the Negro in all other sections will depend upon what it is in the South," but the North will find it increasingly necessary to have its say about the Negroes' status in the South. The North cannot well afford any longer to let the white Southerners have their own way with the Negroes as completely as they have had.

The national compromise has lasted for two generations; it may now be approaching its end, at least relatively. Ten years from now this period in the history of interracial relations in America may come to look as a temporary *interregnum*. The compromise was not a stable power equilibrium. Signs of its end have been frequent during the 'thirties: a whole set of Supreme Court decisions, the New Deal in the South, the increasing activity of federal agencies to stamp out peonage, the agitation for a federal lynching law and for an abolition of the poll tax by Congress, the repeal of the two-thirds majority rule for the nomination of the Democratic candidate for the Presidency, and so on.

The Negro problem is becoming national in scope in a different sense than was meant when white Southerners expressed a belief that the Negro migration to the North would give the North more of a share in the trouble of having Negroes as neighbors and that then the North would understand the racial philosophy of the South better. The Negro vote and the labor vote in the North also have considerable weight in checking Southern conservatism and have increasing power to do so. But aside from all that, national planning cannot leave out the South or humor too much its irrationality. As a matter of fact the South, particularly its agriculture and its population pressure, will continue to remain one of the main national worries.

Because of this development, spurred by the war crisis and the coming peace crisis, it seems justifiable to predict a growing tension between the two regions, one which will not be restricted to the Negro issue. There is not going to be a civil war, of course. The South is this time relatively much weaker in all respects. The North will probably not become more considerate if the interracial tension in the South gets out of hand and results in bloody clashes. As recourse to civil war is out of the question and as things thus have to be settled by political means, the fact becomes of importance that the white South is not united against a redefinition of the Negro's status. The South has been, and is, changing rapidly, and Southern liberalism has been coming to be a force though it was practically nowhere in political power and today is fearfully timid on the Negro issue. Even the ordinary conservative white Southerner has a deeply split personality. In the short run this can be suppressed, and the tension can lead to violent reactions. But in the long run it means that the conservative white Southerner himself can be won over to equalitarian reforms in line with the American Creed.

INTERNATIONAL ASPECTS

What has actually happened within the last few years is not only that the Negro problem has become national in scope after having been mainly a Southern worry. It has also acquired tremendous international implications, and this is another and decisive reason why the white North is prevented from compromising with the white South regarding the Negro. The situation is actually such that any and all concessions to Negro rights in this phase of the history of the world will repay the nation many times, while any and all injustices inflicted upon him will be extremely costly. This is not yet seen clearly by most Americans, but it will become increasingly apparent as the War goes on.

We mentioned in passing that the American Negro cannot help observing the color angle to this War. He is obviously getting vicarious satisfaction out of this perspective, and he is also testing some vague feelings of solidarity and allegiance to the cause of other colored peoples involved in the world conflagration. But this is a minor part of the international implications. The American Negro is thoroughly American in his culture and whole outlook on the world. He is also loyal to America, and there is no danger that he will betray it. This is at least certain in the short-range view, which covers this War and the coming peace. How the Negro would react if he were left dissatisfied and if later a new war were to be fought more definitely along color lines is more difficult to predict.

The main international implication is, instead, that America, for its international prestige, power, and future security, needs to demonstrate to the world that American Negroes can be satisfactorily integrated into its democracy. In a sense, this War marks the end of American isolation. America has had security behind the two protecting oceans. When now this isolation has been definitely broken, the historians will begin to see how it has always greatly determined the development of America. Statesmen will have to take cognizance of the changed geopolitical situation of the nation and carry out important adaptations of the American way of life to new necessities. A main adaptation is bound to be a redefinition of the Negro's status in American democracy.

It is commonly observed that the mistrust of, or open hostility against, the white man by colored people everywhere in the world has greatly increased the difficulties for the United Nations to win this War. Many old sins and stupidities are today staring back upon the white man, and he continues to commit them, though he now knows better. The treatment of the Negro in America has not made good propaganda for America abroad and particularly not among colored nations. That good American who has acquired such a rare understanding for the Asiatic people's mind, Pearl S. Buck, comments:

> Japan . . . is declaring in the Philippines, in China, in India, Malaya, and even Russia that there is no basis for hope that colored peoples can expect any justice from the people who rule in the United States, namely, the white people. For specific proof the Japanese point to our treatment of our own colored people, citizens for generations in the United States. Every lynching, every race riot, gives joy to Japan. The discriminations of the American army and navy and the air forces against colored soldiers and sailors, the exclusion of colored labor in our defense industries and trade unions, all our social discriminations, are of the greatest aid today to our enemy in Asia, Japan. "Look at America," Japan is saying to millions of listening ears. "Will white Americans give you equality?"

And she assures her compatriots:

> We cannot . . . win this war without convincing our colored allies—who are most of our allies—that we are not fighting for ourselves as continuing superior over colored peoples. The deep patience of colored peoples is at an end. Everywhere among them there is the same resolve for freedom and equality that white Americans and British have, but it is a grimmer resolve, for it includes the determination to be rid of white rule and exploitation and white race prejudice, and nothing will weaken this will.

This is perhaps an exaggeration. Perhaps the War can this time be won even without the colored people's confidence. But the absence of their full cooperation, and still more their obstructive activities, will be tremendously costly in time, men and materials. Caste is becoming an expensive luxury of white men.

It seems more definitely certain that it will be impossible to make and preserve a good peace without having built up the fullest trust and good-will among the colored peoples. They will be strong after the War, and they are bound to become even stronger as time passes. For one thing, this is certain in so far as numbers are concerned. During the short span of the last three centuries, which includes almost the entire epoch of white power expansion, the peoples of European stock increased sevenfold, while the others increased only threefold. The whites grew from a bare 100 millions, or a fifth of the globe's total, to over 700 millions, or a third of all mankind. The increase for the whites was fastest during the last century when they gradually became able to control deaths but had not as yet brought births under control. The whites are, however, now in the second phase of this dynamic sequence: the white birth rate is falling so fast that it is catching up with the relatively stable death rate. The population expansion of the whites is now slowing down, absolutely and relatively. Many of the Western nations, including America and all those other peoples on the highest level of industrial civilization, will probably start to shrink in population numbers within the next few decades. The colored nations, on the other hand, are just entering the first stage where expansion is likely to be pushed by an increasingly improved control over death, and it is unlikely that the increase in birth control will keep pace with the improvement of the control over death. The whites will, therefore, from now on become a progressively smaller portion of the total world population. If we except the Russian peoples, who are still rapidly increasing, the rapid change in proportion stands out still more dramatically.

Another broad trend is almost as certain, namely, that the "backward" countries, where most colored people live, are going to become somewhat industrialized. The examples of Japan and, more recently, of Russia and China give support to the view that in the future we shall see many backward countries industrialized at a tremendously more rapid rate than were the pioneer Western countries, who had to find out everything for themselves. The same examples illustrate also how such backward nations can advantageously use the newly created industrial apparatus for producing war materials, and they illustrate, too, how they can fight with them.

Particularly as Russia cannot be reckoned on to adhere to white supremacy, it is evident from these facts—though nobody in our countries seems to take it seriously—that within a short period the shrinking minority of white people in our Western lands will either have to succumb or to find ways of living on peaceful terms with colored people. If white people, for their own preservation, attempt to reach a state in which they will be tolerated by their colored neighbors, equality will be the most they will be strong enough to demand.

History is never irredeemable, and there is still time to come to good terms with colored peoples. Their race pride and race prejudice are still mostly a defensive mental device, a secondary reaction built up to meet the humiliations of white supremacy. This is apparent in the case of the American Negro. It probably holds true even for other colored people who have not yet had a taste of power. A Chinese propaganda leaflet assures the Americans:

> Chinese nationalism or race-consciousness is essentially defensive in character. It has developed out of continuous fight for freedom, and has never been offensive.

It should be apparent that the time to come to an understanding on the basis of equality is rapidly running out. When colored nations have once acquired power but still sense the scorn of white superiority and racial discrimination, they are likely to become indoctrinated by a race prejudice much more akin to that of the whites—a race prejudice which can be satisfied only by the whites' humiliation and subjugation.

CHAPTER XII

Minorities: The General Case

THE position of the Spanish-American minority portrayed in the following selection is typical of the broad racial problem in America. It is an example of racial or ethnic discrimination which has not been carried as far as a caste barrier. It happens that in the Southwest of the United States, this discrimination hits the Spanish-American segment of the populace. At different times, however, and in different parts of the country, the Irish-Americans, the Polish-Americans, the Italian-Americans, and a host of other minority groups have presented a similar spectacle.

THE MINORITY CITIZEN*

For two years or more, the Spanish-language paper in the *colonia* has carried on a campaign against the refusal of certain rights and privileges to Americans of Mexican extraction. "Discrimination," in this sense, has no exact equivalent in Spanish; it has to be translated "abusos contra los derechos civiles" or "prejudicios raciales en contra de los Mexicanos," [1] both of which phrases more exactly describe the situation than "discrimination." For, according to dominant Descanso, discrimination is just a little social quirk or idiosyncrasy, an expression of personal taste which could not possibly have legal implications. From this premise, Descanso proceeds to argue that moves to curtail discriminatory practices constitute infringements of personal liberty. The personal liberty of the dominant group is meant, of course, for the personal liberties of other groups are not a factor, from this point of view. Descanso tries to place a dislike for seeing little Americans of Mexican descent in a public swimming pool in the same class as a dislike of seeing onions on the dinner table. It has not only so rationalized its breaches

* From *Not with the Fist* by Ruth D. Tuck, copyright, 1946, by Ruth D. Tuck. Used by permission of Harcourt, Brace and Company, Inc. Pp. 197–207, 210–222.

[1] Abusos contra los derechos civiles: abuses of civil rights; prejudicios raciales en contra de los Mexicanos: racial prejudices against Mexicans.

of civil trust for itself. It has, in the past, succeeded in convincing many a Mexican-American that fighting for equal privileges constituted a social error, a simple case of bad manners—pushing yourself in where you weren't wanted.

There are few legal bars, as such, against the Mexican or American of Mexican descent. He is counted on the white side of miscegenation statutes, as a rule. No Jim-Crowism is part of his life, even in the sovereign State of Texas. School segregation is put upon a basis other than the ethnic, officially. Courts have held that the non-Caucasian clauses of restrictive residence covenants do not include persons of Mexican ancestry. If he is a citizen, he is not barred from the polls. These are advantages which the dominant community is quick to point out, particularly when it is trying to wedge between the Mexican-American minority and other minorities less favored. In some ways, this position is an asset, but in other respects it is a liability. It makes the job of fighting the extra-legal discrimination all the more difficult. Rather than having the job of battering down a wall, the Mexican-American finds himself entangled in a spider web, whose outlines are difficult to see but whose clinging, silken strands hold tight.

For many years, the immigrant and his sons made no effort to free themselves. They burned with resentment over a thousand slights, but they did so in private, or among others of their kind. "Docility" was the most admired characteristic of the Mexican immigrant, by the dominant group, who often added "cowardly" to the description. The immigrant was not a coward, but he was bewildered, leaderless, and desperately in search of security. "Don't go where you're not wanted," "Keep your mouth closed and you won't give yourself away," and "Don't get *la raza* in trouble" were some of the admonitions he gave himself and his children. Violations of civil rights were likely to be greeted in the *colonia* with an apathetic, saddened shrug and the comment, "Yes, that is how they treat us Mexicans." The man who submerged himself in *Mexicanismo* was a more admired figure than the man who stood up for his rights and so "got us all into trouble." Perhaps this passivity is the mark of any minority which is just emerging from severe exploitation, but the immigrant and his sons seemed to remain in this stage a long time.

In the end, it was the war which really awoke Descanso's *colonia*, as it did many another Mexican colony in the Southwest. In a world in which the heroic sacrifice of Americans of Mexican descent at Bataan and Corregidor could be followed, in eighteen months, by riots against Americans of Mexican descent in Los Angeles, passive accommodation lost much of its value. It has become trite to make this observation, but there is force and clarity in the triteness. The immigrant mother in the *colonia,* who had lost a son in battle, felt quite simply that his little brothers should be able to attend a public plunge or an unsegregated school.

The incident in the *colonia* which fired it to social action made such a direct connection between sacrifice in war and civil rights. The son of one of the prominent men in the *colonia* was killed in flight training and the body was shipped home for military burial. Wishing the best last resting-place possible, the father bought a lot in a near-by "memorial park." The man in charge thought him an Italian, it was later explained. When the father returned with the mother and her relatives to view the lot, his money was returned and the purchase refused with the explanation, "Oh, we didn't know you were Mexican. We don't bury Mexicans here." The military funeral was eventually held elsewhere. Now, this sort of thing had been happening for years. It still happens, and the bodies concerned are often in uniform, to be interred with American flags. But the fact that it took place in such a dramatic fashion, involving such a shock to a grief-stricken mother, striking such an exemplary, *gente decente* family, aroused the whole *colonia*. The story is still told by indignant women in the *colonia,* written in letters to relatives in Mexico, and recounted on visits there. Every *nacional* (imported contract worker) eventually hears it. As a nullifier of "good-will" policies, it and stories like it are potent forces.

Indignation coalesced in the formation of the Defense Committee and the successful fight to open the public plunge to the public, regardless of national or ethnic origins. The plan for the committee originally embraced a series of such court cases, based on concrete situations, and touching one after another of the spheres in which Mexican-Americans encountered discrimination. The *colonia* had its steam up. Instead, however, of finding another concrete case like that of the public plunge, it ran into a network of half-defined, nebulous situations. All of them involved discriminatory practices, but none of them provided the explicit detail needed for legal action. In some cases, the city, having no mind to be caught flat-footed again, had hastily put in a little legal window-dressing.

The display of "white trade only" signs and the refusal of service to persons of Mexican descent was to have been a target for the committee. The city council quickly made the display of such signs illegal, but scarcely a month passes when some Mexican-Americans are not refused service in a bar or café. Techniques for doing so are facilitated by the plethora of customers in these establishments. The tables are all filled, and none ever seems to empty for Mexican-Americans—those people who were let in ahead had "reservations." Or the ethnically undesired customer is seated, but gets no service—for as long a period as two hours. Or it just happens to be "club night" in a certain establishment, and the management is very sorry that it cannot serve those without a card. Or, if the case is finally brought to court, the judge may blandly rule that no "demand" for service was made, regardless of the evidence presented. The *colonia* leaders have learned that the best place to press a case is the federal court, if jurisdiction can be obtained, and that the most experienced and expensive legal talent is none too good.

Segregated schooling was also on the agenda of the Defense Committee. The school board quickly forestalled possible action by doing away with segregation in the *barrio pequeño*. About the school situation in the West End, the board wrings its hands, protesting, "But, you see, no amount of re-districting will improve this. It's just an unfortunate situation our predecessors wished on us. Anyway, it's the fault of the Mexicans. They all like to live in the same place." Any admission by *colonia* leadership that the situation is difficult and that the concentration of Mexican population does not improve it, is seized upon by administrators as proof that the *colonia* approves segregation—hence nothing should ever be done about it.

Contrary to the wishful thinking of Descanso, all Mexican-Americans do not like to live "in the same place," particularly if that place represents the most inadequate, ramshackle, crowded housing in the city. Volumes have been written about the poor housing of the Mexican-American throughout the Southwest; Descanso is no exception to the general picture. A quick look at the County Housing Authority's map is all that is necessary to confirm this fact. Two dark-brown sections, labeled "sub-standard," stand out—they are the *colonia* and the *barrio pequeño*. They represent *the* sub-standard housing for the city. They also represent the areas of greatest population density.

The history of any family who had an income beyond a subsistence level usually contains an incident somewhat like the following: "When my father got to be assistant foreman, he decided to look for a better house. He answered the ads in the paper, but the people just said flatly they wouldn't rent to Mexicans. Then he decided he'd buy, but it was the same thing there. The house we wanted wasn't much, and it was only about four blocks the other side of the tracks. The sale was all ready to go through, when the owner backed out. The neighbors had been raising hell about selling to Mexicans. So finally my father just bought another shack, next door to the one we already had, to have room for his family. It's the one where my married brother lives now." A college student said, "The sociology courses can't teach me anything about 'invasion.' One of the first things I remember is the time we tried to rent a house just north of here. We'd been there for two weeks when the agent came around to say that we'd have to move at the end of the month—the neighbors had protested to the owner. That evening, some teachers—Anglo-Americans who were friends of my father's—came down to talk about the 'Mexican problem.' The real Mexican problem, the one that had mother in tears, they couldn't do anything about."

The housing bars against the Mexican-American have been exactly this sort—invisible ones. While there are restrictive covenants in many a deed in the north of town, they are thought of as applying to Negroes or Orientals. Actually, about fifty families of Mexican extraction live outside the *colonia,* and thirty-five of them have moved across the tracks in the last two years. Some families, of "high type" pseudo-Mexican or "Spanish" origin, have always lived outside the *colonia;* this group usually includes the consular officials and their families. Once a Mexican-American family is settled in a neighborhood, there is little friction. Sometimes there is active good will and friendliness, if the neighbors happen to be Catholic also. The friction arises when another family of Mexican extraction tries to move into the same general neighborhood. "We don't want any more Mexicans on this street," is the slogan, applicable no matter how "high type" and "Spanish" the invaders may be. If a number of families of Mexican extraction begin to move into a neighborhood, it may suddenly develop that there are no houses for sale for miles around. Owners have just changed their minds about selling, say the agents, and what can one do? Thus, without recourse to anything so crude as a restrictive covenant, a quota system is actually set up for movement away from the *colonia.*

The less desirable the Anglo-American neighborhood the smaller the quota is. The professional man of good income may encounter little difficulty in moving near the country club, but the workingman who wants to move five or six blocks east of the *colonia* is likely to find no takers for his down payment. This has the effect of bottling up those families who are most in need of improved housing. The result is to multiply shack upon shack on the crowded streets and narrow lots west of the tracks.

Descanso has, in the past, turned a deaf ear to any sweeping proposals for slum-clearance and decent low-cost housing. Nice, civic-minded ladies have actually talked in favor of retention of the slum areas. "You know, I'd hate to see Barbarita Street [a crowded alley known in social-work circles as 'Delinquency Row'] go. It's just like a bit of old Mexico, with the cactus fences and tiny houses covered with roses. When I have visitors I always take them down to see it." The number of Mexican-American families buying in the north and east of Descanso, however, has recently given such civic-planners pause. "With money in their pockets," says Descanso, "they'll all be trying to move into our part of town. It may be that better housing, privately financed if possible, in that end of town, would keep them where they belong." There is even talk of making everything terribly "old Spanish" and picturesque, with rows of oleanders and mission arches; and the Confederation of Mexican Societies, with its plans for a *Casa de la Colonia,* is helping segregation along. "See," say the civic planners, "even those prominent Mexicans would rather stay in the West End. They're happier among their own kind."

It is true that about 60 per cent of the *colonia* either owns its homes or is buying them; this is as true in the meanest streets as in those where housing is not sub-standard. Most of the purchases have involved hard work, sacrifice, and considerable planning. A man like Juan Pérez may not have received much for his money, by the time interest charges are counted in, but to him it means a degree of security. He will not be willing to give it up unless he is sure that he will get at least as much security in return. Neither will he be happy in a barracks-like apartment structure, no matter how scientifically planned. He likes to have a small yard, a few fruit trees and flowers, and some chickens. "It's obvious," said a housing authority on a tour of the *colonia,* "that the pattern for Mexican-American rehousing should be the cottage community type—with fences for every front yard!" Give Juan Pérez a chance at such a home, even outside the *colonia,* on some rental or purchase basis which will guarantee him tenure, and he would jump at the chance. He gets a hungry gleam in his eye when he sees pictures of the bright, clean homes of Swedish workers' villages, and he would not be at all reluctant to see his children farther away from the *cantinas* and drunks of Monticello Avenue.

Certainly some of the elderly, to whom ownership of anything—even a board-and-batten with the battens off and the roof leaking—represents a miracle, would be difficult to move. Much of their stubbornness is fear of falling into the hands of another *explotador.* The *padre,* too, would probably represent an obstacle. Sincerely anxious as he is for better living conditions for his parishioners, he is not eager to see them dispersed. The colony scoffers say, "If the flock ever scattered, he'd never collect it again." His plans for a parochial school in the *colonia* depend upon new generations of Mexican-Americans being born there. To date, he has seemed to incline strongly toward privately erected family units, no slum clearance, and oleanders.

The second generation, however, has little nostalgia for the *colonia*. "Sure, maybe it's picturesque," said a high-school boy, "to Anglo slumming parties who can live anywhere they want to. Maybe they'd feel differently if they tried it here for a while. I don't want to lose touch with my family, but, if I make any wages at all, I'm sure going to get out of this sink-hole." "No kids of mine are going to be brought up there, if I can help it," is another very general comment. Only one thing, apparently, will hold the second generation in the *colonia*. "Maybe I should get out, for my children's sake," said a young father, "but I'm afraid of losing touch with my people, while they still need help. It's a question many of us face—whether it's better to move across town and show, by example, what can be done, or to stay here, in the middle of things, and help more of our people move eventually."

In housing, as in other matters, there are no obvious barriers, legally labeled as such, before the Mexican-American. But the invisible barrier can be just as impenetrable and far more tantalizing. Its operation is often more effective than if it had been embodied in law, because it is difficult to isolate and fight. To a group as distinguished by sensitive pride as the Mexican-American, such techniques are cruelly effective. An honest insistence on a basic right can be made to look like a mere social faux pas, "pushing in where you aren't wanted." To a few elite, the hope is always held out that, if they are sufficiently "high type" and willing to cut themselves off from the rest, the invisible barrier can be broken. The dominant community can always pretend that its right hand does not know what its left hand is doing. "Why, we haven't any discrimination—we have a Mexican in the Elks."

As a last resort, the Mexican-American can always be encouraged to ponder how much better off he is than the Negro or the Oriental. This tactic has the added advantage, from the point of view of the dominant group, of setting one minority against another. If it can divide minority action on such an issue, for example, as a permanent Fair Employment Practice Committee, it can say, "The very people who would profit from this are squabbling among themselves. If they will cut one another's throats for advantage, what can you expect the poor employer to do?" On questions of educational facilities, access to public facilities, relief budgets, and even unionization, the same dividing tactic is used time and time again. One minority group is offered a little *atole con el dedo,* and off it trots, wagging its tail. The Mexican-American group has certainly fallen for this bait repeatedly, to the ill-disguised amusement of those who proffered it.

Many of the problems of the Mexican-American are different than those of the Negro or the Oriental. He has an advantage in that the caste is not closed, completely, at the top for him. With this advantage, the Mexican-American could easily constitute the spearhead for advance in all minority gains. He has a freedom of action and movement often denied to other minority members; he can attempt things impossible for them. But the gains he would make for all minorities would be gains for him, too. Desperately as the Mexican-American has pretended—particularly under snobbish, self-seeking leadership—that he is better off than *los tintos,*[2] he knows that the difference is one of degree rather than of kind. Whatever the ethnic niceties of the situation may be, that is the way the sociological cards fell, from 1910 on.

The same sensitive pride which makes the Mexican-American wince unduly under slights also makes him too anxious to please—to be judged favorably by the dominant group. When *la plebe* says, of its prejudices toward *los tintos* and others, that "they are things we learned from you people," it is not far from the truth. Los Conejos offered little scope for race prejudice. Members of the *gente decente* felt themselves, in general, superior to the few Negroes or Chinese they encountered; but the preoccupation with race, the allergy to a darker skin, the thousands of status-weighted allusions to it, was something they had to learn here. In states like Texas, it was in the very air they breathed. There was no surer way to please an Anglo than to slight a Negro, and much of the early accommodating leadership among Mexican immigrants made ample use of this technique.

The *colonia,* apparently, has a divided mind on the subject. Among its top leadership, there are at least two individuals who openly proclaim and practice minority solidarity. A third recognizes the necessity of working with Negro groups, particularly in politics, but adds a few private reservations about "knowing them socially." The others, pushed in some cases by *gente decente* families, would like to cling to the advantage of being "better than *los tintos,*" even in public action. The second generation, even among its leaders, is uncertain in regard to public action with Negro groups—for the most part, it is uninformed regarding their objectives. Friendships and alliances in school activities, among them playground fights, occur between Mexican-American and Negro youth, but they are seldom sustained after school hours. There is little contact of an intimate

[2] Los tintos: slang for colored, usually applied to Negroes.

social sort between the *colonia* families and the Negroes who have moved in at its east edge, save among very young children. (In the *barrio pequeño,* however, where families of the two groups have lived side by side for several years, there are not only friendships among children but visiting and sociability among families of the two groups.) However, for all the distance between the two groups in the *colonia,* there is instant, quick sympathy for the Negro who is obviously exploited or mistreated by dominant groups.

In regard to the Orientals, there is still remoteness, but of a slightly different sort. To *la plebe,* the Oriental businessman—market owner, nurseryman, "herb doctor," or vegetable wholesaler—represented an economically advantaged person, sometimes a potential employer. He was not, as the Negro often was, a competitor in the same labor market. He could be admired for his acumen and success; to do him credit, he apparently did not take undue advantage of his position. There was genuine sympathy in the *colonia,* for the exiled Japanese-Americans, several of whom lived and had businesses within the *colonia.* Even the Mexican-Americans who occupy Nisei-owned property have no theoretical objections to their return, although, should return coincide with a housing shortage, there might be friction. Nor do families who have lost sons in the Pacific area confuse the issue of the Japanese enemy with that of the loyal resident or citizen of the United States—a rather remarkable achievement, considering the radio and press campaign to which they have been exposed. With regard to the Japanese-Americans, there seemed to be cognizance by *la plebe* that mistreatment of this minority threatened other minorities. However, aside from respect for the Oriental's financial success and sympathy for his minority status, there is little closeness between the two groups in the sense of friendship or intermarriage. Both disapprove such closer connections, although they are able to live side by side in harmony.

In speaking of people and their groupings, one must be very careful—as Descanso is not—to distinguish between (1) the tendency of persons of like interests, background, and taste to cluster together and (2) the refusal of basic rights, such as access to education, public facilities, or employment, by one group to another. It is the latter which is "discrimination." That it may have originally grown out of the former does not justify its existence, as Descanso appears to think. No one should know better than Descanso that "natural" tendencies, uncurbed, fast develop into vices! It is something the *colonia* could consider before, out of a desire to curry favor, it copies the vices. . . .

ON BEING A CITIZEN

There is a large potential voting population in the *colonia,* and it is getting larger every year. The *colonia's* vote could easily swing the ward of which it is a part, because, although the ward is large, population density at its upper end is slight. Any group which composes 12 per cent of the population is a force on the ballot, if it is active. If the *colonia* is not aware of this, there is certainly awareness elsewhere. The Mexican-American vote is watched carefully, by men with political "know." Those who would like to maintain the status quo draw a long breath when it shows its customary apathy.

Politics in the *colonia* is incredibly lily-white and naive, compared to that in the rest of the city. What activity exists is conducted just the way the civics books say it should be, with the result that it is often as far removed from reality as the civics books. In many ways, this high-principled behavior is an asset. An honest vote, if it could be registered in quantity at the polls, would advance the *colonia* much farther than attempting to play fancy games with the old hands on the other side of town. To date, the Mexican-American vote in Descanso is not "sold," nor can it be "delivered." The cynics and the disappointed among the Anglo-Americans say that is because it just cannot be aroused. But whenever it shows any activity at all, there is considerable excitement on the other side of town; and the activity is likely to be interpreted as being more significant than it really is.

The *colonia* leadership is aware that voting power is potential strength, but it has not yet learned the techniques, nor is it willing to do the hard foot-work necessary to turn it out, precinct by precinct. A special ward election produced the Liga Cívica, an attempt in this direction, but too hastily organized to count for much in the election it was supposed to influence. Most of the persons thus registered voted in the national primaries, though. Registration of additional voters proceeded sporadically throughout the spring and early summer, with the result that the national election produced what county officials considered a record Mexican-American vote of 73.90 per cent in this ward, not too far below the city average of 79.75. It is, however, a general and dangerous tendency of masses everywhere in the United States to display political activity only once every four years. The Mexican-American will have to learn, along with many other groups, that it is unceasing vigilance at the polls—all the way from Congressional primaries down to school board and water district elections—which counts.

Jury duty presents a startlingly biased picture in Descanso. No Mexican-

Americans serve on juries, nor are they apparently wanted—although several Negroes do serve. The story is an interesting one. In Descanso, for county jury duty, the judges draw up lists of prospective jurors, to whom the clerk then sends questionnaries. On the basis of the returned questionnaires—and by judgments which include such items as "neatness of handwriting"—lists of jurors are formed. These lists are constantly revised, and one of the bases for removal of a juror's name is his continued unacceptability to lawyers trying cases before the Superior Court. "In a big county like this, we can't keep calling people in, at five cents a mile, if the lawyers won't take them when they get here."

In 1942, after prodding from some quarter or other, it was decided to include Mexican-American names for the first time on the judges' lists. Ten names were obtained, some of them, apparently, from the police. The incident of "the nicest little Mexican housewife, who wrote such a good hand, but was found to have been a shoplifter" may have been a by-product of the method of selection. Several others were eliminated because they were found "not mentally alert" or "just too ignorant." Inasmuch as the *colonia* contains several persons with college degrees and a hundred or so, all perfectly bilingual, with high-school diplomas, it rather appeared as though the original selection had been faulty. However, the real slaughter apparently came through the attorneys. "The attorneys just would not permit them to serve," said a minor court official. "We had a lot of criminal cases involving Mexicans that year, and attorneys just would not have Mexicans on the jury for these cases." That was the end of Mexican-American jury service; there are no Hispanic names on the jury lists today.

However, Negro jurors serve in comparatively large numbers, and attorneys like to have them on juries for criminal cases involving Negroes. This may be the hand of the National Association for the Advancement of Colored People—or it may be something quite different. "You see," explained an attorney, "the Negroes who serve are all old-timers here in town. We know them and they know us. They're all good, conscientious people. We don't call any of these excitable new Negroes." At one time, jury lists contained as many as fifteen Negro names for 500 white names, a figure which made the unofficial quota of one-half of one per cent of the Negro population look rather badly ciphered. Inasmuch as registered voters may apply for jury duty and the inclination of the judges, who have to maintain reasonable rotation of names, is to consider those applications, the *colonia* has a job before it. There are plenty of mentally alert and well-educated merchants who could afford to let the relatives run the *tienda* for a day and numerous respectable housewives, innocent of the slightest thought of shoplifting, who would make intelligent jurors. Jury duty may be a bore and an inconvenience, but it is a "must" for a minority.

THE POLICE AND THE PRESS

With this brief glimpse of the exit end of the judicial hopper, it might be well to turn to its intake department, that of law enforcement. The Mexican immigrant in the United States has been accused of having an unusually high rate of crime and delinquency; and the doings of some of his children, tagged as "zoot suiters" or *pachucos,* have furnished copy for sensational journalistic imaginations to an extent not even exceeded by Hollywood. To Descanso's press, any scared fifteen-year-old who falls into the hands of the police on Monticello Avenue is a "zoot suiter," complete with knife, bicycle chain "knuckles," and a criminally mature philosophy. Furthermore, he is a *Mexican* "zoot suiter," a *Mexican* "gang member," or a *Mexican* delinquent, regardless of the fact that he was born in the United States. The press, in Descanso and elsewhere, has succeeded in building up a body of highly spiced misinformation in the public mind, whereby a Mexican colony is peopled entirely by vicious youth with criminal tendencies. The presence of a few Mike Maldonados and Jimmy Garcías idling on a street corner is sufficient to send a thrill of eager horror up the spines of a slumming party. "See—*pachucos!*"

As has been pointed out, the number of Mexican-American youth who have any degree of criminal maturity is small. Still, the number of arrests of juveniles of Mexican extraction is large, compared to the proportion of the population their group represents. The *colonia* and the *barrio pequeño,* with 12 per cent of the population of Descanso, furnish 28 per cent of juvenile arrests. It must be remembered that bad housing and slum conditions, whatever the population concerned, are conceded to account for a 15 per cent rise in delinquency rates. Not only are these two areas *the* slums of Descanso, but they have been notably lacking, to date, in public recreation facilities. It is certain, furthermore, that the prejudices, conscious or unconscious, of law enforcement officers provide further impetus to frequent arrest. The average Descanso police officer is not an unkindly man—the flagrant abuses of justice and decency toward minorities which are routine in some cities occur here only sporadically. Police officers simply share the run-of-the-mill biases of the dominant group; they are in a position to act on them oftener. Untrained in the philosophy of juvenile work in general, they certainly have no special equipment for the delicate business of handling second-generation youth. To such an officer, the youthful population of the West End is likely to appear as "jail bait."

If the arrest pattern of juveniles points to one moral, it is that the young Mexican-American leaves himself statistically unprotected by his habit of idling on street corners. The places at which arrests most commonly occur and the times at which they are made point up the picture vividly. Mike Maldonado and his pals are gathered at the corner of Sixth and Monticello, with no more criminal intent than that of "watching what is going on." If they are noisy, when the police car comes around at 9:30 P.M., they are "disturbing the peace." If they move a hundred feet in one direction or another, they are "loitering in the vicinity of a pool hall." If they have succeeded in getting some liquor from one of the disreputable *cantinas,* they may be "drunk and disorderly," by the time of the next appearance of the police car. At a later hour, a few may have committed "malicious mischief," out of idleness and curiosity. If they drift over to a municipal dance, their very appearance in a body may lead to further disturbance of the peace. The tragedy of juvenile misbehavior everywhere is its essential unplanned, undeliberated nature. Even serious offenses have their genesis in aimless drifting; the criminal action is so spontaneous that it surprises even the doer. "We was just standing around and we saw this car with the keys in it," has been the inception of many a juvenile case of grand theft, among all groups. The boy of Descanso's *colonia,* in following the village pattern of recreation set by his elders—that of idling and conversing on the streets—puts himself in further jeopardy.

The average boy who gets arrested in the colonia is not a recidivist. Few boys are arrested twice within a year's time, but new little fish swim into the net all the time. Their home addresses correspond, with terrifying exactitude, to those areas designated by housing authorities as most sub-standard. Their offenses run much higher during the winter months, when these homes seem more crowded and unattractive. Not all such boys, by any means, come from the disorganized fringe of the *colonia,* but most of them come from homes where the parents know little of American life. It might be added that, say what you will for the cloistering of girls, it has a positive effect on delinquency statistics. Practically *no* Mexican-American girl is ever arrested by the police. The old tradition of male freedom at adolescence, however, is certainly a contributing factor to the difficulties of the *colonia's* boys.

Rarely is a Mexican woman in difficulties with the law, either, and still more rarely does she slip into prostitution. Adult males, however, contribute more extensively to arrest records than do their sons. The offense which leads to their involvement with the law is always the same one, repeated with monotonous regularity over acres of police blotters. It is drunkenness, as a rule uncomplicated by any other charge. The offenders are, largely, the laborers of middle age and over. They stagger coming out of a *cantina,* they go to sleep in parks, or they relieve the demands of nature at a picket fence. They are arrested, they pay fines of ten or fifteen dollars apiece, and they start the whole cycle over again the next week or month. They represent, with amazing fidelity, those families in the lower disorganized fringe of the *colonia.*

The *colonia* is not proud of these befuddled oldsters, but it has a certain sympathy for them. "Those police cars are like *zopilotes.*[3] They circle these streets. It doesn't make any difference how quiet a man is. If he is alone on the streets at night, he is stopped. If he has had a drink or two, he is drunk." One old man proudly described a certain function he performs for his neighbors. "I have lived here forty years and the police know me for a good man. Anyway, it now upsets my stomach to drink. But I go with my friends and when we come home, I keep the edge of the sidewalk. The police car stops and I say, 'Good evening, Mister Policeman, it is just me, Tomás Valdes, and these boys here are my nephews.' They make a joke and go away. But it is very dangerous to be on the streets at night if you do not know the police." The police frankly admit that they arrest any Mexican, particularly a laborer, who seems to have been drinking, while they would exercise greater leniency toward other groups in other places; they feel that the person of Mexican extraction has a greater propensity for "getting into trouble" after having a few drinks. They also admit that this vigilance has no appreciable effect in reducing adult arrests for drunkenness—nor to their recollection, did prohibition. Total adult fines, from this district, average as much as $500 to $700 monthly, particularly during the winter months. Like the young, the adult male seems to be more law-abiding during the summer. One repeated offender of middle age, asked why he never got in jail during the summer, replied, "It's warm at home in summer, but, when it rains, the *cantina* is more comfortable."

The question of what to do with the old, ill-adjusted, discouraged laborer who has no place to go except a *cantina* is not a simple one. Perhaps he is as difficult of rehabilitation socially as he is vocationally. But the question of what to do with a fifteen-year-old who has no place to go except the streets is comparatively easy. Descanso has proved, in a small way, that solution is possible; unfortunately, it has shown little interest in following

[3] Zopilotes: buzzards.

the matter up. During the summer of 1943, delinquency was appreciably lowered by a night-park program of ball games held on a vacant lot one block north of "Delinquency Corner." During the summer of 1944, the same program reduced delinquency to zero for six weeks and to a previously unknown low for the remainder of vacation. Winter recreation admittedly involves more resource, equipment, and personnel, but that is scarcely an excuse for its non-existence. The very fact that the *colonia* has no entrenched gang organizations, little recidivism, and juvenile delinquency chiefly of a casual and accidental type argues that recreational therapy would work well. If decent housing were added to the cure, recovery might very well be complete.

"The same old stuff," says Descanso when it hears about recreation and housing as solutions of juvenile problems. The trouble is not that they are the "same old stuff," but that they have never been adequately tried. If a quarter of the energy Descanso has expended, in the last three years, in solemn conclaves on "the delinquency problem" had been turned to getting decent recreation on the West Side, it would now have less to talk about. If a sixteenth of the energy expended in shuddering over headlines about "zoot suiters" and mongering rumors about girl *pachucas* with knives secreted in their pompadours had been so turned, it might have nothing at all to talk about. The inescapable conclusion is that Descanso prefers to keep delinquency as a conversation piece.

In that decision, it gets considerable assistance from its press. The Descanso *Reporter* is not a yellow sheet, by any means; nor does it entirely reflect the entrenched reaction of a great deal of the national press. It usually curbs sensationalism and scandal sharply in its pages. Sporadically, it espouses a liberal point of view, much in the manner of a swimmer putting a toe in a cold plunge. Most of the time, however, it attempts to keep in exact step with the prejudices and biases of the communities it serves—or, more exactly, with the points of view held by the powerful groups in those communities. This, its editors sincerely believe, is "reflecting public opinion." On the question of the Mexican-American minority, it has not been guiltless of helping to form those biases and prejudices.

A specific incident will serve as an example. At one of the municipal dances, a group of sailors made passes, verbally and otherwise, at some Mexican-American girls. Their boy friends protested—the sailors persisted, saying, "Do you want to make something of it?" In the fight that ensued, a fifteen-year-old Mexican-American boy slashed a sailor's wrist with a penknife. No one in the excited crowd gave first aid, and the sailor lost considerable blood. The next afternoon—a Sunday—a crowd of servicemen gathered in the park near the municipal auditorium, and there was talk, apparently, of a "march on Monticello Avenue." The military authorities, grown wise in such matters, promptly canceled leaves for a ten-day period. There—except for the trial of the boy who, outnumbered by older and heavier opponents, had unwisely used a knife—the matter might have rested, as the sailor recovered very promptly.

The *Reporter,* however, ran headlines in its city section, and followed them by some very imaginative misstatements. Not a word was said about the provocation given the Mexican-Americans. Phrases like "undeclared war between servicemen and zootsuited Mexican youths," "a gang of twenty-five Mexican *pachucos* attacked four service men," "The zoot suiters fled in the darkness at the approach of officers," and "military authorities ordered a ten-day state of emergency" worked the city up to the boiling point. Rumors of all varieties circulated over every bar and soda fountain. The sailor had died, and the Mexican community had begged the *Reporter* to suppress the news for fear of reprisals. Nine *pachuca* girls with knives in their hair had been arrested and had confessed to a pact to seduce and murder sailors. A Mexican-American youth had been discovered hanged. Armed *pachucos* from other communities were planning a "march on Descanso."

As if to nullify the prompt quieting action taken by military authorities, the *Reporter* published a long interview with a man who described himself as head of the Fathers of Fighting Sons. "It is not right that our sons are denied the right to freely walk the streets of the country while criminals and lawless elements are permitted to roam at large at all hours," said this dignitary, who was privately characterized by his familiars as a "Texas crackpot." The police, meanwhile, were arresting Mexican-American youths for questioning. The paper published the names and addresses of all of them and made no retractions when it was clear they had nothing to do with the knifing. Ironically enough, the boys and girls who had been the focus of the disturbance were in no sense *pachucos.* They came from good homes, on the upper levels of the *colonia,* and had good school and employment records. The fifteen-year-old who wielded the knife had not come with them. He had inserted himself, gratuitously and certainly unwanted, into the fracas, apparently to show off. Nothing about the whole incident connoted gang organization or "criminal and lawless elements."

The matter of securing a fair hearing for the boys who had done no knifing, but had merely defended girls of their group, proved to be a complicated matter. At the first hearing, the presiding judge acted as though he had been doing too much newspaper reading. It took the expenditure of considerable money, the hiring of an attorney outside the area, and another hearing to bring out the real facts of the case. Those facts received no newspaper headlines, needless to say, nor even any mention. Dominant Descanso is still convinced that twenty-five "Mexican *pachucos*" wantonly attacked some heroic men in uniform. When it goes to Monticello Avenue to eat "Spanish food," it imagines every shadowy street peopled with lurking, stealthy criminal figures, armed with "razor-sharp four-inch blades" (the *Reporter's* journalese for "pocketknife").

Why a respectable, civic-minded man like the editor of the *Reporter*, which normally foreswears the sensationalism of metropolitan journals, lent himself to a display of this sort is difficult to imagine. There is complete evidence by now—of which he must have been aware—that, if you want a riot, this is the way to produce it. Descanso certainly displayed riot psychology for three or four days. The *colonia* says, "Oh, he just wanted to sell some more newspapers," or, more perceptively, "Maybe he got mad at something and he felt like taking it out on the Mexicans." Anyone who believes in the essentially dualistic nature of man would have been fascinated, during those three days in Descanso, in watching normally kind, friendly faces display sadism, fear, and spite. It was impossible to believe that these average citizens, too, did not have something they wished to "take out" on a scapegoat—perhaps their own frustrations, insecurities, and self-mistrust.

The damage worked by one of these incidents lasts a long time. The public mind seems to have a genius for retaining dramatic untruths. It desperately wants to blame somebody or something else for situations which arise from its own shortcomings. The editor of the *Reporter* has annulled much of his courageous stand on slum-clearance and improvement of conditions in the West End. "Why give those people anything?" say the shrill voices of Descanso's citizenry. "They're criminals and foreigners and generally low!" As if finally aware of this, the *Reporter's* editorial page, some months later, carried eight paragraphs headed "True Americans." After listing the names of boys of Mexican ancestry who had died in battle, the editorial made a plea for "plans for the postwar era" which would take into account "the part these young Americans of Mexican ancestry are to play in our tomorrow." The editorial might have added: "These young men are exactly like those other youngsters—no better, no worse—whom we were mistakenly calling criminals three months ago. Two of those youngsters are now in the service. Let us hope that, when they are in battle for us, they will remember us with a charity which we do not deserve."

ARMED SERVICE

That its young men of Mexican extraction are coming back from the wars with a "new concept of life"—to quote the editorial—Descanso has no doubt. It is a little nervous about the situation. In public offices and places of influence, one hears constantly repeated the idea that "these things will really be problems when all the Mexican boys who've seen service get home." Will these boys be docile track laborers and orange pickers? Will they want to live in a shack in the *colonia?* Can they be refused service at bars and cafés? Will they be satisfied to "stay in their own part of town"? Will they insist on "social equality," with its connotation of friendship and intermarriage? Will "once a Mexican, always a Mexican" still hold true?

Descanso is inclined to think it will not, but of how such a change will come about it has no idea. "Gradually," it says, or "by education." It shows, by every action, that it hopes the day of reckoning will be far in the future. It maintains, meanwhile, the old barriers against the mothers, fathers, sisters, wives, and little brothers of Mexican-American veterans. Does it imagine that it can "do something" for these veterans which will not include their families, their communities, and the very climate of opinion of Descanso itself? Does it fancy that "doing something," in the honest sense of granting full integration with American life, will not involve reconstruction of its whole status-system, with the corollary cheap labor complex? If the expressions of its leading citizens are any criteria, this is exactly what it does fancy. It wants to make a gesture and still preserve the status quo. Like an unwilling horse, it feels itself dragged, by national and international events, toward a goal it sniffs suspiciously.

There is scarcely a home in the *colonia* which did not have a son in service; many had three or more. The big families the social workers used to frown on have their uses in time of war. By and large, the experiences of the *colonia's* youth in the services have been satisfying ones. Unlike the Negro youth, they have not found, in uniform, a denial of the democracy for which they are asked to fight. Few are commissioned officers, but many have had the satisfaction of working up to the top of non-commissioned ranks. They have made close friends among Anglo-Americans. They have, in some cases, married into Anglo-American families from other parts of the country and have found that the social prejudices of Descanso did not exist. They have found that they can do things well, that they can command and take responsibility. Even the misfits and comparative failures feel that they have been judged, not as "Mexicans," but as individual men, by the same standards as other men. The successful have had the heady experience of accomplishment free of the tag "pretty good for a Mexican." They are, as they say, "all steamed up."

A pharmacist's mate said: "The years on the ship are the best ones I ever spent. When you learn to get on with a thousand men and do your work and hold your own without ever hearing 'Mexican,' you get on to a lot of things. In a way, I wish I could stay with the Navy. I hope they don't discharge me right now on account of this leg. If I came back to the colony now, I think I'd blow up after a few months. Two weeks is bad enough. It's like breathing good, clean air—salt air, maybe,—and then getting back to a swamp. I'd like to finish the war. Then there'll be a lot of us back together." A former corporal in the ground forces said: "I've had a swell time and I've been treated swell. The rest of the United States isn't like Descanso, I've found out. I'd like to live in the East—I've got a girl there. But you couldn't move my mother, and I've got to help her until the kids are grown. My girl says she wouldn't mind living in the *colonia,* but she's just dumb. She thinks it's romantic or something. I'd sure hate to risk it." A discharged private in the infantry said: "I'm glad I'm going to have one of those little buttons to wear in my coat. And a flock of foliage to put on my uniform for Armistice Day parades. I'm going into politics. There's seven or eight of us, all from Southern California, who've talked it over. Things are going to happen in these colonies, and we're going to see that they do."

It is true that great potential leadership developed among Mexican-American youth in the armed forces. If it keeps its drive, many barriers may go down before it. Its effect on the youngsters still in school is already great. The caustic comments of the returned veteran on *Mexicanismo* make it seem what it really is—a ridiculous, antiquated day-dream. Accommodating leadership is just a way of getting yourself fooled, to the veteran. Being a *pachuco* is just being a little punk. Getting an education is all-important. "Why, if I'd had a decent education, I bet I'd have been a captain." And as for the other side of town—but here the fresh voice of confidence and direction wavers.

The alert and mature veteran realizes that, in spite of all he can do and say, dominant Descanso *is* dominant. When he walks down Monticello Avenue, he feels the pressure of all the old childhood patterns of restriction, defeat, and helplessness. He feels, as one young ex-sergeant said, "as if something was being taken away, like I wasn't myself the way I am in camp." If there is a severe depression, followed by a fascism which takes it out on minority groups, where would the veteran who has returned to the *colonia* be? He is already handicapped, en masse, by insufficient education. Would he be one of the discouraged, broken cynics, like many a veteran of the first World War—at home only in a bar? Would he be a contributor to a crime wave like that which followed the last war? Or would he be like the youthful European veteran of 1918, rioting in the streets? The steam is up. The veteran knows the channels into which he would like to have it go: a good job, a happy family life, and full status in American life for his group. Where it actually goes is something dominant Descanso and the nation of which it is a part will determine. By the portents now observable, the veteran is not going to be put off with *atole con el dedo;* but sometimes he mistrusts, not only life and the times, but the power of his own newly acquired manhood to hold out against pressure.

CHAPTER XIII

Japanese-Americans: The Meaning of Citizenship

The readings on the treatment of the Americans of Japanese ancestry are included as a particularly illuminating case of the general question of race in American society. In general, the status of this group has been more nearly that of the non-Negro minority groups. During World War II, however, the feeling about these people gained in intensity overnight and furnished a textbook case of the manner in which frustrations in our society find an outlet in activity of this kind.

WHAT ABOUT OUR JAPANESE-AMERICANS? *

In the spring of 1942, we in the United States placed some 110,000 persons of Japanese descent in protective custody. Two out of every three of these were American citizens by birth; one-third were aliens forbidden by law to be citizens. Included were three generations: Issei, or first-generation immigrants (aliens); Nisei, or second-generation (American-born citizens); and Sansei, or third-generation (American-born children of American-born parents). Within three months after removal from the west coast had been ordered, this entire group of men, women, and children had been lodged in temporary assembly centers, under military guard, awaiting transfer from the area. No charges had been filed against these people nor had any hearing been held. Evacuation was on racial, or, perhaps more accurately, on ancestral grounds. Germans and other enemy aliens were not removed. Nor were Chinese and Koreans, who belong

* Reprinted, courtesy of the Public Affairs Committee, Pamphlet No. 91, *What About Our Japanese-Americans,* by Carey McWilliams, 1944, pp. 1–29.

to the same race as the Japanese. But all persons having any Japanese blood, however slight, were forced out.

In the excitement of the moment, the evacuation of the Japanese seemed merely a minor incident of the war. But as the shock of finding ourselves at war gradually abated, the nation began to be uneasy about many aspects of the evacuation. They began to ask whether it squared with our democratic ideals. If the issues were unclear at the outset, they became increasingly involved with each new step of the program. As the danger of an invasion of the west coast receded, measures were taken which no one had urged at the height of the excitement. Internment, for example, had not been planned originally by the authorities: merely removal from the area. And rather to our amazement, we discovered that after every person of Japanese ancestry had been removed from the west coast and placed in protective custody, agitation against them increased instead of subsided. The evacuation was seized upon as proof of disloyalty and used to justify further measures against the west-coast Japanese group. Each step in the program began to involve entirely unforeseen consequences. Now in the third year of war, it is possible to review the entire proceeding and to ask a number of questions, such as: Why were these people removed from the west coast? Are the measures which have been taken against them actually related to the reasons advanced for their removal? What has happened to this group of 100,000 men, women, and children? What are the likely consequences of this program?

BEFORE PEARL HARBOR

The Japanese were a late immigrant group. They arrived, for the most part, in the years between 1900 and 1910. Most of the early immigrants were single men who married fairly late in life, so that the second-generation group did not appear in large numbers until after 1920. In 1940, the average age of the Issei, or alien group, was around fifty years of age; that of the Nisei, or citizen group, around nineteen or twenty years of age. The Issei had lived in the United States, on an average, for thirty-five years. Of 126,947 Japanese in this country in 1940, 112,353 lived in the three west-coast states. Nearly 80 per cent were in California. Unlike some immigrant groups, the Japanese did not do much spreading out. They were more densely concentrated on December 7, 1941, than they had been twenty years previously. Their concentration was not merely geographical but occupational: 43 per cent of the gainfully employed west-coast Japanese were in agriculture, more particularly, in the production of fresh vegetables and small fruits for the large urban west-coast markets. An additional 26 per cent were to be found in the wholesale and retail trade, which was largely confined to the distribution of Japanese-grown produce. Both external and internal pressures had tended to set the Little Tokyo settlements apart from the larger communities of which they were a part. Many of these settlements, both rural and urban, were located near important strategic areas.

Within this rather narrow orbit, the Japanese had done reasonably well. Their farm lands and buildings, in California alone, were valued at $65,781,000. In 1941, the Japanese turned out 42 per cent of the truck crops raised in California, and their production was valued at $30,000,000. In the same year, the thousand or more Japanese-operated fruit and vegetable stores in Los Angeles employed nearly five thousand people (mostly Japanese) and did an annual business of about $25,000,000.

Unlike other immigrant groups. Not only were the Japanese a late immigrant group, but they were racially different from the others and were also set apart by sharp cultural differences. Noting that the rate of assimilation for the Japanese was somewhat slower than for other immigrant groups, west-coast residents hastily concluded that the cultural difference was to be accounted for in terms of race. It must be remembered, however, that the American-born or Nisei generation had not, by December 7, 1941, assumed the leadership of the Japanese communities, although they would clearly have done so in another decade. In 1930, slightly more than half of the Japanese in America were foreign-born; but in 1940 the ratio had declined to slightly more than one-third. In other words, the war struck the west-coast communities just at the moment when the American-born and American-educated generation was beginning to displace the alien generation in positions of social and economic leadership.

Thus there existed on the west coast, on December 7, 1941, a deep fissure in the social structure of the region. This fissure separated the relatively small Japanese minority from the rest of the population. Like the earthquake fissures that run along the Pacific Coast, this particular fissure was deeper in some areas than in others; it had been dormant for some years, but it was still potentially active. As fifty years of prior social history had shown, almost any jar or shock was capable of disturbing it. The attack on Pearl Harbor was more than a jar; it was a thunderous blow, an earthquake, that sent tremors throughout the area in which the fissure existed. The resident Japanese were the victims of this social earthquake.

This is the root-fact, the basic social fact, which precipitated the mass evacuation of the west-coast Japanese—which has been accurately described as "the largest single forced migration in American history."

THE EVACUATION

Before discussing *why* evacuation was ordered, it may help to give a brief log-of-events. On December 11, 1941, the Western Defense Command was established and the west coast was declared a theater of war. General J. L. DeWitt was designated as military commander of the area. On December 7 and 8, 1941, the Department of Justice arrested, on presidential warrants, all known "dangerous enemy aliens." Subsequently, by a series of orders, the Department of Justice ordered the removal of all "enemy aliens" from certain designated zones or so-called "spot" strategic installations, such as harbors, airports, and power lines. The deadline fixed for this "dress rehearsal" of the larger evacuation to follow was February 24, 1942. Following the appearance of the Roberts Report on Pearl Harbor, the public temper on the west coast noticeably changed and by the end of January, 1942, a considerable press demand appeared for the evacuation of all Japanese. In the excitement of the moment, it was not generally noted that the Roberts Report referred to *espionage* activities in Hawaii but was silent on the question of *sabotage*. For months after the release of the Roberts Report it was generally assumed, on the west coast, that acts of sabotage had been committed in Hawaii, despite absolutely conclusive proof from the most authoritative sources that no such acts had been commited.

Executive Order No. 9066. The moment this press campaign for evacuation was launched, the west-coast delegation in Congress held a meeting in the offices of Senator Hiram Johnson and, on February 13, 1942, recommended to the President "the immediate evacuation of all persons of Japanese lineage." The report suggested that this might be accomplished without the necessity of a declaration of martial law such as had been proclaimed in Hawaii on December 7. On February 19, the President signed Executive Order No. 9066 authorizing the War Department to set up military areas and to exclude any or all persons from these areas. The next day Mr. Stimson delegated this responsibility to General DeWitt. On March 2, General DeWitt, by proclamation, established Military Areas Nos. 1 and 2, and on March 27 he prohibited all persons of Japanese ancestry from leaving these areas.

Then by a series of 108 separate orders, General DeWitt ordered all

Japanese removed from Military Areas Nos. 1 and 2 (embracing all of Washington, Oregon, and California, and a portion of Arizona). By June 5, 1942, all persons of Japanese ancestry had been removed from Military Area No. 1 (the coastal area), and by August 7, 1942, Military Area No. 2 (the eastern part of the three west-coast states) had likewise been cleared of all Japanese. It will be noted that it was General DeWitt and the west-coast congressional delegation who recommended mass evacuation. The President and the Secretary of War naturally relied upon General DeWitt's appraisal of the situation. In the last analysis, it was General DeWitt who had to make the decision since the responsibility generally was vested in him. Now *why* did he order mass evacuation?

"Military Necessity." The explanation given at the time was that mass evacuation was ordered "as a matter of military necessity." The nature of the military necessity itself was not defined. With the issuance of General DeWitt's final report on evacuation (dated July 19, 1943, but not released until January, 1944), it now becomes possible to grasp rather clearly what was embraced within the catch-all phrase, "military necessity." First of all, the report established that the west coast was in imminent danger of invasion after Pearl Harbor. Guam was captured on December 13; Hongkong fell on December 24; Manila on January 2; Singapore in February. Our fleet had been badly crippled at Pearl Harbor, and for a time the disposition of the enemy's fleet was not known. On February 23, 1942, a Japanese submarine shelled the California coast near Santa Barbara. Unquestionably, the risk was serious, and General DeWitt's responsibility was certainly great.

Military commanders must make quick decisions. They have to act on the basis of possibilities as well as probabilities; they cannot weigh considerations with the nicety of a scientist working in a laboratory. General DeWitt must have been haunted by the specters of Admiral Kimmel and General Short, who had been charged with neglect of duty in Hawaii. Yet after making all of these allowances, it is now apparent that the conclusions drawn by General DeWitt were not justified by the evidence.

The threat of sabotage. In his final report, General DeWitt stresses the danger of sabotage and espionage. But by February 14, 1942, he knew that no acts of sabotage had occurred in Hawaii. And General DeWitt even goes so far as to cite the absence of sabotage as "confirming indication that such action will be taken." While the risks of spies was real enough, this risk is not related to the presence of Japanese-Americans on the west coast. Who are some of the individuals who have been arrested either for espionage activities in behalf of Japan or for being unregistered agents of Japan?

They are all native-born white Americans: John Farnsworth, Harry Thomas Thompson, Vincent Williams, David Warren Ryder, Arthur Clifford Reed, Heizer Wright, Ralph Townsend, and Joseph Hilton Smyth. For some years prior to Pearl Harbor, a Los Angeles police captain had received money, from time to time, from the local Japanese consul, in payment for his services in spying on local Japanese-Americans who were distrusted by the consul! Moreover, it has been pointed out that, after Pearl Harbor, Japan relied almost entirely on non-Japanese agents, and for obvious reasons. On June 14, 1943, the Office of War Information revealed that the persons who did the actual signaling at Pearl Harbor were Nazi agents. No Japanese-Americans, either in Hawaii or on the mainland, have been convicted of either sabotage or espionage. This itself is strong proof that the General was looking in the wrong corner for agents.

Protection against mob violence. General DeWitt also said that he acted to protect the west-coast Japanese from mob violence. He notes, however, that most of the reports of attacks against them, upon investigation, "either were unverified or were found to be cumulative." Actually, there are only two reported instances of violence. On December 27, 1941, a fight occurred between Filipinos and local Japanese in Stockton, California; and on January 1, 1942, unknown persons fired several shots at a Japanese in Gilroy. Despite the shock of the attack on Pearl Harbor, there was *no hysteria* on the west coast. Such experienced observers as Chester Rowell, Dr. Eric Bellquist of the University of California, Selden Menefee, and the reporters for *Time, Life,* and *Fortune* have all testified to this fact. Some of the west-coast papers made the same admission. If there was a real danger of mob violence, then why did the military authorities on the west coast take no steps to allay hysteria—such steps, for example, as were taken in Hawaii—and why were no authoritative statements issued to disprove the widely spread rumors of sabotage in Hawaii? These rumors still circulate on the west coast.

Disloyal Japanese known. Undeniably there were dangerous individuals among the resident west-coast Japanese. But these individuals were well known to the authorities. They were promptly arrested on December 7 both in Hawaii and on the west coast. For over five years there had been a constant check on both the Issei and the Nisei. Our intelligence services were fully informed. The fact that the military authorities had never contemplated mass evacuation until public agitation began to develop in favor of the idea indicates that they did not regard the risk as serious. In an article that appeared in *Harper's Magazine,* a Naval Intelligence officer in Southern California declared that in his opinion mass evacuation was not necessary and that the overwhelming majority of the people were loyal.

Racial considerations. General DeWitt's report makes it clear that his interpretation of "military necessity" involved a judgment on sociological grounds. "The continued presence," writes General DeWitt, "of a large, unassimilated, tightly knit racial group, bound to the enemy by strong ties of race, culture, custom, and religion, constituted a menace which had to be dealt with." There is at least some question as to whether the task of weighing these "ethnic affiliations" was a proper assignment for a military commander. Sociologists, who had been studying the problem for years, have drawn an entirely different conclusion from the same facts. The prompt arrest of all "dangerous enemy aliens" and the fact of war itself had served to cut whatever ties had bound the west-coast Japanese communities to their homeland. If these "ethnic affiliations" were deemed so dangerous on the west coast, why were the same affiliations in Hawaii regarded as unimportant? There has been no mass evacuation of the Japanese in Hawaii, where they constitute 37 per cent of the entire population, and all the authorities agree that, there, the local Japanese have conclusively demonstrated their loyalty.

Racial considerations were evidently regarded as part of the "military necessity" requiring mass evacuation. "The Japanese race," states General DeWitt in his report, "is an enemy race, and while many second- and third-generation Japanese born on United States soil, possessed of United States citizenship, have become 'Americanized,' the racial strains are undiluted. . . ."

Testifying on April 13, 1943, before the House Naval Affairs Subcommittee, he also volunteered this remark:

> . . . (The Japanese-Americans) are a dangerous element, whether loyal or not. There is no way to determine their loyalty . . . it makes no difference whether he is an American; theoretically, he is still a Japanese and you can't change him. . . . You can't change him by giving him a piece of paper.

This reference to citizenship as "a piece of paper" and the frank admission that "loyalty" was not even a factor certainly indicate that the racial consideration was uppermost in General DeWitt's mind. This same consideration was uppermost in the minds of the influential public officials who were mobilizing public opinion in favor of mass evacuation and who were bringing pressure to bear directly upon General DeWitt. Governor Earl Warren of California (then Attorney-General) told the Tolan Committee early in 1942 "that when we are dealing with the *Caucasian race* we have methods that will test the loyalty of them," but that no such determination could be made in the case of the Japanese. The many demonstrations of the loyalty of the west-coast Japanese were apparently regarded as an immaterial consideration. Racial distrust was the chief factor prompting mass evacuation.

Evacuation held proof of disloyalty. It would be idle, at this late date, to review the pros and cons of mass evacuation were it not for the fact that mass evacuation has placed the entire resident Japanese-American minority under a cloud of suspicion. The fact that evacuation was ordered, for example, is now being cited as *proof* of the disloyal character of the entire group. Actually, there is no basis whatever in the available evidence for such an inference. It is also interesting to note that some of the groups that were most active in California in urging evacuation of every person of Japanese ancestry from the west coast were, at the same time, strenuously opposed to the evacuation of a single person of Japanese ancestry from Hawaii! Some of these groups, moreover, had a freely acknowledged economic interest in mass evacuation. Immediately after Pearl Harbor, the Shipper-Grower Association of Salinas, California, sent Mr. Austin E. Anson to Washington to lobby for evacuation. "We're charged with wanting to get rid of the Japs for selfish reasons," said Mr. Anson. "We might as well be honest. We do. It's a question of whether the white man lives on the Pacific Coast or the brown man."

Voluntary removal fails. At the outset, it was merely the *removal* of all persons of Japanese ancestry that was contemplated by the authorities. There was no thought, at the time, of *internment.* Between February 19 and March 27, 1942, the Japanese were free to depart voluntarily from the area. During this period, 10,231 left Military Area No. 1, but of this number, 4,825 merely moved into Military Area No. 2. Not only were the Japanese moving too slowly—as viewed by the military—but many of them did not have enough money to leave the area. They did not know where to move, and they were meeting with opposition even while in transit. For example, Governor Payne Ratner of Kansas stated that "Japs are not wanted and not welcome in Kansas" and directed the state police to turn back any Japanese trying to enter the state.

As they sought to retreat eastward, evacuees met with many unpleasant incidents. Signs posted in shops read: "This restaurant poisons rats and Japs"; barber shops carried signs reading "Japs shaved: Not Responsible for Accidents"; signs were placed in automobile windshields reading "Open Season for Japs"; filling stations, restaurants, and hotels refused to serve evacuees. Realizing that some agency would have to be established to assist in evacuation, President Roosevelt, on March 18, 1942, issued Executive Order No. 9102 creating the War Relocation Authority. Early in April, the director of the authority met with the governors of the western states in Salt Lake City. These governors, with one exception, refused to accept responsibility for the maintenance of law and order unless evacuees were placed under military guard. These developments compelled the government to stop further voluntary evacuation and to undertake a program of planned relocation.

The evacuation centers. As "E-Day" approached—the date fixed by the Army for removal—the Japanese-Americans reported to civil control stations where they were escorted to hastily improvised "assembly centers" —usually race tracks, parks, and pavilions. Some of these centers were good-sized communities; there were over 18,000 evacuees in the Santa Anita center. In many instances, the evacuation started before the centers were prepared to house and feed the evacuees. Yet within a period of 137 days over 100,000 people had been moved into the centers, the gates had been locked, and sentries had established their patrols.

The speed with which this vast movement of people was accomplished is unquestionably a tribute to army efficiency; but it is also a remarkable demonstration of the loyalty of the Japanese-Americans themselves. Secretary Stimson has pointed out that "great credit is due our Japanese population for the manner in which they responded to and complied with the orders for exclusion." In no single instance did they fail to cooperate with the authorities. On the contrary, they helped install most of the facilities in the centers and immediately relieved the authorities of a major share of the administrative burden of providing food and shelter for 100,000 people.

THE RELOCATION CENTERS

The evacuees were hardly settled in the assembly centers before they were transferred to the ten relocation camps established by the War Relocation Authority (W.R.A.) in Utah, Arizona, California, Idaho, Wyoming, Colorado, and Arkansas. By November 1, 1942, this second major migration had been completed. Some 110,000 were lodged in the relocation centers. These included a small group from Alaska, some 1,073 Japanese removed from Hawaii, 1,300 Japanese paroled from the internment camps (the so-called "dangerous enemy aliens"), and a few Japanese who, although living outside the western defense command, had voluntarily moved into the centers.

Although the relocation centers are an improvement on the temporary assembly centers, they can hardly be considered as satisfactory living quarters. Evacuees are housed in barracks with one family per room and, in many instances, more than one family is housed in a single room. Community toilets and washrooms have been set up for each block, and evacuees are fed in community messhalls at a cost to the government of between thirty-four and forty-two cents per person per day. No one has starved in these centers, and no one has frozen; but this is about as much as can be said in defense of the centers as housing projects. No fair-minded person who has visited the centers will believe, for one moment, that the evacuees are being "coddled" or "pampered."

Constitutional rights maintained. As far as is possible under the circumstances, W.R.A. has sought to maintain the constitutional rights of the evacuees. The citizens among them continue to vote in the areas in which they were formerly residents. There is no censorship of mail. Virtual freedom of religious worship is maintained. Open meetings may be held in the centers, and outspoken newspapers are published by the evacuees in most of the centers. A degree of self-government is also permitted. Obviously, it would be an exaggeration to say that evacuees exercise their constitutional rights in the centers with the same freedom from restraint that prevails outside the centers; but it will be noted that most basic rights have been maintained. Approximately 90 per cent of the employable residents are employed by W.R.A. on various work projects and in the messhalls, hospitals, farms, etc., in the centers. Evacuees receive a cash allowance of $12, $16, or $19 a month according to the nature of their duties. Food, shelter, and medical care are provided without charge. There are 30,000 Japanese-Americans of school age in the centers for whom educational facilities, from kindergarten through high school, have been provided.

Relocation outside the centers. Originally, W.R.A. intended to make these centers genuine relocation projects, but the centers had no sooner been established than outside interests, such as the sugar-beet industry, began to clamor for labor to meet the manpower shortage in agriculture. Naturally desirous of meeting this demand, W.R.A. began, in the summer of 1942, to release evacuees on seasonal permits and were meeting with enthusiastic praise from their employers. This unforeseen development encouraged W.R.A. to devise a permanent release program and to shift its emphasis from relocation within the centers to permanent relocation outside the centers. This shift in policy has led to a cutting-down of work projects in the centers and a definite drive to relocate the evacuees before the end of the war. Early in 1943, W.R.A. opened employment offices throughout the Middle West and began a real campaign to find jobs for the evacuees. By the second anniversary of the W.R.A., some 19,000 evacuees (85 per cent of whom are Nisei) were relocated outside the centers over a wide area of the Middle West, East, and South. Chicago alone has 3,500, while fairly large numbers of them have found jobs in such cities as Detroit, St. Paul, Madison, Denver, Salt Lake City, St. Louis, and Cincinnati. The problem now faced by W.R.A. is to persuade more of the evacuees to relocate.

Segregation. The relocation centers are not normal communities. They are institutions and they breed a type of "prison complex." The men, women, and children who were suddenly moved by the thousands into these partially constructed Little Tokyos isolated in mountain desert areas were not in a normal frame of mind on their arrival. They had but recently undergone a profoundly disturbing experience. The vast majority of them regarded evacuation as a wholesale rejection by their fellow Americans. Living in a center is, at best, an extremely irritating experience. Over-crowding is universal; there is no privacy whatever, and people wait in lines to eat, to wash, to be interviewed. In the centers most of the evacuees read the west-coast newspapers and worry incessantly about their future. They are plagued by every imaginable type of fear and anxiety. With much time for gossip and talk, rumors sweep through the centers like wildfire. It must be remembered that *all kinds of persons* are to be found in these centers—old and young, rural and urban, aged farm laborers and sophisticated young artists. There are individuals in the centers who do not look Japanese, do not speak or write Japanese, have never been to Japan, and who had, prior to relocation, never lived among other Japanese. Parental discipline tends to break down in the centers: the family, as such, is robbed of its traditional functions. There is, also, every conceivable shading of political opinion to be found among the evacuees. The isolation of the centers—in time and in space—is extremely depressing. The barbed-wire fences and the lookout towers and the armed sentries are constant reminders of the hostility of American public opinion. When all of these factors are considered, it is not surprising that minor disturbances, such as those which broke out in the Manzanar, Poston, and Tule centers, should have occurred.

The loyalty test. Since these disturbances were clearly the work of a minority of the evacuees, W.R.A. determined to segregate the loyal from the disloyal. While plans for segregation were being considered, the President announced on January 28, 1943, that the Army had decided to form a Japanese-American combat team on a volunteer basis. Since the Army proposed to send a recruiting team to the centers, W.R.A. decided to conduct a general registration of all persons in the centers 17 years of age and older. This registration was conducted in the centers with little or no advance preparation, under the most confused conditions. As part of the registration, evacuees were asked to answer a so-called "loyalty" question. Even the *alien* group was asked Question 28, which read:

> Will you swear unqualified allegiance to the United States of America and foreswear any form of allegiance or obedience to the Japanese Emperor or any other foreign government, power or organization?

It should be remembered that *alien* Japanese are ineligible for citizenship under our naturalization laws. Yet these aliens were asked to answer a question which, if answered affirmatively, would automatically strip them of the only citizenship they possessed without at the same time making it possible for them to become American citizens. The impossibility of this situation became apparent to W.R.A., and a revised question was finally submitted to the aliens, but only after much damage had been done.

These aliens knew that west-coast groups were conducting a powerful campaign for their deportation at the end of the war. If there was a danger of deportation, then obviously they would be in a difficult position if they renounced Japanese citizenship. Many of the Nisei resented the questionnaire because it assumed that they had a divided loyalty—a proposition which they have never conceded. Demagogic pro-fascist elements in the centers took full advantage of the confusion that prevailed in all of the centers during registration. In some centers, actual violence and intimidation occurred. The effects are shown both in the appeal for enlistment and in the registration itself.

In Hawaii, the Army called for 2,500 volunteers for the combat team and nearly 10,000 promptly volunteered. In the relocation centers only about 1,200 volunteered. The resentment of the evacuees to the questionnaire was indicated by its peculiar results. Although 87 per cent answered the loyalty questions affirmatively, only 74 per cent of the male *citizen* group answered affirmatively and 96 per cent of the male *alien* group answered favorably. The rather surprising difference in the response of the two groups seems to be due to the resentment which the Nisei felt over the entire evacuation program and to a group of Nisei who were educated in Japan. While segregation was unquestionably desirable, a questionnaire was hardly the way to determine loyalty. A Japanese agent, for example, would certainly not show his hand by failing to answer the loyalty question satisfactorily.

Tule Lake. Once the registration had been completed, W.R.A. announced that all of the "disloyal" elements would be concentrated in the Tule Lake Center in Northern California. Between September 15 and October 15, 1943, the "loyal" Japanese-Americans were removed from the Tule Lake Center and distributed among the other centers, while all the "segregants" were transferred to Tule Lake. In all, four classifications of evacuees were sent to the Tule Lake Center: (1) all evacuees who had requested repatriation to Japan were automatically sent to Tule Lake; (2) the "no-nos," that is, those who had answered the loyalty questions negatively, were sent to Tule Lake after a hearing at which they had an opportunity to change, modify, or explain their answers; (3) all evacuees regarding whom the various intelligence services had evidence indicating possible disloyal inclinations were sent to Tule Lake; and (4) close relatives of those in the foregoing categories who expressed a desire to remain with the segregants rather than disrupt family ties. After the first major exchange was effected, the number of "disloyal" segregants in Tule Lake was 13,540, divided into the following categories:

Repatriates and expatriates	5,127
Registration segregants	4,222
Other segregants	4,191

The commonly held idea that this group is composed of really disloyal persons is at least open to serious question. Investigation revealed, for instance, that 28 per cent of the evacuees who went to Tule Lake from the Manzanar Center were children under 18 years of age. The proportion was higher in other centers. These children were not asked to fill out the registration form. In view of the haste with which the registration and segregation programs were conducted and of the widespread confusion that prevailed, the utmost care must be taken if a lasting injustice is not to be committed against the American-born minors in the Tule Lake Center. Segregation cut across family lines and caused the most tragic personal complications in more than one case.

Among the adults, approximately 80 per cent of those who requested repatriation actually answered the loyalty question affirmatively. In most cases, they had requested repatriation solely for family reasons. One, for example, was a widower with four children. Two of his sons are in the United States Army, but his two daughters were sent to Japan to live with relatives after the death of the mother. The father explained that, while feeling complete loyalty to the United States, he nevertheless believes that his primary duty is to be with his minor daughters in Japan.

THE AFTERMATH

Mass evacuation has created a host of problems. Since they were not created by the people but by the government, they must be accepted as a national responsibility. The evacuation program was so uncertain at the outset and so sudden when it came that the evacuees did not have time to dispose of their property in a fair and orderly manner. Altogether, their west-coast holdings were valued at around $200,000,000. While W.R.A. now has established a property division designed to assist the evacuees, a satisfactory system of property custodianship was lacking when evacuation was ordered. Huge losses were suffered through hasty, forced sales. Since the majority of the evacuees have been cleared of even the suspicion of disloyalty, it would seem only fair for the government to make some compensation. This can probably best be accomplished through the creation of a claims commission in the postwar period to pass upon the thousands of claims that will unquestionably be filed. The volume of litigation that is likely to arise would in itself seem to require the setting up of such an agency.

Was evacuation Constitutional? One of the worst features of mass evacuation was that a particular minority was subjected to unusually harsh measures solely on the grounds of race or ancestry. Only those persons having Japanese blood were included within the order; and all were included who had any Japanese blood, however slight. It is apparent that this presents a constitutional problem of the gravest possible character.

On June 21, 1943, the Supreme Court decided the case of *Hirabayashi vs. United States*. Mr. Hirabayashi had been convicted of violating both the curfew order and the evacuation order. While the court held that the curfew order was a valid exercise of the war power, it pointedly refused to pass on the question of the constitutionality of the evacuation order. A study of the several opinions filed in the matter makes it clear that the Supreme Court entertains serious doubts as to the constitutionality of the evacuation procedure so far as the Nisei, or citizens are concerned. For example, Mr. Justice Murphy said that the curfew order "goes to the very brink of constitutional power"; while Mr. Justice Douglas, in a concurring opinion, wrote the following words: "Detention for reasonable cause is one thing. Detention on account of ancestry is another."

In a later case, *Korematsu vs. United States,* the court has passed directly on the constitutionality of evacuation. A still more serious legal question arises in connection with the Tule Lake segregants. While the Tule Lake evacuees are termed "segregants," it is apparent that they are really prisoners of war. The center is under heavy military guard and censorship. A bill to divest the citizens in this group of their American citizenship met defeat in Congress by a narrow margin.

Prospects for relocation. Assuming that W.R.A. is permitted to carry through its present policies, what are the prospects for the future? By March, 1944, some 19,000 evacuees had been released from the centers and relocated outside the western evacuated area. The W.R.A. may succeed in relocating an additional 20,000 by the end of 1944. But even this will still leave in the relocation centers, not including Tule Lake, about 50,000 evacuees. The most energetic, the best trained, and the most highly skilled evacuees have already been relocated. Individual relocation is certain to proceed more slowly after 1944. There will be left in the centers, in any case, a permanent "residue" population, made up of the lame, the halt, and the blind—old Issei bachelors, orphans, aged Issei couples without children. Strong pressures may still be found in most of the centers against relocation. Evacuees fear the "outside." They are uncertain about the type of treatment and reception they will meet. They lack confidence in their ability to succeed in areas with which they are not familiar. Having adjusted to center life, they do not want to face still another dislocation. And, lastly, there is the hope in many minds of an eventual return to the west coast. It is quite likely that most of the evacuees would leave quickly if the ban against return to the west coast were to be lifted.

Return to the west coast? Relocation might be speeded up enormously if evacuees could be granted permission to return to the west coast for periods of from thirty to ninety days for the purpose of disposing of such holdings as they still retain and arranging for the shipment of personal belongings to other areas. The changed military situation would seem to justify relaxation. The danger of actual invasion has passed; many of the emergency measures have already been relaxed both on the west coast and in Hawaii; the west coast is no longer a theater of war but a base of operations.

In no case would there be a mass return of the evacuees to the west coast. Many of them have already been relocated elsewhere; others are being relocated every day; and, in many instances, there is nothing for the evacuees to return to on the west coast. Among the Nisei, in particular, there is a strong current of feeling against the west coast, and many of them have no intention whatever of returning permanently. If the ban on the west coast were lifted entirely, it would mean that the last restriction on the rights of the Nisei had been removed. This consideration alone would go far toward improving the morale of all the evacuees who have remained in the relocation camps.

Permanent camps? Already W.R.A. has announced that it intends to close one of its Arkansas relocation centers as soon as possible. If relocation proceeds at the 1943 rate, it is possible that other centers can be closed before the war is over. It would also seem feasible to convert one, possibly two, centers into genuine relocation projects which could eventually be turned over, on a cooperative basis, to the evacuees who will not leave the camps.

THE DEMOCRATIC POTENTIAL

While mass evacuation was a harsh measure, it should be recognized that the relocation program does carry democratic possibilities. The concentration of most of the Japanese-Americans on the west coast in ingrown communities was by no means a healthy situation. The American-born Nisei were experiencing great difficulties in finding employment opportunities to which their skills entitled them. They had not succeeded in outgrowing the dominance of their elders or in breaking away from the strong social ties which held them in Little Tokyo.

For many of these younger and more enterprising Nisei, relocation has been a genuinely liberating experience. They have found opportunities in areas outside the west coast for which they had been seeking for years prior to their removal. They have moved out of the narrow, airless world of Little Tokyo into the main stream of American life. The experience they have undergone has shattered some of their illusions, but it has given a new value to such concepts as "liberty" and "freedom." As a group, they are showing a more active and healthy concern with the problems of other racial minorities. In many other fields, they are demonstrating an alert awareness of the kind of world in which they live. To appreciate this development, one must recognize that the Japanese on the west coast, and particularly in California, occupied an economic niche considerably above Negroes, Chinese, Mexicans, and Filipinos. Evacuation was a shock to their pride, but it has not been without its healthy, if unforeseen, consequences. This observation, however, would not be true of the entire group nor even of all the Nisei. For many, evacuation has involved nothing but bitterness and a feeling of frustration.

It may be healthy, moreover, that the "Japanese Problem," which has echoed on the west coast for nearly fifty years, has now ceased to be a local and has become a national problem. It is now definitely related to the problem of the other racial minorities. This is important since it is evident that we shall never solve any of these problems until we have solved all of them.

The all-Japanese combat team. The most constructive step taken by the government in dealing with the Japanese-Americans was its decision, in January, 1943, to form an all-Japanese combat team. Previously, the Nisei had been classified as ineligible for military service. Today this stigma has been completely removed. The Nisei now have an opportunity to demonstrate their loyalty, and they are doing so in the most concrete manner. Today there are over 8,000 Japanese-Americans in the Army. They were among the first troops to land on the beaches of Salerno, where their conduct was singled out for special praise by General Mark Clark. Casualties in the 100th Infantry Battalion, made up entirely of Nisei, amounted to more than 40 per cent. In addition, Nisei soldiers are serving as interpreters and as intelligence officers with our units throughout the Pacific and in India. As interpreters, they have played, according to Lieutenant-Colonel Karl Gould, "an indispensable role" in the war. (At the time of the attack on Pearl Harbor, there were approximately six hundred people in the United States, not including the Japanese-Americans, who had a workable knowledge of spoken and written Japanese!) Over two hundred Japanese-Americans are serving in the Merchant Marine and quite a number of Nisei girls have joined the WAC.

Sergeants Kazuo Komoto and Fred Nishitsujii have been cited for gallantry in the Southwest Pacific. Sergeant Ben Kuroki, of Hershey, Nebraska, has taken part in over twenty-five combat flights over Hitler's Europe. He participated in the raid on the Ploesti oil fields and wears the Air Medal with four Oak Leaf Clusters. "I want the people to know," he said in a recent interview, "that we're loyal Americans, just like anybody else." As a group, the evacuees in the centers have demonstrated their loyalty by every means available to them. They have purchased war bonds; conducted drives for the Red Cross; organized volunteers-for-victory committees; made radio transcriptions for the O.W.I. and, within the limitations of detention, have done all in their power to further the war effort. When word was released of the execution of the American flyers in Tokyo, the Nisei soldiers in training at Camp Shelby bought $100,000 in war bonds in a single day to demonstrate how they felt about this act of barbarism.

Earning the right to citizenship. The magnificent spirit shown by these people, both here and in Hawaii, where they have been very largely responsible for the success of the defense effort, cannot fail to win the admiration of the American people. Faced with such conclusive proof of loyalty—all the more remarkable in view of the evacuation program itself—

the agitation currently being fostered on the west coast for the deportation of the parents of these soldiers seems unfair. In the days, weeks, and months to follow, the Nisei will be steadily earning the right to fair treatment, to full citizenship, just as the loyal Issei will be establishing, by their excellent conduct under the most trying circumstances, a right to the chance to become American citizens after the war.

If the relocation program is ended at an early date with most of the evacuees relocated outside the centers, the program itself will show constructive results despite the hardships, expense, and needless suffering which it has involved. It may be justified as an extension of democracy and not merely defended as "a harsh but necessary" impairment of the democratic process. We need not apologize for the program as a "detour from democracy," for it has a strong democratic potential as many of the Nisei themselves now recognize. The bitterness and resentment that it has provoked can be wiped out—the Nisei themselves are anxious to forget the entire experience—provided only that we insist that the program serve a genuinely democratic purpose. If, on the other hand, race bigotry gets the upper hand in this program, it can spell disaster. Already there is a dangerous tendency to regard the war in the Pacific as a racial war. Already Japan has made effective use of the evacuation program throughout the Far East, where it is constantly being cited as proof of racial bigotry in America. As long as the relocation centers are full of evacuees, we, as a nation, will be in a strange position: attempting to instill a respect for democracy behind barbed-wire fences; advocating principles that we fear to trust in action; trying to administer democratically a program that produces, in the centers themselves, antidemocratic cross-currents and tendencies.

A challenge to America. Many of the basic issues of the war and of the peace to follow are bound up in the ten relocation centers, from California to Arkansas, in which some 80,000 people of Japanese ancestry are living today. "If," as John Embree has said, "administrative problems involving a hundred thousand people cannot be intelligently and democratically solved, how are we to solve the complex postwar problems of, say, Southeast Asia with its mixed population of a hundred millions?" The welfare of the center residents actually becomes of minor importance when measured against the vastly greater issues that are involved in this seemingly unimportant wartime "episode."

"It is doubtful," writes Dr. Robert Redfield, "if any deprivation of civil rights so sweeping and categoric as this has ever been performed under the war powers and justified by the courts." The very center of the problem, he points out, "lies in the fact that the evacuation and confinement were done on a racial basis." The ultimate effects of this action will be felt outside our country—in Asia, in the Pacific, throughout the vast area around the rim of the Pacific where a new world is emerging from this war. Whether we are to save these "young Americans with Asiatic faces," for the democratic way of life involves the vastly more important question of whether we are to extend and deepen this same way of life throughout the Pacific. For our relations with this small group of 80,000 American citizens are, in miniature, a sketch or blueprint of our relations with the people of a postwar Japan.

President Roosevelt's message to Congress of September 14, 1943, may be regarded as an official statement of federal policy on the relocation program:

> With the segregation of the disloyal evacuees in a separate center, the War Relocation Authority proposes now to redouble its efforts to accomplish the relocation into normal homes and jobs in communities throughout the United States, but outside the evacuated area, of those Americans of Japanese ancestry whose loyalty to this country has remained unshaken through the hardships of the evacuation which military necessity made unavoidable. We shall restore to the loyal evacuees the right to return to the evacuated area as soon as the military situation will make such restoration feasible. Americans of Japanese ancestry, like those of many other ancestries, have shown that they can, and want to, accept our institutions and work loyally with the rest of us, making their own valuable contribution to the national wealth and well-being. In vindication of the very ideals for which we are fighting this war, it is important to us to maintain a high standard of fair, considerate, and equal treatment for the people of this minority, as of all other minorities.

This statement should be construed, not as a mere statement of policy by this administration, but as a solemn pledge spoken by the President in the name of the American people.

PART SIX

Education and Public Opinion

CHAPTER XIV

The Public-school System

THE elaborate division of labor characteristic of our society both complicates and makes especially crucial the problem of training successive generations to carry out the essential activities. The important role of the family in the socialization process will be discussed in another section; but the demands of a democratic and industrial system require that the family's efforts be supplemented, and to a great extent be replaced, by agencies specializing in education. What agencies shall have responsibility for this function, what place the educational personnel will have in the total social structure, who shall determine the content of education—these are important questions to which there is no pat answer. Some of the major efforts of our own society to deal with them are described in the following sections.

Although free and compulsory formal education tends to be regarded today as a natural and inevitable part of the social scene, this was by no means always the case. The historical development of, and struggle over, the public school system is the subject of the following selection from E. P. Cubberley.

SOME OF THE ISSUES *

The second quarter of the nineteenth century may be said to have witnessed the battle for tax-supported, publicly controlled and directed, and non-sectarian common schools. In 1825 such schools were the distant hope of statesmen and reformers; in 1850 they were becoming an actuality in almost every Northern State. The twenty-five years intervening marked a period of public agitation and educational propaganda; of many hard legislative fights; of a struggle to secure desired legislation, and then to hold what had been secured; of many bitter contests with church and pri-

* Cubberley, Ellwood P., *Public Education in the United States* (New York: Houghton Mifflin Company, 1919), pp. 119–123, 125–127.

vate-school interests, which felt that their "vested rights" were being taken from them; and of occasional referenda in which the people were asked, at the next election, to advise the legislature as to what to do. Excepting the battle for the abolition of slavery, perhaps no question has ever been before the American people for settlement which caused so much feeling or aroused such bitter antagonisms. Old friends and business associates parted company over the question, lodges were forced to taboo the subject to avoid disruption, ministers and their congregations often quarreled over the question of free schools, and politicians avoided the issue. The friends of free schools were at first commonly regarded as fanatics, dangerous to the State, and the opponents of free schools were considered by them as old-time conservatives or as selfish members of society. . . .

ARGUMENTS FOR AND AGAINST FREE SCHOOLS

Both sides to the controversy advanced many arguments for and against state tax-supported schools, the more important on each side being the following.

I. Arguments for public tax-supported schools.

1. That education tends to prevent pauperism and crime.
2. That education tends to reduce poverty and distress.
3. That education increases production, and eliminates wrong ideas as to the distribution of wealth.
4. That a common state school, equally open to all, would prevent that class differentiation so dangerous in a Republic.
5. That the old church and private school education had proved utterly inadequate to meet the needs of a changed society.
6. That a system of religious schools is impossible in such a mixed nation as our own.
7. That the pauper-school idea is against the best interests of society, inimical to public welfare, and a constant offense to the poor, many of whom will not send their children because of the stigma attached to such schools.
8. That education as to one's civic duties is a necessity for the intelligent exercise of suffrage, and for the preservation of republican institutions.
9. That the increase of foreign immigration (which became quite noticeable after 1825, and attained large proportions after 1845) is a menace to our free institutions, and that these new elements

can be best assimilated in a system of publicly supported and publicly directed common schools.

10. That the free and general education of all children at public expense is the natural right of all children in a Republic.
11. That the social, moral, political, and industrial benefits to be derived from the general education of all compensate many times over for its cost.
12. That a State which has the right to hang has the right to educate.
13. That the taking over of education by the State is not based on considerations of economy, but is the exercise of the State's inherent right to self-preservation and improvement.
14. That only a system of state-controlled schools can be free to teach whatever the welfare of the State may demand.

II. Arguments against public tax-supported schools.

1. Impractical, visionary, and "too advanced" legislation.
2. Will make education too common, and will educate people out of their proper position in society.
3. Would not benefit the masses, who are already as well cared for as they deserve.
4. Would tend to break down long-established and very desirable social barriers.
5. Would injure private and parochial schools, in which much money had been put and "vested rights" established.
6. Fear of the churches that state schools might injure their church progress and welfare.
7. Fear of the non-English speaking classes that state schools might supplant instruction in their languages.
8. The "conscientious objector" claimed that the State had no right to interfere between a parent and his child in the matter of education.
9. That those having no children to be educated should not be taxed for schools.
10. That taking a man's property to educate his neighbor's child is no more defensible than taking a man's plow to plow his neighbor's field.
11. That the State may be justified in taxing to defend the liberties of a people, but not to support their benevolences.
12. That the industrious would be taxed to educate the indolent.

13. That taxes would be so increased that no State could long meet such a lavish drain on its resources.
14. That there was priestcraft in the scheme, the purpose being first to establish a State School, and then a State Church.

THE WORK OF PROPAGANDA

To meet the arguments of the objectors, to change the opinions of a thinking few into the common opinion of the many, to overcome prejudice, and to awaken the public conscience to the public need for free and common schools in such a democratic society as ours, was the work of a generation. With many of the older citizens no progress could be made; the effective work everywhere had to be done with the younger men of the time. It was the work of many years to convince the masses of the people that the scheme of state schools was not only practicable, but also the best and most economical means for giving their children the benefits of an education; to convince propertied citizens that taxation for education was in the interests of both public and private welfare; to convince legislators that it was safe to vote for free-school bills; and to overcome the opposition due to apathy, religious jealousies, and private interests. In time, though, the desirability of common, free, tax-supported, non-sectarian, state-controlled schools became evident to a majority of the citizens in the different American States, and as it did the American State School, free and equally open to all, was finally evolved and took its place as the most important institution in our national life working for the perpetuation of our free democracy and the advancement of the public welfare.

For this work of propaganda hundreds of School Societies and Educational Associations were organized; many conventions were held, and resolutions favoring state schools were adopted; many "Letters" and "Addresses to the Public" were written and published; public-spirited citizens traveled over the country, making addresses to the people explaining the advantages of free state schools; many public-spirited men gave the best years of their lives to the state-school propaganda; and many governors sent communications on the subject to legislatures not yet convinced as to the desirability of state action. At each meeting of the legislatures for years a deluge of resolutions, memorials, and petitions for and against free schools met the members. . . .

SUPPORT FROM ASSOCIATIONS OF WORKINGMEN

Workingmen, too, through their newly formed organizations, also took a prominent part in the propaganda for the establishment of public tax-supported schools. Among the many resolutions adopted by these wage-earners the following are typical:

At a General Meeting of Mechanics and Workingmen held in New York City, in 1829, it was:

> *Resolved,* that next to life and liberty, we consider education the greatest blessing bestowed upon mankind.
>
> *Resolved,* that the public funds should be appropriated (to a reasonable extent) to the purpose of education upon a regular system that shall insure the opportunity to every individual of obtaining a competent education before he shall have arrived at the age of maturity.

At a meeting of workingmen held in Philadelphia, in 1829, it was declared that:

> No system of education, which a freeman can accept, has yet been established for the poor; whilst thousands of dollars of the public money has been appropriated for building colleges and academies for the rich.

Each candidate for the state legislature was formally asked to declare his attitude toward "an equal and general system of Education." In 1830 they adopted a long *Report* on the conditions of education in Pennsylvania, demanded schools, and declared that there could be "no real liberty in a republic without a wide diffusion of real intelligence."

In 1830 the Workingmen's Party of Philadelphia included, as the first plank in its platform:

> *Resolved,* that the time has arrived when it becomes the paramount duty of every friend to the happiness and freedom of man to promote a system of education that shall embrace equally all the children of the state, of every rank and condition.

In 1830 an Association of Workingmen was formed at New Castle, Delaware, and in their constitution they provided:

> Let us unite at the polls and give our votes to no candidate who is not pledged to support a rational system of education to be paid for out of the public funds.

At a Boston meeting of "Workingmen, Mechanics, and others friendly to their interests," in 1830, it was:

> *Resolved,* that the establishment of a liberal system of education, attainable by all, should be among the first efforts of every law-giver who desires the continuance of our national independence.

In 1830 the "Farmers', Mechanics', and Workingmen's" Party of New

York State, in convention at Salina, included as one of the planks in its platform the following:

> *Resolved,* that a scheme of education, more universal in its effects, is practicable, so that no child in the republick, however poor, should grow up without an opportunity to acquire at least a competent English education; and that the system should be adapted to the conditions of the poor both in the city and country.

In 1835 the workingmen of the city of Washington enumerated as one of their demands the establishment of "a universal system of education," and in 1836 the "General Trades Union" of Cincinnati, in an "Appeal to the Workingmen of the West," urged that they try to elevate their condition by directing their efforts toward obtaining "a national system of education."

THE PRESENT SITUATION IN THE SCHOOLS *

As an enterprise in mass management, public education is one of the largest of all public businesses. Its plant, its personnel, its annual expenditures all rank it among the largest governmental functions. By 1930 the total value of the property and endowments of the public schools had reached the impressive sum of $6,674,445,000. Their annual expenditures, including interest and capital outlay, were at a level of about $2,300,000,000. Drastic reduction in expenditures, followed by partial recovery, has occurred since 1930; in 1935–36 the schools were maintained with enrollments substantially above those of 1930 through the expenditure of about $2,000,000,000.

As an enterprise in human relations, the schools deal in the human lives of the future Nation. Enrollments in all public elementary and secondary schools reached a total of 26,367,098 in 1935–36. Enrollments in elementary schools reached their peak in 1930 and have since declined slightly because of the smaller number of children in the total population. In 1935–36 enrollments in public elementary schools were 20,392,561. High school enrollments continue to expand as a larger proportion of all youth enter the high schools. Youth to the number of 4,399,422 were enrolled in public high schools in 1929–30; by 1935–36 the number had increased to 5,974,537. . . .

* *Report of the Advisory Committee on Education,* 75 Cong., 3 Sess., House Document No. 529, pp. 3–7, 8–11, 12–22.

Following a half century of laying of foundations between 1830 and 1880, and a second half century of rapid expansion ending in 1930, it may well be that America is now entering upon a period of evaluation—a period in which will be determined more accurately what educational policies are best suited to a modern democracy and how best they may be realized in practice.

GENERAL CHARACTERISTICS OF THE PUBLIC-SCHOOL SYSTEM

When the work of evaluation is undertaken, it is immediately apparent that an intense localism is at once the strength and the weakness of American schools. Local interest and support have been the major factors in the development of the most democratic system of education in the world. Our folk-made schools have given us many great benefits. We also bear the burden, however, of many grave disadvantages that trace back directly to local responsibility for public education. We have in this country a considerable number of the best public schools in the world. We also have far more than our share of those of very inferior quality.

The strong public-school centers in the United States are found most frequently today among the small and middle-sized cities. The school boards in these cities are usually free from unwise forms of political interference and tend to be made up of competent citizens, although those citizens are frequently more representative of business and the professions than of other groups in the community. Administrative control is effective and the local tax base in most such communities is adequate to support a liberal measure of educational service without reliance upon any other source of support. The leadership by school administrators is in general as good as can be found in any phase of governmental service, and in many cases reaches a very high level. The classroom teachers in those cities typically are well prepared, are seldom without experience, and are both interested in their work and desirous of improving it.

Under such conditions, schools can give effective attention to stimulating the maximum development of the children. The courses of study are adaptable and can be adjusted to changing conditions. Textbook teaching is still the rule, but some use is being made of reading materials other than textbooks. Health, welfare, and noncommercial recreational activities are provided to some extent. School and community activities are frequently blended to provide a more inspiring curriculum and to achieve other values.

The school systems in the middle-sized cities are capable of much further improvement, but their great virtue lies in the fact that improvement is going on at a rather rapid rate. They have the necessary resources and enough autonomy for leadership to function. They may well continue to provide much of the educational leadership for America. Every effort should be made to encourage them to do so.

The school situation in the great metropolitan areas is often less satisfactory. Their wealthy and autonomous suburban areas have perhaps the finest public schools in the United States, but the large cities themselves present another picture. They unquestionably have the financial resources for good educational programs, and in many cases provide educational service at a high expenditure level. They suffer, however, from the chronic handicaps of mammoth urbanism. In all cases they adapt to changing conditions only at a slow rate. They have not yet found techniques by which to instill a progressive spirit throughout the entire personnel of centralized school systems, each as large as those of many whole nations in other parts of the world. In some cases they suffer from the most flagrant applications of the spoils system and other phases of corrupt political action.

The least-satisfactory schools in the United States are now to be found for the most part in rural areas. The rural schools are better than they were formerly, but under present conditions there is no prospect that the rural areas will be able through their own resources to lessen the wide gap between rural and urban levels of educational service.

In 1935–36 the average expenditure per pupil in average daily attendance in all public schools, urban and rural, was $88.30. The numbers of urban and rural children in average daily attendance were approximately equal—11,406,380 urban and 10,892,387 rural. The average expenditure per pupil in average daily attendance in urban schools was $108.25, and in rural schools $67.40. The rural figure includes town and village schools as well as those in the open country. Expenditures in the schools of open country areas are much lower, although statistics of average expenditure in such schools are not available.

Low expenditure levels in rural areas are reflected in poorly paid and relatively untrained teachers, reliance on stereotyped forms of textbook instruction with inadequate provision of supplementary books and other instructional materials, school terms averaging a month shorter than those in cities, and a general lack of the health, welfare, guidance, and other services in addition to instruction that are needed by children in schools. . .

In 1930 there were 810,000 children between the ages of 7 and 13 who were not going to school at all. Most of those children were in the poorest rural areas.

The continued maintenance of large numbers of one-teacher rural schools with extremely small enrollments is responsible in many areas for both a low level of educational service and a high tax bill for the service that is provided. A study completed in 1934 recorded nearly 44,000 schools in which the attendance per school ranged from 3 to 17 pupils, and average costs per pupil ranged from $200 to $80, although the level of service provided was markedly inferior to that found in many town and village schools operating at cost levels around $40 per pupil in attendance. . . .

Throughout the Nation in rural schools with a single teacher, nearly a fourth of all the teachers have had no preparation beyond a high-school education and seven out of eight have had no more than 2 years of education beyond high school. Considering the circumstances, the amount of good accomplished by these teachers is large, but the results are still inadequate.

The administration of the school system in the United States is more highly decentralized than any other public function, primarily because of the small size of most rural school districts. Data collected in 1934 show that there are approximately 127,000 separate and independent school districts and other types of local school jurisdictions. Each of these local jurisdictions is free to decide on the type and quality of education offered, subject only to general State laws and regulations and to the limit of available funds. Altogether there are about 424,000 school board members; in 12 States they outnumber the teachers. More efficient administration would be possible in many areas if some rural districts were consolidated. Larger districts could afford professionally trained superintendents who are beyond the reach of a small rural district.

The schools generally both in rural and in urban areas are deficient in their facilities for necessary services other than routine instruction. Training for preprimary children has only begun to be introduced. Facilities for physical education, for health education, and for recreation are extremely limited in the schools attended by a majority of the children in this country. . . .

Some 2,500,000 children of school age in the United States are handicapped in some way that necessitates facilities in addition to those provided for other children. Not more than 325,000 are receiving the attention necessary to make their education a success. A majority of the children with defects of sight, hearing, speech, and other functions can be made capable of supporting themselves and of living useful lives in the community if they are given a fair chance to obtain an education. To neglect this opportunity, as is now being done in most of the cases, is to impose an unfair burden on the children themselves and an expense on the community throughout their lives. Twenty-six States have laws concerning special classes for some types of handicapped children, but no State is providing funds large enough to meet the requirements. In rural areas the available information indicates that practically nothing is being done in the way of providing suitable education for these children.

In most of the States where there are separate schools for Negroes, the schools for white children are below the national average, yet Negro schools are only about half as well supported as white schools. Because of the intimate economic relations that necessarily exist between the two races, the low level of education among Negroes is a severe burden not only on themselves but on all who must employ them or have dealings with them. Even in Northern States, the large influx of Negroes from the South makes the quality of their previous training a matter of vital importance to the localities where they live and work. All the statistics for length of school term, average attendance, educational qualifications of teachers, type of school buildings, and other factors indicate that a wasteful neglect is characteristic of the treatment of Negro school children in most of the areas where they are required to attend separate schools. . . .

PUBLIC HIGH SCHOOLS

Education at the secondary level in this country was for a long time considered a special privilege, available only to a few on the payment of tuition fees, and designed chiefly as a preliminary preparation for certain professions. During the latter part of the nineteenth century the growing realization of the implications of democracy led to the development of the high school as a part of the common school system.

In retrospect, nothing in the evolution of American education is more striking in its sweep than the development of the secondary school. Nothing like it has ever happened before in any other country. As late as 1890 in the United States only 3.8 percent of the number of young people 14 to 17 years of age were enrolled in public high schools; at present more than 60 per cent of the population of high-school age are enrolled in public high schools. In 1937 for the first time the number of graduates from high schools in a single year passed the million mark. There are now some 25,000 public high schools in which over 230,000 teachers instruct almost 6,000,000 boys and girls, by means of a curriculum that is gradually, although inadequately, being adapted to meet the individual and social needs of American youth.

For the country as a whole, the period of phenomenal high-school expansion appears to be drawing to a close. The effects of the decline in birth rate which began some years ago are already beginning to be shown in the size of the youth population; about 1940 the number of youth of high-school age will begin to decrease. With 60 percent of the number of youth in the 4-year high-school age group already attending high school and with a decline in the total youth population, it will no longer be possible for the high-school enrollment to double each decade as it often has during the past half century.

Expansion will not stop abruptly, however; all existing trends indicate that a considerably higher percentage of those of high-school age will attend high school in the future, particularly in areas where high-school enrollments are still low.

School attendance beyond age 16 is not usually required by law, and many States have not accepted fully the obligation of making a high-school education universally available. The limitations on existing facilities are indicated by a wide variation among States with respect to the percentage of youth of high-school age who are enrolled in high schools. . . .

With the radical changes in social life, brought on by the development of present industrial and economic conditions and by the rapid growth of cities, the schools have been swamped with new duties. These new duties have come along with the great increases in high-school enrollments and changes in the composition of the groups of students enrolled. School administrators have often been too busy with pressing immediate tasks to think through fundamentally the necessary changes in their programs. Yet there is now no possible doubt that the school system must supply many new kinds of training, particularly in the secondary schools.

Education for citizenship, for example, can no longer be properly confined to a formal study of the structure of government, leaving the pupil innocent of all idea as to what really happens at the City Hall or in Washington. Students should learn something of the economic causes of political pressure, the nature of propaganda, the democratic treatment of honest difference of opinion, and the technique of cooperation.

Most high schools offer some types of training designed specifically to prepare for employment, but programs in the vocational field are relatively undeveloped. . . .

For adequate occupational preparation, many young people need special vocational training, but consideration should also be given to the far greater importance of general training for useful employment. Underlying each particular specialized trade or calling must be the basic skills and habits—accurate arithmetic, careful use of the language, and responsibility and conscientious work. Both elementary and secondary schools need better facilities for giving the basic training which will prepare a young person to learn a job quickly and, if the job vanishes in the course of technological change, to shift over without serious trouble to some new type of work. . . .

The complex opportunities and pitfalls of modern life make it practically impossible for most high-school pupils to make a wise choice of future occupation on the basis of casual observation of the world around them. Yet only a few schools are providing educational and vocational guidance under trained and capable counselors. In the absence of suitable provision for guidance, much of the high-school education now provided fails to meet the needs of the pupils. More attention to guidance is needed, with a more realistic definition of the requirements for ultimate employment and a better supply of data as to relative opportunities in the various fields. . . .

The high schools must also assume far greater responsibility than at present for part-time educational and related services for out-of-school youths and adults. Most of the 900,000 young people who drop out of high school each year without being graduated are in need of further educational service, and many of them would respond if suitable part-time programs were provided. Adults also have increasing needs for the services of the schools to supplement the education they received earlier in life, for vocational retraining, and for constructive leisure-time activities. In many areas the community facilities will not be complete until the high schools become true community centers for educational, recreational, and cultura aspects of community life. . . .

PRIVATE SCHOOLS

In 1933–34 there were about 12,000 private elementary and secondary schools in this country. Nearly two-thirds are controlled by the Catholi Church, and about one-sixth are under other church auspices. Privat schools enroll about one-tenth of the total number of elementary-schoo pupils and about one-sixteenth of the total number of high-school pupils Most States . . . grant tax exemption to such of them as are nonprofit making in character. . . .

SUPPORT OF EDUCATION

Over three-quarters of the annual cost of public education is me through taxation of property, chiefly by local jurisdictions. Because of thi situation, the fortunes of education rise and fall with the ability and willingness of real estate owners to pay taxes. No other great social service is dependent so largely upon so unsatisfactory a tax base.

The implications of providing most of the financial support of education through local taxation become more apparent when consideration is given to the 127,000 local school jursidictions, most of which raise their taxes separately. Frequently real estate values in school districts are entirely out of proportion to the number of children. The larger the number of districts in a given area and the smaller their average size, the less likely is there to be any reasonable relationship between wealth and children. In Iowa, for example, the most prosperous school district has been estimated to have 275 times the wealth per child of the poorest district. In a number of States, the most able local units could provide $100 or more per child for every $1 provided by the least able units.

Differences in educational opportunity are not so great as might be supposed from these differences in economic ability, because the least able districts in most States tax themselves much more heavily than the most able districts, and also because most States provide part of the cost of education through State distributive funds raised through State taxation. Nevertheless, the amount of inequality in educational opportunity within States is very great. Children living in the poorer districts within States can have suitable educational opportunities only if a large share of school support comes from outside the present boundaries of those districts.

EXPENDITURES FOR SCHOOLS BY THE VARIOUS STATES

The same types of differences as to educational opportunity that exist within States also exist among States. There is no single entirely satisfactory measure that can be applied to determine differences in educational opportunity, but in general there is a very high correlation between expenditures per pupil and the quality and amount of service provided. Marked differences exist in the amounts which the various States spend for the education of each school child in average daily attendance. . . .

In three States, the amount expended per pupil [in 1935–36] in average daily attendance was less than $30; in three others at the opposite extreme, expenditures were above $115 and were thus nearly four times as large. . . .

The great disparities among States in the support of education are not due to a lack of interest or of effort on the part of the States that provide the least support. . . . Those States having the least adequately supported schools are, in general, the ones putting forth the greatest effort. . . .

Teachers' salaries are the largest single item of educational expense. In 1935–36 the average compensation of teachers, supervisors, and principals in all public elementary and secondary schools was below $600 in three States, while it was above $1,800 in three others at the opposite end of the scale. . . .

States differ markedly in the average length of the school term they provide. In 1935–36 the average length of the school year for public schools was 173 days. In two States, the average length of the school year was under 140 days; in nine States, it was above 180 days. These differences correlate closely with the differences in expenditures. . . .

It should be noted that although the States differ greatly in their average expenditures for education, even greater differences can be found by comparing expenditures in units smaller than States. A number of States can be found in which expenditures per classroom unit for education are 12 to 15 times as high in some districts as in others. In many States the range within those States is represented by ratios higher than 6 to 1; in only a few States having State distributive funds of substantial size does the ratio drop as low as 3 or 2 to 1.

The problem of inequality within States is no less important than the problem of inequality among States. Both problems may be traced back to the same causes of unequal distribution of resources. Inequality within States can be lessened through vigorous action by State governments, but for reasons discussed later in this report, there are definite limits to State action in reducing inequalities of educational opportunity.

LACK OF BALANCE IN THE EDUCATIONAL LOAD

Financial support for education through State and local taxation would produce more equitable results if the lack of balance in the educational load were not so great. The educational load is distributed very unequally among regions and States and between the rural and urban population. . .

The productive workers of the Southeast carry a burden of child care and education about 80 percent greater than that carried by the similar age group of adults in the Far West. In 9 States, of which 6 are in the Southeast, there were in 1930 over 600 children 5 to 17 years of age per 1,000 adults 20 to 64. In 6 States—New York, Illinois, Nevada, Washington, Oregon, and California—there were fewer than 400 children 5 to 17 years of age per 1,000 adults 20 to 64 years of age.

The high ratios of children to adults in the Southern States are not due in any large degree to the age distribution of the Negro population in those States. In a number of Southern States, there are more white children per 1,000 white adults than there are Negro children per 1,000 Negro adults. For the Southeast as a whole, however, in 1930 there were 591 white and 632 Negro children 5 to 17 years of age per 1,000 adults 20 to 64 years of age in the respective races.

The differences among States and regions, in the ratio of children to adults, to a large extent reflect differences in the ratio of rural to urban population in the various States. . . .

In substantially every State, the adult group in the rural population is carrying an educational load, in terms of number of children to be educated, that is far in excess of the load carried by the adult group in urban areas. In rural-nonfarm areas—the small towns and villages under 2,500 population—the relative number of children is about 40 percent greater than in urban centers of 100,000 population or more. The heaviest load of all, however, is carried by the rural farm population, with nearly twice the number of children in proportion to adults that is found in large cities.

The farm population not only has a disproportionately heavy educational load; it must carry the load on a per capita income markedly less than that of the nonfarm population. In 1930 the farm population was responsible for the care and education of 31 percent of the children, but the farmers received only 9 percent of the national income. In the Southeastern region this disparity was still greater, the farmers of that region having the care of approximately 4,250,000 children age 5 to 17, with only 2 percent of the national income. At the other extreme the nonfarm population of the Northeast, with approximately 8,500,000 children age 5 to 17, had 42 percent of the national income.

The problem of inequality of educational opportunities is to a large extent a problem in rural urban differences in educational load and economic resources. If the rural and urban population were distributed among the States substantially in the same proportions, inequalities of educational opportunity could be minimized through the operation of equalization funds in the various States. The urban population, however, is concentrated in a relatively small number of States; more than half of the States are predominantly rural. . . .

THE ABILITY OF THE STATES TO SUPPORT SCHOOLS

About 20 percent of the children of school age in the United States live in States where with no more than average effort more than $75 per child could be provided for education, while another 20 percent live in States where not more than $25 per child could be provided without more than average effort. An expenditure of $50 per child would be deemed low in comparison with the typical urban standards of any region, yet more than 60 percent of the children live in States that on a State-wide basis could not provide $50 per child for public schools without more than average effort. . . .

The general pattern of expenditures, by States, is similar to that of financial ability, but in some States actual expenditures are considerably less than the amounts that would be available with average effort, whereas in other States the reverse is true. Although the levels of expenditure cover a wide range, they do not differ so widely as do the levels of financial ability. The States of more than average financial ability are, in general, making less than average effort to support education, while the States of less than average ability are with few exceptions making considerably greater than average effort to support education.

It is to the credit of the States of low financial ability that with few exceptions they rank at the top in the percentage of their income devoted to schools. Nevertheless, they rank at the bottom with respect to the quality of the schooling provided. Although the States having the least ability to support education tend to make the greatest effort in proportion to ability, even with such effort they are unable to support education at anything like the level attained, with less than average effort, by the more able States.

EDUCATIONAL IMPLICATIONS OF INTERNAL MIGRATION

No American can view with satisfaction or even complacency a situation in which large areas and population groups are retarded in their educational development through circumstances beyond their control. Moreover, no American can escape the results of this situation if it is allowed to continue. . . .

Notwithstanding the high rate of natural increase of the farm population, the net migration from farms between 1920 and 1930 was so large that the total farm population declined by more than a million. On the other hand, the previous low rate of natural increase in cities dropped still further; a larger part of the great increase in urban population between 1920 and 1930 was provided by migration from rural areas.

The cityward movement of the population was dominated by youth under 25 years of age and by migration from the farming areas of the South. Of the children between 10 and 20 years of age living on farms in 1920, approximately 40 percent were living in towns and cities in 1930.

About 60 percent of the net migration of all ages from farms was from farms located south of the Mason and Dixon line.

The depression checked the movement of population from farm to city, but by 1935 that movement was again definitely on the increase. For many years, at least, there is little reason to expect any permanent alteration in the general pattern of migration. Technological advance is materially reducing the demand for agricultural workers, and in a number of populous rural areas there is an intense pressure of population on the resource structure. From these areas youth in large numbers may be expected to migrate in search of economic opportunity.

Few urban areas now have rates of natural increase sufficient to maintain their present populations. If American cities, large and small, are to grow or even to maintain their population at the present level, they must look to the rural population as a source of recruitment.

The movement of youth in large numbers from farm to city, across State lines, and from region to region raises educational problems of the first magnitude. It is a fact of no slight importance that large numbers of youth who will constitute much of the future population are being reared in communities that are now able to provide only the most restricted educational opportunities.

States and regions favored by fortune cannot afford to be indifferent to the educational opportunities provided for youth in the States and regions from which they will draw many of their future citizens. Of the 10 States now most able to support education, 7 are not rearing children in numbers large enough even to maintain their present populations without replacement from other areas.

THE SCHOOLS AND CONFORMITY *

The answers to the author's questionnaire reveal interesting differences in attitude toward teachers' expression of ideas on controversial subjects. In many communities merely believing in unpopular causes creates difficulty, if it is known. Other communities do not object to unconventional views unless they are extremely radical, provided the teacher does not talk about them publicly. In other places the teacher may go still farther and discuss unpopular ideas in class, provided he himself does not support them. He may maintain strict neutrality or he may oppose them, but he

* Beale, Howard K., *A History of Freedom of Teaching in American Schools* (New York: Charles Scribner's Sons, 1941), pp. 237–247, 249, 251–252, 264–268.

must not express approval. In some towns a teacher may not only discuss controversial subjects in class, but, in the course of that discussion, may express personal views on the unpopular side, provided he does not try to convert anybody to his own unorthodoxy. There are usually exceptions to this rule—certain extreme beliefs that it would be unsafe for a teacher to let his pupils know he favors. In a few places a teacher may openly propagandize in class for unpopular causes. He may usually propagandize if he supports the popular side of the controversy. In some communities he may even do so on the unpopular side. In theory he is freer to advocate unpopular causes outside class than inside, but in practice the advocacy of unpopular causes in the community gets him into trouble more quickly than doing so in school. There are exceptions to this rule. In many communities particular subjects arouse great feeling and must be entirely avoided. While usually a teacher is freer to believe in an unpopular cause than to discuss it even impartially, just the reverse is true in regard to certain extreme points of view. Many communities reported in 1933 that a teacher might discuss communism, cancellation of war debts, recognition of Russia, or the necessity of revolution by force to bring social justice, but may not believe in any of these things himself. On the other hand, birth control, the non-existence of God, and evolution are not deemed fit subjects even for impartial discussion in class in many places, where a teacher may believe in them himself. In the South certain points of view, such as censure of Southern leaders for not accepting the results of the Civil War, usually may not even be raised in class. . . .

The country as a whole is still somewhat sensitive about criticism of its own past actions. About one teacher in four is afraid to express the belief that the United States committed a wrong against Mexico in the Mexican War or to defend Germany's position in the World War or Britain's in the American Revolution. One in three is afraid to agree with modern historical research in its deflation of some of the heroes of American history.

On economic questions, popular or generally accepted points of view or opinions that please wealthy and powerful members of the community can be expressed without criticism. There is also a class of economic questions on which teachers are fairly free to express even views on the unconventional side, namely, support of high income taxes, the belief that labor is pitifully underpaid, advocacy of low tariffs for revenue only, support of government ownership of public utilities, belief that "peaceful reform" of the capitalist system is necessary, and support of a capital levy.

But opinion on the unorthodox side of economic issues is usually more restricted than on international, sectional, or "patriotic" questions.

One teacher in four is afraid to censure labor union leaders in sections where labor is well organized. A good deal of objection is raised to advocacy of confiscatory inheritance taxes, belief that "all unemployed have a moral right to support from Federal relief," denunciation of the "profit system," and the charge that "our courts are corrupted by big business." Support of teacher membership in labor unions is frequently impossible. Dangerous, indeed, is disapproval of the practices of local business men like coal operators, utility owners, merchants, lawyers, or manufacturers.

Teachers are less free to take the peace side of the war issue than the unpopular side of economic questions. Most teachers may advocate a large navy or oppose an embargo on the shipment of arms to warring nations. Veterans' appropriations and military training in the schools are dangerous subjects whichever side one takes. Usually, however, it is opposition to war that teachers feel they are not free to express. Many are afraid to advocate total disarmament or to criticize the Supreme Court for its refusal to admit pacifists to citizenship. Still more dare not declare that our entry into the World War was a mistake or praise war-time "conscientious objectors." Most dangerous of all is swearing never to bear arms.

Criticism of the Government is dangerous. One teacher out of three was afraid even to criticize President Hoover for using the army to drive the bonus men out of Washington or to accuse state officials of corruption. It is more dangerous, however, to express censure of the President of the United States on other grounds, or of the local courts for unjust decisions, or of local officials for corruption.

Political questions are still more restricted unless one is on the orthodox side. One in every three or four teachers thinks it unsafe to voice opposition to the "Buy American" movement or to denounce the Ku Klux Klan. Between a third and a half are afraid to censure the Federal Government or local police for prosecuting Communist hunger marchers for parading, or to criticize the activities of the D.A.R., the American Legion, or the Confederate Veterans. Some teachers object to a pledge of loyalty and an oath of allegiance because these imply a pledge to bear arms in any war whatsoever whether just or unjust; but nearly two-thirds of the teachers report it impossible to express this opposition.

Support of radicalism is still more dangerous, though most teachers are free to express opposition to radicalism. One in three is afraid to approve socialism. A majority feel it unsafe to approve communism, criticize the breaking up of a meeting of "Reds" by local police, or suggest that revolution by force is necessary in order to establish justice.

Ideas on social problems are dangerous to unorthodox teachers. In spite of the popular vote for repeal shortly thereafter, only six teachers in seven felt it safe in 1933 to favor rigid enforcement of the Eighteenth Amendment, while it was frequently unsafe to support repeal. In the South it is unwise to express approval of anything more than nominal political equality for Negroes, but in the North teachers are usually free to favor full equality. Approval of social equality for Negroes, however, is dangerous even in some Northern communities and is impossible in the South. Expression of belief in birth control or companionate marriage is impossible. In fact, in the great majority of schools neither subject can be discussed even impartially in its proper place in the curriculum.

Religion is the most restricted of all subjects. Here teachers generally are not free to express approval even of conservative tenets because there are certain to be liberals in the community who will object. Between a third and a half of the teachers are afraid to express acceptance of the theory of evolution, even if they make no effort to persuade their pupils. In the great majority of schools favorable views must not be expressed on either the fundamentalist or the modernist interpretations of the Bible. It is unsafe to let the class know that one believes it dangerous to elect a Catholic to office. Almost nowhere can one admit to a class that he does not believe in the existence of God.

These comparisons are based on a teacher's freedom to express views . . . in . . . class discussion provided he does not try to convert students. There is much less freedom in advocating these same things outside of class and still less in propagandizing for them in class. While this picture portrays the relative degree of freedom in these various realms of ideas, it greatly underestimates for several reasons the extent of actual restrictions. In the first place, the South responded poorly and the freer parts of the country well, thus weighting the questionnaires in favor of freedom. It was harder, also, to get replies from small towns and rural schools than from large cities, where there is the greatest freedom. The teachers most interested in answering were those where there is a good deal of freedom but where teachers want more. An effort was made to reach those who had thought most about freedom and therefore could answer most adequately, and therefore the questionnaire was sent to a selected list of teachers. Still, even of this selected group, probably half reported that they had freedom merely because they had not thought enough about most of the questions to realize how little they really did have. In many cases, freedom seems to exist only because the subject under consideration is not an issue in the particular community. In such a situation, this apparent freedom could be replaced by rigid restriction if and when people became really interested in the subject discussed. Many teachers frankly reply that most of these controversial topics are unknown in their schools and that they do not know what the attitude is. In certain cases a well-organized group of Catholics, laborers, or business men will prevent or create restrictions on some subject that throw it entirely out of line with other attitudes in that community. Freedom to discuss military training depends largely upon whether it is offered in the school in question. The replies of teachers in the great number of schools that offer none overbalance the rigid restrictions against criticism of it in schools where it does exist. This makes freedom in the matter appear much greater than it actually is in schools where military training is an issue at all. Here, then, the restrictive forces are much more powerful than is revealed.

FREEDOM IN CONDUCT

Conduct outside the school gets more teachers into trouble than do ideas expressed in the classroom. Teachers since the World War have been allowed to do many things that would once have caused instant dismissal. Theater-going and dancing are now usually permitted to teachers, though a surprising number of places still forbid dancing. Smoking by men teachers is widely permitted. In many places even women teachers smoke. In some larger cities drinking is at least not punished, even when not specifically permitted, though it is usually not publicly confessed. Divorce is no longer always fatal to the teacher, though it still is dangerous. Freedom is now permitted in dress, in conduct, in habits that would once have been considered "immoral" by a stricter prewar generation. Church attendance and teaching a Sunday school class are still widely expected of a teacher, but much less generally so than formerly. For a time, continuing to teach after marriage was more extensively permitted than formerly. Now that is again rigidly restricted in communities that had come to accept it. The restriction is now based on economic grounds, however, not on moral scruples or views about the woman's place in the home.

Comparisons of detail make a teacher look much freer in 1939 than in 1900. Actually, it is questionable whether the teacher's position in relation to the rest of the community has changed much except in large cities. American standards of conduct have changed. Popular ideas of what is moral and respectable were revolutionized by the War. All sorts of inhibitions were broken down. The change in the position of women in American life has brought release to many a school teacher. The significant fact is not, however, that teachers here and there smoke whereas it would have meant instant dismissal in 1925. The significant fact is that the teacher is still subjected to all sorts of regulations and prohibitions that are not applied to members of the community in other callings. It is the community mores that have changed, not the relation of the teacher to the community. . . .

SOURCES OF PRESSURE UPON TEACHERS

Generalizations for the country as a whole are unsafe, because pressure upon the teacher varies with the type of school and type of community. In public schools, however, public opinion wins first place among pressures by a large margin except in cities of 100,000 or more. There the force of public opinion is not so great as a number of other influences. In private schools in smaller places, public opinion is an important restraint, but in those in large cities it counts even less than in public schools.

The other really great pressures come from parents, superintendents, principals, and school board members or trustees. So nearly equal are these pressures that no generalization is possible for the country as a whole. In private schools, since there is no superintendent, the principal exerts the greatest pressure and parents rank next. Private schools in large cities are usually so organized that the board of trustees, if there is one at all, does not count heavily in the teacher's life. In private schools in smaller places trustees usually exercise large control. In private schools run by individual owners all power is concentrated in this head of the school, except in so far as he in turn is subject to various pressures. In public schools the relative importance of these elements depends upon the size of the town. In cities of over 100,000 the principal ranks below public opinion but above the superintendent. Parents and school boards are weighted almost equally after the superintendent, school boards running a little ahead in cities of over 1,000,000 and parents a little ahead in cities of 100,000 to 1,000,000. In suburban communities parents outrank all the other pressures. School boards come next, then superintendents, and principals last. In cities of 2500 to 100,000 the superintendent is, after public opinion, the most important restrictive force, with the school board next, and principals least important. In rural communities, the principal is still less important; the school board and superintendent outrank parents; but the school board instead of the superintendent becomes the great restrictive force. Next in importance among pressures on teachers come other teachers and students. Except in private schools in large cities and in public schools in rural communities the power of other teachers over a teacher is greater than that of students.

In this group of important restrictive pressures teachers also name business men, politicians, and religious groups. In private schools business men of the community and politicians have little power, but because of the religious connections or traditions of many of these schools, religious groups exert considerable influence. In public schools of great cities politicians outrank the other two, but both business and religious groups are important and exert almost equal pressure, largely because of the active Roman Catholic elements in the great cities. In rural communities, too, and in towns of 2500 to 25,000 the religious groups are much more powerful than business men or politicians. In the great number of American cities that have between 25,000 and 1,000,000 population, religious forces have much less power over teachers than do business men and politicians, and business is more influential than politics. In suburbs of great cities religious groups and politicians are alike unimportant in comparison with business interests.

Lesser but important pressures are exerted by particular organizations and individuals. Generalization is even more difficult here because a group active in one town may not happen to be organized in another town of the same size and type. On the whole, however, the American Legion seems to be the most important. Next come benefactors of the school, the D.A.R., the Chamber of Commerce, and "other patriotic organizations," including in the South the United Daughters of the Confederacy. In private schools benefactors of the school have great influence and the other groups very little. The peace organizations and the Ku Klux Klan share honors for the place of next importance with bar associations not far behind. In private schools and in the Northeast, none of the three has great influence. In the Middle West the bar associations are much less important that the Klan and peace organizations. A few teachers felt that other groups exert such an important pressure that they wrote them into the questionnaire—newspapers, the W.C.T.U., the principal's wife or secretary, and school supervisors. . . .

EFFECT OF THE SIZE OF THE COMMMUNITY UPON FREEDOM

Teachers in large cities on the whole have much greater freedom than elsewhere. There are several reasons for this. They are usually well organized into unions or other groups. They have obtained better tenure laws.

A unified community opinion does not exist. Groups that in smaller places would control the schools are counterbalanced by opposing groups. The struggles of one group against another over the schools have left the teacher free from interference other than politics and favoritism. In the great city there is more teacher interest in controversial subjects than exists in the smaller places, and there are numerous "radicals" in the system. Yet the warring groups in the great city have learned from necessity to live and let live. City dwellers have become indifferent to much that seems important to the small town. Many other matters would still interest small-town folk removed to the large city, if there were still opportunity for interference. But the minute a teacher leaves the school building he is lost in the big city. Neighborly gossip is impossible, where one does not know his neighbors' names or faces. Parents of any two children under the same teacher seldom know each other. Finally, cosmopolitanism has created greater understanding and tolerance on many of the subjects that do vitally matter to city people. . . .

FREEDOM IN THE VARIOUS SECTIONS OF THE COUNTRY

Throughout this study sectional differences in freedom have been indicated. In general, teachers seem to have greatest freedom in the Northeast, except Pennsylvania. The Middle West and Far West have less, the Border States still less, and the South least of all.

The greater degree of freedom in the Northeast is explained by several factors. We have seen that large cities offer greater freedom than small places, and the Northeast is highly urbanized. Industrialization may or may not be an aid to freedom. In Southern mill regions and in the mining and industrial sections of the Border States and Pennsylvania, industrial communities live under a feudal system that usually crushes out freedom. Industrialized life in its more mature stages in the Northeast has been made somewhat more civilized in its industrial relations by the fact that labor is highly organized to protect itself. In these regions industrialization increases rather than restricts freedom. The Northeast, too, lives in the midst of a great diversity of ideas, creeds, manners, and cultures, and this very diversity leads to the necessity of tolerance of strange ideas and customs. The Northeast has long been used to a discussion of social and economic problems, of which other sections of the country have only recently become conscious. Large foreign populations have created a certain cosmopolitanism that other sections lack. . . . Furthermore, many of the better private schools of the Northeast allow, within limits, a great deal of freedom; wealthy men want for their own sons a free education that they are unwilling to grant to poorer men's sons in the public schools they dominate; and the practice of private schools in the matter influences other schools. Besides, the fact that many of the children of the "better class" go to private schools means that men of this class, who often interfere in the schools in other sections, know less about public schools than they would if their own children were in them. Progressive education, too, has established itself in many communities of the East, with its inevitable augmentation of a teacher's freedom of ideas. Then, too, the Northeast, though it has plenty of provincialisms of its own, lives in more direct communication with the rest of the country and the rest of the world, and this tends to create greater freedom. Yet the small town in New England, especially if controlled by two or three mill-owning families, *can* restrict freedom as rigidly as similar small towns elsewhere. . . .

FREEDOM IN PROSPERITY AND DEPRESSION

The last ten years of depression have nearly wrecked the schools in many parts of the country and have had serious effect upon the teacher's freedom. In matters of overcrowding, overwork for the teacher, and lack of materials, economies have put schools back where they were before the World War. Many of the improvements in educational method, gained through a long and slow process of educating the public to their need, have been destroyed at one blow. Salary scales, which in many places were at last coming to be adequate, have been slashed until thousands of teachers are reduced to poverty and financial stress that make talk of freedom meaningless. Many of the best and most progressive modern features of school systems have been swept aside and abolished as "frill and foibles." School terms have been cut savagely. Some schools have been closed altogether. Taxpayers' leagues all over the country have attacked the schools and cut them to the bone instead of eliminating the graft, waste, and unsocial practices from which politicians and some of these wealthy and "respectable" citizens profit. So little public sense of the value of education had educators created that when depression came the schools were among the unessentials first sacrificed to economy. In one large city where an active Citizens' Committee had opposed state legislation that would have enabled the payment of teachers' back salaries, and had wanted to eliminate teachers' pensions, teacher leaders believed that every recent appointee to the board of education had been forced to promise that he would follow the dictates of the Citizens' Committee.

Behind these attacks on the schools are not only the usual greed and selfishness of business and large taxpayers but an underlying popular feeling that education is a non-essential, upon which altogether too much is being spent anyway. This is another sign of the revolt against intelligence. Economies could have been made with benefit to all concerned; but they were the economies of elimination of political corruption in the schools, and that still goes on. Chicago sat by and watched some of its teachers driven to poor relief and others, still employed, forced to the brink of starvation, all for the sake of "economy," while the spoilsmen still gorged themselves on school money, and Chicago did nothing, because in the minds of Chicagoans, in fact if not in theory, education and the integrity of the teaching profession had no really vital part in the "progress" that Chicago was celebrating on the lake front. Many another city can duplicate Chicago's story.

The effect upon freedom of this starving of the schools is obvious. Teaching methods are no longer chosen because of their educational values. Teachers use whatever teaching methods they can under the depleted revenues. Furthermore, security is gone. "There had been a sense of security until alarming state legislation was passed this year," wrote a Des Moines teacher in 1933. At Ann Arbor, Michigan, in 1933, a section was inserted into contracts providing that authorities were not bound by a salary clause if the money ran out. Teachers have been dismissed in wholesale fashion. Contracts, tenure laws, teachers' unions are of little avail in the face of the necessity of "economy." Most of these long-fought-for guarantees of security have been lost—perhaps permanently. The Tenure Committee of the National Education Association reported on July 6, 1934:

> During the past three years the seriousness of the financial problems of our public schools has tended to hide the invasion of politics into the schools of certain communities, the increase in the discharge of competent experienced teachers to make room for cheaper, inexperienced teachers, or for personal friends or relatives of board members, the elimination of important school subjects and activities, the overloading of classes, the injection of fear of unjust discharge into the consciousness of teachers. In many communities teaching morale is being destroyed; the building of a teaching profession has been halted.

Married women have been dismissed from many of the school systems in which they had won places, and are being hired in almost no schools. Teacher after teacher wrote on the questionnaire, "Married women are not hired, but this is only since the depression." This means a reversion to the spoils ideal of teaching. In the South, it is certain that, where economy is necessary, the Negro schools suffered first and most. In Georgetown and Clarendon counties, South Carolina, for instance, Negro schools were closed entirely for a time in order that white schools might stay open.

Much more devastating to freedom, however, than anything actually done to the schools has been the effect of uncertainty and fear that have seized teachers as they wait for further results of "economy." A teacher who lost his position in better days had some chance of getting another. Now being dropped means joining the unemployed. Furthermore, with all rules off and almost certain budgetary cuts ahead, teachers feel that those who do not conform, those who express their own opinions or argue with authorities, those who by word or deed win the slightest official displeasure will certainly be marked for dropping when the next "economy" comes. Insecurity and fear have cowed even courageous teachers and have gone far to destroy freedom. One New York teacher wrote in 1933, "The past three months have silenced any possibility of any kind of protest. Every one has the jitters due to Zangara's attempt on the President, the banks' closing, worry over salaries and unemployment. One knows enough to walk softly." In these troubled times, moreover, public criticism of the politicians or of the bankers' and taxpayers' attacks on the schools is almost certainly fatal to teachers. Powerful teachers' unions have usually been able to fight to save the schools. They have done so in Atlanta, Chicago, and New York. In depression times there have been vigorous attacks upon teachers' unions themselves. Several teachers have pointed out that the only interest of the persons at present attacking the schools is saving themselves tax money, but that these people quickly grasp any unconventional idea of a teacher as an effective weapon in this tax campaign against the schools. They add that one reason the repression of freedom is not worse is that these men know and care too little about the schools to be aware of what is actually going on in them.

VOCATIONAL EDUCATION *

The Committee believes strongly that there are few educational problems now before the American people to which they should give more earnest thought than the need for sound and adequate programs of vocational education. In these days of economic insecurity there are few phases of

* House Document No. 529, *op. cit.*, pp. 48–52, 67–70, 72–74.

life more vital to young people than getting and holding jobs. All schools, and particularly all secondary schools, must seek to improve the preparation they give for the world that awaits their pupils beyond the classroom.

The schools for many centuries have furnished the basic training for certain occupations. The traditional program of the secondary school was largely a preliminary preparation for the professions of law, medicine, and theology. Subjects such as Latin were originally included in the curriculum because they were the indispensable tools of the learned professions of the day. As times changed and those subjects no longer were needed for clearly vocational reasons, they came to be defended by those with vested interests as necessary for general educational purposes, and were retained in the general curriculum.

With the great expansion of recent years in high-school enrollments, the traditional program has become clearly unsuited to the needs of the majority of the pupils, most of whom will not enter the professions. The schools have not moved rapidly in making the necessary changes in their programs, although gradually they have recognized the necessity for instructional facilities designed to give young people preliminary preparation, not only for the professions, but also for a wide range of nonprofessional occupations.

Vocational education may be broadly defined to include all those experiences whereby one learns to carry on a useful occupation. All education serves this end to a certain extent, although it is customary to distinguish between instruction that is directly related to the vocational objective of an individual and that which is general or non-occupational in its purpose. The importance of this distinction is often overstressed, particularly when vocational education is defined narrowly to include only the specific preparation applicable to a relatively highly specialized type of employment. The important fact is that education for the individual is a unitary process, not to be sharply differentiated into that which is solely for vocational ends and that which is general in purpose.

Particularly in a democracy, based on the absence of class distinctions, is there need to maintain unity in the educational system. European educational organization, based on a two-class system of society, furnishes no appropriate model for the schools of the United States. The dual type of school system maintained by most of the countries of Europe, with one set of opportunities for young people who are to enter the professions and another for the working classes, must be avoided in this country if the purposes of American democracy are to be achieved.

The only satisfactory organization for schools in the United States is a unified educational program that will offer each pupil the opportunities best suited to his particular abilities. In other words, the plan of education should be broad enough to provide the necessary opportunities for vocational education without sharply segregating them and setting them up under separate organization.

For 20 years vocational education of an intensive and specialized type has been promoted in the public secondary schools of this country by Federal grants that increased to $10,377,581 during the fiscal year ending June 30, 1937. Under new legislation which recently became effective, the Federal grants now authorized amount to $21,785,000 annually. The grants have been authorized for vocational education in home economics, agriculture, trades and industries, and the training of teachers for these fields. Beginning in 1937–38, training for the distributive occupations is also included.

Home economics until recently has had only a small percentage of the total Federal funds for vocational education in public schools. Some funds were provided for home economics even in the original Smith-Hughes Act of 1917, however, and a Federally assisted program has existed since then for home economics instruction in the schools. . . .

Much content of a social nature is now included within the field of home economics. The evidence points clearly to improved offerings and an increased demand for instruction in home-making in the future.

The teaching in vocational education for agriculture is in general of good quality. Emphasis in the past has been too much on production techniques and too little on the economic and managerial phases of the subject, but a new and enriched course of study is slowly emerging.

The most conspicuous weakness in the provision for agricultural education results from an unsatisfactory relationship to the work of the Cooperative Agricultural Extension Service. While there appears to be full cooperation between local teachers of agriculture and extension workers in many areas, relationships at the State level are unsatisfactory in a number of States, and the respective groups of Federal officials appear to have little cooperative contact with each other. Their relationships up to the present have been concerned mainly with delimiting their respective jurisdictions rather than with developing fields of possible cooperation. . . .

The program of agricultural education fails to reach a majority of those who need such service. Provisions of the Federal statutes and activities of the Federal officials both appear conducive to a type of instruction that is expensive and not easily adapted to the conditions of small rural high schools. Some of the States have developed simpler and less expensive programs that can be adapted to the schools in which a majority of the rural high-school pupils are enrolled, but these programs are not eligible for Federal aid.

The program of education for trades and industries has been well administered in some States and localities, but has been developed and carried on in many instances without sufficient regard to the best interests of the future group of workers. This is especially true with respect to the courses offered for young full-time and part-time high-school pupils. . . . [Such courses have] been too narrowly conceived. In most cases children have been enrolled without adequate introductory guidance and exploratory courses. The very great importance of vocational guidance in connection with vocational education has not been given sufficient recognition. In many cases, programs for the skilled trades have been organized and carried on without sufficient regard for the alternative possibility of cooperating in apprentice training under the direct auspices of industry and labor.

During the depression years local programs of so-called vocational education in industrial plants were organized by the schools in certain areas, with little regard for the important social factors involved, for the benefit of industrial establishments migrating into the communities. Federally aided vocational education was used as a means of securing cheap labor by employers leaving labor markets where standards had been established, by bankrupt employers deserting their creditors and employees, and by contractors for prison labor who had been driven out of penal institutions by legislation. The production of unpaid "students" was sold in the open market, foremen became "teachers" paid from public funds, and speed-up methods became "vocational education."

The abuses in plant-training programs have been somewhat reduced in extent through a recent legislative provision to the effect that "no part of the appropriations herein authorized shall be expended in industrial plant-training programs, except such industrial plant training be bona-fide vocational training, and not a device to utilize the services of vocational trainees for private profit." The Office of Education is attempting to enforce this provision, but has had some difficulty in obtaining complete cooperation.

Devices other than plant training have also been utilized to secure the services of vocational trainees for private profit. Numerous unsatisfactory situations have developed in connection with the placement of vocational students in industry on a part-time basis at the initiative of the schools. Cases have been brought to the attention of the Committee in which federally aided schools have arranged for the employment of pupils in privately owned establishments at wage rates below any appropriate minimum level. In some cases these trainees work for as many as 20 hours a week without any wages whatever. . . .

The most common type of unsatisfactory situation consists of recruiting excessive numbers of trainees into highly specialized trade-training classes. Once training has been set up for a trade such as printing, heating and plumbing, automotive repair work, or electrical work, there is constant temptation to expand enrollments without regard to the possible number of trainees who can be placed in the trade after their training in the school is completed. This tendency to excessive recruitment appears to have been stimulated by the emphasis placed upon increases in enrollments by the United States Office of Education and the agencies responsible for allocation of funds in the States. It has been furthered by the lack of adequate occupational outlook information on a Federal, State, or local basis.

In some cases trade-training classes result in the production of finished merchandise sold on the open market. This has been particularly true of training for the textile industries, but in some cases trade schools offering extensive programs in the building trades have taken contracts for the construction of small houses in order to obtain full-scale training projects. Since the trainees usually are unpaid and materials are purchased as school supplies, the finished product can be and frequently is sold with little regard to normal costs. The unfair competition resulting in such circumstances has been a source of complaint in a considerable number of instances on the part both of employers and of employees in competitive business. In no case should the products of the work of vocational pupils be sold below prevailing market prices.

The deficiencies here cited are merely examples of a general neglect of labor and industrial problems related to vocational education. There seems to be a lack of sufficient understanding of those problems among administrators and teachers in the trade and industrial program. In some areas trade training in the schools appears to be dominated by antiunion employer groups. . . .

The sources of a great deal of the criticism of the trade and industrial training programs would disappear to a considerable extent if intensive types of training were moved up more rapidly to a higher age level of pupils. Training for a specific trade or industrial occupation is likely to be premature for most high school pupils 14, 15, or even 16 years of age. Pupils of these ages should be enrolled for vocational education only in introductory courses of an exploratory type.

Intensive preparatory training can best be given immediately before entrance into an occupation. The occupations for which intensive preparation is needed are now seldom open below age 18, and many are open only at higher ages. Much of the training can also well be given on a part-time basis after employment. As noted previously, the training offered for out-of-school youth and adults has been relatively the most satisfactory part of the existing program. The Committee does not wish to leave the impression that these difficulties have been universal even in that program. In many areas excellent work is being done in the trade and industrial classes. It should also be remembered that trade and industrial training is only one of four types of vocational education for which Federal aid is now provided. Of the other three, agricultural and home economics education have previously been discussed. Federally aided vocational education for distributive occupations is new, and experience is not yet available on the basis of which it can be evaluated. . . .

AN OCCUPATIONAL OUTLOOK SERVICE

The great problem in the education and adjustment of youth is one of facilitating the flow of young people from the schools into the various occupations among which they should be distributed as adults. Under present conditions, attention must be concentrated upon the gap between school and work, and measures of amelioration must be concentrated upon narrowing that gap by any available means.

The problem, however, is not merely one of transferring the young person from some kind of a school to some kind of a job, with as little delay between as possible. In the later years of high school and in college, every young person should have at least a general idea of the type of occupation he will eventually be able to enter. His occupational interests should serve to give integration and reality to his educational experience. The schools should adapt their programs accordingly. Finally, when the youth leaves school, there should be appropriate facilities to assist him, not merely to find a job, but to find the right job.

At present, no one can advise young people with any assurance as to the relative opportunities in the various occupational fields to which their abilities may be suited. The available information is scattered, fragmentary, and frequently unreliable. Moreover, the lack of adequate information makes it impossible for schools to plan their offerings of vocational courses in accordance with prospective outlets for graduates. The lack of information is also the basis of much conflict between employer and labor groups, particularly in connection with matters of apprenticeship and of vocational training of all types.

An occupational outlook service is needed that will provide a clear description of each of the major occupations or groups of minor occupations, the kind of a life each occupation offers, the character of the preparation essential to enter it, the numbers employed and the trend of employment, the numbers of new employees taken on each year, and the numbers of youth in each year of college or secondary school preparation who have the intention of entering the occupation if possible. Such information presented in its historical, geographical, and technological setting would go far toward providing individuals with a broad objective and factual basis for making the choice of an occupation and deciding upon the kind of training to pursue.

If steps were taken to fill in the gaps and to organize the data around the problem, it would be possible to construct a forecast or occupational outlook from statistical and other data most of which are now available. The task would be somewhat similar to the preparation of the agricultural outlook reports that have been issued for many years by the Department of Agriculture. The preparation of the occupational outlook would in some ways be more difficult than the preparation of the agricultural outlook, but in other respects it might be simpler. In the beginning it would be possible to concentrate effort upon forecasting the demand and supply situation in the major occupations. It would be less important to achieve accurate estimates of immediately prospective employment in those occupations than to obtain reliable information as to relative opportunities and as to trends likely to operate over a period of years. . . .

VOCATIONAL GUIDANCE, COUNSELING, AND PLACEMENT

In few fields of endeavor are the existing social facilities more inadequate than in vocational guidance. The ever-increasing complexity of our industrial economy emphasizes the need of young persons for vocational guidance in choosing and preparing for occupations that will be suited to their respective abilities, needs, and interests, and in which they will have opportunity to secure employment.

For the young person in school educational guidance and vocational guidance overlap and are inseparable. Educational guidance to assist individuals to select their courses of study in school is an essential part of an adequate vocational guidance program. Throughout the period of a child's secondary education vocational guidance should give focus and significance to the knowledge gained in school work. Before any specialized training for a specific occupation is undertaken, vocational guidance should be available to encourage an intelligent choice of occupation on the part of the pupil.

For years school authorities have recognized the need for the provision of vocational-guidance service throughout the secondary school period. Studies for this Committee indicate, however, that in at least half of the cities in the United States of 10,000 or more population there are no vocational-guidance programs in the public schools. Vocational-guidance service is much more frequently found in cities of 50,000 or more population than in smaller cities.

Guidance service until recently was almost wholly lacking in the high schools of rural areas. Larger rural high schools are now giving increasing attention to guidance, but only in rare instances have they been able to develop adequate guidance services. The lack of vocational-guidance service for large numbers of rural youth is particularly serious in view of the fact that about one-half of the youth population of the country resides in rural areas, and normally one-third or more of the rural young people go to the cities for employment.

Not only are many communities, both rural and urban, without any program for vocational guidance, but where such a program is in effect the guidance work is often carried on by persons without special training for or previous experience in this specialized type of service. Frequently they devote only part time to the work, and receive little or no supervision from specialists in guidance. The studies for the Committee indicate that in more than half of the cities reporting vocational-guidance programs, the only persons giving attention to guidance service were classroom teachers, assigned part time to guidance work. . . .

VOCATIONAL TRAINING IN INDUSTRY

Traditionally, young people have learned to perform the tasks of industry and to adjust to vocational requirements through actual employment as beginners. It is only within the last generation that the schools generally have undertaken the function of preparing young people for specific employment in nonprofessional occupations. Schoolmen themselves have been divided as to the appropriateness of this task as a function of the schools.

Now that it is generally admitted that the schools must assume greater functions in the vocational field, it is time to review the situation with respect to the division of labor between schools and industry. Clearly the schools can and should provide educational and vocational guidance that will assist young people to select their future occupations and to prepare for them. The schools also should in all cases provide training in the basic skills and general knowledge useful in a wide variety of employment situations. In this way they would give young people a broad base from which to build up their training for specialized occupations. For many specific occupations, particularly those such as homemaking and agriculture, in which large numbers of adults are employed, the schools should provide at least introductory courses. Finally, the schools can and perhaps should provide intensive preparation for a limited number of occupations for which training can be carried relatively far at a reasonable cost, with equipment that can be installed in the schools.

When all of this has been done by the schools, and it will not be accomplished soon, a very large amount of vocational preparation will still be furnished by industry. In a country as diversified as the United States, with between 20,000 and 25,000 distinct occupations subject to classification, it is idle to think that the schools will to any important extent relieve industry of its major responsibilities and necessities in the field of specific vocational training for particular jobs. In order to care for its own needs industry must continue to provide a wide variety of training opportunities. . . .

WHO GETS EDUCATED? *

The American high school was inaugurated more than a century ago, and it has become an increasingly vital element in national life, especially during the last generation. Yet it was 1945 before the census provided data making it possible to appraise the utilization of the high school by various social strata. . . . Hitherto the closest approximation to such an analysis was a comparison of school attendance in prosperous and in poor states.

The association of school grade attained by children with the social status of their families may be estimated from the newly prepared census data. Rental value of home, known to be closely related to income, reflects social class position and is here used as an index of class. For each of seven

* Anderson, C. Arnold, "Social Class Differentials in the Schooling of Youth Within the Regions and Community-Size Groups of the United States," *Social Forces,* Vol. 25 (May, 1947), pp. 434–436, 439–440.

rental groups the census tabulates the distribution of number of school grades completed against each of the following items: sex, race (native white and Negro), census region, community-size group, and single years of age from 7 through 17. Farm dwellers are omitted because the rental values of their homes are indeterminate. . . .

SCHOOLING BY RENTAL GROUP, REGION, AND SIZE OF COMMUNITY

The American people had taken long strides toward their ideal of universal secondary education when the average 17 year old white boy in 1940 had completed 9.7 and his sister 10.1 years of schooling. But these averages conceal important variations among the regions, sizes of community, and social classes of our heterogeneous country. Seventeen year olds in the western region achieve the highest grade and those in the north do nearly as well, but the averages for southern children are consistently lowest. Within each region the means for larger communities exceed those for the smaller places, though the three categories of cities are not far apart; villages show up especially poorly.

Differentials in schooling among social classes or rental groups are considerably greater than those between regions or communities. The range covered by the means of the regions is 1.0 years for boys and 0.8 year for girls. The range of the means among community-size groups is 1.1 years for boys and 0.7 year for girls. Among rental groups, however, the range is more than twice as great (boys, 2.5; girls, 2.3). The superior accomplishment of girls over boys increases as we go down the rental scale, especially in the South.

The "universal high school" is not yet universal. In communities of all sizes and in all regions schooling attained is greater in high status than in low status groups. The mean grades completed decrease progressively from one rental group to another—and, especially among boys, at an accelerating rate. Seventeen year olds from the upper economic groups average about eleven years of schooling irrespective of region or size of community. The status group differences are especially marked in the South, which more than holds its own in educating children from homes at the higher rental levels. It drops behind the other regions, however, as we descend the income scale, until in the least prosperous families southern children lag one or one and a half grades. Within the South, the differences between the means of the top and the lowest rental categories exceed three years. Differences in the West are only slightly over two years and in the North 1.5 years. This regional contrast is of more than ordinary importance, because the lower rental groups contain a larger proportion of the total children in the South than in other regions.

The South would be even more unlike other regions if one could allow for regional variations in rentals paid for equivalent housing. Thus, if the $15–19 rental group in the South were set against the $20–29 group in the North, the apparent handicap of southern children would be greater.

It is possible to adjust partially for the pronounced divergences in rental distributions between communities and regions. To do this, we divided each rental distribution of families into four quarters. This enabled us to compare the mean grade completed by 17 year olds in the fourth of southern families paying the highest rents with that of children from the top fourth in northern large cities.

The typical 17 year old American white boy in the wealthiest quarter of families in 1940 had completed 1.8 grades more than his fellow in the poorest quarter of families, the respective means being 10.5 and 8.7 years. For girls the comparable means were 10.7 and 9.1 and the difference 1.6 years. None of the children in the highest rental quarter in any region completed less than ten grades and none of the northern nor western children in the lowest rental quarter less than nine years. But southern children from homes in the lowest quarter of rentals averaged less than 8.5 years (and boys in villages and smaller cities less than 7.5 grades). The advantage of boys from prosperous families over those from poor families was signally largest in the South (3.0 years), least in the North (1.1), and intermediate in the West (1.6); among girls the differences were respectively 2.7, 1.0, 1.5. At comparable social positions the schooling of girls exceeds that of boys.

Although the larger communities within each region tend to have a higher level of schooling at each equivalent-rental level, the disparity between villages and the smallest cities is the most noticeable. There is some tendency for these differences between communities and also between regions to be greater at the lower than at the upper rental levels.

Certain contrasts between the South and the other regions are brought out more distinctly when we use these adjusted rental classes. In particular, the disadvantage of the lower half of families in the small cities of the South and that of the lower three-quarters of families in southern villages is revealed. We may conclude that in the upper half of the economic distribution (or the upper quarter only, in villages) 17 year old southern children average as many grades as residents elsewhere, but that, among those in the lower half of the rental distribution, the nonsouthern children have considerably better educational attainment.

CHILDREN ATTAINING HIGH LEVELS OF SCHOOLING

Differences in mean years of schooling great enough to affect the careers of a large segment of the population have thus been observed among the several social classes in communities of every size in each region of the country. In attempting to probe behind the averages we chose to compare the percentages of 17 year old youth who had completed eleven or more grades. Individuals in this upper academic category presumably will finish high school and many of them will enter college. . . .

Only one 17 year old out of ten had completed eleven grades in some region-social class-community components of the population, while in other components more than eight persons in ten had progressed that far. For the whole nation, two-fifths of the boys and half of the girls had completed eleven grades. The South trails the other regions by about ten percentage points.

Among the communities of different size the larger cities show up best, but only the villages diverge markedly from all other places. Contrasts among social classes overshadow community and regional differences. Taking all the nation's 17 year olds together, 70 percent of the boys and 79 percent of the girls from families in the highest economic bracket completed at least eleven grades. At the other end of the status scale only 19 percent of the boys and 27 percent of the girls met this standard. This sharp gradient of schooling with economic level marks every size of community in each region, most definitely in the South and least definitely in the North. Within each separate rental group, however, small communities have about as large a proportion of children progressing through eleven grades by age 17 as do larger places, and in the South the smaller communities excel the larger.

Judged by the indexes used in this study, the South clearly is not educating its children as well as the other regions when the regions are compared as blocs. True, southern children from the more prosperous families are not handicapped. In terms of aggregates of population affected this qualification is not important, however, since so large a proportion of southern children are to be found in the lowest rental groups. The West also lags behind the North at the lowest economic level. . . .

CHILDREN ATTAINING LOW LEVELS OF SCHOOLING

We shall look now at the other side of the picture and examine the variations in percentages of children who have not completed more than eight years of schooling by age 17, again viewing these percentages as primarily measures of chances in life related to social class position. . . .

Two-thirds of the 17 year olds in some segments of our population had not completed more than eight grades while in other localities or classes all had done so. Taking all the groups together, 21 percent of the boys and 17 percent of the girls had not finished as many as nine grades. Among regions the disadvantage of the South is again brought out, especially at the lower rental levels and regardless of community size. The southern (weighted) averages are 33.5 percent for boys and 27.9 percent for girls, as against northern averages of 17.9 and 14.2 percent. Once more the western states lead with averages of 14.7 percent and 11.0 percent.

Differences between various sizes of cities, as in the case of high attainment, were not large, but the rural villages (and western small cities) had appreciably larger proportions of children with slight education. Southern village children were particularly handicapped. Whether we consider high or low levels of school completion, the extreme cases are western large cities with the best record and southern villages with the poorest.

The disadvantages suffered by youth in smaller communities and in the South partly reflect lower rental levels. Disparities among the economic levels far outweigh the community and regional variations. For the whole United States, only 4 percent of the boys and 3 percent of the girls in the group of families paying $75 or more rental had not completed over eight grades by age 17. At the lower end of the economic scale the comparable percentages were 48 and 42. The West shows up better than the other regions in each rental class except the lowest. The South surpasses the North (though not the West) in the top three or four rental categories; in the lower economic groups the southern performance is distinctly the poorest. . . .

In conclusion, our study indicates that higher income families in the South are as diligent as similar families in other parts of the nation in educating their children. At the same time we find that the amount of schooling received declines more sharply with falling income in the South than in other parts of the country. This lower level of attainment by southern children from poorer families cannot be attributed to the lack of schooling among Negroes since we are dealing with white only. (The poor showing of the lower rental groups in the West, however, may reflect the presence of the Spanish-Americans.)

Should we then question the frequent assumption that regional poverty combined with a dual school system explains the lower amounts of schooling received in the South? Perhaps policy, attitudes, inertia of depressed groups, and similar factors should be considered along with financial limitations. Our data cannot be focused upon these questions directly.

SOME IMPLICATIONS OF DIFFERENTIAL EDUCATION*

The amount of schooling which children undergo foreshadows, and some would say determines, their future earning capacity and the level of society on which they will find their life. A crude selection, then, goes on in the schools, a social selection of those destined to fulfill certain predetermined social functions.

Partly it is the schools themselves which select. The native intelligence of children sets certain absolute limits to their achievements. No amount of schooling can make the moron perform satisfactorily above his fated level. The schools, by their curriculum which must be mastered before the student can pass on, sift and resift their human materials, selecting on the basis of intelligence chiefly, but allowing considerable weight to other qualities such as a pleasing manner, emotional stability, and diligence.

The schools must sort all the human material that comes to them, but they do not subject all children to the same kind of sorting process. Other things being equal, the schools tend to bring children at least up to an intellectual level which will enable them to function in the same economic and social stratum as their parents. The children of the rich are carried by express elevators of prep schools which do not stop below the college level. The most stupid, indeed, sometimes fall off the elevator, but even these may ultimately ascend to the higher floors by dint of much tutoring and the offices of friends. But the children of the poor tend to drop out early, and very frequently for reasons quite other than incapacity to learn; they drop out because their labor is needed at home, because they are ashamed to attend school in shabby clothes, because there is no tradition in their group of going beyond the literacy stage in education. Equally important

* Reprinted by permission from *The Sociology of Teaching,* by Willard Waller, published by John Wiley & Sons, Inc., New York, 1932, pp. 20–22.

with economic factors are the social assets of a family, its standing in the community, its level of cultural participation, its traditions and ambitions—these factors likewise limit social mobility.

It is clear enough that the native qualities and abilities of students are not the only factors determining their progress in school. Yet the showing that a child makes on the school yardstick, however that showing may itself be determined, usually proves roughly accurate as a measure of further achievement. In casting up our reckoning it is necessary to allow for a number of factors, for the large number of self-educated, for great and not measurable differences in the assimilation of the same subject matter, for the outside factors which affect the operation of the school as a sorting machine; but when we have made all these qualifications it still seems to hold true that the sorting process of the schools produces results which roughly conform to the (cultural or inherent) qualities of the individuals sorted, and it also seems that there is a high degree of correspondence between the point to which one progresses in school and the level on which he functions in society. One of the functions of the school is, then, to sort out individuals with reference to their fitness for certain occupations and social positions. Sorokin goes so far as to say that this distributive function is the essential social function of the school. Hornell Hart demonstrates that we have recently made progress in our utilization of the abilities of individuals.

The functions of the school as an agency of the cultural process and as a channel of vertical mobility are sometimes blended; indeed, these two functions in their individual reference are often indistinguishable. Education brings one into touch with the main stream of culture. The aspiring student embraces this wider cultural participation in the hope that it will make of him something somehow different. Yet this being different is indissolubly connected with having a different place in society. A university confronts a gifted freshman as a vast array of cultural riches; he may appropriate these and realize himself in learning to use them. The cultural process, which must start anew with every generation, automatically assigns men to their proper posts. The manner and extent to which they assimilate the cultural heritage determine the niche they will fit into in the social structure.

One of the important things that the school does is to separate individuals into classes corresponding roughly to certain occupational and social strata. When the matter is pragmatically considered, that conclusion seems inescapable. One is tempted to inquire whether this view of education corresponds with that social philosophy which is known as democratic theory and which is regarded as the fundamental orientation point for discussions of social policy in our society.

If the democratic theory is an egalitarian theory, then this doctrine that the sorting of individuals for given social duties is a necessary function of the schools is most incongruous with it. But egalitarianism is not essential for democracy. Perhaps the better view of the democratic ideal is essentially Platonic, that it is a social arrangement that attempts to use each person in the social function for which his ability best fits him. Competition is the soul of democracy, competition which brings out all the differences of men. But it must be a fair competition, and not a competition of which the result is biased by the hereditary rank or the economic resources of the family. And the competition must be relevant to function, if it is to produce good effects. A democracy is not a society without classes, but a society of open classes. There must be the possibility that the person born in the humblest position may rise to the highest. Each generation must be resifted on its own merits. Theoretically, vertical mobility would be very high in a democracy.

THE EDUCATORS*

Every state in the Union suffers from a shortage of qualified teachers. Despite the end of World War II, the public school system is still unable to secure sufficient teachers to educate the millions of boys and girls attending our elementary and secondary schools.

Everywhere the story is the same: the supply of teachers is inadequate, and conditions are growing increasingly worse. In many instances school superintendents, desperate and at wit's end, have hired taxicab drivers, mechanics, telephone operators, or retired janitors to become teachers. As never before, all communities, both rural and urban, are scraping the bottom of the barrel.

In a sense, Peter is robbing Paul to keep the schools open. Cities of more than 500,000 reach down to the communities of 200,000. By paying more money, the former can secure teachers for their systems. The cities of 200,000, in turn, look to those with 100,000 population, and so it goes, until the small town has to knock on the door of the little rural hamlet. Many communities, especially the rural or poorer ones, have no one from whom to steal.

* From *Our Children Are Cheated* by Benjamin Fine. By permission of the publishers, Henry Holt and Company, Inc. Copyright, 1947, by Benjamin Fine. Pp. 12–14, 16–19.

The teacher shortage is caused by a number of factors, not the least of which is low salaries. But money alone will not bring teachers back into the fold. Teachers object to the community restrictions that they face in many sections of the country, particularly in rural areas. They dislike to lead the lives of Grade-B citizens, always at the beck and call of the town fathers. They are strongly opposed to the political interference that oftentimes keeps them at the mercy of the community. They want to be free political agents.

Even before the war many schools did not have enough teachers. However, in some of the larger cities long waiting lists of eligibles served as a backlog for the systems. Even though their salaries were cut and other restrictions imposed upon them, the teachers remained in the profession. Many eligibles waited year after year, with no place to teach. New York City, for example, had nearly 5,000 on the eligible lists. There they remained for five, ten, and even fifteen years. Chicago experienced a similar condition. Some drifted into other jobs; the rest clung on, hoping to get placed so that they could get regular appointments instead of eking out an existence on a day-to-day teaching basis.

Then came the war. Immediately the demand for help of all kind, skilled and unskilled, zoomed sky-high. The teachers who were still waiting for appointments found it unnecessary to wait longer. They took jobs with the government, with business and industry, or in the military services at much higher salaries than they could hope to earn in the classroom. Instead of the "no vacancy" signs on their doors the schools put up frantic calls for help.

Teachers soon found that they could make more in one week in a factory than they could in a month at school. So they left the classrooms and put on overalls. Thousands of others found good office jobs with the government or in civil service. Never before in our history has such an exodus of teachers taken place.

Their leaving created a vacuum that has been filled with second-rate teachers. Or, in many instances the vacuum, defying the laws of physics, has not been filled. Rural towns and large urban cities say quite frankly that they do not have enough teachers to run their schools efficiently. Moreover, they have no idea where they can get them. Whether in the North, South, East, or West, the same story emerges: the schools are understaffed. Although someone is usually found to take over the classes, that "someone" may often be incompetent or emotionally unsuited to teach. Often the new teacher cannot meet even the minimum requirements of the state.

The cry for more teachers is so universal as to be almost commonplace. I talked with school superintendents and other top educational leaders in such representative cities as New York, Boston, Philadelphia, Providence, Chicago, Detroit, Denver, San Francisco, Oakland, Los Angeles, New Orleans, Baton Rouge, Atlanta, and Washington. I also visited scores of small towns and villages where I talked to leading county and district superintendents, principals, and teachers.

Almost without exception the educators and responsible officials said that their paramount problem was the inability to secure teachers. The shortage exists on both the elementary and secondary levels. Primarily, though, the greatest need for teachers is within the elementary grades. Superintendents just can't find enough experienced or even partially trained men and women to take jobs in the primary grades. . . .

Superintendents in all parts of the country are advertising for teachers. Philadelphia needs 700. Chicago cannot find substitutes to replace teachers who are absent. As a result, sometimes high school girls have to take over the classes. The rural communities are ready to sign up anyone who is able to call the roll and come to class.

"We no longer ask whether an applicant can read or write," a state commissioner said with more than a trace of irony. "If she looks as though she is able to breathe, we will take her."

School after school throughout the country repeats the same story. Name any state at random—Massachusetts, Maine, Illinois, Ohio, Utah, Louisiana, California, North Carolina, Washington, Oregon—and you will find an acute teacher shortage. The hoped-for postwar improvement has not taken place, and this shortage has worked havoc with the schools. Sometimes the damage is intangible; at other times it is tangible. Yet the harm, whether tangible or intangible, is real and lasting. . . .

The public, although still unaware of the gravity of the problem, is gradually becoming concerned with the plight of the schools. A commission, established by President Harry S. Truman, has made a far-reaching survey of the nation's school crisis. The Advertising Council of New York, in co-operation with leading school groups, has embarked on a nation-wide campaign to raise the prestige of the teaching profession.

Almost all of the states find that teaching is an unwanted profession. Whereas a generation ago it was considered a mark of high respectability and some prestige to be a teacher, today the teacher's post is scorned.

"We are in the midst of a first-rate teacher crisis," Dr. John K. Norton, Teachers College, Columbia University, comments.

To this Dr. Ralph McDonald, executive secretary of the National Education Association's department of higher education, adds:

"To say that American education is facing a crisis is an understatement. The teacher shortage has gripped every state with unprecedented intensity. Our schools, as a result, are rapidly disintegrating."

School systems turn in vain to the teacher-training institutes for help in filling vacancies. Typical of conditions found elsewhere is this comment by Dr. Arthur Linden, placement director of Teachers College, Columbia University:

"Of the requests that were made to us for teachers over the past two years we've been unable to help in 40 to 50 per cent of the cases. We have practically no people in the teaching field at present training for the elementary or primary level."

Educators complain that young people are not convinced that teaching can be an exciting job. As a result, the students turn to other professions, side-stepping education; and millions of children are receiving an inferior education, cheated of their rightful heritage, denied an adequate preparation for American citizenship.

"Such a situation would be bad at any time; to deprive children of good teaching is always bad," the Council on Cooperation in Teacher Education asserts. "But in such times as ours the situation is especially serious. As a people we face unprecedented national and international problems. Never in history have we so needed to mobilize all our powers. If we are to hold our place in the world and play our proper part in creating a better world, we must develop all of our intellectual and moral resources, we must give our children a better education than ever before. We cannot do this with teachers of substandard grade.

"The crisis in teaching is, then, a crisis in American life. It is not just a problem for the educational profession: it should deeply concern all of the people of the United States. All should understand the severity of the crisis and what it means for children and adults alike. All should know why the crisis arose and why it continues. All should understand what must be done to save the situation. Then all must act."

Reports from various sections of the nation indicate that the action is slow and scattered. The teacher shortage will not be ended overnight. If all the students now attending teacher-training colleges in Florida were to go into teaching, the total would be less than 10 per cent of the needs, for the next four or five years, of that state. The District of Columbia needs 300 teachers. The 1947 graduating class of the District's teachers' college contained thirty students; of this number only ten indicated that they expected to teach.

CHAPTER XV

Radio, Print, and the Movies

THE schools, the subject of the last chapter, are not the only source from which people derive their ideas, knowledge, and attitudes. In addition, the family [1] and other small groups (some of them not specialized solely or even mainly for education) have always played an important role in socializing the young. In modern times, moreover, still another source for acquiring ideas and imbibing attitudes has come into existence—what is now generally called "the media of mass communication." So important is the political and cultural influence of these mass media (radio, press, and moving pictures) that they have been the subject of much debate and considerable control. The first aim of a political dictatorship is to gain control over the media of mass communication; the aim of a democracy is to keep them as free as possible.

The readings that follow treat primarily the problems of mass communication in our democratic society. Focused in turn on the three major media, they consider to what extent financial interests control the quality and content of what is communicated, to what extent the people themselves are responsible, how the media achieve their results, and what the shortcomings are. Although the role of each medium could profitably be the subject of several books, it is hoped that the short readings in this chapter will raise some of the basic issues with respect to mass communication in modern American society.

A GENERAL VIEW *

Private enterprise in the field of communications has great achievements to its credit. The American press probably reaches as high a per-

[1] For the family's role in socialization see Chapter XXIV below.

* The Commission on Freedom of the Press, *A Free and Responsible Press* (Chicago: The University of Chicago Press, 1947), pp. 52–68.

centage of the population as that of any other country. Its technical equipment is certainly the best in the world. It has taken the lead in the introduction of many new techniques which have enormously increased the speed and the variety of communications. Whatever its shortcomings, the American press is less venal and less subservient to political and economic pressure than that of many other countries. The leading organs of the American press have achieved a standard of excellence unsurpassed anywhere in the world. It is necessary to keep these general comments in mind in order to see the criticisms which follow in the proper perspective.

The economic logic of private enterprise forces most units of the mass communications industry to seek an ever larger audience. The result is an omnibus product which includes something for everybody.

The communications industry, in building this omnibus, has not introduced new material into communication. It has transferred to mass communication what had formerly passed from person to person as gossip, rumor, and oral discussion. The oldest mass medium of which we have record, the *Acta diurna,* an official bulletin board publishing the news in the Rome of the first Caesars, was an omnibus vehicle including sports, crime, and other sensational events as well as news regarding public affairs and official propaganda. So, too, in England, when newspapers were strictly limited to serious intelligence for a small reading public, there was a literature of handbills and pamphlets specializing in crime news.

The American newspaper is now as much a medium of entertainment, specialized information, and advertising as it is of news. A solid evening of radio adds up to something like the reading of a mass-circulation newspaper except that the percentage of reporting and discussion of public affairs is even lower. It goes as low as zero in the case of some local stations, as low as 2 per cent in many, and up to 10 per cent in some network affiliates. The magazines of largest circulation provide a mixed menu of print, pictures, stories, articles, and gossip, to entertain and inform persons of all ages and tastes, with advertising occupying half or more of each issue. The motion picture, as everybody knows, has developed mainly and avowedly as a medium of mass entertainment.

We see, then, that information and discussion regarding public affairs are only a part, and often a minor part, of the output of the communications industry. On the other hand, such information and discussion as are included reach a far larger audience because of the low price which advertising and mass circulation make possible.[1]

[1] The commercial impulse is not the only one which drives the communications industry toward larger and larger audiences. Anybody who has anything to say wants to say it to as

Information and discussion regarding public affairs, carried as a rider on the omnibus of mass communication, take on the character of the other passengers and become subject to the same laws that governed their selection: such information and discussion must be shaped so that they will pay their own way by attracting the maximum audience.

SCOOPS AND SENSATIONS

Hence the word "news" has come to mean something different from important new information. When a journalist says that a certain event is news, he does not mean that it is important in itself. Often it is; but about as often it is not. The journalist means by news something that has happened within the last few hours which will attract the interest of the customers. The criteria of interest are recency or firstness, proximity, combat, human interest, and novelty. Such criteria limit accuracy and significance.

The eager pursuit of these qualities is undoubtedly captivating to the participants, but to the world at large it seems often to lead to unfortunate excesses. The unauthorized "scoops"—at the end of the war, with announcements prematurely made only to be awkwardly withdrawn by the press associations and radio networks—unsettled people's confidence in the dependability of these news sources and marred the generally good war record of the press in safeguarding important announcements.

To attract the maximum audience, the press emphasizes the exceptional rather than the representative, the sensational rather than the significant. Many activities of the utmost social consequence lie below the surface of what are conventionally regarded as reportable incidents: more power machinery; fewer men tending machines; more hours of leisure; more schooling per child; decrease of intolerance; successful negotiation of labor contracts; increase of participation in music through the schools; increase in the sale of books of biography and history.

In most news media such matters are crowded out by stories of night-club murders, race riots, strike violence, and quarrels among public officials. The Commission does not object to the reporting of these incidents but to the preoccupation of the press with them. The press is preoccupied with them to such an extent that the citizen is not supplied the information and discussion he needs to discharge his responsibilities to the community.

The effort to attract the maximum audience means that each news

many people as possible. Countries with government-owned radio, for example, tend to adopt the device of an omnibus product, with simplified and dramatized content.

account must be written to catch headlines. The result is not a continued story of the life of a people, but a series of vignettes, made to seem more significant than they really are. The sum of such discontinuous parts does not equal the whole, because the parts have not been represented in their actual size and color in relation to the whole.

This was illustrated at the San Francisco Conference. This gathering necessarily followed a course governed by protocol; it involved proposal and counterproposal, preparation of texts, amendments and revisions, and eventual agreement by compromise.

On many days during the weeks the Conference was in session there was nothing to report. But the reporters had to send in their stories. Somehow there had to be news. The result on the lower levels was a series of personal items modeled after the Hollywood fan magazine and on the higher levels a distorted account of what took place. Because drama and tension were demanded by the editorial desks back home, drama and tension were manufactured at San Francisco. Hence calm was turned into the calm-before-the-storm. Silence became the silence-of-impending-conflict. The passage of time became a portentous period of delay. So completely was the task of manufacturing suspense performed that, when after some weeks an acceptable charter was signed, the effect on newspaper readers was one of incredulous surprise. . . .

The worst offenders in this direction are to be found among the newspaper columnists and radio commentators. The members of this craft have come to perform an indispensable function in American public discussion. But they must attract the maximum audience, too. Some of them have thought that the way to do this is to supply the public with keyhole gossip, rumor, character assassination, and lies.

THE PRESSURE OF THE AUDIENCE

People seldom want to read or hear what does not please them; they seldom want others to read or hear what disagrees with their convictions or what presents an unfavorable picture of groups they belong to. When such groups are organized, they let the press know their objections to remarks concerning them. The press is therefore caught between its desire to please and extend its audience and its desire to give a picture of events and people as they really are.

The motion picture industry offers the most elaborate example of accommodation to the pressure of the audience. (The Motion Picture Code is described in a study by Ruth Inglis, a member of the Commission staff, published by the Commission under the title, *Freedom of the Movies.*) This accommodation may not have gone quite so far as the present Code executive says it would have to go to satisfy all protestors: it has not limited the villain of the screen to "a native-born, white, American citizen, without a job, and without any political, social, religious, or fraternal affiliation of any kind." But pressure groups, because they have or are thought to have influence on attendance, have shaped the motion picture to their desires. Hollywood's efforts to develop the documentary film may be thwarted by its habit of yielding to this kind of intimidation.

Every branch of the communications industry is subject to the same sort of pressure. Publishers who stick to their guns have suffered for it. The managing editor of one of the principal papers of the country testified before the Commission that in his opinion his publication took a drop of more than 50,000 in circulation because of a policy displeasing to a well-organized pressure group.

It would be a mistake to assume that pressure is always bad just because it is pressure. Testimony before the Commission reveals that pressure groups often correct unconscious bias or mistakes and bring into view neglected areas of discussion. But the power of these groups and the importance of the mass media raise a serious question, to which we shall later return: How can a medium of communication which almost by definition must strive to please everybody perform the function which it should perform today?

THE BIAS OF OWNERS

The agencies of mass communication are big business, and their owners are big businessmen. The American consumers just prior to the war paid the forty thousand mass communication establishments nearly two and a half billion dollars for their services, representing one dollar out of every twenty-seven spent that year for all goods and services. The press is a large employer of labor. With its total wage and salary bill in the same year nearly a billion dollars, it provided about 4 per cent of the country's total salary and wage expenditures. The newspapers alone have more than 150,000 employees. The press is connected with other big businesses through the advertising of these businesses, upon which it depends for the major part of its revenue. The owners of the press, like the owners of other big businesses, are bank directors, bank borrowers, and heavy taxpayers in the upper brackets.

As William Allen White put it: "Too often the publisher of an

American newspaper has made his money in some other calling than journalism. He is a rich man seeking power and prestige. He has the country club complex. The business manager of this absentee owner quickly is afflicted with the country club point of view. Soon the managing editor's wife nags him into it. And they all get the unconscious arrogance of conscious wealth. Therefore it is hard to get a modern American newspaper to go the distance necessary to print all the news about many topics." In the last thirty years, in Mr. White's opinion, newspapers "have veered from their traditional position as leaders of public opinion to mere peddlers and purveyors of news . . . . the newspapers have become commercial enterprises and hence fall into the current which is merging commercial enterprises along mercantile lines."

The same point is made with equal force by another distinguished editor, Virginius Dabney of the *Richmond Times-Dispatch* writing in the *Saturday Review of Literature*: "Today newspapers are Big Business, and they are run in that tradition. The publisher, who often knows little about the editorial side of the operation, usually is one of the leading business men in his community, and his editorial page, under normal circumstances, strongly reflects that point of view. Sometimes he gives his editor a free hand but far oftener he does not. He looks upon the paper primarily as a 'property' rather than as an instrument for public service." The typical American publisher, Mr. Dabney continues, "considers the important part of the paper to be the business management, and is convinced that so long as high salaries and lavish expenditures are made available to that management, the editorial department can drag along under a schedule of too much work and too little pay. Of course, such a publisher sees that the editorials in his paper are 'sound,' which is to say that they conform to his own weird views of society, and are largely unreadable."

Neither indictment is of universal application nor was it intended by its author to be so. There are, as Mr. Dabney says, "brilliant and honorable exceptions." But another highly respected editor, Erwin D. Canham of the *Christian Science Monitor,* thinks upper-bracket ownership and its big-business character important enough to stand at the head of his list of the "short-comings of today's American newspapers."

The published charges of distortion in the press resulting from the bias of its owners fall into the categories that might be expected. In 1935 the American Newspaper Publishers Association condemned the proposed Child Labor Amendment. The A.N.P.A. action with regard to the child labor provision of N.R.A. was characterized by the *St. Louis*

Star-Times as "a disgrace to the newspaper industry." Bias is claimed against consumer co-operatives, against food and drug regulation, against Federal Trade Commission orders designed to suppress fraudulent advertising, and against F.C.C. regulations affecting newspaper-owned broadcasting stations. Other claims involve affiliations with suppliers of raw paper stock and their affiliations with electric power companies. Still others arise from the ownership of outside businesses by the owners of the press. Many people believe that the press is biased in matters of national fiscal policy.

ADVERTISING AND SALES TALK

One of the criticisms repeatedly made is that the press is dominated by its advertisers. The evidence of dictation of policy by advertisers is not impressive. Such dictation seems to occur among the weaker units. As a newspaper becomes financially stable, it becomes more independent and tends to resist pressure from advertisers.

A recent illustration indicates the kind of pressure that may be exerted and the place it is likely to be applied. The American Press Association, advertising representative for about four thousand weeklies and small-town dailies, obtained from the United States Steel Corporation and American Iron and Steel Institute a big order of "policy" advertising in connection with the steel strike last winter, which was placed in fourteen hundred small-town newspapers. The advertising representative, thereupon, wrote a letter to the fourteen hundred publishers saying: "We recommended that your newspaper be put on their [Steel Institute] schedule, as the best territory; and we are counting on you to give them all the support that your good judgment dictates. This is your chance to show the steel people what the rural press can do for them. Go to it, and pave the way for more national advertising." [2]

The radio industry has peculiar problems in relation to advertising. Fewer than a hundred and fifty advertisers now provide all but 3 or 4 per cent of the income of the radio networks, and fewer than fifty provide half the total. The concentration of radio sponsorship goes further than that. Commissioner Durr of the F.C.C. is authority for the statement that in 1943 one-eighth of N.B.C.'s business came from one advertiser, that two advertisers supplied one-fourth and ten advertisers 60 per cent of N.B.C.'s income. One advertiser gave the A.B.C. network one-seventh of its income;

[2] It should be added that, according to *Editor and Publisher*, fewer than 15 per cent of the papers receiving this advertisement carried editorials or news stories on the subject.

two gave it a quarter, and ten more than 60 per cent. In 1945 five companies accounted for nearly a quarter of the network income.

The large advertisers on the air use a small number of advertising agencies; a dozen and a half provide about half the income of the three networks reporting these facts. These agencies not only place the contracts, but also write, direct, and produce the programs. The great consumer industries—food, tobacco, drugs, cosmetics, soap, confectionery, and soft drinks, which in 1945 gave the networks three-quarters of their income—determine what the American people shall hear on the air.

Although the station owner is legally responsible to the government for what goes out over his station, he gets a large part of it from the networks. The networks get their programs from the advertising agencies. The advertising agencies are interested in just one thing, and that is selling goods. We are all familiar with the result, which is such a mixture of advertising with the rest of the program that one cannot be listened to without the other. . . .

Advertising forms almost half the subject matter of the three media which carry it. It serves a useful purpose in telling people about goods that are for sale. Sales talk relies heavily on sheer repetition of stimuli, presents favorable facts only, exaggerates values, and suggests a romantic world part way between reality and a materialistic utopia. It does not discuss a product. It "sells" it.

Much of what passes for public discussion is sales talk. At its best, however, public discussion can be a two-way process, with listening, response, and inter-change, in which some at least of the participants are genuinely seeking for answers and feeling their way toward those answers which are supported by the weight of the evidence. The American faith is that this is the way public opinion should be formed; it should not be manufactured by a central authority and "sold" to the public.

People are used to these different kinds of discourse and often have no difficulty in distinguishing between them. They do not expect to rely on unnamed "medical experts" indorsing a toothpaste as they would upon a named authority writing a serious article on a medical subject in a serious publication. But if this distinction is to be maintained, sales talk should be plainly labeled as such; whether for toothpastes or tariffs, cosmetics or cosmic reforms, devices for reducing waists or raising prices. It should be separated from material which is not advertising or advocacy; and the control of the two kinds of content should be, so far as possible, in separate hands.

MUTUAL CRITICISM

One of the most effective ways of improving the press is blocked by the press itself. By a kind of unwritten law the press ignores the errors and misrepresentations, the lies and scandals, of which its members are guilty. The retraction by John O'Donnell in the *Washington Times-Herald* and *New York Daily News* of his widely resented statement that the victim of General Patton's slapping incident was a Jewish soldier and that because of this the General's later removal from area control in Germany was urged by prominent American leaders, also Jews, was mentioned by only one other daily newspaper in New York. Mayor LaGuardia, when he was in office, freely criticized the press and was as freely quoted in the New York papers. After he became a columnist and commentator, he specialized in criticism of what he regarded as the inaccuracy and misrepresentation of the press. But he ceased to be news. He was met with almost complete silence.

If the shortcomings of the American press can best be overcome by the efforts of the press itself, the abandonment of the practice of refraining from mutual comment and the adoption instead of a resolute policy of criticism of the press by the press are indicated.

THE NEED AND THE PERFORMANCE: QUANTITY

Of the towns in the United States with a population of 1,000 or more, all are reached by newspapers, mail, telephone, and telegraph, and almost all have motion pictures and direct mail service. This is a notable record of achievement. Radio falls far short of this. Although almost all these communities have secondary radio service, only one in fifteen has primary service.

Quantity is in some ways the enemy of the kind of service the country needs. Radio and motion pictures, and to some extent newspapers, tend to offer the fare which will appeal to the largest number of people. But there are large minorities who desire the fulness of a newspaper of record and the distinguished quality of the best foreign motion pictures. These, as well as the omnibus product, should be available for all who want them. At present they are obtainable only in a few metropolitan centers.

Outside the United States the coverage of mass communications is much less complete than it is in this country. Whole populations are cut off from the interchange of news and discussion by poverty, by censorship, and by poor physical facilities for intercommunication. Invention in the field of communications is plainly on the side of more words and pictures going farther at lower costs. But the full use of the new instruments to build a world community will require a clear national policy and a great joint effort on the part of government and private agencies. . . .

THE NEED AND THE PERFORMANCE: QUALITY

Our society needs an accurate, truthful account of the day's events. We need to know what goes on in our own locality, region, and nation. We need reliable information about all other countries. We need to supply other countries with such information about ourselves. We need a market place for the exchange of comment and criticism regarding public affairs. We need to reproduce on a gigantic scale the open argument which characterized the village gathering two centuries ago. We need to project across all groups, regions, and nations a picture of the constituent elements of the modern world. We need to clarify the aims and ideals of our community and every other.

These needs are not being met. The news is twisted by the emphasis on firstness, on the novel and sensational; by the personal interests of owners; and by pressure groups. Too much of the regular output of the press consists of a miscellaneous succession of stories and images which have no relation to the typical lives of real people anywhere. Too often the result is meaninglessness, flatness, distortion, and the perpetuation of misunderstanding among widely scattered groups whose only contact is through these media.

As we have said, the American press has great technical achievements to its credit. It has displayed remarkable ingenuity in gathering its raw material and in manufacturing and distributing its finished product. Nor would we deny that extraordinarily high quality of performance has been achieved by the leaders in each field of mass communications.[3] When we look at the press as a whole, however, we must conclude that it is not meeting the needs of our society. The Commission believes that this failure of the press is the greatest danger to its freedom.

RADIO AND PUBLIC OPINION *

We study the past in order to master the future. Nothing is more urgent for us at this moment than to reconcile the tremendous economic

[3] The periodic awards for excellence in each medium repeatedly go to the same newspapers, stations, producers, writers, and directors.

* Lazarsfeld, Paul F., "The Effects of Radio on Public Opinion," in *Print, Radio and Film in a Democracy,* edited by Douglas Waples (Chicago: The University of Chicago Press, 1942), pp. 66–78.

and technical centralization of contemporary society with our beliefs in individual freedom and dignity. We know that conditions cannot remain as they were during the laissez faire period before the first World War. At the same time we are horrified at the violent solutions which some European countries have attempted. We feel that public opinion can be as dangerous when it is set against any social change as when it is too subservient to authoritarian forms of control. Thus we look at radio and its effects upon public opinion as a possible means of steering safely between these two dangers. Has it made, or can it make, us more amenable to social change without making us thoughtless and intolerant victims of propaganda stereotypes?

CONSERVATIVE ELEMENTS IN AMERICAN RADIO

By and large, radio has so far been a conservative force in American life and has produced but few elements of social progress. There are three factors which go far to explain this conservatism.

1. Broadcasting derives its funds from advertising; hence its commercial function is conspicuous. To attract large audiences and to be a successful sales force, programs must avoid whatever deviates too sharply from what the listener already accepts. Two examples may show how the broadcaster helps to maintain the *status quo* in social policies by his concentration on sales effects.

Each day millions of women listen to the so-called daytime serials. Dramatizations of events in the lives of fictitious middle-class people are broadcast for years in succession; and the enraptured listener, who is closely tied to her small domestic circle, becomes familiar with hundreds of characters. Many studies have shown how intensely women listeners take the plays to heart; how they wait eagerly from one day to another to learn how things turn out; and how much they are inclined to pattern their own behavior upon the solutions for domestic problems that appear in the serials. About three hundred such radio plays each day present a continuous account of people who get into trouble and then get out again. What a unique opportunity for radio to influence public opinion!

But actually the "soap operas" (the name reflecting their sponsorship mainly by manufacturers of soap and other household commodities) carefully refrain from exercising any such influence. The settings are middle class—conforming to the environment of the listeners. In forty-five serials carefully followed up for three weeks, not one character was found who came from the laboring class. Inasmuch as they are upper-class characters, they are used to lend glamour to the middle-class settings rather than to play a role of their own. All problems are of an individualistic nature. It is not social forces but the virtues and vices of the central characters that move the events along. People lose jobs not for economic reasons but because their fellow-men lie or are envious. A simple black and white technique avoids any insoluble conflicts. Even the everyday activities of the characters are patterned according to what the listeners presumably do themselves; reading, for instance, is something which is rarely done in these plays. No other effect than the reinforcement of already existing attitudes can be expected from such programs.

Our second example comes from a study of the foreign-language programs on local American stations. About fifteen hundred hours of such programs are used by sponsors who wish to sell their goods to people who still speak the language of some European country; many of the advertisers are leading American manufacturers. The original purpose of the survey was to see whether the programs are used for subversive propaganda. Almost nothing of the sort was found. Yet it may be said that very likely the advertising portion of the programs has a highly nostalgic effect. In an effort to increase sales, all the commodities are presented with some reference to the home country. American merchandise is praised as being "as good as" that left behind; home-country habits are strengthened by statements that the merchandise will remind the consumers of old times or be of the type they were used to. Patronage by people of the same nationality is much emphasized. Again the programs exert a strongly conservative influence by restricting the listeners to their own language groups and retarding the process of adjustment to the new environment.

2. The conservative character of American radio programs is further explained by what one may call the self-selection of audiences. By and large people tend to listen only to programs with which they agree. Wherever a program might influence the opinions of certain sections of the population, the likelihood of such influence is reduced by their tendency to turn off the radio whenever this possibility becomes apparent. Among farmers, for instance, it frequently appears that they consider the tuning-out of unpalatable doctrines a moral obligation toward their own ideals. Similar observations have been made during political campaigns, where people are more likely to listen to their own candidates than to those of the opposition. Even so-called educational programs are not free from this tendency. Some time ago there was a program on the air which showed in different instalments how all the nationalities in this country have contributed to American culture. The purpose was to teach tolerance of other nationalities.

The indications were, however, that the audience for each program consisted mainly of the national group which was currently being praised. There was little chance for the program to teach tolerance, because the self-selection of each audience produced a body of listeners who heard only about the contributions of a country which each already approved.

Generalizing these experiences into a somewhat paradoxical formula, one may say that radio programs of this kind have most effect upon those who do not listen. For when those who are not "naturals" for a specific program just happen to listen (because they tune in by chance or because they have to listen with other people), then indeed one will find appreciable effects. The candidate to whom one is opposed, the educational program which under ordinary circumstances one avoids, have changed many minds. But, as a general rule, the preselection of the audience must be added to the concentration on advertising effects as a second factor tending to reduce the effectiveness of radio in communicating social ideas.

3. At this moment, and indeed during the last ten years, there is a third factor which contributes to radio's conservatism. The control of radio as a whole is divided between the owners of the facilities, who must be classified as "big business," and a New Deal governmental agency with its well-known progressive tendencies. For technical reasons only a limited number of radio stations can exist in one country. This distinguishes radio from all other mediums of communication, which are open to anyone with sufficient capital to utilize them. The Federal Communications Commission, a governmental administrative agency, has been instituted by Congress to regulate the physical side of broadcasting and to license station-owners. It is inevitable that a certain amount of control extending to the content of broadcasting should accompany such licensing power. However carefully legislation tries to rule out all censorship, as soon as a governmental agency undertakes to direct broadcasting in the public interest, this agency must decide what is in the public interest and what is not. As a result, radio is probably at this moment the most neutral and fairest institution in the country. The businessmen who own it and the civil servants who watch over it balance each other very well. Radio has doubtless given less support to economic royalism than has any other large business institution; but also, like other large businesses, it has been reluctant to place its potential influence behind progressive social ideas.

Since such conservative elements operate in all program policies, it is not surprising that no studies have yet discovered any major changes in public opinion which can be attributed to radio. (It should be remembered that we are not here discussing radio's effect upon people's buying habits.)

And yet this is only part of the picture. To appraise the entire situation properly, one must ask what the effects of radio upon public opinion might be if the division of power were somewhat different. The potentialities can best be appraised by references to studies which have indicated three major types of situations in which radio has definitely affected public opinion.

CONDITIONS OF EFFECT

1. We speak very often of current social trends without being fully aware that such trends do not come about of themselves. They result from a highly complex interaction between human beings and the social institutions and technological inventions they create. If a new invention like radio comes into prominence, we may feel that it merely continues a trend which already exists. But one of radio's effects is to accentuate such a trend and to introduce new phases. In this sense, one of the effects of radio is to bring into sharp relief certain tendencies in our industrial society. One such tendency is to make "cultural goods" the property of the broad masses of the population, with certain inevitable changes in the quality of such goods.

Take, for example, the character of our daily news. One hundred and fifty years ago it would have taken many weeks for an event to become known all over the country. It would have reached the interested individuals in the elaborate details of the reporters' observations. With the development of the telegraph and the modern newspaper, the observations were reduced to abstracts and headlines. The radio has carried the condensation one step further and has created the "flash," an important event tossed over the air in a few words. A similar development occurred in the field of general reading. Not so long ago the only book read and re-read by the pioneers of this country was the Bible. Then the English classics of the nineteenth century came with their large tomes and more diversified fare. When more people wanted to read and more publications became available, digests were supplied to reduce the bulk. The final step is that now in listening to a few questions of Professor Quiz the average listener gets enough data to serve him in conversation the next day. Thus one of the effects of radio is to carry on the trend from detailed information—suited to the interests of a small, well-educated minority—to the barest essentials of current news—designed for the larger masses of people, who are not interested in the details. There are many other fields in which the effect of radio is to increase prevailing trends toward standardization and simplification of communications.

In the political field this effect of radio probably makes people more class conscious. If people for the most part listen to what fits their own frames of reference, and if radio brings more material to their attention, then the effect should be to make their own political decisions more consistent with their class situation and less dependent upon incidental local issues. In an elaborate study of the last presidential campaign, conducted by the Office of Radio Research, it was surprising to see how, as the campaign progressed, the political decisions of most of the people were determined more and more by a few of their social characteristics—religious affiliation, amount of schooling, and economic level.

This should be a good point at which to stress one of the great difficulties in all studies of radio's social effects. The statement just made, like all generalizations, is only partly true. There are exceptions here and there which do not invalidate the statement. The exceptions may, however, affect the course of civilization. Presidents in this country are often elected by a 1 or 2 per cent margin of the popular vote. A general finding about radio's effects may very well have just this small margin of uncertainty which would upset the predicted outcome of an election and the role which radio would play in it. But in this paper we are more concerned with describing basic conditions than in solving specific problems.

A corollary of this trend effect of radio is a new "radio type" of consumer in many cultural areas. Radio has helped to bring to the attention of the American people the important events in Europe and thus has contributed to the generally increased interest in news. However, it has been shown in special studies that this new type of news-consumer created by radio has a more hazy knowledge and a less acute interest in those events than the traditional and smaller groups of people with long-established news interests. A similar audience has been developed in the field of serious music. There is no doubt that the broadcasting of good music over hundreds of stations in this country has enlarged the number of those who like it. Still, a more detailed study of their tastes and attitudes has shown that the musical world of these new music lovers is different, if not inferior, to that of the musical elite of past decades and as judged by classical standards.

2. The second group of situations in which an effect of radio can be traced are those in which radio is used to supplement other forms of influence, especially face-to-face contact. Experiences in the field of educational broadcasting, for instance, have definitely shown that programs are most effective when they promote the activities of organizations like farm bureaus or adult education groups, which have an independent status of

their own and use radio to supplement other means of promoting their aims. The technical term applied to this co-operation between social institutions and radio for cultural purposes is "audience-building." For one intending to use radio for promotional purposes of any kind, nothing is more important than to know that it is most effective when used in conjunction with other stimuli for which radio provides, so to say, the background.

We have examples from several studies. The study of people whose interest in music has been developed through radio has shown that by no means does the effect come about simply as a result of exposure to the musical programs. What happens instead is that a great number of molecular pressures are set working upon an individual at the same time. His social success, or his acceptance by high-spirited friends, may depend upon his tolerance of classical music. By following up the biographies of such new music lovers, it can easily be shown that such face-to-face pressures help to sustain their attention to the radio's programs of good music. It works both ways: The cultural, molecular pressure would not be effective if it did not have the regular supply of good programs; and the radio would not be successful if it were not supported by the face-to-face contacts.

Although no specific studies can be cited to prove it, the success of a radio orator who came to prominence a few years ago was doubtless due not directly to radio but was contingent upon a network of local organizations which provided the necessary face-to-face complement or soundingboard for his radio speeches. The local organizer who lacks the training and the personality to promote doctrines may yet induce people to listen to the program and so expose them to ideas which in turn increase his own prestige.

The mediated effect of radio deserves much further study. In the presidential-campaign investigation it was found that in the county studies about 15 per cent of the citizens acted as so-called opinion leaders. It was they who listened to the radio and read the newspapers and then through various forms of personal contact conveyed what they learned to the large masses of the population. The opinion leaders need not necessarily have social prominence in the community; a temperamental aptitude for the role of go-between is sufficient.

3. The last group of effects may be called the monopolistic effects of radio. Such have attracted most public attention because of their importance in the totalitarian countries. If a government monopolizes the radio, then by mere repetition and by exclusion of conflicting points of view it can determine the opinions of the population. We do not know much about

how this monopolistic effect really works, but it is important to note its singularity. No inference should be drawn regarding the effects of radio as such. It is often forgotten that Hitler did not achieve control through radio but almost despite it, because at the time of his rise to power radio was controlled by his enemies. The monopolistic effects have probably less social importance than is generally assumed.

For obvious reasons, there are not many examples of radio monopoly in the United States. Probably the closest approach is the use of radio to popularize "popular" songs. The conflict between the American Society of Composers, Authors, and Publishers (A.S.C.A.P.) and the radio industry is very revealing from this point of view. The publishers of popular songs have built up in radio a Frankenstein monster which has finally turned against them. For the past decade the music publishers relied exclusively for their success upon what is called "plugging." A new functionary was created—the song-plugger—whose task it was to induce band leaders and station executives to play the songs of his employer. This went so far that, with few exceptions, one could predict which would be the most popular songs in the country, because success depended essentially upon the publisher's ability to obtain for his song a certain fixed number of performances on the air. Special studies have shown that the indices of popular acceptance, like the number of copies of sheet music sold, follow regularly the peak of performances on the radio. When the dispute finally occurred between A.S.C.A.P. and the radio industry, the latter plugged only the songs of their own creation; and the songs which were believed to be dear to the heart of the population disappeared. About one month after the A.S.C.A.P. songs went off the air, surveys showed that the most popular songs throughout the country were already being taken from the lists of the competing organization, which, of course, used radio to promote them.

There are, then, three major types of radio effects upon public opinion which have been studied to date: trend effects, background effects, and monopolistic effects. Such effects remain potential for the reasons we have noticed. Radio tends to refrain from interfering with public opinion. As a matter of fact, each of the three conditions under which radio might influence public opinion dovetails with one of the three factors which make for radio's neutrality. The trend effect does not occur, because there are no programs which consistently express new social ideas. The self-selection of radio audiences works consistently because there are few social movements which stimulate the followers of such movements to listen to the radio for certain programs. Finally, the balance of control between the government and business interests has prevented the monopolistic use of radio by either of any two contending parties.

The question however remains whether this is a fortunate situation. Here of course is where research ends and speculation begins. But it is precisely for the purpose of checking guesses about the future and of placing speculation on a sounder basis that we need studies of the past effects of institutions like radio. Americans committed to the idea of social progress will not voluntarily see radio eliminated as a means to this end. But to those who want radio to be socially more active, equally well-meaning people answer that it is safer to neutralize radio than to unleash the powers of evil it might command. Our analysis raises the question whether, in the long run, such an ostrich policy will work. Radio's neutrality rests on rather incidental grounds, whereas its potential effects derive from its basic characteristics. A change in federal administration, a new depression, the merging of aggressive antidemocratic movements, might easily upset the present balance. It is hard to believe that a policy of appeasement now will be of help when times become more tumultuous. It is better to work out a social policy for radio now, which may be tried out and accepted in relatively quiet times, than to leave the social uses of radio to a more anarchic development. The probability that radio one day will be used to influence public opinion is so great that it is better to plan for it now—and peacefully.

As usual in such questions of policy, the main problem is this: Who shall be made responsible for opening up radio more widely to public discussion and for using it more systematically to communicate the new social ideas which the immediate public interest so evidently requires a larger part of the population to grasp?

PRACTICAL SUGGESTIONS

It is with great hesitation that certain suggestions are repeated here, and none of them is offered as an ideal solution. The following proposals should instead be taken to represent the more substantial opinions in the field.

(a) The commercial setup of radio should probably be left unchanged, not because it is particularly good, but because no definite proof has been offered that government ownership would be better; in such a situation a recommendation of radical change is not justified.

(b) The commercial setup, however, is useful for entertainment programs only. Here competition leads to improvement, because the ever larger audience provides a simple criterion of success. In the case of educational programs it is different. Programs with only a small audience might, in the long run, be the socially more important ones. The danger is that commercial agencies would not dare to put on these programs as long as some competitors were able to catch the audience with less socially minded program policies.

(c) The time devoted to sustaining programs on all networks and independent stations should be handled by regional radio councils. They should be public administrative agencies, organized like planning boards or courts, with the members appointed for fixed periods of time. The members of each council should come from political parties, educational and social institutions, the radio industry, and listener-and-consumer organizations wherever they exist. The organization and administration should be regulated by law.

(d) It will be the task of such regional radio councils to plan sustaining programs on all radio stations. By being completely fair to all radio interests, the council should manage to present programs without reference to the promotional interests of any network or station.

(e) The regional councils will need public funds at their disposal like the funds available to boards of education. Such funds will be mainly devoted to three purposes: (1) the employment of a professional staff; (2) program experiments on noncommerical stations, so as always to have a supply of desirable programs on hand; (3) vigorous efforts to promote the programs among the general public by all appropriate methods of audience-building.

(f) The statutes of such councils must protect the right of all minorities in each region to be presented on the air, regardless of their representation on the council. This minority provision should be so formulated that a minority which feels neglected may have a very short, easy, and inexpensive means of appeal.

(g) How much time the regional councils may have at their disposal, what particular times they may have, and what influence the councils should have on competing programs broadcast at the same times as their own, are questions which should be covered periodically by special rulings. All sorts of experiments should be possible without binding the future to previous faulty decisions.

Such a middle-of-the-road proposal invites attacks from both sides. People committed to government ownership will feel that the proposal makes too many and too decided concessions to the industry. The industry will feel that it gives the devil of government control the little finger which has its proverbial dangers. Perhaps some other solutions will work better in the end. But one thing is sure: It will not be possible to run radio on a complete laissez faire basis, because it is itself one of the outstanding technological changes which have brought about our modern economy, with its absolute necessity for large-scale social planning. To be the masters and not the victims of radio, we must create institutions whereby we can channel its effects upon public opinion.

THE MOVIES *

There is nothing in a medium of communication that limits the content it may carry. You can teach relativity by radio or plug a song in the press; you can put sex over from the lecture platform or religion in a movie. And information of all sorts can be conveyed by every means of communication. The limitation lies not in the carrying capacity of the medium but in the expectation of the audience. One of W. S. Gilbert's clowns complained bitterly that he had only to say "Pass the mustard" to send his dinner companions off into gales of laughter. The same thing would happen if W. C. Fields earnestly and honestly advocated temperance.

Some sixty million people spend from two to four hours in motion-picture theaters every week. Because they pay an average of twenty-three cents in cash for the privilege, the lowest-income groups are represented only sparsely in the audience. The highest-income groups also are sparsely represented, probably because of the competition of more expensive or exclusive ways of achieving similar types of satisfaction. In the sixty million there are more women than men, more under thirty than over. Many habitually spend a certain night each week at a local theater; some are drawn only by certain pictures, stars, or types of promotion.

What the large habitual audience expects is not known with a very high degree of accuracy. The motion-picture industry says the audience expects entertainment. And though that may be true, we have to look with suspicion at the statement because of its source. For the only product the industry manufactures well is entertainment. Exhibitors will tell you that audiences don't want controversy. That, too, may be true; but again the source is suspect. For the exhibitor as an individual is not eager to have his opinion changed. And as theater manager he doesn't want to risk a fight.

* Slesinger, Donald, "The Film and Public Opinion," *ibid.*, pp. 82–83, 87–90.

If you ask him to define controversial material, he will say that it is anything counter to the prevailing view of the local community. A Nazi film is no more controversial in Yorkville than a Republican one is in Westchester.

It is the exhibitor who snips controversy out of the newsreel. An enterprising company may go out of its way to present popular and unpopular views, only to have the theater manager black out what he doesn't want to see. For example, take the great government classic *The River*. It was considered controversial only because it was the controversial New Deal which was developing flood control. Therefore, though it was available free of charge and had a national distributor handling it, screen time was denied it again and again. Yet all reports from the theaters in which it was shown indicated a good deal of audience enthusiasm. . . .

The theatrical motion picture has only one aim. Mr. Hays says it is to entertain, but by that he only means that in the judgment of his colleagues entertainment pays. The sole function of the motion picture is to make money for the production-distribution-exhibition complex. If propaganda made money, producers would make propaganda. If education paid directors $1,000 a week, producers would make education. They are guided only by the little red and black lines that are drawn at the bottom of their account pages. As the producer in *What Makes Sammy Run* puts it: "After all, pictures are shipped out in a can. We're in the canning business. Our job is to make sure that every shipment will make a profit."

Those of us who are interested in education like to dispute Mr. Hays's judgment, but it is hard to refute him on the few facts available. The habitual audience is a seldom failing backlog, and for all we know it consists chiefly of people who are coming in out of the cold. Fortunately that audience is not large enough to make the industry pay its way, and the success of any film is dependent, therefore, on the number of occasional theater-goers it attracts to it. It would be pleasant to assume that more of the 25 per cent of the population who, though physically and financially able, rarely attend the movies, would come to the theater if a more meaty fare were served. But, while they flock in great numbers to *Gone with the Wind*, they stay away in almost equally large numbers from *Dr. Ehrlich's Magic Bullet*. . . .

Let us . . . accept for the moment the fact that the mass theater audience expects entertainment. How can the entertainment motion picture influence public opinion?

From the sweaters worn in summer resorts, we can readily deduce the fact that the motion picture influences fashion. It is equally apparent to anyone with an adolescent son or daughter that the motion picture affects manners and what used to be known as "line." But even those effects fall within definable limits. A Hollywood star may quickly popularize a current fashion. But, if she consciously tried to create a new fashion—for instance, to popularize the wearing of short skirts in a long-skirt era—she probably would lose her own box-office power. Nothing so quickly dates a picture as the style of women's clothes worn in it. Women's clothes two or three years ahead of their time would seem so bizarre as to make an audience uncomfortable. The same thing is probably true, although it would be difficult to prove, of motion-picture manners. As long as they are merely the extremes of recognizable trends, they will not be offensive. When they go counter to those trends, they become, in the words of the industry, "box-office poison."

But a motion picture, or at least some motion pictures, has more to it than manners and clothes. A few of them actually contain ideas. However, when we remember the fact that the primary purpose of the film is to make money and that the accepted way of making money is to appeal to a mass audience, it will be readily inferred that the theatrical motion picture will follow rather than lead fashions in ideas. A case study of a film like *Dr. Ehrlich's Magic Bullet* would give us valuable information about the relation of new ideas to box office. Common-sense students of that film reported time and again that, while the word-of-mouth publicity played it up as dramatic and interesting, many young men declined to take their girls to a film about syphilis.

There are, of course, more subtle ways of putting across perhaps not an idea but a feeling through the motion picture. At a time like the present, a great many movie villains may look and talk a little like Germans or Russians (the latter because most of the current releases were shot before 1941). On the positive side, a great many films in the last half-dozen years have shown in a favorable light priests and members of the Catholic church and Catholic ceremonial. And it is scarcely by accident that, in this largely Protestant country, there will be very few among the millions of movie-goers who do not know how a good Catholic worships, marries, and dies.

When we consider those more subtle ways of affecting public opinion through the entertainment film, it is apparent, in the first place, that the idea presented must be relatively acceptable and, in the second, that it must be reiterated in film after film. A single anti-Nazi film, no matter how dramatically and effectively presented, will scarcely have any long-term effect on the motion-picture audience. For the film-goer like the radio listener has only one exposure. Very few people see a film a second time and practically nobody a third. It is apparent, then, that anyone who wishes to use the entertainment film to modify public opinion must be very powerful indeed or must appeal to a sentiment that is powerfully stimulated in other ways.

PART SEVEN

The Separation of Church and Society

CHAPTER XVI

Varieties of Religion

WITH reference to religious matters the United States has two distinctions. First, it is the country with the least connection between government and religion; even Russia, which allegedly opposes religion, controls religious belief and practice as part of the Party dictatorship. Second, the United States is the country with the greatest number of different religions. The Federal Census of Religious Bodies in 1936 found no less than 256 religious denominations. Some of these are minor and recent, many are basically similar, but still there are great differences between some very large groups. Approximately half the population is listed as a member of some church. Of these about 23 million are said to be Catholics; nearly 5 million are Jewish, and over one million are Eastern Orthodox. Although the total number of Protestants exceeds any of these, they are divided in a multiplicity of comparatively small denominations. Two hundred of the religious denominations in America comprise only 5 per cent of the total church membership. The Catholic church is the strongest single church in the country—a fact that is rather recent in American history.

In this and the next two chapters some varieties of religious life in America, and some problems concerning the relation of religious belief and action to American values, are presented. The aim is not to disparage or praise any religious group—not to espouse the point of view presented in any of the selections—but to present certain facts and opinions that seem relevant to the problem of stability and change in American society. It often happens that, from the point of view of believers in a particular religious system, discussion of their actions by others is construed as unfair criticism and possibly as an infringement of their religious liberty, but to understand the role played by religion in the United States today it is necessary to consider major currents of opinion among different religious groups.

FATHER DIVINE AND HIS MOVEMENT *

The growth of the Father Divine Peace Mission Movement in New York City has been one of the phenomenal occurrences in the history of the Negro in the North.[1] In the metropolis alone there are more than a score of extensions, as the branches of the movement are called. Services are held at one time or other in all of these, but it is in the larger ones, where there are public auditoriums, that the most important occurrences take place.

There are similar branches in other cities and states throughout the Union, chiefly in the North and West, and even in other parts of the world.

ORGANIZATION

In the Father Divine Peace Mission Movement, Father Divine is the organization.

There are no assistants, no assistant leaders, no directors, vice-presidents, vice-chairmen, or elders. Whatever directive is carried out, no matter where it may be, has been issued or is assumed to have been issued by Father Divine.

The reason for such an organizational situation is not far to seek. Father Divine is God. He is everywhere, knows everything, sees and hears all things. Even though he dwells in New York City or Philadelphia a decision made by a follower in California could not have materialized independently, but must have been the result of spirit wireless directly from Father Divine.

In order to perform all the tasks devolving upon him in the metropolis, Father Divine is surrounded by secretaries, most of them women, white or Negro, who write down every word he utters and transmit his wishes to his followers near and far throughout the world.

The question naturally arises how any consistent work is accomplished if there is no organizational responsibility. The fact is there is tremendous

---

* Fauset, Arthur H., *Black Gods of the Metropolis* (Philadelphia: University of Pennsylvania Press, 1944), pp. 55–67.

[1] Since the transfer of the main headquarters to Philadelphia a similar growth is noted in that city where, according to the Negro press, the Father Divine Peace Mission Movement is "fast becoming the largest group of property owners among Negroes in the city." (1943)

organizational responsibility; it is so tremendous and so forceful that followers strain themselves in their efforts to keep attuned to the spirit of their leader, whether he is present or absent, in order that they may know whether or not they have heard his call.

How intimately the leader is involved in every activity of each member of the cult is symbolized by Father Divine's service at the banquet table, known as the Holy Communion. Every dish on which food is placed passes at least once through his hands. When a platter of meat is to be sent around, Father Divine places the serving utensil upon the platter with his own hands. He places the ladle in the tureen of soup; he cuts the first slice of cake, pours the first glass of water, introduces the serving spoon into each container of ice cream. He is thus part of every activity of the feast.

While theoretically there are no subordinates, actually there are certain figures who are recognized as important or outstanding in this general pattern. John Lamb, the very efficient and ubiquitous personal secretary of Father Divine, is one of these. Father Divine's wife, known as Mother Divine, is a ranking member. In the various cities and the different extensions one is likely to find some member who assumes a leading role; this is usually with the knowledge and consent of Father Divine.[2]

Such leadership is not always achieved with the explicit consent of Father Divine, because although Father Divine is God and is supreme and all-wise, nevertheless a branch can begin without his direction.[3] It frequently happens that the first intimation of a new branch extension to reach Father Divine arrives long after the extension has been established. Even at such a late moment, however, the extension becomes a matter for his consideration and approval. Father Divine may approve or disapprove of the organization; he may approve or disapprove of the immediate direction of the extension; he may approve or disapprove of the content and method of instruction or method of operation. Unless the work meets with his unqualified endorsement, it bears no relation to him and he will repudiate it even though it bears his name; in fact he will emphasize his repudiation for the very reason that it does carry his name.

Thus, for thousands of his followers, Father Divine is the immediate as well as final arbiter. He meets scores of them daily, in one of his offices

[2] In Philadelphia, at the main extension at Broad and Catherine Streets, this figure is known as Job Patience.

[3] In the *New Day* catalogue of extensions throughout the world there is appended this note: PARTIAL LIST—Because of the unknown number of FATHER DIVINE connections.

in New York City or Philadelphia, but frequently too in outlying extensions where he makes it a point to hold court, as it were, hearing requests, complaints, and grievances.

While much of the routine work must be delegated to secretaries, Father Divine is not too busy or too important to give personal consideration to what might seem to others the most trivial matters, such as a request of a member to take a trip from Philadelphia to Trenton, or to purchase a new suit of clothes, or to change living accommodations. He visits extensions and makes suggestions and criticisms; he goes out to the farms of the Peace Mission, in the "Promised Land,"[4] and consults with or advises those members who have become farmers; he enters a Peace Mission restaurant or shoeshine parlor, or dress shop, and assays its services in terms of his requirements.

The numbers of the followers in this movement have been estimated from a few thousands to several millions. Either figure probably is extreme. After speaking to scores of Divinites, listening to hundreds of them give public testimony, and noting the character of that testimony, the author is of the opinion that there is a considerable secret, one might say unconscious, following of Father Divine which probably exceeds the many thousands of public followers who might be assembled in a huge convocation. These are chiefly those persons who are influenced by the real followers of Father Divine, although they do not themselves come under his direct and immediate influence. Father Divine himself probably will never know of the actual existence of many of these secret followers, yet they come under the influence of the Father Divine Peace Mission Movement, and to a certain degree they are subject to the discipline of the leader, i.e., indirectly they fall into his organizational scheme. If this is true, the function of this movement on the socio-economic-political level becomes more significant. . . .

MEMBERSHIP

One fact which makes it difficult to speak with finality about membership in this group is that any person, whether a member or not, is admitted to practically every activity of the cult. Thus, although I was not a member (in fact in some respects I was *persona non grata* because of Father Divine's aversion to writers), I entered an extension at Greenkill Farms outside of Kingston, New York, where I was cordially received and was allowed to partake of all the privileges of a member (and of course

---

[4] Name given to choice extensions located in the Hudson River Valley.

observed all rules which a member would be required to adhere to). The only apparent difference in my treatment and that of members was that I was required to pay a fee of two dollars a week for lodging, and approximately fifteen cents a meal for my board. Otherwise everything was absolutely free.

There appear to be two types of members. A great many members merely subscribe to the beliefs and practices of the cult, but otherwise live their lives normally as citizens of their community. These are commonly known as brothers and sisters.

The other type of member seems to have gone a step farther. He has renounced the things of this world completely. He no longer plans his own life, but lives it completely in accordance with the instructions of Father Divine. If he is the possessor of worldly goods, he disposes of them in a manner agreed upon between him and the leader. He does not choose his own vocation or business, but places himself at the disposition of the Father, making himself completely subject to Father Divine's suggestion, instruction, or command. Literally everything which such a member receives, the bread he eats, the raiment he wears, his lodging and work, whatever personal remuneration he may receive, comes through the direction of Father Divine. Such members are the true angels of the cult.

I must emphasize that these are judgments formed as the result of conversations with dozens of Divinites from many walks of life. It does not answer completely the question of membership, which I believe can be answered only as a result of a rather long experience as a member in the cult. Neither does it fully answer the question which is uppermost in the minds of many people who inquire about this movement: Where does Father Divine get the resources to carry on his work? But it does indicate that the movement possesses a mechanism by which it can be self-supporting, yet on the score of democracy can give considerable freedom to persons who wish to be members but prefer to live outside the sphere of complete dependence on the cult. . . .

SACRED TEXT

The sacred text of the Father Divine Peace Mission Movement is not the Bible, but the *New Day,* a weekly periodical issued by the organization. Followers invariably refer to his book rather than to the Bible when they wish to speak with authority.

The only time I ever saw a Bible in a Peace Mission meeting was when Father Divine announced that he had had his secretaries bring in two huge Bibles in order that any visiting preachers who were in the audience might feel at home. The remark produced laughter in the audience.[5]

Father Divine discourages reading the Bible, as statements of members included in this study will reveal. Some members say Father Divine *is* the Bible, so why read it? Certain it is, the Bible of the Peace Mission Movement is the *New Day*. It is read at all meetings. It contains every speech uttered by Father Divine, and many other pertinent speeches and facts.

The *New Day* is the outcome of the *Spoken Word,* a periodical which appeared for the first time in 1934. Then it consisted of a few pages of printed matter, chiefly speeches by Father Divine, and a scattering of advertisements. The copy of the *New Day* which I have before me as I write contains 132 pages, many of them filled with the words and deeds of Father Divine, and with more than 350 advertisements, including some from such well-known commercial houses as F. W. Woolworth Company, Loft Candy Corporation, Fuller Brush Company, McCrory Five and Ten Cent Stores, Daniel Reeve Company, and Lerner Shops. Every advertisement includes somewhere within its text the injunction: "Peace!" Frequently there is added, "Thank you, Father!"

A few headings of speeches by Father Divine, and other data contained in copies of the *New Day* are enlightening in regard to the general nature of the content and the philosophy of the movement:

1. FATHER'S LOVE HAS CAUSED YOU TO DO THINGS THE GOVERNMENT TRIED TO GET YOU TO DO: STOP COMMITTING VICE AND CRIME AND SIN AND DEBAUCHERY OF EVERY KIND

2. IF YOU HAPPEN TO BE A LAW VIOLATOR, A LAW BREAKER, AND A PROFANE PERSON, MY SPIRIT, MY LOVE AND MY MIND WILL GO OUT AND GET YOU

3. WHATEVER I DO AND WHATEVER I AM ALLOWING TO BE DONE, ENDORSEABLE, IT IS FOR THE BENEFIT AND BETTERMENT OF ALL OF YOU

The headings to three photostatic copies of letters by war industries to Negroes who had applied for work with these concerns are indicative of the cult's political orientation:

1. AMERICAN RED CROSS WRITES DOCTOR THAT ONLY

---

[5] This is no longer true. On the lectern of the main auditorium in Philadelphia there now rests a huge Bible (1943).

W—— [6] CITIZENS ARE ELIGIBLE FOR THE DOCTORS-FOR-BRITAIN PROJECT

2. U. S. NAVY DEPT WRITES APPLICANT SEEKING ENLISTMENT IN NAVAL COMMUNICATION RESERVE THAT C—— PERSONS ARE TAKEN ONLY IN THE MESS ATTENDANTS BRANCH OF THE SERVICE

3. CURTISS WRIGHT TECHNICAL INSTITUTE INFORMS APPLICANT THE AIRCRAFT INDUSTRY WILL NOT EMPLOY MEMBERS OF THE SO-AND-SO RACE

BELIEFS

We have seen how the Moors believe that Noble Drew Ali was Allah's divinely-inspired prophet, and the present Noble Drew Ali is the reincarnated form of the prophet; how her followers believe Bishop Ida Robinson is ordained by God; how Prophet Cherry received his mantle directly from God in a vision; how Bishop Grace is the very "grace" of God about which the Scriptures speak.

In the Father Divine Peace Mission Movement, Father Divine *is* God. This fact is accepted without question or cavil by his followers. They believe this emphatically and unequivocally. There are no ifs, ands, or buts, and this is as much the case with the most highly cultured follower as it is for one who was formerly an illiterate share-cropper.

What is to occur should anything happen to Father Divine is an unintelligible question to any follower in the movement. Nothing can happen to Father Divine. He will never die; he is God.

It is impossible, through the written word, to convey the full import of this concept, just as it is impossible to describe the impression which comes over an outsider who listens to a highly intelligent, sophisticated, and cultured young follower averring this fact with a degree of quiet assurance which defies the imagination. The bare fact remains: For the followers of Father Divine, he is God.

Father Divine has come in his present form because the Negro is one of the lowliest of creatures on the earth. God prefers to bring salvation to the lowly.

There is an end of "prophets" of God. There will be no more prophets, because God has wearied of the way people on earth have repudiated

[6] Note the use of W—— for "white," C—— for "colored," and "so-and-so" for Negro. Father Divine forbids the use of terms denoting distinctions of color and race.

former prophets. Therefore, in these latter days, God has returned to the world in person.

Heaven is on earth. Only a select few will be saved.

There is no more baptism with water. Now that God has come, baptism in his spirit is available to every believer.

The Holy Communion is to be celebrated around the banquet table. Instead of wine and bread, "the abundance of the fullness" should be enjoyed, that is, all varieties of food and non-intoxicating drinks are to be served.

No follower should refer to the passage of time with reference to Father Divine, because that constitutes interference with him.

Dates and places of past events must be put out of mind, because they are associated with human living and take the mind off matters of the soul.

Preachers are suspect. Father Divine nevertheless criticizes no creed or cult.

The righteous man is the reincarnation of the expressions, versions, ideas, and opinions of God. The closer a man lives to true evangelism, the more nearly will he approach the appearance of God.

A true follower of Father Divine will never die. Death is the last weakness which the faithful are to overcome. If even those of great faith fail to conquer death, the spirit enters another body and continues thus to live.

Illness is a sign that you have strayed from the faith which Father Divine requires. Somewhere you have failed to live evangelically. If you continue in this way, you will die.

To receive all possible blessings from God, one must give up all.

In times of doubt and trouble, the faithful must think only of Father Divine. They must say, "Thank you, Father," and then they will arrive at the solution of their difficulties. Through belief in Father Divine, any good wish may be materialized.

To live evangelically, one must refrain from stealing, refusing to pay just debts, indulging in liquor in any form, smoking, obscene language, gambling, playing numbers, racial prejudice or hate of any kind, greed, bigotry, selfishness, and lust after the opposite sex.

It is not impossible for a woman to conceive and have a child, but if she has been living evangelically, such conception will be the result of a spiritual union. In the absence of proof, it would be assumed that the birth of a child was the result of a violation of the evangelical code.

TYPICAL SERVICE

In the auditorium are a number of Negroes of both sexes, and a sprinkling of whites. The men and women usually are separated, although occasionally couples are seated together. Some of the members are on the platform in the front of the auditorium, and from time to time one of these arises, or a member from the floor mounts the platform and begins to sing or to testify. At this particular meeting there is no musical accompaniment, though usually there is a band of musicians including piano, drum, saxophone, and possibly a stringed instrument. Job Patience, a West Indian, is chairman of the meeting, and he rises to address the group. He refers to Father Divine's Righteous Government. He speaks of the fourteen planks in the Righteous Government platform. He points to the placards that adorn the meeting place, which likewise are reminders of the Righteous Government, and also to the placards which decry the action of a certain judge who is accused of prejudice against Father Divine in a recent issue which came up in the courts. Now he is leaning heavily on the lectern, on the front of which is engraved a crown surmounted with the letters A D F D, meaning "Anno Domini Father Divine." The leader exhorts the followers to come up and express themselves. Various members respond, including prominent professional people or politicians. These speak generally of the good effect of Father Divine on the morals and behavior of members of the community. The testimony is interrupted from time to time as an individual in the audience breaks into song, which often leads to dancing.

Suddenly a woman enters the hall and whispers to someone. "Father is here!" is the message. A stir is noticeable throughout the place. More people are streaming in. Additional musicians, a clarinetist, cornetist, take up the song. A general, lively expectancy fills the place, with the horns and drums contributing their part to the excitement. There is a spontaneous burst of hand-clapping. People rise, wave handkerchiefs, and cheer. Father Divine is entering the room.

He is an extremely short man, certainly under five feet, and although presumably he has lived many years, his stride and manner are as vigorous and buoyant as a youth's. His clothes are perfectly tailored, displaying a subdued flashiness and bearing no semblance to the usual priestly garb. His dark brown head, nearly bald, is strong and round. A glance at his eyes reveals native shrewdness and a keen sense of humor, but should there be any reason for his returning the glance, they seem unusually keen and penetrating. His powerful body was intended for limbs considerably longer than those on which he moves jauntily up the aisle, making more emphatic the suggestion of great power of will, determination, and command written in the firmly modeled full lips and widespread nostrils.

He walks briskly forward, followed by a corps of secretaries, and selects a seat at the rear of the platform. There he remains for a time somewhat sequestered. Soon he joins in the singing, at the same time kicks his feet against the floor, swaying his body to and fro, and clapping his hands lustily. More testimony and more singing follow when suddenly Father Divine leaps up, strides to the lectern and says a brief word of greeting. He resumes his seat and the singing and testimonials continue.

A short while afterwards, Father Divine again rises and proceeds to speak. He announces he will not do much speaking "yet," but instead he will let the pictures do the talking. (It is a service which is to culminate in motion pictures.) There is much groaning throughout the hall because he is not going to speak at length. Soon the movies are shown. There is a children's picture, a picture of Roosevelt's third inaugural, one on the life of St. Paul, another depicting scenes from the life of Father Divine at one of his farms, and then an industrial film issued by one of the large corporations of the country. While the movies are being shown, Father Divine leaves the room, but it is rumored that he will return at midnight, when there will be a feast in the banquet hall.

PRACTICES

There are no food taboos.

Intoxicants are strictly forbidden.

Dancing with members of the opposite sex is strictly forbidden.

Speaking in tongues is tolerated but not essential.

Business enterprises are encouraged.

Any display of racial intolerance is strictly forbidden. Where white and Negro members live together, arrangements should be made so that they eat and sleep together and not separately.[7]

[7] Of all the cults observed in this study, the Father Divine Peace Mission Movement is most insistent about breaking down all barriers of race and color. It is said that no law is more rigidly enforced than the one which forbids any kind of racial discrimination. On this account it would appear that the Father Divine movement has little chance to spread in the South. It is true that most of its operations are at present confined to the North and West. Nevertheless, the laws regarding sex separation and sex purity are also so strict that it is conceivable that even in the South little objection would be found to the movement. In fact, it may be that the very strict sex taboos have been designed, in part, to overcome the southern objections to the growth of the movement should it ever make encroachments on that part of the country.

The terms "Negro," "white," "black," and "colored," are strictly forbidden. The term "other expression" is employed, also "so-and-so."

There is no marriage; consequently there can be no divorce.

In the case of married couples who enter the cult, divorce is unnecessary since man and wife automatically separate when they become brother and sister in the cult, thereafter to have no regard for any member of the opposite sex.

A true follower will forget all else save Father Divine and his teaching. If he has mother, father, sister, brother, wife or children, he will forsake these, unless they choose to come with him and follow Father Divine. An exception is made for minor children. A parent must be concerned about the rearing of his children, irrespective of membership in the Peace Mission Movement.

A frequent question of the author's whenever he was near Father Divine's banquet table at Rockland Palace, New York City, was how the various followers seated around the table were selected, since there were thousands of additional followers seated outside in the main auditorium who presumably were not invited to the banquet table. The answer from members usually was, "If you are supposed to sit at the banquet table, you will receive a message from the Father. When that message is coming, you will know it. Then you will go to the table and a place will be ready for you."

At one of the Sunday night communion services at Rockland Palace, Father Divine said, "Do not stray from my teachings. There was a member here who, for a price, was arranging for people to sit at my communion table. I warned that member, but she continued her evil practice. She got ill, and then they had to take her to the hospital. Not long after, she passed." In a movement where eternal existence is dependent upon living "evangelically" on this earth, the compulsion of such an admonition is not hard to understand.

The followers of Father Divine view him with the greatest awe and the most profound devotion, yet they feel very close to him, and are free to approach him with any question, opinion, or request. A frequent expression to be heard among his followers, male and female, is "He's so sweet!"

Should a follower have to wait unduly long before seeing Father Divine, or should he fail altogether to communicate with him, such is the internal discipline of the movement that the follower will not question the integrity of his leader, or even of some individual in the movement who may have stood in the way. Instead he will assume that the proper spirit of harmony with Father Divine has not been established. Consequently he will look within himself to find what is lacking to establish the contact.

The comings and goings of Father Divine are signals for the wildest demonstrations among the members. The writer was in Nazi Germany at the beginning of Adolph Hitler's rule, but he saw nothing in the enthusiasm and fanatical worship of Hitler's followers to surpass in intensity the enthusiasm and devotion of the followers of Father Divine.

RELIGION AND THE NEGRO *

In their highly revealing study of religion among American Negroes, Mays and Nicholson have disclosed that if we choose to be guided by the proportion of Negroes and whites in the United States who attend church, Negroes can scarcely be considered more religious than whites.[1] Actually the proportion of white men attending church is higher than that for Negroes. The following figures refer to all church members in America over the age of thirteen years:

Negro women: 73%	Negro men: 46%
White women: 62%	White men: 49%

Thus it becomes apparent that more than 40 per cent of Negroes never attend church at all; and this compares with the total nonchurch going population of America which according to Mays and Nicholson is 42 per cent; but what is more significant, considerably less than half the Negro men attend, and this is below the proportion for white men. Nevertheless the opinion of the universality of religious attitudes among Negroes, as contrasted to whites, persists. . . .

THE NEGRO CHURCH AS AN AMERICAN INSTITUTION

There can be no doubt, of course, that the church, and consequently to a degree religion, have played conspicuous roles in the loves of a vast majority of American Negroes, today and in the past. This degree of influence does not find its exact counterpart in the white man's religious experience.

---

* Arthur H. Fauset, *Black Gods of the Metropolis* (Philadelphia: University of Pennsylvania Press, 1944), pp. 97–101.

[1] Mays and Nicholson, *The Negro's Church,* p. 201, based on U.S. Government religious census of 1926.

As far as the Negro is concerned, Mays and Nicholson properly have pointed out that

> . . . relatively early the church, and particularly the independent Negro church, furnished the one and only organized field in which the slaves' suppressed emotions could be released, and the only opportunity for him to develop his own leadership. In almost every other area he was completely suppressed. . . . Thus, through a slow and difficult process, often involving much suffering and persecution, the Negro, more than three quarters of a century prior to emancipation, through initiative, zeal, and ability, began to achieve the right to be free in his church. He demonstrated his ability to preach; and this demonstration convinced both Negroes and whites that he was possessed of the Spirit of God. . . .[2]

The point to be noted is that the development of the Negro's church came as a result of the Negro's need in America for a place to express himself in various ways; it did not result from some inexorable law peculiar to his nature; neither did such a law, or as Herskovits expresses it, a "drive," constrain the Negro then or later "to turn to religion rather than to political action or other outlets for his frustration."

The two "nationalist" cults in this study are the clues in a consideration of Herskovits' assumption. What kind of people struggle politically? Obviously people who have certain political concepts. Such concepts, to result in action, cannot be divorced from life, but like the religion of the Negro according to Herskovits' characterization, it must bear an "intimate relation to life," involving the "full participation of the communicants."

Stated in political terms, in order for a people to act politically there must be political concepts, and these concepts must be made concrete by means of a political organ or organism, such as a political organization (party) or a political identity (nation). Political struggles of a national group inevitably involve that group's national identity. The struggle then becomes one in terms of that national identity, national homeland, or national unity.

It is just this quality of national identity which until very recently has been lacking in the psychology of the Negroes in America. Perhaps every other sizable group in America does have such a national identity, but because of the historical factors involved in the transfer of the Negro people from Africa to America, and possibly because of the infiltration of blood from practically all the other groups in America into the veins

---

[2] Mays and Nicholson, *op. cit.*, p. 3.

of the Negro group, with a corresponding confusion of national emphases, the Negroes in the United States have not been conscious of those national roots which are so marked in the thinking and traditions of such elements in the American nation as the Germans, Poles, or Irish.

The Black Jews and the Moorish Americans understand some of this. The Black Jews would remind American Negroes of their ancient name and their ancient land. "Without a national name," they say, "there can be no future for a people. Therefore you must not be called Negroes, colored, jigaboos, etc." Having sounded this political note, they are impelled by the logic of their thinking to emphasize the political aspect of their life in America, even though essentially they are a religious group.

The Moorish Americans go even farther than the Black Jews. After positing the fact that the "name" is the first prerequisite, they go so far as to claim the American continent for themselves, contending that this land is merely an extension of Africa. "For a people to amount to anything," they maintain, "it is necessary to have a name, nation, and a land." Although this assumption of the American continent as an extension of their own Africa may be nothing more nor less than a political expedient, we may assume that the words fall short of action only because the Moors do not have the means to make their beliefs real.

Most American Negroes, however, have not been influenced by such convictions. Consequently they have lacked strong political motivation. For such as these, Africa has not been their land, since they were uprooted spiritually as well as physically. They were not bothered by the names attached to them; if they were called Negro, colored, Afro-American, black, it was all pretty much the same thing. But neither has America been their land, since it was all too obvious to them that they were merely second-rate citizens. Inevitably in the past these great masses of Negroes have been relatively inert politically.

In recent years, however, there has been developing, more and more, the conviction among the masses of Negroes that America *is* their land. Today many Negroes point with pride to the fact that not even the Pilgrims may claim priority to them as settlers in the land.[3] Impressed by the increasing strength of their numbers, and beginning to appreciate the potential position of power which inheres in being the largest so-called minority group in the country, the conviction is growing among the

---

[3] The first Negro slaves arrived at Jamestown, Virginia, in 1619.

masses of Negroes that they, as well as the Italians, Poles, Jews, Germans, and any other national groups in America, are Americans.[4]

Pari passu with this developing national pride, political consciousness and enormously increasing political action are manifesting themselves. It is no mere fortuitous circumstance that with the decline in the proportion of orthodox churchgoers indicated by Mays and Nicholson, there is an increase in the proportion of Negroes who are entering the trade unions, organizing by means of consumer cooperatives, economic boycotts, protest groups of various kinds, and those who are otherwise girding for political action.

This latter trend is no more the result of "temperament" or "bent" than is the association with religious attitudes which scholars so often ascribe to the Negro. Clearly it signifies that because of the exigencies of the times, affecting not only the Negro but the entire nation, the need for wholesale political action at last is being felt and understood among the masses of Negroes.

A mechanism for action would logically follow. It is only natural for such a mechanism to utilize the religious organization as one means of bringing about the desired end. What we witness here would seem to be a continuation of the very kind of adaptation of an institution to a given need against which the slaveholders hoped to safeguard themselves by forbidding Negroes to congregate even for purposes of religious worship. Consequently, it should come as no surprise to find in the cults, as Reid pointed out,[5] particularly in those like the Moors, the Black Jews, and the Father Divine Peace Mission Movement, leaders who are aware of these pressing needs and allow the sails of their religious barks to be trimmed accordingly. Thus the Negro church maintains its American tradition.

JEHOVAH'S WITNESSES *

The mature Witness takes on certain definite habits and attitudes that mark him as a true believer. For example, he must not be a philanthro-

[4] Such organizations as the National Association for the Advancement of Colored People, the National Negro Congress, the International Brotherhood of Sleeping Car Porters, and movements like the Black Star movement of Marcus Garvey, are replete with historical evidences of this development of a national consciousness which has been increasing rapidly in recent years.

[5] Ira De A. Reid, *In a Minor Key*, p. 85.

* Reprinted from Herbert H. Stroup, *The Jehovah's Witnesses*. Copyright 1945 by Columbia University Press, pp. 105–108, 121–122, 147–150, 153–157.

pist, except to the Society. When I asked a group of Witnesses if they would contribute to a private institution for the aged, they refused. I reminded them that many elderly people are housed in institutions dependent in large part upon private contributions. If the contributions were not forthcoming, I told them, the lives of these old people would be seriously threatened. To this the Witnesses replied that they could not contribute. No matter how seriously the lives of the old people were endangered, it was more important for Witnesses to employ their resources in spreading the Witness message. Hence the organization is not officially concerned in caring for the needs of others. In 1924 the Society did ask for old clothes for the poor, but the event is unique.[1] The Witnesses believe that the course of history has been downward, that it has reached its lowest depths, and that nothing in our present world merits salvaging.

Officially the Witnesses follow the Fundamentalist Protestants in their stand against smoking and drinking liquor. They hold that these two practices have been proved evil by scientific experimentation, and are taboo not only to the believer by reason of their inherent impurity, but especially because the Bible specifically prohibits their use. The least indulgence in either is considered a "habit." Witnesses in rural areas denounce the "temperance" movement as condoning "moderation"; they refuse to support any "earthly" organization permitting anything short of "total abstinence." This means that if a Witness allows himself to smoke even once or to take any sort of alcoholic drink, even in medicines, he has sinned. The literature is replete with examples of persons who were "cured" of either drinking or smoking by their conversion.[2] In 1924 Mr. Rutherford announced that he strongly favored "the Prohibition Act."[3] While total abstinence prevails among Witnesses in rural areas and in small towns, and especially among those who have strong Fundamentalistic propensities, this does not hold true in the larger cities. In one home where I attended a house meeting, the host served "Swedish punch" after one meeting, and after another, served us coffee containing some sort of liquor. In this particular home, liquor was served after almost every Witness meeting. Sophisticates like these sometimes jibe at the provincialism of rural Witnesses. . . .

In recent years smoking has become more common and in the rural areas some of the Witnesses chew tobacco. Russell's strictures were either forgotten or conveniently not applied. Some who had been with the or-

[1] *Watch Tower*, July, 1924.
[2] *Ibid.*, June, 1882.
[3] *Ibid.*, November, 1924.

ganization since the old days have written to Mr. Rutherford protesting the extended use of tobacco among "younger" Witnesses. In order to appease these old-timers and to be in harmony with the original principles of the movement, Mr. Rutherford restated the Society's position on the use of tobacco, but in a much milder form. A Witness who smokes was not declared untrue to his religious beliefs; Rutherford even argued that the use of tobacco is "clean," and condemned it solely because the Witnesses "should have something better to do with their time and money."

Another of the original teachings which has lapsed into a "blue" law, although never officially denied, is that of "spiritual healing." The early literature refers to many cases of healing as the direct result of right belief. . . .

Such cures are seldom claimed by the Witnesses today, although it is not denied that they do take place as a result of true belief. Present-day Witnesses are so impressed with the idea of the end of the age that they are unable to see and unwilling to grant importance to any other aspect of religion. A few believe that to summon a doctor is evidence of a "superstitious" nature, and therefore refuse medical attention when they are ill, confident that "if Jehovah God wants me to be well, he will keep me so." The majority, however, accept medical services.

The Witnesses of the larger cities attend motion picture theaters; seldom do they attend plays. The ideal Witness, however, does not visit motion picture houses too often, since to do so would be to deprive the service work of an adequate share of his spare time. Sometimes it is not easy for a Witness to decide how many movies he may attend. Once when I was returning from a Witness court trial with two Pioneers, who were sisters, one expressed an inclination for a movie while the other said that she felt that they had been attending too many. After discussing the matter, the first sister decided that she would not be "robbing the Lord of his time" if she went, but the other felt duty-bound to begin her service work as quickly as possible.

In the smaller towns, however, and in the rural areas, there are Witnesses who hold that attending a motion picture theater is a sign of being under the control of Satan. Rural Witnesses have told me that they think the motion picture theaters are bait used by the Devil to ensnare "the Lord's people." The theaters are considered by these Witnesses to be part of "Satan's organization," distracting people from their daily hardships and responsibilities and tending to replace God by offering a substitute solace for their cares. . . .

The Witnesses are thoroughly pessimistic about any form of "social uplift." They believe that it is wiser to reject the evil world and to concentrate upon saving individuals from it for the future, perfect world. This view was conceived first by Mr. Russell and was developed to its logical conclusion by Mr. Rutherford. Mr. Russell surveyed some of the grave social ills of his time—unemployment, war, divorce—and came to the conclusion that all of these problems are "corporately beyond human power to regulate." [4] Any attempt to improve the living conditions of men was considered "unscriptural and erroneous." [5] He argued that only two possibilities were open to religiously minded people (like most doctrinaires he seldom found more than two alternatives). The first of these was: conversion of the whole world en masse to the basic principle of Jesus; the other, the direct intervention of superhuman power.[6] The Witnesses still agree that for them the only solution of world evil is the second. The Witness lives in two worlds; he seeks, however, to live only in one. The world in which he would like to live is more compellingly attractive than the one in which he actually finds himself. His conception of the "kingdom" at the end of history is not that of William Blake, for example, who dreamed of establishing God's kingdom upon "England's green and pleasant land." The Witness kingdom is earthly only in the sense that it supposedly will be established here on this planet and not on any other. The future society has no connection with or resemblance to that of the present. The Witnesses find it difficult to cooperate with national governments, for these are diametrically opposed to the one which will be established in the future. . . .

THE ENEMY WITHOUT

To the observer, the Jehovah's Witnesses seem to have made "hate a religion." [7] Whatever else the Witnesses may believe, they do somehow feel that the whole world is arrayed against them, and respond with resentment, hatred, and bitterness. They believe they owe the world nothing, and from the world they want nothing, for it is evil and not in any sense a positive part of the divine purpose. The list of the resentments is long; actually it includes all of "Satan's organization" which in turn may be defined as any institution or person opposed to "the Lord's organization." By "the Lord's organization" the Witnesses generally mean the Watch

[4] Russell, *Studies in the Scriptures,* IV, p. 381.
[5] *Ibid.,* p. 172.
[6] *Ibid.,* p. 311.
[7] Stanley High, "Armageddon, Inc." *Saturday Evening Post,* Sept. 14, 1940.

Tower Bible and Tract Society of which Charles T. Russell was the founder and Joseph Franklin Rutherford the late head. Any individual or institution not in harmony with "the Lord's organization" is inspired of Satan and is to be hated to the utmost by all true believers.[8]

Those who have met with actual opposition in the pursuance of their duties have readily made known their experiences to other Witnesses, who in turn have spread the information to many others. In this way stories circulate among them of various persecutions in all parts of this country and indeed throughout the world. If these stories are of sufficient interest to the entire flock they are published on the back cover of *The Watch Tower*. The greatly increased number of "field experiences" of this kind carried by *The Watch Tower* in recent years signifies the degree to which the Witnesses have been subjected to violent opposition. . . .

The Records of the Society and of the American Civil Liberties Union show that in 1940 these two groups reported to the Department of Justice over 335 cases in which Witnesses were subjected to mob violence. . . .

The newspapers in some cities and towns have violently opposed distribution of Witness literature. Residents of these communities undoubtedly feel that a kind of sanction for mob violence is given them by such opposition. In some localities the police have failed to intervene. At Litchfield, Illinois, for example, the law officers refused to quell an unruly crowd attacking a group of Witnesses until the mobsters began to beat the women. . . .

The American Civil Liberties Union has offered rewards of $500 for the arrest and conviction of any persons persecuting the Witnesses, and on the whole the results of this offer have been beneficial. In cases where local authorities have been unable or unwilling to handle the situation, the Union and the legal staff of the Society have appealed to the Department of Justice. The Federal Bureau of Investigation has examined about one hundred cases in which the local authorities failed to prevent or stop persecutions, or even took part in them. . . .

To counteract persecution, the Witnesses throughout their history have devised theoretical distinctions between themselves and their foes. These make the enmity more understandable and bearable to the ordinary Witness. Mr. Rutherford used a common religious technique of classifying people and applied it relentlessly. He said: "The two classes are clearly and distinctly marked out by the Scriptures, one doomed to abso-

[8] Guy A. Aldred, *Armageddon, Incorporated,* p. 26.

lute and complete destruction, the other having a possibility of recovery."[9] These two groups are the familiar "saved" and "unsaved." All Witnesses are "in the true light"; while those who do not believe will be completely destroyed. This formula was seized upon eagerly by the Witnesses and for years has been one of their dominant ideas. It provides them with an overly simple technique for examining—and judging—the ideas and relations of others.

The stress upon impassable differences between believer and nonbeliever has welded the organization together into a single fighting unit. Witnesses differing in financial and social status, in color, and even in creed, unite in the face of a common foe and seek by all means both to protect those of their own special group and to advocate the complete destruction of the common enemy. Thus many Witnesses work with monumental courage against the forces seeking their defeat. . . .

Witness wrath turns upon the American Legion as a minority group of superpatriots who "attempt to make and enforce their own laws, which deny the rights of the people."[10] The attitude of individual Witnesses against the American Legion is more bitter than that officially expressed in the literature. The various flag-saluting laws, as well as those compelling military service, are laid by the Witnesses to the door of this organization.

The Jews also are hated by the Witnesses. Although this feeling is common among them, it appears strange at first glance, inasmuch as the movement appeals to many Jews. But all who have joined "the Lord's organization" are precious in the sight of Jehovah and are fellow members of a special human group; thus, converted Jews are made welcome, often with the idea that they are "the chosen people." The official literature terms the Jews outside the movement "blind" because they do not accept "the truth."[11]

Prevalent among the Witnesses is the notion that all Jews are rich. Even refugees who have escaped to this country from persecution abroad are believed to have brought "scads of money" with them. One Witness told me fantastic tales about the apparent luxury within some of the homes of Jewish refugees that he had visited. The affluence of the refugees, according to this Witness, is hidden from most people because they do not have the opportunity which he and his fellow workers have of visiting all kinds of homes.

In spite of this generally unfavorable attitude, which is, indeed, some-

---

[9] Rutherford, *Angels,* p. 56.

[10] Rutherford, *Armageddon,* p. 38.

[11] Rutherford, *Jews,* pp. 8–9.

times shared by Jewish Witnesses themselves, the movement is able to satisfy its Jewish members, who find in its theology the natural, developed expression of essential Judaism. . . .

The mistrust of all religions is one of the prime factors in the efforts of Witnesses to convert others. It also explains in part their relations with an important area of society, namely, religious institutions. In a time when religious organizations are feeling the threat of a common foe, whatever it may be called—paganism, naturalism, force, irreligion—the Jehovah's Witnesses have consistently refused to join with those who would be their friends. The Society is not represented, for example, upon the Board of Directors of the American Bible Society, an organization which exists solely for the publication and distribution of the Bible. It will have no part in the Federal Council of the Churches of Christ in America, and believes that group to be one of the "tools of Satan."[12] On the same ground, the Jehovah's Witnesses refuse to support local churches or such groups as the Y.M.C.A. or the Y.M.H.A.

An especial animosity is directed toward the Roman Catholic Church as a world-wide organization, although the Witnesses are in no sense tolerant of Protestants. Indeed, Mr. Rutherford believed that the Protestant nations are more responsible for present conditions than are the Roman Catholic.[13] Even the Fundamentalists or conservative Protestants are held in derision. . . .

The clergy of both Roman Catholicism and Protestantism enjoy "indolent ease."[14] The Witnesses suggest that the clergy have devised religion as a source of cash income and of control over the people to whom they minister. Of all clergy, however, the Roman Catholic priests are most evil. Said a Witness: "I rejoice that the wicked Hierarchy is being stripped naked and exposed in all her shame so that all honest men may flee from her."[15] Moreover, Christians in general fail to demonstrate the love which their creeds proclaim. As one Witness said: "We find infidels who treat us better than these so-called Christian people whose God is Satan."[16]

Not only is religion one of the three major evils of our time; commerce is another; politics is the third. The three are intimately interlinked, so that each does the bidding of the others, and the success of one is the success of all.

[12] Rutherford, *Jehovah's Witnesses: Why Persecuted?*
[13] Rutherford, *The Kingdom*, p. 13.
[14] Russell, *Studies in the Scriptures*, IV, 63.
[15] *Watch Tower*, June, 1936.
[16] *Ibid.*, May, 1930.

THE POSITION OF THE JEWS*

Many people believe that the Jewish population of the United States is reliably known. "Some even labor under the illusion that the figures have been determined by a federal census." Actually, however, the federal census does not inquire into religious affiliation; and when to this is added the well known difficulty of defining a "Jew," the prevailing ignorance of Jewish demography is well understood. The book edited by Sophia M. Robison, *Jewish Population Studies,* though it does not deal with the whole Jewish population of the United States, nevertheless contributes more reliable data on Jewish demography than any other volume; and some of the facts it reveals are of great significance in comprehending the dynamic process of accommodation and assimilation now under way.

The book includes nine studies of the Jewish population in ten American cities: Trenton, Passaic, Buffalo, Norwich, New London, Pittsburgh, Detroit, Chicago, Minneapolis, and San Francisco. Made by different authors for various purposes, these studies exhibit a wide variety of research techniques. The interesting thing, however, is that despite the variety of methods used and cities studied, the general findings are remarkably similar. And since the Jews are primarily an urban group, these findings may be taken as quite representative of the group as a whole.

The studies give careful documentation of a fact already known—namely, that the Jews constitute to some extent an occupational caste. They are concentrated in trade, especially wholesale and retail. In Detroit, for example, the proportion of all Jewish workers in trade is approximately three times the proportion for the rest of the population; and in wholesale and retail trade it is more than three times the proportion. In Trenton the Jewish proportion is more than three and a half times the non-Jewish proportion. Correspondingly, the percentage in certain other occupations is much lower than in the general population. In no city is "the ratio of Jews in manufacturing and mechanical industries, in public service, in domestic service, in skilled and unskilled occupations anywhere near that of the ratio in the total population." This suggests that when the Jewish immigrants came to this country they did not start as unskilled or semi-skilled laborers as did many other immigrant groups. Instead they

* Adapted from a review of Robison, Sophia M. (ed.), *Jewish Population Studies* (New York: Conference on Jewish Relations, 1943) by Davis, Kingsley, *Journal of Legal and Political Sociology,* Vol. 2 (April, 1944), pp. 154–155.

started in wholesale and retail business. They began, therefore, as a middle class group.

The figures show, however, that they are experiencing at the present time a sharp upward movement in social mobility. They are climbing out of the middle class into an even higher rank. For instance, the second group of occupations in which they are disproportionately represented is composed of the professions. In Trenton, for example, the proportion of gainfully occupied Jewish males in the professions is approximately three times that of the non-Jewish population. Of all physicians and surgeons practicing in this city, two-thirds of them are Jewish; and of all the lawyers and judges, four tenths of them are Jewish. In Passaic, half the members of the medical profession, and more than eight-tenths of the lawyers and judges, are Jewish. That this trend toward the professions is a recent phenomenon is shown by the fact that it is greater in the native than in the foreign-born ranks of the Jews. The foreign-born show a greater concentration in trade, and a lesser concentration in the professions, than do the native-born. Apparently the Jews began with trade, and with the income derived from this source are educating their children for the professions. The data show the proportion of Jewish children in high school and college is greater than the proportion of the non-Jewish children. Success in trade has thus furnished the basis for movement into a still higher social stratum.

The Jews, however, are paying a price for their social rise. It is well known that one of the characteristics of socially mobile persons is their low fertility. Every one of the studies under consideration shows that the proportion of young children in the Jewish population (no matter whether native or foreign-born) is less than that in the non-Jewish population. In Chicago the net reproduction rate for native-born Jewish women is 64, and for foreign-born Jewish women, 68. This is lower than that for any comparable group of non-Jews, and it is, of course, far below replacement level. Since there are few Jews outside of the cities, such low fertility means that Jewish reproduction is far below that of Catholics and Protestants in the country as a whole. The Jews marry later and less frequently than the general population, and their women have babies less often. Consequently, the only conclusion to be reached is that they have been living off borrowed demographic capital. In most cases, their numbers in American cities grew faster than the cities themselves. But this growth was due to immigration, not to natural increase. They were recruiting from high-fertility areas in Europe. Now, if immigration becomes negligible, a continuation of the present fertility pattern will in a fairly short time inevitably begin reducing their numbers. They will become a dying element in the American population.

THE JEWISH SYNAGOGUE IN THE UNITED STATES *

[There are] a number of significant facts which prompt the conclusion that the Jewish religion as a social institution is losing its influence for the perpetuation of the Jewish group in America. What are these facts?

1. The existence in the country of a large number of Jewish settlements without congregations.

2. The small-town and rural Jewish population, as far as institutional worship is concerned, is almost entirely religionless.

3. The present demographic trends within the Jewish population of the United States point toward a wide and very thin dispersion over the countryside of America, away from the cities with organized Jewish religious life.

4. The number of children receiving a religious Jewish education is, in proportion to Jewish adult population, many times smaller than is the case with any other creed, big or small, in America.

Only 871 urban and rural places have reported Jewish congregations in the United States in 1926, according to the Census of Religious Bodies for that year. For the rest of the hundreds and thousands of towns and villages of the United States in which Jews live no congregations were recorded. . . .

The large number of Jewish communities without a single synagogue or temple is a new situation in the life of the Jewish people and is fraught with much social meaning for the future of the Jew in America. The fact that these communities have small Jewish populations does not make them less important from the point of view of the Jewish religion. By historical experience the Jew is a town-dweller. In the numberless villages and small towns of Podolia, Volhynia, Poland, Lithuania, Rumania, and Austria, whence the majority of the Jewish immigrants came, Jewish life centered around the congregation. A synagogue was always the first institution organized, no matter how small the settlement was, as it could always be set up with a small expenditure of money. The need to worship together

* Engelman, Uriah Z., "The Jewish Synagogue in the United States," in *The American Journal of Sociology*, Vol. 41 (July 1935), pp. 44–48, 50–51.

was a great factor of national cohesion. Communal worship was not only a religious but a social function. It was the *sine qua non* of Jewish existence. What effect congregationless Jewish communities will have on the future of American Jewry deserves close observation. For the immediate future one may foretell a large increase in the number of these communities. This increase will be caused by the following factors: (a) the growing dispersion of the Jews over the countryside of America; (b) the indifference of the Jewish masses to organized religion; and (c) the present-day habits of conspicuous worship.

The present trend of the Jewish population is toward decentralization, toward a wider distribution over the land. According to the survey of the American Jewish Committee, Jews have penetrated into every town of more than 25,000 population, while in cities of 25,000 or less the Jews have a representation in 87 per cent of them. In the rural areas the penetration of Jews has only begun. Of the 12,908 incorporated rural places recorded by the census of 1920, Jews were found to dwell in 3,943, or 30.55 per cent of them; while of the 44,565 unincorporated rural places Jews were registered to live in 3,292, or in only 7.39 per cent. Under pressure of economic need the American Jew is beginning to tap the countryside, where by dint of much initiative, energy, and little capital one may, it is still believed, succeed in escaping the unwelcome lot of the city proletariat. . . .

Will the Jew, while migrating into the rural sections and small towns of America, carry over with him the old revered congregation? So far he has not done that. Out of the 2,269 rural and small-town settlements with permanent Jewish residents, only 85 have organized congregations—and this despite the fact that Jewish worship requires no ordained salaried priests (anyone who so desires may perform all the functions of the synagogue) and that the synagogue itself may be, and usually is, housed in a hired hall or in a private room. It is a matter of record that almost half of the Jewish congregations in America even as late as 1927 had no edifices of their own and worshiped in hired halls. Undoubtedly, the light density of the Jewish population in the rural places and small towns is to be regarded as an important contributory cause for the lack of congregations in them. But as the present shifting of the Jewish population into the rural areas is toward wider spread rather than greater density, one may expect in the coming years an increase in the number of Jewish settlements without synagogues or temples. The Jews are leaving the big population centers because of the competition of "big business"; and in the search for a chance to retain or gain his economic independence, the prospective Jewish settler cares little whether or not he finds in his new place of residence co-religionists. This fact is corroborated by the very thin scatter of the Jews over the countryside of the United States. Thus, 66,087 Jews were reported to live in the 44,565 unincorporated places, and 43,513 Jews were registered in the 12,908 incorporated settlements of America in 1927, forming respectively 0.15 per cent and 0.48 per cent of the total populations.

Many of the Jews who are lured into the rural districts and small towns are erstwhile proletarians, who are trying to lift themselves out of the wage-earning class. Their attitude to Jewish organized religion is, as was revealed in a report on a recent convention of the Central Conference of American Rabbis, that of complete indifference—at best, tepid sympathy.[1] Obviously, they form part of a social stratum unlikely to yield devotees, much less pioneers, of Jewish religious organizations.

Another factor that militates against establishing congregations in the rural areas is the present-day desire for conspicuous and expensive worship. The well-to-do villager will rather belong to some magnificent temple-palace in the nearby town than aid in forming a small congregation in his locality. This circumstance may be inferred to have partly contributed to the rise in the average cost of a Jewish house for religious worship. In 1916 the average cost was $35,000, while the present average is above a quarter-million, with many buildings costing a million or more. The synagogue had lost its old usefulness as a place where the Jew communed with his Maker. The high dues and initiation fees keep out the worker and the small shopkeeper. The new function of the temple is that of the rich man's club to provide a proper background on which to set off the members' material prosperity. . . .

The perpetuation of the Jewish synagogue in the United States, all things considered, will depend on continued membership, which in turn will depend on the extent and quality of the religious instruction given to the Jewish children. In 1926 the adult Jewish population of over thirteen years of age numbered 2,995,635; the enrolment in the Jewish religious schools (Sunday and weekday schools combined), 242,841, or 8 per cent. This Jewish ratio of religious school enrolment to population is from three to fourteen times less than that of any other creed in the United States. A private inquiry, conducted by the author in 1929 for the *Menorah Journal,* March, 1929, pages 230–42, on the prevalence of the Hebrew language in America, revealed a similar situation. Out of the total New York Jewish school population of 350,000, almost 270,000 were never

---

[1] *Central Conference of American Rabbis,* XXVIII (1928), 295–310.

shown the Hebrew alphabet, or instructed in the fundamental tenets of the Jewish religion. In other cities the percentage of "Jewish illiteracy" was only slightly lower. During the depression, according to much available information, many Jewish schools were closed, and the total enrolment in the Jewish religious schools decreased. The Jews have no national agencies for the promotion of Hebrew education in America. The Jews in every city organize and maintain their own schools. Only a few cities have bureaus of Jewish education.

As to the immediate future of the Jewish church, all signs tell of an intensification and continuance of the present trends. The effects of the present low ratio of Jewish religious school enrolment to adult population will assert themselves only in the next decade, when the present Jewish school population has become the adult one of the next generation. As a result of this, and the other factors mentioned—the thousands of congregationless communities, the seepage of the Jews into the rural areas—the conformist and assimilationist influences, cumulative in their effects, will become very strong within the Jewish group, and, if unchecked, might cause the total eclipse of the Jewish church in the United States.

CHAPTER XVII

Religious Pressure Groups

In a sense religion and government compete as agencies of social control. It follows that organized religion frequently attempts—sometimes successfully, sometimes unsuccessfully—to influence political bodies and officials to take certain lines of action. Like all pressure groups in a democratic society, those that are religious in character are open to scrutiny and discussion as to their methods. Their aims and techniques also reveal, to a degree, the nature of the religious group and the strength of its organization as distinguished from the sheer size of membership. The readings in the present chapter are designed to do little more than serve as a basis for discussion of some of the problems raised in American society by the activity of religious pressure groups.

HISTORY AND PRESENT TRENDS *

Religions drift into a country. The churches of Chicago are the result of four great . . . migrations to the city.

The first migration was that of the period from 1830 to 1860, and was to a large extent from the eastern seacoast or from the British Isles. This period planted the Methodist, Presbyterian, Episcopal, Baptist, and Irish Catholic churches in Chicago.

The second period was marked by heavy migrations from north continental Europe. They planted the great Lutheran churches and the Catholic churches which root in the populations of Northern Europe.

The third period, beginning about 1890 and continuing to 1914, witnessed migration from Southern Europe resulting in great Catholic growth, with churches of the Polish and Italian Catholics growing to sometimes as high as 20,000 members.

* Holt, Arthur E., "Organized Religion as a Pressure Group," in *The Annals of the American Academy of Political and Social Science,* Vol. 179 (May 1935), pp. 43–49.

With the coming of the World War and the shutting off of European migration, labor began to drift in from the South and the American farms, and Chicago entered a period of Protestant growth with large accessions of Negroes to the Methodist and Baptist denominations.

What is true of Chicago is to a large extent true of the whole United States. The distribution of organized religion roots in various population waves which have distributed themselves over the country.

The 1926 census showed 232,000 local churches in the United States. The number of public school buildings is only a little larger, there being 256,000 of these. These churches are divided into 212 denominations. The largest denomination is the Roman Catholic, with 13,300,000 members over 13 years of age. The second largest in the United States is the Methodist Episcopal Church, with 3,700,000. It is followed by the Southern Baptist Convention, with 3,300,000 adult members. The Jewish congregations have 2,930,000 members 13 years of age and over. The Negro Baptists and the Methodist Episcopal Church South each have more than two million adult members. The United Lutheran Church has 860,000 members and other Lutheran groups add 700,000.

The total church membership over 13 years of age in the United States was roughly 44,380,000 for 1926. The adult population of the United States for 1926 was almost exactly 80,000,000. If 44,380,000 of these people are on church rolls, 55 out of each 100 adults are enrolled as church members.[1]

MAJOR POSITIONS REGARDING POLITICAL PARTICIPATION

The behavior of organized religion as pressure groups will be predetermined by the attitudes of these churches toward the social order. There are at least four easy-to-recognize groupings of the American churches, based on their social theories.

There is first what may be called the apocalyptic group, whose social point of view is similar to that of the New Testament community, which anticipated an early divine intervention in the social order. They "dynamited" the prevailing social order with the doctrine of the Second Coming of Christ. The fact that the social order was evil brought them more consolation than it did anguish. This evil made them certain that the coming of Christ was near at hand. Strange to say, this point of view prevails, not in a majority group, but in a very large group of the American churches. They are not to any great extent interested in improving the social order,

[1] C. Luther Fry, *The United States Looks at Its Churches* (New York: Institute of Social and Religious Research, 1930), pp. 19 f.

and do not bring any great amount of pressure to bear on the state or other social institutions.

The second point of view is that reflected in the historic attitude of the Lutheran Church. To quite an extent this church has accepted the state as God-given and not to be improved or publicly disapproved by the church. The Lutheran group of churches has been very loath to participate in any movements which would seem to go beyond this point of view.

The third view is that held originally by the Calvinistic churches—the theory that it was good Calvinism to cause trouble for the political state. This these churches have not failed to do. They have considered that their religious commitments were in the direction of political participation.

The fourth attitude is that of the Roman Catholic churches, which is not so far removed from the historic point of view of the Middle Ages. The Catholic Church still believes in subordination of the state to the Church, although there is also a tendency to define the state as a separate entity, and an unwillingness to see that duty to Church and duty to state may conflict.[2]

---

[2] The theory of the Catholic Church can be seen in the following quotation from the *Course of Religious Instruction,* Institute of the Brothers of the Christian Schools, Manual of Christian Doctrine, quoted by Garrison, W. E., *Catholicism and the American Mind* (Chicago: Willett, Clark & Co., 1928), p. 190.

Question: Why are the qualities of the Church superior to those of civil society or the State? *Answer:* Because the Church is a religious and supernatural society, while the State is temporal and natural. The Church is a universal, immutable and immortal society, while the State is particular, variable and temporal.

Q. Why is the Church independent of the State? *A.* Because its origin, authority object and end are not from the State; because Christ himself willed that his Church like himself, should be independent of all earthly power.

Q. Why is the Church superior to the State? *A.* Because the end to which the Church tends is the noblest of all ends.

Q. In what order or respect is the State subordinate to the Church? *A.* In the spiritual order and in all things referring to that order.

Q. What right has the Pope in virtue of this supremacy? *A.* The right to annul those laws or acts of government that would injure the salvation of souls or attack the natural rights of citizens.

Q. What more should the State do than respect the rights and liberties of the Church? *A.* The State should also aid, protect and defend the Church.

Q. Has the State the right and the duty to proscribe schism and heresy? *A.* Yes, it has the right and the duty to do both for the good of the nation and for that of the faithful themselves; for religious unity is the principal foundation of social unity.

Q. When may the State tolerate dissenting worship? *A.* When these worships have acquired a sort of legal existence consecrated by time and accorded by treaties or covenants.

Q. May the State separate itself from the Church? *A.* No, because it may not withdraw from the supreme rule of Christ.

Q. What name is given to the doctrine that the State has neither the right nor the duty

HISTORIC POLITICAL THEORIES

So long as the dominant political theory of America was that of a theocracy, and so long as there was only one political party, participation of the Church as a pressure group in the political situation was direct and simple. No one challenged the right of the Church to participate. However, with the triumph of Jefferson and the development of the theories inaugurated by Roger Williams, there came the separation of Church and State and a change of attitude with reference to the right of the Church to participate in politics. This development was furthered by the fact that two political parties of equal standing were now operating in all the American communities, and this created a very practical problem for the Church whenever it tried to give its backing to one or the other. It was liable to lose the support of its own members; and this, few churches were inclined to do. As a result, the period following the Jeffersonian development found the churches very loath to participate in social and political affairs, and a period of social futility on the part of the Church developed.

There now developed what someone has called the "intermediate" organization whereby the Church may participate in political issues. This intermediate organization is exemplified by some of the early organizations for the promotion of temperance legislation and the antislavery societies. These agencies have since developed into the nonpartisan leagues which deal with particular issues, have a political outreach, and are only informally related to the churches. Generally the churches give a hearing to the representatives of these organizations, although no church member is in any way committed to support them.

The outstanding representative organization of this type was the Anti-Saloon League, which claimed to be organized religion in battle with the saloon. Whatever we think of its accomplishment, it proved to be one of the most effective agents for church participation in political reform that have ever been devised in this country. . . .

PARTICIPATION IN INDUSTRIAL CONFLICTS

In the economic controversy following the war between the states which culminated in the Populist Revolt of the nineties, the churches of

to be united to the Church to protect it? *A.* This docrine is called *Liberalism.* It is founded principally on the fact that modern society rests on liberty of conscience and of worship, on liberty of speech and of the press.

Q. Why is Liberalism to be condemned? *A.* 1. Because it denies all subordination of the State to the Church. 2. Because it confounds liberty with right. 3. Because it despises the social dominion of Christ, and rejects the benefits derived therefrom.

the industrial northeast followed to quite an extent the tradition of the churches which backed up the Federalist regime in the time of the conflict between Hamilton and Jefferson. The New England and New York clergy accused the Western farmers of being debt repudiators, and since the clergy of the industrial areas were the more articulate, organized religion to a large extent played the game of the industrial classes. However, again the churches of the frontier furnished some valiant leaders in the person of Senator Kyle and others less noted. The Democratic philosophy of the churches of the frontier was also heavily drawn upon by men like William Jennings Bryan.

In the controversy between labor and capital which was staged largely inside the industrial area, the Protestant churches, closely affiliated with the industrial forces, continued to perform in the traditional pattern established by the early New England clergy. Rockefeller, Armour, Hill, and Morgan were all devoted church members. The *Independent Magazine* in 1887 said that the strike "is a system of pressure applied to society —the most withering despotism that has yet showed itself to the world is the strike and the boycott." The *Congregationalist* rejoiced that Governor Altgeld "has been hanged in effigy by the indignant citizens of Illinois for pardoning two men convicted after the Haymarket Riot." Lyman Abbott from his pulpit called Governor Altgeld "the crowned hero and worshiped deity of the anarchists of the northwest."

MODERN SOCIAL CREEDS

All of the three major representatives of organized religion in the United States have issued social pronouncements on those issues which seem to them of the most vital concern to the ethical commitments of these groups. These modern social creeds are generally issued in the name of the total group, but probably represent a minority point of view struggling to achieve majority status. That of the Jewish group is entitled "Program of Social Justice, Central Conference of American Rabbis, 1932"; that of the Roman Catholics is the Encyclical *Quadragesimo Anno,* Pius XI, May 1931; and that of the Federal Council of Churches, "Social Ideals of the Churches, 1932." The last mentioned was adopted at Indianapolis, December 8, 1932, and is as follows:

The Churches should stand for:

1. Practical application of the Christian principle of social well-being to the acquisition and use of wealth; subordination of speculation and the profit motive to the creative and coöperative spirit.

2. Social planning and control in the credit and monetary systems and the economic process for the common good.
3. The right of all to the opportunity for self-maintenance; a wider and fairer distribution of wealth; a living wage, as a minimum, and above this a just share for the worker in the product of industry and agriculture.
4. Safeguarding of all workers, urban and rural, against harmful conditions of labor and occupational injury and disease.
5. Social insurance against sickness, accident, want in old age, and unemployment.
6. Reduction of hours of labor as the general productivity of industry increases; release from employment at least one day in seven, with a shorter working week in prospect.
7. Such special regulation of the conditions of work of women as shall safeguard their welfare and that of the family and community.
8. The right of employees and employers alike to organize for collective bargaining and social action; protection of all in the exercise of this right; the obligation of all to work for the public good; encouragement of coöperatives and other organizations among farmers and other groups.
9. Abolition of child labor; adequate provision for the protection, education, spiritual nurture, and wholesome recreation of every child.
10. Protection of the family by the single standard of purity; educational preparation for marriage, home-making and parenthood.
11. Economic justice for the farmer in legislation, finance, of agriculture, transportation, and the prices of farm products as compared with the cost of machinery and other commodities which he must buy.
12. Extension of the primary cultural opportunities and social services now enjoyed by urban populations to the farm family.
13. Protection of the individual and society from the social, economic and moral waste of any traffic in intoxicants and habit-forming drugs.
14. Application of the Christian principle of redemption to the treatment of offenders; reform of penal and correctional methods and institutions and of criminal court procedure.
15. Justice, opportunity and equal rights for all; mutual goodwill and coöperation among racial, economic, and religious groups.
16. Repudiation of war, drastic reduction of armaments, participation in international controversies; the building of a coöperative world order.
17. Recognition and maintenance of the rights and responsibilities of free speech, free assembly, and a free press; the encouragement of free communication of mind with mind, as essential to the discovery of truth.

The value of these pronouncements is largely to be found in their educational value; many of the organized religious groups have made them the basis of textbooks and discussion-group materials with which to educate their own members, who in turn have brought pressure on government agencies in the direction of the declared goals of these social pronouncements.

PROCEDURES OF ORGANIZED RELIGION

When organized religion confines itself to educational methods . . . there can be no valid objection to it. The organization of the emotions of the people around values is the very stuff out of which society is made, and the question as to whether the Church has the right to join in discovering, defining, and defending that which is worthy of supreme devotion ought no longer to be debatable. When the state tries to monopolize this function, organized religion will fight it.

However, when members of these groups vote for men and issues not with reference to the value of the issues but with reference to the advantage which this issue or these men can bring to the religious group, organized religion becomes a national menace. When Protestants refuse to vote for Catholics because they are Catholics, or when Catholics do the same, religion is playing the game of group selfishness, and becomes the last and the toughest piece of national obscurantism.

Organized religion commits a misdemeanor when it allows an interest in one particular issue to obscure all other issues. Probably this error was committed by Protestant churches in their zeal for national prohibition. Organized religion, however, has the right to deal with those matters of public opinion which are vital to its life and to its programs of ethical interest. . . .

BIRTH CONTROL AND THE CATHOLIC CHURCH *

Prior to 1936 the conveyance of contraceptive materials or information was forbidden in the United States, even to medical men. This had been the situation since 1873, when the Comstock law banning traffic in obscene and pornographic literature was passed.[1]

---

* A discussion compiled and adapted from various sources, as indicated in footnotes, by a colleague.

[1] Birth control is subject to legislation by the states as well as by Congress. Actually, however, the laws of but one state in 1934 forbade physicians to prescribe contraceptives and druggists to dispense them—and this law was not enforced. See *Hearings* on H.R. 5978, 73rd Congress, 2nd session, January 18–19, 1934.

At the time the Comstock legislation went into effect, contraception was already practiced in the United States, but not nearly so extensively as now. Although some efforts were soon made to inform the American public about the subject and to diffuse contraceptive information, the real struggle began in 1914 with the indictment of Margaret Sanger in New York for violating the postal regulations based on the Comstock law. The ensuing twenty-three years saw Mrs. Sanger fight, with unusual perseverence, to secure modification of the Comstock legislation.

During World War I Mrs. Sanger publicized the right of women to voluntary motherhood. In 1921 she organized the American Birth Control League. In 1928, noting that public opinion had become much more favorable, she decided to press Congress and the state legislatures for modification of restraints on birth control. Accordingly, a year later, she formed the National Committee on Federal Legislation for Birth Control, for the purpose of amending the laws so as to legalize the transportation of contraceptive materials and information by and for medical practitioners. Under the auspices of this organization ten bills were introduced in Congress during 1930–36, hearings being held on the first five.[2] Although none of these bills was passed, the discussion initiated by them had a great educational and propagandistic effect.

Victory for Mrs. Sanger and her movement came in 1936, when a favorable court decision was rendered in a test case instituted by the National Committee. The Federal Government had seized a package of Japanese pessaries, claiming they had been imported contrary to Section 305 (a) of the Tariff Act of 1930 based on the 1873 Comstock act. The United States District Court, where the case first came up, held that the pessaries had been imported lawfully, thus in effect repealing the anti-birth-control provisions. On appeal to the District Court of Appeals the decision, on December 7, 1936, was upheld. The ruling *inter alia* was that:

> While we may assume that Section 305 (a) of the Tariff Act of 1930 exempts only such articles as the Act of 1873 excepted, yet we are satisfied that this statute, as well as all the acts we have referred to, embraced only such articles as Congress would have denounced as immoral if it had understood all the condition under which they were to be used. Its design, in our opinion, was not to prevent the importation, sale, or carriage by mail of things which might intelligently be employed by conscientious and competent physicians for the purpose of saving life or promoting the well-being of their patients.

[2] See H. C. Benjamin, "Lobbying for Birth Control," *The Public Opinion Quarterly*, Vol. 2 (1938), pp. 48–60.

After this decision, Mrs. Sanger's National Committee disbanded, its task accomplished.[3]

ORGANIZED OPPOSITION TO BIRTH CONTROL

The opposition to birth control in the United States has come primarily from pressure groups. It has not come from the people themselves. Between 1914 and 1931 sentiment in favor of birth control, as revealed by American newspapers and magazines, steadily increased.[4] Already by 1931 probably two-thirds of the American people favored the legalization of contraception. A 1935 poll taken by the American Institute of Public Opinion found 70 per cent of the public in favor of legalizing birth control information, the state percentages ranging from 53 in South Dakota to 90 in Arizona and Nevada. A poll by *Farm and Fireside* of its 13,000 rural readers in 1930 found two-thirds of them favoring birth control. Subsequent polls by other journals yielded large majorities for birth control. In short, the approval of voluntary parenthood was already an integral part of American mores at the very time that Congress was refusing to liberalize its anti-birth-control legislation.

What pressure groups stood out against the public will in this matter? Careful study of the hearings on the first five anti-Comstock bills indicates that nearly all the opposition came from organized Catholicism—not from the general membership of the Church but from a small number of priests and professional lay Catholics claiming to represent the general membership.[5] The arguments presented at the hearings closely resemble the arguments frequently reiterated in the Catholic press. They are primarily *ad hominem* in character, and only secondarily even quasi-rational. Temperate and pertinent discussion is conspicuously absent.

Of the *ad hominem* arguments, two stand out. First, the Catholic spokesmen repeatedly pasted the labels of paganism, communism, and immorality upon those favoring liberalization of the birth control legislation. Second, they constantly stressed the voting power of the Catholic popula-

[3] See *Concluding Report* of the National Committee on Federal Legislation for Birth Control (New York: 1937), pp. 39–41. Later copies of *Marriage Hygiene,* a journal published in India, were confiscated, but the Government lost this case too, it being decreed that literature on birth control can be mailed to doctors and other responsible persons.

[4] Hornell Hart, *Recent Social Trends* (New York: McGraw-Hill, 1933), Vol. 1, pp. 414–15.

[5] See, particularly, hearings on H.R. 5978 (January 18–19, 1934), on H.R. 11,082 (May 19–20, 1932), and on S.R. 4436 (May 12, 19–20, 1932, and January 18, 1933) with report.

tion, implying that any congressmen supporting more liberal laws would be penalized at the polls. The effectiveness of these techniques is shown by the large number of Congressmen who either refused to commit themselves or opposed the bills, and by the fact that but one of the ten bills was even reported out of committee.[6]

Of the quasi-rational arguments, the following gives the substance. Birth control is immoral, animalistic, and sinful. It frustrates the natural end of marriage and of man's generative power. It undermines the health of women and results in deformed children. It deprives "future generations of the right to be born." It will, if practiced, reduce industrial and agricultural prosperity and increase the burden of old-age dependency. Finally, it is unnecessary anyway, because control through continence will sufficiently curtail population growth, and because poverty is in any case the result of the maldistribution of wealth rather than the result of population pressure. No supporting factual or theoretical evidence was presented.[7]

THE CATHOLIC COMPROMISE

The arguments presented in the Congressional hearings against bills to liberalize birth control legislation suggest that Catholics not only disapprove of contraception under any circumstances, but also refuse to practice it. In reality, however, the behavior of Catholics in this regard is very similar to that of non-Catholics. This fact is demonstrated by several types of evidence.

Samuel A. Stouffer, in a careful statistical study, shows that in northern and western urban centers of the United States the Catholic birth rate is declining more rapidly than the non-Catholic birth rate.[8] A further study by G. K. Robinson not only corroborates this finding, but indicates that the decline of Catholic fertility will become even more pronounced as a result of diminished immigration and of a consequently more normal

---

[6] Benjamin, *op. cit.*, p. 60. One of the bills was referred to another committee; the others were buried in committee.

[7] See reports on hearings listed already. The same arguments appeared in the Catholic press in the 1920's and 1930's. For more recent discussions see the publications of the Catholic Truth Society; the weekly *America* (June 3, 1939), p. 170, (August 6, 1938), p. 411, (May 1 and 22, 1937), pp. 75, 147, and Vol. 47 (1937), p. 461; *New York Times* (January 1, 1936), p. 16, (February 23, 1936), II, p. 1, (August 9, 1936), iii, p. 10, (April 17, 1937), ii, p. 1, (June 11, 1937), p. 20, (December 28, 1937), p. 30, (April 14, 1938), p. 21.

[8] "Trends in Fertility of Catholics and Non-Catholics," *American Journal of Sociology*, Vol. 41 (1935), pp. 143–66.

age distribution for Catholics.[9] The rolls of American birth control clinics reveal a sizable Catholic clientele. Pearl found that in the 1920's and 1930's more than one-third of the Catholic mothers were making contraceptive efforts.[10]

As a result of the demand by the Catholic rank and file for birth control (other than continence), the Church has found it necessary to sanction it. But it has sanctioned contraception in a peculiar way—by maintaining that only one method (in addition to continence) is right, the so-called "natural" or "rhythm" method. Both lay and ecclesiastical Catholic writers have recommended this particular method, writing numerous books and articles on it and using all the arguments that the proponents of birth control in general have advanced. Among the Catholic arguments favoring birth control by the "rhythm" method are the following:

1. The unemployment situation (this was during the depression) makes birth control necessary.

2. Even in prosperity, poverty compels many couples to limit their fertility so that they can provide for themselves and their offspring.

3. People must not be denied the right to marry simply because they cannot afford offspring, because early marriage is a good thing.

4. The practice of continence is impractical for the masses and often has a deleterious effect upon the spouses.

5. Health conditions—general, kidney, heart, etc.—require many women to prevent pregnancy.

6. The use of the Catholic method of birth control will reduce the number of abortions and deaths traceable to abortion.

7. Catholic birth control will free women of the fear of pregnancy and the unbearable psychic burdens of childbearing, burdens such as "uncontrollable fear, anxiety, irritability, of rebellion against God and His Church for seeming to make demands beyond human Nature, beyond human powers to endure."[11]

Plainly, the Catholic position is a compromise, but one that seems illogical to many Americans. The Church sanctions birth control in

---

[9] "The Catholic Birth-Rate: Further Facts and Implications," *ibid.*, pp. 757–66. Catholics themselves recognize that family size among Catholics is declining as a result of birth control practice. *E.g. Commonweal*, (December 29, 1933), p. 242.

[10] Raymond Pearl, *The Natural History of Population*, (New York, 1939), pp. 234–44.

[11] These arguments are taken from L. J. Latz, *The Rhythm;* Coucke and Walsh, *The Sterile Period in Family Life;* Father J. A. O'Brien, *The Church and Birth Control*, with a supplement on "helpful and practical information for married persons." These works are distributed by Our Sunday Visitor Press, Huntington, Indiana, which has also published anti-birth-control pamphlets. See also F. A. Smothers, "New Light on Birth Control," *Commonweal* (March 8, 1933); and hearings on H.R. 5978, pp. 231–243.

principle and yet insists that no one, Catholic or non-Catholic, be allowed to use any other method than continence or "rhythm." If the "rhythm" method were more efficient than all other methods, there might be some justification for this insistence; but in fact it is not as reliable.[12] The Church has placed itself in the position of defrauding its own members and of insisting that the rest of the population be defrauded as well, by law.

---

[12] Norman E. Himes, *Practical Birth Control Methods,* (New York, 1938), p. 123.

CHAPTER XVIII

Religion and the Schools

EVERY religious group, in order to hold and increase its membership, attempts to teach its faith to the children of its members. Many groups attempt to do more—to attract youth and indoctrinate them even if their parents are adherents of some other faith. In a democratic country such as the United States the public school system would offer, if it were controlled by a particular religious group, a perfect opportunity for mass indoctrination in favor of one religion and against all others. This is the case in some countries, such as Spain and Argentina. But in the United States the Federal Constitution long ago decided the issue by laying down that the public schools, state supported and governmentally controlled, should be free from control by any church. Nevertheless, in one way or another, the basic law is occasionally controverted or brought to a test, as the readings below illustrate. The university, not only because it teaches the young, but also because it advances the frontier of knowledge, is also of concern to religious groups.

THE SEPARATION OF CHURCH AND STATE: ITS MEANING *

What do we mean by the separation of state and church? The subject is clouded with much confused thinking among Protestants . . . as well as among Roman Catholics. This, as we pointed out, is largely caused by the fact that writers on both sides do not check their use of the formula with the Constitution.

Let us take a good look at the Constitution. The opening words of the first amendment dealing with this question read: "Congress shall make no law respecting an establishment of religion, or prohibiting the free

* Reprinted by permission of *The Christian Century* from the issue of November 26, 1947. From an editorial in Vol. 64, pp. 1447–1448.

exercise thereof." It is this double limitation upon the state that gave rise to the formula, "separation of church and state," in the American system of government. What does the first amendment mean? First note certain things that it does not mean.

It does not mean the separation of *religion* and the state. The state, through its representatives, can act from religious motives as well as from economic or political or other motives. In a word, there is nothing in the Constitution that forbids the state to perform a religious act. And it does perform such acts.

Nor does it mean the separation of the church and *politics*. The church has full liberty to engage in political action, either as a body or through its members in the discharge of their democratic responsibility as citizens. The church has the same right in this respect as a labor union, or the National Association of Manufacturers, or a political party, or any other group of citizens. The only inhibition on the church at this point arises from its own conception of itself as a church.

Nor yet does the first amendment mean the separation of *religion* and *politics*. As Dean Weigle well says: "The religious freedom of the citizen includes his right to hold the state itself responsible to the moral law and to God, and the right to labor to this end through appropriate judgments, witness and constructive participation in the activities of citizenship." . . .

The first amendment is precise in what it does: it separates—sharply separates—*church* and *state*, a concept wholly different from any of those referred to above. The church is the organized institution of religion, as the state is the organized institution of political life. It is these two institutions that are to be kept separate. But it is a separation which leaves room for moral and spiritual and political interaction and responsiveness. In what respect, then, are these two institutions to be kept separate? They are to be kept separate—completely separate—in their institutional or official functioning. The official functioning of the state must be kept separate from the official functioning of the organized church. There must be no interlocking of their respective institutional processes by law or the administration of law. This is the constitutional basis of religious liberty.

Look again at the Constitution. It does two things. It forbids Congress to make any law (1) respecting an establishment of religion or (2) prohibiting the free exercise thereof. The first clause is sharply specific; the second states a general principle. Consider the second clause first: "Congress shall make no law prohibiting the free exercise of religion." No religion is to be put under a ban by the state. No religion, on the other hand, may be given a special recognition by the state, for this obviously would have the negative effect of hampering all other religions; they would have to take a subordinate place in the shadow and operate against the prestige of the religion that was given special recognition. The plain design of this clause is to set all forms of religion free, to let them stand on their own feet and flourish or perish by the strength or weakness of their own faith. This is religious liberty. . . .

Two distinguishing features characterize an establishment of religion. One is the power of control over the church by the state, or by the church over the State. This may be a limited control, but insofar as it exists and is exercised at all by one over the other, it is potentially unlimited. The other feature inherent in an establishment of religion is that the church derives its institutional or temporal support, in whole or in part, from taxes levied on all citizens. This is in contrast to a church which is self-supporting, that is, which derives its total support from the voluntary gifts and services of its members, or by other means than government aid. When the fathers drafted the first amendment they had in mind this concept of an establishment of religion.

At first glance it seems that the fathers chose a rather awkward way of phrasing the prohibition of a religious establishment. Why did they not say merely, and more forthrightly, "Congress shall not establish any religion by law"? The key to the answer is in the word "respecting." "Congress shall make no law *respecting* an establishment of religion." This word means something. It meant something to the drafters of the first amendment. It means "pertaining to," or "tending toward," an establishment of religion.

The first amendment is more sweeping and radical than would have been the case had it merely prohibited the establishment of religion. The formula as adopted takes account of the possibility that a religion might come to be established by a gradual process: a law might be enacted which, though it fell far short of establishing a religion, nevertheless would contain the principle of such an establishment. Such a law would become a precedent for the enactment of further legislation pointing in the same direction, thus gradually creeping up to the goal of a full and complete establishment of religion.

The first amendment strikes at the root of the matter. It forbids the making of any law *"respecting"* such an establishment, that is, pertaining to, or tending toward, such an establishment. Congress is thus put on the alert against the making of any law in which the *principle* of union of church and state is implicit. . . .

We set out in the present writing to formulate a definition of separation of church and state. Such a definition has already appeared in our exposition of the Constitution. It should, however, be stated once more and in full. By the separation of church and state is meant the constitutional provision which forbids the making of any law, and therefore the taking of any executive action, that involves the interlocking of the official functions of the state with the official or institutional functions of any church. The all-inclusive function of the state is to make and administer law. And the Constitution forbids the making of any law the effect of which is to establish an interlocking relationship between the two institutions of church and state. Such an interlocking relationship is what is meant by the establishment of religion, in principle or in full actuality. . . .

This uniquely American solution of an age-old problem has been hailed by historians and political philosophers as marking the most significant and fruitful advance in this realm since the beginning of the Christian era. Lord Bryce, in his great work, *The American Commonwealth,* declares that "half the wars of Europe, half the internal troubles that have vexed the European states have arisen from the rival claims of church and state." He continues:

> This whole vast chapter of debate and strife has remained virtually unopened in the United States. There is no established church. All religious bodies are absolutely equal before the law, *and unrecognized by the law,* except as voluntary associations of private citizens. [Italics ours.] Religion, so far from suffering from the want of state support, seems to stand all the firmer because, standing alone, she is seen to stand by her own strength. . . .

If a particular measure involves an interlocking of the official functions or processes of the state with those of any church by the use of tax funds for the benefit of any church, or by the meshing of the diplomatic processes of the state with those of any church, or by any other entanglement of their respective functions, it is unconstitutional. If it does not, the principle of separation of church and state is irrelevant to its consideration.

THE NORTH COLLEGE HILL CASE *

A quiet suburb of Cincinnati offers today a preview of what may happen all over America in the not distant future. Outwardly North

* Reprinted by permission of *The Christian Century* from the issues of May 28, 1947, Fey, Harold E., "Preview of a Divided America," pp. 682–684; and of July 2, 1947, Fey, "They Stand for Free Schools!" pp. 824–825.

College Hill is a peaceful community of small homes. Inwardly it is trembling on the verge of an open outbreak of civil strife. Already violence has occurred. Its 5,000 people are savagely divided into two hostile camps. Lifelong neighbors refuse to speak to one another or to permit their children to associate. Property values are falling sharply, although there is no such slump in communities near by, and real-estate dealers have more houses on their hands than they can sell. People even divide their purchases in accordance with the communal difference which has split the town in two, and several undeclared boycotts are in force. This splitting apart of an American town has resulted from what the National Education Association, after an investigation on the spot, calls "probably the most serious school situation now current in the nation." . . .

The trouble began in 1940 with the incorporation of the St. Mary Margaret parochial school into the educational system of North College Hill. This was done after Roman Catholics secured a majority of one on the local board of education. By the vote of the board the community was obligated to pay salaries to the nuns who operated the parochial school and to pay rental for the schoolrooms in the building. The basement was reserved for the use of the parish, which continued to run highly profitable bingo games there. Within a short time after the original action, the rental and salaries were substantially raised. This overreaching brought a reversal of opinion among the voters of the community. The result was that the Catholics lost the election of 1942. The new school board terminated the arrangement with the parochial school. . . .

In 1945 however the normal Protestant majority of about 200 votes relaxed its vigilance and lost the election by 35 votes. The total population of 7,500 in the school district, which is a little larger than the town, should have around 3,000 electors. Only 2,600 electors registered, and between 2,300 and 2,400 voted. The main issue in the balloting was again the incorporation of the parochial school into the public system. The Citizens School League, the local organization supporting the Catholic candidates, used as their strongest talking point the promise that the inclusion of the parochial school would increase the amount of aid received from state school funds. According to Ohio law, a subvention from the state is available to schools in proportion to the number of pupils attending. In this district, the amount was not large, but it was made to look like a mountain to a few penny-pinching taxpayers. These allied themselves with the Roman Catholics, who were lured by the prospect of unloading their heavy parochial school costs on the public, and decided the election.

Tension developed almost immediately between the Catholic majority on the school board and Dr. William A. Cook, the superintendent of schools. It did not revolve around the incorporation of the parochial school with its eight-nun teaching staff into the public system. The superintendent accepted the voters' decision on that. But it soon became evident that the Catholic majority was determined to place the entire system under the domination of the church. . . .

A long series of crises ensued which involved the budget of the school district, the administration of school buildings, relations between the superintendent and the teachers, and the ever present question of teachers' salaries. On the surface the dissension had the appearance of an ordinary row between a conscientious school executive and an ignorant and overbearing school board majority. Underneath everybody knew that it was a struggle between the American and the Roman Catholic conceptions of education. The real question was whether the public schools of the community could maintain their integrity once they had admitted the parochial school into the public system.

The conflict reached its climax over the issue of who should nominate new teachers for the public schools. If the Catholic board members could get control of this function, which is placed by law in the hands of the superintendent, they could flood the schools with Catholic teachers and so put the entire system into the hands of the church. Realizing this, Superintendent Cook took his stand. He refused repeatedly to turn over to the board his confidential files of teacher applications and the correspondence relating to them. He was threatened with dismissal and with legal proceedings, but he stood his ground. In this action he was supported by almost all the teachers and a majority of the community.

Thereupon he was charged with "insubordination" and at the February 1947 meeting of the board the Catholic majority voted not to renew his contract when it expires in July. This dismissal of a competent superintendent came after the minority had been given only ten minutes to state its case and to present petitions signed by more than 1,200 taxpayers and others asking for renewal of his contract. This high-handed action inflamed the crowd of several hundred who were present. The next day students of the public schools attempted to strike, but were dissuaded by the superintendent. He managed to keep them in school until the March meeting of the board, when an attempt to win reconsideration of his dismissal failed by the usual vote of three to two. The next morning the student strike was on. The N.E.A. investigated three days later. Its report roundly criticized the school board and upheld the superintendent and his staff. . . .

With the majority in the community circumvented at every turn, the school board met on April 15 in a highly inflammatory atmosphere. Both the Schools Improvement Association, which supported the Protestant minority on the board, and the Citizens School League, which supported the Catholic majority, had urged citizens to attend. They came, over 1,000 in number, crowding a school gymnasium. First an attempt was made by a member of the minority to present more petitions in support of the superintendent and to move reconsideration of his dismissal. This failed. Then the secretary of the board read, one by one, letters of resignation from 29 of 33 teachers in the system. The cumulative effect of these letters on the impressionable students produced an amazing scene.

When they realized what was happening, all over the room these youngsters began to cry. By the time the last letter was read, literally hundreds of people, students and their parents, were in tears. One man who was present told me that not 200 people in the room were dry-eyed, and he said the only way he kept control of himself was by leaving the room. "I never saw anything like it," Superintendent Cook said to me. "I have seen children cheer for their schools, parade for their schools and work for their schools, but I never before saw hundreds of children cry for their schools." At the end of the reading a minority member once more attempted to get the superintendent reinstated as the only way the teachers could be retained. This failed and a majority member stood and said, according to the report given me, "Well, now I hope you understand that Dr. Cook is not going to be your superintendent any longer."

This was too much for one citizen, who jumped to his feet. "How can you be so heartless?" he cried. "Don't you see how much these children care? Can't you see their tears?"

"I don't see any tears," retorted the majority member. The protesting citizen immediately took the arms of the two nearest high school pupils and marched them down the aisle to the platform. "Now can you see?" he demanded. (Newspaper photographers were present, and this scene appeared the next day in Cincinnati papers.)

"All I can see," shouted the majority member, "is that your Dr. Cook is not going to be superintendent of this school system any longer.". . .

In that emotionally tense situation this taunt was more than could be borne by some persons, said to include a number of veterans, who were sitting near the front of the crowd. They leaped across the intervening seats to the platform and struck the board member. A fracas ensued which the police, who were present all the time, could not suppress for some time. When they finally managed to get the majority members out, the offending man had part of his clothes torn off and a black eye. Others had saved themselves by getting under a table. The meeting was never formally adjourned, but broke up at this point.

Four hours later, at about two o'clock in the morning, five persons were arrested and charged with assault with intent to commit murder, riotous assembly, aggravated assault and battery. Significantly, these persons were the husband of the woman taxpayer who had filed a suit to stop payments of public funds to the Archbishop of Cincinnati, a nephew of hers, two persons of families which had left Catholic churches to join Protestant churches in the community, and a minor. The bail was set at $5,000 in cash or $10,000 in property. The accused were locked up without being given opportunity to call counsel. A lawyer who had learned of what happened, however, arrived and secured their release. The grand jury later dismissed charges against three for lack of evidence and held the other two for trial on charges of simple assault and battery. . . .

Before more than 1,000 citizens, the three-man Roman Catholic majority on the school board bowed to the will of the people and handed in their resignations. The Protestant minority, which had twice proposed this solution, also resigned.

This development at North College Hill throws the entire administration of the schools into the hands of Probate Judge Chase M. Davies of Cincinnati. Judge Davies' first act was to announce a public hearing on the appointment of a superintendent of schools. The Schools Improvement Association, which had backed the minority on the board in their defense of the integrity of the schools, urged the reappointment of Dr. William A. Cook. . . . Only the retention of Dr. Cook would keep the teachers, they maintained, or make possible reconstruction of North College Hill's ruined school system. . . .

On June 23 Judge Davies announced his decision. It was to offer to re-employ Dr. Cook as superintendent of schools for a three-year term. Dr. Cook immediately accepted. The teachers who had resigned when the superintendent was forced out withdrew their resignations and were reinstated at salary increases of from $300 to $600 a year. A decision will be reached later as to whether the district's lease of the local parochial school from the Roman Catholic archdiocese of Cincinnati is to be renewed. It is expected that it will be terminated. If that occurs, the nuns will resign as public school teachers and henceforth will not be paid from public funds. Thus the school board's decision to resign opened the way for the schools to recover their integrity and for the community to reconstruct its shattered unity.

One important factor in bringing about the resignation of the Roman

Catholic majority was the action of the National Education Association in blacklisting the school system of North College Hill. This unprecedented action followed a similar move by the Ohio Education Association, which also broke precedent when it declared that the local system was "an unprofessional place for teachers to work." The N.E.A. ban, which was announced on the day the board resigned, was to continue "for as long as the present school board majority remains in control.". . .

The national teachers' organization condemned the majority in an eight-point indictment. Standing first in this indictment was the majority's refusal to re-employ Dr. Cook, "an action unwarranted by Dr. Cook's record and standing." Also included were efforts to re-elect a former principal, "demoted for sufficient cause"; "secretive and tyrannical" conduct of school affairs; ignoring protests "of the great majority" of students and teachers and "strong demands" of parents and citizens. The N.E.A. charged the majority with thwarting community efforts at peaceful solution of the issue, causing wholesale teacher resignations and a strike of 700 pupils. In the final count it was charged that the Catholic majority had conducted "the affairs of the board in such a way that large sections of the community have been divided on religious grounds."

Another factor in producing these resignations was a taxpayer's suit filed in Common Pleas court. It seeks to enjoin the district from carrying out the contract entered into by the majority to pay Archbishop McNicholas of the Roman Catholic diocese of Cincinnati $6,000 a year rental for the use of the local parochial school, which the church continues to use. One of the first actions of the majority when it took office on January 1, 1946, was to unload the parochial school on the public treasury. It not only incorporated the school into the public system but also signed an agreement to pay from public funds the salaries of the eight nuns who teach in that school. Concerning this the N.E.A. said: "This school enrolled only Catholic pupils and was taught largely by Catholic sisters, wearing the garb of their religious order. It was conducted as a sectarian school, but paid for out of public funds. Sectarian religious instruction was given each day as a regular part of the school program. The symbolic decorations of the building were of a sectarian nature. The sisters were paid from public funds under contract with the local board of education.". . .

A third factor leading to the resignation of the school board was the united action of Cincinnati Protestantism. On April 28 the Council of Churches of Greater Cincinnati held a meeting to discuss the situation which had developed at North College Hill. Of the more than 200 present, 60 per cent were laymen. Following presentation of the situation, which included a discussion of the taxpayer's suit, the council of churches voted to commend those who had brought the suit. It also authorized its headquarters committee "to initiate such action as it deems necessary to carry out the implications of aforesaid action." One of these implications, as the meeting recognized, would require the council to finance its opposition to the use of public funds "for the establishment and maintenance of sectarian religious schools or the teaching of sectarian religious belief or practice in public schools." This was approved unanimously. The council then issued a public statement which has been distributed throughout the Cincinnati area. It said, in part:

> The principle of the separation of church and state was established on the basis that any state support, however slight, for any church or religious establishment would lead first to bitter wrangling between the adherents of different religions for tax favors and ultimately to that worst of all tyrannies, religious persecution. As President Madison pointed out in his famous 'Memorial Against Religious Assessments,' the first step towards church support, direct or indirect, from tax funds is the first step towards a return of the Spanish Inquisition. Recent disorders in North College Hill prove the soundness of the prophecy of bitter feelings when tax support for any church becomes a public issue. We dare not wait to see whether the rest of Madison's prophecy is sound. . . . The principle of separation of church and state is not a worn out slogan to be evaded by legal fiction. It is the keynote of our religious freedom. As such, it is worth protecting. For that reason, we shall support wholeheartedly the move to stop tax support for any church school, in North College Hill or any other place.

STATE AID TO PARISH SCHOOLS *

Dr. V. T. Thayer, "for eighteen years educational director of the Ethical Culture Schools in New York City," has written a book[1] which is advertised as "valuable ammunition in the war that must constantly be waged against encroachments on freedom of religion." Substantially a brief for naturalistic education, it does not speak out clearly on all the issues involved; but it does suggest that the nation would fare better if all training in supernatural religion were eliminated. The author definitely opposes the equalizing of privileges in public schools and in parish schools, and also the compensating of parents for education given at their expense

* McSorley, Joseph, "State Aid to Parish Schools," in *The Catholic World,* Vol. 165 (May, 1947), pp. 131–135.

[1] *Religion in Public Education.* New York: The Viking Press, $2.75.

in legally established parish schools; either of these concessions he would regard as a breach in "the traditional wall of separation between Church and State."

Here then is a new contribution to a discussion that is exciting the interest of every type of citizen from the expert in constitutional law to the taxpaying village storekeeper. The discussion discloses interlocking issues and tangled interests; yet, as the book before us reveals, the chief disputes revolve around the simple question: "May the State impose an educational pattern (including theories about religion) upon all the children?" Totalitarians of course answer "Yes"; and Catholics answer "No." But then, many non-totalitarians also answer "Yes"; and many non-Catholics answer "No." It will clarify matters, therefore, if everyone who discusses the matter begins by making clear to himself and to others his own inner convictions with regard to two points:

1. Should a democratic State recognize the right of private non-profit schools to give a civil education that conforms to legal standards together with a religious education that conforms to parental wishes?

2. May the State, by unequal distribution of privileges, put pressure on parents to withdraw their children from religious schools and send them to public schools where they will be indoctrinated in a naturalistic theory of religion?

As to the first question the majority of Americans would agree. Legally established religious schools have existed from the beginning of our national life. Nevertheless, there are citizens who would like to see this type of school suppressed; and on some occasions they have made their weight felt throughout the country. It is chiefly with regard to the second question, however, that division and confusion prevail; and, by way of helping in the forming of a balanced opinion on it, we shall recall some facts which supplement certain inadequacies in Dr. Thayer's presentation.[2]

Roughly speaking, the history of education in the United States may be divided into three periods: From the birth of the nation to the second quarter of the nineteenth century; From then until 1900; From 1900 to the present time.

During the first of these periods most of the schools were private and

---

[2] *Public Funds for Church and Private Schools,* by Richard J. Gabel (Washington, D.C.: The Catholic University of America, 1937), is a treasury of information and should be available in every library. Incidentally, the book was cited in the recent Supreme Court decision on the New Jersey School Transportation Case, both in the opinion of the Court and in the dissenting opinion delivered by Mr. Justice Rutledge. Another invaluable book is *Naturalism in American Education,* Geoffrey O'Connell. New York: Benziger Bros., 1938.

religious, and most of them received aid from the States; for neither the Founding Fathers nor the next generation of Americans regarded this arrangement as incompatible with the First Amendment to the Constitution excluding "an establishment of religion." Several influences combined to terminate this period of co-operation. One factor was disputes among religious schools over their respective shares of public money; another was the attitude taken by Horace Mann, pioneer of the free public school system, and champion of what he called "non-sectarianism." The establishment of the Massachusetts Board of Education in 1837 and of the New York City Board of Education in 1842 marked the beginning of a new era. Before long the refusal of aid to a religious school came to be urged as a necessary means of preserving separation of Church and State.

The second period saw the rapid spread of the public school system and a growing inclination to withdraw State aid from religious schools. With the slogan "Keep Church and State separate," pressure groups pushed through the legislatures of various States a welter of statutes, often contradictory to one another, which, although theoretically impartial, helped the public schools to indoctrinate the population with "unsectarianism." In the hope of cutting off aid to religious schools at its source, an attempt was made in 1876 to enact a Constitutional Amendment which would prohibit payment of public funds to any institution that taught "sectarian" tenets. But in that same year an article (possibly by Father Hecker) in *The Catholic World,* commenting on President Grant's opposition to the support of "any sectarian schools," pointed out that, if the law were impartially applied, not one dollar would go to the public schools, which were teaching "sectarian, pagan, and atheistical dogmas" (Vol. XXII., p. 438).

As time passed, religious schools, except among Catholics and Lutherans, dwindled to the vanishing point. A writer in *The Catholic World* (again, perhaps, Father Hecker) had already, in 1870, called on Protestants to unite with Catholics in defense of religious education on the ground that the secularist invasion of the public schools was striking not only at "all Christian faith and Christian morals, but at the family, the State, and civilized society itself" (Vol. XI., p. 105). In 1873 a group of leaders in the Protestant Episcopal Church, proclaiming that any equitable division of school money among Church schools would do no violence to the Constitution, lamented that "the great majority have not yet learned to conceive that minorities have rights even in matters of conscience"; and in 1887 Dr. Hodge of Princeton commended the stand of the Catholic Church. Yet, on the whole, the defense of religious education was left almost entirely to Catholics; and almost every anti-Catholic movement included an attack on parish schools.

In the third period, seeds planted in the preceding century bore fruit. John Dewey, who has been called "the most influential thinker in contemporary American education," together with William Kilpatrick, Harold Rugg, Edward Thorndyke and their countless disciples, dominated the public school system; and, under the cloak of "unsectarianism," they converted it into a powerful propaganda machine for the theory that there is (1) No Personal Creator; (2) No Absolute Truth; (3) No Certainty (except in physical science). In 1934 President Nicholas Murray Butler of Columbia University, after reaffirming separation of Church and State as a fundamental principle in the American political order, declared that in the field of education "this principle has been so far departed from as to put the whole force and influence of the tax-supported school on the side of one element of the population, namely that which is pagan and believes in no religion whatsoever." [3]

The advocates of this one-sided "unsectarianism" have persisted in their attempts to cripple or destroy the Catholic school system by the tendentious interpretation of existing laws and by the passing of new legislation. Pleas to keep Church and State separate and references to the First Amendment are frequent; and most persons overlook the reminder of Secretary Fisher (of President Taft's Cabinet) that the First Amendment prohibits the establishment of a State Church and the support thereof, but not appropriations for religious purposes.

The trend toward totalitarianism in the field of education has become aggressive. On three occasions, within a quarter-century, the Supreme Court of the United States intervened to defend the constitutional rights of Catholics.

In 1922 the State of Oregon passed a law obliging all children to attend public schools. The Society of Sisters of the Holy Name, claiming that the law violated the Fourteenth Amendment, obtained an injunction from a United States District Court. Governor Pierce then appealed the case to the United States Supreme Court, which ruled that the Oregon Compulsory Education Act "unreasonably interferes with the liberty of parents and guardians to direct the up-bringing and education of children under their control." [4]

---

[3] *Columbia University Bulletin of Information,* December 15, 1934. P. 22.

[4] Pierce *v.* Society of Sisters, 268 U. S. 534.

In 1928 the State of Louisiana passed a law directing the State Board of Education to provide "school books for school children free of cost to such children." Certain taxpayers brought suit to enjoin the Board of Education from so doing on the ground that the legislation violated State laws and also the Fourteenth Amendment of the Federal Constitution. A State court refused to issue the injunction; and, on appeal, this judgment was affirmed, first by the Supreme Court of Louisiana, and then by the Supreme Court of the United States, with Mr. Justice Hughes delivering the opinion.[5] The decision of this case obviously resulted in giving considerable indirect aid to the religious schools of the State.

In 1941 the State of New Jersey passed a law authorizing local school districts to provide children with free transportation to and from all non-profit schools. A taxpayer, Arch R. Everson, challenged the law as a violation of both the State and the Federal Constitution. A State court decided in his favor; the New Jersey Court of Errors and Appeals reversed that decision. The case was then appealed to the United States Supreme Court which, in February, 1947, by a 5 to 4 decision, upheld the New Jersey statute of 1941.[6] Mr. Justice Rutledge (who cites Dr. Thayer's book), in his dissenting opinion, held that the First Amendment to the Constitution prohibits any sort of State aid to schools which teach religion; and he declared that he would never sustain any appropriations by a State unless "it can be found that in fact they do not aid, promote, encourage or sustain religious teaching or observances, be the amount large or small." Mr. Justice Black, who delivered the opinion of the Court, pointed out that the implication of this dissenting view would justify a State in cutting parish schools off "from such general Government services as ordinary police and fire protection, connection with sewage disposal, public highways and sidewalks."

The American mind seems to be in a muddled condition with regard to the relation between religion and the schools. Several fundamental legal problems remain unsolved; there is grave confusion about ethical principles. On the one hand, some non-Catholics, like Dr. Thayer, invoke the Bill of Rights against such minor concessions as "the released time plan"; but other non-Catholics, like Professor William Adams Brown, see no objection to "the teaching of religion on school premises and during school hours,

[5] Cockran *v.* Louisiana State Board of Education, 281 U. S. 370 (1930).

[6] Everson *v.* Board of Education, Supreme Court of the United States, No. 52, October Term, 1946, decided February 10, 1947.

if this can be done without expense to the State and under conditions which guarantee educational efficiency and safeguard religious equality." [7] Even more significant is the clash of views between the two Supreme Court Justices in the New Jersey School Transportation Case. Some of the arguments advanced by Mr. Justice Rutledge logically imply that the First Amendment would invalidate a State's purchase of land from a parish, if and because the transaction would be of benefit to the parish. To most men that seems unreasonable. But, if a State may purchase land from a parish, may it not with equal reason compensate a parish for giving civil education to children whose training would otherwise be a charge upon the State?

There remain two important considerations which throw a favorable light on the parish school:

1. The civil education given in Catholic schools represents an annual burden of some $300,000,000 lifted from the shoulders of the taxpayers of the country and borne by the Catholic people.

2. What is far more important, the education given in Catholic schools forms one of our nation's best bulwarks against a grave danger pointed out by many clear thinkers.

The following may serve as examples: In 1936 Professor Louis J. A. Mercier declared: "What our most prominent American educational leaders have been doing in the last thirty-five years is to formulate and propagate such doctrines as must inevitably undermine American institutions and prepare the advent in the United States of atheistic totalitarianism." In 1940 Dr. Mortimer Adler, addressing the Conference on Science, Philosophy and Religion, asserted that most of the professors in American colleges and universities teach positivism, the essential point of which "is simply the affirmation of science, and the denial of philosophy and religion." He said, furthermore, that "the most serious threat to Democracy is the positivism of the professors, which dominates every aspect of modern education and is the central corruption of modern culture. Democracy has much more to fear from the mentality of its teachers than from the nihilism of Hitler."

It would appear to be a patriotic duty then, for Americans to go as far as they legally can in favoring, rather than in hampering, the activities of the parish school.

---

[7] *Church and State in Contemporary America.* New York: Charles Scribner's Sons, 1936. P. 273.

THE IDEAL UNIVERSITY *

In our opinion, the study of philosophy is not only a preparatory discipline for those who are attracted by higher learning, it is a necessary guidance in the attainment of this learning itself. The faculty of philosophy should act as a sort of compensation bureau or "clearing house" in the midst of the intermingling activities of all other faculties and schools. It is evident that a course of philosophy which would be a mere study of all intellectual errors and theories of men since the beginning of civilization, could not accomplish the mission we are advocating. Besides, we educationists consider it our duty to shield the young minds entrusted to us from dangerous intellectual experiences, to which their lack of maturity would surely expose them. Therefore, a doctrine, a system of thought is necessary: the Catholic universities have selected the philosophy of St. Thomas of Aquinas, which is, as you know, the philosophy of Aristotle, christianized, considerably augmented, and fully adapted to the needs of our day. This system is not purely ecclesiastical: it can be described as the "natural philosophy of the human mind."

There is a danger for many students, that of clinging to the *sensible* without ever rising to the *thinkable*. Philosophy will show them how this can be avoided. "The soul and life of university training lies in this process. A university is a laboratory of thought, the home of abstract science, pure theories, fundamental principles, rethought and examined in all the breadth of their spiritual dimensions: there, we can learn what is the hierarchy of essences, what is the being, unfolded in all its modalities and measured according to its limits generically, specifically and differentially."

I must apologize for so obscure a phraseology. But let me, once more, use this abstract language to give a few examples of the practical utility of philosophy. Without it, I cannot see how a student could judge of materialism, pragmatism, and phenomenism, for instance; of naturalism in pedagogics; in mathematics and physics, what could he think of Einstein's relativism and the theories of evolution; in psychology, what of determinism; in social economy, what of the new forms of Marxism; in political science, what of so many systems, fascists, or others?

---

* Mauralt, Monsignor Olivier, "What Is Our Idea of a University," *The Rice Institute Pamphlet,* Vol. 26 (July 1939), pp. 113–118, 122–123.

Natural sciences become more and more popular amongst us. A sound philosophy will, above all, maintain in this particular realm the fundamental principle of finality as the formal bond of experience and the conducting wire of scientific thought, opposing to the so-called scientist the necessary existence of primary causes.

Science is privileged with complete autonomy in its methods and conclusions. But philosophy has the right to criticize science; and it is philosophy that points out to us the exact sense, the nature, and reach of laws and formulas.

To quote again Cardinal Villeneuve, Chancellor of Quebec University: ". . . the true University man is the one who does not simply possess a good knowledge and a fair culture in science and arts but who, moreover, knows their major principles. . . . Philosophy alone links the different teachings on a common ground and provides the root and strength of every science. In other words, philosophy alone gifts the thinker with intellectual power and transcendency, thus enabling him to consider the problems of truth as a *universalist;* philosophy alone creates the University mind apt to judge truth universally, and trains the genial specialist who finally conquers the élite. . . ."

Philosophy ranks first because it possesses the power to organize the different branches of human knowledge and to show the hierarchy in which they stand. But in our estimation, the noblest of all our Faculties is theology, whose object is God Himself.

* * *

"The supreme glory of a Catholic university and its sturdiest rampart against doctrinal error is to add to the gleam of natural lights the splendid rays which come from Above; to pursue its researches in the brightness of this double focus and to penetrate its teaching with the principles of Divine Revelation. Then sacred theology, by its incomparable nobleness as well as by the absolute certainty of its object, surpasses all other knowledge. It associates the earthly man to the eternal science of God Himself." . . .

In Montreal, our faculty of theology has taken the means of propagating theological doctrines among laity and putting higher religious teaching within the reach of the man on the street. It has organized public classes on liturgy, canon law, Holy Scriptures, morals, Catholic action, and pontifical doctrine. The late Pope Pius XI has been, in recent years, the champion of Catholic action.

Catholic action is a lay move sponsored by ecclesiastical hierarchy; it tends towards a renovation of society under the impulse of a live faith and zeal. Its leaders require a thorough training and deep convictions; they will find them in the teachings of our new Institute. . . .

On the occasion of the golden jubilee of the Catholic University of America, His Holiness Pius XI wrote words which can be listened to and understood by every Christian educationist worthy of the name. Here they are: "Through the University, it will be possible to bring to bear upon the most pressing problems of the day the full force of those principles of justice and charity in which alone they will find their solution. In the course of Our Pontificate, we have had occasion to treat these problems more than once in our Encyclical Letters; here We wish only to point out the solid basis upon which Our teaching rests. Since the sciences of civics, sociology, and economics deal with individual and collective human welfare, they cannot escape from the philosophical and religious implications of man's origin, nature, and destiny. If they ignore God, they can never hope to understand adequately the creature which He formed in His own image and likeness, and whom He sent His own Divine Son to redeem. Christian teaching alone, in its majestic integrity, can give full meaning and compelling motive to the demand for human rights and liberties because it alone gives worth and dignity to human personality. In consequence of his high conception of the nature and gifts of man, the Catholic is necessarily the champion of true human rights and the defender of true human liberties; it is in the name of God Himself that he cries out against any civic philosophy which would degrade man to the position of a soulless pawn in a sordid game of power and prestige, or would seek to banish him from membership in the human family; it is in the same Holy Name that he opposes any social philosophy which would regard man as a mere chattel in commercial competition for profit, or would set him at the throat of his fellows in a blind, brutish class struggle for existence."

IMPERSONALIZATION OF RELIGION *

The years following the War between the States saw rapid cultural changes in the two principal revivalistic Churches, the Methodists and the Baptists. At the beginning of the nineteenth century, the educational and cultural chasm between the Churches which had a college-trained

* Sweet, William Warren, *Revivalism in America* (New York: Charles Scribner's Sons, 1944), pp. 163–174, 177–180.

ministry and those in which the educational standards for the ministry were practically non-existent was deep and wide. The end of the century saw that gulf considerably lessened. Clerical culture and learning were no longer a monopoly of the Congregationalists, the Presbyterians, and the Episcopalians. Education, refinement, and dignity now characterized the ministry and services of many Methodists, the Baptists, and the Disciples, equally with those of the formerly elite churches. Indeed the Methodists in the towns and cities by the end of the century began to get out robes and prayer books which had been carefully put aside in the early years of the Church's independent existence, and many of them in form and ritual went far beyond Presbyterianism and Congregationalism.

There was a corresponding change also in the cultural and educational status of the laity of the revivalistic Churches. The denominational colleges following the Civil War grew with amazing rapidity, and the Methodist and Baptist institutions outnumbered all others. The result was the mounting numbers of college graduates sitting in Baptist, Methodist, and Disciples' pews. This does not mean necessarily that revivalism and education were mutually exclusive, but it did mean that an excessive emotional appeal would no longer be effective. . . . Where there are educated persons in any congregation and an educated minister in the pulpit, there is small chance that an extreme emotional revivalism will arise. On the other hand, a congregation made up of people with little education or critical training may easily be led into emotional excess by a revivalistic preacher, who gives way to his own deep feeling, who shouts and gesticulates wildly, while tears stream down his face as he speaks. Highly emotionalized revivalism has always made the greatest appeal to persons of little education. The emotions of such persons "pass swiftly and impulsively into action."[1] In pioneer communities, where the emphasis was placed upon bodily development at the expense of mental equipment and where there were no people of educational attainment, revivalism of the extreme emotional type naturally flourished. It was the changing cultural climate that was responsible for the elimination of much of the extravagant type of revivalism.

The great number of old Methodist camp meeting grounds to be found all over the United States, still owned by the Conferences or camp meeting associations but now turned into middle-class summer resorts or meeting places for summer conferences, are mute witnesses to the social,

[1] F. M. Davenport in his *Primitive Traits in Religious Revivals*, chapter i. See also Elizabeth K. Nottingham, *Methodism and the Frontier, Indiana Proving Ground* (New York, 1941), chapter ix, "Revivalism in England and America."

religious, and cultural change which has taken place in American Methodism. The conditions which gave rise to the camp meeting have passed. With the construction of larger and more adequate church buildings, and the introduction of the protracted meeting type of revivalism held during the winter months, the need for the great summer gatherings in the woods, as harvest time for souls, gradually disappeared.

During the seventies and eighties, and on to the end of the century, what were called camp meetings continued to be held but their nature underwent swift change. At Chautauqua, New York, the old camp meeting ground was transformed (1874) under the leadership of John H. Vincent, later a bishop of the Methodist Church, into an institution whose influence spread all over the nation. Starting as a movement to increase the effectiveness of Sunday School instruction, with courses on Sunday School management and Bible teaching, it expanded within a few years into a veritable university. In 1878 home-study courses in literary and scientific subjects were introduced. The following years courses were offerred for secular school teachers, and in rapid succession Schools of Science and Mathematics, Library Training, Domestic Science, Music, Arts and Crafts, Physical Education, and, in co-operation with Cornell University, a School of Agriculture (1912) were formed. Large lecture halls, a theatre, club houses, a library, and a gymnasium were erected; and between 1924 and 1932 forty-five thousand people attended the general assembly each year, where they heard famous preachers and lecturers, attended concerts, and in other ways absorbed culture.[2]

By the end of the century little Chautauquas had sprung up all over the country and many of them were utilizing old camp meeting grounds. It was a poor town indeed that did not have at least a week of lectures and entertainment some time during the summer months. After 1900 the traveling Chautauquas appeared and companies were formed to supply talent, while college boys were utilized as advance agents to sell the courses to the communities and later to put up the tents and perform the other necessary menial tasks. Such has been the strange development of the camp meeting, a by-product which the old camp meeting preachers would doubtless have hotly repudiated, but a transformation which was inevitable in the light of the change in the cultural and religious climate.

The astonishing growth of American cities from 1880 to the end of the century was one of the marvels of the age. This growth was due to the attractive power of manufacturing centers, drawing population from

---

[2] J. L. Hurlburt, *The Story of Chautauqua.*

the small towns and rural communities, and to an even greater degree from the overcrowded countries of Europe. Between 1880 and 1890 the rural population declined not only in the old New England states, but in such states as Ohio, Indiana, Illinois, and Iowa. During the last two decades of the nineteenth century, the foreign-born population of the great cities reached such proportions as to cause grave apprehension that the basic American ideals and principles would be completely swamped by the great mass of the foreign-born. From the close of the Civil War to 1900, no less than 13,260,000 foreigners of all kinds entered the United States, more than double the population of New England. Following the turn of the century the number entering this country was even larger. In the year 1889, sixty-eight of the towns of Massachusetts, including the largest, were governed by the Irish. The flocking of these newcomers to the cities, both native-born as well as the foreign-born, created problems of all sorts, not alone affecting politics and social conditions but also religion. Thus again a religious crisis was created through mass immigration, comparable to that of the early part of the last century as a result of the western movement of population. Again great masses of people were cutting themselves loose from their old homes, their churches, their schools, and their old neighbors to find new homes in the rapidly developing American cities. In the cities religion had to meet a type of competition which it had never before experienced, in the cafes, beer-gardens, shooting galleries, amusement parks, saloons, theatres, and, in more recent times, moving pictures, night clubs, prize fights, professional baseball, and a host of other types of entertainment.[3] In the light of the kind of competition it had to meet, it becomes clear how and why a new type of spectacular city revivalism arose.

It was the city which gave rise to the professional revivalist. There had been a few men, such as Asahel Nettleton, in the early part of the nineteenth century who devoted all their time to revivalism, but the vocational evangelist came into existence with the rise of the city. The greatest of all the professional revivalists was undoubtedly Dwight L. Moody. His evangelistic career began immediately following the Civil War, and ended with his death in the very midst of a great meeting in Kansas City in 1899. All his great meetings were city campaigns conducted in Brooklyn, Philadelphia, New York, Chicago, Boston, St. Louis, San Francisco. Conservative in theology, a literalist in his interpretation of Scripture though never a bigot, with a flat voice, often ungrammatical in speech, with

[3] A. M. Schlesinger, *Political and Social Growth of the United States, 1852–1933* (New York, 1933), 226, 281–282. See also A. M. Schlesinger, *Rise of the City.*

sermons preached over and over again, Moody's success in pointing men to the Christian way of life was truly astonishing. In 1875, on his return from his first great evangelistic campaign in England, he said to a friend: "I am the most overestimated man in this country. By some means the people look upon me as a great man, but I am only a lay preacher and have little learning." One newspaper reporter, covering his meetings in a certain city, stated that there was never a moment when he was eloquent; that he cared not a whit for logic; that he murdered the English language; and yet he stated there was not another man in America that could have filled the vast auditorium day after day. He held, during these meetings, forty-eight thousand people in the hollow of his hand, and they wept and smiled as he willed. . . .[4] The impression he left was that there was truth behind the man greater than he. . . .

The city evangels who followed Moody—Reuben Torrey, Wilbur Chapman, B. Fay Mills, Sam Jones, George Stuart, W. E. Biederwolf, and Billy Sunday—were all more or less in the Moody tradition, though none ever equaled him in the total and lasting influence which they exerted. They, too, were all conservative in their theology, the majority of them being Presbyterians. Some of them, as Reuben Torrey, were college graduates; others, as Billy Sunday, were without formal schooling. All preached a simple, easily-understood gospel message. Some of them were dramatic in their preaching, and all were assisted by evangelistic singers who not only performed themselves but organized great choirs made up of local talent for the period of the meeting. In the latter years of this type of city evangelism, there was great emphasis placed on highly organized machinery set up by business agents, who demanded that great sums of money be subscribed before the meetings could begin. "Billy" Sunday carried the "big time" evangelism to an extreme equaled by none of his contemporaries. He utilized almost to perfection the techniques of big business in organizing his campaigns and very large sums of money were subscribed to carry them forward. He claims to have preached to eighty millions of people during the course of his career. He always rated large headlines in the newspapers and in other ways attracted the attention of the public generally. This technique, however, by the middle of the nineteen-twenties had begun to pall on the public and during the last years of his life his influence and popularity had greatly declined.

The vocational evangelists reached thousands of people who had lost

[4] Gamaliel Bradford, *Dwight L. Moody, A Worker in Souls* (New York, 1927). See also W. W. Sweet, *The Makers of Christianity from John Cotton to Lyman Abbot* (New York, 1937), 266–278.

contact with the churches; they fought the grosser sins common to city life and they lifted moral standards. None seems to have effected any large social reform, except as that was brought about through reformed lives. Billy Sunday, however, did have a determining influence in bringing in the dry era.

Growing more or less directly out of the Moody influence was a new type of college and university revivalism, very different from the older type which had followed the usual patterns. This new college revivalism, carried on through the medium of college Y.M.- and Y.W.C.A.'s centered in an appeal for the dedication of young life to the cause of converting the world in a generation. Thus religion, with a definite and challenging task to perform, was brought to hundreds of college campuses through the medium of such dynamic leaders as John R. Mott, Robert E. Speer, and Sherwood Eddy. As a result of their labors and influence, literally thousands of students went out from the colleges and universities of the land as crusaders for the cause of bringing in the reign of Christ throughout the world. Student Volunteer Bands were formed in the colleges constituting living centers of religious influence.[5]

During the very years when Moody revivalism was at its height, the Salvation Army was introduced from England to America. It made its appearance here just two years after its establishment in England (1878). In ten years it had marched across the continent and was carrying on its work in every large city in America. Using the old revivalistic methods, with preaching based upon the reality of sin, the divinity of Christ, and his atoning death, and the awful reality of hell, its primary concern has always been and still is to reach and convert people who have met defeat in the struggle of life. They believe that the love of God is as wide as the world; the atoning sacrifice is as universal as human need. Combined with their revivalism they carried on a tremendous work in social service. In 1936 there were 1,088 corps; 103,083 officers and soldiers; and nearly forty millions of property. It conducts working-men's hotels, food depots, industrial homes, farm colonies, second-hand stores, children's homes, employment bureaus, day nurseries, slum settlements, distributes free ice and coal among the poor, gives outings to mothers and children. In short, it fully lives up to its "Articles of War" which pledges every soldier to fight unendingly against all sin and sinful conditions in our cities.[6]

Occupying a position at the opposite pole from the Salvation Army

[5] William M. Beahm, "Factors in the Development of the Student Volunteer Movement for Foreign Missions" (Typed Ph.D. thesis, University of Chicago, 1941).

[6] Of the 1,088 Salvation Army churches, 1,067 are urban (Census of 1936).

is the Oxford Group Movement, fathered by an American Lutheran, Frank Buchman. This is a type of revivalism which has appealed especially to large numbers of students in universities and colleges, and to persons in the upper economic and cultural levels. It is a very personal type of approach, and its early converts were won by personal talks with students at Oxford and Cambridge. Its principal emphasis is upon the guidance that God can and will furnish for every individual; it teaches that God has a plan for every life, but when through personal sin that plan is spoiled "God is always ready with another." To lead the kind of life God has planned for us a person must be willing to surrender "will, time, possessions, family, ambitions." Theologically, Buchmanism is entirely orthodox; it has been characterized as "orthodoxy galvanized into new life in modern conditions." . . . In America the influence of Buchmanism has been primarily exerted among Episcopalians. It has been suggested that just as the Salvation Army was formed to deal with the "downs and outs," the Buchman movement is primarily concerned, and has had its largest success, with the "ups and outs."

Still another type of city revivalism is that which has been carried on by revivalistic cults such as the International Church of the Four Square Gospel. It was founded by Aimée Semple McPherson, an unusual woman who began her career as an evangelist at seventeen years of age and after extensive evangelistic work in the United States, Canada, England, and Australia, came to Los Angeles in 1918. Here her star rose rapidly and in 1921 she had gained a sufficient following to erect a great auditorium seating five thousand (dedicated, 1923) called the "Angelus Temple Church of the Four Square Gospel." She acquired the ownership of a radio station and established a Bible College called the "Lighthouse of International Four Square Evangelism," where Four Square Gospel ministers receive their training. The Angelus Temple with the Bible College constitute a most effective organization for the carrying on of the old type of revivalism with all the showmanship of the most modern kind. For membership, evidence of "born again experience" is required. In 1936 two hundred and five branch organizations were reported throughout the country with a total membership of some sixteen thousand, of which more than eighty per cent are found in cities. . . .[7]

The Churches which have the largest membership today are those bodies which in the past have profited most from revivalism, a type of

[7] *Religious Bodies, 1936* (Washington: United States Department of Commerce, Bureau of the Census, 1941), Vol. II, Part I, 739–746. Of the 205 churches reported in 1936, all but 54 were urban.

religion that is dominantly personal. Revivalism tends to disappear when the impersonal becomes dominant over the personal. Charles Sumner once remarked to Julia Ward Howe, the author of the "Battle Hymn of the Republic," that he no longer was interested in individuals, but only in causes. To that remark Julia Ward Howe replied, "God Almighty has not gone that far, yet." It would seem that in a democracy the personal emphasis in religion would naturally find its largest development. And so it has been, and it would seem that it should remain so. The emphasis in our American democracy upon the freedom of conscience gives personal religion its opportunity, and the great evangelical Churches are living witnesses to what extent that opportunity has been appropriated. . . .

In the last fifty years the great American Churches and their leaders, like Charles Sumner, have grown less and less interested in individuals and more and more concerned with the advancement of causes. No doubt what we call the Social Gospel emphasis has been partly responsible for this growing trend. Gaius Glenn Atkins has remarked that the Social Gospel saved the Protestant pulpit, meaning that it gave preachers live subjects to treat in their pulpits, when the old-time subjects, due to liberal trends in theology, seemed to be outworn. But, at the same time, it undermined the personal in religion. Social and economic justice became the principal theme of all the Social Gospel preachers: the Harry Emerson Fosdicks, the Ernest F. Tittles, the Albert E. Days, the Charles C. Morrisons, and others of their kind, and all the lesser Social Gospel preachers followed in their train. When I was a student in the seminary, we were going to save the world by becoming proficient in sociology and many of us rushed over to Columbia University to take graduate courses in sociology under Giddings. The Social Gospel advocates insisted that you cannot make a better world by "snatching brands from the burning," by proceeding with the conversion of people one by one. They insisted that the Church must deal with society as a whole, with basic causes for sinful living. In their enthusiasm to save society they overlooked sinners. Revivalism, they held, was ineffective, out of date, and must therefore be discarded. . . .

Then came the first World War furnishing other great impersonal themes for the pulpit, such as the saving of democracy. Then came the Treaty of Versailles and the peace crusade which followed its tragic failure. The peace theme furnished the greatest preachers in the land with sermon subjects for a decade and more. If they were not preaching world peace, they were occupied with race discrimination; bettering international relations; furthering international justice. All interesting subjects and many great sermons were built around them, but under such preaching few in the pews ever felt singled out. Many who sat under such preaching no doubt were in full agreement with the preacher and agreed that something ought to be done about it, but as far as they themselves were concerned there was little urge for them to be better men and women. They felt no personal responsibility in the matter, and nothing particularly happened. A few economic royalists got mad and stormed out of the church, leaving their pews vacant; others changed their membership to churches whose ministers preached the "old-fashioned" gospel where they could be at ease in Zion.

Added to this has been the growing influence of religious education, stressing the Horace Bushnell emphasis upon Christian nurture. Thus religion came to be, especially in the large town and city churches, more and more a matter of learning and less and less a matter of feeling. . . . Here too the emphasis has been upon the person's relationship to society, rather than his relationship to God; upon the evils of society rather than upon personal selfishness. In its reaction against the old revivalism, with its overemphasis upon the emotional and the personal, the Church has tended to establish an impersonal and institutional pattern of salvation almost as rigid as that represented by the state Churches of Europe in the seventeenth and eighteenth centuries.

PART EIGHT

Recreation: Leisure and Escape

CHAPTER XIX

Work and Nonwork

As men have been increasingly successful in their struggle for subsistence, an ever-larger proportion of their time has been freed from preoccupation with merely remaining alive. The total supply of "surplus" time made available by cultural development has, to be sure, never been distributed equally—some groups are more nearly a "leisure class" than others—but in modern America the per capita amount of leisure is probably greater than in any other known society, past or present.

What men do with their leisure is of significance to the student of society for several reasons. In the first place, the differential allocation of leisure, like the allocation of all scarce things, follows and reflects the society's system of values. In the second place, the re-creation of social solidarity and of personal freshness and vigor are uses of leisure that are necessary for both societal and individual efficiency. In the third place, recreational activities—what men do in their "spare time"—may provide a clue to the kinds of pressures, strains, and "needs" generated in the normal routine of role-playing: the kinds of drama enjoyed by Chinese are different from the kinds demanded by Americans, and the difference may reflect great variations in social values, frustrations, and dreams. Or, the recreation of coal miners is not that of college professors, and the difference may be symptomatic.

In the present section of our readings we present only a few illustrative discussions of this too-little-analyzed field of recreation. A general statement of some of the issues is given first, and this is followed by a descriptive analysis of leisure-time practices in a typical mid-Western community. Finally, we have chosen some suggestive discussions of the recreational significance of one of America's favorite leisure-time pursuits, the movies.

THE NEW LEISURE *

The problems of leisure have come increasingly into the foreground in recent years for two principal reasons. First, the amount of leisure time has been constantly increasing and seems destined to even more rapid increase in the near future. Secondly, urban civilization and mechanical devices, such as the automobile, the motion picture, and the radio, have disrupted traditional leisure pursuits and the individual's control over his own spare time. . . .

Labor leaders exhibit charts showing the reduction of the working week from eighty-four hours in 1840 to fifty hours, or less, in 1930. Since that time the forty-hour week has, in theory at least, been accepted. In addition, more than one-third of our population consists of children, from 40 to 50 percent of whose waking hours is leisure time. Another fifth of the population, engaged as housewives, has been largely released from the drudgery of long hours by the changing role of the home, as well as by the revolution in the technique of housekeeping. Not only has the number of children per family decreased but the mother's responsibility for education and rearing has been largely assumed by the community. Household conveniences (gas, electricity, water supply, and sewers) as well as simplifications in methods used in the preparation of food and clothing have greatly lessened the labor of millions of women.

Add to this large number of women and children, the "retired" and the "leisure" classes, and some idea of the enormous amount of leisure which exists in a modern community may be secured. The production of the material necessities of life, which has for centuries been the dominant concern of nearly the whole population, including women and children, is today carried on by a relatively small number of people. The "gainfully employed," a class which includes the producers of luxuries (in goods and services) as well as of necessities, today comprise only about two-fifths of our population. In the face of such facts and with even more striking prospects for the future, it is not surprising that Nicholas Murray Butler declares that "guidance in the right use of leisure is vastly more important than what is now known as vocational guidance."

The great increase in the amount of leisure for the masses of men is, however, only one aspect of the new problem. The very changes which

---

* Reprinted from G. A. Lundberg, M. Komarovsky, and M. A. McInerny, *Leisure: A Suburban Study*. Copyright 1934 by Columbia University Press. Pp. 4, 6–8, 15–18.

caused shorter working hours also disrupted to a large extent traditional leisure pursuits. . . . For example, spontaneous and informal neighborhood life, which formerly provided a chief use of leisure, has largely disappeared as a result of the tremendous mobility of modern urban society. Neighborhood life depends upon relative stability; it cannot flourish where a substantial part of the population moves every year or two. In the city, furthermore, occupation tends to supplant geographic location as a basis of fellowfeeling and association. Congested living quarters and the disappearance of the yard and other outdoor facilities have further shifted recreation to the school, the club, and the commercial recreation place.

These new conditions under which spare time is spent have also altered profoundly the uses of leisure. Home and neighborhood games and sports are supplanted by billiard "parlors" and public dance halls. Huge stadia offer a vicarious satisfaction for the urges which conditions no longer permit us to fulfill directly. Instead of singing around the piano, we turn on the radio. The innumerable petty activities of barn, pasture, and garden, many of them heavily mixed with recreational elements, are foreign to the apartment dweller. Even the "job" of the ordinary man was formerly often fraught with variety and high adventure and therefore had its own recreational aspects. There is little possibility of dramatic developments or variety in the operation of a punching machine. The former type of work might leave one tired, but not taut; restful sleep was its remedy. The latter type results in a craving for explosive stimulation as a relief. Add to these considerations the exploitative aspects of advertising, salesmanship, and the modern facilities of communication, and we secure some idea of the altered conditions of leisure.

Professor Jacks has summarized the situation of the modern city dweller as follows:

> On every side he is surrounded by artful operators who have studied his weak points, often with the aid of psychology, and beset him with the offer of ready-made pleasures to be purchased at a price. . . . Even those of us who are immune from the attractions of the cinema, the race-course and the public-house are not masters of our leisure time, at least to the extent we should like to be. We are largely at the mercy of our neighbors, who have facilities of getting at us unknown to the ancient Greeks or even to our grandfathers. Thanks to the telephone, motor car and such-like inventions, our neighbors have it in their power to turn our leisure into a series of interruptions, and the more leisure they have the more active do they become in destroying ours. Nor are we less active in destroying theirs. We spend a great deal of our leisure in mutual botheration. In whatever

conditions you place a man, the use he can make of his own leisure will always be limited by the use that other people are making of theirs.

We are confronted, then, with radically altered conditions under which to spend our leisure and a greatly increased amount of leisure to spend. What will people do under these conditions?

COMPETITIVE CONSUMPTION AS A LEISURE PURSUIT

"It began to be recognized," says the President's Committee on Recent Economic Changes, "not only that leisure is 'consumable' but that people can not 'consume' leisure without consuming goods and services, and that leisure which results from our increasing man-hour productivity helps to create new needs and broader markets." Here we have very excellently revealed the current preoccupation of economists with the productive aspect of their subject. From this point of view the problem of leisure is a problem of increasing man's consumption of material goods so that business and profits may be bigger and better. This, apparently, is the highest and final object of endeavor. Increased sales bring increased employment and higher wages. Purchasing power is thus increased, which in turn makes possible still bigger business. If as a result of big business, improved methods of production are devised by which a task that used to require four days now requires only two, the chief significance of this development, in current theory, is that in the time saved, the laborer will be able to consume some goods and services for which he has hitherto not had time to develop an appetite. Herein we have the modern version of the fascinating experience of growing more corn to feed more hogs, to make more money, to buy more land, to grow more corn, to feed more hogs, and so on. This exhilarating round, at an ever-increasing tempo, represents, apparently, the highest aspiration of Western civilization.

There is no denying the hypnotic centripetal power with which the increasing rapid swirl of this circle is capable of holding man. As a method of bridging the gap between birth and death, *keeping occupied,* it has much to be said for it. It undoubtedly keeps many out of mischief. The people most completely in its sway are not infrequently the pillars of society. Among other things, it prevents philosophic meditation and other morbid reflections which tend to afflict some preachers, professors, artists, and others who won't work according to the formula. Nevertheless, the charmed circle is unpleasantly suggestive of a squirrel cage and its activities suitable rather to the brain of a squirrel than to that of man.

What is the alternative? It is conceivable that under another system of ideals and education men might prefer to utilize at least part of the leisure which the machine has won for them in some form of self-activity which would not greatly affect economic production or profits. We might, for example, hold up what men are rather than what they buy as a standard of worth. On this theory the greatest satisfactions of life, as well as the best balanced personalities, come from the acquisition and exercise of skills and activities of various sorts not necessarily of economic significance. The consumption of blue sky, sunshine, and sylvan solitude, or the amateur dabbling in the fine arts is of this nature. Merely as a method of killing time and consuming energies it may be no more absorbing than the frantic game of keeping up with the Joneses. The justification for this substitute, therefore, must be based on other grounds.

The value of leisure-time activities, play, and recreation is usually conceded to lie in the nervous release which they afford from the customary and coercive activities which the social order imposes upon us. To the extent, therefore, that the pursuits of our leisure time tend to become organized under conventional patterns determined by competitive consumption they lose their unique and primary value as recreation and so become merely another department of activity devoted to the achievement of prestige or status. Is it true that at present a great many leisure-time activities, dictated as they are by the dominant economic motive of the age, partake of this nature? Says Joad: "If the business man plays golf, it is, as he will tell you, to keep himself fit for business; if he takes a holiday he is submitting to boredom for the same reason." Is it true that an increasing number of people find themselves coerced by such considerations into a meaningless round of "recreational," leisure activities, which they heroically endure but which are devoid of capacity to minister to release of nervous tensions and to the development of personality which constitute the true purposes of recreation? Explosive and orgiastic "parties" are the pathological substitutes for the leisure pursuits which are the normal release of the tensions resulting from the job. Orgies have almost become a social obligation. As one girl put it, "Without cocktails the pleasures of life would be insupportable." While on a visit to Coney Island Maxim Gorky remarked: "What an unhappy people it must be that turns for happiness here." What shall we, in fact, say of a civilization which has so encumbered life that one of every twenty of us is destined actually to be committed to a hospital for mental diseases? How shall we appraise a prosperity which insures that one out of every ten of us will suffer such mental impairment as to make us eligible for psychopathic institutions?

The indictment of current leisure-time activities, then, rests not upon the mere fact that they are different from what they used to be or that they tend to be increasingly commercial. Nor should our criticism rest upon the *a priori* generalizations of artists and aesthetes regarding "higher" and "lower" forms of activity. The charge is that leisure or recreation of a certain type is neither leisure nor recreation in any basic biological or psychological sense. Slavish pleasures and mechanical leisure are contradictions in terms. That the shorter working day necessarily means more leisure of a desired or desirable kind is a *non sequitur* which is almost universal but is palpably false. All it necessarily means is more time for other pursuits, or for simple boredom. Boredom is receiving increasing attention as a factor in mental disease. As Edman has said, "Leisure is an affair of mood and atmosphere rather than simply of the clock. It is not a chronological occurrence but a spiritual state. It is unhurried pleasurable living among one's native enthusiasms."

RECREATION IN MIDDLETOWN*

Whatever may be affirmed or denied as to the economic basis of all human societies, Middletown clearly operates on the assumption that the roots of its living lie in the acquisition of money. The churches formally deny this, papers before its women's clubs and even occasional "inspirational" speakers before Rotary stress the primacy of the "higher things" of life, and one of the last things Middletown's formal training of the young stresses is how to "make money." But everywhere one runs upon the culture's commitment, implicit and explicit, to the necessity for and goodness of hard work in the acquisition of property. Not only do the leaders who "run the town" run it to "maintain prosperity" and "to attract new industries," but at many points, less formal than the operations of the business control group, one encounters this dominant commitment to the basic assumption of the primacy of economic interests, with all life built upon hard work for a livelihood, and with "success" in work—measured in dollars earned—as the goal and as the validation of the social utility of the individual's work. One hears the mayor declaim at a public dinner in the spring of 1929, "We have pride in our homes and elation in our schools, but the pulse of our city's life is in our industries." One reads in a business-class editorial that "While marrying for money alone

* From *Middletown in Transition* by Robert S. Lynd and Helen Merrell Lynd, copyright, 1937, by Harcourt, Brace and Company, Inc. Pp. 242–245, 252, 254, 256–257, 264–265, 265–267, 269–271, 273–277, 280–283.

is not advisable, there is probably nothing more important to domestic happiness in the world." And one hears in conversation the simple acceptance of his city by a workingman on the ground that "Of course we like [Middletown]; it's where we get our living."

The fabric of speech touching every aspect of activity sets forth the same philosophy of scarcity, of the need for hard work, of the value of success, and of money as the measure of success: The "good provider" is the "successful" family man; "It *pays* to send children to college"; "The church has made America prosperous. . . . Godliness is profitable even from a business standpoint"; "Jobs are the main issue. . . . There is but one convincing argument for the average voter—one which appeals to his pocketbook"; "It is desirable to *spend* leisure *profitably.*" Thus, not only does the community's activity center in getting a living, but the very symbols of group speech swing around economic values. The culture is repeating insistently that work is an inherently honorable thing by which other activities are measured; that no amount of labor is sufficient to wrest adequate sustenance from a niggardly environment; that group welfare is measured in terms of money prosperity; and that too much leisure for "the common man" is to be feared as deleterious to his character and retarding to the welfare of the whole group.

One of Middletown's most central cultural concepts, more deeply rooted historically even than such things as "Democracy" and "Christianity," is "Scarcity." It still conceives the central conflict and the grand adventure of its culture as that with man's oldest enemy: Scarcity. It has carried over intact the pre-Industrial Revolution emotional sanctions for the necessity for continuous hard work, the danger of too much leisure, and the essential moral goodness of individual striving to "get ahead" as the best way of doing one's personal bit toward the welfare of the group. It is characteristic that one feels at home in Middletown in reading a writer like Malthus. One might almost be listening to a speaker in a Middletown civic club when one reads in Chapter V of the *Essay on the Principle of Population* (1st ed., 1798): "Suppose that by a subscription of the rich, the eighteen pence a day which men earn now, was made up to five shillings. . . . [This] would make every man fancy himself comparatively rich, and able to indulge himself in many hours or days of leisure. This would give a strong and immediate check to productive industry; and in a short time, not only the nation would be poorer, but the lower classes themselves would be much more distressed than when they received only eighteen pence a day."

Even within such an economically dominated scheme of things, however, one must distinguish at the outset the functional significance of leisure to the business class and to the working class. It is not irrelevant or by accident that businessmen in this culture are wont to speak of the "business game," and it is also not by accident that Middletown's machine operators and laborers do *not* talk of the "factory game." Business-class status in Middletown comes from the amount of money one makes, which in turn comes from the job one holds. The amount of money a businessman may make is theoretically unlimited at its upper end, and actually tends to reach in good times for a substantial number of businessmen into a local economic stratosphere which, though, for most of them, modest in terms of the "big" business world, is none the less remotely beyond the cruising range of Middletown's working-class men. Work, in this business-class universe, offers to the fortunate when business is zooming something of the element of exhilaration and adventure associated in our physically unprecarious culture with play activity: one's winnings depend upon one's drive, ingenuity, thrift, and skill, plus a substantial sporting element of luck. It is conceivable that the lack of ingenuity exhibited by these men as regards their leisure is not unrelated to the fact that their ingenuity is so largely and absorbingly—at least in the case of the pace-setting leaders—focused elsewhere. On the other hand, the wives of the business class, gaining nowadays relatively little status from the arts of the housewife, throw themselves into leisure and have become the leisure-innovators of the culture. In this business-class world in which the job itself is so important to status and invites an endlessly "repaying" expenditure of energy, leisure among men is secondary to work: men work not to get leisure but to get money, to "get ahead," to "get up in the world." The resulting spectacle—of some of the ablest members of society, the men best educated, best "off" financially, and conceivably best able to live rich, many-sided lives, spending themselves unremittingly in work, denying themselves leisure and bending fine energies to the endless acquisition of the *means* of living a life they so often take insufficient leisure to live—is one factor leading certain contemporary psychiatrists to remark on the masochistic tendencies in our culture. If the leisure of such men tends to be used instrumentally to further their primary business of getting ahead, it also becomes easy under the driving pressure of the "business game" for the business-class wife to make the leisure of the family contribute to her husband's business activity.

Facing this business-class world is that of the six to seven in ten of the city's population who compose the working class. . . . Nominally their economic ceiling is as high as that of the business class, but Middletown's workers are apparently coming to believe in slowly increasing numbers that, as one of them expressed it, "That's just another one of the fairy tales the Chamber of Commerce feeds you." Status in the workingman's world, where skill is yielding to the machine and "getting ahead" is increasingly beyond the workers' reach, is not often derivable from the kind of job one does, or, with the blurring of the line between "skill" and "nonskill," from the difference between what one earns and what other workers earn. You have a job—if you're lucky—and you work. If you are trying to send your children to college you may be working for that; . . . So you work. Someday you're going to die. Meanwhile, leisure assumes a simple, direct, and important place in your scheme of things: *it's* when you *live,* and you get all of it you can—here, now, and all the time.

Only by understanding this different focus upon leisure of the lives of those living north and south of the tracks can one appreciate the tenacity with which the workingman clings to his automobile. If the automobile is by now a habit with the business class, a comfortable, convenient, pleasant addition to the paraphernalia of living, it represents far more than this to the working class; for to the latter it gives the status which his job increasingly denies, and, more than any other possession or facility to which he has access, it symbolizes living, having a good time, the thing that keeps you working. And again, only by understanding how these two groups weigh the importance of work and leisure can one understand the exasperation of the businessman over the workingman's frequent preference for his car rather than for the slow, painful process of saving for the future.

In all that follows, therefore, it must be borne in mind that statements regarding "Middletown's leisure" are peculiarly open to error in that leisure tends to symbolize at certain vital points different things to the man who has a business and to the man who operates a machine. . . .

HOW MIDDLETOWN READS

Reading played a relatively larger part among Middletown's informal, unorganized leisure activities during the depression than before. The public library circulation figures show in general that Middletown reads more books in bad times and fewer in good times. Circulation failed even to keep up with population growth in the busy years from 1925 to 1929, increasing by only 15 per cent during these four years while the population was growing by 25 per cent. With the depression, circulation jumped by 20 per cent above the 1929 total in the first year, 1930; 1931 surpassed 1930 by 24 per cent; 1932 rose 26 per cent above 1931; and the peak year, 1933, was 11 per cent above 1932. Combined, these gains show a total rise of 108 per cent between 1929 and the peak year of circulation, 1933, while the city's population rose by only 5 per cent to its peak in 1931–32, and in 1933 fell off to only 3 per cent above 1929. Stated in terms of per-capita circulation, the average number of books borrowed annually from the public library by each person of all ages within the city fell from 6.5 in 1925 to 6.0 in 1929, rose to 7.0 in 1930, to 8.5 in 1931, to 10.7 in 1932, and to 12.2, or more than double the 1929 average figure, in 1933. . . .

Shifts in the kinds of adult nonfiction reading may be of special significance as a reflection of new interests, more time for old interests, and the temporary spurring forward of effort to understand the perplexing changes in Middletown's overturned world. The outstanding fact observable from an analysis of the circulation of different kinds of nonfiction in a sample month for the years 1925–35 is that all types of books rose together to peaks in 1932 or 1933 and all fell off after 1933. The increases in Sociology (including Economics and Government), Science, Travel, and Biography are most striking, while History registered the least spectacular gain. . . .

Clearly, Middletown's library [filled] a larger place in the city's life during the depression, as an agency serving the people's leisure, providing morale-building interests, vital information, and, if we are to believe a local editorial, providing an indispensable check to local radical tendencies. In May, 1933, when the fear of radicalism was at its height, this editorial commented on the closing of the public library in a neighboring city for reasons of economy, and added: "It cannot be doubted that the public libraries in Middletown have proved a safety valve for the insurgent spirits of thousands in Middletown. . . . The last public institution ever to be closed, except those which supply food and warmth and shelter to the needy, should be the public library." . . .

RADIO AND AUTOMOBILES

The presence in Middletown of [a] local broadcasting station with membership in a national chain operates in two directions. Like the movies and the national press services in the local newspapers, it carries people away from localism and gives them direct access to the more popular stereotypes in the national life. It is this space-binding emphasis that probably helps to account for such new elements in Middletown today as the popularity of a highly sophisticated syndicated press column like Walter Winchell's "On Broadway," with its heavily localized New York lingo and subject matter. In the other direction, the local station operates to bind together an increasingly large and diversified city. A small city station has an especially heavy and direct financial stake in featuring local matters that will attract and hold local listeners against the pull of other stations. The station accordingly, early in its career, seized upon the local enthusiasm for basketball. The games of the high-school "Bearcats" are broadcast, with a heavy group of local commercial bidders for the advertising involved in sponsoring the programs, and this has helped very materially to build up the following of the station. Commencing in June, 1935, the station utilized the large auditorium of the Masonic Temple for the first local amateur program; the program was sponsored by the X family's department store and brought together within the auditorium the employees of the store and of their factory, while a host of friends listened in at home. The significance for the social cohesion of the city of this focusing of otherwise highly scattered citizens upon an evening of hilarious in-group enjoyment is potentially very great. In addition to such large programs, the station runs a steady stream of smaller local programs: a series of talks by professors at the local college, and talks by local ministers, clubwomen, and businessmen. These home-town programs tend to augment the "we" sense among all elements of a no longer small-town community.

If the word "auto" was writ large across Middletown's life in 1925, this was even more apparent in 1935, despite six years of depression. . . . No formal effort has been made by the relief authorities to discourage car ownership and operation, and, . . . people on relief who own cars have been encouraged to use them in various ways to pick up small earnings. Even at the time of the labor-union fervor under N.R.A., local organizers tell one disgustedly, many Middletown workers were more interested in figuring out how to get a couple of gallons of gas for the car than they were in labor's effort to organize. While some workers lost their cars in the depression, the local sentiment, as heard over and over again, is that "People give up everything in the world but their car." According to a local banker, "The depression hasn't changed materially the value Middletown people set on home ownership, but *that's* not their primary desire, as the automobile always comes first." A local paper estimated in June, 1935, that "10,000 persons leave Middletown for other towns and resorts every fine Sunday." . . .

Car ownership in Middletown was one of the most depression-proof elements of the city's life in the years following 1929—far less vulnerable, apparently, than marriages, divorces, new babies, clothing, jewelry, and most other measurable things both large and small. . . . The passenger-car registrations in Middletown's entire county not only registered scarcely any loss in the early years of the depression but, both in numbers and in ratio to population, stood in each of the years 1932–35 above the 1929 level. Along with this tough resistance of Middletown's habit of car owning to the depression undertow, went a drop of only 4 per cent in the dollar volume of gasoline sales in Middletown between 1929 and 1933, suggesting little curtailment in mileage of cars. . . .

"BRIDGE" AND AMERICAN CULTURE

While dancing is a popular and fairly constant recreational activity the year round for the young, bridge is adult business-class Middletown's way *par excellence* of "putting in an evening" with friends. On every hand one encountered statements that its vogue had increased notably since 1925 and that there is today considerably more playing for money. The game is now an obligatory social skill among the business class. It has increased markedly among high-school children, and has even reached down through the high school to children in the sixth grade. Leaders of local girls' work, such as the Girl Reserves, complain today of bridge as a definite hindrance to interesting girls in other activities. Bridge was very little played among the working class in 1925, but partly through the contagion of the younger group inoculated in high school, it is reported to be growing in popularity south of the tracks, spreading there first through the women's groups and then more slowly to a more resistant group of men, who prefer their pinochle and poker.

No one has analyzed the reason for the vogue of bridge in American life. It is conceivable that it never would have been anything but the sport of an esoteric few, had its growth depended entirely on the male world. Its development, however, has been primarily in the hands of women. It is the supreme hostess technique, supplying the best inexpensive guarantee our culture has discovered against a "dull evening" when friends "drop in." Social talking presents far more risks to a hostess, as it is a much more personal type of relationship liable to run on the rocks of monotony, vacuousness, gossip, or outright antagonisms. Middletown's business class shies off talk of a continuous sort addressed to a single subject or problem. It has in its genteel tradition, fostered by its women in their study clubs, certain vague canons as to "worth-while" things to discuss, and these also involve uneasy inhibitions as regards an evening of gossip and talking personalities. There is no tradition of facile talk for its own sake, for cleverness in such things tends to be confusing, and therefore annoying. "Worth-while" talk is accordingly "serious" talk, and most people have but a spotty fund of knowledge with which to carry on a prolonged conversation without becoming "heavy" or disputatious. All of this tends to make the effort to carry on an evening of talk overstrenuous and likely to be judged in the end as "not having got anywhere." Into this problematic situation has come bridge, the hostess' best friend and the universal social solvent: safe, orthodox, and fun. Men and women who are not interesting talkers can still be good bridge players. Most people's lives involve but a meager amount of sheer fun; they are busy and preoccupied and perplexed as to what to do to make living more fun. And most people, particularly men, in an urban culture crave more human contacts out of business hours with people they like in an atmosphere that liberates spontaneity. Neither the movies nor reading supply this sense of social participation. What bridge has done is to institutionalize fun-in-small-social-groups, at the same time that it is tending to drain serious talk from Middletown's leisure. It is an unparalleled device for an urban world that wants to avoid issues, to keep things impersonal, to enjoy people without laying oneself open or committing oneself to them, and to have fun in the process.

For Middletown's non-bridge-playing population there are pinochle, pedro, knock-rummy, and poker in the lodges and South Side homes, and, exclusively for the males, gambling in the poolrooms and cigar stores. . . . This situation is roughly familiar to every man in town, though the women are wont to think of "the awful places down on the Court House square and on South Walnut Street" as, like prostitution, just one of the unfortunate things that happen and that no one can do anything about. The location of the gambling houses has been the same for many years and their patronage continued strong throughout the depression. Local gambling is not usually a matter of big stakes and noisy scandals but, rather, one of the steady commercialized forms of leisure offered to the workingman of small income—a place to meet the boys, have a good time, and maybe pick up a little something on the side. When a cleanup drive occurred early in 1930, a local editor protested against the mayor's "interference with card playing in cigar stores for checks 'good on the house.' They should not be banned any more than women's bridge games. They play an important part in the social life of this factory city."

ALCOHOL IN MIDDLETOWN

No description of the informal means of spending leisure since 1925 would be in focus without consideration of the larger place occupied by drinking. . . . On every hand, the testimony in 1935 was that "There is much more drinking here now than ten years ago." To which one reliable person, in close touch with the high-school generation for the past fifteen years, added: "And there is much more 'passing out' in public now. Some people seem to regard it as the thing to do." . . .

In April, 1933, the afternoon paper ran a story about the city's "speaks" which suggests the place they occupied in the leisure life of the city:

> The very conditions [the strength of the W.C.T.U., Anti-Saloon League, and the churches] that made prohibition enforcement more vigorous in [this state] than perhaps in any other state, have molded local drinking houses into a veritable institution. Under such conditions, any great investment in a drinking establishment was not a thing to be seriously considered. To survive, those who sold drinks by the glass perforce had to avoid display of any kind. . . . These difficulties made [Middletown's] speakeasies what they are today—private homes to all appearances. . . . Virtually all of Middletown's liquor sellers live in unpretentious homes in the poorer sections of the city. . . . Most of these houses have no more than three rooms in which drinks are served. [Everybody is introduced by the host to everyone else present, the story went on to recount, with the result that] the shell of eternal suspicion which surrounds most persons in their business relations sloughs away when they enter the portals of the liquor houses. The atmosphere is one of genuine friendliness. . . . Except for the difference in the size of the houses, one Middletown drinking place can scarcely be distinguished from another. All have a front room furnished with overstuffed furniture. Conversation is sprightly, but somewhat subdued. Close harmony is banned unless the house is in a very isolated location. Each place has a regular clientele. Everyone knows everyone else. And the houses move to a new location every few weeks as a precaution.

The speakeasies, like their now legal successors in Middletown, the "taverns," performed a dual function: as a physical place of meeting new people, and, psychologically, as an environment conducive to spontaneous human association. The first of these is a relatively more acute need for the working class, who are more sparsely served than the business class in Middletown with institutions facilitating the meeting with and coming to know new people. It is easy for one with a business-class point of view to fail to realize the deterrents to human association, and the resulting isolation, loneliness, and even in some cases the mutual suspicion, that not infrequently characterize the lives of these working-class people. These deterrents are both physical and psychological, including shabby household furniture, too little money, no place to go and no money to go with, newness in a neighborhood, relatively fewer telephones than the business class for "telephone visiting," and the presence of family problems one does not want one's sharp-eyed, gossiping neighbors to know about. The relatively high residential mobility of the working class . . . aggravates this greater tendency of the working class to become socially isolated. One has only to compare the way a working-class population leaves its church services in South Side churches, lingering to talk in the aisles and on the steps, and the brisk dignity with which the business class leave their Presbyterian Church, with their heads full of plans for the afternoon, to sense some of this differential need for places and occasions of social meeting.

On the psychological side, most urban people, particularly the less aggressive personalities, need the facilitation of spontaneity in social intercourse which an institutionalized agency of informality provides. The speakeasy and tavern, like bridge playing for the business class, help to institutionalize spontaneity. Here one sees a cityful of people, with little chance in their workaday lives to be directly personal in a spontaneous sense, finding out a way in their leisure to circumvent the strait-jacket set for them by their culture. The speakeasy and tavern mean being with people in a mood where one takes people on one's own terms and they take one in the same spirit; one can sit silent, or one can talk with a degree of animation and intensity that would make one feel silly and self-conscious in the more constrained environment of one's own parlor with one's neighbors about. In these informal places of conviviality one can be as spontaneous or silly as one pleases without needing to feel self-conscious about it. And an institution that can do this for people loaded with the sober constraints of convention, monotony, and fatigue is an institution for which people are apt to be willing to vote and to fight.

Men ordinarily turn to liquor in such a culture, not to get drunk but in order to ease themselves of enough of these conflicting outside pressures-to-conform to enable them to live for a few hours in a freer mood in which they are less fundamentally alone and constrained. . . .

THE PERSISTENCE OF CLUB LIFE

As one passes from these unorganized ways of spending leisure—gardening in one's back yard, going to the movies, listening to the radio, driving about in one's car, or reading, playing bridge, or drinking—nothing about the organized life of Middletown at play strikes the returning investigator more forcibly than the hardy persistence of the city's club life. Asked about any changes in local club life, a veteran Middletown woman exclaimed, "Goodness! We have more than ever."

In the humbler homes of the business class and all through the working class the same types of women's clubs, many of them the same clubs with the same names, thrive today as in 1925. The Jolly Club members still meet in one another's homes to play bunco for prizes of pillow covers and ash trays, while the notes in the "Society" columns of the press describing the meetings of the Silver Cloud Club, the All Star Pedro Club, the Friendship Club, the Why Not Club, the Sans Souci, the Kill Kare Club, the Moonlight Savings Club, and their scores of sister organizations suggest that this department of life, at least, has gone on its neighborly way despite the depression.

Uptown, their business-class sisters still go to the Federated Club of Clubs in its various departments. Here one still witnesses the most significant indigenous adult literary and artistic strain of the city in the meetings of the Conversation Club (organized in 1894), the Mary-Martha, the Entre Nous, the Martha Washington, the Philomathean, the Riverside Culture, the Round Table, and the other women's "study" clubs.

In 1925 a slow shift was noted as taking place among these veteran study agencies, from the almost exclusive preoccupation with "literature" as the heart of things worth studying toward more active interest in the life of Middletown. This trend, then apparent in comparison with the 1890's, has developed little further in the ten years since 1925. There is somewhat more attention paid to general world events; one "improves one's mind" on a fare somewhat less exclusively literary and artistic; but both current national issues and notably Middletown's own life are but thinly represented in the programs. With the exception of a series of four talks in one club in the winter of 1934–35 on various aspects of the New Deal by local male guest speakers from the college and high school, and an occasional paper in other clubs on such a topic as the Reforestation Camps or "Democracy under Strain," the depression has not appeared in the printed program announcements. Program papers and discussions fall chiefly into the following six classes: artistic and literary; historical; international affairs; travel and the ways of foreign countries; book reviews of novels, biographies, and outstanding recent nonfiction; and a wide miscellaneous group ranging from the Bible to astronomy, the "new Negro," and problems of the home. On the whole, the topics of these last six years exhibit somewhat less wrestling with recondite historical topics, less emphasis upon local patriotic subjects (including the poets, painters, scenery, and similar aspects of Middletown's state), less emphasis upon the Bible, and somewhat more emphasis upon international affairs and upon current books of the serious-popular type.

Middletown feels that the 1925 study painted, as one clubwoman expressed it, "a little too hard a picture of [Middletown's] intellectuals." The intelligent daughter of an educated and decidedly superior woman, in commenting on this local feeling, said:

> "I think the picture is a little hard. The thing is that these women here have to be self-sufficient, with not much outside stimulus, so there is little talking back and forth about what they read and think. My mother belongs to a little group who are reading together such things as Hart Crane, E. E. Cummings, Gertrude Stein, and Vincent Sheean. They steer clear of most of the poets tinged with economic radicalism, but are well read on the symbolists. Yet I don't think they derive a great amount of personal satisfaction from their reading."

This last sentence may touch the core of the situation. As the business-class woman's role in the family has come to include less of the earlier unremitting dawn-to-dark toil, she had been forced, with less housework and fewer children to bear and rear, to find a socially and personally self-justifying role. The traditional attribution by this culture of finer sensibilities to women has prompted her to act as though she had wide and strong interests in the "finer things of life." This role assumption on her part has been accepted by the preoccupied males as giving some semblance of body to certain highly prized symbols of the culture such as "progress" and "culture" (in the artistic sense). The heavy concentration of "culture" in the refined, artistic sense in the female side of the community is the result. Actually, no population reared under our system of high-school education, including a wide diversity of temperaments and abilities, and aggregated into groups on a social rather than an interest basis, can have anything other than an uneven interest in being proficient in this—to Middletown in its daily concerns—largely symbolic world of "the finer things of life." It is no reflection on the business-class women of Middletown, thus herded into a stereotyped role for their sex, that their "study" clubs with their programs of reading "good" books and discussing "broadening" topics are earnestly pursued rather than reflecting the spontaneity of acute personal interests; and that the programs are scattered and casual rather than characterized by concentration of enthusiasm. The world of refined knowledge is today far too wide to be attacked successfully without the aid of the selective factor of interest in specific problems. It is unlikely that even half of the women in any of the city's study clubs read the foreign Associated Press dispatches in the local press with any consistency, care, or real interest. When such a club puts on a series of programs on "international affairs," it becomes for most of the members something of an intellectual *tour de force*. The following program of one study club for the winter of 1934–35 is a natural outgrowth of this sort of effort to reach for the cultural moon. Each member was assigned a country (other than the United States) and in successive meetings each reported for her country on the following: location and boundaries, legends, climate and seasons, population and language, music and sports, housing, war heroes, Christmas observance, economic prosperity, manners and customs, form of government, education, holidays and feasts, art and literature, exports and imports, its greatest social problem, religion.

ALCOHOL AND COMPLEX SOCIETY *

For the individual, alcohol can reduce tension, guilt, anxiety and frustration. For the individual, alcohol can also reduce operational efficiency below the minimum necessary for social existence, or even for existence at all. In relation to the total society, alcohol can make possible association and interpersonal activity which may ordinarily be barred; it can permit variations in ideas and activities also, although this is a minor point; and it can allow an escape valve for socially frustrated individuals, an escape which can be relatively safe. Alcohol can also break down individual participation in associations, thus weakening them. It can impair the exactitude and rhythm of behavior patterns and socially valuable ideas, and it can impair foresight and the results of previous foresight.

We may thus liken alcohol to other discoveries or inventions of dynamic character, such as the wheel, electricity, techniques of organization, political and scientific concepts, dynamite, gases, and so on. It is a human artifact of great power. How it is used or misused is, of course, a very different matter. . . .

From [the] extraordinary specialization [of modern America] has sprung the greatest amount and variety of food, shelter and clothing the world has ever experienced. There is protection against sickness, there are facilities for recreation and many other values which go beyond anything even imagined by the sages of primitive groups. There are also some other results of or concomitants to this process which have not been an unmixed blessing. . . .

Money is a very important concomitant of increased specialization; it is needed because of the great difference between the specialists and because all the specialists need the goods and services of the others. This

* Bacon, Selden D., "Alcohol and Complex Society," in *Alcohol, Science and Society* (New Haven: *Quarterly Journal of Studies on Alcohol*, 1945), pp. 179, 181, 183–194.

problem is *immediately,* but only *immediately,* settled by two steps: one, the translation of every object and service into terms of a common denominator, an invention in the realm of ideas; two, a material invention, a representation of that symbolic denominator by tangible objects. In other words, running an elevator, preparing a person to meet death, growing corn, telling jokes, and organizing public health measures, must all have a common denominator, and that denominator must be represented by a tangible and transferable and carefully trade-marked object. The immediate answer is money, but although this is a brilliant adjustment, it carries problems in its wake—problems unknown to less specialized societies and also problems known of old but enhanced and complicated because of money.

One use made of money is the denial of intergroup dependence. People refuse to admit they are dependent on other groups and individuals and nature. The only thing they depend on is money. Rather than organize their lives and their efforts to satisfy their needs around activities and interpersonal relationships, many individuals attempt to organize their lives around an adjustment between themselves and money.

Lest anyone underestimate what I mean by individuals organizing their lives around money, let me illustrate. As basic needs of man I first suggested food, shelter, and clothing; I take it for granted that you realize that we Americans, about 95 per cent of us at least, meet these needs through money—not only city apartment dwellers, but farmers and cattlemen and fishermen. They buy equipment and pay taxes and get clothes and medical service and paint and nails and seed and education for their children, and food and shelter, and much else, with money.

But there are other needs. Affection, friendship and prestige, pleasant inter-personal relations. We get these primarily through family and friendship groups. In complex society, money plays a tremendous role in maintaining position in such groups. Its function in this role is largely a limiting, negative force rather than a determining, positive force. That is, even enormous amounts of money cannot guarantee entrance into groups, but just small decreases can force one out. Friendship and clique membership is a two-way affair. If the Joneses serve food to you at their house, you have to reciprocate. If the Joneses' daughter takes your daughter to the movies or buys her an ice cream cone, your daughter has to reciprocate. If your friends and neighbors keep their places in good order, which requires money, you have to do likewise. Amongst your friends you cannot be the only one who does not have a car, send the children to a private school, invite the others to a meal, have a clean shirt every morning, or participate in the ways of the clique whatever they may be. Studies made of the unemployed during the depression show that the threat to or actual loss of social position was one of the most painful blows suffered. It was felt by the husband, the wife, and the children. They lost their friends.

Still another very important value to the individual is that of maintaining some degree of control over his own existence and of the situation immediately pressing him. That money has influenced the satisfaction of this desire is obvious. But to what degree does it operate? The answer is that it exerts a controlling interest. An enormous number of persons in our commercial, industrial and personal-service life can exert control of their own lives only through a weekly or daily wage. Whether or not they will receive that wage is dependent upon forces beyond their understanding and control. Effort and ability are important, but are not controlling. For the member of the less specialized society, this situation does not exist. Food and shelter and respect of others are subject, of course, to outside, uncontrollable factors (weather, fire, insects, personal and group enemies, disappearance or diminution of species of food animals and fish, and the like), but there is no danger of having perfectly satisfactory environmental conditions plus willingness and ability to work accompanied by the inability to get food, shelter, and protection. Our millions of unemployed were quite unable to live and support families by farming, hunting or fishing. Nor could the millions whose standards were lowered by receiving $20 a week rather than $30 make up the difference by return to such direct ways of existence. Their way of directing their lives is by acquiring wages. They get the wages from persons over whom they have little control, with whom they have little in common. Furthermore, the wage payers are often quite uncertain as to how much money will come in from which they can pay wages. The complexities of the flow of money need only to be recognized by us as existing. The relevant point now is that in the specialized world the worker's control of his life is, to a great extent, controlled by money, and he cannot control money. Moreover, he faces this problem every week, every day. It can control his whole life continuously. He cannot plan ahead without it, and he cannot be assured of what he will have.

This utilization of money in the specialized society has two important aspects for our consideration. The first is that different groups of persons who are heavily dependent on each other are enabled to avoid contact and to avoid mutual understanding and cooperation. To put it conversely, it allows mutually dependent groups to fight each other bitterly in a completely impersonal way. To dramatize this possibility let us note how money can allow persons to hold utterly incompatible ideas. The example is purposefully extreme. If one man should go to another man's house, a member of the group but a stranger and an inoffensive one to him, and should take away his food, his furnishings, ruin his friendships, force his children to stop school, prevent his family from having medical care and recreation, we would violently disapprove, no matter how the story was told. If this one man, by manipulating prices, credit and wages, achieves the same result on many other men, strangers and inoffensive to him, but makes money for himself and some others, then, depending on how the story was told, we might feel he was a very able person. This incompatibility of ideas is one of the great questions to be solved in American life today. Note that the interposition of the idea of money between the two parties makes an extraordinary difference. This magic symbol is able to relieve the guilt, is able to take away the viciousness and aggressiveness which otherwise would be observed. Many writers have pointed this out in contemporary literature: When the farmer is pushed off his land, when the city tenant is evicted, when the borrower of small loans is forced to pay three to four times the amount he received, it always appears that no one is being aggressive or unpleasant; it is just fate, the magical turn of the financial wheel. Nor can the aggrieved party find out who hurt him. The sheriff points to the finance company, the finance company to the bank, the bank to financial holding companies, the latter to stockholders, and all of them are terribly sorry if they happen to hear about it.

This brings us to the second point, which is that money is an artificial, that is, a humanly invented idea, represented by paper and metal objects. Like all powerful and brilliant ideas or inventions—dynamite, political parties, electricity, unions, the family—it is very, very useful, and very, very dangerous. Instead of always insuring that specialized effort will be possible and that all the specialists will get all the specialized goods and services, it sometimes happens that it has very different results. It gets completely out of control. A lot of people can have no money at all and no prospect of getting any. A much larger number suddenly may have a great deal less than usual. And nobody knows what to do about it, although many are certain that the other fellow's ideas are crazy.

INDIVIDUALISM

[Another] concomitant of this process of specialization is individualism. To describe this process we must consider another facet of complexity, namely, mobility. The physical possibility of mobility was enormously increased by the technological revolution of the last 150 years. The need for such mobility rose from the specialization process and its concomitants.

Individualism refers, first, to the increased value of each individual to other individuals. Association is always of great value to every human being, and so other persons are always valuable, but in a world of specialists this value is extended and enhanced. For example, when bakeries first emerged in the colonies, the specialist baker was hardly an indispensable person. If one did not have cash or did not like shop-made products, one made one's own bread at home. This was possible because one had flour and other ingredients sufficient for the purpose at hand, one had utensils, basic equipment, oven space, a kitchen; one had the skill, the time, and the feeling that it was right, proper, and natural to bake one's own bread. Specialization has its values, however, and bakeries became integrated into the way of life. . . .

If you have no money, you get no bread. If you do not like the baker, you can only go to another baker. You may not know the baker personally, but he is very important to you. So are the telephone linesman, the personnel at the sewage disposal plant, the shoemaker, the laundryman, the bus driver. This means that power adheres to individuals which was not present in the simpler society. If, in the more primitive group, John Jones decided to quit work, it was not just a matter of his starving to death; it did break up the pattern of life considerably, especially for John's family, but it did not directly and immediately threaten a large percentage of the group, and it was possible, although irritating, for someone else to take up the slack. John's work was as hard and as easy, as dignified and as undignified, as most other persons' work. Not many of us, however, could take on someone else's job today. Nowadays the Jack-of-all-trades is further characterized as being master of none. Furthermore, there are many jobs we would consider as below our respective dignities. More and more individuals have become clothed with a type of power unknown before. This aspect has a reverse side also. If the specialty becomes outmoded or if the specialty requires almost no skill or training at all, then the person seems to have less power than any individual in the more primitive group. For the most part, however, the individual's social power has been increased by specialization just as the individual's physical power has been increased by the automobile and the gun.

A second consideration on this score is that the individual specialists or participants in a particular specialty have worked hard to extend this automatic importance and power. The bakers, the doctors, the tool-and-dye workers, the teachers, the shoemakers, and so on have endeavored to enhance and to guarantee their positions. They have a private stake in this process.

Another aspect of individualism is the person's lessened need for close social participation. The rise of money and mobility has had a great deal to do with the emancipation of individuals from tight, all-encompassing social organizations. Not having to depend on the parents, on the priest, on the neighbors, as did the member of the more primitive society, the individual can withdraw from their control. He can look forward to making money, living in another place, having radically different ideas, doing what he wants without their meddling. For the member of the primitive society such attitudes or actions meant death. Without father, brothers, cousins, children, who would do business with you, who would back your side of an argument, who would protect you? The answer was clarion clear—"No one." That was why banishment was such a terrible sentence. It meant some form of death, not quite determined how, when, or where, but fairly soon and very sure. Today the young man leaves his home town "to make something of himself." He will adjust to strangers through money, through his drive and skill and luck in his specialty. He is "on his own," a great value in our society, although a death penalty among primitive groups. Not that he stays "on his own" very long. He joins groups, but more and more they tend to be specialized groups. Whereas the person in the simpler society worked, played, worshiped, gossiped, and, in general, lived with about the same group of persons, the individual in the modern complex society may belong to several groups with different personnel. The church group, the school group, the neighbors, the men at the shop, office or store, the three or four close friends, may form half a dozen groups with varying personnel. These, in turn, may have slightly, even greatly, different ideas of what is proper, permissible, interesting or desirable. Most important, the individual can shift from one group to another. This means that a wider range of behavior is open to him. The sanctioning power of any one group is, of course, potentially weakened by the varying norms of the others. What is of greater importance is the fact that these are specialized organizations and that a group having over-all societal interests does not command the individual's loyalty, as it could in a simple society. One result of this situation is the commonly observed fact of a single individual following incompatible moral codes. A man can show aggressiveness, slyness, laziness in his occupational morality which he would bitterly reject in his home circle. He can pray in one direction and vote in another. His life being somewhat compartmentalized, such relative variety of behavior is possible. This emancipation from a solid, unified, omnipresent group sanction has many assets for both individual and society. It also has many liabilities. There is a loss of security in personal relationships. A wide field is opened up for fraud. Many groups are exceedingly shortlived and competition between them is continuous, often bitter. A strong, widespread morality is more difficult to maintain. The greater freedom of action for the individual puts a heavy burden upon him; he has to face questions and problems that hardly exist in a simpler, more uniform, less specialized society. . . .

SOCIAL COMPLEXITY AND ALCOHOL

With these attributes of complex society described, we may consider the significance of social complexity for the part played by alcohol both in relation to society as a whole and in relation to the life of the individual. . . .

[One] function of alcohol has been its use in social jollification. Although the distinction between the needs of the society as separate from those of the individual is occasionally difficult to perceive, in this instance a fairly clear discrimination can be made. The maintenance of order and of unity within the society is imperative for the survival of the society. The feeling that the individuals are a "we-group" as opposed to "others," the feeling that it is pleasurable to be one of "us," the restatement of the fundamental mutuality of the members, these values are attained by meetings of pleasurable purpose. In any society there will be stresses and strains which tend to break the unity; certain individuals will be unsatisfied, will be more ambitious than achieving; certain groups will be antagonistic. Meetings in which such ambitions and frustrations and resentments are irrelevant, in which purely rewarding pursuits are at hand, will help restore or enhance the integrating principles.

As we have seen, one of the concomitants of complexity is stratification, another is ignorance of other subgroups, a third is the increased aggression allowed by the widespread utilization of money, a fourth is increased individualism. The need for integrating mechanisms in a more and more complex society is a phenomenon whose existence can hardly be challenged. The difficulty of effecting such mechanisms is apparent. One of the best ways, aside from great external danger, is through amusements. They present an activity or interest which can be neutral to conflicting interests and personalities; they can be stimulating, they can be rewarding, and they hold small threat of punishment.

Theoretically we would expect an increase of pleasure meetings in a complex, competitive, individualistic civilization, and in our society this theoretical expectancy is fully met. There has been a development of both commercialized and noncommercialized pleasure rituals which would seem extraordinary to the members of the simpler society. From organized spectacles which operate 8 to 16 hours a day every day to the informal tea, cocktail, and card-game gatherings, the members of our society are almost surfeited with recreational association. As would be expected, activities connected with occupational specialty are generally held taboo at these meetings. Specialization and specialists, however, have infiltrated this area of behavior as they have almost all others.

With this extension and elaboration of recreation, alcohol's part in jollification or in pleasure association has become enhanced. Note the role of alcohol in these situations. We have, on the one hand, a society whose individuals are often (1) more self-contained and independent, (2) more ignorant of each other's interests and activities, (3) more separate from each other, (4) more prone to aggressive and competitive relationships; on the other hand, there is a need for unsuspicious, pleasant, relatively effortless joint activity. How can one put these together? One way is to transfer the ordinary, diverse, specialized attentions of the individuals to one neutral object interesting to all—a spectacle, for example, or a chess game. The trouble with this adjustment is that it does not allow much interpersonal activity. Another way is to relax all the people. All of us here have undoubtedly experienced meetings intended to be recreational and found them stiff, uncertain, tense. Intermixture does not take place. Despite the need to spread interaction, individuals remain aloof, or little groups of previous acquaintance maintain their own safe little cliques. The organizers have to break down the hostilities, the indifference, the ignorance, and the suspicions. To do this they try to get the individuals to relax. Alcohol is a quick, easy, fairly sure means of accomplishing this end. It may have other, less desirable effects; at the moment, that is irrelevant.

The conclusion on this point, whether reached by deduction from principles or by observation of our own society, is that the stratification, individualism, intergroup ignorance, and internal competitive tradition, all engendered by the complexity of society, enhance the function of alcohol. Complexity results in a need for greater integrative functioning; relaxation of tension, uncertainty and suspicion is necessary for this function; alcohol has been found useful in its accomplishment.

In addition to the need of the society for greater integration, there is also the need of the individual to make contacts, both occupational and recreational. In a mobile, multistratified world, this is more difficult than in a stable, less-stratified world. In a specialized, competitive world, recreational devices for the individual seem more essential. Yet the factors just discussed make difficult the attainment of that easy, trustworthy, noncompetitive friendship situation which is requisite for interpersonal relaxation. The traveling salesman is an extreme example. His role is highly competitive and is lived in a world of strangers. Alcohol is obviously functional for achieving the relaxation of suspicion, of competitive tension, of the barriers usually present in our society between strangers.

In contrast, then, to the effect of a complex society on the medical, food, and religious-exaltation functions of alcohol is the effect of the complex society on alcohol's function of promoting recreational and other association. This function is definitely enhanced.

ALCOHOL AND TENSION

We now approach the more important, perhaps the fundamental function of alcohol for individuals. As you are all aware, alcohol is a depressant. Alcohol allows, through its depressing function, a relaxation of tension, of inhibition, of anxiety, of guilt. There is no need to define narrowly the meanings incorporated in these words. You have heard a good deal about them and are aware of the sort of behavior and attitude which is implied. I will consider, however, the areas of behavior and attitude which are most commonly colored with these emotional characteristics. The listing I shall present is only suggestive, grows out of reading, training, and observation; the order of appearance is quite arbitrary. Around what personal problems of adjustment do anxiety, tension, guilt, and the like, arise?

I would suggest the following: (1) the individual's opinion of himself; (2) gaining and holding the respect and the affections of others; (3) conflict with others, through self-assertion, through criticism, through out-and-out aggressions; (4) over-all security, as to ownership, prestige, personal safety, as they are tied up with money; (5) responsibilities accepted in the achievement of specific goals; (6) sexual matters.

This is a purely descriptive listing. It may seem to imply that these six are totally separate matters. They are not! The list is merely a convenient set of handles by which one can pick up and examine the package labeled "one human being." The handles alone are meaningless.

In a complex society these areas of behavior and attitude are more greatly challenged, are more difficult to live through or adjust to than they are in a simpler society. For a very simple example, take the matter of self-assertion or the exhibition of aggression. In a world of extraordinary dependence on others, aggression is very dangerous. To make an oversimplified analogy—an airplane engine in which the cylinders are at war with each other or with the spark plugs is a dead engine. You may want to tell your client, your parishioner, your landlord, or your boss, what you think of him. But it is very, very dangerous. So you refrain from doing it. You have been trained since infancy not to do it. We have all been trained not to lose control of our tempers, not to attack others, not to be too self-assertive. Does that mean that we do not feel aggressive? It does not. We just cover it up. Sometimes we can train ourselves so well that we do not even recognize that we are angry, but our emotions do not stop operating. In a complex, specialized, stratified society we are continually in situations where we are dependent on others and the others do not seem to care much about us. Elevator operators, waiters, salespeople, clients, partners, all of them have it in their power to frustrate us. By the very nature of the system they must frustrate us somewhat, since they serve 50 or 500 other people in addition to us, and we must take our turn; that is ineradicable in association. So we get angry. But we cover it up. The complexity of society increases the incidence of aggression-provoking situations. The complexity of society renders the expression of aggression ever more dangerous.

Consider the matter of prestige, of recognition from others. In a society in which there is great homogeneity of activity, where most people do about the same things in the same way, the range of prestige is smaller. Either you are a good or a mediocre or a bad workman. Furthermore, in a simple society the tangible marks of success, such as conspicuous consumption or ownership, are also limited in variety and quantity. But in a complex society the situation is dramatically different. There is an extraordinarily refined hierarchy of prestige. Much of the prestige goes with the position rather than with the individual's talent or exertion of effort or pleasing personality.

Furthermore, recognition and prestige depend more and more on obvious, often tangible, symbols. In the simple society, it is easy to tell who is an efficient, pleasant person. In the stratified, specialized society, it is not easy. People are more and more inclined to give recognition according to conspicuousness and wealth. There is not the time, there is not the knowledge, there is not the personal interaction on a variety of levels of experience, for people to judge.

Let me give an example of this that took place at football practice on the Yale field when I was a freshman; probably it occurred many years earlier and surely has been going on ever since. One of the players, utilizing the accepted technique of "talking it up," was always calling his roommate's name whenever the latter did anything that was even passably good. "Come on Johnson," "Attaboy Johnson," "Take him out, Johnson," and so on, and so on. The only purpose was to fix the name Johnson in the coach's mind. In any other situation he called his roommate Brad. The coaches were faced with about 140 persons from whom they would pick 25 for the first team. They very soon were aware of Johnson. Even though the coaches know of this system, it still works. It works in the army, it works in the factory, it works in getting into Who's Who. In a simpler society, it just will not work.

Yet, despite this weakness, the need to get good persons for specialized positions is pressing and in this impersonalized competitive society the goal of gaining prestige is enhanced. The result, of course, is increased apprehension, increased sensitivity, increased tension.

In a complex society where personal relationships are more and more specialized, impersonal and competitive, and where various specialties are not understood by others, recognition and respect and prestige are more intensely desired, are more difficult to attain, and are, perhaps, more suspect, than in simpler societies. This results in frustration, envy, aggression and anxiety which do not appear in such marked form from this source in simpler societies.

The increased complexity of our social existence has increased social responsibilities. As a simple example, consider General Eisenhower or the president of a large corporation. One of the outstanding characteristics of high position in any of our ways of life is an increase in responsibilities. For many hierarchies we may say that the taking on of higher office is matched by an increase in the anxieties a person carries. One of the earmarks of the executive is his ability to assume anxiety with understanding and with poise. The person in the lowest rank carries very little anxiety about the function of the organization. At 5 P.M. he quits work and forgets about it, although he still carries personal anxieties. The high-ranking man carries his anxiety concerning the whole organization all the time. The one has little or no prestige and little or no anxiety on this score; the other has much prestige and much anxiety.

The general over-all security represented by money in a complex society has already been dealt with. The increased anxiety from this source reflects through all of the significant emotional areas that were listed, in addition to possessing a ranking of its own. Although it weighs most obviously on the people in the lowest economic ranks or in marginal positions, it can be equally oppressive to people who, while not threatened with starvation, are threatened as to their social position and prestige.

Time forbids dealing with the other emotional areas. It is, or should be, sufficiently clear that interpersonal relationships and personal satisfactions are more difficult, are more anxiety-provoking, are more exhausting, in a complex society.

The advantages of a complex society are manifest. But there is a price to pay. That price is intangible, difficult to measure or define. It can be roughly labeled as emotional insecurity for the individual. Since alcohol can reduce the impact, can allow escape from the tensions, fears, sensitivities, feelings of frustration, which constitute this insecurity, its role will be more highly valued. . . .

DYSFUNCTIONAL ASPECTS

Now we come to the results of societal complexity on what might be called the socially and individually dysfunctional aspects of alcohol. The potentialities of alcoholic beverage consumption remain the same but are to be viewed in a different light. We could speak of dynamite in the same way; its properties do not change, but its effects on human beings can be of a tremendously constructive or tremendously destructive nature.

The complex society presents great rewards to individuals; two factors balance these rewards, are a sort of fixed charge: (1) break-down of any part is far more dangerous than in the simple society; (2) there must be a more exact fulfillment of function than was previously necessary on the part of every sub-group and every individual. To put this in a more general way: the need for imagination and perception, for control over responses, for timing and balance, is greatly increased by the complex culture; just to get things done is a more delicate task, and the penalty for not getting things done has far greater social implications than in the simpler society. Do not illustrate this in your minds by the sole picture of a person driving a car or tending a machine. One tendency of our material culture has been to dominate our thinking in just such a narrow way. Think rather of relations between groups of people, employer and employee, principal and agent, people of different social classes; think rather of the foresight necessary in a production schedule, in bringing up children, in establishing governmental procedures. These activities in a complex society demand greater sensitivity, greater efficiency in action, greater imagination and greater caution than in a simpler society. Alcohol lowers sensitivity, efficiency, and caution. It deteriorates balance and timing. Personal aggression and irresponsibility are far more dangerous in a complex society, and, as an adjustment to this, child-training in complex society lays heavy emphasis on self-control, indoctrinates inhibitions and repressions on aggression and irresponsibility; alcohol allows release of these inhibitions. Regularity of behavior is as essential in a complex society as in a complex machine. Alcohol can wreck regularity of behavior. I need not expand on this point. The conclusion is apparent. The need of the society for regularity, precision, individual responsibility, and integration through self-control and cooperation, is increased by complexity. The achievement of these values is directly threatened by alcohol in proportion to its depressant action.

A further societal complication is to be seen in the means of control. It has been pointed out that specialized and formal groups have become more powerful and have extended their functions while all-purpose and intimate groups have been weakened. If the drinking of alcohol and its effects were limited to the area of one of these specialized groups, sanctions could be efficient. Or if the society were simpler, more homogeneous, more dominated by some all-purpose, personally intimate and significant association, sanctions could be significant. The drinking of alcohol and its effects, however, infiltrate all manner of acts and associations and ideas. The attempt to exert sanctions over this wide, loosely organized area will be met with opposition, argument, and relatively unabashed violation. The sanctioning authority will not be recognized. The ideology behind the attempt will be challenged. Social classes, minority groups, religious groups, locality groups, and other categories will not have the identity of purpose, understanding and experience which would allow such action to proceed smoothly. The complexity of society is of manifest significance on this point. Furthermore, the question of control can itself create further disorganization in the society. This, of course, is quite irrelevant to the physical and psychological properties of alcohol.

In a society already impersonal, competitive, individualistic and stratified, the effect of excessive drinking on the individual is dramatic. You have heard, and presumably will hear, sufficient on this subject to make any treatment here quite superfluous. I would only draw attention to the fact that the complexity of the society, and the concomitants of that complexity as here described, exaggerate and speed the deterioration process in the maladjusted person.

CHAPTER XX

Hollywood Entertainment

MOVIES AND VALUES *

A SIGNIFICANT question for the study of any institution is the degree to which it reflects the values of the society. From the study of many cultures, we have learned to expect a greater gap between behavior and values in rapidly changing societies than in more stable ones. We assume that movies will reflect values and goals, as folklore, the theater, and literature (both "fine" and "popular") have always reflected them. In a period of rapid change and conflict within the value system it will be of interest to note which values are most stressed by the movies. . . .

Culture and institutions do not operate in an impersonal vacuum. A society consists of people as well as institutions. The problem is a double-edged one—that of the impact of the movies on the people who see them, and the impact of people on the movies. Part of the problem has been so oversimplified as to lose validity. Would-be reformers, looking for easy solutions, regard the movies as a prime cause of delinquency, crime, and drunkenness. But these are symptoms of social and individual pathology, with a complex history. As anthropologists, we are more interested in the normal than in the pathological. What is the effect of the movies on the vast audience who are not criminals, delinquents, or drunkards? How do movies influence their concepts of human relations, their value systems, their notions of reality? . . .

RELATIONSHIP OF MOVIES TO OTHER INSTITUTIONS

Movies have a number of functions. They are one of several forms of mass communication, functioning primarily on the emotional level through their production of daydreams. They are entertainment, which of course, in any form, is never "pure," but always has hidden or open psychological and educational subfunctions. They are a form of art—that of telling a

* Powdermaker, Hortense, "An Anthropologist Looks at the Movies," *The Annals of the American Academy of Political and Social Science,* Vol. 254 (November, 1947), pp. 80, 81, 83–86.

story. All these operate within the structure of big business, which in turn becomes another function of movies, with profits as a goal. The relationship to the theater and the novel is easily seen, for they too are concerned with the telling of stories, with tales of the conflicts between men and the resolution of the conflicts, with man's unfulfilled wishes and their fulfillment.

Although not made by the folk and quite different from folk art, the movies have some resemblance to it in their repetitive use of well-known themes or formulas which is so characteristic of primitive folklore. At the same time, the movies strive for the new, and in their efforts to be timely they resemble the newspapers. Many writers and producers eagerly scan the papers for "inspiration" for stories, and theirs is the newspaper attitude of the "scoop," the first picture on the latest newspaper interest. Many times the latest "scoop" is set within a well-known formula used in the past, and in this way the seeming contradictions between the old and the new are harmonized. . . .

In a society such as ours, with its rapid rate of change, various sections of the population are in different stages of change. In times of change, values usually lag behind behavior. There is an inherent contradiction in our value systems stemming from diverse historical traditions. The movies, as well as other institutions, choose certain values over others for emphasis.

For instance, love is a major theme and value stressed in the majority of movies. There is an almost obsessional emphasis on "romantic love," love as the end and be-all of existence. Making money, work, friendships, one's place in the world, are all secondary. In an increasing number of contemporary movies, the setting of the story is married life, with a beautiful, rich, neurotic heroine threatened by a loss of love object. Her response usually takes an extreme form, such as alcoholism or murder. In the picture "Smash-Up" we are presented with a married couple supposed to be very much in love with each other. The husband is shown so insensitive as to be completely unaware of his wife's emotional need to be a part of his everyday life. Nor does he appear to have any psychological need to bring her into his life. His insensibility is carried to the point of his being completely unaware that his efficient secretary is very much in love with him and that his wife is jealous. The wife's response to the situation is to become an alcoholic.

In another recent picture, "Unfaithful," where an unusually sincere attempt is made to understand a woman's being unfaithful to her husband while he was overseas during the war, the heroine kills her former lover. Then, she seems more concerned with concealing her relationship with the dead man, so that her husband will not be "hurt," and to keep his love, than with the fact that she has killed a man who was her lover over a period of time. Guilt feelings are indicated only briefly in one sequence immediately following the killing. Nor does she seem concerned over whether or not she will be punished by the courts. But her obsessive anxiety is, will her husband find out that the dead man was her lover, and will he therefore stop loving her? Both of these examples are characteristic of innumerable other films, in which the portrayal of love has very little psychological validity.

Disproportionate stress. Actually, it puts a heavy burden on love to make it carry the entire weight of living. The excessive nature of the burden which love carries in our society is one of the major problems of human relationships. The movies exaggerate this problem to the utmost. Love is an important part of life, literature, and art. And it is one of the major ways for an individual to relate himself to life. But it is not the only one. Work is another. In the pictures just mentioned, "Smash-Up" and "Unfaithful," both women had had successful careers before marriage. Yet neither one turned to work or any other interest when the husband was, in one case, neglecting her, and, in the other, away. In our everyday life, almost everyone works, and work is important not only as a means of earning a living, but also as a way of relating to society. Yet the importance of work or the satisfactions to be gained from it are rarely shown in movies. The love object is all that matters, and if he is lost there is no further point to life. Murder, alcoholism, insanity, are movie solutions to this problem. In real life, people do lose a love object, but go on sanely living, sometimes to love again. We think that the majority of our adult audience know this as well as the anthropologist.

There is much that could be written on the nature of love as shown in the movies, but in this brief discussion we pass on to another theme, or rather the absence of one theme. Rarely do we find the making of money glorified or regarded as an end in itself. We can remember no movie in which the hero is interested just in profits. A man interested only in profits is more likely to be the villain. Looking at our movies, one would gather that making a living, or making a lot of money, is secondary to the one and only important thing in life—love. This emphasis on love and lack of emphasis on making money are also essentially true of other mass mediums of communication, such as radio, and popular and pulp magazines; and the problem, therefore, goes far beyond the movies.

It is strange to find this in a society where profits and making a living are among the chief incentives and goals for the majority of people. It is interesting to find this in the daydreams manufactured by men in an industry primarily concerned with profits. Obviously, our manufactured tales do not reflect our lives in the manner in which the folk tales of the Kwakiutl and Blackfoot Indians reflect theirs.

Contradictory values. [One explanation] may lie in the contradiction of values within the very core of our society. We have not been able to lose the early Christian beliefs that making profits is antithetical to salvation and that money-making by itself is not a legitimate goal of life. Somewhere in our superego lingers a belief in the sinfulness of money, while in our behavior the accumulation of money is a main goal. This is an inherent contradiction in society which has never been fully realized on a social or individual level, and in Hollywood it is accentuated by the huge sums of money made by the successful people in the movie industry. Rich individuals in our culture attempt to solve the conflict through giving large sums to charity and by other "good works"; and society has attempted some regulation of profits through taxation and other controls. But the conflict is still there. In general, our manufactured daydreams do not recognize the conflict, and choose to ignore the motivation of much of contemporary behavior and exaggerate the romantic theme. . . .

THE AUDIENCE

We . . . know something about the audience through its organized groupings. There are, for instance, the "fan" clubs and magazines. The fans, usually a relatively young group, are obsessively and possessively interested in their particular stars. The star system of the studios, combined with the close-up shots on the screen, helps to satisfy and further exploit this interest. The close-up of the star reveals intimately every eyelash, the detail of the hairline, the curve of the lips, and every shade of expression. This view of the star, plus the details given by columnists of what the star eats for breakfast and whether or not he sleeps in pajamas, gives not only the fan but the regular movie-goer and reader of newspaper movie columns a feeling of great personal knowledge about his favorite actor.

This need, which has been so well exploited by the studios, we relate to one of the significant changes in our society, namely, the increasing loneliness of man. This is in part due to the development of urbanism as a way of living, with a resultant increase in the number of face-to-face contacts, which, however, become more and more impersonal. . . . Modern man is lonely, desperately in need of personal relationships. He goes to the movies, and for two hours he has the illusion of close, intimate, personal contact with exciting and beautiful people. His loneliness is briefly assuaged. There are obviously other reasons for the success of the star system, which in this brief article cannot be discussed.

MOVIE THEMES AND PLOTS *

This paper presents part of a larger study of contemporary American movies in which we analyzed the content of 67 Hollywood movies released in New York City between September 1, 1945 and September 1, 1946. These were all the grade-A movies with a contemporary American urban setting. Our study intends to ascertain the Hollywood variants of the love and hostility themes which pervade the dramatic plots of western culture. The study also aims to relate these variants to actual patterns in American life.

Our interest is not to compare the movie world with the real-life world so as to ascertain to what extent the movies reproduce existing conditions or deviate from them. We are rather concerned with the ways in which movie plots express psychological dispositions of the culture in which they are produced and consumed. Limitations of space prevent us from presenting all the major recurrent movie plot structures in this vein. To illustrate our approach, we shall discuss only some aspects of the treatment of love in our films.

UNCONVENTIONAL MEETINGS

A major tendency in the treatment of love in contemporary American films is the attempt to combine the appeal of the conventional and unconventional in a single relationship. This is expressed in the manner in which the hero and heroine become acquainted. There is a marked preference for showing the first meeting as a self-introduction, frequently occurring between the hero and heroine in complete isolation, or in an impersonal milieu surrounded by strangers. Such unconventional meetings are preferred in the pictures analyzed to formal introductions in a ratio of about three to one.

The manner and place of the first meeting underscore its unconventionality. One third of the self-introductions are pickups. Usually initiated by the man, they take place mainly on the street, in trains, or in cheap places of entertainment. Equally frequent is the sudden irruption of one partner

* Wolfenstein, Martha, and Leites, Nathan, "An Analysis of Themes and Plots," *op. cit.*, pp. 41, 44–48.

into the life of the other. One third of the self-introductions take this form, again with a predominance of male initiative. The hero of "Somewhere in the Night," fleeing from his underworld pursuers, breaks into the dressing room of the startled heroine, a night-club singer. In "The Kid from Brooklyn," the hero rushes into the heroine's bedroom to telephone for a veterinary obstetrician for his parturient milk wagon horse. In one of the exceptional cases of female initiative, the heroine forces her way into the apartment of the hero, her favorite mystery story writer, to urge him to help her solve a mystery ("Lady on a Train").

Professional contacts also provide a basis for self-introduction. However, the professional contexts or incidents are usually out of the ordinary. For instance, the hero may meet the heroine in the course of his work as a private detective, in an atmosphere of danger and pursuit. Other occasions for self-introduction are head-on collisions and rescues of women in distress. Least frequently self-introductions occur in a context of normal social life. . . .

CONFLICT BETWEEN SACRED AND PROFANE LOVE

The combination of sacred and profane love in a single relationship constitutes one of the major pervasive themes of American films. The possibility of developing a conventional relation from unconventional beginnings is one illustration of this theme. Of deeper significance is the emergence of a group of heroines who combine the charms of good and bad girls.

Freud has pointed out that the difficulty of choosing between a good and a bad girl constitutes one of the major problems in the love life of western men. The difficulty is that of fusing two impulses in relation to the same woman. On the one hand, there are sexual impulses which a man may feel to be bad and which he may therefore find it hard to associate with a woman whom he considers fine and admirable. The image, and the actuality, of the "bad" woman arise to satisfy sexual impulses which men feel to be degrading. On the other hand, there are affectionate impulses which are evoked by women who resemble the man's mother or sister, that is to say, "good" women. A good girl is the sort that a man should marry, but she has the disadvantage of not being sexually stimulating.

SOLUTIONS TO CONFLICT

In the Nineteenth Century. There are various possible solutions to this conflict. The attempt may be made to satisfy one of these impulses at the expense of the other, to satisfy them both but with different women, or to combine the two impulses in a single relationship. For instance, in Victorian England the major approved solution was to renounce profane love in favor of the sacred variety. A rebellion against this Victorian ideal is expressed in Swinburne's "Dolores," an attempt to go to the opposite extreme of sexual satisfaction unmingled with affection. A different solution was the pattern supposedly frequent in France and Italy, in which a man would keep both a wife and a mistress. The frequent nineteenth-century fantasy of the saintly prostitute, of the Camille type, represented an attempt to combine sex and affection, to imagine a woman toward whom both feelings could be expressed.

In Hollywood Films. The solution favored by current American films is another variant of the combination of sex and affection in a single relationship. The image of what we may call a "good-bad girl" has been created. The good-bad girl differs from the saintly prostitute of the last century in that she is not really bad, but only appears bad. After her apparent badness has been sufficiently established to make her sexually exciting, it is explained away as a false impression, created by ambiguous circumstances, and the hero is left with a warm-hearted, loving girl whom he can marry and settle down with. At the same time she retains the glamorous appearance and bold manners which made it so easy to believe in her wickedness.

Usually the good-bad girl appears to be promiscuous, or to be involved with a bad man (a gangster or Nazi). Occasionally she appears guilty of theft or murder. In "Gilda," the title character (after whom the Bikini bomb was named) is the most thoroughgoing example of a heroine who looks wildly promiscuous through the greater part of the film, and who in the end turns out to be a faithful and devoted woman who has never loved anyone but the hero. Gilda and the hero had been lovers before the action of the film begins, and had separated because of his jealousy. When they meet again the hero has become the right-hand man of a big gambler and international schemer; Gilda has become the gambler's wife. The hero is tortured not only by seeing Gilda as his boss's wife, but also by her strenuous flirtations with other men. Eventually the boss disappears and is considered dead. Gilda has tried to persuade the hero of her continued love for him, and he now agrees to marry her. But he still does not believe in her. To punish her for her apparent infidelities to the boss and to himself, he holds her a virtual prisoner. His strong-arm men follow her wherever she goes and forcibly dissuade her admirers. One night Gilda appears at the swank night club adjoining the gambling casino which the hero now runs. She sings and dances with great seductiveness and finally begins stripping off her clothes (she doesn't get much farther than her long black gloves) while men from the audience rush forward to assist her. The hero, who enters just in time to get an agonizing glimpse of the climax of the performance, sends his men to carry her out. While episodes of this sort present vividly the image of the beautiful promiscuous woman, they are interspersed with other occasions when Gilda pleads with the hero to believe that she has never loved anyone but him. In the end it turns out that what the hero thought he saw was a deceptive appearance, and what Gilda told him was entirely true. An understanding police official, who interests himself in their affairs, persuades the hero of this. All of Gilda's carryings-on with other men have been motivated by her love for the hero, whom she wished to hold by making him jealous. Once this has been explained to the hero by an impartial observer, he finally recognizes her for what she is: a good girl who loves only him.

In other cases the good-bad girl is not so completely free from taint, but still she turns out to be less bad than she had seemed, or there are strong extenuating circumstances for a lapse which is in any case temporary. The heroine of "Strange Love of Martha Ivers" manifests a complicated combination of real badness, seeming badness, and goodness. The girl has just come out of jail, to which she had been sent for stealing a fur coat. She explains to the hero that the coat was given to her by a boy friend who later disappeared. Thus she did not really steal the coat, but wasn't she rather friendly with the thief? In another episode she is forced by the wicked district attorney, who is still pursuing her for the crime she did not do, to play a trick on the hero. She induces him to go with her to a café where, by prearrangement, a man comes up and claims to be her husband. The pretendedly outraged husband demands that the hero come outside and fight. The hero is then forced into a waiting car in which several thugs beat him up. The heroine later has a chance to explain the whole thing to the hero; she really has no husband, and so on. In this series of bad appearances and virtuous explanations, one or two bad things remain that are not explained away. However, since the girl repeatedly turns out to be so much better than she seemed, there is probably the illusion that with a few more explanations, for which perhaps the film did not have time, she could be shown to be completely good. An atmosphere is created in which both the affirmation and the denial of the girl's badness have a strong emotional impact. They do not entirely cancel each other out, since it is more satisfying to believe both.

In Foreign Films. The good-bad girl seems to be a peculiarly American solution to the problem of two types of women. A comparison with films of other countries seems to indicate certain marked differences. A recent British film, "Madonna of the Seven Moons," deals with the two-types problem in a different way. The heroine is a dual personality. Most of the time she is a rather prim and stately wife and mother, devoted to her family and to good works, but every so often her other personality takes possession of her. She completely forgets her usual life, assumes a gypsy-like costume and abandon, and runs away to join her lover, a dark and passionate underworld character. The development in this good woman of a wild character is attributed to a girlhood seduction at the hands of a dark vagabond. The British film seems to say rather gallantly that it is the fault of a bad man if the sexy potentialities of a good woman are brought to the surface. The same woman can be both good and bad, but she does not have both characters in relation to the same man. This contrasts with the American good-bad girl pattern, according to which the girl always appears to the same man in both her aspects. The bad component appears much more disassociated and alien in the British version than in the American. It is significant that the fiery lover is an Italian. There is much less feeling in the American films of the irretrievable harm that men can do to women if they are not careful. The American good-bad girl survives her adventures unharmed. The British heroine can only escape her double life by dying.

French films seem to persist in maintaining the separation of good and bad women. The hero, placed between a good and a bad woman, is more attracted to the bad one. Attempts at fusion tend to take the form of having the bad woman converted from perennial promiscuity to true love by the right man. In a recent French film, "Macadam" (1947), a young sailor is shown pursuing a promiscuous friendship with a rather severely good girl. A young prostitute seduces the sailor, and he immediately loses interest in the good girl, even treating her quite rudely. The prostitute at the same time falls in love with the sailor, and a stable relationship is established between them. In this and other French films, the promiscuous woman is shown as not being bad at heart. This is what redeems her. No attempt is made, as in the American films, to explain away her promiscuity as merely apparent.

German pre-Hitler movies seem to have expressed an even stronger duality of good and bad women. The man moves between the good woman who is safe, domestic, and dull and the bad woman who will lure him to his destruction.

THE DISAPPEARANCE OF THE VAMP

The good-bad girl of the recent American films has put the old-style vamp out of business. The vamps of the twenties were dangerous women who unscrupulously used their sexual appeal to ruin men. Men were fascinated and bound by these women who alone could offer them the dizzy excitement of sex. Sex in those days was more mysterious, a dark rite of which the wicked woman was the priestess. It retained some of the aura of Biblical sin. One has only to recall, for instance, Greta Garbo in "Flesh and the Devil," the story of the fatal woman destroying the friendship of two fine men by becoming the mistress of one and the wife of the other. As the old preacher explains to the hero, when the devil cannot find any other way to tempt a man, he sends a beautiful woman. This image of the dangerous woman has disappeared. In the good-bad girl the hero can find sex and a square deal at the same time. Bad girls still remain, but they have mainly lost their hold on men. They have become rather a pathetic lot, hankering after heroes for whom they have no appeal.

The issue between the two types of women appears mainly in the films which one may call "male melodramas," revolving around the love and hate problems of a central hero. In films of this type, 80 per cent have a good-bad girl as the main female character. In about 50 per cent of the cases, the good-bad girl is opposed to a straight bad girl, over whom she regularly wins out. In approximately 30 per cent, the good-bad girl occupies the center of the stage alone. In only 20 per cent is the issue one between a bad girl and a simple good girl, a contest in which the good girl does not always win.

The difference between the bad and the good-bad girls is mainly that the bad girls really are what the good-bad girls only seem to be, that is, promiscuous, involved with bad men, and criminal. In "Blue Dahlia," the hero returns from the war to find his wife drunk in the midst of a wild party, and on terms of obvious intimacy with an older man who later turns out to be a gangster. After the party has dispersed, she completes the alienation of her husband's affections by admitting that their baby was killed in an auto accident caused by her drunken driving. In "The Big Sleep," the bad sister of the heroine is a nymphomaniac who has killed a man who repulsed her advances. In "Strange Love of Martha Ivers," the bad woman has a long list of crimes to her credit, including murder and theft. In each of these cases, the bad girl loses out to a good-bad girl who is equally alluring and less harrowing to have around.

The majority of bad girls fail to win the love of the men they want. Frequently they experience the frustrating combination of being repulsed by the men they love and pursued by men whom they dislike. Only a small minority are happy in love. The good-bad girl, on the other hand, always gets her man. She is frequently pursued by other men as well, who help to provide an atmosphere of desirability.

The disappearance of the vamp is further evident if we compare movie spy types of World War I and World War II. The earlier beautiful spy, like Mata Hari, for instance, was an irresistible woman who lured men from the opposite side to betray their secrets to her. She was quite cold and ruthless until the day when she fell in love with one of her victims. At this point her employers always had to shoot her; like a horse that has broken a leg, she was no longer useful. This spy legend was another version of the prostitute ennobled by love. In contrast to this, World War II women spies are shown as clean-cut American girls doing a patriotic job. They do not have to be redeemed by love since they are good all along; and they are always in love with men on their own side. The enterprising girl from home is thus substituted for the alluring foreign woman.

MOVIE TRENDS AND OTHER CULTURE TRENDS

The tendency to combine all satisfactions in one relationship, symbolized by the figure of the good-bad girl, may be related to various other trends in American culture. The ideal of monogamy still persists, but hedonistic demands, developing in part from an economy of abundance, urge the satisfaction of every need. The combination of these two trends leads to the expectation of finding one person who will satisfy every wish. The strength of this expectation is attested by the high divorce rate. Disillusionment with a marriage partner cannot be mitigated by supplementary satisfactions on the side. The longing is to begin all over again and try to find the perfect person.

The uncompromising demand to have everything seems to be more marked in Americans than in Europeans. There is little readiness to accept compromises, much less to make renunciations. The more characteristically European solutions of the two-types problem seem to express an underlying resignation. There is more the feeling that one can't have everything, that life is necessarily haunted by regrets for missed opportunities, that a certain amount of frustration is inevitable, that the attempt to get too much is likely to involve fatal conflicts. The American feeling seems to be less tragic. The belief that you can eat your cake and have it still seems strong. The hero of the American films happily survives the conflicts of love and hate which have so often been fatal for dramatic heroes of other times and places.

The real-life counterpart of the good-bad girl has probably developed with the increasing sexual accessibility of good girls. Terman, for instance, pointed out the continuously increasing trend in women toward premarital sexual relations. With this development, the prostitute becomes less necessary, and the sheltered innocent less frequent. The two corresponding images tend to lose their hold on imagination. On the one hand, the seductress, more or less glorified, tends to fade out. On the other hand, the sweet helpless girl, whom the good man had to protect against the roué, also disappears.

Another real-life development, related to the disappearance of two-typism, seems to be that an increasing number of urban women try, and succeed more or less, to remain glamorous looking for an indefinite length of time. To have an appearance which proclaims the comfortable homey wife and mother is felt as a failure. The image of a mother is being transformed in the direction of a continuity between mother and glamour girl. This is illustrated in a recent series of advertisements featuring "model mothers," i.e., professional models who continue their careers after becoming mothers, and who appear no less glamorous when they have one or two pretty children in the picture with them.

Another relevant real-life factor may be that educated parents have been trying to be more moderate in imposing sexual taboos on their children. Possibly the impression of the extreme badness of sex has been less firmly implanted in childhood than was formerly the case. This would weaken the adult tendency to conceive of sex as something shady, secret, and separate from the rest of life.

The movie image of the good-bad girl expresses the feeling that sexual needs can be satisfied by a good girl, that they no longer require involvement with a dangerous bad woman. However, the split in the good-bad girl image suggests that the sexual component is not entirely assimilated. In order to be sexually stimulating, the good girl must retain a semblance of badness, particularly in the form of seeming to be involved with other men. A lingering association of sex and wickedness remains.

PART NINE

Modern Marriage and the Family

CHAPTER XXI

American Family Organization

ALTHOUGH the family is often referred to as the "basis of society" and "the most fundamental institution," surprisingly little attention is paid to it in scientific circles. Whether in college curricula or in social science journals, it receives only a fraction of the attention that is given to economic and political matters. This learned neglect, however, is not matched on the popular level, for in the stories and novels that people read, the movies they see, and the gossip they transmit, family relations receive an astounding amount of attention. Love, courtship, sex, marriage, divorce—these are the things that capture the public imagination and the popular interest.

As between the two attitudes—scientific neglect on the one hand and popular interest on the other—the second is of course right. We know that the family is of extreme importance in the formation of personality, in the determination of mental balance, in the determination of happiness. The neglect of the family in social science is a kind of blindness, now being slowly overcome. When we undertake to view American society as a totality, the central importance of the family cannot be denied. The readings given in this and the next three chapters make clear that there is a close relation between our family organization and the rest of our social system. For example, the family offers a key to our class organization; it contains the basis of some of our major conflicts; it helps to determine our national character structure; it provides the source of our current population trends; and it forms the subject of much of our religion and many of our reforms. In view of these considerations the space given to the family in the present work seems justified.

THE FAMILY'S LOSS OF FUNCTIONS *

The functions of the family have been declining very rapidly since the invention of the factory run by steam. . . . In the agricultural era which preceded this industrial age, the functions performed largely by the family were six—affectional, economic, recreational, protective, religious, and educational. Spinning, weaving, sewing, the production of food, the preparation of food, laundering, the production of soap, and many other economically productive functions have all left the aegis of the family in whole or in part, changing the nature of the employment of men and women, and particularly taking away from women their ancient employment. The loss of economic functions is most noticeable in the large modern city among apartment-house dwellers, less developed among families in the smaller towns and in the country.

Other functions of the family have similarly declined. Recreation is found outside the home. In earlier times education, very broadly conceived, was in large part a function of the family, including physical education, manual training, domestic science, and vocational education. To-day very few of these forms of education remain in the home. In feudal times the protection of the home, the women, children, the aged and dependent kin, was in part a function of the father and male relative. The loss of these functions has been due in large part to the mechanical inventions resulting in the growth of cities and factories. . . .

The losses of functions may mean that the spindle and the loom have now completely disappeared as symbols of home life, and the laundry tub, the sewing machine, family games and the prayer book are following them. Indeed the cooking stove, the broom and even the cradle seem to be taking flight also! The invention and diffusion of methods of birth control must take rank with steam and the multi-family dwelling as significant inventions affecting the family. It has been particularly the means of a great reduction in the number of children, which has cut down the activities of the family in a purely quantitative way so that they are comprised in a very short period.

Some of these functions which are an integral part of social life have not disappeared but have simply shifted from the family to other social agencies, especially to the industries, with their welfare work, and to the

* Taken from Ogburn, W. F., "Social Heritage and the Family," in Rich, Margaret E. (Ed.), *Family Life Today* (New York: Houghton Mifflin Company, 1928), pp. 30, 31–33, 35–37, 38–39.

state, that is, all the organs of city, county, state, provincial and national governments. . . .

Moreover, the trend in the loss of functions shows little slackening and no tendency to turn and move in the opposite direction. Manufacturing is growing much faster than agriculture. Women are entering industry at a greater rate than the growth of population. The schools are taking the children at earlier ages. Protective legislation and paternalistic government activities are increasing. Recreation is becoming more commercialized and finds expression outside the family. These trends are effective for rural homes and in the towns as well as among city dwellers.

It is very difficult to predict the future, particularly in the social sciences. Furthermore, prediction is accurate usually in inverse ratio to the length of time it covers. So, for the immediate future one may simply observe that the trends seem to be moving as they have in the past. One may further speculate that as many of these changes in the family have been due to mechanical inventions which produced factories and cities, so new mechanical inventions may in the future, again quite change the course of the family. But what the new inventions will be cannot be told. . . . The cheaper and wider distribution of electricity, if accompanied by certain mechanical inventions, might tend to restore industries to the home. New inventions again may revolutionize the family in opposite directions. . . .

The tremendous loss of functions by the family is an established fact that may promise some good or some bad outcome, depending on the adjustments that are made. If the schools can be made to educate children better than the family can, then this shift of functions is a net gain. So also if other social agencies, such as the State and industry, can carry on their activities better than the family once did, the loss to the family is a gain to society.

But when these many activities are shifted from the family to other social groups, what will happen to the family? I believe that it is quite possible, even probable that the family will emerge a more harmonious institution, though such an end is hardly conceivable to those whose eyes are turned backward. The family is a little group of persons who stay together because of certain attractions or bonds or ties; otherwise they would move and live apart. These bonds are—or have been—the economic bond, the protective, the educational, the religious, the recreational and one other very important one, the affectional. All these common activities helped to keep the family intact as a group, though they have not been strong enough, however, always to hold family groups wholly together, for aside from death, some families everywhere have been disrupted by separation or divorce. As all these bonds, except the tie of affection, have been materially weakened during the past century, it is natural that the family would fall apart more frequently. The loss of these functions means then that the family largely must look to one bond alone to hold it intact, namely, the bond of affection.

Surely this is not so dismal a prospect as some of our calamity howlers think—a prospect of families based on affection. When the family was a business partnership affection may never have existed, or it may have been turned into hate or irritation or suffering between husband and wife, and indeed the affectional relation between child and parent may have been overlaid by cruelty and authority, by restricted personality, by a domination that left no freedom. Yet with affection gone, a family group had to continue because of external ties.

With the changed conditions, the family must rely much more on affection. With birth control, with women working outside the home, with fewer children, and with more frequent divorce, it seems very probable that much more attention will be given to the affectional element. And while separation and divorce may be more frequent, it is quite probable that the average quantity of affection (to use a statistical concept) per family unit remaining intact or founded anew after divorce will be much higher than was the case when the family was held together by many other bonds. This may not be the case, however, for there are many forces in modern life that produce nervousness, and nervous men and women find it more difficult than others to find suitable mates. The conditions of modern life also present certain strains on affection.

There are some who think that affection is not a solid enough foundation on which to build the family structure, but these I think are also people whose eyes are turned backward. Yet in taking opposition to their views, we must not be dogmatic or let our wishful thinking dictate our conclusions. In truth, science has as yet very little to tell us of the causes and habits which build affection. The topic has been taboo. Yet it seems very probable that science and the subsequent diffusion of what it will discover about affection and the learning process will do much to make affection between all the members a more frequent affair in the family. Those who would solve family problems and try to direct the course of evolution of the family toward better channels must work to discover as much as possible about the science and art of affection for parents and children as well as husbands and wives and to disseminate these fundamentally important discoveries as widely as possible. . . .

How shall these new and better adjustments be made? Not by clinging to the old beliefs and customs, for the old conditions of agriculture and home industry cannot be brought back with culture as it is, nor the mores that grew up with them. The family will have to work out new adjustments to the small family, to a family with reduced production in the home for women, to a family which is not to be held together so much by economic and social bonds, but which is to be based on affection. To make these adjustments the family will have to make new inventions and utilize new researches in the psychology of personality, utilize new knowledge regarding the habits and practices of affection, and the new discoveries regarding the training of children. It does not seem probable that the family will recover the functions it has lost. But even if the family doesn't produce thread and cloth and soap and medicine and food, it can still produce happiness, which does not seem such a very bad thing to do, after all.

CONTEMPORARY FAMILY TYPES *

Reduction of the family in the United States in size and function has reached an extreme degree. Protestant and secular, urban and mobile, scientific and educated, Americans have forsaken the extended kinship group as an important social unit and have stressed the married-couple nucleus. Moreover, this nucleus has shown, in the world's highest divorce rate, a tendency to dissolve. Women have come as near achieving equality with men, and children emancipation from parents, as in any nation. The idea of immediate personal happiness as the primary aim of matrimony is widespread; even college courses on marriage and the family, by advertising themselves as a "guide to happiness," . . . foster it. Mass romanticism —the deification of romantic courtship—has reached its pinnacle in the preoccupation of motion pictures and popular literature with the affairs of adolescent love. The ideal of a separate unit (room, apartment, or house), as private for each couple as walls and separate conveniences can make it, has achieved a new peak. The use of contraception has become ever more effective, and the number of children has decreased sharply. Ceremony and religion have almost disappeared from the family as a unit, and conflict of opinion among the population has reduced the uniformity and certainty of family mores. Individuation of family members, in short, has reached a point beyond which it can seemingly go no farther.

* Taken from Davis, Kingsley, "Changing Modes of Marriage: Contemporary Family Types," in Hill, Reuben, and Becker, Howard (Eds.), *Marriage and the Family* (Boston: D. C. Heath and Company, 1942), pp. 108–110, 111–115.

THE MIDDLE-CLASS FAMILY

The urban middle class, both because of its size and because of its social and economic dominance, determines the standard American family. It is toward this standard that the family in other classes, and indeed in other nations, seems to be moving, at least for the present. . . .

The popular sociological view is that because of the factory system, urban living, mobile transportation, rapid communication, social climbing, public education, etc., the family has lost many of its functions, but that the affectional functions—sexual gratification and child rearing—still remain. The present writer, however, has raised questions as to the accuracy of this interpretation. Since institutions are functionally and structurally integrated, it seems unlikely that one institution could lose most of its functions and still retain the others in the same form as before. The high reliance on romantic love and the quest for happiness in marriage, plus virtual divorce by mutual consent, have considerably weakened the emotional security which marriage once afforded, and have in turn affected the provision of a stable milieu for children. Objective evidence of the breakdown of the child-rearing function is afforded by the birth rate. During the five years preceding the 1940 census, for example, our cities were replacing their population by births to the extent of only 74 per cent. This means that with the same fertility and mortality they would, unless aided from outside, ultimately lose 26 per cent of their population per generation. [The prewar and postwar boom in the birth rate, which brought even the cities above replacement, is believed by demographers to be a temporary phenomenon.]

In so far as it fails to perform its essential functions, the middle-class urban family stands a good chance of being replaced. Whether this will come through foreign conquest, class revolution, or new population policies, nobody knows. Most nations, now more closely knit and better able to control private behavior, may follow the example of France, Belgium, Germany, Sweden, Japan, and Russia in starting policies designed to influence the number and quality of the population. In such case the peak of individualized marriage will have been passed and some sort of regimentation will have taken its place. . . .

THE AMERICAN FARM FAMILY

Of all groups in the American population, the farming contingent has changed least since colonial days. It best represents, in family matters, the traditional attitudes of Protestant America. Whereas in Europe the usual mode of agricultural settlement had been the village, in America it was the open farm which the frontiersman had cleared himself and on which he settled with his family. This mode of settlement fostered an intensely isolated type of familism, the farm family becoming more self-sufficient, conservative, stable, and fertile than the urban family. But the very isolation of each family and the possibility of moving to new land farther west prevented strong clan solidarity from developing. Eventually, therefore, the farm family showed many of the signs of individualism which have typified urban middle-class family life for many years.

Marriage for the farmer is the foundation of a business partnership. The wife's labor is not only necessary but is also functionally integrated with that of the husband and children. Obedience of wife and children to the man was required in the pioneer farm family, not because of an abstract principle of male superiority but because of the necessities of the situation. "The common and paramount interest of family members in the outcome of the farm enterprise necessitated agreement on all matters. . . . There was need for an executive in each family who could give direction to the process of living. The natural executive was the father, hence our usual judgment that the farm family was patriarchal." But the wife was so essential that she had, and has today, considerable "say" about the farm, particularly about domestic matters. On southern tenant farms, for example, the usual pattern is for the wife to do everything inside the house, for the man to do everything in the field (with the wife occasionally helping at busy times), and for both to share the intermediate duties of the back yard and barn. The wife's work within the house consists partly of child tending, partly of housekeeping (cooking, cleaning, washing, sewing, canning). At least one crucial problem which plagues the urban wife has never arisen for the rural woman; namely, the question of whether or not she should work. The farm wife has always worked; there has been no conflict between her child-rearing and housekeeping activities on the one hand and her economic activities on the other, for both can be conveniently accomplished and integrated in and about the home. Only under urban conditions, with the exclusion of the family from economic functions, does the problem of female "emancipation" arise.

Since the interlocking system of tasks, assigned on the basis of sex and age, turns the farm family into a close-knit productive unit, it is small wonder that about 10 per cent more of farm than of city people get married, or that the average farm couple marries about a year earlier than the average urban couple, that they are about twice as fertile, and that they are about twice as likely to remain married.

In addition to the value of children as young workers and companions, the persistence of traditional mores explains the high fertility on the isolated farm. In 1935–1940, when the net reproduction rate of the city stood at only 74, the rate for the farm was 144, which under stable conditions would mean an increase of 44 per cent per generation. The most fertile farmers, however, are not those who own their farms, but rather those who simply labor on them. As in the city, there is an inverse differential birth rate which, though present today, may not be a usual accompaniment of rural life. . . . The inverse differential fertility of farm classes in America may reflect . . . the penetration of urbanism into rural regions. Another fact—the greater fertility of subsistence farmers as against commercial farmers—bears out the interpretation, and indicates that if farming continues to become more of a business enterprise, farm fertility will continue to decline. In the past, fertile farm families have furnished cities not merely with food but with human beings as well. Though this has been a tremendous burden because the offspring leave just at their most productive age, it is really a blessing because it prevents the accumulation of population in an occupation for which the demand is steadily diminishing. The "burden" to the farmers, therefore, is simply the burden common to all parents who rear large families in our society; and the question is, How much longer will they continue to shoulder it?

Despite its high fertility, the American farm family has not attained [Old-World] continuity. . . . The opportunity for farm youth to move to a city or to move to new lands in the West has taken them away from home and broken the family ties. There has been of course inheritance of property, but with children away, with few limits on selling, parceling, or willing land, the farm has not remained identified with a particular family through generations. The farm, with cash crop and capital tools, has become the servant of a money economy, a cog in a commercial system, rather than a sacred way of life. With better communication, a growing population density, and a heightened educational outlook, all of which lessen the farm's isolation, the tendency of the farm family to approach ever more closely the secular, urban type may be expected to continue.

THE NEGRO FAMILY

His African culture having been destroyed, the American Negro had to acquire our civilization from the peculiar and unfavorable angle of the slave. More than three fourths of his entire history in America have been spent in bondage. His "freedom" has lasted for only two and a half generations and has been marred by extraordinary difficulties. After emancipation, for instance, he was left foot-loose and confused in a demoralized South, pitied or despised by his erstwhile masters, pampered or neglected by his Yankee deliverers. Slowly he found himself re-enslaved in a pariah caste, the lower layer of a rigid two-race system. Later, trying desperately to escape this caste prison, he found his opportunity during the labor shortage of World War I, when industries were booming but immigrants were no longer arriving. His trek to the cities during this period, however, was but the pursuit of another mirage, for he was strangely unaccustomed to and hence maladjusted in the city environment. Throughout the postwar depression he found himself at the bottom of the economic ladder, unemployed, badly housed, despised, diseased, and disorganized. Only slowly and painfully has he adjusted himself to the city, where his high mortality and low fertility still augur ill for him.

The Negro's tragic history left scant opportunity for permanence in his family relations. Whether or not he could marry, and once married could remain with wife or children, was not a matter of his own but of his master's will. Slave mating, indeed, was hardly marriage because it lacked some of the qualities essential to wedlock, above all the quality of durability. The footloose period after the Civil War freed the Negro family from the master's arbitrary will, but it provided no organized community controls over behavior; and after the former slave had settled down to a new status—the status of an outcaste—the norms of the white community were largely meaningless to him, because lack of education, lack of income, and lack of self-determination made it impossible to develop these norms in his own circle. Finally, during the period of migration to the cities the Negro's pariah adjustment, worked out mainly in rural regions, left him helpless before all the urban forces tending to create family instability. The Negro family is still the most loosely organized and easily broken in the United States.

Back in the days of slavery it was the father's rather than the mother's authority that was primarily usurped by the master. The master had the privilege of having sexual relations with the slave, of disciplining her, of determining her residence, and of owning and controlling her children—all privileges which the husband would normally have. She was left largely in control of her own cabin, however, and within this abode her mate, deprived of his authority, was likely to take orders from her. Since she, not her mate, was essential to rearing the children, the master protected her in her domestic privileges; and since mates might come and go in her life, while the children belonged to her master anyway, she was independent of any particular male who might presume to be her husband. Thus began the Negro matriarchal pattern.

In the reconstruction period the maternal advantage continued, but at a terrible cost. Whereas formerly the master had guaranteed the Negro mother economic support, now the waywardness of the Negro male left her to support herself and her offspring alone. She paid dearly for her matriarchal position, while the male reaped the advantage of sexual freedom and irresponsibility. Throughout the Negro's subsequent history this pattern of maternal dominance at home and male irresponsibility abroad has persisted. In the country and city alike these inconsistencies have given rise to extremely high rates of desertion, illegitimacy, and venereal disease. The relation between mother and children, however, has been constant and devoted. Indeed, Negroes have experienced greater ease in tracing their ancestry through their mothers than through their fathers, because of the closer relation with the mother.

The absence of permanence in family relations implies, at bottom, a lack of social control over sexual impulse. The privileges of masters and masters' sons during slavery, the tendency to "breed" slaves as if they were animals, the subsequent mobility of the reconstruction period, the privileges of white men under the two-caste system, the inability to raise one's caste status by virtuous conduct, and the anonymity and lack of status in the city—all have contributed to alienate Negro behavior from Puritan sex standards. Furthermore, ignorance and poverty have prevented the Negro from evading the consequences of sexual irregularity; hence the high rate of illegitimacy, venereal disease, abortion, and sterility. Negroes produce only one eighth of all births in the United States but they contribute over one half of the illegitimate births. The colored rate is generally seven to eight times that of the white rate. For syphilis Negroes had, during 1927–1936, an attack rate of 2870 as against 796 per 100,000 for the whole United States. It has been claimed that twenty in every hundred southern Negroes show a positive blood Wassermann, and of these 14.4 per cent result from congenital syphilis. Negroes in an Alabama county reached the "saturation point," with 39.8 per cent of those tested showing a positive Wassermann. Venereal disease, combined with bad diet and hard working conditions, produces among the Negroes thousands of spontaneous abortions, stillbirths, and cases of sterility. The resulting lowered fertility constitutes an exception to the usual inverse correlation between fertility and social status in our society. The low fertility of the Negro, together with his high mortality, gives him a very low net reproduction rate of approximately 107—barely enough to maintain a stationary population.

With all of this, however, perhaps the outstanding characteristic affecting the family patterns of the American Negro is his consciousness of skin color. In his choice of a mate the Negro is strongly influenced by this consideration, which only incidentally enters the mind of the white man. The Negro, placed in a racial caste which is really mixed, inevitably attaches a high value to possession of blood from the superior caste. Other things equal, he wishes to secure as light a mate as possible. Above all, the successful Negro male wants a light mulatto if he can get her. Thus racial miscegenation still goes on within the colored group, white blood filtering downward, Negro blood filtering upward.

Our delineation has blurred the class distinctions within the Negro group. Actually, with the mass movement of Negroes into cities, there has developed a Negro middle class, brilliantly described by Frazier.[1] Although more superficialities than profundities have been copied from the white (for example, divorce, childlessness, conspicuous consumption) and although undoubtedly some features of the Negro heritage still cling to the *nouveaux arrivés,* the divergences from the white urban middle-class pattern are surprisingly small.

STATISTICS ON THE FAMILY *

MARRIAGE

Half of the men in this country who marry for the first time do so before their 25th birthday and half of the women before their 22nd birthday, according to data from the 1940 Census. More specifically, the median age at first marriage for men was 24.3 years and for women, 21.6 years. The average couple marrying 50 years ago was a little older than the average couple in current times. Results derived from the 1890 Census showed that the median age at first marriage was 26.1 years for men and 22.0 years for women at that time. Thus, the average married man of 1940 was his wife's senior by about three years, whereas his grandfather was likely to have been senior by four years.

The decline since 1890 of nearly two years in the median age of men at first marriage may be attributed in part . . . to the more widespread knowledge today of means of family limitation. In the earlier period post-

[1] Frazier, E. Franklin, *The Negro Family in the United States* (Chicago: University of Chicago Press, 1939), Chaps. 19 and 20.

* Glick, Paul C., "The Family Circle," *American Sociological Review,* Vol. 12 (April 1947), pp. 165–169, 171–172, 174.

ponement of marriage was probably more often relied upon as a means of limiting family size.

It should be recognized, of course, that not all couples establish a separate home when they marry. In ordinary times, approximately one couple out of every five moves in with relatives or lives in rented rooms as lodgers for a while after marriage. The proportion of couples living in this manner declines sharply until middle age and reaches a low point of about 3 per cent for couples in their 50's.

Over a considerable period of time there has been a growing tendency for married couples to make their homes with an established family. There is evidence in unpublished data from the Censuses of 1930 and 1910 that smaller proportions of couples at these earlier dates than in 1940 were failing to maintain their own households. A survey made in June, 1946, showed an increase of only 9 per cent since 1940 in the number of private households as compared with an increase of 40 per cent in the number of couples living doubled up in private households. The latter increase developed, no doubt, as a consequence of the lack of housing facilities to accommodate the great numbers marrying during, or since the end of, the war.

CHILDBEARING

Following marriage, about a year elapses before the average mother bears a child. This interval has not varied greatly since 1917, when the Bureau of Census first published national figures on children by order of birth. The median age of mothers bearing their first child in 1940 was 22.6 years. In 1890 it probably was about 23.0 years. Between 1940 and 1942 it remained practically unchanged in spite of a rather large increase in the proportion of first births among all births.

For women who had married and had reached the end of their reproductive period (45 to 49 years old) by 1940, the average number of children born per woman was approximately 3.1. Statistics on children by order of birth indicate that these 3.1 children were born about two years apart, hence a period of only about four and one-half years elapsed between the birth of the first and the last child, as a rule. The typical mother, had, therefore, borne her final child at the (median) age of 27.2 years.

Because families were so large two generations ago, the average woman at that time had twice as long an interval between the birth of her first and last child as does the woman of today. She had borne 5.4 children with an estimated interval of 9 years between the first and the last. Not until the age of about 32 years had she given birth to the last child.

At this point it is appropriate to mention in passing, at least, those women who have never borne any children. Among women who had married and completed their period of fertility (45 to 49 years old) by 1940, 15.4 per cent had had no children. For 1890 the corresponding figure was only half as large, 7.9 per cent.

CHILDREN LEAVING HOME

From the time the last child is born until the first child leaves home, the size of the family usually remains stable. Probably a majority of children depart from the parental home for a new permanent place of residence within less than a year from the time they marry.

Let us assume as a reasonable approximation, therefore, that the average (ever-married) woman of completed fertility (45 to 49 years old) in 1940 had had three children who grew to maturity, married, and left home at the same age that their parents married. The decline in the number of children living at home would accordingly have taken place when the mother was between the ages of 45 and 50 years. By way of comparison, the average woman of her grandmother's era would have been 47 to 55 years old, if she had lived as long as that, when her five surviving children were leaving home.

DISSOLUTION OF THE FAMILY

This brings us to the final stage of the family cycle, when first one then the other of the parents is expected to die. For the average couple who married in 1940, the chances are 50–50 that, under mortality rates observed at that time, they will survive jointly for about 39 years. At the end of that period the wife would be 61 years old and the husband 64. They would have lived together for 11 years since the last of their three children married. By comparison, the typical couple of two generations ago could have expected to survive together for only 31 years after marriage, that is, until the wife would have attained age 53 and the husband 57. This is two years short of the time when their fifth child would have been expected to marry.

Thus, the decline in size of family and the improved survival prospects of the population since 1890 not only have assured the average parents of our day that they will live to see their children married but also have made it probable that they will have one-fourth of their married life still to come when their last child leaves the parental home. This represents a remarkable change since 1890. It is one of the most dramatic, and at the same time one of the most significant changes from the viewpoint of the life experiences of the parents, of all changes in the family cycle in the last 50 years. It has a multitude of social and economic implications.

The wife would ordinarily be expected to survive longer than her husband, partly because she is usually younger and partly because mortality rates are more favorable for women than for men, age for age. In the typical situation, therefore, the period of joint survival of husband and wife is terminated with the death of the husband. In this case, the average wife would be expected, under present conditions of mortality, to live on after her husband's death for about 13 years, to age 74; 50 years ago, she could have looked forward to living until age 68. In the less common situation, the period of joint survival is broken by the death of the wife. In that case, the average husband, under mortality conditions of today, would be expected to live on for 6 years, to age 70, whereas 50 years ago he would have been likely to live until age 66.

RESIDENTIAL SHIFTS

In ordinary times, about four out of every five couples establish a home apart from their parents when they marry. Furthermore, many of those who have established a home are likely to move to another location with more adequate living space when the size of their family increases. It should not be surprising, therefore, that only 41 per cent of the heads of husband and wife families were living in the same house in 1940 as in 1935. Generally because of job considerations, 13 per cent had shifted their place of residence still greater distances; that is, they had crossed county lines (or the limits of cities of 100,000 or more) or had come to this country from abroad.

These overall averages, interesting enough in themselves, conceal some striking differentials among couples in the several stages of the family cycle. For instance, only 16 per cent of the family heads under 35 years old in 1940 were living in the same house or apartment they had been living in five years earlier. The other 84 per cent had moved. By way of contrast, among families with the husband in the upper age range, 55 years old and over, 64 per cent were in the same home and the other 36 per cent were not. These statistics make apparent the high degree of correlation between population movement and age.

Families of young couples are not only more likely to move within a county but are also more likely to migrate between counties. Those in which the husband was under 35 years of age in 1940 were more than three times as likely to have moved into another county (or city of 100,000 or more) during the preceding five years as the group 55 years old and over.

HOME OWNERSHIP

Closely related to residential shifts is tenure of home. In fact, a large part of the movement of families is occasioned by the purchase of a home. Few indeed of the young couples in separate living quarters own their homes. Only 12 per cent of those under 25 years of age were home owners in 1940 but by the age period 35 to 44 years more than three times that proportion, or 39 per cent, were home owners. At each advancing age of the family head the proportion owning homes increased until, at age 65 and over, 69 per cent were owners.

FAMILY INCOME

The pattern of change in family income for wage-earner families very closely resembles that of rental value. Husband and wife families in which the husband was under 25 years old in 1940 had just about half as large a median family income during 1939 as those aged 45 to 54, the latter representing the peak group. Families in which the husband was in the oldest age group, 65 and over, had a median family income approximately 25 per cent below that in their prime. The largest median incomes were generally found among those groups of families in which the chief earner had attained the age when he could perform with the maximum skill and usefulness in his trade or profession. Furthermore, higher family earnings were found, other things being equal, among those groups of families in which adult relatives were most common. The earnings of these relatives helped to make possible larger payments for housing accommodations and thus also help to explain the correlation between the rental value and family income curves.

All but one or two per cent of the family heads under 45 years old in 1940 were classified as members of the labor force. At ages 55 to 64, nearly 90 per cent were still working or looking for work. Above the age of 65, only slightly over half, 52 per cent, of the husbands who were family heads reported themselves as workers. Of those in this oldest age group who were still employed, more than 40 per cent were farmers or farm laborers.

Among the wives of family heads in 1940, 12 per cent were actively engaged in work for pay or profit, other than home housework, or were seeking such work. The maximum percentage of wives in the labor force,

16.5 per cent, was found among those whose husbands were 25 to 29 years old. At each succeeding age thereafter the proportion of wives in the labor force steadily declined. At ages of husbands above 65, only about 5 per cent of their wives were reported as workers.

CHAPTER XXII

Courtship and Mate Selection

To understand the American family and its problems, one must know how the individual family is formed. It is in the process of formation—in mate selection, courtship, and engagement—that subsequent events in wedlock and parenthood have their origin. So important, indeed, is the process of forming a family that the community and the society at large take a serious interest in it. Society regulates the family by controlling its formation. For this reason the mode of mate selection is intimately tied with the class structure, the economic order, and the educational system. Courtship behavior is strongly involved with religion and morality, with fashion, literature, and art. The readings below explore both the actual behavior of courtship in America and the institutions that consciously or unconsciously control it.

THE OLDER MORES *

Our formal mores of courtship are reasonably clear. . . . A young man and a young woman must not speak to each other without first being formally introduced. After the introduction, it is the privilege of the young man to make such advances as would lead to further acquaintance; he asks the young woman whether he may call, or invites her to attend the theatre or movies or to go to a dance with him; on such occasions the young man pays all expenses. The participation of the young woman in furthering the association is quite limited; she may invite the man to her home for dinner, or invite him to call; more rarely, she may invite him to a social occasion at her home or that of a friend. . . . In theory, much of the courtship takes place in the young woman's home. It is understood that a girl

* From Waller, Willard, *The Family: A Dynamic Interpretation* (New York: The Dryden Press, Inc., 1938), pp. 177–179.

should have a place in which to entertain her friends, and her parents usually, in America, vacate the parlor or sitting-room for her. If the girl visits the boy's home 'to meet his parents,' the parents do not leave the parlor. In such relations, the young people are supposed to remain on rather formal terms with one another, and sexual advances or even proffered caresses are supposed to be insulting to the girl. Anything which puts the girl under too great obligation to the young man is tabooed; she may not accept expensive gifts from him; likewise she may not accept gifts of a highly personal nature. During the early period of such associations, late hours and long automobile rides are not supposed to be *comme il faut*. If the persons involved are quite young, their parents usually regulate such associations minutely.

The relationship goes into a new phase when it becomes what is known as an engagement. The young man formally proposes marriage to the girl, accompanying this proposal with a declaration of affection. If the proposal is accepted, the couple associate from then on in a different way because it is understood that they are soon to be married. They accept a certain mutual exclusiveness, and neither one is supposed to have social engagements with other members of the opposite sex. More expensive presents and presents of a more personal nature may now be given by each to the other; typically the young man gives the young woman a diamond which is to be worn on the third finger of her left hand. Caresses and other forms of mutual endearment are now permitted by even the most rigid morality, although the young people are still supposed to observe the custom of premarital chastity. The young people are, however, left alone a great deal. As the date of the marriage approaches, the girl is inducted into a round of ceremonies, showers, and parties; the man shares in this only slightly, although there is some tradition in favor of a bachelor party on the night before his marriage. . . . It is understood that a relationship should not continue too long or become too intimate without eventuating in an engagement and ultimately a marriage. If a young man consorts with a girl for a considerable period of time and does not propose marriage, a male relative of the girl is privileged to inquire as to his intentions, whether they are honorable and serious.

These social usages brought well-bred young men and well-bred young women together; they likewise arranged it so that genteel young ladies would be likely to have little contact with ineligible men and eligible men would not be likely to marry young women of the wrong class backgrounds.

ROMANTIC LOVE AND COURTSHIP *

The American mode of marital selection is extremely individualistic. Nothing indicates this better than our concept of romantic love. This concept, more than any other, stresses the cult of the individual. It emphasizes choice on a strictly personal basis, apart from all ulterior considerations. But in spite of its free character, this romanticism, this cult of the individual in marital selection, is a product of our own social structure. In both cases we are dealing with a social reality that is causally connected with the rest of society.

> Romantic love as it exists today, with all the varying perturbations it occasions, is as definitely a sign of specific historical conditions as are big battleships with turbines, internal-combustion engines, and electrically driven machines. It would be as sensible to treat the latter as effects of a single psychic cause as to treat the phenomena of disturbance and conflict which accompany present sexual relations as manifestations of an original single psychic force or *libido*.[1]

It should be noted that romantic love is chiefly limited to *pre*marital rather than marital relations. It is a phenomenon connected with "courting" in the strict sense of the term. It is, in short, the supreme expression of our particular mode of relationship between the unmarried. The theory is that two people become attached to each other by virtue of purely personal qualities, all other considerations being thrown to the winds. This personal attachment sweeps them off their feet, they vow eternal fidelity, and they get married as an external expression of the inner sentiment they share. Thus having successfully expressed their overpowering inner feelings, they of course live happily ever after.

Essential ingredients of such romantic love are idealization, anticipation, uncertainty, skill, and competition. By idealization is meant the human tendency in some situations to regard the part as representative of the whole, and to react to the whole as if the unknown parts were as perfect as the known part. When the person has a preconceived notion of what the ideal whole should be, he is apt to see only the best qualities. Furthermore, if it is a courtship relation, he is likely to be *shown* only the best qualities. Seeing

* By the senior editor, from an unpublished manuscript.

[1] John Dewey, *Human Nature and Conduct* (New York: Modern Library, 1930), pp. 153–154.

these good parts, he is often content to remain ignorant of the rest, for by the simple use of imagination, stimulated by his need to find his heart's desire, he can imagine the whole object as being as perfect as the part he sees.

The statement that love is blind refers specifically to this idealization—for in his desire to have his ideal, the lover may remain stubbornly oblivious to the plainest of facts, seeing only what he wants to see. The love affair of Keats must surely have been of this character. Even when unsavory facts are admitted, the person may still be emotionally unable to attach significance to them or guide his conduct in the light of them. Thus Phillip in *Of Human Bondage* understands in a factual sense the shortcomings of the waitress of whom he is enamored. They give him no end of torment. She has only a beautiful profile, everything else being mediocre and tedious. He knows this, and yet he cannot detach his attention from her. Her bad qualities virtually ruin his life as he continues in a hypnotic state of irresistible idealization. He can understand, but he can never *feel* that she is as trivial as she really is. He searches unremittingly for that perfection which unconsciously he assumes must be there.

The powerful motivation that manifests itself in romantic attachment—motivation which, as in the case of Phillip, pushes the individual beyond all bounds of common sense—must itself be explained. Why is a man driven so irresistibly, let us say, to idealize a woman? The answer lies in two circumstances, both inherent in the character of our society. First, romantic love exists among us as a cultural compulsive, a collective representation. It is a pattern of behavior that is handed down to each new generation by every form of communication—in conversation, in moving pictures, in story, novel, play, and song. Any given individual in our society is therefore provided with an ideal conception of the opposite sex, is taught to look for perfection, to stake his emotional happiness upon finding it, and to infer from certain manifestations—such as a pretty face or a delicate manner—that perfection is somehow there. He is taught to long for expressions of affection from the perfect creature, to respect her, to do or die for her. The cultural example would not be sufficient, however, if there were not in the second place another factor operating—the taboo upon premarital intercourse but not upon premarital contact. This has the effect, if the taboo is observed, of stimulating the lovers sexually at the same time that it denies gratification. Thus the libidinal energy of the sex urge, guided by the romantic tradition of the culture, is accumulated like an electric charge and is turned loose only through the channel of idealization, giving to the idealization an astonishing impetus.

Another ingredient is of course anticipation. The courtship process is fairly slow, ultimate consummation being usually a good way off with many intervening trials and tribulations. The very taboos themselves create this condition. We know that any object if sufficiently desired and adequately withheld will be romanticized—i.e. conceived as perfect; it will be dwelt upon in thought and dream, will cause loss of appetite, will grow more valuable as anticipation continues. The younger the person the more vivid the imagination, and hence the more pronounced the anticipatory idealization. The child who has long wanted red-topped boots may, when he gets them, insist upon wearing them to bed; he simply cannot get enough of them. Romantic love is one kind of emotional experience associated with poignant anticipation. The sexual object being greatly desired but being unobtainable over a period of time, anticipatory pleasure is built up, so that the lover thinks that the intimacy of marriage would be sheer bliss forever; he cannot conceive of getting enough of the love object. Romantic love is more frequent and more intense in youth and young adulthood, not simply because imagination is more active at this time, but also because the sexual urge is stronger and the cultural ideals more unalloyed by experience.

Allied with anticipation is the element of uncertainty. The outcome of courtship is not only important to the individual, but also problematical. Hence the popular interest in romantic love is undoubtedly a part of the universal gambling interest, which arises in situations where the outcome is both important and uncertain. The uncertainties of choosing a life-mate capture the attention in the highest degree. There is a conflict of wills and aims (obstructing the course of true love), calling for manipulative skill (all is fair in love and war), courage (faint heart never won fair lady), and persistence (all's well that ends well). The outcome, at the same time that it is uncertain, is highly important, for it may mean a happy or an unhappy life. Thus all the elements creating an intense gambling interest are present, and this would seem to account for the fact that where romantic courtship exists there is a tremendous amount of attention in popular literature and art devoted to it. Movies, stories, novels—every form of narrative art—run on this topic endlessly. The public never seems to tire of it, any more than it tires of horseracing, detective novels, or business enterprise. This interpretation is borne out too by the frequency with which magic appears as an aid in courtship. Magic, according to the theory of Malinowski and others, is employed in important endeavors where the outcome is both uncertain and important. Its frequent use in courtship bears out our interpretation of the interest element in romantic interaction.

But why should courtship be fraught with such uncertainty? One reason lies in the fact that romantic love supposedly rests upon sheer impulse—upon the whim and fancy of two persons; and any trivial incident, any quirk of circumstance, may serve to deflect the inner feeling in another direction. Another reason is that in courtship two wills with conflicting interests are intimately involved; the parties are not pursuing some common goal outside of their relationship, but rather they are pursuing each other—so that the conflict of interest as between man and woman is a perpetual threat to harmony. Still another reason lies in the competitive nature of free courtship. In courtship the suitor does not have complete possession; in fact in the early stages he has practically no rights over the woman at all. His proprietorship is continually threatened by the presence of rivals, and the situation is as uncertain as any highly competitive situation. Furthermore, it is often to the interest of the other party to exaggerate and utilize the competitive circumstances in which the suitor finds himself, in order to gain a dominant position in the relationship. It is small wonder that the suitor leads a hard life and sometimes resorts to magic in a desperate effort to cinch the outcome. Skill is essential, and this lends a workmanlike interest in the technique of handling women, but at the same time, there being many eligible competitors and many chance factors beyond control, success is seldom assured.

The free courtship of individualized America, then, is associated with the romantic complex, which involves idealization of the love partner on the basis of scanty knowledge, a cultural compulsive, and unsatisfied sexual urge, and which involves the glow of anticipation, the danger of competition, and the agony of uncertainty.

By now the romantic complex in America has changed slightly from that described above. We already think of the old-fashioned romanticism as somewhat ridiculous. A lover writing stilted verses about a girl he has hardly seen and certainly does not know, and praising her for virtues she probably does not have, seems a bit foolish, especially if he makes no real attempt to get better acquainted with her. Such "pale-and-wan" romanticism, based on rather strict separation of the sexes and on sexual puritanism, is rapidly giving way to a new kind of realism. Nowadays, with coeducation, female employment, urban freedom, moral relativism, and automobile transportation, boys and girls mingle so regularly and so intimately that they cannot nourish many idealistic illusions about each other Their relation, and hence their conception of love, has a more matter-of fact quality. It is more of a personal attachment than an idealized passion and is more frankly attributed to sex than to God or the Universe. The physical bonds between the lovers are more substantial. The lover is not satisfied with a peep at his ideal in church on Sunday; he wants a date whenever he asks for it, and usually insists on "necking," possibly on "petting," and perhaps on sexual intercourse. In these circumstances some of the elements that formerly contributed to the romantic complex no longer persist in their pure form.

This is not to say that romantic love has disappeared, or that it has lost all of its irrationalities. The ideal, the traditional conception, still has a remarkable vitality, and people occasionally lose all common sense in following it out. If love in America has grown more realistic, it has also grown more competitive. If it has become less controlled, less ritualized, it has also become more problematical. It has become heavily involved in the whole question of sexual experimentation and sexual desire. Guilt feelings, aroused sexual passion, fear of consequences—all have been added to the already turbulent emotion of love. Sexual desire is in itself an anarchic thing; when it is freed from traditional controls without the development of a unified system of new norms, it becomes a source of emotional disturbance for the young people caught in the toils of social change and amorous activity. In so far, then, as romantic love thrives on problems, on uncertainty and competition, it will continue to manifest itself in our society. In so far as it thrives on distance and sexual repression, it will decline. Be it noted that in a huge, complex society most of our social contacts are mechanical and impersonal. Each individual is thrown upon his own to synthesize out of the multifarious social contacts some sort of pattern, some organization of his life. Above all, he must find, as best he can, that rare and precious thing, a close personal tie with someone in an ocean of impersonal ties. Our society, more than any other, makes a sharp distinction between personal and impersonal relations. Moreover, it sets personal relations adrift. They are increasingly a matter for the individual to decide, not the organized groups of which he is a member. Thus, as between a man and a woman, there is an increasing tendency to let them define the relation as they see fit. At the same time the relationship is important to them because so much of their life is spent in an impersonal atmosphere. The intimate relationship offers a refuge, for in it they can get outside themselves, can merge their aims and desires, can feel the confidence and security of depending on someone else. Finding this intimate, satisfying personal relationship is not an easy thing for the individual; our social organization does not guarantee it in any way, but simply leaves the matter open to competition and individual effort, and therefore makes it profoundly problematical. Furthermore, with the multiplicity of contacts and the absence of firm social controls, an intimate relationship once established is not secure. A rival may at any time come to take away what seems precious beyond everything else. Thus love in our culture has not grown placid simply because it has grown more realistic. It has not lost the quality of a search for an ideal. It has not lost its capacity to consume the interest of the individual or to furnish the motif of fiction. It is still the turbulent romantic complex, but in a new and more intricate form.

ROMANTIC LOVE AND MARRIAGE

Our ideal of marriage is that of a close personal relation, formed and maintained because the two individuals love one another. But love is at bottom a very anarchic thing, impatient of social restraint. Consequently, in attempting to base marriage on this emotion, our society has necessarily chosen to sanction a high rate of marital instability. In the stricter society of a century ago, love was more unrealistic and romantic, and hence constituted a poor basis for matrimonial solidarity. But in other ways marriage was more rigidly controlled. The realistic love of modern courtship is more compatible with marriage, and hence contributes more to marital stability; but on the other hand, most of the other social controls over marriage have weakened, so that wedlock is more purely dependent on personal feelings. In this situation the anarchic character of sexual love, whether of the romantic or the realistic kind, outweighs in many cases the binding character of mutually adjusted habits and common experience, and leads to desertion, separation, or divorce. The high rate of divorce in the United States, which many people profess to disapprove, is intimately connected with our ideal conception of the basis of marriage (romantic love), which many people seemingly approve. Here then is an example of inconsistency in our value system and in our social organization.

THE RATING AND DATING COMPLEX *

The mores of courtship in our society are a strange composite of social heritages from diverse groups and of new usages called into existence by the needs of the time. There is a formal code of courtship which is still nominally in force, although departures from it are very numerous; the

* Waller, Willard, "The Rating and Dating Complex," in *American Sociological Review*, Vol. 2 (October 1937), No. 5; pp. 727–734.

younger generation seems to find the superficial usages connected with the code highly amusing, but it is likely that it takes the central ideas quite seriously. The formal code appears to be derived chiefly from the usages of the English middle classes of a generation or so ago, although there are of course many other elements in it.

The usual or intended mode of operation of the formal mores of courtship—in a sense their "function"—is to induct young persons into marriage by a series of progressive commitments. In the solidary peasant community, in the frontier community, among the English middle classes of a few decades back, and in many isolated small communities in present-day America, every step in the courtship process has a customary meaning and constitutes a powerful pressure toward taking the next step—is in fact a sort of implied commitment to take the next step. The mores formerly operated to produce a high rate of marriage at the proper age and at the same time protected most individuals from many of the possible traumatic experiences of the courtship period.

The decay of this moral structure has made possible the emergence of thrill-seeking and exploitative relationships. A thrill is merely a physiological stimulation and release of tension, and it seems curious that most of us are inclined to regard thrill-seeking with disapproval. The disapproving attitude toward thrill-seeking becomes intelligible when we recall the purpose of such emotional stirrings in the conventional mores of courtship. Whether we approve or not, courtship practices today allow for a great deal of pure thrill-seeking. Dancing, petting, necking, the automobile, the amusement park, and a whole range of institutions and practices permit or facilitate thrill-seeking behavior. These practices, which are connected with a great range of the institutions of commercialized recreation, make courtship an amusement and a release of organic tensions. The value judgment which many lay persons and even some trained sociologists pass upon thrill-seeking arises from the organizational mores of the family —from the fact that energy is dissipated in thrills which is supposed to do the work of the world, i.e., to get people safely married.

The emergence of thrill-seeking furthers the development of exploitative relationships. As long as an association is founded on a frank and admitted barter in thrills, nothing that can be called exploitative arises. But the old mores of progressive commitment exist, along with the new customs, and peculiar relationships arise from this confusion of moralities. According to the old morality a kiss means something, a declaration of love means something, a number of Sunday evening dates in succession means something, and these meanings are enforced by the customary law, while under the new morality such things may mean nothing at all—that is, they may imply no commitment of the total personality whatsoever. So it comes about that one of the persons may exploit the other for thrills on the pretense of emotional involvement and its implied commitment. When a woman exploits, it is usually for the sake of presents and expensive amusements—the common pattern of "gold digging." The male exploiter usually seeks thrills from the body of the woman. The fact that thrills cost money, usually the man's money, often operates to introduce strong elements of suspicion and antagonism into the relationship.

With this general background in mind, let us turn to the courtship practices of college students. A very important characteristic of the college student is his bourgeois pattern of life. For most persons, the dominant motive of college attendance is the desire to rise to a higher social class; behind this we should see the ideology of American life and the projection of parents' ambitions upon children. The attainment of this life goal necessitates the postponement of marriage, since it is understood that a new household must be economically independent; additional complications sometimes arise from the practice of borrowing money for college expenses. And yet persons in this group feel very strongly the cultural imperative to fall in love and marry and live happily in marriage.

For the average college student, and especially for the man, a love affair which led to immediate marriage would be tragic because of the havoc it would create in his scheme of life. Nevertheless, college students feel strongly the attractions of sex and the thrills of sex, and the sexes associate with one another in a peculiar relationship known as "dating." Dating is a sort of dalliance relationship. In spite of the strength of the old morality among college students, dating is largely dominated by the quest of the thrill and is regarded as an amusement. The fact that college attendance usually removes the individual from normal courtship association in his home community should be mentioned as a further determinant of the psychological character of dating.

In many colleges, dating takes place under conditions determined by a culture complex which we may call the "rating and dating complex." The following description of this complex on one campus is probably typical of schools of the sort:

> X College, a large state-supported school, is located in a small city at a considerable distance from large urban areas. . . . There are few students who live at home, and therefore the interaction of the young is but little influenced by the presence of parents. The students of this college are predominantly taken from the lower half of the middle classes, and constitute

a remarkably homogeneous group. . . . Nevertheless, about half of the male students live in fraternities. . . . There is intense competition among the fraternities. The desire for mobility of class, as shown by dozens of inquiries, is almost universal in the group and is the principal verbalized motive for college attendance.

Dating at X College consists of going to college or fraternity dances, the movies, college entertainments, and to fraternity houses for victrola dances and "necking"; coeds are permitted in the fraternity parlors, if more than one is present. The high points of the social season are two house parties and certain formal dances. An atypical feature of this campus is the unbalanced sex ratio, for there are about six boys to every girl; this makes necessary the large use of so-called "imports" for the more important occasions, and brings it about that many boys do not date at all or confine their activities to prowling about in small industrial communities nearby; it also gives every coed a relatively high position in the scale of desirability; it would be difficult to say whether it discourages or encourages the formation of permanent attachments. Dating is almost exclusively the privilege of fraternity men, the use of the fraternity parlor and the prestige of fraternity membership being very important. Freshman men are forbidden by student tradition to have dates with coeds.

Within the universe which we have described, competition for dates among both men and women is extremely keen. Like every other process of competition, this one determines a distributive order. There are certain men who are at the top of the social scramble; they may be placed in a hypothetical Class A. There are also certain coeds who are near the top of the scale of dating desirability, and they also are in Class A. The tendency is for Class A men to date principally Class A women. Beneath this class of men and women are as many other classes as one wishes to create for the purpose of analysis. It should be remembered that students on this campus are extremely conscious of these social distinctions and of their own position in the social hierarchy. In speaking of another student, they say, "He rates," or "He does not rate," and they extend themselves enormously in order that they may rate or seem to rate.

Young men are desirable dates according to their rating on the scale of campus values. In order to have Class A rating they must belong to one of the better fraternities, be prominent in activities, have a copious supply of spending money, be well-dressed, "smooth" in manners and appearance, have a "good line," dance well, and have access to an automobile. Members of leading fraternities are especially desirable dates; those who belong to fraternities with less prestige are correspondingly less desirable. I have been able to validate the qualities mentioned as determinants of campus prestige by reference to large numbers of student judges.

The factors which appear to be important for girls are good clothes, a smooth line, ability to dance well, and popularity as a date. The most important of these factors is the last, for the girl's prestige depends upon dating more than anything else; here as nowhere else nothing succeeds like success. Therefore the clever coed contrives to give the impression of being much sought after even if she is not. It has been reported by many observers that a girl who is called to the telephone in the dormitories will often allow herself to be called several times, in order to give all the other girls ample opportunity to hear her paged. Coeds who wish campus prestige must never be available for last minute dates; they must avoid being seen too often with the same boy, in order that others may not be frightened away or discouraged; they must be seen when they go out, and therefore must go to the popular (and expensive) meeting places; they must have many partners at the dances. If they violate the conventions at all, they must do so with great secrecy and discretion; they do not drink in groups or frequent beer-parlors. Above all, the coed who wishes to retain Class A standing must consistently date Class A men. Cressey has pointed out that the taxi-dancer has a descending cycle of desirability. As a new girl in the dance hall, she is at first much sought after by the most eligible young men. Soon they tire of her and desert her for some newer recruit. Similarly the coed has a descending cycle of popularity on the campus which we are describing, although her struggle is not invariably a losing one. The new girl, the freshmen coed, starts out with a great wave of popularity; during her freshman year she has many dates. Slowly her prestige declines, but in this case only to the point at which she reaches the level which her qualities permanently assure her. Her descent is expedited by such "mistakes," from the viewpoint of campus prestige, as "going steady" with one boy (especially if he is a senior who will not return the following year), by indiscretions, and by too ready availability for dates. Many of the girls insist that after two years of competitive dating they have tired of it and are interested in more permanent associations.

This thrill-dominated, competitive process involves a number of fundamental antagonisms between the men and the women, and the influence of the one-sex group accentuates these. Writes one student informant, a girl, "Wary is the only word that I can apply to the attitude of men and women students toward each other. The men, who have been warned so repeatedly against coeds, are always afraid the girls are going to 'gold-dig' them. The coeds wonder to what degree they are discussed and are constantly afraid of being placed on the black list of the fraternities. Then too they wonder to what extent they can take any man seriously without being taken for a 'ride.'" Status in the one sex group depends upon avoiding exploitation by the opposite sex. Verbatim records of a number of fraternity "bull sessions" were obtained a few years ago. In these sessions members are repeatedly warned that they are slipping, those who have fallen are teased without mercy, and others are warned not to be soft. And almost all of the participants pretend a ruthlessness toward the opposite sex which they do not feel.

This competitive dating process often inflicts traumas upon individuals who stand low in the scale of courtship desirability. "While I was at X College," said a thirty-year-old alumnus, "I had just one date. That was a blind date, arranged for me by a friend. We went to the dorm, and after a while my girl came down and we were introduced. She said, 'Oh, I'm so sorry. I forgot my coat. I'll have to go get it.' She never came down again. Naturally I thought, 'Well what a hit I made!' " We have already seen that nonfraternity men are practically excluded from dating; it remains to note that many girls elect not to date rather than take the dates available to them. One girl writes as follows: "A girl's choice of whom to fall in love with is limited by the censorship of the one-sex group. Every boy that she dates is discussed and criticized by the other members of the group. This rigid control often keeps a girl from dating at all. If a girl is a member of a group in which the other girls are rated higher on the dating scale than she, she is often unable to get dates with boys who are considered desirable by her friends. In that event she has to decide whether to date the boys that she can and choose girl friends who would approve, or she must resign herself to not dating."

Since the class system, or gradient of dating desirability on the campus, is clearly recognized and adjusted to by the students themselves, there are interesting accommodations and rationalizations which appear as a result of inferior status. Although members of Class A may be clearly in the ascendant as regards prestige, certain groups of Class B may contest the position with them and may insist upon a measuring stick which will give them a favorable position. Rationalizations which enable Class D men and women to accept one another are probably never completely effective.

The accommodations and rationalizations worked out by one group of girls who were toward the bottom of the scale of campus desirability are typical. Four of these girls were organized in one tightly compact "bunch." All four lived off campus, and worked for their room and board. They had little money to spend for clothes, so there was extensive borrowing of dresses. Members of the group co-operated in getting dates for one another. All of them accepted eleventh hour invitations, and probably realized that some stigma of inferiority was attached to such ready availability, but they managed to save their faces by seeming very reluctant to accept such engagements, and at length doing so as a result of the persuasion of another member of the bunch. The men apparently saw through these devices, and put these girls down as last minute dates, so that they rarely received any other invitations. The bunch went through "dating cycles" with several fraternities in the course of a year, starting when one of the girls got a date with one member of the fraternity, and ending, apparently, when all the girls had lost their desirability in that fraternity.

Partly as result of the unbalanced sex ratio, the boys of the group which we are discussing have a widespread feeling of antagonism toward the coeds. This antagonism is apparently based upon the fact that most of the male students are unable to date with coeds, at least not on terms acceptable to themselves. As a result of this, boys take great pride in the "imports" whom they bring in for house parties, and it is regarded as slightly disgraceful in some groups to date a coed for one of the major parties. Other men in the dateless group take on the role of misogynists—and read Schopenhauer.

During the winter term the preponderance of men assures to every coed a relatively high bargaining power. Every summer witnesses a surprising reversal of this situation. Hundreds of women school teachers flock to this school for the summer term, and men are very scarce; smooth, unmarried boys of college age are particularly scarce. The school teachers are older than the boys; they have usually lost some of their earlier attractiveness; they have been living for some months or years within the school-teacher role. They are man-hungry, and they have a little money. As a result, there is a great proliferation of highly commercialized relations. The women lend their cars to their men friends, but continue to pay for repairs and gasoline; they take the boys out to dinner, treat them to drinks, and buy expensive presents for them. And many who do not go so far are available for sex relations on terms which demand no more than a transitory sort of commitment from the man.

The rating and dating complex varies enormously from one school to another. In one small, coeducational school, the older coeds instruct the younger that it is all right for them to shop around early in the year, but by November they should settle down and date someone steadily. As a result, a boy who dates a girl once is said to "have a fence around her," and the competition which we have described is considerably hampered in its operation. In other schools, where the sex ratio is about equal, and particularly in the smaller institutions, "going steady" is probably a great deal more common than on the campus described. It should be pointed out that the frustrations and traumas imposed upon unsuccessful candidates by the practice of "going steady" (monopolistic competition) are a great deal easier to bear than those which arise from pure competition. In one school the girls are uniformly of a higher class origin than the boys, so that there is relatively little association between them; the girls go with older men not in college, the boys with high school girls and other "townies." In the school which is not coeducational, the dating customs are vastly different, although, for the women at least, dating is still probably a determinant of prestige.

True courtship sometimes emerges from the dating process, in spite of all the forces which are opposed to it. The analysis of the interaction process involved seems to be quite revealing. We may suppose that in our collegiate culture one begins to fall in love with a certain unwillingness, at least with an ambivalent sort of willingness. Both persons become emotionally involved as a result of a summatory process in which each step powerfully influences the next step and the whole process displays a directional trend toward the culmination of marriage; the mores of dating break down and the behavior of the individuals is governed by the older mores of progressive commitment. In the fairly typical case, we may suppose the interaction to be about as follows: The affair begins with the lightest sort of involvement, each individual being interested in the other but assuming no obligations as to the continuation of the affair. There are some tentatives of exploitation at the beginning; "the line" is a conventionalized attempt on the part of the young man to convince the young woman that he has already at this early stage fallen seriously in love with her—a sort of exaggeration, sometimes a burlesque, of coquetry—it may be that each person, by a pretence of great involvement, invites the other to rapid sentiment-formation—each encourages the other to fall in love by pretending that he has already done so. If either rises to the bait, a special type of interaction ensues; it may be that the relation becomes exploitative in some degree and it is likely that the relationship becomes one in which control follows the principle of least interest, i.e., that person controls who is less interested in the continuation of the affair. Or it may be that the complete involvement of the one person constellates the other in the same pattern, but this is less likely to happen in college than in the normal community processes of courtship.

If both persons stand firm at this early juncture, there may ensue a series of periodic crises which successively redefine the relationship on deeper levels of involvement. One form which the interaction process may assume is that of "lover's quarrels," with which the novelists have familiarized us. A and B begin an affair on the level of light involvement. A becomes somewhat involved, but believes that B has not experienced a corresponding growth of feeling, and hides his involvement from B, who is, however, in exactly the same situation. The conventionalized "line" facilitates this sort of "pluralistic ignorance," because it renders meaningless the very words by means of which this state of mind could be disclosed. Tension grows between A and B, and is resolved by a crisis, such as a quarrel, in which the true feelings of the two are revealed. The affair, perhaps, proceeds through a number of such crises until it reaches the culmination of marriage. Naturally, there are other kinds of crises which usher in the new definition of the situation.

Such affairs, in contrast to "dating," have a marked directional trend; they may be arrested on any level, or they may be broken off at any point, but they may not ordinarily be turned back to a lesser degree of involvement; in this sense they are irreversible. As this interaction process goes on, the process of idealization is re-enforced by the interaction of personalities. A idealizes B, and presents to her that side of his personality which is consistent with his idealized conception of her; B idealizes A, and governs her behavior toward him in accordance with her false notions of his nature; the process of idealization is mutually re-enforced in such a way that it must necessarily lead to an increasing divorce from reality. As serious sentimental involvement develops, the individual comes to be increasingly occupied, on the conscious level at least, with the positive aspects of the relationship; increasingly he loses his ability to think objectively about the other person, to safeguard himself or to deal with the relationship in a rational way; we may say, indeed, that one falls in love when he reaches the point where sentiment-formation overcomes objectivity.

THE MARRIAGE MARKET AND ITS IRREGULARITIES *

To use the term "market" in connection with marriage may suggest something sordid. Perhaps here lies our first exercise in realism. The term is used to analyze certain aspects of marriage; it is helpful in our intellectual understanding of the situation. . . .

Marriage involves a market as does every other human process where there is a free seeking and choosing, by multitudes of individuals, of good things which are limited in quantity. There is demand and there is supply, whether we look at it from the standpoint of men or of women. The individual who falls in love and marries may feel that this course of events

* Taken from Folsom, Joseph Kirk, "Finding a Mate in Modern Society," in Folsom, Joseph Kirk (ed.), *Plan For Marriage* (New York: Harper & Brothers, 1938), pp. 73–79. Copyright, 1938, by Harper & Brothers.

is something unique and personal, which was predestined to happen to him and his partner. Yet in sober reality, the romance and marriage of this young couple were governed by the social circumstances and conditions surrounding them.

It will be helpful to bear in mind certain general facts about the marriage market in the United States. About 90 per cent of both men and women marry eventually, that is, if they live to be fifty-five or more. In the case of women, all but two or three per cent of those who will ever marry have done so by the age of thirty-five; in the case of men a somewhat larger proportion wait until after that age. If the man is in the early twenties, the average tendency is for him to marry a girl about three years younger than himself; the average groom of thirty-five takes a bride six or seven years younger. Because of the usually greater age of men when they marry and the fact that women on the average outlive men by two or three years, there are many more widows than there are widowers. Young men of the professional classes marry on the average at twenty-seven or twenty-eight years of age, while those of the laboring and farming classes tend to marry at twenty-five or less. . . .

One of the most important irregularities in the marriage market is the geographically and socially uneven distribution of the two sexes. The number of boys born is very slightly greater than that of girls. While Nature provides a partner for almost everyone, human beings do not stay where Nature puts them. Migration removes adolescent girls from the farm to the village or small city more than it does boys. But it also takes men and boys to the West, to large cities and to industrial communities. The farms, the large cities, metal-working industrial cities, and the West tend toward excess of males; suburbs, small cities, textile cities, and the South and New England tend toward excess of females. In *wealthy* suburbs there are only three single men to four single women, whereas in industrial suburbs there are four single men to three single women. In New England the sex ratio of the approximately total marriageable population (i.e., single, widowed, and divorced persons aged fifteen and over) is 89, and in the Pacific states it is 125.

No one knows how much our marriage rate is cut by these local irregularities in the distribution of the sexes, but it is certainly a factor of considerable moment. In the industrial suburbs as in the working class areas of large cities and in the West generally, it is the men who must compete vigorously for partners; the women are in the favored position, being fewer in number. In prosperous residential suburbs and among the more educated classes women must compete for men. This is a very rough picture of the situation, because the real competition is based not merely on the sex ratio of the whole population, or of the unmarried adult population, but more particularly upon the sex ratio within specific social horizons. Many of the excess males in the larger cities are itinerant workers or foreign-born, who would not normally be accepted in marriage by most of the resident women. In such cities there may be an actual shortage of men in the class within which the native American women, for example, would be willing to marry. . . .

Puzzling as it may seem, women are more affected than men by the sex ratio of their community. A certain irreducible percentage of men seem to remain bachelors anyway regardless of the sex ratio. They do not marry even when there is a surplus of women from which to choose. It is probable that these men remain bachelors either for financial or personality reasons and that many of them should so remain. On the other hand, when the men are in great preponderance in a community, almost every woman marries, there is no great residuum of spinsters. Thus if we examine the population of about forty years of age of the wealthy suburb of Brookline, Massachusetts, and the western industrial city of Pueblo, Colorado, we find that the percentage of men who remain single at this age is about 18 in both communities. On the other hand, the women of this age are 33 per cent single in Brookline, which has a huge excess of women, and only 9 per cent single in Pueblo, which has a large excess of men. Since women are more affected by the surplus or deficiency of men than the men are affected by a surplus or deficiency of women, it would seem that the woman's fate in the marriage market is relatively more a matter of opportunity or circumstance and less a matter of her own personality or personal competence. This means that there are probably many married women who are not well fitted for marriage, and many unmarried women who would make admirable wives. The same statement would not be true to so great a degree about men. It also follows from these facts that there are probably more frustrations among women than men because of wanting to be married and not succeeding. These are further intensified by the fact that men are still more free than women to secure a substitute for one aspect of married life, the sexual.

In general, then, it would seem that the marriage market presents a greater problem to women than to men. . . .

A closely related problem of the marriage market is what Dr. Popenoe calls the "mating gradient." This means that men on the average marry "downward." . . .

In one California study the average IQ of husbands was found to be about 8 points higher than that of their respective wives. Two-thirds of the men in another sample were found to have married women with lower IQ's than their own. Yet the average IQ of *all* males is the same as that of *all* females! In a third study 43 per cent of the men had wives with fewer years of formal education and only 24 per cent of them had wives with more schooling than their own. Several studies made by the writer's students, taking inventory of hundreds of married couples known to them personally, brought the same result as regards education. A sizable proportion of college men marry non-college women, but practically no college women marry men below college grade.

The surpluses of women in the wealthy suburbs and in the wealthier areas of cities are another phase of this same pattern. In the rougher and coarser social areas of a community or of a country, where men earn their living by the sweat of their brow, they are undersupplied with women. In the more privileged areas of a community or of a country, women outnumber men. The extra women are drawn in largely because of jobs peculiarly open to women, existing in those areas: domestic service, clerical work, school teaching, nursing, and so on. Thus social forces conspire to produce a pattern similar to that found in the majority of primitive and historical societies: polygyny at the top of the social scale, monogamy at the middle, and polyandry at the bottom. In our traditional culture, however, the surplus women at the top have chosen spinsterhood and celibacy rather than polygyny. There are indications, however, of a weakening in this acceptance of celibacy. Triangles of the one man and two women type develop; sometimes these are tolerated by the wife; in other cases the man changes partners by way of divorce, and we have "serial" rather than "simultaneous" polygyny. At the bottom of the social scale we find relatively more polyandrous relations, including prostitution.

A study in Philadelphia showed that people are about three times as likely to marry partners in their own occupations as pure chance would allow. Yet a large percentage of the educated women go into occupations where there is a shortage of men, such as school teaching, library work, and so on. Among the professional women in *Who's Who in America* only 22 per cent of the librarians are married, 36 per cent of the educators, 38 per cent of the physicians, 64 per cent of the actresses, 67 per cent of the musicians, and 75 per cent of the social workers. Popenoe points out that every year that an educated young woman delays marriage, her chances grow less. Her standard for a husband rises continually, while the number of unmarried men meeting this standard diminishes more rapidly than the number of unmarried women who desire such a standard. The eligible men are marrying other girls of less education.

Thirty years ago the probability of eventual marriage for the graduates of eastern women's colleges was only 50 to 60 per cent. These same colleges, however, have been steadily advancing their marriage rates until now it may be roughly estimated that their average graduate has a 75 or 80 per cent chance of eventual marriage. About the same may be said of the women graduates of all kinds of colleges today. This figure, let it be noted, is still substantially less than the figure for women at large (90 per cent).

Many educated women when they come to an age when marriage seems no longer probable develop a certain devotion to their work, together with a very impersonal attitude toward men, which tends to reduce what little chance they still have to marry. For many persons this is good mental hygiene. It is often better to renounce an objective completely as soon as its attainment appears improbable, than to cling for years to a hope whose periodic revivals are likely to be followed by new and bitter disappointments.

UNROMANTIC COURTSHIP *

The material following is a description of the sexual relations found among the second-generation Poles in a Western Massachusetts village of some three thousand population. The Poles constitute the main ethnic-group in the village, but there are many French-Canadians and Northern and Southern Irish: of the old Yankee stock there is but a small residue left. The village is non-farm, and the factory which was its reason for being has been shut down completely for over five years. The youth of the village are faced by an economic stone-wall.

THRILL-SEEKING THROUGH CASUAL DATING

There are three public dance-halls in the vicinity which are much frequented by the local youth. Not all the Polish girls accept dances from strangers and chance-acquaintances, but many do.

---

* Green, Arnold W., "The 'Cult of Personality' and Sexual Relations," in *Psychiatry: Journal of the Biology and Pathology of Interpersonal Relations,* Vol. 4 (August, 1941), No. 3, pp. 344–348.

The local boys usually drive to the surrounding towns and villages for their pick-ups, so that the Village's Main Street is the hunting ground for out-Village boys. The following is a scene that is many times almost duplicated every night of good weather.

> Three girls are parading Main Street in all their finery, keeping a sharp although carefully screened look-out for the cruising automobiles. A car slows to a stop. One of the three male occupants announces, "Isn't it a nice night." One of the girls draws up short with feigned surprise, snaps out a cool "Is it?"
>
> The other girls simulate anxiety to continue their walk, but apparently resign themselves to the whim of their bolder companion, albeit with poor grace. Then the conversation becomes general, the boys adopting a blatant pose of sophistication, the girls a tone of mockery.
>
> By silent, subtle communication the girls agree that the boys are sufficiently attractive, and, since none of them has previously had a distressing experience with one of the boys, they place their feet on the running-board of the car.[1] The conversation continues, loud and raucous; the boys disparage the size of the Village, the girls counter with wisecracks gleaned from the movies and radio. Finally, the girls enter the car. One of the boys announces he is not feeling well, cannot drink any beer, so they go for a ride.[2] The car is soon parked in a secluded road for a period of necking.

After the initial group-date, the most impressed boy may attempt to date one of the girls individually, either at a dance, on the street, or, rarely, by calling at the girl's home. If she is willing to continue seeing him, on that night or shortly thereafter, he tries to seduce her. The girl either submits or struggles, on a physical basis.

This is the social jungle, where frustration of the male calls forth aggression in the form of violence, the justification for which is this: that the girl has made her person in some degree accessible, and since there is no known code to which she can refer him as reason for resisting his advances, then it must be in slighting terms of personal dismissal, a flagrant affront to the boy's ego. In such a situation, rape is not uncommon.

In this type of behavior, members of one sex group exhibit no interest in members of the other as persons. Rapport is crude and unorganized,

---

[1] A local boy explained the significance of this act: "When 'they' put their feet on the running-board of your car; you know you've got 'em."

[2] For the girl, this type of behavior does not offer the opportunity for economic exploitation that dating affords the middle-class girl. Usually it takes the combined resources of two or three lads to gasoline a car for an evening's entertainment.

based upon sexual excitation.[3] Each sex group manifests a profound distrust of the other. The boys consider themselves gulled and derided when refused intercourse. The girls travel together as a sort of mutual aid society. As between them and the boys there is little feeling of friendliness, but rather a situation approximating open warfare.[4]

EXPLOITATIVE RELATIONS

This type of courtship is the continued going together of a pair, both of whom usually live in the Village. It is more general than casual dating, claiming many more of the Polish youth. Its greater frequency is occasioned by the girls' preference and the shortage of funds among the boys. Continued going together constitutes an exploitative relation, for it redounds even more certainly than casual dating to the control of the boy.

Usually, the girl who goes steadily with a boy is more reserved, less promiscuous and foolhardy than those who date indiscriminately. For any of a complex of reasons she does not flaunt her person on the open street or freely invite the attentions of strangers.

Status on the basis of occupation is denied the girl, for the local region offers nothing better than the sweat-shop or domestic service in a near-by city. Intense boredom and irritation are her lot in a home where privation rules, and where Polish speaking parents do not understand her or her problems.

The girl is not inculcated with the cult of personality, which is largely dependent upon the family for imposition, but she has taken over all of the superficialities of American life. She reads American magazines, attends an American school, wears American clothes, speaks the latest American radio slang, and has become an American swing-addict.

She is conversant with a world that her parents do not know, but which they suspect, and against which they attempt to retaliate by using the coercive measures the girl knows are not sanctioned in the American culture. While for the most part conforming outwardly, the girl holds the dictates of her parents in either tolerant or bitter contempt.

Her milieu fails to offer her the steady, uncompromising set of habits

[3] Neither the community nor the Polish ethnic-group offer any patterns for social relationships between the young of opposite sexes except on the basis of dating or "going together."

[4] The printable terms used to refer to members of the opposite sex by the boys include "bag," "squash," "pig." These terms constitute aggression-releases. They are used with special relish by social rejects, who thus express contempt—a hate derivative—for recalled blocking of the sexual impulse.

of purposeful industry, unreflecting loyalty to family welfare, which rural-familism affords, nor, the cheap commercialized amusement available in cities, nor yet, a new purposeful life-organization to supplant that which cared for her parents.

One result of this *impasse* has been the burgeoning of in-groups among the girls whose main activity is the reading and discussion of romantic fiction and true-confessional magazines. So much time spent in vicarious experience of idealized love has made the romantic interest paramount in the girl's life.

In the eyes of her companions she gains status by attracting and holding the attention of some young man. Losing him means losing face for there are no other interests to which to turn, no work that can be made important as a defense. And her bargaining position is such that she is allowed to have no one in reserve.

Most important of all, she cannot disparage the relationship to her sex in-group, or declare herself not really involved, for she has already, naively, made an open confession of deepest involvement. She does not have the bourgeois trait of close-mouthedness, of training in secrecy, which is invaluable to efficient competition and bargaining.

When her young man makes sexual demands of her, threatens to terminate the relationship if refused, she is literally caught in a trap. The ultimatum creates a problem for her, but very little moral indignation is aroused for her training has not led her to expect kindliness and deference. Pride and the fear of becoming the butt of cruel jokes prompt her to yield.

To her, marriage is the only available career, and she is hoping the boy will ultimately marry her so that she may escape her conflict-ridden home. The loss of her 'virtue' does not compare with the disaster that non-marriage would bring. And since she is not an economic asset to her parents, they also are anxious that she marry; they would make her life considerably more uncomfortable than it is if she sent the boy away. Because the lack of understanding in her home precludes a familial discussion of the problem, she follows the line of least resistance.

The question might be raised whether the nature of her romantic interest, fed by love-story book and magazine, does not lead her to expect noble sacrifice and idealism in her own romantic relationship, and thus prompt her to refuse the boy's demands. Such is not the case. The boys whom she knows exhibit little differentiation of personality. They are unemployed or unskilled laborers, have a uniform small amount of formalized education, similar outlook on life, similar backgrounds, the same narrowly circumscribed set of interests, and they all conform to the dead level of mediocrity demanded by the Village.

For this reason her state of in-loveness attaches easily, almost impersonally seeks out a love-object. Instead of idealizing the personality of the love-object, she continues to idealize the ideal. Since the transition to the idealization of the person is not made, since her love-phantasies are projected out of sight, that is, are not applicable to any of the boys she knows, the boy's ultimatum does not force her to hate him or to revise her set of values.

The boy, in contradistinction to the girl, is usually involved in both types of courtship at the same time. It is legitimate to speak of the attitude and value complex he brings to the courtship arena as a constant factor; it will not be necessary to introduce even a crude descriptive dichotomy such as was used in sorting the girls.

The boy has a reduced success drive. He does not exercise the caution, foresight, and repression of impulse that the middle-class boy must use in courtship, as in all other relationships, to ensure that the channels of vertical mobility be kept open to him. In terms of social and economic betterment, the local Polish boy has little either to gain or lose by marrying: he gains a better opportunity of holding a job, since, locally, single men are the first to be laid off; and his chances of securing work on the WPA, or getting on relief, are bettered. He loses freedom of action in sexual adventure.

Thus a passive-resistant, uncalculating attitude is maintained toward marriage. Its coming soon or late means little to the boy's life organization: while contraceptives are always carried during casual dating, he often grows careless in steady dating. Most of the marriages in the Polish Parish are precipitated by premarital pregnancy.

He maintains an aggressive-sexual attitude toward women, is not interested in them as persons. He does not have the romantic concept of love. Three indices illustrate this:

The boy, of whatever age, scornfully rejects the love-theme in his reading matter. From the local Library he secures adventure, detective, and mystery yarns. Not only "love stuff," but any book which deals with emotional problems irritates him.

At the local movie hour, when the hero pauses in pursuit of the villain to proffer the heroine a tender sentiment, whistling and foot-stamping greet his fall from grace; and the lights go up, the old janitor scampers about aimlessly, pleading for quiet amidst the deafening uproar, when a movie approximating the problem-play is presented.

Over the beer-bottles, in tavern and club, the code of toughness is eulogized. Sexual exploits, actual and imaginary, are discussed in terms of successful hunting. Imputed failure to bring an affair to its natural conclusion is met with caustic ridicule. Because sexual success is a sure road to status, the sexual interest is almost as important to the boy as the romantic interest is to the girl.

It is doubtful that the boy is capable of falling in love, if love be considered a striving toward a person, generating ideation and emotion to overcome cultural blocks. His background does not foster idealization of the other's personality. Any block he encounters he personalizes. His milieu prompts and enables him to exploit the girl sexually. He is only too well aware of the strength of his bargaining position. He makes the most of it.

RESULTANT MARRIAGES

There are two polar points of view which may be adopted in making an evaluation of the marriages resulting from the courtship practices described: first, that of society, which is interested in seeing that a marriage remains legally unbroken, that divorce or desertion does not occur; second, that of the person, who is primarily concerned with satisfying his own physical, psychic, and social needs.

The Polish Parish has had but one divorce and two cases of desertion in the past five years. Ethnic-group solidarity is still strong enough in this rural community to enforce outer conformity.

Yet, one might wonder why the local marriage remains unbroken when it is entered by a reluctant boy, by a girl who has been coerced during courtship, by a couple who do not feel the ecstatic "oneness" which typically precipitates middle-class marriage. The answer is that while the cult of personality offers many psychic satisfactions, some of which have been mentioned, in this instance its *absence* fosters institutional stability!

Like members of the middle-class, the local couple yearn for ego-gratification, but on a different level. Attacks and unreflective self-assertions of the other that would bring a "hurt response," and the necessity for a re-definition of the situation in a middle-class marriage, do not mean significant changes for the local marriage. Precisely because the pair are not "one," as demanded by middle-class ideology, the marriage can bear up under insults, vulgarities, aggressions, that would utterly ruin a middle-class marriage.

The local couple have not idealized a tremendous expectation for their marriage. The marriage relation is not intensive. There is not a ceaseless seeking-out of the other's motivation, no rigid set of expectations to which the other must conform, with the feeling of betrayal if the other does not conform. Conflict is concrete, specific, limited in time and area of interaction, and while violent, rarely summatory, typically subsiding, through sheer lack of further momentum, with no new definition of the situation.

The cult of personality, in courtship and marriage, demands its price: a psychic defenselessness against real or putative attacks on the ego by the beloved, a quivering sensitivity which, without moralizing, might be posited as a luxury the poor can ill afford.

The local couple, having largely renounced the success-drive, are spared the frustrations the middle-class husband experiences in striving to advance himself when he is blocked, and the pique the middle-class wife feels in being married to such a man.

MARRIAGE BETWEEN RACIAL CASTES *

In the southern part of the United States, where white and black constitute two distinct racial castes, no intermarriage is legally or morally permitted. The rationale of the prohibition is strikingly revealed in the usual legal definition of a Negro. A favorite legislative formula is that a Negro is anyone who has one-eighth or more of Negro blood in his veins. Georgia bans marriage between a white person and persons having an "ascertainable trace of either Negro, African, West Indian, Asiatic Indian, Mongolian, Japanese, or Chinese blood in their veins." Such laws indicate one thing: that the racial integrity of the upper caste is to be strictly maintained, to the degree that all persons of mixed racial qualities shall be placed unequivocally in the lower of the two castes. To permit intermarriage would be to give the hybrid offspring the legal status of its father, and would soon undermine the very basis of the caste order. Hence either intermarriage must be strictly forbidden or racial caste abandoned. Thirty states forbid intermarriage and thus align themselves legally on the side of racial caste.

Even in those states where intermarriage is legal it seldom occurs, being against custom.

* Davis, Kingsley, "Intermarriage in Caste Societies," in *American Anthropologist,* Vol. 43 (July–September, 1941), No. 3; pp. 388–389.

CLASS ENDOGAMY IN THE UNITED STATES *

Our courtship system is analogous to our economic system. We have an open-class economic order. Each person begins in the class rung to which he is born, but he may subsequently rise or fall according to his achievements. Similarly in courtship each person starts in terms of his involuntary social background, but since the courtship process is highly competitive, he has a chance to attain a different result according to his personal charm, skill, and achievements. Yet the social background and the social limits to competition mean that most Americans marry within their own social class. It is not surprising to learn, as Davie and Reeves found, that "practically no intermarriage (3.9 per cent) occurred between areas far removed in social, economic, and cultural traits."

Romantic love does militate against class endogamy, because, as we have seen, it places a high evaluation upon the person as a person, independently of his social circumstances. Hence, in theory at least, qualities that do not count for much in the class system—such as beauty and amorous skill—count for a great deal in courtship. A man of high position may supposedly fall in love with a waitress, actress, or other woman far beneath him socially. But in practice, since the personality is so largely a product of past social experience, there is no such thing as "the person" apart from all social circumstance. Inevitably some of the factors that go to create the intrinsic person with whom one falls in love are class factors. Bernard Shaw's play, *Pygmalion,* well illustrates these points. As long as the heroine retained her original class characteristics, she was not a fit person for the young aristocratic speech professor to fall in love with. But as soon as he had altered her habits to conform with upper class standards, she was such a fit person. Hence, though romantic love theoretically makes possible interclass marriage, the courtship process works out so that relatively little of it occurs. . . .

PROPINQUITY AND MATE SELECTION

The urban society of today has no rules prescribing exogamy or endogamy on the basis of local area; but marriages occur most frequently

* By the senior editor, from an unpublished manuscript.

between those who have a high degree of proximity to each other. Three excellent studies have been made, one by Bossard in Philadelphia, another by Davie and Reeves in New Haven, and a third by Daniel Harris, with respect to the residential propinquity of couples just prior to their marriage.[1] In these studies the investigators tabulated marriage license applications according to the place of residence of the applicants, and measured in terms of city blocks the distance between the residences of the two applicants in each case. Bossard found that in 12.64 per cent of the cases the couple lived at the same address, in 17.18 per cent they lived within one block or less of each other, in more than 30 per cent they lived within five or less blocks of each other, and in more than 50 per cent they lived within twenty or less blocks of each other. He also found that in only 17.8 per cent of the cases did one of the contracting parties live outside of the city at the time of application, and that the percentage of marriages decreased steadily and markedly as the distance between the residences of the contracting parties increased. Propinquity may play a larger role than these figures indicate, for the author reminds us that it was not possible to determine the number of cases in which the parties, living far apart at the time of application, formerly lived nearer to each other. In view of what is so often said about the mobility and unneighborliness of urban life, these findings are fairly striking, especially when it is borne in mind, as Dr. Bossard points out, that the greater the area taken into account, the larger is the number of potential mates.

The study by Davie and Reeves found the role of propinquity to be strikingly similar in New Haven. For the most part, only minor differences were discovered, *viz.* (a) the proportion of couples whose premarital addresses were less than three blocks apart was not so great in New Haven as in Philadelphia; (b) the number of couples residing from three to twenty blocks apart was proportionately greater in New Haven; (c) the proportion of spouses living more than twenty blocks was lower in New Haven than in Philadelphia; and (d) the number of couples in which one of the parties resided outside the city was greater in New Haven than in the other town. The only striking difference was that in the Connecticut city only 6.42 per cent of the couples gave the same address for both parties, whereas the figure was 12.64 per cent in the Pennsylvania

[1] James H. S. Bossard, "Residential Propinquity as a Factor in Marriage Selection," *Amer. J. of Sociology* 38 (Sept., 1932), pp. 219–224; Maurice R. Davie and Ruby Jo Reeves, "Propinquity of Residence Before Marriage," *Amer. J. of Sociology,* 44 (Jan., 1939), pp. 510–517; Daniel Harris, "Age and Occupational Factors in the Residential Propinquity of Marriage Partners," *Journal of Social Psychology,* Vol. 6 (May, 1935), pp. 257–261.

city.[2] "It is quite remarkable that in each city 51 per cent of all cases fall within the twenty-block radius." Furthermore, "an almost identical pattern emerges in the two cities when twenty blocks or more intervene between the two addresses."

The authors of the New Haven study went further than Bossard; they attempted in ecological terms to answer the question, to what extent is propinquity of residence an index of cultural similarities in the backgrounds of the contracting parties. From the marriage licenses alone they discovered that closely propinquitous marriages (i.e. within five blocks) showed, first, an unusual number of atypical matings (e.g. groom younger than bride, groom very young or very old, both parties marriage repeaters, bride widowed or divorced, civil rather than religious ceremony), and second, a high degree of racial and national homogeneity, being especially frequent among Negroes, Jews, and Italians. By plotting the propinquitous marriages in terms of the natural ecological areas of New Haven, the authors found that in 43.4 per cent of all the cases the marriage-contracting parties lived in the same ecological area.

> This is especially significant in view of the small size of most of the areas. They range in maximum distance from four to thirty-two blocks (only two areas show a maximum distance range of twenty or more blocks), and they average about eleven blocks. If to these cases are added those of individuals marrying within like areas (30.2 per cent), then nearly three-quarters (73.6 per cent) of all persons marrying within the city chose mates residing in the same type of neighborhood. Practically no intermarriage (3.9 per cent) occurred between areas far removed in social, economic, and cultural traits.

The authors conclude, therefore, that residential propinquity in marriage is a result of two factors: (a) the tendency of people with similar class status to congregate in urban areas; (b) the tendency of people living near each other to have more contact and hence a greater tendency to marry. The latter factor, however, as both studies suggest, is an important factor per se, since the applicants tended to select mates from near at hand rather than from a distance within the same area, and did not select mates very frequently from similar areas further removed.

---

[2] There may be a flaw in these cases. The same address may be given as a matter of convenience, and thus increase the number beyond what it actually should be. On the other hand, one would expect a contrary error in the marriage licenses—namely, that if a couple have been residing together as man and wife, they would hesitate to give the same address on the license but would invent a separate one for one of the parties, which would tend to make the apparent figures *lower* than they should be.

RELIGIOUS ENDOGAMY IN THE UNITED STATES *

Practically every religion recruits its new members primarily by birth. Intermarriage therefore not only threatens the sect with the possible loss of an adult member, but the possible loss of new child members. For this reason intermarriage must either be forbidden or so regulated that the allegiance of the children is guaranteed.

JEWISH ENDOGAMY

Jews have always frowned upon intermarriage with non-Jews. The Mosaic prohibition of marriages between Israelites and Canaanites was extended to all the pagan nations with whom the Jews had contact. Ezra's ordinance that the Jews returning from the Babylonial exile put aside their alien wives was added to the Mosaic prohibition, and furnished authority in the time of the Maccabeans and of the Roman wars for Talmudic and codified interdictions against matrimonial connections between Jews and all gentiles. Exception was made by some rabbis in case the non-Jew became a proselyte. In later times, as the Jews became increasingly a part of Western civilization and hence merely another sect in a welter of religious groups found in this civilization, the prohibition against intermarriage was relaxed somewhat. . . . The Jewish synod convened by Napoleon in 1807 declared that when contracted in accordance with the civil code, marriages between Israelites and Christians were valid. Such marriages, of course, could not be solemnized by the religious rites of Judaism, but they were no longer punishable by ritual anathema. The Rabbinical Conference of Braunschweig in 1844 went further and declared that intermarriage of Jews with Christians or with other adherents of monotheistic religions was not forbidden, provided the parents were permitted by the law of the state to rear the offspring in the Jewish faith. This abandonment of the Talmudic position, however, aroused strong criticism even from the advocates of reformed Judaism. The majority of Reform Jewish rabbis have maintained the orthodox position that intermarriage is a threat to Judaistic survival. In spite of the feeling against intermarriage, however, it has always taken place. It has varied in amount according as the relations of the state and religion have varied. Where the state has been

* By the senior editor, from an unpublished manuscript.

dominant and has left religious matters alone, intermarriage has been high. This was the case in Germany before the Third Reich, as it is the case in France and America today. But where the state has concerned itself with religion, either to take sides with one faith (as in pre-revolutionary Russia) or to set up a new faith of its own (as in the Nazi regime), then the pressure against intermarriage, both internally and externally, has increased. In addition, since the Jewish group has some of the earmarks of a caste, it seems true that the more open and mobile a given social organization has been, the more numerous the intermarriages between Jew and non-Jew.

CATHOLIC ENDOGAMY

Christianity has matched the Jewish endogamous rule with prohibitions of its own against the marriage of Christians to Jews. Indeed it has gone further and set up impediments against the marriage of Christians to non-Christians, whether the latter be Jews, Pagans, Moslems, or what not. Christianity has softened its endogamous rule only where by the marriage conversion to Christianity appeared possible. When the conversion seemed hopeless, marriage to a pagan was forbidden. Similarly, by the famous Pauline privilege, if one's mate became a proselyte to another religion, he could be divorced.

With the coming of the Reformation, Catholic councils and synods extended the prohibition to apply to Protestants, and the Popes inveighed in strong language against intermarriage with them. The Protestants retaliated by forbidding intermarriage with Catholics.

Today, the increasing secularization of life, growing individualization in courtship, and rising dominance of state law over religious law in the regulation of marriage, have all diminished the force of church impediments. Yet within the religious community the endogamous rules are still in effect, especially so far as Catholics are concerned.

The revised code of canon law of 1918 reiterates the prohibition of marriages between individuals of "mixed religion and disparity of cult," but as a concession to the increasing laxness in the rigid enforcement of the impediments it permits such marriages if the non-Catholic party promises in writing that he will not interfere with the religious worship of the Catholic and if both parties promise that the children of both sexes will be baptized and reared in the Catholic religion. These conditions were rigidly insisted upon in 1932 in a letter issued by the church authorities who set as punishments for violations the annulment of the marriage, exclusion from participation in church activities, the denial of a church funeral and in extreme cases public excommunication.[1]

Today the interesting feature of these religious injunctions is that they have no legal force. The law is an instrument of the state, and the state has not seen fit in most countries to bar intermarriage between religious sects. Indeed, through its recognition of civil marriage and its licensing system, the modern nation generally treats marriage as a nonreligious phenomenon. In some instances, the effort of religious associations to restrict the marriage choice of their members by contractual agreements has been prosecuted as illegal because it offends the law that no contracts may be made in restraint of marriage.

A question has arisen as to the legal effects of the ante-nuptial promise to rear the children in the Catholic faith which the Church requires of anyone marrying a Catholic.[2] Such a promise, if carried out plainly minimizes the threat of mixed marriage to the Church itself, for if the children are reared in the Catholic faith, the irregularity is restricted to one generation only; whereas if the children are reared in the faith of the non-Catholic parent, the procreative power of the Catholic parent is lost to the Church. But, as might be expected, the English and American courts have generally refused to give to the ante-nuptial promise the standing of a legal contract. There are no statutes covering the matter, and the leading cases which have set the precedent in common law have held that a father, by virtue of his position in the family, has the right to determine the religious education of his children and cannot restrict this right by a contract with the wife, who has in this matter a subordinate position.[3] Rev. White tries to demonstrate that this ground is obsolete in view of the modern equality between man and wife, and that the other reasons in the cases supposedly setting precedents have been extraneous to the main issue, the cases having been decided on grounds of jurisdiction, age of the children, delay in bringing suit, etc. He attempts to show that the ante-nuptial promise should and will stand in law, and he goes so far as to provide a model form which should be used in reducing the promise to writing, with appropriate legal wording, witnesses, and duplicates. The promise, he believes, is a real contract by the usual legal definition. The Catholic party acquires the right to

[1] *Encyc. of Soc. Sciences,* VIII, p. 152.

[2] See Robert J. White, *The Legal Effect of Ante-Nuptial Promises in Mixed Marriages* (Philadelphia, 1932). This is an excellent treatise on the subject from the Catholic point of view.

[3] White, *op. cit.,* pp. 4–26.

have the children baptized and reared in the Catholic religion, in return for which she is willing to marry the other party.

In spite of the cogency of the Reverend White's legal reasoning, however, there are probably extra-legal factors which will continue to bring adverse decisions from the courts relative to these promises. One of these is the unexpressed but popular ethical view that a marriage is in itself an agreement which demands a great deal from both parties, and that to ask one party, in addition to the ordinary sacrifices, to give up the right to rear the children in his own religion, is asking too much to be fair. Stated differently, it may be said that in a nation where different religious groups have a comparatively equal status, it goes against the grain to have one receive all the advantages, the other all the disadvantages of a mixed marriage. Thus the Protestant is likely to say that he dislikes mixed marriage as much as a Catholic does, but that he is not so unfair as to demand that when a mixed marriage does occur the children are to be reared exclusively in the Protestant faith. . . .

PROTESTANT ENDOGAMY

At times the Protestant sects have been quite militant against intermarriage. An act of 1697 in Ireland provided that no Protestant woman who possessed or was heir to real property to the value of £500 should marry a Papist under penalty of losing her total property. Another law of the same country in 1725 made it a felony for any Papist priest or unfrocked clerk to perform a mixed marriage. But in 1932, shortly after the restatement of the Catholic demands on the subject, the Federal Council of Churches of Christ in America contented itself with asserting that "where intolerable conditions are imposed . . . persons contemplating a mixed marriage should be advised not to enter it." All Protestant creeds have brought some pressure upon their adherents to prevent intermarriage into other religious groups.[4] In the present day, however, the pressure is not great, especially as between different Protestant sects.

---

[4] *Encyc. of Soc. Sciences,* VIII, p. 153.

CHAPTER XXIII

Women in the Labor Force

One of the great problems of modern industrial society is how to use women economically at the same time that they perform their function of bearing and rearing children. Formerly, in an agricultural setting, economic production and human reproduction could be performed simultaneously. The home and farm constituted the economic unit where the woman could perform those duties most compatible with her role as wife and mother. Nowadays, however, economic production has moved out of and away from the home. If a woman is to be economically employed, she usually has to leave her home for the greater part of the day. This necessarily interferes with child-rearing, which, especially with the new scientific techniques of child care and child training, is a 24-hour-per-day task. The development of the small family pattern has further complicated the matter in one sense; for it means that usually there are no relatives living with the family who can care for the child while the mother is away working. On the other hand, the small family pattern has enabled women to have fewer children and to have them in a smaller portion of the reproductive span. This has freed many women for economic productivity during a good part of their lives. The problem of getting the two functions together has not been solved, however, and its ramifications will continue to cause our society much concern.

EMPLOYMENT OF MARRIED WOMEN *

Whenever unemployment is in the public mind, there is likely to be some controversy over public policy regarding the employment of married women. At such times there is usually a demand for government

* Durand, John D., "Married Women in the Labor Force," *The American Journal of Sociology,* Vol. 52, (November, 1946), pp. 217–223.

and industry to [get] married women out of the labor market in order to make more jobs available to men. This and other reductions in the labor force are proposed as alternatives to increasing employment opportunities so that all persons wanting work can be employed.

The economics of paring down the labor force as a way of getting "full employment" is questionable, to say the least. But those who favor this policy fortify their case with arguments on noneconomic grounds. They argue that even if there were no danger of mass unemployment, the nation could benefit more from women's services in keeping house and bringing up children than it could from their employment in producing economic goods. They say that the increase in the number of married women working for pay—a trend which has been going on in this country for many decades—undermines the American home and threatens to destroy the population itself by reducing the birth rate. The question of public policy involved in this argument is particularly pertinent at the present time because the number of married women in the labor force increased very greatly during the war and has not, at least not yet, returned to normal.

TABLE I *

PER CENT OF MARRIED WOMEN IN THE LABOR FORCE, BY AGE: 1890 AND 1940

Age	*Per Cent in Labor Force*	
	1890	*1940*
Under 25 years	6.4	18.0
25–34 years	4.7	20.0
35–44 years	4.4	17.1
45–54 years	3.8	12.4
55–64 years	2.9	7.7
65 years and over	2.1	3.0

* Census figures adjusted for comparability; 1940 figures obtained by adding to published data for married women (husband present) estimates for married women (husband absent) based on an unpublished tabulation for a small sample of the census returns, made available to the author by the Bureau of the Census.

In 1940, according to the census, about 16 per cent of all married women were in the labor force. The corresponding figure for 1890, adjusted so far as possible for comparability, was 4 or 5 per cent. As far as one can tell from the census figures the percentage rose steadily, decade by decade, during the half-century interval. There is some doubt on this score because the figures from successive censuses are not exactly comparable, and all of them, except possibly the 1910 figures, were probably too small to represent the whole number of married women in the labor force at the census dates. But without any doubt the trend has been sharply upward for a long period of time.

An age by age comparison of 1890 and 1940 percentages of married women in the labor force, which is shown on Table 1, indicates that there has been an increase in every age group for which data are available. The increases were relatively greatest for women in the childbearing ages. . . .

THE BIRTH RATE AND THE EMPLOYMENT OF WIVES

Without any doubt this trend is connected with the decline of the birth rate. What is the nature of the causal connection? We have some 1940 census data which throw light on this question.

The percentages of married women (husband present) in the labor force in 1940, classified by number of children under ten years old, are shown in Table 2. In the age group eighteen to twenty-four years, the percentage in the labor force was almost four times as high for women who had no children under ten as it was for women who had one such child. The percentage for mothers with one child, in turn, was nearly twice as high as that for mothers with two or more children. In the older groups the differentials were smaller, but even in the group forty to forty-four years old the percentage for women with no children under ten was twice as high as the percentage for women with one such child.

The younger the children the smaller is the probability that the mother will be in the labor force. This is shown by 1940 labor force percentages for married women (husband present) who had only one child under ten, standardized for age of the women, and classified by age of the child. The percentage of mothers working was only two-thirds as great if the child was under five as it was if the child was five to nine years old. Children over ten years of age also tend to keep their mothers out of the labor market. Among wives of family heads who had no children under ten years old, the standardized labor force percentage was about three-fourths as great if there was a child ten to seventeen years old as it was if there was no such child. It is evident that the percentage of married women in the labor force at a given time is related to the trend of the birth rate during at least two prior decades. Most important in this connection is the trend in the proportion of women who bear no children at all, but, for those who become mothers, the age at which they bear their children is also very important in relation to employment, and the number of children is of some importance.

TABLE 2*

PER CENT IN THE LABOR FORCE FOR MARRIED WOMEN (HUSBAND PRESENT) EIGHTEEN TO FORTY-FOUR YEARS OLD BY NUMBER OF CHILDREN UNDER TEN YEARS OLD: 1940

Age (years)	*Women with No Children under Ten*	*Women with One Child under Ten*	*Women with Two or More Children under Ten*
18–24	27.2	7.2	4.3
25–29	36.1	11.5	7.4
30–34	31.1	11.9	8.2
35–39	23.3	10.0	7.2
40–44	16.9	8.2	6.5

* Census figures adjusted.

The causal relationship is not simple. Having a child evidently reduces very greatly the probability that the mother will be in the labor force. At the same time being in the labor force reduces the probability that a woman will bear a child within a given period of time. Having children involves an economic sacrifice to the parents in any case, but the sacrifice is doubly great when the wife must give up her job to become a mother. Furthermore, trends in fertility and in the employment of married women are jointly related to other factors. Gainful employment and family limitation may both be means of attaining the same objectives: a higher level of living or more independence and a broader sphere of interests for the wife. In many cases women also work in order to save money so that they can afford to have children.

Therefore, no one can say exactly how much of the increase in employment of married women has been caused by the decline of the birth rate or how much of the decrease in fertility has been due to increased employment of potential mothers. But it is possible to estimate the maximum effect of changes in fertility on the trend in employment of married women, and vice versa. . . .

Declining fertility has probably had a substantial effect on the percentage of married women in the labor force, but the increase in that percentage has been the result mainly of other factors. Likewise, the decrease in fertility has been caused mainly by factors other than increasing employment of married women though the employment trend has probably been a substantial contributing factor.

In the future a further decline of the birth rate because of factors other than increasing employment of married women would probably contribute substantially to the growth of the female labor force, but the trend will depend primarily on other factors. Conversely, a further rise in the percentage of married women in the labor force would probably tend to depress the birth rate in the future, but the trend of the birth rate will be governed mainly by other factors.

URBANIZATION AND THE EMPLOYMENT OF WIVES

A review of factors other than fertility which are likely to affect the future trend in employment of married women indicates that the trend is likely to continue upward in the long run, regardless of any probable change in the birth rate. One of the reasons why more working wives can be expected in the future is the progress of urbanization. In the past this has been an important reason for the growth of the female labor force as well as a substantial factor contributing to the decline of the birth rate.

The importance of urban-rural distribution in relation to the employment of married women is indicated by these standardized percentages from the 1940 census for married women (husband present) eighteen to sixty-four years old: The percentage in the labor force was about 16½ per cent in metropolitan districts of 100,000 or more and other urban areas as compared with 13 per cent in rural-nonfarm areas and only 6 per cent in rural-farm areas outside of metropolitan districts of 100,000 or more. The low percentage for rural-farm women is related to their comparatively high birth rate; but even when women without any children under ten are considered separately, the percentages in the labor force for metropolitan and urban areas are very much higher than those for rural-farm areas. The differential is partly a result of differences in employment opportunities. As a rule it is not customary in the United States for women to do farm work except for light chores and certain kinds of seasonal labor; and in the outlying, rural districts there is not much other gainful work which they might do. Besides, attitudes regarding the propriety of paid work for married women are different in farm and nonfarm areas. The idea that a woman has almost as much right to a job as a man is a comparatively new one, and it penetrates slowly into the more conservative rural communities. . . .

In the future there can hardly be any doubt that urbanization, or, at least, sub-urbanization and the spread of the urban attitude regarding gainful employment of women, will continue. It will be an important factor tending toward a further increase in the percentage of married women in the labor force.

CHANGING OCCUPATIONAL PATTERNS AND OTHER FACTORS

Closely related to urbanization are certain trends in the occupational composition of the demand for labor which are favorable to the employment of women in general. In the long run there is a widening field for the employment of professional workers; clerical, sales, and other white-collar workers; and semi-skilled industrial operatives—occupations for which women are well suited. These occupational trends are rooted in continuing changes in methods of production and in the demands of consumers. They can be expected to continue in the future. . . .

Also important among these "other" factors is the development of household conveniences and commercial services which, together with the declining birth rate, have helped to lighten women's home duties and to free them for outside work. Washing machines, mechanical refrigerators, vacuum cleaners, and automatic central heat are among the labor-saving conveniences which have helped to shorten the housewife's working day. Laundries, bakeries, clothing factories, and restaurants are among the commercial establishments that have transferred much of her work to the sphere of gainful activity. The development of such conveniences and services has by no means reached its limit. For example, an extension of the frozen food industry, providing complete, precooked meals frozen on disposable dishes, seems to be in prospect. Eventually institutional facilities for the care of children may be developed on a large scale. The final result might be virtually to eliminate the home as a place of work and housewives as a functional group of the population.

All signs indicate that the opportunity for married women to work will continue to improve in the long run, even without a further decline of the birth rate. There is more doubt about future developments affecting their desire to work. The motive, of course, is mainly financial, though other considerations also are important, especially in the case of professional women. If peace and full employment can be maintained in the future, the United States can look forward to an era of prosperity and rising per capita income. Under such conditions, how will women's economic motive to be in the labor force be affected?

TABLE 3*

PER CENT OF MARRIED WOMEN IN THE LABOR FORCE IN 1940, BY HUSBAND'S WAGE OR SALARY INCOME IN 1939 AND NUMBER OF CHILDREN UNDER TEN YEARS OLD

Wage or Salary Income of Husband	*Women with No Children under Ten*	*Women with One or More Children under Ten*
$ 1– 199	33.1	16.6
$ 200– 399	28.5	13.9
$ 400– 599	26.9	12.3
$ 600– 999	24.8	12.1
$1,000–1,499	21.5	8.9
$1,500–1,999	14.0	5.6
$2,000–2,999	12.1	3.3
$3,000–and over	8.5	2.8

* Married women (husband present) eighteen to sixty-four years old, in metropolitan districts of 100,000 or more population, whose husbands received less than $50 of income more than wages or salaries. Percentages based on adjusted census figures, standardized for age of women.

According to the theory which most economists hold at present, the proportion of people who offer their labor on the market tends to diminish as the level of real wages rises, other things being equal, but there is not enough statistical evidence to show whether this is true or not, at least so far as married women are concerned. The 1940 census statistics show that the wives in the poorest families are the ones most likely to be in the labor force. This is indicated by the figures in Table 3, which shows standardized percentages in the labor force in 1940 for married women (husband present) eighteen to sixty-four years old, in metropolitan districts of 100,000 or more, whose husbands had less than $50 nonwage income, classified by husband's wage or salary income in 1939 and standardized for age of the women. The concentration of working wives in the lowest income brackets is evident, especially in the case of the wives who had children under ten years old. But this correlation between income of husband

and employment of wife is a static one and does not prove that there is a similar dynamic relationship between *changes* in the level of real wages and *changes* in the percentage of wives who work, or who desire to work, over long periods of time. The urge to add to the family's income presumably depends not so much on how much income the family has as on the width of the gap between actual income and desired income. No one knows whether the rise in the level of real wages in the United States has been accompanied by a greater or smaller rise in the desired living standard. It is only possible to observe that the percentage of married women in the labor force has increased in the long run while real wages rose and that the increase apparently continued fairly steadily through decades of prosperity and decades of depression. Perhaps it is a justifiable inference that this trend will continue in the future regardless of general economic conditions.

THE VALUE OF MARRIED WOMEN'S EMPLOYMENT

In summary, the long-established upward trend in the percentage of married women working for pay is likely to continue in the future, once the abnormal conditions caused by the war have disappeared. The reasons why it can be expected to continue are largely independent of the future decline of the birth rate which most students of population expect in the long run. Increasing employment of potential mothers will probably tend to make the birth rate lower than it would otherwise be if no public action is taken to counteract its depressing effect on fertility. But the future course of the birth rate will depend mainly on other circumstances.

There has been a great deal of able discussion of public policy toward employment of married women in relation to population policy. Two points in it should be emphasized. In the first place, married women's employment is a great economic advantage, often amounting virtually to a necessity, for their families. It is also an economic benefit to the nation since it makes possible a higher income per capita of the population and a greater total economic product. In the second place, public policy in this matter, if any, does not necessarily involve a choice between more children and greater material wealth. Only a minority, even of the married women who have no children, is in the labor force. Increasing gainful employment of married women is not necessarily incompatible with a rising birth rate, as shown by our experience during the war when the number of wives in the labor force rose to an unprecedented figure while the birth rate shot upward.

With a proper distribution of responsibilities for producing economic goods on the one hand and for bearing and rearing children on the other, the nation could enjoy the benefit of a much fuller utilization of married women as a labor resource without an adverse effect on the birth rate. The problem of public policy arises from the fact that such a rational distribution of functions is not likely to come about of its own accord. To achieve it with economic justice to those who assume the burden of parenthood, and without violating individual freedom, is a task of social engineering which this nation may yet have to face if it should embark on a program of raising the birth rate.

CHAPTER XXIV

Adolescence and Parent-child Relations

AMERICA is notoriously a place where parent-child relations are subject to stress and strain. The reasons are numerous, but they all revolve around the role of the family in modern society. The transfer of functions from the family and the reduction in the size of the household have left a situation in which conflict would seem inevitable. A centrifugal force is affecting the home and making the mutual adjustment of parent and child a difficult process. This is why American parents spend so much time thinking about their parental problems, and why adolescence in our culture is a period of emotional turmoil. The selections below are meant to illuminate some of the major stresses and strains. They deal with the problems of the adolescent in American society and with the conflict between children and their parents.

ADOLESCENCE AND THE SOCIAL STRUCTURE *

Whether recognized as a separate status or not, the adolescent period seemingly has one outstanding peculiarity—namely, that it is a time when the individual is attaining physical maturity without necessarily attaining social maturity. In terms of growth, strength, fecundity, and mental capacity, full maturity tends to be attained only a short time after puberty; but socially the adolescent still has a long way to go, in most cases, before full status is reached.

This tendency for the adolescent to be more mature physically than socially is most pronounced in settled and traditionalized, and also modern, societies, but it is a condition that is to some extent inherent in the nature of all human society. Evolving through uncounted millennia, culture has developed a complexity of principle and a fullness of content that require a

* Davis, Kingsley, "Adolescence and the Social Structure," *The Annals of the American Academy of Political and Social Science,* Vol. 236 (November, 1944), pp. 8–15.

long time for the individual to master. At the same time it has made possible a type of social organization in which power and advantage are dependent on social position, knowledge, experience, and reputation, rather than brute strength or innate cunning. In so far as these things have anything to do with age, they are more likely to come with middle age, or even old age, than with adolescence. There has grown up, therefore, a situation in which the adolescent, despite his physical equality with or even superiority to the older person, is nevertheless placed in a socially subordinate position. The result is a sort of disharmony which, in times of social disorganization, *sometimes* expresses itself in conflict between the generations.

If mental and physical maturity came between 30 and 35 years of age, instead of between 15 and 20, there would be a much longer period of youthful plasticity during which an enormously enhanced amount of culture could be absorbed. As it is, especially in modern society, the individual must keep on learning after his capacity to do so has already begun to decline. Even though his mental *capacity* has reached its peak during adolescence, his acquired knowledge, judgment, insight, and self-reliance are generally far from their peak.

The great extension of the average length of life in modern times, while it has afforded more scope and rationale to post-adolescent learning, has not lengthened the adolescent period itself. Instead, it has prolonged the duration of adulthood, and has consequently made adolescence a smaller fraction of the average life-span.

Also helping to make the complex heritage of modern culture possible is specialization. Each individual is not required to learn the entire culture, but only that part of it which concerns him. The mechanism, however, like the extension of the length of life, has its limitations, as one can readily see by imagining a society with no general language but merely a separate language for every occupational group.

Societies of course differ as to how freely they permit young people to accumulate knowledge and experience. Frequently in order to transmit first the ideal elements of the culture, the elders select the cultural content that is given to children and protect them from contrary experiences. To the extent that this happens, it postpones social maturity to some stage beyond adolescence. In modern society, because of this protectiveness as well as other factors, even middle-aged people are commonly accused of being emotionally immature.

In addition to the increasing complexity of culture and the consequent length of time required for socialization, social evolution has progressed to the point where power does not ordinarily depend on physical prowess. Even an army, which presumably depends par excellence on physical skill and strength, is controlled by elderly generals and colonels. The adolescent, despite his achievements in battles, sports, and tests, has long been forced to defer to older persons whose biological capacities are less than his. The latter, by virtue of having held a position early in life, are able, in a stable society, to continue to hold it later in life, and by virtue of it to acquire other positions of even greater influence. Furthermore, because of the endlessness of the educational process, they are in a way better qualified for responsible positions. Their qualification, however, is a socially acquired and not a biologically maturing qualification. It is based on knowledge and experience, both necessary for successful political and administrative decisions.

Thus in a sense (the physical sense) the community does not utilize its great men until they are already past their prime; but in another sense (the social sense) it utilizes them at the peak of their greatness—in what one might call their administrative or sociological maturity. The principle of seniority, therefore, is no accident, no empty form. The charge is frequently made that the old hang onto their positions as vested interests, and that this is the explanation of the subordination of youth to age. That older persons seek to hold what power they have is generally true, but their desire does not explain the fact that they *can* do so. They are able to hold their power because they have a kind of superiority—a superiority developed and buttressed by an organized society, but a superiority nonetheless.

If our hypothesis is true, then adolescence is ordinarily the time when the lag of social development behind physical development first becomes pronounced. As society grows more complex the lag becomes greater, and adolescence, as socially defined, extends farther into organic adulthood.

MAJOR POINTS OF ARTICULATION

Sociologically, it is necessary to get behind the kaleidoscopic array of customs in different societies and to examine the alternative principles which *any* human society, as a functional and structural system, has at its disposal in utilizing the adolescent generation. Between the adolescent stratum and the rest of the social structure there are numerous points of articulation where alternative principles may be employed. Indeed, anyone unfamiliar with the anthropological literature is likely to be surprised at the number of junctures in which adolescence must somehow be handled but in which the mode of handling is open to several divergent possibilities.

In what follows, only four such points of articulation will be discussed, viz.: occupational placement, reproductive control, authoritarian organization, and cultural acquisition. These correspond to four major foci of institutional organization, namely: the economic, the familial, the political, and the educational. In each case the alternative employed by any given society depends primarily on that society's total structure.

Occupational placement. Since every society involves some specialization of function, an important matter is the selection of individuals for various occupations. This selection may be made by ascription or by choice. If by choice, it can be made at any time, but if much training is required, it needs to be made by the time of adolescence at the latest, because this period represents the last stage of rapid learning. The earlier the choice is made, the more intensive can be the training. On the other hand, the later it is made, the more it may rest on a true evaluation of personal talent and preference.

It is probably no accident, therefore, that the most complex societies (i.e., modern Occidental ones) on the whole defer the final decision until adolescence and provide most of the specialized training during that period. Less complex societies, such as that of classical India, may decide the matter at birth and provide what training is necessary during the entire childhood. In simpler societies the division of labor may be so slight that the question, except perhaps as regards the positions of chief and shaman, may be unimportant. In a complex but changing society the decision as to occupation tends to be deferred until late adolescence or early adulthood, because occupational possibilities are altering so fast that decisions made earlier may be subsequently rendered inadvisable; yet it is precisely in such a society that an elaborate training, and hence an early decision, are necessary.

The handling of occupational placement plays a significant role in determining the status of the adolescent. If in a simple and stable society the occupation is ascribed or chosen early in life, if the training extends through childhood or is relatively simple in character, adolescence does not stand out occupationally as a period of any particular importance. By the time he reaches adolescence the individual may in fact be practicing his occupation, and may be looked upon in this regard as an adult. If on the other hand the society is complex and changing, adolescence tends to become a time of difficult choosing and intensive training, and hence to acquire a pronounced importance as a socially recognized, eventful period of life. If there is a gradation within each occupation, the adolescent generally starts at the bottom rung. This tends to give him a distinct subordinate status.

If the element of competition is introduced, it acts as an individualizing force that makes of adolescence a period of strain and perhaps of deprivation, at the same time that it raises the level of general achievement.

Reproductive control. In its determination of the adolescent status, every society must somehow recognize the fact that the reproductive capacity first appears at the inception of adolescence. One crucial question is whether the adolescent shall be permitted to gratify his sexual desires through normal heterosexual intercourse or whether such gratification must be postponed. A second is whether the gratification, if permitted, shall be in marriage or in premarital relations; and if the latter, whether the illegitimate children shall be killed, disposed of to relatives, or kept by the girl. Finally, there is the question of whether marital choice is free or is controlled by others, and whether marriage establishes a separate household or merely an extension of the parental menage.

Among most peoples of the world, at least until recently, there was some variation of a recurrent pattern. Either marriage occurred shortly after puberty or premarital intercourse prevailed. The choice of a marital partner was generally in the hands of parents or kinsmen, though the right of veto, in theory at least, supposedly belonged to the parties to the marriage. Wedlock did not usually imply a separate household, and did not convey full emancipation from the parents. Although there were countless variations on this generalized pattern, the underlying theme was extremely widespread. Its main characteristic was that it gave a sexual and reproductive function to the adolescent but carefully controlled the exercise of this function.

By way of contrast, American society is unusual, though not entirely unique, in the following ways: It maintains the ideal of premarital chastity in the face of a long period of postponement of marriage after puberty. In connection with this, it upholds the freedom of marital choice and fosters competition and the doctrine of *caveat emptor* in courtship. Finally, it emphasizes the independence and separateness of the wedded couple. As a consequence, the adolescent period becomes one of considerable strain. The young person is permitted to associate closely with the opposite sex but is put on his honor to remain virtuous, is supposed to choose his own mate independently but is in many ways still under the authority of the parents, and is forced to compete for love in a rating and dating system that interferes and gets entangled with his fortunes in that other competitive system, the occupational. The strains are somewhat different for boys and for girls, but only as two different sides of the same situation.

Authoritarian organization. Whereas American youth think that getting a job and getting married entitle them to independence, the case is quite different in many other societies. In old India, Ireland, China, and Japan, for example, the authority of the parent tended to continue until death. The end of adolescence did not mean a significant change in authority, and hence the adolescent phase, for that reason at least, did not stand apart as a separate period. In addition, there was little conflict over authority, not only because complete emancipation did not occur, but also because such emancipation as did occur developed by well-grooved, mutually accepted, publicly ritualized steps.

In modern society, by contrast, the child is supposed to become completely emancipated from the parental power, but the exact time, manner, and cause of such emancipation remain uncertain, a subject of dispute, recrimination, and remorse. The individual may become a full-fledged wage earner as early as childhood or as late as adulthood. Marriage is often postponed so long that there tends to arise a distinction between the adolescent and the unmarried adult. Neither employment nor matrimony, therefore, may be accepted as a standard criterion of emancipation. There is no such standard criterion. Each family must virtually settle the matter for itself as a result of private interaction. This in spite of the fact that the emancipation, once it does come, is relatively more complete than in most societies.

In Peter Blos's book, *The Adolescent Personality,* one of the three major goals of adolescence is claimed to be "emancipation from the family." Achieving this goal is viewed as a long and hard psychic struggle. Yet in most societies it either comes in the normal course of affairs or never comes at all. Among us, it comes as a struggle because the adolescent needs the protection of his family at the same time that he rebels against its authority, because he dreads to leave the glamorous irresponsibility of youth for the humdrum cares of adulthood, and because he has no standardized steps by which emancipation can be automatically and publicly achieved.

In relation to older persons outside his family, the adolescent, if he has a separate status at all, usually has a subordinate one, because of the sociological reasons for the seniority principle already discussed. The adolescent boy is most likely to be accorded full adult status in simple, mobile, warlike societies, where physical prowess is emphasized as a societal necessity. Even so, it is only during the latter part of the adolescent period, say between the ages of 18 and 22, that he achieves virtual parity. The Comanche culture, for example, prior to the coming of the whites placed considerable emphasis on youth but the older men nevertheless retained a superiority in magic which partially compensated them for their loss of prestige due to physical decline.

In our society, even apart from the family, the adolescent finds an absence of definitely recognized, consistent patterns of authority. Because of the compartmentalization of the culture he is defined at times as an adult, at other times as a child. Furthermore, he is subjected to a confusing array of competing authorities, of which the school is the principal but not the happiest one.

Cultural acquisition. In most social systems the child acquires the rudiments of the culture informally. Any definite instruction by parents or elders is of short duration and limited scope. Only the highly civilized societies possess specialized educational establishments professionally staffed and forming a separate phase of life, and even they until recently reserved these establishments primarily for the upper social ranks (as in most of Latin America today).

For inculcating modern culture, the universal and specialized school system is a necessity. Its concentrated and abstract curriculum, professional staff, physical separateness, and internal organization all give a rapid and systematic grounding in the principles of the civilization, and remarkably facilitate the educational process. But by virtue of the very qualities that make it efficient in teaching abstractions, it tends to divorce itself from the facts and experiences of everyday life. For years the pupil is drilled in principles, on the assumption that he will subsequently apply them in actual life. His childhood is thus treated as the preparation for life, not as real life itself.

The difficulty, of course, is that not everything can be taught in school. The person often emerges with a hoard of abstract knowledge, but with little knowledge of the concrete situations he must negotiate in order to get along. The harder he studies, the more unfit he becomes for ordinary day-to-day existence. Above all, there is such a long interval between learning and application that the incentive to learn often flags and must be bolstered by an amazing system of planned competition and artificial rewards.

Out of ennui and practical necessity the average pupil finally begins to participate in a more vivid world, the world of youth culture. This, in its adolescent phase, is characterized by irresponsibility, "having a good time," athletics, sex attraction, and the repudiation of adult control. One reason it takes this form is that it is "denied status by society at large, and is regarded primarily as a destructive and undesirable, a foolish and queer expression of the impulses of young people." It has, in other words, no avowed function in the institutional structure, but is interstitial, officially purposeless, a phenomenon seldom found in other societies.

No wonder the cry of unreality is raised against the school system, and reforms are proposed which have in view the reintegration of education and life. Some of the reforms, however, have missed the point. They have overlooked the efficiency of systematic instruction and have attempted to make education "grow out of real life situations," not realizing that since modern culture rests on abstract knowledge, to confine all instruction to the applied and the concrete would soon produce stagnation.

The root of the difficulty apparently lies in the fact that while the young person is going to school he is doing little else of a responsible and productive nature. Therefore, the remedy is, perhaps, to give him an essential function in the world outside of school—i.e., to let him work—and to relate his schooling to this function. He could then receive his reward not solely in terms of grades, diplomas, honors, and degrees, but also in terms of wages and things accomplished. Thus the learning of principles would be attached to actual situations, not by the radical method of reducing all learning to a clumsy empiricism and thereby bankrupting the culture, but by making the young person a citizen who produces to the limit of his natural and acquired capacities.

The objection that a thorough grounding in basic principles leaves little time for participation in economic and political activity is valid. But there are three directions in which this obstacle may be overcome: first, the invention of new educational technology; second, the elimination of irrelevancies from the curriculum; and third, the overhauling of the incentive mechanism. New educational technology, such as the recent methods of improving reading habits, may make possible the absorption of the same amount of knowledge in a much shorter time. As to irrelevancies in the curriculum, it seems clear that they are there because the purpose of schooling, both for the society and for the individual, is not clear. One way of eliminating them would be to define more clearly the fundamentals in our culture and thus reduce the number and the variety of "liberal arts" subjects. An additional way would be to eliminate applied subjects, such as manual training and shorthand, except in so far as they relate to the pupil's known vocation. This would require specialization earlier in the school career than is now in fashion, and would have the disadvantage of requiring the choice of an occupation when the individual is still young and hence incapable of choosing wisely; although under a planned economy, vocational guidance by experts would be required in any case. Early specialization would allow the school work to be tied to actual life, because the child would enter the first stages of his occupation while already going to school. This, in turn, would help to solve the incentive problem. If a child were already launched on the first stages of his occupation, if his school subjects had specific application to his job, so that his wages, advancement, and so forth, depended on them, he would be more disposed to study.

CAUSES OF PARENT-YOUTH CONFLICT *

Why does contemporary western civilization manifest an extraordinary amount of parent-adolescent conflict? In other cultures, the outstanding fact is generally not the rebelliousness of youth, but its docility. . . . What, then, are the peculiar features of our society which give us one of the extremest examples of endemic filial friction in human history?

Our answer to this question makes use of constants and variables, the constants being the universal factors in the parent-youth relation, the variables being the factors which differ from one society to another. Though one's attention, in explaining the parent-youth relations of a given milieu, is focused on the variables, one cannot comprehend the action of the variables without also understanding the constants, for the latter constitute the structural and functional basis of the family as a part of society.

The first important variable is the rate of social change. Extremely rapid change in modern civilization, in contrast to most societies, tends to increase parent-youth conflict, for within a fast-changing social order the time-interval between generations, ordinarily but a mere moment in the life of a social system, becomes historically significant, thereby creating a hiatus between one generation and the next. Inevitably, under such a condition, youth is reared in a milieu different from that of the parents; hence the parents become old-fashioned, youth rebellious, and clashes occur which, in the closely confined circle of the immediate family, generate sharp emotion. . . .

THE BIRTH-CYCLE AND DECELERATING SOCIALIZATION

Note, however, that rapid social change would have no power to produce conflict were it not for two universal factors: first, the family's dura-

* Davis, Kingsley, "The Sociology of Parent-Youth Conflict," *American Sociological Review*, Vol. 5 (August, 1940), pp. 523–535.

tion; and second, the decelerating rate of socialization in the development of personality. "A family" is not a static entity but a process in time, a process ordinarily so brief compared with historical time that it is unimportant, but which, when history is "full" (i.e., marked by rapid social change), strongly influences the mutual adjustment of the generations. This "span" is basically the birth-cycle—the length of time between the birth of one person and his procreation of another. It is biological and inescapable. It would, however, have no effect in producing parent-youth conflict, even with social change, if it were not for the additional fact, intimately related and equally universal, that the sequential development of personality involves a constantly decelerating rate of socialization. This deceleration is due both to organic factors (age—which ties it to the birth-cycle) and to social factors (the cumulative character of social experience). Its effect is to make the birth-cycle interval, which is the period of youth, the time of major socialization, subsequent periods of socialization being subsidiary.

Given these constant features, rapid social change creates conflict because *to* the intrinsic (universal, inescapable) differences between parents and children it adds an extrinsic (variable) difference derived from the acquisition, at the same stage of life, of differential cultural content by each successive generation. Not only are parent and child, at any given moment, in different stages of development, but the content which the parent acquired at the stage where the child now is, was a different content from that which the child is now acquiring. Since the parent is supposed to socialize the child, he tends to apply the erstwhile but now inappropriate content. . . . He makes this mistake, and cannot remedy it, because, due to the logic of personality growth, his basic orientation was formed by the experiences of his own childhood. He cannot "modernize" his point of view, because he is the product of those experiences. He can change in superficial ways, such as learning a new tune, but he cannot change (or *want* to change) the initial modes of thinking upon which his subsequent social experience has been built. To change the basic conceptions by which he has learned to judge the rightness and reality of all specific situations would be to render subsequent experience meaningless, to make an empty caricature of what had been his life.

PHYSIOLOGICAL DIFFERENCES

Though the disparity in chronological age remains constant through life, the precise physiological differences between parent and offspring vary radically from one period to another. The organic contrasts between parent and *infant,* for example are far different from those between parent and adolescent. Yet whatever the period, the organic differences produce contrasts.

Most societies avoid the potential clash of old and young by using sociological position as a neutralizing agent. They assign definite and separate positions to persons of different ages, thereby eliminating competition between them for the same position and avoiding the competitive emotions of jealousy and envy. Also, since the expected behavior of old and young is thus made complementary rather than identical, the performance of coöperative functions is accomplished by different but mutually related activities suited to the disparate organic needs of each, with no coercion to behave in a manner unsuited to one's organic age. In our culture, where most positions are *theoretically* based on accomplishment rather than age, interage competition arises, superior organic propensities lead to a high evaluation of youth (the so-called "accent on youth"), a disproportionate lack of opportunity for youth manifests itself, and consequently, arrogance and frustration appear in the young, fear and envy, in the old.

ADULT REALISM VERSUS YOUTHFUL IDEALISM

The decelerating rate of socialization, when taken with rapid social change and other conditions of our society, tends to produce certain differences of orientation between parent and youth.

Though both youth and age claim to see the truth, the old are more conservatively realistic than the young, because on the one hand they take utopian ideals less seriously and on the other hand take what may be called operating ideals, if not more seriously, at least more for granted. Thus, middle-aged people notoriously forget the poetic ideals of a new social order which they cherished when young. In their place, they put simply the working ideals current in the society. There is, in short, a persistent tendency for the ideology of a person as he grows older to gravitate more and more toward the status quo ideology, unless other facts (such as a social crisis or hypnotic suggestion) intervene. With advancing age, he becomes less and less bothered by inconsistencies in ideals. He tends to judge ideals according to whether they are widespread and hence effective in thinking about practical life, not according to whether they are logically consistent. Furthermore, he gradually ceases to bother about the *untruth* of his ideals, in the sense of their failure to correspond to reality. He assumes through long habit that, though they do not correspond perfectly, the discrepancy is not significant. The reality of an ideal is defined for him in terms of how many people accept it rather than how completely it is mirrored in actual behavior.[1] Thus, we call him, as he approaches middle age, a realist.

The young, however, are idealists, partly because they take working ideals literally and partly because they acquire ideals not fully operative in the social organization. Those in authority over children are obligated as a requirement of their status to inculcate ideals as a part of the official culture given the new generation.[2] The children are receptive because they have little social experience—experience being systematically kept from them (by such means as censorship, for example, a large part of which is to "protect" children). Consequently, young people possess little ballast for their acquired ideals, which therefore soar to the sky, whereas the middle-aged, by contrast, have plenty of ballast.

This relatively unchecked idealism is eventually complicated by the fact that young people possess keen reasoning ability. The mind, simply as a logical machine, works as well at sixteen as at thirty-six.[3] Such logical capacity, combined with high ideals and an initial lack of experience, means that youth soon discovers with increasing age that the ideals it has been taught are true and consistent are not so in fact. Mental conflict thereupon ensues, for the young person has not learned that ideals may be useful without being true and consistent. As a solution, youth is likely to take action designed to remove inconsistencies or force actual conduct into line with ideals, such action assuming one of several typical adolescent forms —from religious withdrawal to the militant support of some utopian scheme—but in any case consisting essentially in serious allegiance to one or more of the ideal moral systems present in the culture.[4]

---

[1] When discussing a youthful ideal, however, the older person is quick to take a dialectical advantage by pointing out not only that this ideal affronts the aspirations of the multitude, but that it also fails to correspond to human behavior either now or (by the lessons of history) probably in the future.

[2] See amusing but accurate article, "Fathers Are Liars," *Scribner's Magazine,* March, 1934.

[3] Evidence from mental growth data points to a leveling off of the growth curve at about age 16. For charts and brief explanations, together with references, see Shuttleworth, F. K., *The Adolescent Period,* Monographs of the Society for Research in Child Development, III, Serial No. 16 (Washington, D.C., 1938), Figs. 16, 230, 232, 276, 285, 308.

Maturity of judgment is of course another matter. We are speaking only of logical capacity. Judgment is based on experience as well as capacity; hence, adolescents are apt to lack it.

[4] An illustration of youthful reformism was afforded by the Laval University students who decided to "do something about" prostitution in the city of Quebec. They broke into eight houses in succession one night, "whacked naked inmates upon the buttocks, upset beds and otherwise proved their collegiate virtue. . . . " They ended by "shoving the few remaining girls out of doors into the cold autumn night." *Time,* October 19, 1936.

A different, usually later reaction to disillusionment is the cynical or sophomoric attitude; for, if the ideals one has imbibed cannot be reconciled and do not fit reality, then why not dismiss them as worthless? Cynicism has the advantage of giving justification for behavior that young organisms crave anyway. It might be mistaken for genuine realism if it were not for two things. The first is the emotional strain behind the "don't care" attitude. The cynic, in his judgment that the world is bad because of inconsistency and untruth of ideals, clearly implies that he still values the ideals. The true realist sees the inconsistency and untruth, but without emotion; he uses either ideals or reality whenever it suits his purpose. The second is the early disappearance of the cynical attitude. Increased experience usually teaches the adolescent that overt cynicism is unpopular and unworkable, that to deny and deride all beliefs which fail to cohere or to correspond to facts, and to act in opposition to them, is to alienate oneself from any group, because these beliefs, however unreal, are precisely what makes group unity possible. Soon, therefore, the youthful cynic finds himself bound up with some group having a system of working ideals, and becomes merely another conformist, cynical only about the beliefs of other groups.

While the germ of this contrast between youthful idealism and adult realism may spring from the universal logic of personality development, it receives in our culture a peculiar exaggeration. Social change, complexity, and specialization (by compartmentalizing different aspects of life) segregate ideals from fact and throw together incompatible ideologies while at the same time providing the intellectual tools for discerning logical inconsistencies and empirical errors. Our highly elaborated burden of culture, correlated with a variegated system of achieved vertical mobility, necessitates long years of formal education which separate youth from adulthood, theory from practice, school from life. Insofar, then, as youth's reformist zeal or cynical negativism produces conflict with parents, the peculiar conditions of our culture are responsible.

PARENTAL AUTHORITY

Because of his strategic position with reference to the new-born child (at least in the familial type of reproductive institution), the parent is given considerable authority. Charged by his social group with the responsibility of controlling and training the child in conformity with the mores and thereby insuring the maintenance of the cultural structure, the parent, to fulfill his duties, must have the privileges as well as the obligations of authority, and the surrounding community ordinarily guarantees both.

The first thing to note about parental authority, in addition to its function in socialization, is that it is a case of authority within a primary group. Simmel has pointed out that authority is bearable for the subordinate because it touches only one aspect of life. Impersonal and objective, it permits all other aspects to be free from its particularistic dominance. This escape, however, is lacking in parental authority, for since the family includes most aspects of life, its authority is not limited, specific, or impersonal. What, then, can make this authority bearable? Three factors associated with the familial primary group help to give the answer: (1) the child is socialized within the family, and therefore knowing nothing else and being utterly dependent, the authority of the parent is internalized, accepted; (2) the family, like other primary groups, implies identification, in such sense that one person understands and responds emphatically to the sentiments of the other, so that the harshness of authority is ameliorated; (3) in the intimate interaction of the primary group control can never be purely one-sided; there are too many ways in which the subordinated can exert the pressure of his will. When, therefore, the family system is a going concern, parental authority, however inclusive, is not felt as despotic.

A second thing to note about parental authority is that while its duration is variable (lasting in some societies a few years and in others a lifetime), it inevitably involves a change, a progressive readjustment, in the respective positions of parent and child—in some cases an almost complete reversal of roles, in others at least a cumulative allowance for the fact of maturity in the subordinated offspring. Age is a unique basis for social stratification. Unlike birth, sex, wealth, or occupation, it implies that the stratification is temporary, that the person, if he lives a full life, will eventually traverse all of the strata having it as a basis. Therefore, there is a peculiar ambivalence attached to this kind of differentiation, as well as a constant directional movement. On the one hand, the young person, in the stage of maximum socialization, is, so to speak, *moving into* the social organization. His social personality is expanding, i.e., acquiring an increased amount of the cultural heritage, filling more powerful and numerous positions. His future is before him, in what the older person is leaving behind. The latter, on the other hand, has a future before him only in the sense that the offspring represents it. Therefore, there is a disparity of interest, the young person placing his thoughts upon a future which, once the first stages of dependence are passed, does not include the parent, the old person placing his hopes vicariously upon the young. This situation, representing a *tendency* in every society, is avoided in many places by a system of respect for the aged and an imaginary projection of life beyond the grave. In the absence of such a religio-ancestral system, the role of the aged is a tragic one—sometimes compensated for by an interest in the grandchildren, which permits them partially to recover the role of the vigorous parent.

The essential point is not that there are other authorities—in every society there are extrafamilial influences in socialization—but that, because of specialization and individualistic enterprise, they are *competing* authorities. Because they make a living by their work and are specialists in *socialization,* some authorities have a competitive advantage over parents who are amateurs or at best merely general practitioners.

Let us now take up, point by point, the manner in which western civilization has affected this *gemeinschaftliche* and processual form of authority.

1. *Conflicting norms.* To begin with, rapid change has, as we saw, given old and young a different social content, so that they possess conflicting norms. There is a loss of mutual identification, and the parent will not "catch up" with the child's point of view, because he is supposed to dominate rather than follow. More than this, social complexity has confused the standards *within* the generations. Faced with conflicting goals, parents become inconsistent and confused in their own minds in rearing their children. The children, for example, acquire an argument against discipline by being able to point to some family where discipline is less severe, while the parent can retaliate by pointing to still other families wherein it is firmer. The acceptance of parental attitudes is less complete than formerly.

2. *Competing authorities.* We took it for granted, when discussing rapid social change, that youth acquires new ideas, but we did not ask how. The truth is that, in a specialized and complex culture, they learn from competing authorities. Today, for example, education is largely in the hands of professional specialists, some of whom, as college professors, resemble the sophists of ancient Athens by virtue of their work of accumulating and purveying knowledge, and who consequently have ideas in advance of the populace at large (i.e., the parents). By giving the younger generation these advanced ideas, they (and many other extrafamilial agencies, including youth's contemporaries) widen the intellectual gap between parent and child.

3. *Steps in parental authority.* Not institutionalized, our society provides little explicit institutionalization of the progressive readjustments of authority as between parent and child. We are intermediate between the extreme of virtually permanent parental authority and the extreme of very

early emancipation, because we encourage release in late adolescence. Unfortunately, this is a time of enhanced sexual desire, so that the problem of sex and the problem of emancipation occur simultaneously and complicate each other. Yet even this would doubtless be satisfactory if it were not for the fact that among us the exact time when authority is relinquished, the exact amount, and the proper ceremonial behavior are not clearly defined. Not only do different groups and families have conflicting patterns, and new situations arise to which old definitions will not apply, but the different spheres of life (legal, economic, religious, intellectual) do not synchronize, maturity in one sphere and immaturity in another often coexisting. The readjustment of authority between individuals is always a ticklish process, and when it is a matter of such close authority as that between parent and child it is apt to be still more ticklish. The failure of our culture to institutionalize this readjustment by a series of well-defined, well-publicized steps is undoubtedly a cause of much parent-youth dissension. The adolescent's sociological exit from his family, via education, work, marriage, and change of residence, is fraught with potential conflicts of interest which only a definite system of institutional controls can neutralize. The parents have a vital stake in what the offspring will do. Because his acquisition of independence will free the parents of many obligations, they are willing to relinquish their authority; yet, precisely because their own status is socially identified with that of their offspring, they wish to insure satisfactory conduct on the latter's part and are tempted to prolong their authority by making the decisions themselves. In the absence of institutional prescriptions, the conflict of interest may lead to a struggle for power, the parents fighting to keep control in matters of importance to themselves, the son or daughter clinging to personally indispensable family services while seeking to evade the concomitant control.

4. *Concentration within the small family.* Our family system is peculiar in that it manifests a paradoxical combination of concentration and dispersion. On the one hand, the unusual smallness of the family unit makes for a strange intensity of family feeling, while on the other, the fact that most pursuits take place outside the home makes for a dispersion of activities. Though apparently contradictory, the two phenomena are really interrelated and traceable ultimately to the same factors in our social structure. Since the first refers to that type of affection and antagonism found between relatives, and the second to activities, it can be seen that the second (dispersion) isolates and increases the intensity of the affectional element by sheering away common activities and the extended kin. Whereas ordinarily the sentiments of kinship are organically related to a number of

common activities and spread over a wide circle of relatives, in our mobile society they are associated with only a few common activities and concentrated within only the immediate family. This makes them at once more unstable (because ungrounded) and more intense. With the diminishing birth rate, our family is the world's smallest kinship unit, a tiny closed circle. Consequently, a great deal of family sentiment is directed toward a few individuals, who are so important to the emotional life that complexes easily develop. This emotional intensity and situational instability increase both the probability and severity of conflict.

In a familistic society, where there are several adult male and female relatives within the effective kinship group to whom the child turns for affection and aid, and many members of the younger generation in whom the parents have a paternal interest, there appears to be less intensity of emotion for any particular kinsman and consequently less chance for severe conflict.[5] Also, if conflict between any two relatives does arise, it may be handled by shifting mutual rights and obligations to another relative.

5. *Open competition for socioeconomic position.* Our emphasis upon individual initiative and vertical mobility, in contrast to rural-stable regimes, means that one's future occupation and destiny are determined more at adolescence than at birth, the adolescent himself (as well as the parents) having some part in the decision. Before him spread a panorama of possible occupations and avenues of advancement, all of them fraught with the uncertainties of competitive vicissitude. The youth is ignorant of most of the facts. So is the parent, but less so. Both attempt to collaborate on the future, but because of previously mentioned sources of friction, the collaboration is frequently stormy. They evaluate future possibilities differently, and since the decision is uncertain yet important, a clash of wills results. The necessity of choice at adolescence extends beyond the occupational field to practically every phase of life, the parents having an interest in each decision. A culture in which more of the choices of life were settled beforehand by ascription, where the possibilities were fewer and the responsibilities of choice less urgent, would have much less parent-youth conflict.[6]

6. *Sex tension.* If until now we have ignored sex taboos, the omission has represented a deliberate attempt to place them in their proper context

[5] Margaret Mead, *Social Organization of Manua* (Honolulu: Bernice P. Bishop Museum Bulletin 76, 1930), p. 84. Large heterogeneous households early accustom the child to expect emotional rewards from many different persons. D. M. Spencer, "The Composition of the Family as a Factor in the Behavior of Children in Fijian Society," *Sociometry*, Vol. 2 (1939), pp. 47–55.

[6] Mead, *Coming of Age in Samoa,* 200 ff.

with other factors, rather than in the unduly prominent place usually given them. Undoubtedly, because of a constellation of cultural conditions, sex looms as an important bone of parent-youth contention. Our morality, for instance, demands both premarital chastity and postponement of marriage, thus creating a long period of desperate eagerness when young persons practically at the peak of their sexual capacity are forbidden to enjoy it. Naturally, tensions arise—tensions which adolescents try to relieve, and adults hope they will relieve, in some socially acceptable form. Such tensions not only make the adolescent intractable and capricious, but create a genuine conflict of interest between the two generations. The parent, with respect to the *child's* behavior, represents morality, while the offspring reflects morality *plus* his organic cravings. The stage is thereby set for conflict, evasion, and deceit. For the mass of parents, toleration is never possible. For the mass of adolescents, sublimation is never sufficient. Given our system of morality, conflict seems well nigh inevitable.

Yet it is not sex but the way it is handled that causes conflict. If sex patterns were carefully, definitely, uniformly geared with nonsexual patterns in the social structure, there would be no parent-youth conflict over sex. As it is, rapid change has opposed the sex standards of different groups and generations, leaving impulse only chaotically controlled.

The extraordinary preoccupation of modern parents with the sex life of their adolescent offspring is easily understandable. First, our morality is sex-centered. The strength of the impulse which it seeks to control, the consequent stringency of its rules, and the importance of reproductive institutions for society, make sex so morally important that being moral and being sexually discreet are synonymous. Small wonder, then, that parents, charged with responsibility for their children and fearful of their own status in the eyes of the moral community, are preoccupied with what their offspring will do in this matter. Moreover, sex is intrinsically involved in the family structure and is therefore of unusual significance to family members *qua* family members. Offspring and parent are not simply two persons who happen to live together; they are two persons who happen to live together because of past sex relations between the parents. Also, between parent and child there stand strong incest taboos, and doubtless the unvoiced possibility of violating these unconsciously intensifies the interest of each in the other's sexual conduct. In addition, since sexual behavior is connected with the offspring's formation of a new family of his own, it is naturally of concern to the parent. Finally, these factors taken in combination with the delicacy of the authoritarian relation, the emotional intensity within the small family, and the confusion of sex standards, make it easy to explain the parental interest in adolescent sexuality. Yet because sex is a tabooed topic between parent and child, parental control must be indirect and devious, which creates additional possibilities of conflict.

Summary and conclusion. Our parent-youth conflict thus results from the interaction of certain universals of the parent-child relation and certain variables the values of which are peculiar to modern culture. The universals are (1) the basic age or birth-cycle differential between parent and child, (2) the decelerating rate of socialization with advancing age, and (3) the resulting intrinsic differences between old and young on the physiological, psychosocial, and sociological planes.

Though these universal factors *tend* to produce conflict between parent and child, whether or not they do so depends upon the variables. We have seen that the distinctive general features of our society are responsible for our excessive parent-adolescent friction. Indeed, they are the same features which are affecting *all* family relations. The delineation of these variables has not been systematic, because the scientific classification of whole societies has not yet been accomplished; and it has been difficult, in view of the interrelated character of societal traits, to seize upon certain features and ignore others. Yet certainly the following four complex variables are important: (1) the rate of social change; (2) the extent of complexity in the social structure; (3) the degree of integration in the culture; and (4) the velocity of movement (e.g., vertical mobility) within the structure and its relation to the cultural values.

Our rapid social change, for example, has crowded historical meaning into the family time-span, has thereby given the offspring a different social content from that which the parent acquired, and consequently has added to the already existent intrinsic differences between parent and youth, a set of extrinsic ones which double the chance of alienation. Moreover, our great societal complexity, our evident cultural conflict, and our emphasis upon open competition for socioeconomic status have all added to this initial effect. We have seen, for instance, that they have disorganized the important relation of parental authority by confusing the goals of child control, setting up competing authorities, creating a small family system, making necessary certain significant choices at the time of adolescence, and leading to an absence of definite institutional mechanisms to symbolize and enforce the progressively changing stages of parental power.

If ours were a simple rural-stable society, mainly familistic, the emancipation from parental authority being gradual and marked by definite institutionalized steps, with no postponement of marriage, sex taboo, or open competition for status, parents and youth would not be in conflict. Hence, the presence of parent-youth conflict in our civilization is one more specific manifestation of the incompatibility between an urban-industrial-mobile social system and the familial type of reproductive institutions.

YOUTH TELL THEIR STORY *

EXTENT TO WHICH PARENTS DEPEND UPON YOUTH FINANCIALLY

About one out of every five young persons interviewed reported that he was helping to support, or was completely supporting, his parents. Fifteen per cent stated that, although their help was needed at home, they were unable to contribute anything. In nearly two-thirds of the families, the help of the youth was reported as unnecessary. That the overwhelming majority of the youth were willing to help is indicated by the fact that less than 1 per cent stated that they were unwilling to help at home.

The responsibility for helping the parents financially falls more heavily upon the boys than upon the girls—25 per cent of the boys, as against 13 per cent of the girls, contributing partial or total support.

The extent to which youth are free from the obligation of assisting in the support of their parents also varies with the occupational level of the father.

More than six out of every ten youth (63.6 per cent) whose fathers were farm laborers were called upon to contribute something to their parents' support, and more than half of this number stated they were actually doing so at the time of the interview. At the other occupational extreme, less than two out of every ten (15.4 per cent) whose fathers were on the professional-technical level were called upon to make some contribution, and less than two-thirds of this number stated that they were actually doing so.

A few of the comments that our youth made on this matter of contributing to the support of their parents suggest a wide variety of attitudes.

"I get more than my money's worth. I'm glad to have a home and parents to live with."

"Our parents kept us, now we should keep them."

"I pay seven dollars. That's too much."

* Bell, Howard M., *Youth Tell Their Story* (Washington, D.C.: American Council on Education, 1938), pp. 26–29, 34–48.

"I'm glad I'm able to do it."

"Mother is alone at home with a sick brother. We all keep her off relief, but I can't help much."

"I give my mother everything I make."

"I don't see why he [the father] should get help from us. They have these old age pensions."

"The government should provide for widows. Then I wouldn't have to spend my life in a factory where I earn thirteen dollars a week."

The social and economic implications of these data are obvious. In the low income brackets, one finds youth living under circumstances that tend to force them into some kind of gainful employment at a relatively early age. Examine the families with fathers in the higher occupational and income levels, and one finds youth whose circumstances permit them to look forward to a relatively secure educational and vocational future. As the father's occupational level rises from that of the farm laborer to the professional worker, one finds a progressive decrease in the proportion of their children who are called upon to contribute to the support of the family group.

A youth's obligation to contribute to the support of his parents usually acts as a restriction upon his freedom to plan for his own future. Exactly how much of this obligation, and its consequent restriction, is to be charged to the relatively low income of his father, and how much is to be charged to the relatively large number of his living brothers and sisters (Table 1)

TABLE I

MEDIAN NUMBER OF LIVING CHILDREN IN PARENTAL FAMILY

Father's Occupation	*Median Number of Living Children*
Professional-technical	3.6
Office-sales	3.6
Managerial	4.0
Skilled	4.7
Semi-skilled	4.9
Domestic-personal	4.9
Unskilled	5.6
Farm owner-tenant	6.1
Farm laborer	6.9

is, of course, problematical. At least it is clear that the opportunities for a young person to "live his own life" vary both with the father's occupational and income level and with the size of his parental family.

The problem of providing equality of educational and vocational opportunity for *all* youth presents a number of points of attack. One of these is the obvious one of increasing the wages, and the total income, of economically submerged groups. Another is state supplementation of the income of needy families on the basis of the size of family. Although the underlying motive has often appeared to be more of a military than a social nature, this method has actually been adopted by certain European governments. Another approach to the problem would be a more general practice of family limitation through birth control.

The issue involved in the choice of these possible alternatives is both vital and basic. One of the most precious jingles of the philosophy of democracy is "equality of opportunity." A general increase of the income of economically submerged groups would place the responsibility primarily upon industry. A subsidy program would place more responsibility for the provision of such equality upon the shoulders of the state, while a more general family limitation program would tend to place a larger measure of this responsibility upon the head of the family. An effective solution would doubtless involve all three.

IDEAS ABOUT CHILDREN

There seems to be no very important difference between the boys' and the girls' desire for children—84 per cent of the boys wanted eventually to have at least one, while 89 per cent of the girls expressed the same desire. The fact that this friendly attitude toward the eventuality of being mothers and fathers is stronger among the older members of each sex group than among the younger ones would tend to support the sincerity of their responses to this question. . . .

We not only discovered whether or not our young person wanted, eventually, to have children, but we also found out the number he would like to have "if circumstances were ideal." One thing upon which the great majority of youth agreed: they wanted fewer children than their parents had.

On the basis of the 11,707 youth who indicated the number of children which they considered ideal (including the 1,057 who desired no children at all), we have the following median number of children desired by different groups of youth.

The figures in Table 2 suggest that young people have a way of look-

TABLE 2

MEDIAN NUMBER OF CHILDREN DESIRED

Classification of Youth	*Median Number of Children Youth Desire*
All youth	2.7
Farm	2.8
Village	2.7
Town	2.7
City	2.7
Male White	2.7
Male Negro	2.5
Female White	2.8
Female Negro	2.5
Jewish	3.0
Catholic	2.9
Protestant	2.7
Mixed affiliations	2.7
No affiliation	2.6
Male single	2.7
Male married	2.6
Female single	2.8
Female married	2.7

ing askance upon the size of their parents' families. It will be remembered that the median number of living children in the parental family is 4.7. The "ideal" number for all the groups of youth who expressed an opinion is exactly two less than this number—an extremely significant difference. Whether or not circumstances will permit youth to realize this, along with their other ideals, is, of course, conjectural. About all that seems certain is that generally speaking, they want fewer children than their parents have had. The difference between the median number of children the youth of certain groups desire, and the median number their parents had, may be found by comparing Table 1 with Table 2.

WHERE YOUTH PREFER TO LIVE

"If the opportunity for choice presented itself, where would you prefer to live?" The expressed preferences of the youth responding to this question betray what appear to be some interesting potential trends.

Three of the most obvious preferences, or prejudices, and possibly the three most reliable indications as to future population trends are listed below.

1. There is least satisfaction among residents of villages (2,500 population or less). Village youth seem to welcome few things with as much enthusiasm as the possibility of moving somewhere else. In fact, three out of every four say that they would move if they could.

2. Almost half of the youth living on farms (46 per cent) indicated that they would prefer to live somewhere else.

3. Regardless of whether youth are living on farms, in villages, towns, or cities, the greatest preference is shown for cities and the suburbs of metropolitan areas.

On the basis of the 13,185 youth who expressed a preference, the *net loss* would be 225 for the towns, 168 for the farms, and 1,748 for the villages. The net gain for the city and suburbs represents the sum of all these losses, or 2,141. Reduced to percentages, these figures indicate that, if youth were free to live wherever they wished, the towns (that is, communities with a population of 2,500 to 25,000) would lose 14.5 per cent of their youth populations, the farms would lose 6.2 per cent, and the villages would lose 58.5 per cent, or almost six out of every ten!

So far as these expressed preferences go, it would seem that the urbanization of our population is as yet an uncompleted trend. The "back to the farm" movement may have a powerful appeal to harassed and depression-sick breadwinners, but it seems to have made very little impression on the younger generation.

SOURCE OF SEX INFORMATION

Only three out of every ten youth reported that they received most of their sex knowledge from parents or relatives. Here again there seems to be a stronger inclination on the part of the girls to discuss intimate personal matters with their parents—the difference being almost three to one in favor of the girls (45.1 per cent as against 16.8 per cent). The home is reported as the chief source of sex information about twice as frequently by the white youth (33 per cent) as by the Negro (18 per cent). Considering this matter from the point of view of religious affiliation, it appears that the Protestant home ranks highest with 32 per cent, the Catholic home taking the middle position with 29 per cent, while the Jewish home takes the lowest rank with 17 per cent.

The chief source of sex "education" for the youth of all ages and all religious groups was found to be the youth's contemporaries. Both the amount and the accuracy of this information were influenced, therefore, by the relative immaturity of the youth's friends who volunteered it. Sixty-six per cent of the boys and 40 per cent of the girls reported that what they knew about sex was more or less limited to what their friends of their own age had told them.

After "contemporaries" and the youth's home, the source that is next in importance is the school, from which about 8 per cent of the young people reported they had received most of their sex information. A few, about 4 per cent, reported that they owed most to books, while less than 1 per cent asserted that they had acquired most of their information from movies. Exactly the same proportion specified the church as the chief source of their sex information. . . .

DO MARRIED YOUTH HAVE HOMES OF THEIR OWN?

Perhaps the most significant fact with respect to the conditions under which married youth are living has already been referred to—that almost half of our married subjects (46.4 per cent for young men and 40.2 per cent for young women) were found to be residing with their parents or other relatives. Exactly how much of this "doubling up" has been the result of the depression's pinch, and how much has been voluntary, we do not know. We do know, however, that a substantial number of our young married people regarded the matter of getting a home of their own as their most perplexing personal problem. . . .

It would seem that any plan designed to improve the lot of married youth will have to go deeper than any educational, social, or recreational "programs." Important as these are, it is unlikely that any remedy is likely to be very effective which fails to deal realistically with the need for low-cost housing units for young married people who are unable to enjoy the social and psychological benefits of living independently in homes of their own.

RELATION OF AGE AT MARRIAGE TO FAMILY INCOME

It has already been seen that the lower the family income, the sooner the youth leave school—and the sooner they marry. . . .

Youth whose fathers are unskilled or farm laborers are twice as likely to marry before they are 25 years old as are those whose fathers are engaged in the professions (34.5 per cent as against 15.8 per cent). In fact, there seems to be a clear-cut relationship between early marriages and low family incomes. The fact that the median age of the youth at the time of the interview was practically the same for the children of fathers in all the occupational groups suggests that the economic background of the family operates as an independent factor in determining whether youth marry or not.

It also appears from our data that a relationship exists between the school grades young people have attained and the age at which they marry. Generally speaking, it can be said that the less schooling a youth has had, the sooner he is likely to marry. . . .

SUMMARY

So far as we are concerned, the net effect of these consistent relationships has been to arouse the suspicion that underneath the placid surface of our social scheme of things there operates a striking concurrence of social and economic forces that tends to freeze social levels and groups into a sort of perennial *status quo.*

The idea that such a "conspiracy" may exist in our democratic land will doubtless offend many people who have been nourished on the American tradition of free enterprise, and who have been led to suspect that low beginnings are a sort of open sesame to an abundant adult life. In fact, the suggestion that there can exist any barrier between the vaulting aspirations of the young and the eventual success of the adult may be regarded by some as definitely subversive and un-American.

Yet, a detached and dispassionate consideration of the data that have just been analyzed emphatically points to both the existence of such forces and to the depressing effects they are having on a large proportion of our youth population. How to reduce this cause and effect relationship to a phrase that is neither trite nor meaningless is not an easy task. What it seems to amount to is a sort of vicious circle of economic determinism.

The first step in the business of exploring the circumference of a circle is to choose a point at which to begin. In this "circle of economic determinism," let us begin with the youth's father—the older generation. Let us assume, for this first whirl around the circle, that the father is employed in one of the lower occupational groups. Let us say that he is an unskilled or farm laborer. Although we have acquired no data on the father's income in this study, we know, from a great variety of responsible sources, that the income of unskilled and farm laborers is not only relatively but actually low.

Another significant thing that we know about this low-income father is that he is apt to have a relatively large number of children—about twice as many, in fact, as the father who is engaged in one of the professions.

Follow this chronological circle around to the next generation. At this point, we find youth whose educational and vocational opportunities have been adversely affected by both the low income of their fathers and the relatively large number of their brothers and sisters. These two forces of low income and large families tend to cut short the period in which the youth is encouraged to train for his own future. They operate to force him out of school, into work, and into marriage, at a relatively early age.

Most that has happened to the youth of this large low-income family has tended to hold him in pretty much the same kind of social and economic vise that has gripped his father. He has had comparatively little education, and we know . . . that low grade attainment is associated with low wages. He has married at a relatively early age. Although he has indicated that the "ideal" number of children is substantially less than the number his parents had, it is a presentable assumption that the same social, economic, and perhaps psychological forces that operated to leave his low-income father with a large family will continue to operate with him. And so begins the second dismal swing around the same vicious circle. And so, *ad infinitum*.

As indicated elsewhere, there are at least two ways of blasting this circle. One of these is to recognize the state or community responsibility to the youth in families whose incomes are too low to provide opportunities for such growth and development as is fundamental to a healthy and enduring democracy. And the other is to clarify, through both youth and adult education, the usual consequences that are visited upon the individual child when the family's income and the family's size are inadequately adjusted to each other.

What is clearly needed is more effective educational, vocational, and recreational programs for *all* youth. In the development of such programs there are two points of attack. One of these is toward the development of programs that are more realistically adjusted to the needs and interests of the young people they are intended to serve, while the other is toward a more general equalization of educational, vocational, and recreational opportunities.

Those who are impelled to question the wisdom of building a youth program on so wide and deep a base may recall with profit the fact that many of the social and political structures that ardent lovers of democracy deplore have been reared from the bedrock of a discontented and disillusioned generation of youth.

There are said to be many things that a democracy must have, or die. One of these things, we suspect, is a social order enriched with enough generosity and foresight to provide all its youth with opportunities to grow, and endowed with enough wisdom and courage to make these opportunities worth the taking.

CHILD AND ADOLESCENT LABOR *

It is difficult to comprehend, in 1944, the belief in the rightness of child labor that prevailed in the early period of this country's industrialization—and the ages at which children were employed. No one raised an eyebrow in 1808 when the opening of the Baltimore Cotton Manufactory was announced as follows:

> This Manufactory will go into operation this month, where a number of boys and girls, from eight to twelve years of age are wanted, to whom constant employment and encouraging wages will be given. . . . This being the first essay of the kind in this city, it is hoped that those citizens having a knowledge of families, having children destitute of employment, will do an act of public benefit, by directing them to the institution.

Not until 1813 was the first law affecting working children enacted, and this Connecticut statute merely required that children in factories be instructed in reading, writing, and arithmetic. Another quarter of a century went by before there was concern for the conditions under which children worked. Then, in 1842, Massachusetts specified that children under 12 years should not work more than 10 hours a day. Six years later the first minimum-age law was passed, in Pennsylvania, establishing a 12-year minimum for work in cotton, woolen, and silk mills. This was a high standard, and was followed by a 9-year age minimum in Connecticut in 1855 and a 10-year age minimum in Massachusetts in 1866.

Even the National Child Labor Committee, when it was founded in 1904, was not especially concerned with the worker of adolescent age. The committee thought in terms of, and in legislative halls fought for, the protection of younger children. Completion of grammar school and a 14-year age minimum for employment were "standards" not to be easily achieved;

* Zimand, Gertrude Folks, "The Changing Picture of Child Labor," *The Annals of the American Academy of Political and Social Science,* Vol. 236 (November, 1944), pp. 83–87, 90–91.

an 8-hour day for children under 16 was a goal that had been reached by only three states; the 16-year-old worker was considered a full-fledged member of the adult working world, not even counted separately by the census. . . .

PRESENT STANDARDS

Today, adequate child labor standards, recommended by the 1940 White House Conference on Children in a Democracy and endorsed by governmental and voluntary agencies concerned with juvenile employment, call for:

A minimum age of 16 years for all employment during school hours and for manufacturing at any time.

A minimum age of 14 years for employment outside of school hours.

A minimum age of 18 years for employment in hazardous occupations.

An 8-hour day and 6-day and 40-hour week for minors under 18 years of age, with hours spent in school considered as part of the working day.

Regulation of night work for minors under 18 years of age.

Health examinations for minors under 18 years of age before they are permitted to enter employment.

These standards have by no means been adopted in all states. Children under 14 are still at work and many under 16 are leaving school for employment. Children work long hours, late at night, and at hazardous occupations. Pre-employment health examinations are . . . far short of the recommended standards. . . .

DEVELOPMENT OF FEDERAL LEGISLATION

Those interested in child labor legislation realized . . . that their efforts to raise standards through state legislation were largely unproductive. . . .

It was not until . . . 1916, [however,] that the first Federal Child Labor Law was passed. Based on the interstate commerce power of Congress, it set a minimum age of 14 for employment in mills, canneries, and manufacturing establishments and 16 years for mines and quarries, prohibited night work, and limited working hours to 8 a day for children 14 to 16.

This law was declared unconstitutional in 1918, and a second law, based on the taxing power of Congress, was passed in 1919, embodying the same standards. When this, too, fell under the axe of the Supreme Court, an amendment to the Constitution was introduced giving Congress the specific power to "limit, regulate and prohibit the labor of persons under 18 years of age."

Passed by Congress in 1924, this amendment was ratified by only four states during the next two years, and many legislatures not only refused to ratify but passed motions of "rejection." By 1931 only five states had ratified. But in the early 1930's the spectacle of adults in bread lines while children worked, and the successful though brief experience with Federal regulation of child labor through the industrial codes adopted under the NRA, revived interest in the amendment. By the end of the 1937 legislative season, ratifications numbered twenty-eight. The amendment itself then went before the Supreme Court for a decision as to whether a state which had once rejected it could subsequently ratify, and whether ratification by states was valid so many years after its passage by Congress. The Supreme Court in 1939 held that prior rejection was no bar to ratification, and that the question of the time that had elapsed since its submission to the states was a legislative matter which could be brought to the attention of Congress if and when the amendment achieved ratification by the required number of states.

In the meantime, however, efforts in behalf of the amendment had slackened, and no state has acted since 1937. This is due primarily to three reasons:

1. The passage of the Fair Labor Standards Act (Wage-Hour Act) in 1938 provided Federal protection for a large number of working children, i.e., those employed in interstate commerce industries. It also removed one of the strongest arguments for ratification, namely, the unfair competition that existed between manufacturers in states with high standards and those in states with backward laws.

2. The decision of the United States Supreme Court upholding the constitutionality of this act and specifically reversing its former child labor decision together with other decisions, especially those involving the definition of interstate commerce under the National Labor Relations Act, suggested that certain additional areas of child labor such as agriculture, could be brought under Federal regulation without a constitutional amendment.

3. The nature of the opposition to the Child Labor Amendment, especially on the part of newspapers and some church groups, was such that it did not seem possible to secure eight more ratifications.

PRESENT FEDERAL LAWS

At present there are three Federal laws affecting child labor. The Wage-Hour Act prohibits the employment of children under 16 years in industries whose products are shipped in interstate commerce. Children employed in agriculture when not legally required to attend school are exempt, and the Children's Bureau of the United States Department of Labor is authorized to permit the employment of children 14 and 15 years in work (other than manufacturing or mining) that does not interfere with their schooling, health, or well-being. The act also empowers the Children's Bureau to prohibit the employment of minors under 18 years in hazardous occupations. Under this authority orders have been issued dealing with the manufacture of explosives, work on motor vehicles, in coal mines, in logging and sawmilling, on woodworking machines, and with radio-active substances. This act covers child labor in practically all mills, mines, factories, and canneries, as well as in other industries, such as the telegraph industry, which are held to be interstate in character.

Other Federal laws affecting child labor are: the Sugar Act of 1937, since renewed, which reduces benefit payments to growers who employ children under 14 and 15 years for more than 8 hours a day; and the Walsh-Healey Act of 1936, which sets a minimum age of 16 years for males and 18 years for females in the production of goods made under contract with the Government. The 18-year minimum for females has temporarily been reduced to 16 years for industries engaged on war contracts.

STATE LEGISLATION

Child labor in industries not covered by Federal law is regulated through state legislation. This includes work in trade and service industries, such as stores, offices, laundries, hotels, restaurants, garages, places of amusement, and others. State child labor laws are like a patchwork quilt with forty-eight pieces, no two of which match. . . . They differ widely as to ages and occupations covered, and are riddled with special regulations or exemptions for specific industries or groups of children. . . .

DECLINE IN CHILD LABOR 1910–1940

In 1910 child labor reached its peak, with nearly two million children 10 to 16 years of age gainfully employed—one out of every six of this age group. During subsequent years child labor and school attendance legislation, together with the increasing mechanization of industry, tended to reduce the number. The widespread unemployment of the 1930's brought an even sharper reduction.

The steady decrease in the number of children at work each census year since 1910, and the increase in the number attending school, are shown in Table 1.

Despite this sharp reduction, the 1940 Census listed nearly 210,000 children 14 and 15 years of age, and nearly two-thirds of a million boys and girls of 16 and 17 years as gainfully employed—full time or part time—in industry or in agriculture. Sixty-four per cent of the 14- and 15-year-olds and 83 per cent of the 16- and 17-years-olds were out of school and presumably full-time workers.

EFFECT OF REGULATION ON YOUNG PEOPLE

Most needed in our postwar action on youth employment is greater consistency in our regulations, with more attention to their effect on the individual young people whose employment is regulated. Any organization concerned with child labor receives many letters from young people and their parents, friends, and teachers, complaining about injustices which they believe result from the child labor law. Their number is increasing. . . .

What can be said, for instance, to the parent who complains that in his state a 14- or 15-year-old boy cannot legally take a vacation job in a store or restaurant or in almost any capacity except farm work, although he could if he lived in any other state of the Union?

What about the youth, old enough to leave school, who is refused an employment certificate because he has carious teeth, but who cannot pay to have his teeth filled until he is earning? In a few states he is given a limited certificate and must return at intervals to show that the dental work is being done; in others, he just cannot work.

How can we convince a physician of the soundness of child labor laws when his 15-year-old patient with one eye, whom for therapeutic reasons he had urged to take vacation employment, found a job, got the anticipated psychological "lift," and then was refused a work permit because he was not "of normal development"?

How can we explain to parents why it sometimes takes their children several days with much running around to get a permit for summer employment? or why they must wait in line for hours and are then given a perfunctory one-minute physical examination? . . .

Greater flexibility [is needed]. Child labor, 1900 style, was clearly a social

TABLE I

SCHOOL ATTENDANCE AND CHILD LABOR IN UNITED STATES
1910–40 (U.S. CENSUS)

	1910	*1920*	*1930*	*1940*
Under 14 years				
Population 7–13 years attending school ..	12,146,173	13,869,010	16,398,400	15,034,695 [a]
Population 10–13 years gainfully employed	895,976	378,063	235,328	Not reported
14–15 years				
Population attending school	2,676,465	3,124,129	4,156,378	4,347,665 [a]
Population gainfully employed	1,094,249	682,795	431,790	209,347
16–17 years				
Population attending school	1,573,377	1,644,061	2,669,857	3,361,206 [a]
Population gainfully employed	Not reported	1,712,648	1,478,841	662,967

[a] The basis for determining school attendance in the 1940 Census differed from that of previous years. In 1940, school attendants were those who had attended school during March, the month preceding the census; former censuses included persons who had attended school at any time between the previous September and the census date. The 1940 figures, if on a comparable basis with those of previous years, would therefore be higher than those given.

evil of the first magnitude and called for prohibition—without any "ifs" or "buts." But work for older boys and girls is not, in itself, an evil. On the contrary, work experience is an essential factor in their development, and this may mean paid employment on a part-time, vacation, or full-time basis.

We must strike a proper balance between the dangers of unregulated employment and of overprotection for adolescents. When jobs become less plentiful, the young worker will be at a disadvantage merely because of his youth and inexperience. To add unnecessary restrictions or overcumbersome work-permit procedure, with which employers have little patience in normal times, is to place barriers in the way of young people that may prevent them from securing suitable work experience. We must protect boys and girls from harmful employment, but we must also help them to meet another basic need of the adolescent—"the boy's need to be needed, the need to count in the world, to assert himself as a man among men, to express in action his irrepressible will to serve."

THE MIDDLE-CLASS SON *

PERSONALITY ABSORPTION

How can we define the middle-class child's situation? It has already been said that his personality is "absorbed," and to the extent that it has been absorbed, he is in danger of developing neurotic symptoms. But why is it absorbed?

Perhaps the best way to view his social conditioning is to consider his parents, and their position in relation to him. The father's work takes him far from the place of residence, where most of his associates are only slightly less strangers to him than they are to his family. He is a white-collar worker. As a salesman, office worker, minor bureaucrat, or professional man, his job-techniques revolve around manipulating the personalities of others, instead of tools. Since he has internalized the supreme middle-class value, individual success, he tries to use his associates, education, hobbies, intellectual interests, in terms of their possible value to his career; in fact, he has himself been conditioned to view his associates, education, hobbies, intellectual interests, in terms of their possible value to his career. On the job he views himself not so much as functionally associated with

* Green, Arnold W., "The Middle Class Male Child and Neurosis," *American Sociological Review,* Vol. 2 (February, 1946), pp. 34–41.

others in a common purpose, but as a self-contained unit establishing "contacts" with others. His work relations are not defined in fixed terms of status and role to the extent that they were in the past for he is on the move, or views himself in that way. He has, then, a well-developed tendency to view his relations with others in terms of what he, as a mobile, displaced person, can get out of them.

Yet the modern middle-class father cannot use his child either in the new sense of manipulating others to his own advantage, nor, be it noted, in the ways available in the past. In the old rural-familistic system, the child served well three predominant interests of the father: he would soon work on the farm, or during the earlier days of the industrial revolution, in the factory; . . . he would provide economic security in the father's old age; and finally, he would provide psychological security by preserving the family name. . . .

In terms of dollars alone, the cost of raising a modern middle-class child represents a serious threat to the personal ambition of the father. At the very time when, in terms of his primary success-goal, he should have time and money available for further study if a professional man, money for clothes, entertaining, household furniture and an automobile for purposes of presenting a "front" in any event; at this time when his career is in its initial and hence its crucial stage, the presence of the child represents a diversion of energy and funds. . . . A certain degree of ambivalence directed toward the child is inevitable. . . .

With the advancing individuation of modern society, not only has individual success become a supreme value, but also individual, hedonistic enjoyment. The child again presents an interference with most of the recreation available to the middle-class father, for whether commercialized (movies, sports events, plays) or social (golf, bridge, tennis, dinner parties), these are designed not for family-wide participation, but individual- or couple-participation.

In conjunction with the above factors, the growing middle-class emphasis upon "scientific child care" and the child's higher education, further increases the father's duties and obligations, while his rights steadily diminish. What emerges from his total situation is an ambivalence toward his child which is more or less widespread, though very rarely admitted, even with confidantes. Finally, children interfere with the companion and partner roles of husband and wife, which are more and more displacing the traditional patriarchal and housewife-and-mother roles.

And how about the mother? She enters marriage and perhaps bears a child with no definite role and series of functions, as formerly. Her old role within the patriarchal family, with its many functions, its economic and emotional security, its round of community participations, is lost, but no well-defined role has taken its place. She feels inferior to men because comparatively she has been and is more restricted. If she works after marriage she faces sex discrimination on the job and perhaps her husband's criticism if his traditional role of bread-winner is important to him.

Half-seriously she prepared for a career prior to marriage, half-seriously because a career is regarded by most middle-class girls as insurance against the grim possibility they will not be married; through a "good" marriage (the folk phrase "she married well" refers not to personality adjustment but to the bank balance and career prospects of the husband) the middle-class girl attains far more status than is possible through a career of her own. But the period of phantasy dalliance with a career, or an embarkation upon one, leaves her ill-fitted for the drudgery of housecleaning, diapers, and the preparation of meals. The freedom which the urban apartment and modern household devices have brought the middle-class housewife has been commonly misinterpreted as well as exaggerated. While the Victorian housewife had more work to do, that work was part of a well-integrated system of household and community activities. While the modern middle-class housewife has more leisure-time than either her mother or grandmother, she must still work at a number of household jobs for which she has not been trained, which are usually not an essential part of her value-system, and which are isolated from her social activities. One sociologist has expressed this dilemma facetiously: half her working day is spent doing something she does not like, the rest is spent thinking up ways of getting even with her husband. The resulting boredom frequently leads to a period of indecision early in the marriage over whether to have children or resume the career. . . .

And so it is inevitable that the child shall be viewed with some degree of ambivalence by both father and mother, for he represents a direct interference with most of the dominant values and compulsions of the modern middle class: career, social and economic success, hedonistic enjoyment. . . .

Personality absorption [thus] takes place against a background of parental ambivalence. The mother has little to do, in or out of the home; she is her single child's sole companion. Modern "scientific child care" enforces a constant supervision and diffused worrying over the child's health, eating spinach, and ego-development; this is complicated by the fact that much energy is spent forcing early walking, toilet-training, talking, because in an intensively competitive milieu middle-class parents from the day of birth on are constantly comparing their own child's development with that of the neighbors' children. The child must also be constantly guarded from the danger of contacting various electrical gadgets and from kicking valuable furniture. The middle-class child's discovery that the living-room furniture is more important to his mother than his impulse to crawl over it, unquestionably finds a place in the background of the etiology of a certain type of neurosis, however absurd it may appear.

Under constant supervision, with limited play-area in a house touching other homes on all sides, or in an apartment, and lacking companions, the child's physiological expansiveness, fed by his boredom, persists in getting him into trouble: screaming, running around the apartment, upsetting daddy's shaving mug, rending teddy-bear in two, emptying his milk on the rug to observe what pattern will be formed. This "trouble" is all a matter of definition. Similar behavior, in modified form, would not be interpreted in primitive society as "trouble," and neither would it be by [working-class] Polish parents in rural New England.

Already the parents have made "love" of supreme importance in their relation to the child, theirs for him and his for them, partly because of the love-complex of our time, which is particularly ramified within the middle class, and partly as a compensation for the many sacrifices they have made for the child, long debated before and after its arrival. The child's need for love is experienced precisely because he has been conditioned to need it. That the need is biological seems unlikely. Now, the more ambivalent the parents are toward the child, the more seriously is the "trouble" he causes them interpreted. He should not act in such a way because of the sacrifices they have made in his behalf, and the least he can do is show his gratitude by "loving" them in turn, i.e., keeping out of "trouble." When the trouble inevitably occurs, the most effective punishment imaginable is the threat to withdraw their love from him. He "needs" that love because his personality has been absorbed by these two persons, because he has been conditioned to have a slavish-emotional dependence upon them. Not the need for parental love, but the constant threat of its withdrawal after the child has been conditioned to the need, lies at the root of the most characteristic modern neurosis. Mamma won't like you if you don't eat your spinach, or stop dribbling your milk, or get down from that davenport. To the extent that a child's personality has been absorbed, he will be thrown into a panic by this sort of treatment, and develop guilt-feelings to help prevent himself from getting into further trouble. In such a child a disapproving glance may produce more terror than a twenty-minute lashing in little Stanislaus Wojcik.

The threat of love-withdrawal is usually the mother's technique for controlling the child. At first the father may threaten to withdraw love, but as the child grows older the father finds a more subtle control—the expression of disapproval. The child is limited to his parents for modeling his behavior. While very young, he wants to set the table and sweep the floor "like mummy." In a few years standards of manly conduct are imposed and he wants to do things "like daddy." The father now controls him through the child's new self-conception, and it is not so much the use of "authority" as threatening the child's self-respect. The child is not a person who amounts to very much, how does he ever expect to get along when he gets old enough to go to school, or join the Boy Scouts, or go to college, or get a job? Again, to the extent that the child's personality has been absorbed, he will be made to feel small, insignificant, unworthy. And, feeling absorbed, caught and helpless, must propitiate these combined god-monsters that he needs so desperately. Hence anxiety, guilt-feelings, the sense of inferiority, seek security at all costs for he is living alone and afraid, in a world he never made.

As for authority, its exercise generates neurotic symptoms only under two conditions, both of which must be present; close identification of the child with at least one parent; the effective blocking-off of all avenues of authority-avoidance for twenty-four hours of the day. Neither of these conditions is met in the Polish homes described, and thus while the authority wielded by Polish parents is far more "irrational" (as defined by Fromm) than that likely to be encountered in many middle-class homes, neuroses are not developed. Indeed, it seems unlikely that Fromm's differentiation between rational and irrational authority has much psychological relevance. The child is hardly in a position to understand when authority is ". . . based on the competency of the person in authority to function properly with respect to the task of guidance he has to perform . . ." and when it is ". . . based on the power which the authority has over those subjected to it and on the fear and awe with which the latter reciprocate." Perhaps the Polish children do not experience irrational authority exactly as defined by Fromm, for while they fear parental authority they also are hostile toward and contemptuous of their parents, and thus are not in awe of them. Nevertheless, the important differentiation is not between rational and irrational authority but the extent to which any parental authority succeeds in absorbing the child's personality, which is itself dependent upon factors other than the imposition of arbitrary authority.

COMPETITION AND THE MALE

Yet when we have used the term "personality absorption" we have not by any means explained a neurosis etiology. The personality of the middle-class girl of the late nineteenth century was "absorbed" by her parents, she was subjected to the demands of "love" and unquestioning obedience, at least ideally; nevertheless, the rate of neurosis under those conditions was probably not too high, as nearly as can be judged at this later date. Why? Because she was not faced with inconsistent expectations of conduct on the part of others and herself. Because love and obedience were integrated within a role which changed relatively slightly from childhood into adolescence, courtship, and finally into marriage. In other words, her initial goals and self-conceptions were constantly re-enforced with each new life experience.

The modern middle-class child on the other hand, particularly the boy, who has found surcease from anxiety and guilt by blind obedience and "love" for his parents, is not allowed to stabilize his relationships with others on that basis. His play-group, which may be denied him until he has reached school age, makes him feel a certain shame and inadequacy in attempting to approach its members with familiar techniques. He also early discovers that he is involved in competition with others, as an individual with his contemporaries, and as a representative of his family unit with other families.

If the abstraction "ours is a competitive society" is translated into terms of what happens to the child born to modern middle-class parents, it becomes quite relevant to the present discussion. Before the child has developed a real self-awareness he becomes part of a process of invidious comparison with other families: he uttered his first word two months earlier than the Jones' boy; he weighed so many pounds at the end of his first year. At Sunday School he received the Bible for perfect attendance; at public school his grades in arithmetic were higher than two-thirds of the other members of the class. He may take piano lessons in view of the day when Mrs. Smythe's pupils will be on public exhibition before the parents of the neighborhood. Everything he accomplishes or fails to accomplish becomes an inevitable part of the family's attempt to maintain or improve its standing in the community.

But effective competition demands a certain degree of independence, firmness of purpose, perhaps aggressiveness. Even for the "normal" middle-class child the transition from submission to some degree of independent behavior is made difficult. And for the child whose personality has been absorbed, an especially exacerbated conflict arises. He is expected to "do things," to accomplish, perhaps to lead in some endeavor, like other children, but his earliest social conditioning was dependence, submission, inferiority; his accomplishments, if any, are on a god-scale—in phantasy. He is desperately attempting to stabilize all later relationships on the basis of his earliest conditioning. Any pressure to compete only exaggerates his anxiety, guilt, and feeling of inadequacy. Life in the modern middle-class home insures that he shall feel that pressure.

There are, then, three elements in the etiology of what has been called the most characteristic neurosis of modern society; personality absorption; the reiterated threat to withdraw a love which has been made of paramount importance; a conflict between the resulting initial adjustment of submissive propitiation and the later assumption of goals of achievement and roles of independent action.

The child is not able to establish an integrated self-conception. Propitiation has meant obedience and "love" for the parents, leading to a compulsive repression of self-will. But he soon discovers that propitiation, in the sense of meeting new parental expectancies, means exhibiting independence, self-assertiveness, aggressiveness, outside the home. The father, as the child's mediator of the outside male world, rather than the mother, makes this demand uncompromisingly. . . .

With the new conflicting expectations, on the part of the parents and contemporaries, the child's anxiety reaches new heights, a double set of guilt-feelings appear where previously there was only one: at first he felt guilty only if he failed to love and obey, and this guilt could be assuaged by the propitiation of submission; now, however, the god-monsters will be appeased only by a combination of submission in his role of child-in-family, and assertiveness in his playgroup, school-pupil, and other roles enacted outside the home. An integration of these conflicting roles is impossible. His conception of himself becomes one of abject failure. Any striving is painful for it violates the initial submissive adjustment. But he feels equally guilty for not making the effort to achieve. This is a key to much of his contradictory and self-blocking behavior: His desire to be the last man in the last regiment and his desire to conquer the world; his demand that everyone shall love him, and his settled conviction that no one could love a person as base as he; his inability to erect a hierarchy of values; his endless debate over the value of his own goals. He is damned if he does and damned if he doesn't. He is embraced by a psychological Iron Maiden: any lunge forward or backward only impales him more securely on the spikes. . . .

CHAPTER XXV

Divorce: Its Causes and Effects

ALMOST any foreigner, when asked to comment on the American family, will immediately mention our high divorce rate. For an advanced industrial people, Americans marry early; and they also divorce and separate frequently. The attitude taken toward the phenomenon is usually one of either condemnation or apology, with condemnation enjoying the major limelight. In what follows, however, an attempt is made by various authors to study separation and divorce in America from an analytical and factual point of view, in order to enhance our understanding of their causes and significance.

DIVORCE AND THE CHILD *

Theoretically the problem of the post-divorce child is universal—not only because divorce itself in one form or another is universal, but more profoundly because the child of divorce constitutes a potentially anomalous element in social organization. In most societies this potentiality is not allowed to express itself; instead, social institutions exist which take care of the child without undue turmoil. The peoples of Western civilization, on the other hand, have developed a peculiar institutional system that makes the problem very acute and hard to solve in practice. To understand why this is true one must compare the position of the child after divorce in different societies.

DIVORCE AND THE IMMEDIATE FAMILY

Since it dissolves the immediate family (now generally believed to be always and everywhere a part of society), the act of divorce usually offends the sense of order and fitness in social affairs. Hence it is nearly always

* Davis, Kingsley, "Children of Divorced Parents: A Sociological and Statistical Analysis," *Law and Contemporary Problems* (Durham, N.C.: Duke University Law School, 1944), pp. 700–714, 716–717, 719–720.

tolerated in fact but never approved in principle. When children are involved the antagonism to divorce is greater, because dissolution of the marriage runs counter to the main function of the immediate family—namely, the bearing and rearing of children. Having formed a union which is socially defined, which involves mutual rights and obligations, and which clearly has as its main function the rearing of children, the parents separate and thus deprive the child of its socially prescribed milieu. If he remains with one parent he lacks the other—a real loss, because each parent plays a necessary and complementary role in the child's life. If the parent with whom he stays remarries, the child falls into a stepchild situation. If he is shifted back and forth between the parents, he must adjust to two different domestic milieus, possibly two different stepchild situations, and must therefore run the risk of discontinuity in his emotional and intellectual development.

This description seems extremely obvious, but it appears so only because it describes the situation *in our culture*. To millions of people living in non-Western societies the description would appear ludicrous—not because it fails altogether to fit their social systems, but because it fits them only in an abstract or analytic sense. Although the immediate family is a universal group, it is not instinctive; rather it is a cultural phenomenon, and as such its specific form, and above all its connections with the rest of society, vary tremendously from one social system to another. It happens that in countless societies the immediate family is so interwoven with other institutional groups, that in case of divorce, the children do not constitute a social problem. The break-up of the immediate family is the same as in our society, and the anomaly of the child's position is potentially the same, but actually the parents' relation to other persons—often to clansmen and joint householders—is such that the child continues largely under their care.

DIVORCE IN PRIMITIVE SOCIETY: THE IBO

The success of non-Western societies in solving the problem of the post-divorce child is explained by their wider use of kinship groups other than the immediate family. With them the immediate family is not the sole, nor even the most important kinship unit. Instead the clan, the extended family, and the joint household serve as important parts of social organization and perform functions which with us are left either to non-kinship groups or to the immediate family. Let us take as an example the Ibo society of Southern Nigeria, whose divorce customs have been ably reported.[1]

[1] Wieschhoff, Divorce Laws and Practices in Modern Ibo Culture (1941) 26 Journal of Negro History, 299–324.

The first thing to note is the nature of Ibo marriage. It is not an agreement between the two prospective mates, but rather a contract between the parents and more fundamentally the clans of the mates. Without the prior consent and agreement of the two parental families no marriage could take place. Secondly, the prospective groom or his family must pay a bride-price to the girl's relatives, without which the union would have no legal standing. Thirdly, in spite of the marriage, the husband and wife remain socially and religiously members of their respective clans. The wife joins her husband's family physically but not spiritually. She must participate in the economic activities of his household, and above all she must bear children for his clan. But her underlying allegiance remains with her own family, and she may at any time return to it. The bride-price is the compensation that her parents, having gone to the expense of rearing her, receive for the loss of her services. It is not the price of her person, as such, for she continues to belong to her clan, but the price of her services. In return she has obligations toward her husband and his family. He also has obligations toward her, and unless these are properly observed her services may be withdrawn. She does not share her husband's possessions, inherit any of them after his death, or hold any claim to the children borne by her. Her husband has the right to contract as many marriages as he or his family can afford, and since a man's prestige depends on his wealth, and his wealth is most effectively displayed by the number of wives, he will try to secure as many as possible.

Being a private contract between the two families, a marriage may be revoked at will by either side. If he is willing to forget the bride-price the husband may send his wife back for any cause whatsoever. On the other hand, the wife may not be able to leave her husband even for just cause if her family refuses to refund the bride-price. Only if she has good prospects of remarrying, which means that another man stands ready to pay her family the bride-price (which then is returned to the original husband), may she leave of her own free will.

One of the most frequent causes of the dismissal of Ibo wives is barrenness. If several years elapse without a child being born, the wife may be sent home and the bride-price recovered. If, on the other hand, the wife has fulfilled her duty by bearing at least two children, including one son, it is extremely difficult for the husband to return her to her parents and receive back the bride-price. The charge of barrenness often elicits the counter-charge of impotence. If the wife fails to conceive for some years after marriage, she or her family and possibly her husband may make arrangements for extra-marital relations. A child born under such circumstances is of course the property of the husband and bolsters the position of the wife.

Obviously in Ibo society there can be no question of the custody of the children when a marriage is dissolved. They belong to the husband's family. It was largely for them that the marriage was contracted and the bride-price paid in the first place. The question may be raised as to how they can be taken care of without their mother, but the truth is that the mother's care is not necessary. Since the household usually includes some of the husband's female relatives, perhaps other wives, there is little difficulty about rearing the children.

The case of the Ibo has been chosen because its handling of divorce is, in its major outlines, typical of that in many primitive societies. The marital relation is dominated by lineal kinsmen, and the custody and rearing of the children do not depend on the continuance of the immediate family. The fact that the Ibo are patrilineal in their clan organization means that the child is viewed primarily as a member of the father's clan. This is sometimes thought to be the most difficult case for post-divorce children in kinship societies, because of the young child's physical dependence on its mother. Actually in some patrilineal societies the children do remain with the mother while they are infants and are returned to the father at a later date.[2]

In matrilineal and matrilocal societies the problem is easier. There, after divorce, it is the father who must leave; the child belongs to its mother's clan and hence remains in the mother's household.[3] No conflict arises between the biological attachment to the father. This is one reason why divorce is usually easier in such societies. The following description of the situation among the Khasis is typical:

> "In the event of a divorce the mother is always allowed the custody of the children. Divorces . . . are of common occurrence, the result being that children in many cases are ignorant of the names even of their fathers. For the mother, on the other hand, the children cherish a very strong affection, all their sympathies and emotions binding them closely to their mother's kin. . . . The great drawback attaching to divorce in ordinary communities, i.e. the effect it has on the lives of the children of the marriage, does not apply to the Khasis, for with them the children always live with their mother and their mother's family, which latter would be bound to maintain them."[4]

[2] This is true of the Yaruba, neighbors of the Ibo in Nigeria, and of the Naron people and the Namib Bushmen of South Africa.

[3] Examples are the Pueblo Indians of the Southwest, the Iroquois of the Northwest, the Bush Negroes of Dutch Guiana, the Khasis of Assam, and the Minangkabau of Sumatra.

[4] Gurdon, The Khasis (1914) 80–82.

In societies where the emphasis on extended kin is bilateral rather than unilateral, or in which residence and descent are at variance, or in which other special conditions obtain, almost any conceivable rule may prevail with reference to the custody of children after divorce. Sometimes the children are divided equally, sometimes the boys are given to the father and the girls to the mother, sometimes the mother gets the younger, the father the older children. Generally, however, there is no major problem of adjustment, because, whoever gets him, the child is likely to live in intimate and stable relationship with other relatives, both male and female, who will perform the functions of the missing parent.

Although there are exceptions and occasional lapses, the general rule among primitive peoples may be summed up in a quotation from an article on Sumatran cultures:

> "In Indonesia among strictly patrilineal peoples, such as the Batak and the natives of Nias, all the children of divorced parents remain with the father. . . . Among sibless people the children are divided between the parents at divorce, and among matrilineal peoples they naturally remain with the mother."[5]

THE CASE OF THE CHINESE

Not only primitive but civilized societies may utilize kinship as an important principle of social organization. This was the case in China before the process of Westernization set in. The immediate family was subordinate in nearly every respect to the extended family. The mates were selected and the marriage arranged by the parents, and the couple usually lived with the parents of the husband. The young bride was subordinate to the older females in her husband's extended household, and the husband was subordinate to his grandfather, father, or older brother. The household was frequently quite large, so that the children were surrounded by adults other than their mother and father, notably by uncles, aunts, and grandparents. The husband could divorce his wife for numerous causes, of which one was barrenness and another disregard of his parents. The wife's right of divorce was virtually nil.

Divorce in China did not imply family disorganization in our sense of the word. Since the dominant kinship unit was the extended patrilineal kin, the dissolution of a particular marriage had little significance, for it took more than this to break up the entire kindred or even a particular household. Furthermore, concubinage and polygyny made divorce less dis-

[5] Loeb, *Patrilineal and Matrilineal Organization in Sumatra:* The Batak and the Minangkabau (1933) 35 *American Anthropologist* 16, at 45 ff.

ruptive, because if one consort were divorced the others could maintain the immediate family. In any case the child necessarily remained in the father's household, where he continued to find the milieu much as it had been before. If divorce seldom occurred in Chinese society it was not because the dissolution of wedlock was considered "bad for the child," but because marital harmony did not depend primarily upon personal likes and dislikes.

In a kinship society, whether primitive or civilized, the immediate family is hardly an independent unit. It is the extended family which exercises the main influence, which has the privilege of choosing the mate, determining the residence, controlling the property, watching the morals, and in general managing the affairs of the young couple. The married pair either live with or near their relatives, and the children consequently grow up with the latter. Therefore if one parent is lost through death or divorce the child's domestic environment is not seriously disturbed. He tends to remain in the same household, among the same intimate relatives, feeling just as secure and loved as ever. Also, what might be called the principle of kinship substitution usually operates—the principle that if one kinsman is lost, another is available to take his place. Such a principle is necessary if kinship is to form the basis of social organization, and it is embodied widely in the so-called classificatory type of kinship terminology, which calls different relatives by the same term (e.g. father and father's brother) because they may be functionally equivalent or capable of substitution. The principle means that the child is seldom left without some relative to function as a parent for him. Being familiar with this mechanism, he accepts it as a part of life. Also, since usually it is sociological rather than biological paternity that counts, the "stepchild" situation does not arise. Actually, so far as daily behavior is concerned, the child may have drawn little distinction between his parents and the other adults in the household anyway. It is therefore easy for him to make the adjustment when a parent is lost. Things remain for him pretty much as they were before.

DIVORCE IN THE SMALL FAMILY SYSTEM

One of the outstanding peculiarities of Western civilization, in contrast to the cultures discussed above, is the degree to which kinship has lost its social importance. At first sight this might suggest that divorce itself would have lost its importance, but such is not the case. The decline of kinship has affected the extended, not the immediate, family. The latter has lost some of its erstwhile functions in our mobile, urban, industrial society, but because it is virtually the sole remaining kinship unit it has acquired some of the functions formerly performed by other kinship relations. Its burden has therefore become heavy—perhaps too heavy for its inherently frail structure; and divorce, which dissolves the immediate family, has become a much greater problem, because it represents a threat to the family organization that remains.

With the principle of kinship substitution and the custom of the great household abandoned, the child of a deceased or divorced parent has as a rule nowhere to turn except to the other parent. He does not retain the balanced family life that a child in a kinship society is likely to have. He is therefore a "problem" in a much more pressing sense.

EMOTIONAL TENSION IN THE SMALL FAMILY

Having become the sole important kinship unit, the small family exhibits an unusual emotional concentration within itself. Its members, living apart from other kinsmen and surrounded by temporary acquaintances or strangers, can rely only upon themselves to share the feelings peculiar to blood relationship. The resulting intensity is sometimes extremely great, if not stifling. The loss of non-affectional functions has further increased the importance of the family's emotional bonds at the same time that it has reduced the mutual coöperation in outside matters which would ordinarily support these bonds. Marriages, instead of being arranged by the elders on the basis of objective standards, are formed on the basis of romantic love and maintained on the strength of mutual likes and dislikes. The custom of having only one, two, or three children, plus the isolation of the parents from any other children than their own, increases the uniqueness and hence the emotionality of the parent-child relation. Consequently any marital discord not only affects the mates acutely but also involves the children. Husband and wife, as a compensation for marital unhappiness, unconsciously seek consolation, revenge, release, prestige, security, or what not in the children. The offspring in turn are victims of divided loyalty, emotional insecurity, and parental interference. This is why many experts believe that chronic discord is worse for the child than divorce; but the emotional intensity of the immediate family in modern society complicates divorce itself. It not only makes divorce more probable (because if things go wrong they go very wrong), but it also makes much harder the emotional readjustments of parents and children after divorce.

THE EQUALITARIAN PRINCIPLE AND CUSTODY

Our reliance upon the immediate family is connected with another trait that aggravates the problem of the divorced child—namely, the equalitarian principle in wedlock. In a society where clans exist the child belongs either to his father's or his mother's clan. He cannot belong to both. Consequently in case of divorce there is little question as to the child's custody and residence. But in our system the child does not automatically belong to one parent. Instead he may belong to either one, and it is up to the court to decide which one. Furthermore, because the estranged parents have a potentially equal claim, they often *compete* for the affection and custody (though not for the support) of the child. The court must assume the role of arbiter. It must exercise its "discretion," but finds itself with few rules on which that discretion can base itself. The welfare of the child rather than the claims of the parents is supposed to be the goal, but what is "welfare" to one judge is apt to differ from what is "welfare" to another.[6]

That parents compete for custody of the children is suggested by the results of Marshall and May's study of cases in Maryland and Ohio. They show that the mother generally gets the children, but that this is because she is usually the plaintiff. When the father is the plaintiff he gets custody more often than she, as Table 1 reveals.[7] There is thus a tendency to award

TABLE 1

DISPOSITION OF CUSTODY IN MARYLAND AND OHIO CASES: PERCENTAGES

	Custody to Husband		Custody to Wife	
	Maryland *	*Ohio* †	*Maryland*	*Ohio*
All Actions	10	10	68	75
Husband Plaintiff	30	37	25	34
Wife Plaintiff	2	2	85	86

* Marshall and May, *supra* note 7, at 316.
† Marshall and May, *supra* note 7, at 346.

[6] An investigation made under the writer's supervision by a graduate student (Mrs. Mary Rice Morrow) at the Pennsylvania State College showed in Pennsylvania an almost complete lack of crystallized opinion among judges on this matter. They tended to award custody on the basis of unconscious or vaguely formulated rules of thumb. They seemed usually to believe that general principles could not be applied, because "each case is different." Only one-fourth of the replies admitted that changing customs and social values had any influence on the type of decision rendered. There was, however, a tendency to rely on the advice of social work agencies, which presumably supply more systematic evidence than "interested parties" can supply and contribute a professional definition of the child's welfare.

[7] Marshall and May, *The Divorce Court*, Vol. I, Maryland (1932) 31; Vol. II, Ohio (1933) 346–350.

custody to the "innocent" party, although this apparently has little to do with the welfare of the child. There is also a tendency for the mother to get custody oftener when the children are girls, the father when they are boys—a fairly frequent pattern in other societies. Less than five per cent of the Ohio cases involve division of the children between the parents, although provision is usually made whereby the parent not receiving custody may visit, or be visited by, the children, in which case there is a sort of de facto mixed custody. The facts indicate that a majority of the children of divorced parents in this country are living with their mother. This conclusion is substantiated by a study of high school students whose parents have been divorced.[8] Thirty-two per cent of these students did not remember their father's occupation as compared to only 8 per cent of the students from non-divorced homes, indicating a surprising lack of contact with the father after divorce. Nevertheless, the parents have at the start an equal claim to the children, and the question of custody must be thrashed out anew in every case. The competitive claims of husband and wife also emerge with reference to the support of the child. Since in our culture the father is supposed to support the child and the mother to care for it, the tendency of the court is to continue this division of labor after divorce. The fact that in a money economy a child can be supported at a distance, makes this arrangement seem convenient; but actually it presents an anomalous situation, because the father, deprived of the child's company, is nevertheless held economically responsible for him. The father thus receives an obligation without a reciprocal right. The one-sidedness of the arrangement is reduced, however, by the fact that woman's social role is more closely connected with the family than is that of the male, and that consequently his being deprived of the child's company entails less sacrifice than her being so deprived. Furthermore, the care of children is more burdensome and less easily evaded than their support.

THE FACTOR OF MORAL STIGMA

Although divorce in some form is permitted in all societies but encouraged in none, there are great differences in the degree of disapproval attached to it. American opinion has gradually changed from sharp to rather mild disapproval.[9] The law, however, has retained in theory the

[8] Weeks, "Differential Divorce Rates by Occupation" (1943), *Social Forces*, 334–337.

[9] Several systematic studies document this trend. Barnett, *Divorce and the American Divorce Novel 1858–1937* (1939), finds a gradual transition from the nineteenth-century view of marriage as a divinely ordained end in itself to the twentieth-century view of it as a means to individual happiness, revocable if it does not succeed. Correspondingly there has been a

older attitude; it bans divorce by mutual consent, stipulates that one party must have committed a wrong against the other, and thinks in terms of the "guilty" and the "innocent" partner. The moral condemnation of divorce has made, and still does make, the child's position more difficult than it would otherwise be.

To see the effect of moral stigma one should compare the child whose parents are separated by divorce with one whose parents are separated by death. The obvious difference that in one case only one parent remains alive while in the other both parents do, means that the divorce child may *theoretically* retain the contact and devotion of both parents. But this ideal possibility does not usually work out in practice, because the child, entangled by the closeness and intensity of the family bonds and the guilt complex of the divorce relation, is inevitably involved in the marital conflict. He is, after the divorce, the sole remaining link between the former mates, and consequently serves as the only instrument through which they can express their mutual resentment. The equalitarian principle which gives both of them rights in the child is conducive to his being used in this way, for if he divides his time between the two he must necessarily serve as a means of communication for them. A study of the divorce child in Nebraska showed that "often the part-time child is used as a weapon by one or both parents," that "in a few cases youngsters stated they had procured information for one parent against the other," that the situation afforded "the father an opportunity to find out how his former wife is spend-

---

growing tendency to regard divorce less as a moral and social evil and more as a personal experience, and to find the cause of divorce less in moral fault, with attendant blame of the parties concerned, and more in factors beyond individual control, such as early upbringing, unconscious personality traits, and social conditions. The shift of opinion was particularly noticeable after World War I, but it had been under way before that, and there was an especially marked change in the attitude toward remarriage after divorce. Curiously, the public interest in divorce has gone through four cycles of concern; first, over the very fact of divorce; second, over the effects of divorce on the children; third, over the question of alimony; and fourth, over the problem of post-divorce adjustment. The author, who finds that the first divorce novel by an American writer appeared in 1858, thinks that perhaps divorce as a fictional theme may have spent itself after this cycle of emphasis.

Koster, *The Theme of Divorce in American Drama, 1871–1939* (1942), traces the same shift of opinion in American plays. He too is able to date the striking change of attitude after World War I, and to document the transition from condemnation of an alleged social evil to toleration of a necessary though regrettable fact of individual experience.

Hart, *Changing Social Attitudes and Interests,* Recent Social Trends, Vol. I (1933), pp. 382, 414–417, uses refined indicators of approval and disapproval to gauge the public tolerance of easy divorce as reflected in magazine articles between 1905 and 1931.

In recent years opinion polls, such as that conducted by *Fortune* in April, 1937, and the *Ladies Home Journal* in February, 1938, have shown in a more direct manner the liberalized public attitude toward divorce.

ing his alimony, whom she is 'stepping out with,' and so forth," that "the mother may likewise question the child when he comes 'home' from father," and that in some cases "the child is bribed in order to get this information," and is thus taught by his own parents "to lie, spy, and blackmail." [10]

Playwrights and novelists have seized upon the dramatic element in the situation, usually portraying the child as an innocent victim of parental folly, living an unnatural and lonely life.[11] Some of the sympathy undoubtedly reflects the genuinely difficult situation of the child, but one suspects that a good deal of it also reflects a moralistic bias. Since divorce is sinful, the child's lot must be painted as badly as possible in order to make the sin (in its consequences for the *innocent* offspring) seem as terrible as possible. Thus the moral stigma attached to divorce not only makes the child's position worse than it would otherwise be, but also requires that it be depicted as even more tragic than it actually is.

The child of divorced parents probably runs no greater risk of a step-parent situation than does the bereaved child. But he does run a risk, as the latter does not, of falling into *two* such situations, because both parents may remarry and he may be shifted from one household to the other. Actually this does not happen in a large percentage of cases,[12] but it happens often enough to give point to novels and plays about "part-time children." The parents may have moved far away from each other and remarried in different social circles. The child may thus have to divide his life between two radically different milieus, with a resulting confusion in his personality development. Because of bitterness between the estranged parents, he is apt to be under a taboo upon what he can say concerning events in the other household. Not only must he suppress part of his memories, but he must alter his personal habits and his family terminology each time that a shift is made. The situation is so new in our culture that no adequate terminology exists. What, for instance, is the new spouse of the divorced parent to be

[10] Sullenger and Brownlee, Children of Divorce (1934) 9.

[11] See especially the following novels: Wilson, The Kenworthys (1925); Young, Custody Children (1926); Johnson, Children of Divorce (1927); Wharton, The Children (1928); Sedgwick, Philippa (1930); Spencer, The Incompetents (1933); Savage, Summer Hail (1936); Eliot, Angel's Mirth (1936); and Pope, The Sentence of Youth (1936). For plays see Crothers, Mary the Third (1923) and Susan and God (1937); Ford, What Imagination Will Do (1928); and Atlas, Wednesday's Child (1934). These are all cited and the plots discussed in Barnett, *op. cit. supra* note 10, especially at 96–104, and Koster, *op. cit. supra* note 9, in Chap. 5.

[12] It rarely happens for two reasons: first, probably less than half of the divorced persons who have children remarry; second, even when both parents happen to remarry, the child often remains in one household to the exclusion of the other. Custody is generally awarded to only one parent, though it is hard to say in how many cases the child regularly visits the other parent.

called by the child? "Stepmother" is hardly the correct term, because it implies that the child's real mother is dead. When the child talks to playmates about his father's wife, he accordingly has a hard time describing her, and outsiders frequently make mistakes that embarrass them and consequently him.[13] Finally, he almost inevitably comes to prefer one household to the other, a fact taken by one parent as a breach of affection and an expression of a perverse devotion to the stepparent (perhaps the original correspondent) in the other household.

> "The parents of the little boy who is now five were divorced when he was less than a year old. They were given joint custody. Thus every other week he was shifted from one grandparents' home to the other. From the statements of this little tot it is evident that his paternal grandmother was trying to instill in him a disfavor for his mother, and the maternal grandparents were endeavoring to blacken his father's reputation. However, this particular youngster favored his father's home. (When returned from there he was restless and unruly for several days.)" [14]

One thing that makes any stepchild situation difficult is the mystical importance our culture attaches to biological parenthood. A "real" son or daughter must be one's "own." When the stepchild is the offspring of a person still living, who once had and (even worse) may still have the primary affection of one's mate, then the difficulty of loving the child is increased.

In some ways, therefore, the child of divorced parents is less fortunate than the bereaved child, but the reason lies chiefly in the emotional and moral implications with which our culture surrounds divorce. If spouses would divorce amicably; without blame or recrimination; if the law would cease to search for the guilty party; if the public would accept divorce as a natural occurrence—if, in short, all the attitudes and sentiments which control the institution of the family were abandoned, then the position of the child after divorce would not be anomalous, and writers of fiction would not feel obligated to paint his lot in somber colors. But in such a free and easy society there would be hardly any necessity of marriage, and hence no such thing as divorce. Mating would be on an informal basis, and the children would be cared for by whoever felt inclined, if anybody.

As previously mentioned, our peculiar institutional structure places considerable reliance upon the immediate family. Since this unit has lost

---

[13] There is not even a special term that designates the child of divorced parents. "Orphan" properly refers to a child of deceased parents. Only by a circumlocution, or by a coinage which seems in bad taste (e.g., divorce-child), can the child of divorced parents be designated.

[14] Sullenger and Brownlee, *op. cit. supra* note 10, at 9.

many of its functions it can be broken without disturbing many aspects of society. Such dissolution does, however, affect seriously the rearing of children, which is an extremely important function in any society. Therefore, if the current social system for rearing children is to be maintained, divorce cannot become a matter of absolute indifference. There is, however, good evidence to indicate that easy divorce does not necessarily imply the disintegration of society. Many societies having high divorce rates are every bit as stable as many having low divorce rates. Egypt, for example, has an extremely high divorce rate (much higher than the United States), yet its fertility, the stability of its institutions, and the contentment of its people are apparently as great as they are in India, which has a low rate. In nineteenth-century Japan the divorce rate was much higher than in China, yet Japanese social organization was, if anything, more efficient. There is no reason to believe, therefore, that a highly tolerant attitude toward divorce in the United States will mean the decline and fall of our civilization. In practice we seem to be moving in the direction of easier divorce anyway, and as this movement continues the position of the child of divorced parents should improve. The only necessity is that some sort of social machinery be worked out for rearing the child properly—a necessity hard to supply in our culture. Once this is accomplished the incidence of divorce is of little consequence to the stability of the larger society.

THE NUMBER OF LEGAL DIVORCES

To determine the number of children in the United States whose parents are permanently living apart, we should have to know, first, the number of divorces, annulments, desertions, and informal separations that occur from year to year, and second, the number of children affected by these events. Unfortunately our knowledge is deficient on all these points. The best statistics relate to the number of legal divorces, annulments, and separations, but even these are sadly inadequate, because Congress, although it often inveighs against divorce and frequently reiterates that the family is the foundation of society, does not allot sufficient funds to secure accurate marriage and divorce statistics.[15] No official figures at all are obtainable on desertions and informal separations. Our attention, therefore, will of necessity be confined to legal divorces.

[15] The establishment of a registration area for marriage and divorce has been suggested several times. A comprehensive plan along this line was well under way when it was interrupted by lack of appropriations caused by World War II. See Cohen, *Centralized Collection of Marriage and Divorce Records and Their Uses* (1941) 31 American Journal of Public Health.

As is well known the divorce rate in the United States has risen steadily for as long as any information has been available. In 1940 it stood at two divorces per 1,000 population,[16] the highest rate ever recorded in this country and six times as high as the average rate during the period 1867–1871. Since 1940 the rate has risen still higher. In the accompanying chart the number of divorces per 100 marriages from 1888 to 1945 is shown.

THE NUMBER OF CHILDREN AFFECTED BY DIVORCE

Although the growing divorce rate implies an increasing number of children affected by divorce, it does not mean a proportionate increase. Several factors have combined to prevent this. In the first place, the birth rate has diminished. From 1871 to 1940, for example, when the divorce rate was increasing six-fold, the birth rate was dropping by more than fifty per cent.[17] In the second place, divorce has tended increasingly to occur in the early years of marriage. During the period 1867–1886 the most frequent number of divorces occurred in the seventh year of marriage. After that, from 1887 to 1906, it occurred in the fifth. And during a subsequent period, 1922–1932, it fluctuated between the third and fourth years, with the third holding the upper hand.[18] Today it almost certainly falls in the third year. Naturally, the earlier the divorce the fewer the children, especially since divorce often involves a prior separation (quite long when the "cause" is desertion). In the third place, divorce occurs more frequently and the rate has risen more rapidly in the city than in the country, and it is precisely in the city that birth rates are lowest.[19] In general it has been shown that divorce rates are greatest where birth rates are least.[20] For all of these reasons the increased divorce rate has not meant a corresponding increase in the number of children affected. As a matter of fact the latter is only about one-third the number of persons getting divorces each year.[21] Approximately

[16] *15 Vital Statistics Special Reports* (U. S. Bureau of the Census, 1942) 196.

[17] The estimated average birth rate during 1871–1875 was 37.0 per one thousand population. Lotka, *Modern Trends in the Birth Rate* (1936) 188 *Annals* (of the American Academy of Political and Social Science) 2. In 1940 it was 17.9. *15 Vital Statistics Special Reports* (U. S. Bureau of the Census, 1942) 128.

[18] Cahen, *Statistical Analysis of American Divorce* (1932) 123; *Marriage and Divorce 1932* (U. S. Bureau of the Census, 1934) 5; Monahan, "The Changing Probability of Divorce" (1940) 5, *American Sociological Review*, 536, 543.

[19] Mowrer, *Family Disorganization* (1939) 42–48; Willcox, *Studies in American Demography* (1940) 351–354.

[20] Groves and Ogburn, *American Marriage and Family Relationships* (1928) 378; Li, *Le Divorce en France* (1936).

[21] Cahen, *op. cit., supra* note 21, at 113. For the period 1922 to 1932 the number of persons receiving divorces each year averaged was 117,657, which turns out to be 33.3 per

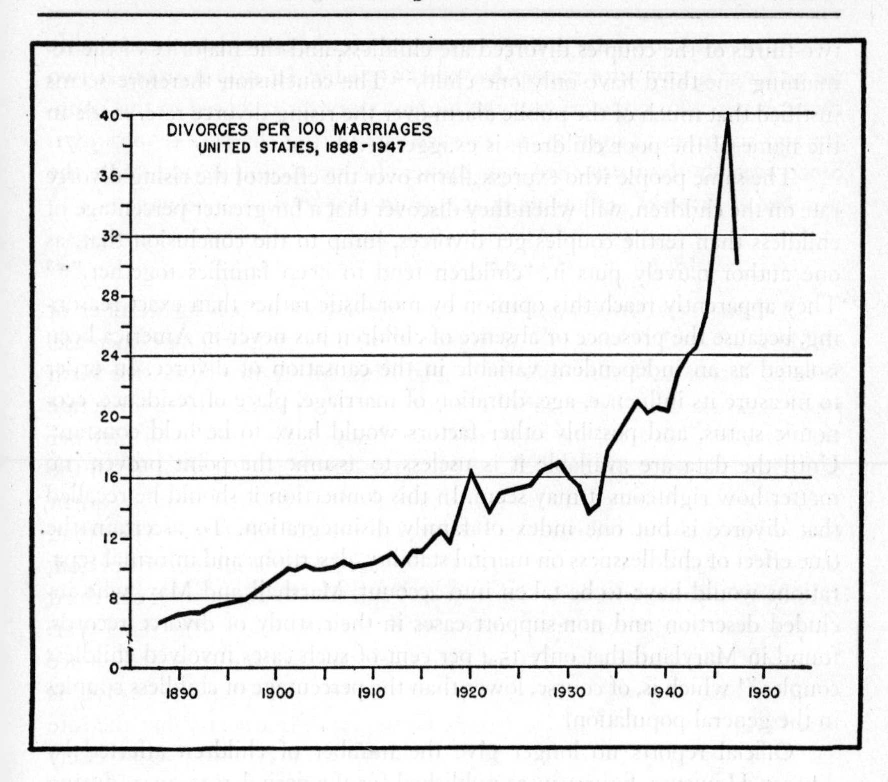

Divorces per One Hundred Marriages

In this chart the divorces are not related to the marriages in the same year, but to the marriages occurring in the previous ten years. That is to say, the chart shows the number of divorces per average hundred marriages occurring each year in the ten years previous to the year in question. This ratio is taken because most divorces represent the break-up of marriages which occurred during the prior ten years. The figures from 1888 to 1939 were taken from Hornell Hart and Henrietta Bowne, "Divorce, Depression and War," *Social Forces,* Vol. 22 (December, 1943), pp. 192–193. For later years they were computed from figures contained in releases from the Bureau of the Census and the National Office of Vital Statistics.

two-thirds of the couples divorced are childless, and the majority of the remaining one-third have only one child.[22] The conclusion therefore seems justified that much of the public alarm over the rising divorce rate, made in the name of the poor children, is exaggerated.

The same people who express alarm over the effect of the rising divorce rate on the children, will when they discover that a far greater percentage of childless than fertile couples get divorces, jump to the conclusion that, as one author naively puts it, "children tend to keep families together."[23] They apparently reach this opinion by moralistic rather than exact reasoning, because the presence or absence of children has never in America been isolated as an independent variable in the causation of divorce. In order to measure its influence, age, duration of marriage, place of residence, economic status, and possibly other factors would have to be held constant. Until the data are available it is useless to assume the point proven, no matter how righteous it may seem. In this connection it should be recalled that divorce is but one index of family disintegration. To ascertain the true effect of childlessness on marital stability, desertions and informal separations would have to be taken into account. Marshall and May, who included desertion and non-support cases in their study of divorce records, found in Maryland that only 15.4 per cent of such cases involved childless couples,[24] which is, of course, lower than the percentage of childless couples in the general population.

Official reports no longer give the number of children affected by divorce. However, figures were published for the period 1922–1932, during which time slightly more than 36 per cent of the cases reported children. Making allowances for possible omissions, the average number of children affected by divorce each year during this period was approximately 117,500. This was an extremely small number compared to the total child population; indeed, it was only 0.27 per cent of the number of children aged 0–18 during the period covered. The average number of offspring per divorce was only 0.67, and it was only 1.8 per case reporting children. Both figures exhibited a remarkable stability during the entire 11-year period, the latter never varying from 1.8 until the last year (1932) when it dropped to 1.7. In view of the stability of the number of children per divorce during the

---

cent of the number of divorcees. This is undoubtedly a lower proportion than data for the nineteenth century, if available, would show, but because of the rise in the birth rate since 1933 it is probably fairly representative of the last decade.

[22] Cahen, *op. cit. supra* note 21, at 113.

[23] Bernard, *American Family Behavior* (1942) 98.

[24] *Op. cit. supra* note 7, at 74.

period, and certain grounds for believing it to be stable since then (e.g. a similar average birth rate), it can be used as a ratio for estimating the number of children affected by divorce in subsequent years, as follows:

1933	110,000	1938	162,000	1943	218,000
1934	136,000	1939	167,000	1944	209,000
1935	145,000	1940	176,000	1945	254,000
1936	157,000	1941	192,000	1946	306,000
1937	166,000	1942	205,000		

The 1940 estimate represents 0.41 per cent of the children aged 0–18 living at that date. Thus the proportion was still less than half of one per cent.

THE TOTAL NUMBER OF CHILDREN WITH DIVORCED PARENTS

The knowledge that 150,000 to 200,000 children are affected by divorce each year in the United States does not tell us how many are living at any one time whose parents have ever been divorced. The latter figure, at any given time, is composed of all those children affected by divorce during the previous 18 years, less those who have died or who have passed age 18. In order to estimate it, actuarial methods must be employed. When this is done the total number for 1940 turns out [25] to be 1,533,000. So far as the writer is aware, this is the only estimate of the kind ever made for the United States. Its accuracy, in view of the paucity of basic data, is only approximate, and it probably errs below rather than over the actual number. If correct, it means that 3.6 per cent of all children in the United States have divorced parents.

Because divorce occurs more often in the early years of marriage, the majority of the children at the time of divorce should fall in the young ages.

FUTURE TRENDS

For predicting a postwar divorce wave, there is a qualitative basis—namely, the instable character of marriages formed under prewar, war, and

---

[25] The age distribution of children affected by divorce was assumed to be that reported in 1 Marshall and May, *op. cit. supra* note 7, at 79. The survival rates from the United States life table (1930) were then applied to each age, and each cohort was followed through until the year 1940 was reached, when a sum was taken of the number remaining in all cohorts at that year. The method, together with the method of estimating other figures in this article, will be more fully explained in a technical article.

postwar conditions. That such marriages are unstable was proved statistically in connection with the last war, it being shown that at least during all the years up through 1933 the marriages formed in 1919 and 1920, and to a lesser extent in 1917 and 1918, gave rise to a disproportionate number of divorces.[26] The causes of the instability are the special motives and conditions that, at such a time, govern mate selection on the one hand, and influence marital relations on the other.

During the preliminary period of preparation for war, young people tend to marry with even less rationality than usual. Sudden prosperity in the form of abnormally large wages gives them financial independence of their elders at a premature age. Increased mobility gives them release from primary group controls. The confusion of patriotism with both sex and love gives them a distorted conception of marriage as at once a duty to the nation and a means of immediate gratification. The pressure of wartime anxieties, such as nostalgia, insecurity, and fear of separation or death, gives them a pathological reliance on sudden marriage as a refuge.[27] The exhilaration of new uniforms and of new and exciting ways in which the sexes are thrown together gives them a tendency to overlook the defects of persons known on short acquaintance. Finally, the boom in marriages itself gives them a collective stimulus toward matrimony. "Once the wave of war marriages gets under way, the movement generates its own motivating fervor," many girls fearing a dearth of men after the rush toward wedlock is over.[28] In short, marriage becomes a fad, if not a craze, and ordinary precautions are thrown aside.

Insofar as rational motives assert themselves, they are likely to represent a mercenary adaptation to war conditions. The prospect of a liberal allowance from the government, of a substantial life insurance policy furnished by the government, and of pensions and bonuses, helps the girl consent. The widespread belief in the early stages that married men will not be drafted prompts many a hasty wedding. Such rational motives as these, plus the irrational ones just mentioned, lead to highly unstable unions; for they mean that the marriage is in many cases treated as a means for reaching an end which will either not exist in peacetime or will not be served by the continuance of this particular match.

Most of these motives and conditions prevail also during the second and third periods of war—the period of actual conflict and the period of

[26] Hall, "The Instability of Post-War Marriages" (1934) 5 *Journal of Social Psychology*, 523–530.

[27] Bossard, "Family Problems in Wartime" (1944) 7 *Psychiatry* 66.

[28] *Ibid.*

postwar readjustment. The marriage rate declines during the second period, but the few marriages that take place are as prone to instability as the earlier ones. Finally, after the war, in addition to the generally mobile and unsettled conditions, there are three factors in particular that contribute to ill-advised unions—first, the emotional and sexual intensity of contact after long separation; second, the feeling of moral and nervous release from war tension, and third the fulfillment of engagements made during the period of conflict. Also, most of the mercenary inducements mentioned above continue in operation.

War marriages are weakened not only by the factors governing the decision to marry and the choice of mates, but also by the conditions that affect them after the union is consummated. The separation of married couples by military service is especially damaging, because it lasts a long time, comes often in the earliest stage of married life (before there has been time for mutual adjustment), and places the two people in extremely different environments (where incompatible habits and points of view are acquired and new ties formed).[29] Also, by emphasizing loyalty to the nation rather than to the family, and courage rather than abstinence, war tends to loosen the controls over sexual morality.[30] This new orientation tends to continue into the postwar era, but without the purpose or discipline of war; and, with the addition of other elements, the jazz-age begins. It is through these troubled times that the great number of marriages formed in the prosperous and exciting years before the period of actual combat must pass. Since their quality was not the best to begin with, a high percentage of them will inevitably wind up as casualties.

As a result of the excessive marriage rate before and after the war, of the hasty and ill-advised character of many war unions, of the adverse effect of war conditions upon them and of the postponement of divorce during the period of actual conflict, the number of divorces during the period of postwar readjustment should, by far, exceed anything previously known in this country. Divorce itself will become almost a fashion. Many couples will want one not because they are really incompatible but because they feel entitled to it. Eventually most of the unsuccessful unions will have been dissolved and the divorce rate will drop. The rate, however, will not drop to the former level, because there is a secular increase that has been going on for decades and that shows no sign, as yet, of faltering.

---

[29] Bossard, *supra* note 27, at 67–71. Bossard, *War and the Family* (1942) in Becker and Hill, Marriage and the Family, 574–577; Waller, War and the Family (1940) 13–15; Hall, *supra* note 26, at 528.

[30] Waller, *op. cit. supra* note 29, *passim*.

CONCLUSION

In the United States, as in other Western nations, the child of divorced parents constitutes a relatively new, acute, and unsolved social problem. This is due primarily to the peculiar social structure that Western peoples have developed. It is not due, as many people believe, to the rising divorce rate. The divorce rate has risen steadily and is likely to rise still more, yet such a trend merely increases the incidence of, but does not create, the problem. There are societies in which the divorce rate is higher than in the United States, but where the problem of the divorced child hardly exists. In primitive or archaic kinship societies the allocation of the child to the mother's or the father's family is usually automatic, and the child has substitute parents and many kinsmen living with or near him; consequently, the adjustment after divorce is quite easy. Our society, on the other hand, has a small family system with little emphasis on extended kinship, with equalitarian rights of the parents in the child, and with intense emotional involvement in both the marital and the parental relationship. As a consequence the child's future must be decided in each divorce case by the discretion of the court, with few principles other than the vague "welfare of the child" to guide it. The parents often use the child as an instrument of mutual conflict. They also compete for his custody, though not for his support. The public exaggerates the disadvantages of the child's situation, and seeks to prove by this means that divorce itself is an evil. In our culture, therefore, the child of divorce is a social problem in the sense that societal machinery for dealing with him does not operate automatically or satisfactorily. Though he is really better off than the child whose parent has died, he is more of a problem because his condition is felt to be somebody's fault, with all that this implies.

With the possible exception of the last two decades, the number of children affected by divorce each year in the United States has not risen as fast as the divorce rate. According to our estimates the number in 1940 was 176,000—only 0.4 per cent of the total number of children in the population. In the same year the number of children whose parents had *ever* been divorced was, by our estimate, 1,533,000, which was 3.6 per cent of the total child population. Such figures are merely approximate, but may be sufficiently accurate to aid social agencies having to deal with the problem. It should be remembered, however, that these estimates relate only to legal divorces. The number of children affected by permanent desertion and separation, independently of the law, is entirely unknown, but the chances are that it is substantially larger than the number affected by divorce—

yet the social problem is essentially the same, and perhaps worse. . . .

The statistics, tentative at best, indicate the numerical extent of the problem. The sociological and anthropological analysis tries to show the causes of it. Neither approach, unfortunately, can give a certain answer to the two great questions of the future: In what ways will the social structure change so as to make the child of divorced parents less of a social problem? And when will the secular increase in the divorce rate reach a turning point? About the only certainty is that both changes are bound to eventuate sometime. It is doubtful if either can be accomplished deliberately by legal means, although the law will likely play a part. Since a high divorce rate does not necessarily threaten societal stability if ways are available for safeguarding the children, it may be that America will eventually have a divorce rate that will seem astounding by present standards. If so, it is safe to assume that the present chaos concerning the children will not then prevail. Some social mechanism will have been envolved for taking care of them. The remedy, therefore, does not necessarily lie in reducing the number of divorces. Divorce is here to stay. Instead, some means of neutralizing the effects of divorce on the child may be found by the creation of new institutional relationships that will replace the kinship bonds of primitive and archaic societies.

DIVORCE LAW IN THE UNITED STATES

LEGAL TRENDS *

The law of divorce in the United States is exceedingly complex. It is also clouded and uncertain. Moreover, it seems to be static. Its principles and aims resemble those of fifty years ago. The changing role of divorce in our culture cannot be attributed to legal shifts, but rather to other changes in our social order. Yet the law is changing, and the changes are significant. Among the major changes that have occurred in the last three decades are the following.

(1) *An increase in the number of legal grounds, and the introduction of certain new "grounds" that violate the traditional theory of divorce law.* Whereas under the old theory one party had to commit an unbearable fault against the other, two jurisdictions (Alaska in 1933 and New Mexico in 1935) have now legislated that "incompatibility of temper" is an adequate

* From *Successful Marriage*, edited by Morris Fishbein, M.D., and Ernest W. Burgess, Ph.D., copyright, 1947 by Morris Fishbein. Pp. 460, 462–465.

ground for divorce. Incompatibility cannot be a fault, nor can it be blamed on one party and not the other. It takes two to be incompatible. A man can commit adultery, but he cannot very well commit incompatibility. In addition, at least five jurisdictions have amended their laws so as to permit divorce because of voluntary separation. Such separation is certainly different from the old-style "desertion." Like incompatibility, it is a mutual matter. "No charge of desertion nor assumption of guilt is necessary; if the parties voluntarily live apart for the given period, either may get the divorce on this ground alone."[1] In short, American law is beginning to permit divorce by mutual consent. It has always done so in practice, as everyone knows, and increasingly as time has gone by, but only recently has it begun to do so in theory.

(2) *Vacillation with respect to migratory divorce.* Competition for the divorce business has led some states to lower the residence requirements to a few weeks or months. This has made migratory divorce easier, though it remains true that such divorces account for only a small portion (something around 3 per cent) of the total. The legal theory is that a divorce granted in one state must be recognized by the other states, provided the state in question has jurisdiction. If the state does not have jurisdiction, the divorce is void. This theory, however, is pure fiction. Divorces are regularly granted by states lacking jurisdiction, and these divorces are treated as valid.

The legal theory is not applied in practice because the basis on which jurisdiction depends, "domicil," is ambiguous.

> Domicil in this country has lost much of the stability it possessed in earlier times, . . . People are in the habit of changing their homes frequently from state to state. In many cases they have homes in several states. Again, married women are permitted to have domicils different from their husbands'. Under present conditions, therefore, it is frequently difficult, if not impossible, to ascertain where the domicil of a person is.[2]

The legal definition is subjective: a bona fide domicil is a place which the person *regards* as home and where he *intends* to stay more or less indefinitely. If an objective definition is employed, then domicil boils down to residence for some specified length of time. In the absence of any federal statute laying down the period of residence necessary to establish domicil for divorce purposes, the states are privileged to make their own rules. The

[1] Folsom, Joseph K., *The Family and Democratic Society* (New York: Wiley, 1943), p. 515.

[2] Lorenzen, Ernest G., "Extraterritorial Divorce—Williams v. North Carolina II," *Yale Law Journal,* Vol. 34 (Dec., 1944), p. 805.

courts, however, prefer the subjective definition and refuse, *in theory,* to accept the objective definition of residence alone. Therefore a state to which the party "has moved immediately prior to the divorce and from which he removes immediately afterwards is uniformly held not to be the domicil of the party in question." [3] Yet this is exactly what most persons getting out-of-state divorces do. Presumably, then, if the law practiced its theory, it would treat nearly all such divorces as void. But it does no such thing. The courts continue to grind out divorces for out-of-state applicants, the persons who obtain these divorces practically never get prosecuted, and when a question is raised about the divorce, the courts in other states refuse to reopen the case because of the doctrines of estoppel and *res judicata.*

Most divorces in the United States (about 95 per cent) are the result of mutual agreement. This does not mean that both parties "want" the divorce, but simply that neither will try to compel the other party to stay married. As a result, after the divorce is granted neither one is likely to challenge the decree, and usually no one else is interested in doing so. This means that in the great majority of cases a decree can serve without penalty as a basis for subsequent conduct. However invalid it may be in theory, it is valid in its consequences. But suppose somebody does challenge it, will the courts then treat the divorce as void? Will they grant another divorce or annulment without reference to the "void" divorce? Will they recognize the first spouse as the legitimate heir in preference to the second, or "spurious," spouse in case of remarriage? Will they refuse to admit the "void" divorce as a valid defense in suits for alienation of affection? The answer is no. "Oddly enough, it is only in the case of a prosecution for bigamy that one can be certain that such results will follow, and prosecutions for bigamy after anything which resembles an effort to obtain a divorce are so rare that, for practical purposes, they may be and are ignored." [4]

The law rationalizes its unwillingness to treat a "void" divorce as void by two devices. First, it invokes the doctrine of estoppel when both parties have appeared in action and have not seriously contested the divorce. Each is, by his participation in the "void" divorce, estopped from subsequently questioning the jurisdiction of the court that granted it. "If either party subsequently avails himself of the divorce by remarrying, he is said to have put himself in a position in which it would be unfair for him to deny the validity of the divorce." Second, the law invokes the doctrine of

[3] Harper, Fowler V., "The Myth of the Void Divorce," *Law and Contemporary Problems,* Vol. 2 (June, 1935), pp. 335–47.

[4] *Ibid.,* p. 339.

res judicata. Even if the person has fought the action and has not remarried, he may nevertheless be forbidden to question the validity of the divorce.

> Whenever the husband and wife appear in a court and a divorce is subsequently rendered, neither party can attack the decree in a collateral proceeding on the grounds that the court did not have jurisdiction to divorce them. This means that for practical purposes any state has jurisdiction to divorce a man and wife who desire to obtain such a decree there. Neither can ever raise the question as to its validity. Property rights are determined quite as though the situation fell within the orthodox rules governing jurisdiction. Children of subsequent marriages will, for economic purposes at least, be legitimate quite as though their parents were not "bigamists." Indeed, to call such subsequent marriages bigamous is completely misleading. They are bigamous only in the rare event that some zealous prosecuting attorney desires to make himself so unpopular that it will be impossible for him again successfully to compete for public preferment . . . It is simply not true that a divorce rendered in a state to which both parties resorted solely for the purpose of obtaining the decree is without legal effect. On the contrary, it has the precise effect which the parties desire.[5]

Seen in this light, the recent case decided by the Supreme Court is merely a rare attempt to apply the legal theory.[6] It is the first time the chief tribunal has addressed itself specifically to the question of domicil. In this case a man and woman went from North Carolina to Reno, stayed there six weeks, secured a divorce in compliance with Nevada law, married immediately thereafter in Nevada, and returned to North Carolina as husband and wife. Neither of the ex-spouses objected to the divorce; one of them subsequently died and the other remarried. But the state of North Carolina prosecuted the couple for bigamous cohabitation. Upon appeal, the Supreme Court justices, by a six to three decision, sustained the conviction. Their argument was that no domicil had in fact been established in Nevada and that therefore the divorce was void. The three dissenting justices, in two separate opinions, maintained that the North Carolina court did not charge the jury correctly, that the burden of proof should have been on the prosecution to prove the illegality of the Nevada domicil, and not on the petitioners to prove its validity. Further, they claimed that the concept of domicil is so indeterminate that it cannot serve as a basis for criminal action in face of the acceptance of domicil by the Nevada court on the basis of Nevada statutes.

The effect of this Supreme Court decision upon migratory divorce is

[5] *Ibid.*, pp. 340–341.
[6] Williams v. North Carolina II, 65 Sup. Ct. 1092 (U.S. 1945).

yet to be seen. I believe it will have little effect, because prosecutions of married couples for bigamous cohabitation are unusual, and because courts will shrink from bastardizing the children of such unions. The next step, obviously, is for the Congress of the United States to define domicil in an exact and uniform manner—perhaps as one year's residence. Only in this way will the confusion finally be dispelled.

(3) *Increased use of social-work aids in divorce cases.* There is a tendency for divorce litigation to be handled by special domestic-relations courts and for these courts to use the results of social investigation in determining the facts.[7] In addition, the legal-aid societies that have been growing in number and scope also are an aid in straightening out divorce tangles. These social-work agencies help not so much with reference to the main issue of divorce as in the ancillary judgments with respect to alimony and custody. The movement in the direction of more systematic case work in connection with divorce litigation will probably continue. This suggests an avenue for increased usefulness on the part of the marriage counselor.

THE MYTH OF THE VOID DIVORCE *

The clue to domicil is home. . . . Home, however, is an extremely flexible and nebulous conception. . . . The touchstone is . . . the intention, . . . [a] subjective element. It is not necessary for the person to intend to make a permanent home in the new dwelling place, but it is necessary that his intention be such as to make the new dwelling place something other than a mere transient place of abode. Certainly, if the person intends to remain only a short time and plans a definite and permanent removal to another dwelling place thereafter, it would be extraordinary to designate as his home the place where he makes his brief sojourn. A state to which the plaintiff, or the defendant, or both, has moved immediately prior to the divorce and from which he removes immediately afterwards, is uniformly held not to be the domicil of the party in question. Thus, the ordinary Reno or Mexican divorce is in contemplation of orthodox legal theory void because rendered in a state which was the domicil of neither party to the proceedings. . . .

---

[7] In Michigan the Wayne County Circuit Court, which has jurisdiction in divorce matters, has since 1929 had attached to it the office of "Friend of the Court," the function of which is to ascertain the facts and bring in evidence of aid to the court. See Edward Pokorny, "Observations by a 'Friend of the Court,' " *Law and Contemporary Problems,* Vol. 10 (Summer, 1944), pp. 778–789; "The Enforcement of Foreign Decrees for Alimony," *ibid.,* Vol. 6 (Spring, 1939), pp. 274–282.

* Harper, Fowler V., "The Myth of the Void Divorce," *Law and Contemporary Problems* (Durham, N.C.: Duke Law School, 1935), pp. 337–341, 344, 346–347.

One would expect . . . that if a divorce is obtained in a state under conditions which do not conform to the rules of jurisdiction, the following results would necessarily follow: a subsequent annulment or divorce action between the same parties should not fail by reason of the former "void" divorce; in proceedings for letters of administration or probate on the death of one of the spouses, the first husband or wife should be recognized as against a spouse by a subsequent marriage; in bills for a widow's allowance or for admeasurement of dower or partition of lands, the first spouse should prevail as against a subsequent one; in an action for alienation of affection which occurred after the "void" divorce, such divorce should not be a valid defense; in actions for ejectment or specific performance between grantees or heirs of the principals to the divorce action, the divorce should be ignored as affecting the rights of the parties; in a criminal prosecution for bigamy, the "void" divorce should not constitute a defense. These results are all implied in the very notion and definition of jurisdiction and obviously follow from the major premise established by the word "void." Oddly enough, it is only in the case of a prosecution for bigamy that one can be certain that such results will follow, and prosecutions for bigamy after anything which resembles an effort to obtain a divorce are so rare that, for practical purposes, they may be and are ignored.

The anomalous character of this situation is evidenced by the variety of legal doctrines which courts have attempted to develop. Thus, the doctrine of "estoppel," a fiction of the first magnitude, is invoked in situations in which both parties appear in the action and the divorce is not seriously contested. So too, although the defendant does not enter an appearance, the plaintiff is estopped to deny the jurisdiction which he has thus invoked. Again, if either party subsequently avails himself of the divorce by remarrying, he is said to have put himself in a position in which it would be unfair for him to deny the validity of the divorce. Solicitation for the second spouse and the children of the second marriage has driven the courts thus to treat the "void" divorce as if it were valid. In actions between the first and second wife for a share of the husband's property, the first spouse will not be permitted to raise the question of jurisdiction if she herself had remarried or if, by consenting to the divorce, she had thus made possible the embarrassing position of the second wife. Something akin to this doctrine is applied in favor of third persons as, for example, in the case in which the first wife sues another woman for alienating her husband's affections by conduct subsequent to a "void" divorce. . . .

In view of these facts, it would seem that a frank and straight-forward formulation of legal rules with respect to jurisdiction for divorce would be entirely at variance with the rules formulated in the books. And yet the most recent authoritative restatement of these rules sets forth the timeworn but false formulae as already indicated with but one reference to the important body of law heretofore discussed. This puts the legal profession very much in the position of telling the candidates for a divorce that they cannot legally go to Nevada or Paris or Mexico and obtain a decree, but, if they do so disregard the law, the judges will be astute enough to find a form of words which will put them in the same position as though they had conformed to orthodox legal precepts. . . .

When the respectable layman hears the legal profession denounce a Reno or a Mexican divorce as "void," but at the same time finds that persons who avail themselves of such decrees achieve legal results which are, for all practical purposes, identical with the results of a "valid" divorce, his respect for law is not apt to increase. It is not surprising, then, to discover the respectable layman himself content to do with a void divorce, convinced as he is that its invalidity is Pickwickian in character.

To characterize such persons as bigamists is to confuse legal theory with facts and to confound legal crime with anti-social conduct. They are bigamists only in the sense that millions of reputable persons are criminals because they indulge in conduct approved by public opinion but forbidden by an official formula. Indeed, whether such persons are law breakers depends solely on the major premise incorporated in one's definition of law. If we adhere to realities, we imply in the word law only that certain governmental functionaries will behave in a manner which conforms to a pattern represented by the content of legal rules. When, therefore, these officials, judges, juries, sheriffs, policemen and others, are confidently expected to act and do act in a manner contrary to a formula, it is in no real sense that the formula represents the "law. . . ."

It may be because divorce has religious and ethical ramifications that we find so much cant and sham in connection therewith. Thinking about divorce and marriage even by supposedly "tough-minded" realists still often proceeds from sentimental assumptions, the validity of which are highly dubious. There is presumed to be some great intangible value in the permanency of wedlock. There is, in addition, for many the infinite value for marriage as a sacrament. It is assumed, therefore, that if divorce is not completely forbidden, it should at least be difficult to obtain. Consequently we find a legal theory which makes divorce available only upon certain fixed "grounds." But the practice both of laymen and judicial tribunals belies the theory. Collusive divorces are the rule rather than the exception. In other words, consent divorces are the most common form in a steadily increasing divorce rate. A case investigation including a fair sampling of the grist of the divorce mills of one state has disclosed only three per cent of the divorces granted that were actually contested. The same study revealed the highly dubious character of the evidence that is required to substantiate cause for divorce. In other words, the whole theory of divorce has very little relation to the decrees which actually sever the marital relation and which serve as a release from an unhappy marriage. The "void" divorce represents an analogous instance in which those who make and state law deliberately close their eyes to the rules which control the conduct of human beings.

It may be that lawyers and legislatures cannot fairly be accused of hypocrisy in these situations. The social effect of flagrant intellectual dishonesty, however, is apt to have quite as corroding an effect upon the ethical sensibilities of the community. There is no merit in clinging to a dogma long after it has ceased adequately to picture that phase of life to which it is pertinent or to serve as an ideal toward which human beings sincerely strive. Neither the theory of divorce nor of jurisdiction to render a divorce accurately portrays the legal phenomena to which it is relevant. Nor does it appear that any of these legal formulae represents a goal which either the legal profession or the community has any genuine desire to reach. It is obvious that under such circumstances legal theories should be revised to conform to legal facts even if it be at the expense of what, in the first instance, undoubtedly represented *bona fide* ideals after which social institutions were sought to be patterned.

CHAPTER XXVI

Stability and Instability in American Society

THREE questions have been uppermost in the present book: First, what is it that unifies the American people, that enables them to act together as a nation? Second, what is it that *dis*unites them, that gives rise to stress, strain, and instability and hence points the way to change in American society? Third, what are the features that are peculiar to American society, setting it apart from other kinds of social order? The same data will provide the answers, of course, to all three questions. Basically, it seems, American unity derives from a common set of values and institutions. Not only do these values and institutions furnish the over-all pattern of social interaction, but also, to the extent that they are peculiarly our own (not to be found in the same combination elsewhere), they supply the key to the uniqueness of American society. At the same time the strains and conflicts in our system, the instabilities that lead to change, can be regarded as conflicts of values, interests, and means. Through one basic set of materials it is therefore possible to derive at least partial answers to the three questions posed.

Since, however, the selections in this book are drawn from many authors and represent diverse outlooks, a final summary of the main findings and implications is now needed. This summary will recapitulate briefly the major elements in our value system and will then deal briefly with the sources of instability and change.

THE AMERICAN VALUE SYSTEM

The term used most often to describe the American value scheme is "democracy." It has a double meaning, referring in one sense to a kind of government and, in a second but related sense, to a kind of social order. In the political sense it means that the people themselves should determine public policy. Democratic government is therefore the institutional machinery for carrying out this ideal, for making the peoples' wishes known to and mandatory upon the political officials, and for rotating official positions among the citizenry. This machinery is highly elaborate in our complex society, including as it does Federal and state constitutions, secret ballots, legislatures, checks and balances, judicial reviews, vetoes, limited terms of office, recalls, referendums, and so forth. The machinery, however, will not work by itself. Too often an attempt has been made to multiply the machinery but neglect the substance of democracy. In order for the system to work there must also be *social* as well as political democracy. Some of the values of social democracy are as follows:

(1) *Ethical equality*. In the Christian view all individuals are spiritually equal, regardless of their material differences. This ethical view is expressed politically in the democratic franchise, in which each citizen, regardless of race, creed, occupation, or wealth, has one vote. It is also expressed in the disapproval of extreme differences of material status, as in the dislike of slavery and indenture. But in the American system it has never been carried to the extent of eliminating material differences. On the contrary, material inequality is an assumption of our value system.

(2) *Equal opportunity*. American society has traditionally been an "open-class" society, in which individuals could advance according to their merit. It has not favored placing all individuals on one level (equalitarianism) or placing them in hereditarily unequal levels (caste). Rather, it has favored "equal opportunity to advance."

Strictly defined, the phrase "equal opportunity" would mean that *all significant* differences were equalized at the start. Each individual would have identically the same chance as every other to advance in the social scale. The only difference in the achievement of one man as against another would be the amount of *effort* he put into it. But the doctrine of equal opportunity obviously does not go this far. It means, rather, that the difference at the start shall not be due to involuntary social factors. At most it can be due to biological factors which, with appropriate effort, the individual can convert into social advancement. Thus the inheritance of wealth violates the doctrine, because the inequalities it produces reflect ancestral achievements rather than one's own. The individual does not *earn* his inherited wealth. True, he does not earn his I.Q. either, but this is not socially controlled.

Even in this modified sense equal opportunity is not provided by our social system. Everybody knows that the son of a doctor and the son of a truck driver, given the same biological capacity, do not have an equal opportunity to become distinguished scientists.[1] It is impossible to eliminate all involuntary social advantages at the start, because other values compete with the goal of equal opportunity—for instance, those associated with the family. As long as we have the institution of the family, the class position of the parents will influence the class position of the child.

This does not mean that the ideal of equal opportunity has no effect in our society. As long as there is *some* opportunity to advance, as long as the ideal is practiced to some extent, every person can *hope* to get ahead, and this hope will have a powerful effect on behavior. No one can deny that the son of a truck driver has some chance of becoming a distinguished scientist. If he exerts enough effort, he may in fact beat out the doctor's son. Indeed, in our philosophy the less the opportunity, the greater is the merit of success. We still admire the virtues of thrift, abstinence, and hard work.

Equal opportunity would be meaningless without material inequalities, because then there would be nothing to strive for. Difference in position and pay in our society is ideally construed as the reward that goes to the individual in proportion to the energy and talent he brings to his societal tasks. The principle of unequal rewards for unequal services is therefore embodied in all branches of our competitive social order. But unequal rewards would be tyranny if the individual had no opportunity to demonstrate his abilities. Consequently the doctrine of equal opportunity balances the principle of unequal rewards; each facilitates and each limits the other.

(3) *Free competition*. The connection between equal opportunity and competition is easy to see. Governmental positions, for example, can be occupied by only a small percentage of the population. If these positions were the fixed monopoly of a par-

[1] For evidence see Visher, Stephen S., *Scientists Starred 1903–1943* (Baltimore: Johns Hopkins Press, 1947), Chs. 8, 10.

ticular group, they would change hands only once per generation and the rest of the people would have no hope of occupying them. Therefore, in a democratic society provision is made for the achievement of temporary political status through the competition for votes. Similarly, equal opportunity in economic affairs implies equal access to the market, that each seller may present his goods and services to the buyers, getting a price commensurate with his efficiency. The only trouble, of course, is that success itself breeds success in competition, and that inevitably some become so powerful that they gain monopolistic advantages. For this reason anti-trust legislation represents a very democratic, if drastic and sometimes quixotic, effort to avoid the undemocratic consequences of democratic laissez faire.

(4) *Separation and balance of interests.* Ideally, democracy visualizes a certain balance of power between the various interests, with no one interest or class combining several forms of power. It is felt that the state, for example, should be limited to governmental functions, and should undertake economic activity only under special circumstances and with unusual safeguards. Private business can then represent an interest of its own and operate as a check on governmental power. Similarly it is felt that the government should favor no one church, and that neither great political nor great economic power should be placed in the hands of ecclesiastics. Only by keeping such major interests as church, state, and business separate and balanced can the democratic values be maintained in practice.

(5) *Public education.* A complex and specialized society requires elaborate education. To be democratic, it also requires that the schools be open to everyone and that they provide for free discussion and free investigation. So important are the schools as testing and sifting devices that to exclude anyone from them is to deny him equal opportunity. Also, if important decisions are to be made by the people themselves, a high general level of education must be achieved. Universal literacy, political awareness, and appreciation of the democratic values are essential to the liberal-democratic system. Consequently, in a democracy education is supported by the community at large out of tax funds. Special interests may try to get hold of the schools for purposes of indoctrination, but according to democratic principle no special interest, whether religious, economic, or partisan, should have the

privilege of using governmental funds for schools of its own kind.

(6) *Freedom of expression.* Intimately linked with the other democratic values is freedom of expression. It includes the right to criticize the government, to report the facts, to pursue science, and to propagate one's own religious beliefs. It is one of the hardest of the democratic freedoms to maintain, because of the almost universal tendency to forbid opinions contrary to one's own. Since the freedom of expression does not include the right to libel, to portray indecencies, to incite to overthrow the democratic system, or to blaspheme, special interests are continually trying to censor the media of communication under the guise of some legitimate ground of limitation. The history of modern dictatorships seems to show, however, that as soon as the channels of communication are controlled, democracy is lost.

(7) *Tolerance.* If all citizens are ethically equal, any differences between them are secondary and may be tolerated. Liberal democracies thus exhibit relatively high tolerance, as exemplified in the freedom of worship and the freedom of opinion.

Religious tolerance is difficult because religion proclaims absolute imperatives and supernatural truths, and therefore is disinclined to tolerate contradiction. The democratic nation accordingly achieves religious tolerance only by a certain amount of secularization. Differences in religion are tolerated either because they are trivial (as among the Protestant denominations) or because they are not intruded into the real affairs of life.

For political tolerance the principle of majority rule has two implications: first, that there is a minority which has been allowed to express its opinion; and second, that the rulers, who are always a minority, do not restrain the judgment of the majority (i.e., the ruled). A free press and radio are therefore essential, because they are the chief avenues for stating and defending conflicting points of view, as well as for keeping the public informed of the actions of its officials. The system works better when the cleavages are not fundamental—when, for example, it is a matter of Democrats *vs.* Republicans, rather than of Communists *vs.* non-Communists. If general over-all agreement prevails, the specific issues can refer to means rather than to ends, and tolerance will come easily. Vertical mobility aids agreement by reducing sharp cleavages between classes. Public education helps by providing a standard indoctrination for everybody.

INDIVIDUALISM: A SUMMARY

Second only to democracy in describing our social system is "individualism." It apparently implies, from the individual's point of view, all that we have been saying about the democratic system of values. It suggests the right of each person to make his own decisions. Of course, we know that each individual cannot make "his own" decision in any absolute sense. He is limited by what he has been taught, by ignorance, by prejudices, and so forth. Also, he cannot with impunity decide to kill his neighbor, burn down his house, or publish obscene literature. All that the term can mean, then, is that the individual has the right, wherever possible and within his own framework, to enjoy a fairly wide range of choices. Thus we feel that a man should be able to choose his occupation as he pleases (as long as it is a legitimate occupation), to choose his mate according to his desire (as long as she is not already married), to choose his religion, to spend his money as he likes, etc. In contrast to the individual in a custom-ridden society, such as that of India or the European Middle Ages, and in contrast to a totalitarian dictatorship, such as that of Russia or Nazi Germany, the American seems remarkably "free." He is certainly controlled by custom and authority, but more indirectly and more voluntarily than are these others. Freer from parental control and kinship obligations, from censorship, from religious intolerance, from a particular occupational and social niche, he has more leeway to move about, to pick his alternatives, and thus to take the responsibility of fashioning his own unique career. Indeed, the notion of a "career," the particular life pattern achieved by the person himself, like the notion of "self-reliance" and of the "self-made man," is peculiarly American.

Ethically, the individualistic ideal is expressed in terms of the "inalienable rights" of the individual, the desirability of self-expression, the "integrity" of the self. The individual is felt to have a value of his own, and therefore to be entitled to uniqueness. This outlook is carried into education, where we have the "elective system" and "progressive" classroom techniques. It is carried into the family ("each must live his own life"), into economics ("private" property and "individual" initiative), into government ("individual liberty"), and into religion ("one's own conscience," "the individual and his Maker").

It appears to be obvious that individualism, thus conceived, is simply the reflection of all the democratic values mentioned above, viewed from the standpoint of the person.

THE CONDITIONS OF STABILITY

These, then, are the main values in which Americans believe. Needless to say, as abundantly shown by the readings in this volume, they are only imperfectly embodied in practice. For this variance there are two main causes: First, although Americans generally will agree on these values in the abstract they do not agree on their application in concrete situations. Second, the conditions of life in the United States have changed to such an extent that the erstwhile means for carrying them out are no longer fully adequate. Disagreement on the application of values explains in large measure the instability in American society.

A necessary condition for social stability is that the different parts of the structure "fit together." So far as the values are concerned, the real test of whether or not they fit together comes only when they are applied. One sign of instability, for example, is the presence of competing definitions of proper conduct *in the same situation*. In the United States, specifically, there is relatively little agreement on the rightness or wrongness of the following: premarital sex relations, industrial strikes, price control, poll taxes, gambling. These are "issues" so long as there is disagreement about them. Fortunately, they are not such fundamental issues that they threaten to split the society into warring factions. They are not comparable to the religious issue in India prior to the partition of that country, or to the Communist issue in France after World War II. Their solution means social change, but not revolutionary change.

Another sign of social instability is the presence of incompatible roles in the same individual. American women, for example, are expected to be well educated and capable of companionship with their husbands, and also to keep house, rear children, and be sweet, feminine, and beautiful. Also, many of them have to help the family and the nation by entering the labor market, which means a conflict between their economic and their reproductive functions. It seems probable, therefore, that our family structure will gradually change in a direction tending to reduce these incompatibilities.

Still another sign of instability is the inculcation of goals from which large segments of the population believe they are debarred by existing institutions. Thus the tendency of Communist propaganda among the laboring classes of the United States is to deny the possibility of a laboring man's getting ahead, educating his children, achieving security, and so forth *under our existing system*. In the South the Negro imbibes our general democratic outlook, and yet he finds he is debarred from political participation, from use of equal public facilities (including education), and from countless other advantages that the white man has. Naturally he resents the actual structure of race relations, because it blocks him from realizing the goals he has been taught to cherish. When large groups think of themselves as being frustrated in this way, whether it be true or not, the social system has the seeds of instability.[2] Social stability prevails only when there is no mass incentive to change the basic social structure.

These are ways in which the social system fails to "fit together." In addition to "fitting together," however, there is another condition necessary for long-run stability—namely, functional adequacy. A stable society is one in which the values of the people motivate them to behave in ways that meet the society's survival needs. If they do not, the social system fails to survive. If democratic individualism leads to such chaotic inefficiency, such pursuit of private interest, and such incapacity for quick and solid decisions that the government cannot maintain order, the democratic system will not survive in that particular country, because a social system requires a minimum of political order. In recent times, dictatorship of one kind or another has often replaced an inefficient democratic system.

---

[2] See Merton, Robert K., "Social Structure and Anomie," *American Sociological Review*, Vol. 3 (1938), pp. 672–682.

ELEMENTS OF STABILITY IN AMERICA

Inasmuch as the United States is a "going concern," it is clear that most of the conditions of stability are somehow being met. Just *how* they are being met is a question seldom considered. Let us discuss it briefly.

One of the outstanding characteristics of the American value system, as we have seen, is its emphasis on individualistic competition for superior economic status. By throwing competition open to all, and by motivating each person to want to have the best job possible, we maximize the chances of getting "the best man in the right job." Now, how well does this aspect of our system "fit" with the other aspects—with the family structure and with the dominant religion, for example?

Americans are supposed to live with their parents *only until capable of fending for themselves economically;* then they are supposed to strike out on their own and establish their own families as units entirely separate from their parental families. Moreover, the father is not supposed to dictate his son's occupational choice. The son not only makes his own occupational decision, but he is encouraged to surpass his father's occupational position if he can. In other words, in his family role the American learns to leave his initial family and strike out on his own just at the point when, in his economic role, he enters the race for superior rewards. Clearly the American family structure is compatible with the American ideal of individualistic competition. It is compatible in a number of other ways, because romantic courtship, companionship marriage, and easy divorce are all closely linked with an individualistic and competitive economic order. Also, it is in the family that the child learns that affection and respect are conditional upon his performance in competition with others. In these ways the American family organization and the American economic system "fit together."

The same is true of religion. The economic and political individualism of the American credo finds its counterpart in the stress upon human dignity in the Christian faith, and especially in the Protestant doctrine of individual responsibility. The Protestant emphasis on active work in *this* world, on the accumulation of wealth for productive but not for luxurious or idle living—the attitude sometimes called "worldly asceticism"—comports very well with competitive capitalism. Moreover, the tolerance of Protestantism for secular science, its sharp separation of religious means from empirical means,[3] strongly favors the development of technology, with its potentiality for enormous productivity and a high standard of living. Its tolerance for birth control also fits well with the emphasis on the material welfare of the individual, since parents can care for a few children better than they can care for many. Thus American Protestantism is an integral part of the American scene.

American society has grown so complex—its division of labor so ramified, its technology so advanced, its cities so large—that certain characteristics emphasized in our value system are essential to its maintenance. For instance, universal public education gives the widest possible training and selection of personnel for the multitudinous kinds of work that must be done. Freedom of expression is closely related to the freedom of scientific inquiry, which is necessary to keep the technology going. Tolerance is essential if large and diverse groups are to live crowded together in great cities. Individual freedom is also advantageous, because it permits people to find their own niches in society by a competitive process with maximum incentives for effort. If people are to have responsibility for finding their own places in society, if in every new generation a widespread reshuffling of status-occupants on the basis of a competition of talent is to occur, then the individual's freedom to make his choices, to go where he pleases, to try what he wishes, must be guaranteed in the legal and ethical system.

In sum, there is an integration in American society. The various parts of the social structure do successfully interlock. The family structure, the economic organization, the class system, education, religion, and politics—these are different aspects of the same total phenomenon, and they mutually reinforce one another.

But, as we have abundantly seen in this book, each of the aspects that we can point to as a stabilizing element also gives signs of potential instability. Consequently, we must now turn to a summary of the elements of instability suggested by the readings.

[3] Summed up, for example, in the popular phrases, "Trust in God, and keep your powder dry," "God helps him who helps himself," as well as in the more secular aphorism, "In God we trust; all others pay cash."

SOURCES OF INSTABILITY

INTERNAL INCONSISTENCIES

Since our democratic values, though usually stated in absolute terms, limit one another, their application in practice always raises the question of relative emphasis. This uncertainty gives a chance for special interests to interpret the values in their own way, while still seeming to remain within the democratic framework.

One of the basic conflicts is between the compassionate (equalitarian) aspect of our value system on the one hand and the competitive (*in*equalitarian) aspect on the other. Competition inevitably means that some people get hurt. They get hurt not only in a material sense but also in an emotional sense. The very fact that they strive hard for comparative advantage means that, when they fail, they suffer severely. In general the average American protects himself by seeming not to care, by good sportsmanship, by diversification of his interests (so that in some respect he is bound to succeed), by rationalizing his failures, by choosing as companions those who do not excel him, and so forth. But the truth remains that an individualistic, competitive social order is hard on some people. This is especially true when urban-industrial conditions have greatly increased the impersonality and enormity of the competitive process. Some individuals find that their "democratic" rights consist mainly in the right to sleep on park benches, to be unemployed, to feel insecure. Naturally there arises a desire for protection against the vicissitudes of the very social order which was supposed to be individualistic and therefore of benefit to the individual.

The same conflict manifests itself in the feeling that material inequalities have exceeded the bounds permitted by ethical equality. The inequalities of wealth have become so great in the United States that it seems unbelievable they could be due solely to a difference in ability. The man whose income is $200,000 per year is surely not 200 times as capable, or as valuable to his country, as the man who gets only $1,000. But regardless of difference in ability, it is felt that a human being should not be allowed to sink into abject poverty and depend on degrading charity. The individual should be shielded against the full effects of competition by minimum wages, unemployment insurance, pensions, job security, free medical attention, low-cost housing projects, and so forth.

But who will do this protecting? Obviously it must be the government, because this is the only agency representing *all* the people. However, if it is to develop a full-scale program of guaranteed benefits to the individual, involving everything from minimum wages to medical attention, the government must become such a complicated bureaucracy and acquire so much power that again the individual finds himself heavily controlled. He must, as a recipient of benefits, follow the rules, fill out the forms, wait in line, and toady to the officials. As a taxpayer he must pay a very large proportion of his income to the government. No longer can he use his money of his own free will, but he must give it to others who use it for him in ways over which he, as merely one citizen among millions, has little control. It was precisely from too much control that the individual revolted in the Reformation, when the democratic, individualistic social order was first inaugurated. Shall the individual now admit that he cannot endure what he fought for? Shall he slip back under surveillance from the cradle to the grave?

The choice would be an easy one if conditions were the same as they were a century ago. The competitive order was then flanked by sufficient kinship, community, and religious solidarity to reduce its untoward effects, so that few Americans would have chosen paternalistic state socialism. But now, under advanced urban-industrial conditions (themselves a product of the successful operation of competitive capitalism), *free* competition, *equal* opportunity, and *individual* enterprise are themselves difficult to maintain. Competition has a tendency to grow into a titanic struggle, not between puny individuals but between giants. Great industrial corporations, business firms, political machines, labor unions, and veterans' organizations compete with each other, and increasingly the individual can advance himself only as a member of these giant combines. This is the natural result of competition, because success breeds success and failure breeds failure, until the differences become enormous. A positive program of breaking down monopoly—of dissolving holding companies, banning the closed shop, and restricting the financial propagandistic activities of organizations—might conceivably bring back a more personal competitive order; but again it would take such a strong governmental organization to execute the program that official bureaucracy would be substituted for private monopoly, and the net gain in individual emancipation would perhaps not be great. In other words, the only way to keep "free" competition under modern conditions is to *control* it, which makes it partly "unfree."

The rapprochement between ethical equality and differential reward, between human dignity and free competition, is thus always difficult in a democratic society. In the United States, now reaching industrial and economic maturity, the issue is becoming even more clearly drawn. The two principles are rallying points for mutually opposed groups and parties. The compassionate sentimentalists call for security and paternalism, the rugged individualists for competition and self-reliance. Whatever the solution, the conflict represents a strong element of instability in our social organization.

THE QUEST FOR SECURITY BY UNDEMOCRATIC MEANS

Despite the differences of opinion in our society, a high degree of stability remains, because most people still believe in democratic procedures for settling controversies. They accept the verdict of the polls, the decisions of the courts; they follow orderly political procedures. But it is uncertain whether some procedures—such as the strike or high-pressure lobbying—are really democratic or not. Some of them seem to represent the exercise of veiled force, and some to represent graft and bribery. Furthermore the quest for security, for shelter against competition through some assured advantage, has led to clearly nondemocratic arrangements in our society. Among the most striking of these are our racial castes, our class inheritances, and our monopolistic practices.

RACIAL CASTES

Previous readings have fully documented the existence of the caste principle in American interracial relations. Its most extreme application is with reference to Negroes, but it is also present in varying degrees with respect to Mexicans, Japanese, and Jews. It has the advantage of giving the white persons (of whatever class) an assured status based on birth and hence independent of what they do. It removes large groups from competition. Yet it is such a clear violation of democratic values that the proponents of racial segregation must find special reasons for their views—e.g., "biological inferiority," national security, maintenance of the American standard of living. Science punctures these rationalizations and forces the proponents virtually into admitting that in this case they do not accept democratic values. This was the situation in the 1948 presidential election when the "Dixiecrats" admitted that they were plainly against *civil rights* for Negroes.

The denial to large groups of those rights stated to be the inalienable rights of man, written into the Constitution, taught in the schools, and maintained in the churches introduces an element of instability in our existing social organization. On the one hand, the groups so denied feel frustrated and naturally seek to change the situation. On the other hand, the groups who monopolize these rights are forced to use undemocratic and often illegal means to maintain their monopoly. The two principles—that of caste and that of open-class—are incompatible; any compromise between the two can at best be merely temporary. As long as they are both present in our society, they will generate instability.

CLASS INHERITANCE

The American family organization is as well adapted to a mobile, individualistic social order as any other known type. But there is a limit to which any family organization can be so adapted and still remain what we would regard as familial. The difficulty lies in the transmission of skills, attitudes, connections, and wealth from parents to children—amounting to the partial inheritance of social status. Such transmission is inevitable if the family is retained. Since the family has a high value in our eyes, Americans do not (as the Soviets once did) propose to abolish it because of this undemocratic influence. Instead, about all they may do is to cut down its undemocratic effects as far as possible.

One obvious way to reduce the family's undemocratic influence is to strike at the inheritance of wealth. Democratic societies have already taken the first step by abolishing primogeniture and systems of entailed property, and by allowing parents to will their property to others besides their own children. Most of them have already taken the second step, which is to levy heavy and graduated inheritance taxes. None of them will pursue this step to the point of confiscation of estates, because of the effect on saving and capital accumulation, but in the United States the amount that now is supposed to go to the government, when the law is not evaded, is very large. Graduated income taxes and gift taxes also tend indirectly to reduce the inheritance of wealth.

Another way to lessen the family's undemocratic influence is one not yet tried—namely, to tax private schools and colleges, using the money for the support of public schools. Private schools are of course the refuge of the rich. Class attitudes are taught there, superior educational advantages are given, contacts are made, and so the class position of the wealthy father is cemented in the child. Wealth employed in supporting private education cannot be employed in supporting public education. Heavy taxation of all private schools—religious or otherwise—with the returns earmarked for public schools, would force the rich to use their money and brains to improve the public schools. More fellowships and scholarships, awarded on the basis of merit, would also help to give the able children of the poor a chance to get ahead of the mediocre children of the rich.

On one front or another, whether in legislation, taxation, or education, the struggle will continue, the upper classes attempting to pass on their advantages to their children, the lower classes attempting to keep them from doing it. The effort is understandable in either case. A father naturally wishes to give his son "a head start" in the competitive struggle by buying him a superior education, by taking him into the family business, by leaving him a large inheritance. If he is wealthy, he can do these things. If not, he is likely to be more receptive to such new ideas as advocating more support of public education, more government control over business, and greater inheritance taxes.

BUSINESS MONOPOLIES

In business the quest for security brings an attempt to capture the market by expanding the firm's size, or to control the price through agreement with other firms. Our previous readings have shown to what extent the control of wealth is centralized in a few hands in the United States. They have not shown to what extent collusive price agreements prevail; and indeed, no one really knows. In any case monopoly, although bred from competition, is contrary to the competitive aspect of liberal-democratic social structure, and is hence a subject of controversy.

Business monopoly is sometimes a subtle kind. Consider, for example, the media of mass communication, which are an essential part of modern democracy. Increasingly the newspapers, broadcasting stations, and moving pictures have been dominated by a few big business houses. This is almost inevitable in view of the heavy capitalization necessary to maintain these enterprises on an economic scale. But as a result the media of mass communication tend to reflect the businessman's point of view. The 1948 presidential campaign found the newspapers of the country almost solidly behind the *losing* candidate. In this case the papers were not reflecting public opinion, they were trying, unsuccessfully, to mould it—and to mould it in favor of a special interest. The same had been true in previous presidential elections. With monopolistic control of the media of mass communication there is always the possibility that people will not get the facts, that free discussion will not prevail. Dissatisfaction of the masses with communication media that do not reflect their interests or values may prove a source of future social change.

UNION MONOPOLIES

The escape from competition is by many paths. In addition to business monopoly, there is the monopoly of labor unions. These generally attempt to fix wages, to restrict employment in a given occupation or industry to their own members, to bar the immigration of foreign labor, and to enforce their demands by strikes in which their members not only refuse to work but attempt to keep anyone else from working in their place. In addition, they usually favor promotion on the basis of seniority rather than ability. Finally, they often oppose technological changes on the ground that these changes endanger their jobs and that, under existing conditions, labor does not share directly in the extra profits accruing from them. Whether we judge these activities as good or bad, there is no denying that they depart radically from the individualistic and competitive kind of democracy we have had in the past.

AUTHORITARIAN GROUPS

A source of potential instability is represented by the groups that seek refuge in an absolute ideology and consider themselves above discussion or criticism by outsiders. These seek to control opinion, education, and scientific inquiry in a way that would enhance the power of the group itself. Such groups would like to capture the school system, to censor all communication media, to suppress all contrary ideologies. Instead of having people make their own decisions, such organizations would *tell* the people what to think and how to vote. In their view the highest authority is not the people themselves but the priests, the party members, the hooded knights, the brown shirts, or whatever the dignitaries of the particular organization are called. Such groups are always ready to gain ground when democratic vigilance weakens.

PERSONALITY AND COMPETITION

Our dynamic, competitive, mobile, and heterogeneous society places a heavy burden on the individual. It constantly forces him to choose between numerous alternatives, to take the responsibility for his choice, to compare himself with others, to wrestle with his own conscience, to abandon his familiar surroundings and old friends in the pursuit of new opportunities. It puzzles him with conflicting judgments as to his proper role, by doubts as to his own worth.

In his family the individual learns as a child to want and need affectional security. Since the family is now usually small, the affection comes mainly from his parents. His parents, however, especially if they are middle class, tend to reward him with affection only if he achieves it by his competitive success. Success in our urban-industrial society comes, however, primarily from the manipulation of other persons. They rather than the forces of nature are the obstacles and the means to one's aspirations. Consequently, the individual is forced to develop toward others the same kind of attitude that his agricultural ancestor developed toward tree stumps, rocks, and insects: an instrumental, impersonal attitude. But if he views others in such a way, he must suspect that others view him similarly. He finds it increasingly difficult to enter into the unsuspecting relationships of affectional intimacy that he learned as a child to crave.

The husband-wife relationship is one of the few in which the modern American is "allowed" to establish an affectional bond. Even this bond, however, is the outgrowth of a competitive courtship and the rating and dating complex. Furthermore, in marriage itself the individual frequently finds that affection is dependent on competitive success. He must "deserve" his spouse's love; and with the marriage bond dissolvable with increasing ease, he cannot be sure that he has permanently "won."

As an adolescent the individual is expected to cut loose from his parents and strike out for himself—the very parents who have made him, as a child, dependent on them for affection. But the exact time, the way in which it should be done, the new rights and obligations—these are not uniformly defined in our culture. Each individual must work it out for himself with his own parents.

Many of the previously examined disharmonies between different parts of our social structure reflect themselves in the personalities of Americans because they are the bearers of the conflicting values. Not only are rates of neurosis and psychosis very high, but many symptoms of mental disorder have their highest incidence in precisely those groups who most clearly conform to the competitive-democratic pattern. Suicide rates are highest among urbanites, among men, and among Protestants; heart disease and stomach ulcers are the typical disorders of the "strivers and strainers."

The individual in America seeks to protect himself against the rigors of the system. He often pretends to take life lightly, refuses to work too hard, and rationalizes his defeats. Above all, he indulges in escapist amusements. He takes his football and baseball more seriously than politics (which itself is a kind of game with him), his vacation trips more seriously than his job itself, and the comic strips more seriously than the business news. Nevertheless, the very frenzy and unreal character of his recreational patterns suggest the severe psychic strain that he is under.

He is the most vacation-minded of any human being, and his vacation must be as far removed from his regular work and regular place of abode as possible. He is often heavily dependent on alcohol for escape, and sometimes upon marijuana and opium. He usually requires stimulants—coffee, tobacco, Coca-Cola—to keep him going. Only the youthful can stand the pace, and consequently he greatly fears growing old.

An escape more powerful than any is that offered by authoritarian movements. It is always easy for the individual to take this exit from the uncertainty and struggle. A church that settles all of one's problems of conscience for one, a government that tells one what to believe, where to work, and how to live, a school that gives not science but eternal truths—these offer succor to the frustrated and the troubled. They give the individual a truth beyond himself, to which he can devote his energies unquestioningly. The only trouble is that, like narcotics, they end by depriving the individual of his self-determination.

CONCLUSION

Perhaps the emphasis of this book has been more on instability and conflict than the facts warrant. An attempt has been made, however, to analyze the main source of integration in American society—namely, the common set of values shared by the people. Social integration does not depend on an absence of change. Indeed, social change is occurring constantly. In a stable society, however, the ultimate values do not change. It is rather the means of carrying out these values that alter with the alteration of the conditions of life. The American value system has remained relatively constant while the country has become urbanized and industrialized. If liberal-democratic values are to continue to hold sway, the social structure will have to undergo further changes in the future. What is a change in keeping with democratic ideals, and what is a change not in keeping with them, is a distinction that every citizen, if he wishes to keep his basic way of life, must learn to make. May this book help him to make the distinction wisely.

Indexes

Name Index

(* Indicates sources from which readings were drawn for this volume.)

J

K

L

M

N

O

Z

Subject Index